(Continued)→

The Little, Brown Handbook

The Little, Brown Handbook

EIGHTH EDITION

H. Ramsey Fowler
University of Memphis

Jane E. Aaron

Daniel Anderson
Technology Consultant
University of North Carolina, Chapel Hill

New York San Francisco Boston
London Toronto Sydney Tokyo Singapore Madrid
Mexico City Munich Paris Cape Town Hong Kong Montreal

Editor-in-Chief: Joseph P. Terry
Senior Development Manager: Arlene Bessenoff
Development Editor: Linda Stern
Supplements Editor: Donna Campion
Marketing Manager: Carlise Paulson
Senior Production Manager: Bob Ginsberg
Design Manager and Text Designer: Wendy Ann Fredericks
Cover Designer: Kay Petronio
Technical Desktop Manager: Heather A. Peres
Senior Manufacturing Buyer: Dennis J. Para
Electronic Page Makeup: Dorothy Bungert/EriBen Graphics
Printer and Binder: RR Donnelley & Sons Company
Cover Printer: Phoenix Color Corp.

The authors and publisher are grateful to the many students who allowed their work to be reprinted here and to the copyright holders who are listed after page 968. Those pages are hereby made part of this copyright page.

Library of Congress Cataloging-in-Publication Data

Fowler, H. Ramsey (Henry Ramsey)
The Little, Brown handbook / H. Ramsey Fowler, Jane E. Aaron.—8th ed.
p. cm.
Includes index.
ISBN 0-321-07507-2
1. English language—Grammar—Handbooks, manuals, etc. 2. English language—Rhetoric—Handbooks, manuals, etc. 3. English language—Textbooks for foreign speakers. 4. Report writing—Handbooks, manuals, etc. I. Aaron, Jane E. II. Title.
PE1112.F64 2000
808'.042—dc21 00–031332

Please visit our Web site at *http://www.awlonline.com/littlebrown*.

ISBN 0-321-07507-2

2 3 4 5 6 7 8 9 10—DOC—03 02 01 00

Preface for Students: Using This Book

The Little, Brown Handbook is a basic resource that will answer almost any question you have about writing. Here you can find out how to get ideas, punctuate quotations, search the Internet, cite sources, or write a résumé. The handbook can help you not only in writing courses but also in other courses and beyond school.

Don't let the size of the handbook put you off. You need not read the whole book to get something out of it, and no one expects you to know everything included. Primarily a reference tool, the handbook is written and arranged to help you find the answers you need when you need them, quickly and easily.

Using this book will not by itself make you a good writer; for that, you need to care about your work at every level, from finding a subject to spelling words. But learning how to use the handbook and the information in it can give you the means to write *what* you want in the *way* you want.

Organization and content

An overview of the handbook appears inside the front cover. Briefly, the book divides into the following sections:

- Chapters 1–4 deal with the big picture: the writing process and paragraphs.
- Chapters 5–7 discuss critical thinking, reading arguments, and writing arguments.
- Chapters 8–11 introduce computer skills for writers: computer literacy, document design, Web composition, and online collaboration.
- Chapters 12–26 cover sentence basics: the system of English grammar and its conventions, errors that affect clarity, and techniques of effective sentences.
- Chapters 27–37 treat two technical elements of sentences and words: punctuation and mechanics (meaning capital letters, underlining, and the like).
- Chapters 38–41 move to words—how to choose them, look them up, learn them, spell them.

- Chapters 42–47 cover research writing from planning through revising, with a complete guide to citing sources.
- Chapters 48–53 introduce writing in the academic disciplines: literature, the other humanities, the social sciences, and the natural and applied sciences.
- Chapters 54–56 contain practical information on taking essay exams, writing business letters and job applications, and delivering oral presentations.
- Two glossaries—one of problem words and expressions, the other of terms—and a detailed index finish the book.

Finding information

Your instructor may assign whole sections of the book and discuss them in class or may use comments on your papers to direct you to particular sections. He or she will certainly encourage you to look things up on your own whenever you have a question. To help you do that, the handbook provides many ways of finding information quickly. Some of these surround the main text:

- The **Plan of the Book,** inside the front cover, displays the book's entire contents. This plan also shows the system of coded headings (explained below).
- The **Contents,** immediately after this preface, gives a more detailed version of the book's plan.
- The **ESL Guide,** inside the back cover, indexes the book's topics for students using English as a second language.
- The list of **Editing Symbols,** also inside the back cover, gives the abbreviations often used to mark papers.
- The list of **Useful Lists and Summaries,** just before the back endpapers, indexes topics that students frequently ask about.
- The **Index,** on the last pages of the book, lists every term and concept and every problem word or expression mentioned in the book. It is very detailed so that you can locate the precise point you seek and the page number where the point is discussed.

Many of the handbook's reference and learning aids appear on the text pages themselves, as illustrated by the samples opposite. Notice especially the code, **15b**, with the section heading near the top of the page and in the blue-green box in the right margin, where the code is accompanied by the symbol **agr**. Your instructor may use the codes or the symbols or both to mark specific weaknesses in your papers—for instance, either **15b** or **agr** on your paper would indicate an agreement problem. To discover just what the problem is and how to revise it, you can consult the plan of the book or the list of editing symbols, or you can thumb the book.

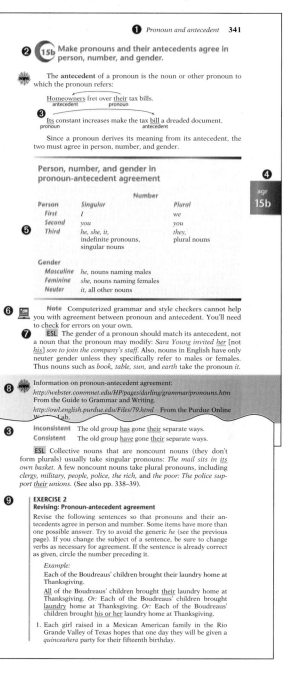

❶ Running head (header): the topic being discussed on this page.

❷ Section heading in blue-green. The circled code (**15b**) consists of the chapter number (**15**) and section letter (**b**).

❸ Examples, always indented. Color underlining highlights sentence elements and revisions.

❹ Page tab in blue-green, containing the nearest section code (**15b**) and the editing symbol for the topic being discussed (**agr**).

❺ Box in pale yellow, containing a summary or checklist.

❻ Computer tip (see the next page).

❼ Pointer for students using English as a second language, flagged with a yellow box.

❽ Web links in a blue-green box (see the next page).

❾ Exercise with gold vertical line.

❶ *Pronoun and antecedent* 341

❷ **15b Make pronouns and their antecedents agree in person, number, and gender.**

The **antecedent** of a pronoun is the noun or other pronoun to which the pronoun refers:

Homeowners fret over their tax bills.
antecedent pronoun

❸ Its constant increases make the tax bill a dreaded document.
pronoun antecedent

Since a pronoun derives its meaning from its antecedent, the two must agree in person, number, and gender.

Person, number, and gender in pronoun-antecedent agreement

❹  

agr 15b

❺

Person	Number: Singular	Number: Plural
First	I	we
Second	you	you
Third	*he, she, it,* indefinite pronouns, singular nouns	*they,* plural nouns

Gender	
Masculine	*he,* nouns naming males
Feminine	*she,* nouns naming females
Neuter	*it,* all other nouns

❻ **Note** Computerized grammar and style checkers cannot help you with agreement between pronoun and antecedent. You'll need to check for errors on your own.

❼ ESL The gender of a pronoun should match its antecedent, not a noun that the pronoun may modify: *Sara Young invited her* [not *his*] *son to join the company's staff.* Also, nouns in English have only neuter gender unless they specifically refer to males or females. Thus nouns such as *book, table, sun,* and *earth* take the pronoun *it.*

❽ Information on pronoun-antecedent agreement:
http://webster.commnet.edu/HP/pages/darling/grammar/pronouns.htm From the Guide to Grammar and Writing.
http://owl.english.purdue.edu/Files/79.html From the Purdue Online W[...] Lab.

❸ Inconsistent The old group has gone their separate ways.
Consistent The old group have gone their separate ways.

ESL Collective nouns that are noncount nouns (they don't form plurals) usually take singular pronouns: *The mail sits in its own basket.* A few noncount nouns take plural pronouns, including *clergy, military, people, police, the rich,* and *the poor: The police support their unions.* (See also pp. 338–39.)

❾ **EXERCISE 2**
Revising: Pronoun-antecedent agreement

Revise the following sentences so that pronouns and their antecedents agree in person and number. Some items have more than one possible answer. Try to avoid the generic *he* (see the previous page). If you change the subject of a sentence, be sure to change verbs as necessary for agreement. If the sentence is already correct as given, circle the number preceding it.

Example:

Each of the Boudreaus' children brought their laundry home at Thanksgiving.

All of the Boudreaus' children brought their laundry home at Thanksgiving. *Or:* Each of the Boudreaus' children brought laundry home at Thanksgiving. *Or:* Each of the Boudreaus' children brought his or her laundry home at Thanksgiving.

1. Each girl raised in a Mexican American family in the Rio Grande Valley of Texas hopes that one day they will be given a *quinceañera* party for their fifteenth birthday.

The handbook's reference aids are meant to speed your work, but you need not use any or all of them. You may of course browse or read this book like any other, with no particular goal in mind but seeing what you can learn.

Special symbols

Frequently throughout the handbook, you'll see the following symbols:

- The computer shown here signals tips for using computers productively for all kinds of writing activity, from discovering ideas through checking spelling or grammar to citing sources. (See the previous page for an example.)

- The Web shown here marks connections between the text and helpful Web sites listed at the bottoms of the same or facing pages. (See the previous page for an illustration.) The Web addresses are as up to date as we could make them before this book was printed, but inevitably some sites will move or disappear. For more current links, see this book's Web site at *http://www.awlonline.com/littlebrown.*
- The symbol **ESL** flags material for students using English as a second language, which is integrated throughout the handbook. (See the previous page for an illustration.) A guide to the ESL topics appears inside the back cover.

Recommended usage

The conventions described and illustrated in this handbook are those of standard written English—the label given the language of business and the professions. (See also pp. 558–59.) Written English is more conservative than spoken English in matters of grammar and usage, and a great many words and constructions that are widely spoken remain unaccepted in careful writing.

When clear distinctions exist between the language of conversation and that of careful writing, the handbook provides examples of each and labels them *spoken* and *written.* When usage in writing itself varies with the level of formality intended, the handbook labels examples *formal* and *informal.* When usage is mixed or currently changing, the handbook recommends that you choose the more conservative usage because it will be acceptable to all readers.

Preface for Instructors

The Little, Brown Handbook always aims to address both the current and the recurrent needs of composition teachers and students. This eighth edition is no exception. Writing and its teaching are changing dramatically because of electronic media, and the handbook has changed in response. At the same time, much about writing does not change, and the handbook remains a comprehensive, clear, and accessible guide to a host of writing situations and challenges.

The Little, Brown Handbook is actually many books in one, and each is stronger in this edition. The revisions—highlighted below with bullets—affect the overall organization and almost every page.

A guide to writing with computers

The handbook's advice for using computers in all facets of writing has increased dramatically:

- More than ninety new **computer tips**, for a total of 150, integrate computer use with all stages of researching, writing, revising, and editing. Signaled by the computer image shown here, these tips explain when computers can help and also when they cannot.

- More than four hundred **Web links** give addresses for helpful sites on every topic covered by the handbook. Related to the text by the symbol shown here, the links appear at the bottoms of the same or facing pages.
- A new Part III, **"Using Computers Critically,"** contains four new chapters on computer skills, encouraging students to use the machines not only efficiently but effectively for their writing situations:

  "Becoming Computer Literate" covers word processing, file management, spelling and grammar/style checkers, e-mail format and etiquette, essential Web skills, and other topics. Nine screen shots illustrate steps and concepts.

  "Designing Documents" connects the principles and elements of design to academic, business, and publicity writing. The ten sample documents include an annotated comparison of effective and ineffective designs.

"Composing for the Web" covers principles of writing and designing Web pages, including tips for using HTML editors. Nine screen shots illustrate the discussion.

"Collaborating Online" introduces the basics of e-mail and Web collaboration, stressing ways to make group work productive. Three screen shots illustrate online discussion and file sharing.

- The Glossary of Terms now includes more than **three dozen computer terms.**

A guide to researching with computers

New or expanded discussions of computers in research bring the handbook up to the minute:

- A new discussion of **finding bibliographic information for online sources** includes an annotated screen shot.
- An expanded discussion of **Web research** includes appropriate cautions and a detailed case study illustrated by four screen shots.
- An extensive section on **other Internet sources** covers the pros and cons of discussion groups.
- An expanded discussion of **evaluating online sources** provides a detailed checklist and new exercises.
- A new section on **acknowledging online sources** addresses issues of copyright and fair use.
- New **electronic documentation models** illustrate all styles: eleven new MLA, three new Chicago, five new APA, and two new CBE.
- A new chapter on **Columbia style for online sources** in the humanities and the sciences provides dozens of models and shows how Columbia can supplement the other styles.
- New **resources for writing in the disciplines** give scores of Web sources for literature, other humanities, the social sciences, and the natural and applied sciences.

A guide to research writing

With detailed practical information and two sample MLA papers, the handbook has traditionally given close attention to research writing. This edition's changes and additions clarify the process and expand key topics:

- Research writing is now **reorganized in four chapters:** planning, finding sources, working with sources, and writing and revising.

- Distinctive concerns of research writing receive added attention:

  Formulating a research question.
  Developing a research strategy, including tapping into one's own knowledge and balancing print and online sources.
  Avoiding plagiarism, with additional examples of paraphrasing and quoting.
  Integrating quotations, including introducing, altering, and interpreting them.
  Documenting sources, a conceptual discussion addressing why disciplines' styles vary.

A guide to the writing process

Several improvements strengthen the handbook's practical approach to invention, the thesis, revision, and other elements of the writing process:

- A new first chapter emphasizes assessing the **writing situation,** includes a detailed checklist, and offers a fuller discussion of **purpose.**
- A new **student work-in-progress** on Internet communication provides examples at every stage, including complete first, revised, and final drafts.
- Ten new **collaboration exercises** encourage students to work together online or face to face in order to generate ideas and solve writing problems.

A guide to critical thinking, reading, and writing

The handbook now links the related subjects of critical thinking and argument, emphasizing them in the new Part II:

- **Reading a Web site critically** is now a key component of reading and writing with a critical perspective.
- Two chapters on argument—one on reading, one on writing—now discuss **Toulmin's model of argument** and integrate it with induction and deduction.
- The discussion of **fallacies** adds false authority and sweeping generalization.
- New material on **organizing an argument** includes a box outlining common patterns.

A guide to usage, grammar, and punctuation

The handbook's core reference material features concise explanations, annotated examples from across the curriculum, and frequent exercises in connected discourse. The changes here are small but significant:

- Dozens of computer tips spell out the uses and limitations of **grammar, style, and spelling checkers.**
- An expanded and foregrounded chapter on **emphasis,** with new exercises, focuses on strong subjects and verbs and movement from old to new information.
- The new **MLA style for brackets with ellipsis marks** receives full coverage and is clearly distinguished from other disciplines' styles.
- **Changes in examples** are now more visible, highlighted with color underlining instead of italics.

A guide for ESL students

The handbook continues to provide extensive rhetorical and grammatical help for ESL students, all integrated into the rest of the book so that students do not have to distinguish between ESL problems and those they share with native speakers. For easy reference, the symbol ESL signals ESL notes and sections, and an endpaper guide pulls all the coverage together in one place.

- **Nineteen new ESL notes**—rhetorical as well as grammatical—bring the total to seventy-six notes and thirteen sections.

A guide to writing in the disciplines

Along with its cross-curricular examples and exercises and its extensive research help, the handbook offers specific advice on academic writing. Two changes in particular improve this material:

- Academic writing is now **organized into five chapters:** general guidelines and then writing about literature, other humanities, the social sciences, and the natural and applied sciences.
- **Chicago, APA, and CBE styles** all receive expanded coverage, and CBE now includes both name-year and number styles of citation.

An accessible reference guide

The handbook has an unusually accessible format, with helpful endpapers, nearly 150 summary and checklist boxes, and a clean page design. In this edition the most noticeable change may be visual:

- **A new design** retains the book's clean, uncluttered format while allowing full-color screen shots and other illustrations.

A reference for college and beyond

With chapters on document design, writing across the curriculum, taking essay exams, writing for business, and making oral presentations, the handbook is a resource that students keep. With a cloth cover and sturdy binding, it is a book that lasts.

Supplements

An extensive package of supplements accompanies *The Little, Brown Handbook* for both instructors and students. An asterisk (*) precedes any item that is complimentary to qualified adopters of the handbook.

For instructors and students

- ***Daedalus Online for The Little, Brown Handbook*** is the next generation of DIWE, the highly regarded Daedalus Integrated Writing Environment, uniting collaborative learning with the inherently cooperative tools of the World Wide Web. This writing environment allows students to explore online resources, employ prewriting strategies, share ideas in real-time conferences, and post feedback to a discussion board. *Daedalus Online* offers instructors a suite of interactive management tools to guide and facilitate students' participation.
- *****The Little, Brown Handbook Online,*** on the Web at *http://www.awlonline.com/littlebrown,* provides a companion site for the handbook. It includes brief reviews of the topics in the text, practice exercises for every topic, and links to resources on writing, research and documentation, document design, and many other subjects. For instructors, the site offers sample syllabuses, teaching suggestions, and downloadable transparency masters.
- ***The English Pages Web site,** located at *http://www.awl.com/englishpages,* provides instructors and students with resources for reading, writing, and research not only in composition but also in literature, technical writing, and basic skills.

For instructors

- ***The Instructor's Annotated Edition,** revised and updated by Janice Okoomian, Brown University, combines in one convenient volume the text of the student edition and essays and annotations for instructors. The IAE contains answers to all exercises (adjacent to the exercises), scores of classroom discussion topics and activities, and helpful essays for both new and experienced teachers. This edition includes more than fifty new suggestions each for computer and collaborative exercises, ninety new reading suggestions, and a thorough revision by Daniel Anderson, University of North Carolina, Chapel Hill, of the essay "Using Computers to Teach Writing."
- *A laminated **conversion guide** helps instructors adapt to new chapter numbering created by the handbook's smaller chapters and added computer material. Sized to be carried inside the cover of the student's or instructor's edition, the conversion

guide shows all seventh-edition codes side by side with their eigth-edition parallels.

- *Two supplements reproduce parts of the student's or intructor's editon for classroom use: a set of **transparency masters** with key boxes and lists from the text; and a separate **answer key** containing all exercise answers.
- **Teaching Online: Internet Research, Conversation, and Composition,*** Third Edition, is an accessible introduction to Internet resources for teaching writing, offering basic definitions and information on Internet access and showing how to integrate a variety of Internet tools in writing courses.
- *An **extensive assessment package** includes diagnostic tests and TASP and CLAST exams. All tests are keyed to the handbook, and all are available both in print and on computer software. In addition, the software versions can be customized and used on a network for online testing.
- **Model Research Papers from Across the Disciplines,*** Fifth Edition, a collection of student papers in the humanities, social sciences, and natural sciences, contains photo-reproducible material that can be distributed to students.
- *The **Longman resources for instructors** include six valuable works: *Teaching in Progress: Theories, Practices, and Scenarios,* by Josephine Koster Tarvers; *Using Portfolios,* by Kathleen McClelland; *Comp Tales,* writing teachers' reports on their teaching experiences, edited by Richard Haswell; and the videos *Writing, Teaching, and Learning,* by David Jolliffe, and *Writing Across the Curriculum: Making It Work,* produced by Robert Morris College and the Public Broadcasting System.

For students

- **The Little, Brown Handbook Multimedia CD-ROM,*** casts the print version of the handbook into a multimedia environment that features both visual and audio explanations, interactive exercises with immediate feedback, rapid searches, highlighting and note-taking functions, and bookmarks and dog-ears for easy reference.
- ***The Little, Brown Workbook,*** Eighth Edition, by Donna Gorrell, St. Cloud State University, parallels the handbook's organization but provides briefer text and many more exercises. This edition includes a new section on writing with computers. A separate answer key is also available.
- ***ESL Worksheets,*** Third Edition, by Dawn Schmid, California State University, San Marcos, provides nonnative speakers with extra practice in the areas that tend to be more troublesome for them.

- ****Researching Online,*** Fourth Edition, by David Munger, gives students detailed, step-by-step instructions for performing electronic searches; for researching with e-mail, discussion groups, and synchronous communication; and for evaluating online sources.
- ****Documenting Sources Across the Curriculum*** is a handy compilation of the handbook's material on preparing a working bibliography and documenting sources in MLA, APA, Chicago, CBE, and Columbia styles.
- *A separate booklet, ***The Longman Guide to Columbia Online Style,*** adds to the handbook's presentation.
- ***Study Wizard Computerized Study Guide*** provides practice and review exercises, with answers explained and keyed to the handbook.
- ***Take Note!*** is a cross-platform CD-ROM that integrates note taking, outlining, and bibliography management into an easy-to-use package.

Additional supplements for students include ***Eighty Readings,*** Second Edition; the ***Literacy Library Series** (*Public Literacy, Workplace Literacy,* and *Academic Literacy*); ****Visual Communication,*** by Susan Hilligoss; ****Analyzing Literature: A Guide for Students,*** by Sharon James McGee; ****Reading Critically: Text, Charts, Graphs,*** Second Edition, by Judith Olson-Fallon; and two guides to collaborative learning, ****Learning Together,*** by Tori Haring-Smith, and ****A Guide for Peer Response,*** by Tori Haring-Smith and Helon Raines.

The handbook may also be packaged with other books at a discount. Two **dictionaries** are available: *Merriam-Webster's Collegiate Dictionary,* Tenth Edition, a hardcover desk dictionary; and *The New American Webster Handy College Dictionary,* Third Edition, a briefer paperback. And the **the Penguin Program,** through Penguin Putnam, offers a variety of Penguin titles, such as Arthur Miller's *Death of a Salesman* and Julia Alvarez's *How the Garcia Girls Lost Their Accents.*

Acknowledgments

We could not keep *The Little, Brown Handbook* fresh and useful without the help of many instructors who talk with sales representatives and editors, answer questionnaires, write detailed reviews, and send us personal notes.

For the eighth edition, we are especially grateful to the many instructors who communicated with us directly or through reviews, drawing on their rich experience to offer insights into the handbook and its instructor's annotated edition: Michael Anzelone, Nassau Community College; Kirstin Ruth Bratt, Arizona Western College;

Cheryl Clements, Blinn College, Bryan; Peggy Cole, Arapahoe Community College; F. Brett Cox, Gordon College; Kathleen Dooley, Tidewater Community College, Virginia Beach; Gloria W. East, St. Petersburg Junior College; Tim Engles, University of Georgia; John F. Healy, Baker University; Diana Laulainen-Schein, University of Minnesota; David McDowell, Anne Arundel Community College; Marta E. Magellan, Miami-Dade Community College, Kendall; Phillip J. Miller, University of Tennessee, Martin; Kay Mizell, Collin County Community College; Kevin Nebergall, Kirkwood Community College; Philip Nel, College of Charleston; Laura Noell, Northern Virginia Community College; Michael O'Connor, Millikin University; Wayne Rambo, Camden County College; Janet Rentsch, Saginaw Valley State University; John Schaffer, Blinn College, Bryan; Allison Smith, Louisiana Tech University; Jessica E. Stephens, Eastern Kentucky University; Frances Stewart, Bessemer State Technical College; Karah Stokes, Kentucky State University; Timothy P. Twohill, Kent State University, Tuscarawas; Kay J. Walter, Blinn College, Brenham.

In responding to the ideas of these thoughtful critics, we had the help of many creative people. Daniel Anderson, University of North Carolina, Chapel Hill, was a superb collaborator as our technology consultant, always as helpful and patient with us as he is shrewd about computer use. And Sylvan Barnet, Tufts University, continued to lend his expertise in the chapter "Reading and Writing About Literature," which is adapted from his *Short Guide to Writing About Literature* and *Introduction to Literature* (with Morton Berman, William Burto, and William E. Cain).

In and around Longman, too, support was unstinting. Arlene Bessenoff sponsored the handbook in-house and responded nimbly to our every need. David Munger gave quick and thoughtful research support. Linda Stern provided astute suggestions on the developing manuscript. Carlise Paulson devised and managed a vibrant marketing effort. Robert Ginsberg, now a longtime colleague and friend, once again saw to it that, against all odds, the manuscript indeed became a book. Kathryn Graehl copyedited to catch our lapses. Wendy Fredericks created the striking new design. Dorothy Bungert worked her usual miracles in page make-up. And Nancy Bell Scott put everything else aside to proofread on a difficult schedule. We are grateful to all these collaborators.

Contents

PART II

PART III

The Little, Brown Handbook

PART I

The Writing Process

CHAPTER 1

Assessing Your Writing Situation

"Writing is easy," snarled the late sportswriter Red Smith. "All you have to do is sit down at the typewriter and open a vein." Most writers would smile in agreement, and so might you. Like anything worthwhile, writing well takes hard work. This chapter and the next two will show you some techniques that successful writers use to ease the discomfort of writing and produce effective compositions.

1a Understanding how writing happens

Every time you sit down to write, you embark on a **writing process**—the term for all the activities, mental and physical, that go into creating what eventually becomes a finished piece of work. Even for experienced writers the process is usually messy, which is one reason that it is sometimes difficult. Though we may get a sense of ease and orderliness from a well-crafted magazine article, we can safely assume that the writer had to work hard to achieve those qualities, struggling to express half-formed thoughts, shaping and reshaping paragraphs to make a point convincingly.

There is no *one* writing process: no two writers proceed in the same way, and even an individual writer adapts his or her process to the task at hand. Still, most experienced writers pass through certain stages that overlap and circle back on each other:

http://www.awlonline.com/littlebrown Links to Web resources on the writing process and the writing situation.

http://www.powa.org/ The Paradigm Online Writing Assistant, featuring writing models and strategies.

http://owl.english.purdue.edu/ The Purdue Online Writing Lab, featuring a searchable collection of more than 130 handouts on writing.

http://webster.commnet.edu/HP/pages/darling/original.htm The Guide to Grammar and Writing, featuring advice on writing at every level, from the essay through grammar.

- *Analyzing the writing situation:* considering subject, purpose, audience, and other elements of the project (pp. 4–17).
- *Developing or planning:* discovering a subject, gathering information, focusing on a central theme, and organizing material (pp. 18–46).
- *Drafting:* expressing and connecting ideas (pp. 49–51).
- *Revising:* rethinking and improving structure, content, style, and presentation (pp. 52–66).

With experience, as you complete varied assignments and try the varied techniques described in this book, you will develop your own basic writing process.

Note Like many others, you may harbor the misconception that writing is only, or even mainly, a matter of correctness. True, any written message will find a more receptive audience if it is correct in grammar, spelling, and similar matters. But these concerns should come late in the writing process, after you've allowed yourself to discover what you want to say, freeing yourself to make mistakes along the way. As one writer put it, you need to get the clay on the potter's wheel before you can shape it into a bowl, and you need to shape the bowl before you can perfect it. So get your clay on the wheel, and work with it until it looks like a bowl. Then worry about correctness.

EXERCISE 1
Starting a writing journal

Recall several writing experiences that you have had—a letter you had difficulty with, an essay you enjoyed, an all-nighter spent happily or miserably on a term paper, a posting to an online newsgroup that received a surprising response. What do these experiences reveal to you about writing, particularly your successes and problems with it? For instance:

Do you like to experiment with language?
Are some kinds of writing easier than others?
Do you have trouble getting ideas or expressing them?
Do you worry about grammar and spelling?
Do your readers usually understand what you mean?

Record these thoughts as part of continuing journal entries that track your experiences as a writer. (See pp. 19–21 on keeping a journal.) Specific suggestions for considering your past work appear in Chapter 1, Exercises 4, 7, and 11; Chapter 2, Exercises 1, 8, and 12; Chapter 3, Exercises 2, 6, and 9; and Chapter 4, Exercises 3, 11, 17, 20, and 23. As you complete writing assignments for your composition course and other courses, keep adding to the journal, noting especially which procedures seem most helpful to you. Your aim is to discover your feelings about writing so that you can develop a dependable writing process of your own.

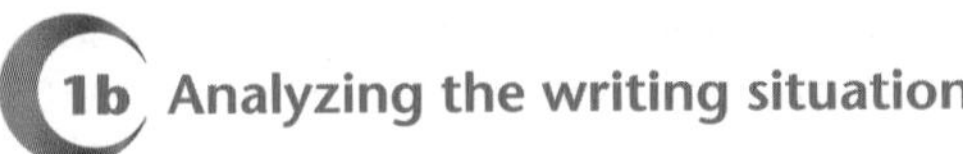

1b Analyzing the writing situation

Any writing you do for others occurs in a context that both limits and clarifies your choices. You are communicating something about a particular subject to a particular audience of readers for a specific reason. You may need to conduct research. You'll be up against a length requirement and a deadline. And you may be expected to present your work in a certain format.

These are the elements of the **writing situation,** and analyzing them at the very start of a project can tell you much about how to proceed. (For more information about these elements, refer to the page numbers given below.)

Subject (pp. 6–9)

- What does your writing assignment instruct you to write about? If you don't have a specific assignment, what do you want to write about?
- What interests you about the subject? What do you already have ideas about or want to know more about?
- What does the assignment require you to do with the subject? (See p. 7.)

Audience (pp. 10–14)

- Who will read your writing? What do your readers already know and think about your topic?
- Do your readers have any characteristics—such as educational background, experience in your field, or political views—that could influence their reception of your writing?
- What is your relationship to your readers? How formal or informal should your writing be?
- What do you want readers to do or think after they read your writing?

Purpose (pp. 15–17)

- What aim does your assignment specify? For instance, does it ask you to explain something or argue a point?
- Why are you writing? What do you want your work to accomplish?
- How can you best achieve your purpose?

Research (pp. 618–65)

- What kinds of evidence—such as facts, examples, and the opinions of experts—will best suit your topic, audience, and purpose?

- Does your assignment require you to consult sources of information or conduct other research, such as interviews, surveys, or experiments?
- Besides the requirements of the assignment, what additional information do you need to develop your topic? How will you obtain it?
- What documentation style should you use to cite your sources? (See pp. 698–99 on source documentation in the academic disciplines.)

Deadline and length

- When is the assignment due? How will you apportion the work you have to do in the available time?
- How long should your writing be? If no length is assigned, what seems appropriate for your topic, audience, and purpose?

Document design

- What organization and format does the assignment require? (See pp. 215–18 on format in the academic disciplines and pp. 902–15 on format in business.)
- Even if a particular format is not required, how might you use margins, headings, illustrations, and other elements to achieve your purpose? (See pp. 201–14.)

Note The elements of the writing situation listed above pertain to traditional academic writing. For some online writing, however, the elements may be different. E-mailing a brief query to a discussion group, for instance, may not involve the particulars of research, deadline, length, and document design. Creating material for the World Wide Web, in contrast, will complicate some elements, especially design. Still, any online writing will require you to consider the essential elements discussed on the following pages: subject, audience, and purpose.

EXERCISE 2
Analyzing a writing situation

The following assignment was made in a survey course in psychology. What does the assignment specify about the elements of the writing situation? What does it imply? Given this assignment, how would you answer the questions opposite and above?

> When is psychotherapy most likely to work? That is, what combinations of client, therapist, and theory tend to achieve good results? In your paper, cite studies supporting your conclusions. Length: 1500 to 1800 words. Post your paper online to me and your discussion group by March 30.

1c Discovering and limiting a subject

For most college and business writing, you will write in response to an assignment. The assignment may specify your subject, or it may leave the choice to you. (If you're stuck, you can use the discovery techniques on pp. 18–29 to think of subjects.) Whether the subject is assigned or not, it will probably need some thought if it is to achieve these aims:

- The subject should be suitable for the assignment.
- It should be neither too general nor too limited for the length of project and deadline assigned.
- It should be something you care about.

1 Pursuing your interests and experiences

Some assignments, such as a physics lab report or a business case study, leave you little room to express yourself. But even these assignments provide some leeway—for instance, in how you conduct and write your research. And many other subjects that may seem inflexible actually allow you considerable freedom. If you are assigned a comparison-and-contrast essay on two people you know, the choice of people and the way you compare them could make the difference for you between simply enduring the writing process or enjoying and learning from it.

When no subject is assigned, find one in your experiences, interests, or curiosities:

- What subject do you already know something about or have you been wondering about? Athletic scholarships? Unemployment in your town?
- Have you recently participated in a lively discussion about a controversial topic, such as a change in relations between men and women or an event in your family's history?
- Do you find a current technological trend, such as the use of cellular phones or e-mail, especially exciting or disturbing?
- What have you read or seen lately? A shocking book? A violent or funny movie? An effective television commercial?
- What topic in the reading or class discussion for a course has intrigued you or seemed especially relevant to your own experi-

http://www.powa.org/whttowrt.htm What to write about, from the Paradigm Online Writing Assistant.

http://webware.princeton.edu/Writing/wc4b.htm Finding and narrowing a subject, from Princeton University.

ences? An economic issue such as taxes? A psychological problem such as depression?

- What makes you especially happy or especially angry? A hobby? The behavior of your neighbors?
- Which of your own or others' dislikes and preferences would you like to understand better? The demand for sport-utility vehicles? A taste for vegetarian cuisine?

2 Matching subject and assignment

When you receive an assignment, study its wording and its implications about your writing situation to guide your choice of subject:

- What's wanted from you? Many writing assignments contain words such as *discuss, describe, analyze, report, interpret, explain, define, argue,* or *evaluate.* These words specify the way you are to approach your subject, what kind of thinking is expected of you, and what your general purpose is. (See pp. 15–17.)
- For whom are you writing? Some assignments will specify your readers, but usually you will have to figure out for yourself whether your audience is the general reading public, your classmates, your boss, the college community, your instructor, or some other group or individual. (For more on analyzing your audience, see pp. 11–14.)
- What kind of research is required? Sometimes an assignment specifies the kinds of sources you are expected to consult, and you can use such information to choose your subject. (If you are unsure whether research is required, check with your instructor.)
- Does the subject need to be narrowed so that you can do it justice in the length and time required? (See "Narrowing the Subject," below.)

3 Narrowing the subject

Because most assignments leave some room for you to shape the subject, they are usually quite general. The same may be true of your first attempts to make the assigned subject your own or to invent a subject. Communication on the Internet, Lincoln's weaknesses as President, federal aid to college students, corporate support for the arts, summer jobs—all these cover broad areas that whole books might be written about. For a brief paper, you'd need a topic much narrower, much more specific, so that you could provide the facts, examples, and other details that make writing significant and interesting.

The following examples illustrate how broad subjects can be scaled down to one of several specific subjects, limited and manageable:

Broad subjects	Specific subjects
Communication on the Internet	The advantages of online communication Whether the government should regulate Internet content Whether the Internet will contribute to social and economic inequality
Lincoln's weaknesses as President	Lincoln's most significant error as commander-in-chief of the Union army Lincoln's delay in emancipating the slaves Lincoln's difficulties in controlling his cabinet
Summer jobs	Kinds of summer jobs for unskilled workers How to find a summer job What a summer job can teach
Federal aid to college students	Which students should be entitled to federal aid Kinds of federal aid available to college students Why the federal government should (or should not) aid college students

Here are some guidelines for narrowing subjects:

- Again, pursue your interests, and consider what the assignment tells you about purpose, audience, sources, length, and deadline (see pp. 4–5).
- Break your subject into as many topics as you can think of. Make a list.
- For the topic that interests you most and fits the assignment, roughly sketch out the main ideas and consider how many paragraphs or pages of specific facts, examples, and other details you would need to pin those ideas down. This thinking should give you at least a vague idea of how much work you'd have to do and how long the resulting paper might be.
- If an interesting and appropriate topic is still too broad, break it down further and repeat the previous step.

The Internet can also help you limit a general subject:

- On the World Wide Web, browse a search engine such as Yahoo! or a catalog such as BUBL LINK that organizes subjects into directories, moving from the general to the specific. As you pursue increasingly narrow categories, you may find a suitably limited topic.

- Browse a newsgroup or Web forum that relates to your general subject, considering the topics discussed and the arguments made.

Once you find a narrow topic you like, test it as described opposite by sketching out the main ideas and estimating their length.

Don't be discouraged if the perfect topic does not come easily or early. You may find that you need to do some planning and writing, exploring different facets of the general subject and pursuing your specific interests, before you hit on the best topic. And the topic you select may require further narrowing or may shift subtly or even dramatically as you move through the writing process.

EXERCISE 3
Narrowing subjects

Following are some general writing assignments. Use the given information and your own interests to find specific topics for three of these assignments.

1. For a letter to the editor of the town newspaper, describe the effects of immigration on your community. Length: two pages. Deadline: unspecified.
2. For a writing course, consider how the World Wide Web could alter the experience of popular culture. Length: three pages. Deadline: one week.
3. For a course in sociology, research and analyze the dynamics of a particular group of people. Length: unspecified. Deadline: four weeks.
4. For a writing course, read and respond to an essay in a text you are using. Length: three pages. Deadline: two weeks.
5. For a government course, consider possible restrictions on legislators. Length: five pages. Deadline: two weeks.

EXERCISE 4
Considering your past work: Discovering and limiting a subject

Think of something you've recently written—perhaps an application essay, a business report, or a term paper. How did your subject evolve from beginning to end? In retrospect, was it appropriate for your writing situation? How, if at all, might it have been modified?

http://yahoo.com Yahoo!, a Web search engine organized by subject.

http://bubl.ac.uk/link/ BUBL LINK, a catalog of academic Web resources organized by subject.

http://www.lii.org A collection of subject-related links compiled by librarians.

http://www.remarq.com A searchable collection of Web discussion forums.

http://deja.com A searchable archive of newsgroup subjects and messages.

EXERCISE 5
Finding a topic for your essay

As the first step in developing a three- to four-page essay for the instructor and the other students in your writing course, choose one of the topics you arrived at in Exercise 3 or some other topic you like. Use the guidelines in the previous section to come up with a topic that is suitably interesting, appropriate, and narrow.

1d Considering the audience

Who are your readers? Why will they read your writing? What will they need and expect from you? These questions are central to writing and will crop up again and again because (except in writing only for yourself) you are always trying to communicate something to readers.

Your audience may be specified or implied in a writing assignment. When you write an editorial for the student newspaper favoring expansion of the college health facilities, your audience is fellow students, who will be reading the paper for information of general and personal interest. When you write a report on a physics experiment, your audience is your physics instructor, who will be reading to evaluate your competence and see if you need help. If no particular audience is specified or implied, then you are free to decide whom you want to address: your classmates? your boss and others at work? those who drive cars? Whatever the audience, it can help you decide what to say about your topic and how to say it.

ESL If English is not your native language, you may not be accustomed to appealing to your readers when you write. In some cultures, readers may accept a writer's statements with little or no questioning. Readers of English, however, expect the writer to reach out to them by being accurate, fair, interesting, and clear.

1 Knowing what readers need

As a reader yourself, you know what readers need:

- *Context:* a link between what they read and their own knowledge and experiences.
- *Predictability:* an understanding of the writer's purpose and how it is being achieved.
- *Information:* the specific facts, examples, and other details that make the subject clear, concrete, interesting, and convincing.

http://www.colostate.edu/Depts/WritingCenter/references/processes/audmod/audmod.htm A guided tour promoting audience awareness for writers, from Colorado State University.

- *Respect:* a sense that the writer respects their values and beliefs, their background, and their intelligence.
- *Voice:* a sense that the writer is a real person.
- *Clarity and correctness:* writing free of unnecessary stumbling blocks and mistakes.

For much academic and business writing, the needs and expectations of readers are specifically prescribed; thus Chapters 48–52 and 55 discuss the special concerns of writing in various disciplines and in business. But even in these areas, you must make many choices based on audience. In other areas where the conventions of structure and presentation are vaguer, the choices are even more numerous. The box below contains questions that can help you define and make these choices.

Questions about audience

- Who *are* my readers?
- Why are readers going to read my writing? What will they expect?
- What do I want readers to know or do after reading my work, and how should I make that clear to them?
- What characteristic(s) of readers are relevant for my topic and purpose? For instance:

  Age or sex
  Occupation: students, professional colleagues, etc.
  Social or economic role: adult children, car buyers, potential employers, etc.
  Economic or educational background
  Ethnic background
  Political, religious, or moral beliefs and values
  Hobbies or activities

- How will the characteristic(s) of readers influence their attitudes toward my topic?
- What do readers already know and *not* know about my topic? How much do I have to tell them?
- If my topic involves specialized language, how much should I use and define?
- What ideas, arguments, or information might surprise readers? excite them? offend them? How should I handle these points?
- What misconceptions might readers have of my topic and/or my approach to the topic? How can I dispel these misconceptions?
- What is my relationship to my readers? How formal or informal will they expect me to be? What role and tone should I assume?
- What will readers do with my writing? Should I expect them to read every word from the top, to scan for information, to look for conclusions? Can I help with a summary, headings, or other aids? (See pp. 201–22 on document design.)

You can download the questions about audience from this book's Web site: *http://www.awlonline.com/littlebrown*. Store them in a file of their own, and duplicate the file for each writing project. Insert appropriate answers for that project between the questions, and print a copy for reference while you develop your paper.

2 Pitching your writing to your audience

Your sense of your audience will influence three key elements of what you write:

- The specific information you use to gain and keep the attention of readers and to guide them to accept your conclusions. This information may consist of concrete details, facts, examples, or any other evidence that makes your ideas clear, supports your assertions, and suits your readers' background, biases, and special interests.
- The role you choose to play in relation to your readers. Depending on your purpose and your attitude toward your topic, you will want readers to perceive you and your attitude in a certain way. The possible roles are many and varied—for instance, portrait painter, storyteller, lecturer, guide, reporter, advocate, inspirer.
- The tone you use. **Tone** in writing is like tone of voice in speaking: words and sentence structures on the page convey some of the same information as pitch and volume in the voice. Depending on your writing situation and what you think your readers will expect and respond to, your tone may be formal or informal. The attitude you convey may be serious or light, forceful or calm, irritated or cheerful.

Addressing a specific audience

Even when you're writing on the same topic, your information, role, and tone may change substantially for different audiences. Both memos below were written by a student who worked part-time in a small company and wanted to get the company to conserve paper. But the two memos address different readers.

To coworkers

Ever notice how much paper collects in your trash basket every day? Well, most of it can be recycled with little effort, I promise. Basically, all you need to do is set a bag or box near your desk and deposit wastepaper in it. I know, space is cramped in these little cubicles. But what's a little more crowding when the earth's at stake? . . .

Information: how employees could handle recycling; no mention of costs

Role: cheerful, equally harried colleague

Tone: informal, personal (*Ever notice; you; what's; Well; I know, space is cramped*)

To management

In my four months here, I have observed that all of us throw out baskets of potentially recyclable paper every day. Considering the drain on our forest resources and the pressure on landfills that paper causes, we could make a valuable contribution to the environmental movement by helping to recycle the paper we use. At the company where I worked before, employees separate clean wastepaper from other trash at their desks. The maintenance staff collects trash in two receptacles, and the trash hauler (the same one we use here) makes separate pickups. I do not know what the hauler charges for handling recyclable material. . . .

Information: specific reasons; view of company as a whole; reference to another company; problem of cost

Role: serious, thoughtful, responsible employee

Tone: formal, serious (*Considering the drain; forest resources; valuable contribution;* no *you* or contractions)

Typically for business reports and memos, the information grows more specific and the tone more formal as the rank and number of readers rise.

If you are writing online—for instance, to an Internet newsgroup or over a network linking the students in a course—you may not know enough about your audience to pitch your writing to particular expectations and needs. Consider, then, providing more information than you otherwise might, assuming the role of an equal (perhaps a colleague), and using a level tone (neither very formal nor very informal, neither hostile nor chummy). When unknown readers respond to your writing, keep in mind that they may represent very diverse backgrounds and interests. If you have written conscientiously and yet find some readers' reactions unexpectedly silly or disagreeable, you should feel free to ignore them. (See pp. 192–97 for more on online communication.)

Writing academic papers

Much of your college writing will have only one reader besides you: the instructor of the course you are writing for. Whether this person knows you well or not, he or she will take a certain approach to your work. In a composition course your instructor is likely to read your work as a representative of a general audience and respond to it in the additional role of helpful critic (see p. 66). That means you should not assume specialized interest in or knowledge of your topic, nor should you expect the patience of a doting parent who fills in what his or her child can't (or won't) express. If something about your topic would need to be said to a classmate or a reader of your local newspaper, say it clearly and carefully.

In academic courses such as literature, psychology, management, and chemistry, your writing will be addressed to a specialized audience of practitioners of the discipline, represented by your instructor. If you are writing a paper on the economic background of the War of 1812 for an American history course, you may assume your instructor's familiarity with the key events, players, and published interpretations. Your job is to show your own command of them and their relevance to your topic while assuming an appropriate academic role and tone.

- Present yourself as a serious and competent student of the subject in which you are writing.
- Demonstrate that you have at least a basic understanding of the discipline's research methods, vocabulary, and principles.
- Be specific.
- Write clearly and concisely.
- Avoid undue informality.

These requirements allow considerable room for your own voice, as these two passages on the same topic prove:

> One technique for heightening the emotional appeal of advertisements is "color engineering." Adding color to a product or the surrounding advertisement can increase sales despite the fact that the color serves no practical purpose. For example, until the 1920s fountain pens were made of hard black rubber. When colorful pens were suddenly introduced, sales rose dramatically.
>
> "Color engineering" can intensify the emotional appeal of advertisements. New color in a product or the surrounding ad can boost sales even when the color serves no other use. In the 1920s, for example, fountain pens that had been hard black rubber suddenly became colorful, and sales shot up.

As you gain experience with academic writing, you will develop the flexibility to write in your voice while also respecting the conventions of the various disciplines.

EXERCISE 6
Considering audience

Choose one of the following topics, and, for each audience specified, ask the questions on page 11. Decide on four points you would make, the role you would assume, and the tone you would adopt for each audience. Then write a paragraph for each based on your decisions.

1. The effects of smoking: for elementary school students and for adult smokers
2. Your opinion of welfare: for someone who is on welfare and for someone who is not and who opposes it
3. Why your neighbors should remove the wrecked truck from their front yard: for your neighbors and for your town zoning board

EXERCISE 7
Considering your past work: Writing for a specific audience

How did audience figure in a piece of writing you've done in the recent past—perhaps an essay for an application or a paper for a course? Who were your readers? How did your awareness of them influence your choice of information, your role, and your tone? At what point in the writing process did you find it most productive to consider your readers consciously?

EXERCISE 8
Collaborating on audience

Either online or face to face, discuss with at least one classmate your experience of how writing for an academic audience differs from other writing situations. What do academic readers expect for subject matter, research, tone, document design, and other elements of writing that, say, readers of personal letters or magazines do not? Bring into the discussion specific examples of academic writing you've done.

EXERCISE 9
Analyzing the audience for your essay

Use the questions on page 11 to determine as much as you can about the probable readers of your essay-in-progress (see Exercise 5). What does your analysis reveal about the specific information your readers need? What role do you want to assume, and what tone will best convey your attitude toward your topic?

1e Defining a purpose

When you write, your **purpose** is your chief reason for communicating something about a topic to a particular audience. Purpose thus links both the specific situation in which you are working and the goal you hope to achieve.

1 Defining a general purpose

Your purpose may fall into one of four general categories: entertainment, self-expression, explanation, or persuasion. These purposes may overlap in a single piece of writing, but usually one predominates. And the dominant purpose will influence your particular slant on your topic, the supporting details you choose, even the words you use.

http://webster.commnet.edu/HP/pages/darling/grammar/composition/purpose.html-ssi How purpose influences writing, from the Guide to Grammar and Writing.

The general purposes for writing

- To entertain readers
- To express your feelings or ideas
- To explain something to readers (exposition)
- To persuade readers to accept or act on your opinion (argument)

In most college or business writing, by far the most common purposes are explanation and persuasion:

- Writing that is mainly explanatory is often called **exposition** (from a Latin word meaning "to explain or set forth"). Using examples, facts, and other evidence, you present an idea about your subject so that readers understand it as you do. Almost any topic is suitable for exposition: how to pitch a knuckleball, why you want to major in business, the implications of a new discovery in computer science, the interpretation of a short story, the causes of an economic slump. Exposition is the kind of writing encountered most often in newspapers, magazines, and textbooks.
- Writing that is primarily persuasive is often called **argument.** Using examples, facts, and other evidence, you support your position on a debatable topic so that readers will at least consider your view and perhaps agree with it or act on it. A newspaper editorial favoring city council reform, a business proposal for a new personnel policy, a student paper recommending more required courses or defending a theory about human psychological development—all these are arguments. (Chapters 6 and 7 discuss argument in some detail and provide illustrative essays.)

2 Defining a specific purpose

Purpose can be conceived more specifically, too, in a way that incorporates your particular topic and the outcome you intend:

To explain how to pitch a knuckleball so that readers can do it themselves

To explain how Annie Dillard's "Total Eclipse" builds to its climax so that readers appreciate the author's skill

To explain why the county has been unable to attract new businesses so that readers better understand the local economic slump

To persuade readers to support the college administration's plan for more required courses

To argue against additional regulation of health-maintenance organizations so that readers will perceive the disadvantages for themselves

To argue for additional gun-control laws so that readers will agree on their necessity

Often, a writing assignment will specify or imply both a general and a specific purpose. For instance, when assigned a report on a physics experiment you've conducted, you know the purpose is to explain the experiment so that your readers can evaluate it. When assigned an editorial presenting a case for or against expanding your school's health facilities, you know the purpose is to persuade readers to support or resist the expansion.

If the assignment leaves purpose up to you, then try to define it soon after you have your topic, to give yourself some direction. Don't despair if you aren't successful, though. Sometimes you may not discover your purpose until you begin drafting, or you may find that your initial sense of purpose changes as you move through the writing process.

EXERCISE 10
Finding purpose in assignments

For each of your narrowed topics in Exercise 3 (p. 9), suggest a likely general purpose (entertainment, self-expression, explanation, persuasion) and try to define a specific purpose as well. Make audience part of your suggestions: what would you want readers to do or think in each case?

EXERCISE 11
Considering your past work: Defining a purpose

Look over two or three things you've written in the past year or so. What was your specific purpose in each one? How did the purpose influence your writing? Did you achieve your purpose?

EXERCISE 12
Collaborating on purposes

Either online or face to face, discuss with at least one classmate the purposes for writing. Each participant should give two or three varied examples of general and specific purposes. How would each example influence the choices made by the writer? What challenges might each present?

EXERCISE 13
Defining a purpose for your essay

For your essay-in-progress, use your thinking so far about topic (Exercise 5, p. 10) and audience (Exercise 9, p. 15) to define a general and specific purpose for your writing.

CHAPTER 2

Developing and Shaping Your Ideas

Once you have assessed your writing situation, or even while you're assessing it, you'll begin generating the ideas and information that will help you achieve your purpose. At some point, too, you'll begin bringing order to your thoughts, focusing and organizing them so that readers respond as you intend.

2a Discovering ideas

For some writing projects, you may have little difficulty finding what you have to say about your topic: ideas will tumble forth on paper or screen. But when you're stuck for what to say, you'll have to coax ideas out. Instead of waiting around for inspiration to strike, use a tcchniquc for generating ideas. Anything that gets your mind working is appropriate: if you like to make drawings or take pictures, for instance, then try that.

The following pages describe some strategies for discovering ideas. These strategies are to be selected from, not followed in sequence: some may help you during early stages of the writing process, even before you're sure of your topic; others may help you later on; and one or two may not help at all. Experiment to discover which strategies work best for you.

Note *Whatever strategy or strategies you use, do your work in writing, not just in your head.* Your work will be retrievable, and the act of writing will help you concentrate and lead you to fresh, sometimes surprising, insights. If you participate in online collaboration to develop topics, your activities will probably be stored electronically so that you can review and use the work. Ask your instructor if

http://webware.princeton.edu/Writing/wc4b.htm Exploring ideas, from Princeton University.

http://www.powa.org/whtfrms.htm Discovery techniques, from the Paradigm Online Writing Assistant.

Techniques for developing a topic

- Keep a journal (below).
- Observe your surroundings (p. 21).
- Freewrite (p. 22).
- Make a list or brainstorm (p. 24).
- Cluster (p. 25).
- Ask the journalist's questions (p. 26).
- Use the patterns of development (p. 26).
- Read (p. 28).
- Think critically (p. 28).

you are unsure of how to reach the online files. (For more on collaborating online, see pp. 243–52.)

ESL The discovery process encouraged here rewards rapid writing without a lot of thinking beforehand about what you will write or how. Some ESL writers find it helpful initially to do this exploratory writing in their native language and then to translate the worthwhile material for use in their drafts. However, this practice does require the extra work of translating not only sentences but thought patterns, and it merely postpones the need to think and create in English.

1 Keeping a journal

A place to record thoughts and observations, a **journal** can be a good source of ideas for writing. It is a kind of diary, but one more concerned with ideas than with day-to-day events. *Journal* comes from the Latin for "daily," and many journal keepers do write faithfully every day; others make entries less regularly, when the mood strikes or an insight occurs or they have a problem to work out.

Advantages of a journal

Writing in a journal, you are writing to yourself. That means you don't have to worry about main ideas, organization, correct grammar and spelling, or any of the other requirements of public writing. You can work out your ideas and feelings without the pressure of an audience "out there" who will evaluate your thinking and

http://207.158.243.119/html/journals___diaries.html Information and resources on journal keeping, from the Journals and Diaries Web site. (In the address, type three underscores between *journals* and *diaries.*)

expression. The freedom and flexibility of a journal can be liberating. Like many others, you may find writing easier, more fun, and more rewarding than you thought possible.

You can keep a journal either on paper (such as a notebook) or on a computer. If you write in the journal every day, or almost, even just for a few minutes, the routine will loosen up your writing muscles and improve your confidence. Indeed, journal keepers often become dependent on the process for the writing practice it gives them, the concentrated thought it encourages, and the connection it fosters between personal, private experience and public information and events.

Usually for the same reasons, teachers of writing and other subjects sometimes require students to keep journals. The teachers may even collect students' journals to monitor progress, but they read the journals with an understanding of purpose (in other words, they do not evaluate work that was not written to be evaluated), and they usually just credit rather than grade the work.

ESL A journal can be especially helpful if you're writing in English as a second language. You can practice writing to improve your fluency, try out sentence patterns, and experiment with vocabulary words. Equally important, you can experiment with applying what you know from experience to what you read and observe.

Uses of a journal

Two uses of a journal are discussed elsewhere in this book: a reading journal, in which you think critically (in writing) about what you read (pp. 121, 791); and a research journal, in which you record your activities and ideas while you pursue a research project (pp. 619–20). But you can use a journal for other purposes as well. Here are just a few:

- Confide your hopes.
- Write about your own history: an event in your family's past, a troubling incident in your life, a change you've seen.
- Analyze a relationship that disturbs you.
- Explore your reactions to current events, movies, television, music, or Web sites.
- Prepare for or respond to a course you're taking by puzzling over a reading or a class discussion.
- Build ideas for specific writing assignments.
- Sketch possible designs for a Web composition you are developing, or track the progress of the site's development.
- Practice various forms or styles of writing—for instance, poems or songs, reviews of movies, or reports for TV news.

The writing you produce in your journal will help you learn and grow, and even the personal and seemingly nonacademic entries

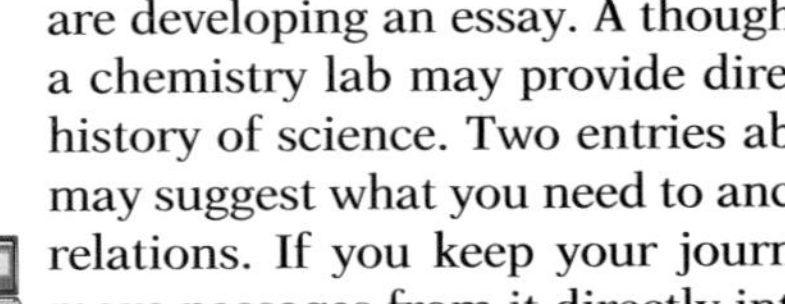

can supply ideas when you are seeking a subject to write about or are developing an essay. A thought you recorded months ago about a chemistry lab may provide direction for a research paper on the history of science. Two entries about arguments with your brother may suggest what you need to anchor a psychology paper on sibling relations.  If you keep your journal on a computer, you can even move passages from it directly into your drafts. (See pp. 184–85 for information on moving text.)

The following student samples give a taste of journal writing for different purposes. In the first, Charlie Gabnes tries to work out a personal problem with his child:

> Will's tantrums are getting worse—more often, more intense. Beginning to realize it's affecting my feelings for him. I feel resentment sometimes, and it's not as easy for me to cool off afterward as for him. Also I'm afraid of him sometimes for fear a tantrum will start, so treat him with kid gloves. How do we break this cycle?

In the next example Megan Polanyis ponders something she learned from her biology textbook:

> *Ecology* and *economics* have the same root—Greek word for house. Economy = management of the house. Ecology = study of the house. In ecology the house is all of nature, ourselves, the other animals, the plants, the earth, the air, the whole environment. Ecology has a lot to do with economy: study the house in order to manage it.

In the next example Sara Ling responds to an experience. (We'll follow Ling's writing process in this chapter and the next.)

> Had an exchange today with a man who just joined the snowboarding forum—only he turns out to be a woman! She says she's been afraid to write to the forum as a woman because the guys there might shout her down. (When she figured out I was a woman, she decided to fess up to me.) She asked about my experiences. Had to admit I'd had problems of the what-does-a-girl-know sort—advised her to keep her gender a secret to see what happens. Wish I'd thought of it myself. Maybe I'll start over with a new screen name.

2 Observing your surroundings

Sometimes you can find a good subject or good ideas by looking around you, not in the half-conscious way most of us move from place to place in our daily lives but deliberately, all senses alert. On a bus, for instance, are there certain types of passengers? What seems to be on the driver's mind? On campus, which buildings stand out? Are bicyclists and pedestrians at peace with each other?

To get the most from observation, you should have a tablet and pen or pencil handy for notes and sketches. If you have a camera, you may find that the lens sees things your unaided eyes do not notice. (When observing or photographing people, though, keep some distance, take photographs quickly, and avoid staring. Otherwise, your subjects will feel uneasy.) Back at your desk, study your notes, sketches, or photographs for oddities or patterns that you'd like to explore further.

3 Freewriting

Writing into a subject

Many writers find subjects or discover ideas by **freewriting:** writing without stopping for a certain amount of time (say, ten minutes) or to a certain length (say, one page). The goal of freewriting is to generate ideas and information from *within* yourself by going around the part of your mind that doesn't want to write or can't think of anything to write. You let words themselves suggest other words. *What* you write is not important; that you *keep* writing is. Don't stop, even if that means repeating the same words until new words come. Don't go back to reread, don't censor ideas that seem dumb or repetitious, and above all don't stop to edit: grammar, punctuation, spelling, and the like are irrelevant at this stage.

The physical act of freewriting may give you access to ideas you were unaware of. For example, the following freewriting by a student, Robert Benday, gave him the subject of writing as a disguise:

> Write to write. Seems pretty obvious, also weird. What to gain by writing? never anything before. Writing seems always—always—Getting corrected for trying too hard to please the teacher, getting corrected for not trying hard enuf. Frustration, nail biting, sometimes getting carried away making sentences to tell stories, not even true stories, *esp.* not true stories, *that* feels like creating something. Writing just pulls the story out of me. The story lets me be someone else, gives me a disguise.

(A later phase of Benday's writing appears on p. 25.)

If you write on a computer, you can ensure that your freewriting keeps moving forward by turning off your computer's monitor or turning its brightness control all the way down so that the screen is dark. The computer will record what you type but keep it from you and thus prevent you from tinkering with your prose. This **invisible writing** may feel uncomfortable at first, but it can free the mind for very creative results. When you've finished freewriting, simply turn the monitor on or turn up the brightness control to read what you've written, and then save or revise it as appropriate. Later, you may be able to transfer some of your freewriting into your draft.

ESL Invisible writing can be especially helpful if English is not your first language and you tend to worry about errors while writing: the blank computer screen leaves you no choice but to explore ideas without regard for their expression. If you choose to write with the monitor on, concentrate on *what* you want to say, not *how* you're saying it.

Focused freewriting

Focused freewriting is more concentrated: you start with your topic and write about it without stopping for, say, fifteen minutes or one full page. As in all freewriting, you push to bypass mental blocks and self-consciousness, not debating what to say or editing what you've written. With focused freewriting, though, you let the physical act of writing take you into and around your subject.

An example of focused freewriting can be found in the work of Sara Ling, whose journal entry appears on page 21. In a composition course, Ling's instructor had distributed "Welcome to Cyberbia," an essay by M. Kadi about communication on the Internet. The instructor then gave the following assignment:

> M. Kadi's "Welcome to Cyberbia" holds that the Internet will do little to bridge differences among people because its users gravitate toward other users who are like themselves in most respects. In an essay of 500–700 words, respond to Kadi's essay with a limited and well-supported opinion of your own: Can the Internet serve as a medium for positive change in the way people of diverse backgrounds relate to each other? If so, how? If not, why not? The first draft is due Monday, April 4, for class discussion.

On first reading Kadi's essay, Ling had been impressed with its tight logic but had found unconvincing its pessimistic view of the Internet's potential. She reread the essay and realized that some of Kadi's assertions did not correspond to her own Internet experiences. This discovery prompted the following focused freewriting:

> Kadi says we only meet people like ourselves on the Internet, but I've met lots with very different backgrounds and interests. Actually, "turned out to have" is more like it, since I didn't know anything about them at first. There's the anonymity thing, but Kadi ignores it. You can be anyone or no one. I can pose as a man if I want (probably should have, to avoid rejection on the snowboarding forum). No one has to know I'm female or Asian American or a student. We're not stuck in our identities. Not hampered by them in expressing our views and getting those views accepted. Communication without set identity, especially physical appearance. This could make for more tolerance of others, of difference.

With this freewriting, Ling moved beyond her initial response to Kadi's essay into her own views of how anonymity on the Internet could improve communication among diverse groups.

4 Making a list

Like focused freewriting, list making requires opening yourself to everything that seems even remotely connected to your topic, without concern for order or repetition or form of expression. You can let your topic percolate for a day or more, recording thoughts on it whenever they occur. (For this approach to work, you need to keep paper or a computer with you at all times.) Or, in a method more akin to freewriting, you can **brainstorm** about the topic—that is, focus intently on the topic for a fixed amount of time (say, fifteen minutes), pushing yourself to list every idea and detail that comes to mind.

Like freewriting, brainstorming requires turning off your internal editor so that you keep moving ahead instead of looping back over what you have already written to correct it. It makes no difference whether the ideas and details are expressed in phrases or complete sentences. It makes no difference if they seem silly or irrelevant. Just keep pushing.

If you are working on a computer, the technique of invisible writing, described on page 22, can help you move forward. So can turning off any bulleting, numbering, or outlining function your word processor may have. (See p. 186 for more on these functions.)

Here is an example of brainstorming by a student, Johanna Abrams, on what a summer job can teach:

summer work teaches—

how to look busy while doing nothing
how to avoid the sun in summer
seriously: discipline, budgeting money, value of money

which job? Burger King cashier? baby sitter? mail-room clerk?
mail room: how to sort mail into boxes: this is learning??
how to survive getting fired—humiliation, outrage
Mrs. King! the mail-room queen as learning experience
the shock of getting fired: what to tell parents, friends?
Mrs. K was so rigid—dumb procedures
Mrs. K's anger, resentment: the disadvantages of being smarter than your boss
The odd thing about working in an office: a world with its own rules for how to act
what Mr. D said about the pecking order—big chick (Mrs. K) pecks on little chick (me)
probably lots of Mrs. Ks in offices all over—offices are all barnyards
Mrs. K a sad person, really—just trying to hold on to her job, preserve her self-esteem
a job can beat you down—destroy self-esteem, make you desperate enough to be mean to other people

how to preserve/gain self-esteem from work??
if I'd known about the pecking order, I would have been less show-offy, not so arrogant

(A later phase of Abrams's writing appears on pp. 38–39.)

When you think you've exhausted the ideas on your topic, edit and shape the list into a preliminary outline of your paper (see pp. 35–38). Working on a computer makes this step fairly easy: you can delete weak ideas, expand strong ones, and rearrange items with a few keystrokes. You can also freewrite from the list if you think some items are especially promising and deserve more thought.

5 Clustering

Like freewriting and list making, **clustering** draws on free association and rapid, unedited work. But it also emphasizes the *relations* between ideas by combining writing and nonlinear drawing. When clustering, you radiate outward from a center point—your topic. When an idea occurs, you pursue related ideas in a branching structure until they seem exhausted. Then you do the same with other ideas, staying open to connections, continuously branching out or drawing arrows.

The example of clustering below shows how Robert Benday used the technique for ten minutes to expand on the topic of creative writing as a means of disguise, an idea he arrived at through freewriting (see p. 22). Though he ventured into one dead end, Benday also circled into the interesting possibility (at the bottom) that the fiction writer is like a god who forgives himself by creating characters that represent his good and bad qualities.

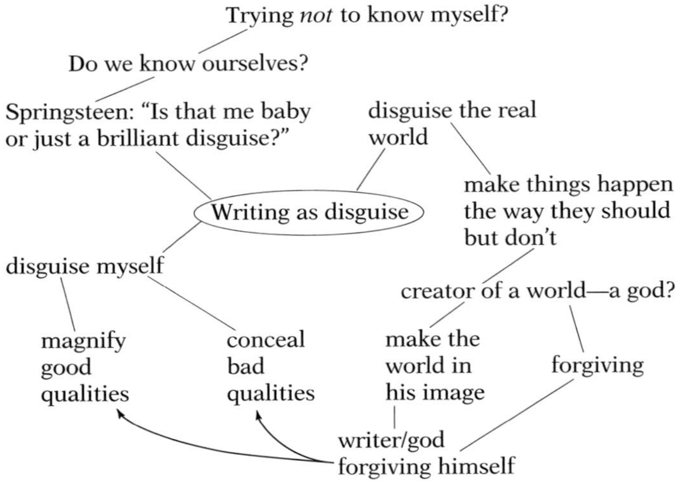

6 Using the journalist's questions

Asking yourself a set of questions about your topic—and writing out the answers—can help you look at the topic objectively and see fresh possibilities in it. Asking questions can also provide some structure to the development of ideas.

One such set of questions is that posed by a journalist with a story to report:

Who was involved?
What happened and what were the results?
When did it happen?
Where did it happen?
Why did it happen?
How did it happen?

These questions can also be useful in probing an essay topic, especially if you are telling a story or examining causes and effects. (See also the next section.)

You can download the journalist's questions from this book's Web site: *http://www.awlonline.com/littlebrown.* Save the list in a file of its own, duplicate it for each writing project, and insert appropriate answers between the questions. Print your answers so they're handy while you develop your paper. You can also move passages from the answers directly into your draft. (See pp. 184–85 for more on word processing.)

7 Using the patterns of development

The **patterns of development**—such as narration, definition, comparison and contrast, and classification—are ways we think about and understand a vast range of subjects, from our own daily experiences to the most complex scientific theories. They also serve as strategies and patterns for writing about these subjects, as illustrated by the discussions and paragraph-length examples on pages 95–104.

To see your topic from many angles and open up ideas about it, you can ask the following questions based on the patterns of development. Not all these questions will be productive, but at least a few should open up new possibilities.

You can download the questions from this book's Web site: *http://www.awlonline.com/littlebrown.* Then use them for each writing project, as suggested above for the journalist's questions.

How did it happen?

In **narration** you develop the topic as a story, with important events usually arranged chronologically (as they occurred in time): for instance, an exciting basketball game or the steps leading to a war.

How does it look, sound, feel, smell, taste?

In **description** you use sensory details to give a clear impression of a person, place, thing, or feeling, such as a friend, a favorite room, a building, or an experience.

What are examples of it or reasons for it?

The pattern of **illustration** or **support** suggests development with one or more examples of the topic (one couple's efforts to adopt a child, say, or three television soap operas) or with the reasons for believing or doing something (three reasons for majoring in English, four reasons for driving defensively).

What is it? What does it encompass, and what does it exclude?

These questions lead to **definition:** specifying what the topic is and is not to give a precise sense of its meaning. Abstract terms—such as *justice, friendship,* and *art*—especially need defining. (See p. 145.)

What are its parts or characteristics?

Using the pattern of **division** or **analysis,** you separate a subject into its elements and examine the relations between elements. The first step in critical thinking, analysis is also discussed on page 129.

What groups or categories can it be sorted into?

Classification involves separating a large group (such as cars) into smaller groups (subcompact, compact, and so on) based on the characteristics of the individual items (the sizes of the cars). Another example: academic, business, personal, literary, and other types of writing.

How is it like, or different from, other things?

With **comparison and contrast** you point out the similarities and differences between ideas, objects, people, places, and so on: the differences between two similar computer systems, for instance, or the similarities between two opposing political candidates.

Is it comparable to something that is in a different class but more familiar to readers?

This question leads to **analogy,** an extended comparison of unlike subjects. Analogy is often used to explain a topic that may be unfamiliar to readers (for instance, the structure of a government) by reference to a familiar topic (the structure of a family).

Why did it happen, or what results did it have?

With **cause-and-effect analysis,** you explain why something happened or what its consequences were or will be, or both: the causes of cerebral palsy, the effects of a Supreme Court decision, the causes and effects of a gradual change in the climate.

How do you do it, or how does it work?

In **process analysis** you explain how the topic is accomplished (how to write an essay) or how it happens (how a plant grows, how a robot works).

As you can see on pages 95–104, the patterns of development also provide a means of introducing information in paragraphs. Further discussion of how the patterns may combine in an essay appears on pages 113–15.

8 Reading

Many assignments require reading. To respond to M. Kadi's essay about the Internet, for instance, Sara Ling had to digest Kadi's work. Essays on literary works as well as research papers also demand reading. But even when reading is not required by an assignment, it can help you locate or develop your topic by introducing you to ideas you didn't know or expanding on what you do know.

Say you were writing in favor of amateur athletics, a subject to which you had given a lot of thought. You might be inclined to proceed entirely on your own, drawing on facts, examples, and opinions already in your head. But a little digging in sources might open up more. For instance, an article in *Time* magazine could introduce you to an old rule for amateur status, or a posting to an online newsgroup could suggest a pro-amateurism argument that hadn't occurred to you. (See pp. 633–65 for techniques of library and computer research that you can use to locate sources on a topic.)

People often read passively, absorbing content like blotters, not interacting with it. To read for ideas, you need to be more active, probing text and illustrations with your mind, nurturing any sparks they set off. Always write while you read so that you can keep notes on content and—just as important—on what the content makes you *think*. (See pp. 119–36 for specific guidelines on the process of active reading.)

Note Whenever you use the information or ideas of others in your writing, you must acknowledge your sources in order to avoid the serious offense of plagiarism. (See p. 686.)

9 Thinking critically

Even if you do not read for information and ideas on your topic, you can still think critically about it. Critical thinking (discussed on pp. 118–36) can produce creative ideas by leading you to see what is not obvious. It can also lead you systematically to conclusions about your topic.

Sara Ling, writing about communication on the Internet, used the operations of critical thinking to explore her topic:

- **Analysis:** What are the subject's elements or characteristics? Ling looked at the ways Internet users can communicate because of their anonymity.
- **Interpretation:** What is the meaning or significance of the elements? Ling saw that the anonymity of Internet users could help them transcend their physical differences.
- **Synthesis:** How do the elements relate to each other, or how does this subject relate to another one? Ling perceived important and hopeful differences between anonymous Internet communication and face-to-face interaction.
- **Evaluation:** What is the value or significance of the subject? Ling concluded that by making people more tolerant of one another, the Internet could help build community out of diversity.

EXERCISE 1
Considering your past work: Developing a topic

In the past how have you generated the ideas for writing? Have you used any of the techniques described on the preceding pages (perhaps not called by the same names)? Have you found the process of generating ideas to be especially enjoyable or difficult? If some writing tasks have been easier than others, what do you think made the difference?

EXERCISE 2
Keeping a journal

If you haven't already started a journal on your own or in response to Chapter 1, Exercise 1 (p. 3), try to do so now. Every day for at least a week, write for at least fifteen minutes about whatever comes into your mind—or consult the list on page 20 for ideas of what to write about. At the end of the week, review and write about your experience and your journal entries. What did you like about journal writing? What didn't you like? What did you learn about yourself or the world from the writing? What use can you put this knowledge to?

EXERCISE 3
Using freewriting, brainstorming, or clustering

If you haven't tried any of them before, experiment with freewriting (p. 22), brainstorming (p. 24), or clustering (p. 25). Continue with the topic you selected in Chapter 1, Exercise 5 (p. 10), or begin with a new topic. Write or draw for at least ten minutes without stopping to reread and edit. (Try using invisible writing as described on p. 22 if you're freewriting or brainstorming on a computer.) When you finish your experiment, examine what you have written for ideas and relationships that could help you develop the topic. What do you think of the technique you tried? Did you have any difficulties with it? Did it help you loosen up and generate ideas?

EXERCISE 4
Sending an online query
When you have spent some time developing your topic, consider any doubts you may have or any information you still need. Send an online message to your classmates posing your questions and asking for their advice and insights.

EXERCISE 5
Developing your topic
Use at least two of the discovery techniques discussed on the preceding pages to develop the topic you selected in Chapter 1, Exercise 5 (p. 10). (If you completed Exercise 3, then use one additional technique.) Later exercises for your essay-in-progress will be based on the ideas you generate in this exercise.

2b Developing a thesis

Your readers will expect an essay you write to be focused on a central idea, or **thesis,** to which all the essay's paragraphs, all its general statements and specific information, relate. The thesis is the controlling idea, the main point, the conclusion you have drawn about the evidence you have accumulated. Even if you create a composition on the World Wide Web, you'll have a core idea that governs the links among pages and sites.

The thesis will probably not leap fully formed into your head. You may begin with an idea you want to communicate, but you will need to refine that idea to fit the realities of the paper you write. And often you will have to write and rewrite before you come to a conclusion about what you have. Still, it's wise to try to pin down your thesis when you have a fairly good stock of ideas. Then the thesis can help you start drafting, help keep you focused, and serve as a point of reference when changes inevitably occur.

1 Conceiving your thesis statement

A good way to develop your thesis is to frame it in a **thesis statement.** The thesis statement gives you a vehicle for expressing your thesis at an early stage, and eventually it or (more likely) a revised version may be placed in the introduction of your final essay as a promise to readers of what they can expect.

As an expression of the thesis, the thesis statement serves three crucial functions and one optional one:

Functions of the thesis statement

- It narrows your subject to a single, central idea that you want readers to gain from your essay.
- It names the topic and asserts something specific and significant about it.
- It conveys your reason for writing, your purpose.
- It often provides a concise preview of how you will arrange your ideas in the essay.

Here are some examples of subjects and corresponding thesis statements (with each statement's topic and assertion highlighted in brackets):

Subject	Thesis statement
1. The pecking order in an office	Two months working in a large government agency taught me that an office's pecking order should be respected. [*Topic:* office's pecking order. *Assertion:* should be respected.]
2. The direct distribution of music to consumers via the World Wide Web	Because artists can now publish their music directly via the Web, consumers have many more choices than traditional distribution allows. [*Topic:* consumers. *Assertion:* have many more choices.]
3. What public relations does	Although most of us are unaware of the public relations campaigns directed at us, they can significantly affect the way we think and live. [*Topic:* public relations campaigns. *Assertion:* affect the way we think and live.]
4. Preventing juvenile crime	Juveniles can be diverted from crime by active learning programs, full-time sports, and intervention by mentors and role models. [*Topic:* juveniles. *Assertion:* can be diverted from crime in three ways.]

Guidance on writing and revising thesis statements:

http://webster.commnet.edu/HP/pages/darling/grammar/composition/thesis.htm From the Guide to Grammar and Writing.

http://www.english.uiuc.edu/cws/wworkshop/tips/thesisstmt.htm From the University of Illinois, Urbana-Champaign.

Subject	Thesis statement
5. Abraham Lincoln's delay in emancipating the slaves	Lincoln delayed emancipating any slaves until 1863 because his primary goal was to restore and preserve the Union, with or without slavery. [*Topic:* Lincoln's delay. *Assertion:* was caused by his goal of preserving the Union.]
6. Federal aid to college students	To compete well in the global economy, the United States must make higher education affordable for any student who qualifies academically. [*Topic:* United States. *Assertion:* must make higher education affordable.]
7. The effects of strip-mining	Strip-mining should be tightly controlled in this region to reduce its pollution of water resources, its destruction of the land, and its devastating effects on people's lives. [*Topic:* strip-mining. *Assertion:* should be tightly controlled for three reasons.]

Notice that statements 4 and 7 clearly predict the organization of the essay that will follow. Notice, too, that every statement conveys the purpose of its writer. Statements 1–5 announce that the writers mainly want to explain something to readers: office pecking order, more music choices for consumers, public relations, and so on. Statements 6 and 7 announce that the authors mainly want to convince readers of something: the federal government should aid college students; strip-mining should be controlled.

ESL In some cultures it is considered rude or unnecessary for a writer to state his or her main idea outright or to state it near the beginning. But readers of English usually expect a clear and early sense of what a writer has to say.

2 Drafting and revising your thesis statement

To draft a thesis statement, ask these questions:

- What conclusion can I draw from the work I have done so far?
- How can I express that idea by naming the topic and making an assertion about it?
- How can I convey my purpose in that assertion?

To answer these questions, you may need to write one or more drafts of your essay. And you may need multiple drafts of the thesis statement itself.

Sara Ling went through a common procedure in writing and revising her thesis statement on Internet communication. In her first try she stated her topic and commented on it:

> Interaction on the Internet differs from face-to-face interaction.

This statement focused on Ling's topic but did not specify the difference between the forms of interaction or the significance of the difference. Nor did it convey Ling's purpose in writing. Realizing as much, Ling rewrote the statement:

> The unique anonymity of the Internet allows new forms of communication, and it could build diversity into community.

This statement solved some of the problems of the previous version: Ling identified the unique feature of the Internet (its *anonymity*), asserted its significance (*it could help build diversity into community*), and implied her purpose (to explain how the Internet could build community). But *new forms of communication* was still vague, so Ling spelled out her meaning:

> The unique anonymity of the Internet lowers the barriers of physical appearance in communication, and it could build diversity into community.

In her final revision, Ling unified the statement by pulling together the two parts separated by *and* into a single assertion:

> By lowering the barriers of physical appearance in communication, the Internet's uniquely anonymous form of interaction could build diversity into community.

When you are writing and revising your thesis statement, check it against the following questions:

Checklist for revising the thesis statement

- Does the statement make a concise *assertion* about your topic?
- Is the assertion *limited* to only one idea?
- Is the assertion *specific* and *significant?*
- Does the statement at least imply your *purpose?*
- Is the statement *unified* so that the parts relate to each other?

Here are other examples of thesis statements revised to meet these requirements:

Original	**Revised**
This new product brought in over $300,000 last year. [A statement of fact, not an assertion: what is significant about the product's success?]	This new product succeeded because of its innovative marketing campaign, including widespread press coverage, in-store entertainment, and a consumer newsletter.
People should not go on fad diets. [A vague statement that needs limiting with one or more reasons: what's wrong with fad diets?]	Fad diets can be dangerous when they deprive the body of essential nutrients or rely on excessive quantities of potentially harmful foods.

Original	**Revised**
Televised sports are different from live sports. [A general statement: how are they different, and why is the difference significant?]	Although television cannot transmit all the excitement of a live game, its close-ups and slow-motion replays more than compensate.
Seat belts can save lives, but now carmakers are installing air bags. [Not unified: how do the two parts of the sentence relate?]	If drivers had used lifesaving seat belts more often, carmakers might not have needed to install air bags.

Note You may sometimes need more than one sentence for your thesis statement, particularly if it requires some buildup:

> Modern English, especially written English, is full of bad habits that interfere with clear thinking. Getting rid of these habits is a first step to political regeneration.
>
> —Adapted from George Orwell, "Politics and the English Language"

However, don't use this leeway to produce a wordy, general, or disunified statement. The two (or more) sentences must build on each other, and the final one must present the key assertion of your paper.

EXERCISE 6
Evaluating thesis statements

Evaluate the following thesis statements, considering whether each one is sufficiently limited, specific, and unified. Rewrite the statements as necessary to meet these goals.

1. Aggression usually leads to violence, injury, and even death, and we should use it constructively.
2. Electronic mail is invaluable.
3. One evening of a radio talk show amply illustrates both the appeal of such shows and their silliness.
4. Good manners make our society work.
5. The poem is about motherhood.

EXERCISE 7
Collaborating on thesis statements

Either online or face to face, discuss the five thesis statements in Exercise 6 with at least one classmate: Which statements did you find satisfactory, and which not? Why? What does the discussion tell you about the qualities of an effective thesis statement? When you have developed the thesis statement for your own writing (Exercise 9, opposite), ask for the reactions of the same classmate(s). Is your statement significantly limited, specific, and unified? How could you improve it?

EXERCISE 8
Considering your past work: Developing a thesis

Have you been aware in the past of focusing your essays on a central idea, or thesis? Have you found it more efficient to try to pin down your idea early or to let it evolve during drafting? To what extent has a thesis helped or hindered you in shaping your draft?

EXERCISE 9
Drafting and revising your own thesis statement

Continuing from Exercise 5 (p. 30), write a limited, specific, and unified thesis statement for your essay-in-progress.

2c Organizing ideas

An effective essay has a recognizable shape—an arrangement of parts that guides readers, helping them see how ideas and details relate to each other and contribute to the whole. You may sometimes let an effective organization emerge over one or more drafts. But many writers find that organizing ideas to some extent before drafting can provide a helpful sense of direction, as a map can help a driver negotiate a half-familiar system of roads. If you feel uncertain about the course your essay should follow or have a complicated topic with many parts, devising a shape for your material can clarify your options.

Before you begin organizing your material, look over all the writing you've done so far—freewriting, notes from reading, lists, whatever. Either on paper or on a computer, pull together a master list of all the ideas and details you think you may want to include. Leave wide margins for additions that will occur to you as you think about shape.

1 Distinguishing the general and the specific

To organize material for an essay, you need to distinguish general and specific ideas and see the relations between ideas. **General** and **specific** refer to the number of instances or objects included in a group signified by a word. The "ladder" on the next page illustrates a general-to-specific hierarchy.

Resources for organizing papers:

http://www.powa.org/orgnfrms.htm From the Paradigm Online Writing Assistant.

http://wuacc.edu/services/zzcwwctr/orgdev_menu.html From Washburn University.

Most general

↑ life form
plant
flowering plant
rose
American Beauty rose
↓ Uncle Dan's prize-winning American Beauty rose

Most specific

Here are some tips for arranging your ideas:

- Underline, boldface, or circle the most general ideas. These are the ideas that offer the main support for your thesis statement. They will be more general than the evidence that in turn supports them.
- Make connections between each general idea and the more specific details that support it. On paper, start with a fresh sheet, write each general idea down with space beneath it, and add specific information in the appropriate spaces. On a computer, rearrange supporting information under more general points. Your word processor may include a Comment function that allows you to add notes about connections. It may also include an Outline function that can automatically indent and resequence information. Note, however, that some writers find the Outline function cumbersome to work with. (See pp. 190 and 189, respectively, for more on these functions.)
- As you sort ideas, respect their meanings. Otherwise, your hierarchies could become jumbled, with *rose* illogically subordinated to *animal,* or *life form* somehow subordinated to *rose.*
- Once you have sorted out general ideas and specific supporting information, delete information that has no place, or fill in holes where support is skimpy.
- Experiment with various arrangements of your general ideas and their supporting information, seeking an order that presents your material clearly and logically. On paper, you can cut the master list apart and paste or tape each general idea and its support on a separate piece of paper. Then try different orders for the pages. On a computer, first save the master list and duplicate it. To move material around, select a block of text and either copy and then paste it where you want it or (a little quicker) drag the selected text to where you want it. (See pp. 184–85 for more on these word-processor functions.)

2 Choosing an organizing tool

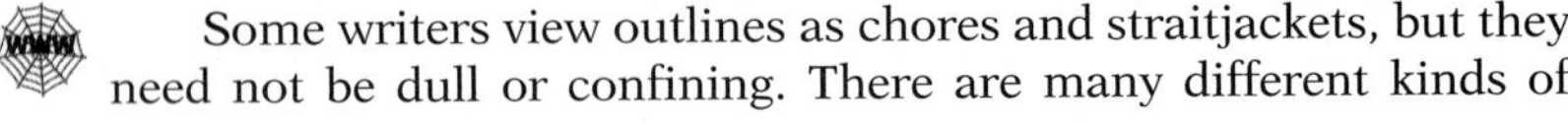

Some writers view outlines as chores and straitjackets, but they need not be dull or confining. There are many different kinds of outlines, some more flexible than others. All of them can enlarge and clarify your thinking, showing you patterns of general and specific, suggesting proportions, highlighting gaps or overlaps in coverage. If your word processor has an Outline function (see opposite), you may want to experiment to see whether it helps you construct an outline.

Many writers use outlines not only before but also after drafting—to check the underlying structure of the draft when revising it (see p. 54). No matter when it's made, though, an outline can change to reflect changes in your thinking. You should view any outline you make as a tentative sketch, not as a fixed paint-by-numbers diagram.

Using a scratch or informal outline

For many essays, especially those with a fairly straightforward structure, a simple listing of ideas and perhaps their support may provide adequate direction for your writing.

A **scratch outline** lists the key points of the paper in the order they will be covered. Here is Sara Ling's scratch outline for her essay on Internet communication:

Thesis statement

By lowering the barriers of physical appearance in communication, the Internet's uniquely anonymous form of interaction could build diversity into community.

Scratch outline

No fear of prejudgment
   Physical attributes unknown—age, race, gender, etc.
   We won't be shut out because of appearance
Inability to prejudge others
   Assumptions based on appearance
   Meeting of minds only
   Finding shared interests and concerns

Ling put more into this outline than its simplicity might imply. Besides working out an order for her ideas, she began sketching their implications. She might have begun drafting from this outline, but she opted to develop her ideas further in a detailed formal outline (see p. 39).

An **informal outline** is usually more detailed than a scratch outline, including key general points and the specific evidence for them. A student's informal outline appears on the next page.

http://owl.english.purdue.edu/Files/132/6-outline.html Using and creating outlines, from the Purdue Online Writing Lab.

Thesis statement

The main street of my neighborhood contains enough variety to make almost any city dweller feel at home.

Informal outline

The beginning of the street
  high-rise condominium occupied by well-to-do people
  ground floor of building: an art gallery
  across the street: a delicatessen
  above the delicatessen: a tailor's shop, a camera-repair shop, a lawyer's office
The middle of the street
  four-story brick apartment buildings on both sides
  at ground level: an Italian bakery and a Latino bodega
  people sitting on steps
  children playing
The end of the street
  a halfway house for drug addicts
  a boarding house for retired men
  a discount drugstore
  an expensive department store
  a wine shop
  another high-rise condominium

Using a tree diagram

In a **tree diagram** ideas and details branch out in increasing specificity. Like any outline, the diagram can warn of gaps, overlaps, and digressions. But unlike more linear outlines, it can be supplemented and extended indefinitely, so it is easy to alter for new ideas and arrangements that you may discover during drafting and revision.

Following is Johanna Abrams's tree diagram, based on her earlier list of ideas on a summer job (pp. 24–25). Each main part of the four-part diagram represents a different general idea about the summer-job experience. Within each part, information grows more specific as it branches downward.

Thesis statement

Two months working in a large government agency taught me that an office's pecking order should be respected.

Tree diagram

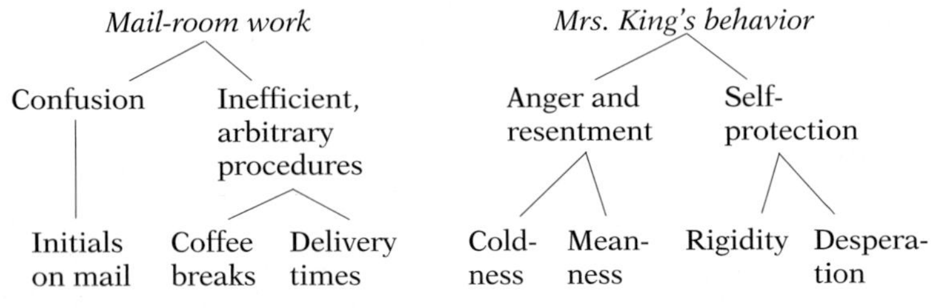

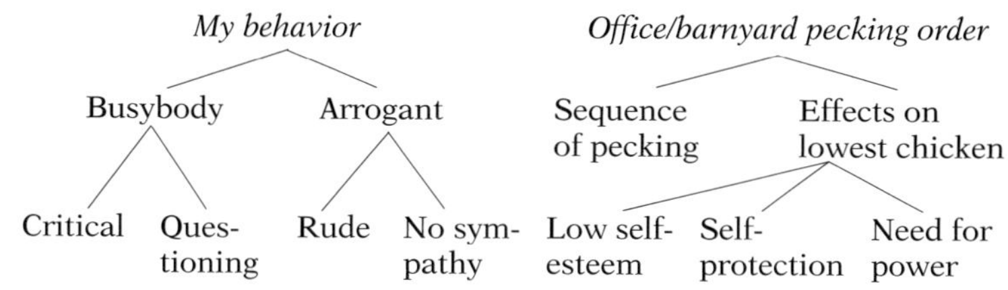

A tree diagram can be especially useful for planning a project for the World Wide Web. The diagram can help you lay out the organization of your project and its links and then later can serve as a site map for your readers. (For more on composing for the Web, see pp. 224–42.)

Using a formal outline

For complex topics requiring complex arrangements of ideas and support, you may want or be required to construct a **formal outline.** More rigidly arranged and more detailed than other outlines, a formal outline not only lays out main ideas and their support but also shows the relative importance of all the essay's elements and how they connect with one another.

Note Because of its structure, a formal outline can be an excellent tool for checking a draft before revising it. (See p. 54.)

On the basis of her scratch outline (p. 37), Sara Ling prepared this formal outline for her essay on the Internet:

Thesis statement

By lowering the barriers of physical appearance in communication, the Internet's uniquely anonymous form of interaction could build diversity into community.

Formal outline

I. No fear of being prejudged
  A. Unknown physical attributes
    1. Gender
    2. Age
    3. Race
    4. Style
  B. Freer communication
  C. No automatic rejection
II. Inability to prejudge others
  A. No assumptions based on appearance
    1. Body type
    2. Physical disability
    3. Race
  B. Discovery of shared interests and concerns
    1. Sports and other activities
    2. Family values
    3. Political views
  C. Reduction of physical bias

Ling's outline illustrates several principles of outlining that can help ensure completeness, balance, and clear relationships. (These principles largely depend on distinguishing between the general and the specific. See pp. 35–36.)

- All the outline's parts are systematically indented and labeled: Roman numerals (I, II) for primary divisions of the essay, indented capital letters (A, B) for secondary divisions, further indented Arabic numerals (1, 2) for principal supporting points and examples. A level of detail below the Arabic numbers would be indented further still and labeled with small letters (a, b). Each succeeding level contains more specific information than the one before it.
- The outline divides the material into several groups. An uninterrupted listing of ideas like the one following would indicate a need for tighter, more logical relationships among ideas. (Compare this example with part II of Ling's actual outline.)

  II. Inability to prejudge others
  - A. Body type
  - B. Physical disability
  - C. Race
  - D. Sports and other activities
  - E. Family values
  - F. Political views
  - G. Reduction of physical bias

- Within each part of the outline, distinct topics of equal generality appear in parallel headings (with the same indention and numbering or lettering). In the following example, points B, C, and D are more specific than point A, not equally general, so they should be subheadings 1, 2, and 3 under it. (See section IIA of Ling's outline.)

  A. No assumptions based on appearance
  B. Body type
  C. Physical disability
  D. Race

- All subdivided headings in the outline break into at least two parts because a topic cannot logically be divided into only one part. The following example violates this principle:

  B. Discovery of shared views
  - 1. Interests and concerns

  Any single subdivision should be combined with the heading above it (as in section IIB of Ling's actual outline), matched with another subdivision, or rechecked for its relevance to the heading above it.
- All headings are expressed in parallel grammatical form (see

Principles of the formal outline

- Labels and indentions indicate order and relative importance.
- Sections and subsections reflect logical relationships.
- Topics of equal generality appear in parallel headings.
- Each subdivision has at least two parts.
- Headings are expressed in parallel grammatical form.
- The introduction and conclusion may be omitted (though not, of course, from the essay).

pp. 443–46 on parallelism). Ling's is a **topic outline,** in which the headings consist of a noun (*fear, attributes, communication, gender, rejection,* and the like) with modifiers (*no, of being prejudged, unknown physical, no automatic,* and the like). In a **sentence outline** all headings are expressed as full sentences, as in this rewrite of part II of Ling's outline:

II. On the Internet, we are unable to prejudge others.
   A. We cannot make common assumptions based on physical appearance.
      1. People with athletic builds must be unintelligent.
      2. People in wheelchairs must be unapproachable or pathetic.
      3. People of other races must hold views different from our own.
   B. We discover shared interests and concerns.
      1. We find common ground in sports and other activities.
      2. We see that we all feel much the same about our families.
      3. We learn the similarities in each other's political views.
   C. The Internet could reduce physical bias in the world.

See pages 748–49 for a complete sentence outline.

- The outline covers only the body of the essay, omitting the introduction and the conclusion (see "Choosing a structure," below). The beginning and the ending are important in the essay itself, but you need not include them in the outline unless you are required to do so or anticipate special problems with their organization.

3 Choosing a structure

Introduction, body, and conclusion

Most essays share a basic shape:

- The **introduction,** usually a paragraph or two, draws readers into the world of the essay. At a minimum, it announces and clarifies the topic. Often, it ends with the thesis statement, making a commitment that the rest of the essay delivers on. (See pp. 107–09.)

- The **body** of the essay is its long center, the part that develops the thesis and thus fulfills the commitment of the introduction. The paragraphs in the body develop the general points that support the thesis—the items that would be labeled with Roman numerals and capital letters in a formal outline like the one on page 39. These general points are like the legs of a table supporting the top, the thesis. Each general point may take a paragraph or more, with the bulk of the content providing the details, examples, and reasons (the wood of the table) to support the general point and thus the thesis.
- The **conclusion** generally gives readers something to take away from the essay—a summary of ideas, for instance, or a suggested course of action. (See pp. 109–11.)

This basic shape applies mainly to traditional essays, less to compositions for the World Wide Web. In a Web project, the first page will probably serve as the introduction (see p. 106). From there, the structure will be flexible, as readers choose how to use menus and which links to follow. And the project will probably not have a formal conclusion (see p. 110). Still, you'll want to arrange menus and place links to emphasize what's most important among your ideas. (See pp. 224–42 for more on composing for the Web.)

ESL If English is not your native language, the pattern of introduction-body-conclusion and the particular schemes discussed below may differ from what you are used to. For instance, instead of focusing the introduction quickly on the topic and thesis, writers in your native culture may take an indirect approach. (See also p. 107.) And instead of arranging body paragraphs to emphasize general points and then support those points with specific details, examples, or reasons, writers in your native culture may leave the general points unsupported (assuming that readers will supply the evidence themselves) or may give only the specifics (assuming that readers will infer the general points). (See also p. 75.) When writing for English speakers, you need to take into account their expectations for directness and for the statement and support of general points.

The body of an essay

In most writing situations at least one of the schemes listed opposite will be appropriate for organizing the body of an essay. These schemes are so familiar that readers expect them and look for them. Thus the schemes both help you arrange your material and help readers follow you.

Schemes for organizing ideas in an essay

- Space
- Time
- Emphasis

General to specific	Increasing importance
Specific to general	Decreasing familiarity
Problem-solution	Increasing complexity

Organizing by space or time

Two organizational schemes—spatial and chronological—grow naturally out of the topic. A **spatial organization** is especially appropriate for essays that describe a place, an object, or a person. Following the way people normally survey something, you move through space from a chosen starting point to other features of the subject. Describing a friend, for instance, you might begin with his shoes and move upward or begin with his face and move downward. The informal outline on page 38 illustrates a spatial organization, moving from one end of the street to the other.

A **chronological organization** reports events as they occurred in time, usually from first to last. This pattern, like spatial organization, corresponds to readers' own experiences and expectations. It suits an essay in which you do one of the following:

- Tell a story about yourself or someone else.
- Explain a process from beginning to end—for instance, how to run a marathon or how a tree converts carbon dioxide to oxygen.
- Recount a sequence of events, such as a championship baseball game or the Battle of Gettysburg.
- Explain the causes that led to an effect, such as a bill passed by the legislature or a car model's design. Alternatively, explain how a cause, such as a flood or a book, had multiple effects.
- Provide the background to a situation—for instance, the separate lives of a group of friends who gather to help in a soup kitchen or the making of a movie that turned out to be a hit.

A chronological organization structures the essay on pages 71–72.

Organizing for emphasis

Some organizational schemes must be imposed on ideas and information to aid readers' understanding and achieve a desired emphasis. Two of these depend on the distinction between the general and the specific, discussed on pages 35–36. The **general-to-specific scheme** is common in expository and argumentative essays that start with a general discussion of the main points and then proceed to specific examples, facts, or other evidence. The following thesis statement forecasts a general-to-specific organization:

> To compete well in the global economy, the United States must make higher education affordable for any student who qualifies academically.

The body of the essay might first elaborate on the basic argument and then provide the supporting data.

Sometimes you may anticipate that readers will not appreciate or agree with your general ideas before they see the support for them—for instance, in an expository essay that presents a novel way of looking at common experience, or in an argumentative essay that takes an unpopular view. In these cases a **specific-to-general scheme** can arouse readers' interest in specific examples or other evidence, letting the evidence build to statements of more general ideas. The following thesis statement could be developed in this way:

> Although most of us are unaware of the public relations campaigns directed at us, they can significantly affect the way we think and live.

The writer might devote most of the essay to a single specific example of a public relations campaign and then explain more generally how the example typifies public relations campaigns.

Many argumentative essays use a **problem-solution scheme:** first outline a problem that needs solving; then propose a solution. (If the solution involves steps toward a goal, it may be arranged chronologically.) The following thesis statement announces a problem-solution paper:

> To improve work flow and quality, the data-processing department should add one part-time staffer and retrain three others in the new systems.

A complete problem-solution paper appears on pages 177–80.

A common scheme in both explanations and arguments is the **climactic organization,** in which ideas unfold in order of increasing drama or importance to a climax. For example, the following thesis statement lists three effects of strip-mining in order of their increasing severity, and the essay would cover them in the same order:

> Strip-mining should be tightly controlled in this region to reduce its pollution of water resources, its destruction of the land, and its devastating effects on people's lives.

As this example suggests, the climactic organization works well in arguments because it leaves readers with the most important point freshest in their minds. In exposition such an arrangement can create suspense and thus hold readers' attention.

Expository essays can also be arranged in variations of the climactic pattern. An essay on the effects of air pollution might proceed from **most familiar to least familiar**—from effects readers are likely to know to ones they may not know. Similarly, an essay on various computer languages might proceed from **simplest to most complex,** so that the explanation of each language provides a basis for readers to understand the more difficult one following.

4 Checking for unity and coherence

In conceiving your organization and writing your essay, you should be aware of two qualities of effective writing that relate to organization: unity and coherence. When you perceive that someone's writing "flows well," you are probably appreciating these two qualities. An essay has **unity** if all its parts relate to and support the thesis statement. Check for unity with these questions:

- Is each main section relevant to the main idea (thesis) of the essay?
- Within main sections of the outline, does each example or detail support the principal idea of that section?

An essay has **coherence** if readers can see the relations among parts and move easily from one thought to the next. Check for coherence with these questions:

- Do the ideas follow in a clear sequence?
- Are the parts of the essay logically connected?
- Are the connections clear and smooth?

A unified and coherent outline will not necessarily guide you to a unified and coherent essay, because so much can change during drafting. Thus you shouldn't be too hard on your outline, in case a seemingly wayward idea proves useful. But do cut obvious digressions and rearrange material that clearly needs moving.

The unity and coherence of an essay begin in its paragraphs, so these two concepts are treated in greater detail in Chapter 4. You may want to consult several sections in particular before you begin drafting:

- The topic sentence and unity (pp. 75–78).
- Transitions and coherence (pp. 80–91, 112).
- Linking paragraphs in the essay (pp. 113–15).

Unity and coherence may seem unimportant in compositions for the World Wide Web, in which entire documents are linked to each other so that it's easy to move among them. However, precisely because the Web is such a fluid medium, you risk losing or confusing your readers if you don't consider unity and coherence. Your project should have a clear purpose and clear ideas relating to that purpose, and the connections between ideas should be spelled out to orient readers. For instance, the opening page of the project can serve as an introduction that lays out the goals, maps the structure and development, and states the thesis. Then other pages can tie into that opening page, specifying connections and forecasting what is to come. (For more on composing for the Web, see pp. 224–42.)

EXERCISE 10
Organizing ideas

The following list of ideas was extracted by a student from freewriting he did for a brief paper on soccer in the United States. Using his thesis statement as a guide, pick out the general ideas and arrange the relevant specific points under them. In some cases you may have to infer general ideas to cover specific points in the list.

Thesis statement

Despite the World Cup competitions held in the United States, soccer may never be the sport here that it is elsewhere because both the potential fans and the potential backers resist it.

List of ideas

Sports seasons are already too crowded for fans.
Soccer rules are confusing to Americans.
A lot of kids play soccer in school, but the game is still "foreign."
Sports money goes where the money is.
Backers are wary of losing money on new ventures.
Fans have limited time to watch.
Fans have limited money to pay for sports.
Backers are concerned with TV contracts.
Previous attempts to start a pro soccer league failed.
TV contracts almost matter more than live audiences.
Failure of the US Football League was costly.
Baseball, football, hockey, and basketball seasons already overlap.
Soccer fans couldn't fill huge stadiums.
American soccer fans are too few for TV interest.

EXERCISE 11
Creating a formal outline

Use your arrangement of general ideas and specific points from Exercise 10 as the basis for a formal topic or sentence outline. Follow the principles given on pages 40–41.

EXERCISE 12
Considering your past work: Organizing ideas

What has been your experience with organizing your writing? Many writers find it difficult. If you do, too, can you say why? What kinds of outlines or other organizing tools have you used? Which have been helpful and which not?

EXERCISE 13
Organizing your own essay

Continuing from Exercise 9 (p. 35), choose an appropriate organization for your essay-in-progress. Then experiment with organizing tools by preparing a tree diagram or a scratch, informal, or formal outline.

EXERCISE 14
Collaborating on organization

Either online or face to face, exchange with a classmate the outline you each prepared in response to Exercise 13. (Include your preliminary thesis statement with the outline to clarify your subject, purpose, and main idea.) Evaluate your classmate's outline for unity and coherence: What, if anything, does not clearly relate to the thesis? Does the thesis seem fully developed? Where, if at all, does the sequence of ideas seem confusing? When you have received your classmate's comments, revise your outline as needed to improve unity and coherence.

CHAPTER 3

Drafting and Revising

The separation of drafting and revising from the planning and development discussed in Chapters 1 and 2 is somewhat artificial because the stages almost always overlap during the writing process. Indeed, if you compose on a computer, you may not experience any boundaries between stages at all. Still, your primary goal during the writing process will usually shift from gathering and shaping information to forming connected sentences and paragraphs in a draft and then restructuring and rewriting the draft.

3a Writing the first draft

The only correct drafting style is the one that works for you. Generally, though, the freer and more fluid you are, the better. Some writers draft and revise at the same time, but most let themselves go during drafting and *especially* do not worry about errors. Drafting is the occasion to find and convey meaning through the act of writing. If you fear making mistakes while drafting, that fear will choke your ideas. You draft only for yourself, so errors do not matter. Write freely until you have worked out what you want to say; *then* focus on any mistakes you may have made.

Starting to draft sometimes takes courage, even for seasoned professionals. Students and pros alike find elaborate ways to procrastinate—rearranging shelves, napping, lunching with friends. Such procrastination may actually help you if you let ideas for writing simmer at the same time. At some point, though, enough is

Advice on drafting and overcoming writer's block:

http://webster.commnet.edu/HP/pages/darling/grammar/composition/brainstorm.htm From the Guide to Grammar and Writing.

http://owl.english.purdue.edu/Files/132/7-draft.html From the Purdue Online Writing Lab.

http://webware.princeton.edu/Writing/wc4a.htm From Princeton University.

enough: the deadline looms; you've got to get started. If the blankness still stares back at you, then try one of the following techniques for unblocking:

Ways to start drafting

- Read over what you've already written—notes, outlines, and so on—and immediately start your draft with whatever comes to mind.
- Freewrite (see p. 22).
- Write scribbles or type nonsense until words you can use start coming.
- Pretend you're writing to a friend about your topic.
- Conjure up an image that represents your topic—a physical object, a facial expression, two people arguing over something, a giant machine gouging the earth for a mine, whatever. Describe that image.
- Write a paragraph on what you think your essay will be about when you finish it.
- Skip the opening and start in the middle. Or write the conclusion.
- Using your outline, divide your essay into chunks—say, one for the introduction, another for the first point, and so on. Start writing the chunk that seems most eager to be written, the one you understand best or feel most strongly about.

You should find some momentum once you've started writing. If not, however, or if your energy flags, try one or more of the following techniques to keep moving ahead:

Ways to *keep* drafting

- Set aside enough time for yourself. (For a brief essay, a first draft is likely to take at least an hour or two.)
- Work in a place where you won't be interrupted.
- Make yourself comfortable.
- If you must stop working, leave a note with the draft about what you expect to do next. Then you can pick up where you stopped with minimal disruption.
- Be as fluid as possible, and don't worry about mistakes. Spontaneity will allow your attitudes toward your subject to surface naturally in your sentences, and it will also make you receptive to ideas and relations you haven't seen before. Mistakes will be easier to find and correct later, when you're not also trying to create.
- Keep going. Skip over sticky spots; leave a blank if you can't find the right word; put alternative ideas or phrasings in brackets so that you can consider them later without bogging down. If an idea

(continued)

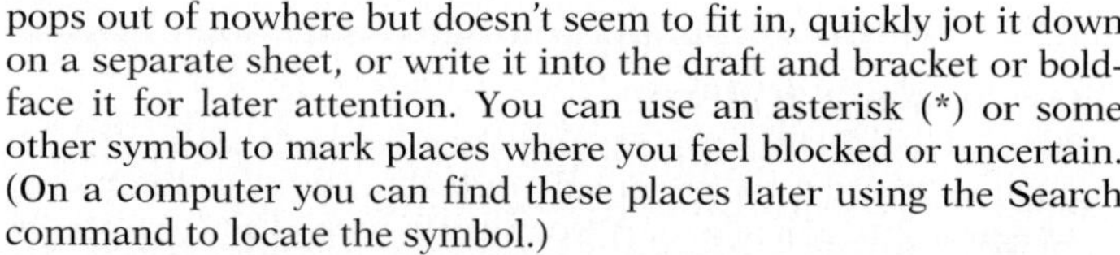

Ways to *keep* drafting
(continued)

pops out of nowhere but doesn't seem to fit in, quickly jot it down on a separate sheet, or write it into the draft and bracket or boldface it for later attention. You can use an asterisk (*) or some other symbol to mark places where you feel blocked or uncertain. (On a computer you can find these places later using the Search command to locate the symbol.)

- Resist self-criticism. Don't worry about your style, grammar, spelling, punctuation, and the like. Don't worry about what your readers will think. These are very important matters, but save them for revision. If you're writing on a computer, help yourself resist self-criticism by turning off automatic spelling- or grammar-checking functions (see p. 186) or by trying invisible writing as described on page 22.
- Use your thesis statement and outline to remind you of your planned purpose, organization, and content.
- But don't feel constrained by your thesis and outline. If your writing leads you in a more interesting direction, follow.

If you write on a computer, frequently save the text you're drafting—at least every five or ten minutes or every couple of paragraphs and every time you leave the computer. (Many word processors will automatically save your text as you're writing. See p. 184.) In addition, back up your drafts on a separate disk, and perhaps even print paper copies (so-called hard copy) in case anything happens to your disks.

Whether you compose on paper or on a computer, you may find it difficult to tell whether a first draft is finished. The distinction between drafts can be significant because creating text is different from rethinking it (see p. 52) and because your instructor may ask you and your classmates to submit your drafts, either on paper or over a computer network, so that others can give you feedback on them (see p. 66). For your own revision or others' feedback, you might consider a draft finished for any number of reasons: perhaps you've reached the assigned length and have run out of ideas; perhaps you find yourself writing the conclusion; perhaps you've stopped adding content and are just tinkering with words.

Sara Ling's first draft on Internet communication appears on the facing page. (Her earlier work appears on pp. 21, 23, 29, 32–33, 37, and 39.) You can also view the draft on this book's Web site: *http://www.awlonline.com/littlebrown.*

First draft

Title?

In "Welcome to Cyberbia," M. Kadi says that the Internet will lead to more fragmentation in society because people just seek out others like themselves. But Kadi ignores the Internet's uniquely anonymous form of interaction could actually build diversity into community by lowering the barriers of physical appearance in communication.

Anonymity on the Internet. It's one of the best things about technology. No one knows your age or gender or race. Whether your fat or thin or neat or sloppy. What kind of clothes you wear. (Maybe your not wearing clothes at all). People who know you personally don't even know who you are with an invented screen name.

We can communicate freely without being prejudged because of our appearance. For example, I participate in a snowboarding forum that has mostly men. I didn't realize what I was getting into when I used my full name as my screen name. Before long, I was often being shouted down with such insults as "What does a girl know?" and "Why don't you go back to knitting?" Then a nice man I had been exchanging messages with wrote me a private e-mail, and he turned out to be a she! This woman had been wiser than me and hidden her gender with her screen name. She hadn't received any of the hostile responses I had, just because no one knew she was a woman. As this example shows, posing as people different from who they really are can enable people to make themselves heard in situations where normally (in the real world) they would be shut out.

We cannot prejudge others because of their appearance. Often in face-to-face interaction we assume we know things about people just because of the way they look. Assumptions prevent people from discovering their shared interests and concerns, and this is particularly true where race is concerned. The anonymity of the Internet makes physical barriers irrelevant, and only people's minds meet. Because of this, the Internet could create a world free of physical bias.

Logged on to the Internet we can become more tolerant of others. We can become a community.

EXERCISE 1
Analyzing a first draft

Compare Ling's draft with the previous step in her planning (her formal outline) on page 39. List the places in the draft where the act of drafting led Ling to rearrange her information, add or delete material, or explore new ideas.

EXERCISE 2
Considering your past work: Drafting

Think back over a recent writing experience. At what point in the writing process did you begin drafting? How did drafting go—smoothly, haltingly, painfully, painlessly? If you had difficulties, what were they? If you didn't, why not?

EXERCISE 3
Collaborating on drafting strategies

Either online or face to face, discuss with at least one classmate the strategies that have helped you start drafting or keep up momentum while drafting. (Include any of the strategies in the boxes on pp. 49–50 that have proved helpful to you.) The next time you're drafting and run into an obstacle, try a strategy suggested by a classmate that seems likely to help you overcome the obstacle.

EXERCISE 4
Drafting your own essay

Prepare a draft of the essay you began in Chapters 1 and 2. Use your thesis statement and your outline as guides, but don't be unduly constrained by them. Concentrate on opening up options, not on closing them down. Do not, above all, worry about mistakes.

3b Revising the first draft

Revision literally means "re-seeing"—looking anew at ideas and details, their relationships and arrangement, the degree to which they work or don't work for the thesis. While drafting, you focus inwardly, concentrating on pulling your topic out of yourself. In revising, you look out to your readers, trying to anticipate how they will see your work. You adopt a critical perspective toward your work (see Chapter 5), examining your draft as a pole-vaulter or dancer would examine a videotape of his or her performance. (Writing teachers often ask students to read each other's drafts partly to train

http://owl.english.purdue.edu/Files/132/8-revise.html Revising papers, with examples and links to additional resources, from the Purdue Online Writing Lab.

the students in using and benefiting from this critical perspective. See p. 66.)

Computerized word processing has removed the mechanical drudgery of revision. With a few keystrokes you can add, delete, and move words, lines, or whole passages. Writers disagree, though, over whether it's better to consider revisions on paper or on screen:

- Paper copy allows you to see the whole draft at once and may be easier to read accurately, but if your work is stored on a computer you then have to key in your changes.
- Working on a computer allows you to see changes as you make them and to experiment with different versions of the same passage, but it can prevent you from seeing your work as a whole.

Whatever your own preference, do take a couple of precautions. First, work on a duplicate of any draft you're revising so that the original remains intact until you're truly finished with it. (You may be able to do without the duplicate if your word processor has a function that shows, or "tracks," changes alongside the original text, allowing you later to accept or reject alterations. See p. 190.) And second, save successive drafts under their own file names in case you need to consult them for ideas or phrasings. (See p. 183.)

1 Gaining distance from your work

Reading your own work critically requires that you create some distance between it and yourself—not always an easy task. The following techniques may help:

Ways to gain distance from your work

- Take a break after finishing the draft to pursue some other activity. A few hours may be enough; a whole night or day is preferable. The break will clear your mind, relax you, and give you some objectivity.
- Ask someone to read and react to your draft. Many writing instructors ask their students to submit their first drafts so that the instructor and, often, the other members of the class can serve as an actual audience to help guide revision. (See also pp. 67–69 on receiving and benefiting from comments.)

- If you compose your draft in handwriting, type it on a typewriter or computer before revising it. The act of transcription can reveal gaps in content or problems in structure.
- If you compose on a computer, print your draft on paper. You'll be able to view all pages of the draft at once, and the different medium can reveal weaknesses you didn't see on screen.

(continued)

Ways to gain distance from your work *(continued)*

- Outline your draft. While reading it, highlight the main points supporting the thesis. Write these sentences down separately in outline form. (If you're working on a computer, you can copy and paste these sentences.) Then examine the outline you've made for logical order, gaps, and digressions. A formal outline can be especially illuminating because of its careful structure. (See pp. 36–41 for a discussion of outlining.)
- Listen to your draft: read it out loud to yourself or a friend or classmate, read it into a tape recorder and play the tape, or have someone read the draft to you. Experiencing your words with ears instead of eyes can alter your perceptions.
- Ease the pressure. Don't try to re-see everything in your draft at once. Use a checklist like the one on page 56, making a separate pass through the draft for each item.

2 Revising, then editing

Strictly speaking, revision includes editing—refining the manner of expression to improve clarity or style or to correct errors. In this chapter, though, revision and editing are treated separately to stress their differences: in revision you deal with the underlying meaning and structure of your essay; in editing you deal with its surface. By making separate drafts beyond the first—a revised one and then an edited one (p. 60)—you'll be less likely to waste time tinkering with sentences that you end up cutting, and you'll avoid the temptation to substitute editing for more substantial revision.

This temptation can be especially attractive on a computerized word processor because it's so easy to alter copy. Indeed, writers sometimes find themselves editing compulsively, spinning their wheels with changes that cease to have any marked effect on meaning or clarity and that may in fact sap the writing of energy. Planning to revise and then to edit encourages you to look beyond the confines of the screen so that deeper issues of meaning and structure aren't lost to surface matters such as word choice and sentence arrangement.

3 Titling your essay

The revision stage is a good time to consider a title. After drafting, you have a clearer sense of your direction, and the attempt to sum up your essay in a title phrase can help you focus sharply on your topic, purpose, and audience.

Here are some suggestions for titling an essay:

- A **descriptive title** is almost always appropriate and is often expected for academic writing. It announces the topic clearly, accurately, and as briefly as possible. The final title of Sara Ling's essay—"The Internet: Fragmentation or Community?"—is an example, as are "Images of Lost Identity in *North by Northwest,*" "An Experiment in Small-Group Dynamics," "Why Lincoln Delayed Emancipating the Slaves," and "Food Poisoning Involving *E. coli* Bacteria: A Review of the Literature."
- A **suggestive title**—the kind often found in popular magazines—may be appropriate for more informal writing. Examples include "Making Peace" (for an essay on the Peace Corps) and "Anyone for Soup?" (for an essay on working in a soup kitchen). For a more suggestive title, Ling might have chosen something like "What We Don't Know Can Help Us" or "Secrets of the Internet." Such a title conveys the writer's attitudes and main concerns but not the precise topic, thereby pulling readers into the essay to learn more. A source for such a title may be a familiar phrase, a fresh image, or a significant expression from the essay itself.
- A title tells readers how big the topic is. For Ling's essay, the title "The Internet" or "Anonymity" would have been too broad, whereas "Lose Your Body" or "Discovering Common Ground" would have been too narrow because each deals with only part of the paper's content.
- A title should not restate the assignment or the thesis statement, as in "The Trouble with M. Kadi's Picture of the Internet" or "What I Think About Diversity on the Internet."

For more information on essay titles, see pages 385 (avoiding reference to the title in the opening of the paper), 535 (capitalizing words in a title), and 207 (the format of a title in the final paper).

4 Using a revision checklist

Set aside at least as much time to revise your essay as you took to draft it. Plan on going through the draft several times to answer the questions in the checklist on the next page and to resolve any problems. (If you need additional information on any of the topics in the checklist, refer to the page numbers given in parentheses.) Note that the checklist can also help you if you have been asked to comment on another writer's draft (see p. 67).

If you work on a computer, you can download the revision checklist from this book's Web site at *http://www.awlonline.com/littlebrown.* Save the list in a file, and duplicate it for each writing project. Then insert your answers to the questions along with re-

Checklist for revision

See also specific revision checklists for arguments (p. 177), research papers (p. 707), and literary analyses (p. 806).

- **Purpose:** What is the essay's purpose? Does that purpose conform to the assignment? Is it consistent throughout the paper? (See pp. 15–17.)
- **Thesis:** What is the thesis of the essay? Where does it become clear? How well do thesis and paper match: Does the paper stray from the thesis? Does it fulfill the commitment of the thesis? (See pp. 30–34.)
- **Structure:** What are the main points of the paper? (List them.) How well does each support the thesis? How effective is their arrangement for the paper's purpose? (See pp. 35–36, 41–45.)
- **Development:** How well do details, examples, and other evidence support each main point? Where, if at all, might readers find support skimpy or have trouble understanding the content? (See pp. 18–29, 93–95.)
- **Tone:** What is the tone of the paper? How do particular words and sentence structures create the tone? How appropriate is it for the purpose, topic, and intended readers? Where is it most and least successful? (See pp. 12–14.)
- **Unity:** What does each sentence and paragraph contribute to the thesis? Where, if at all, do digressions occur? Should these be cut, or can they be rewritten to support the thesis? (See pp. 45–46, 75–78.)
- **Coherence:** How clearly and smoothly does the paper flow? Where does it seem rough or awkward? Can any transitions be improved? (See pp. 45–46, 80–91.)
- **Title, introduction, conclusion:** How accurately and interestingly does the title reflect the essay's content? (See pp. 54–55.) How well does the introduction engage and focus readers' attention? (See pp. 106–09.) How effective is the conclusion in providing a sense of completion? (See pp. 109–11.)

lated ideas for changes. Print the expanded list so it's handy while you revise. (See pp. 184–85 for more on word-processing functions.)

5 Examining a sample revision

In revising her first draft, Sara Ling had the help of her instructor and several of her classmates, to whom she showed the draft as part of her assignment. (See p. 66 for more on this kind of collaboration.) Based on the revision checklist, she thought that she wanted to stick with her initial purpose and thesis statement and that they had held up well in the draft. But she also knew without being told that her introduction and conclusion were too hurried, that the movement between paragraphs was too abrupt, that the example of the snowboarding forum went on too long, and that the fourth paragraph was thin: she hadn't supplied enough details to support her ideas and convince her readers.

Ling's readers confirmed her self-evaluation. A few, however, raised a point that she had not considered, reflected in this comment by a classmate:

> I would have an easier time agreeing with you about the Internet if you weren't quite so gung-ho. For instance, what about the dangers of the Internet, as when adults prey on children or men prey on women? In your third paragraph, you don't acknowledge that such things can and do happen. Also, is a bias-free world (fourth paragraph) really such a sure thing? People will still meet in person, after all.

For her revision, Ling printed out a paper copy and then made changes directly on the draft. The revision begins on the next page. The main changes are explained below and keyed to the revision by numbers (some numbers are used more than once):

1. With a descriptive title, Ling named her topic and forecast how she would approach it.
2. Ling rewrote and expanded the previous abrupt introduction to draw readers into the question she would explore and to give a fuller summary of Kadi's essay.
3. Ling rewrote the transitions between paragraphs to make each paragraph relate clearly to her thesis statement and to make the essay flow more smoothly.
4. At these points Ling added examples to support her general statements. This and the following two categories of changes occupied most of Ling's attention during revision.
5. Ling condensed the example from her experience. Some readers commented that it overwhelmed the paragraph, and Ling realized that she had given more background than needed.
6. In response to her classmates, Ling twice qualified her ideas to acknowledge complexities she had previously ignored. (The first qualification created an overlong paragraph, so Ling broke the paragraph in two.)
7. Ling's energy had flagged when she came to her conclusion, and all her readers found it too rushed. In response, she pulled in the final ideas of the preceding paragraph, spelling one out and qualifying the other, and she summarized her main point more fully.
8. Ling added a work-cited entry for Kadi's essay, using MLA style. (See pp. 698–99 for more on documentation in general and 710–42 for more on MLA style.)

You can also view Ling's revision on this book's Web site: *http://www.awlonline.com/littlebrown.*

Revised first draft

The Internet: Fragmentation or Community? 1

~~Title?~~

We hear all sorts of predictions about how the Internet will enrich our lives and promote equality, tolerance, and thus community in our society. But are these promises realistic? In her essay "Welcome to Cyberbia," M. Kadi argues that they are not. Instead, she maintains, 2
~~In "Welcome to Cyberbia," M. Kadi says that~~ the Internet will lead to more fragmentation, *not community,* ~~in society~~ because *users merely* ~~people just~~ seek out others *with the same biases, needs, and concerns as their own. The point is an interesting one but Kadi overlooks* ~~like themselves. But Kadi ignores~~ the Internet's uniquely anonymous form of interaction, *which* could actually build diversity into community by lowering the barriers of physical appearance in communication.

Writing on the Internet, you can be as anonymous as you like. Unless you tell them, the people you communicate with do not ~~Anonymity on the Internet. It's one of the best things about technology. No one~~ know~~s~~ your age or gender or race. Whether *you're* ~~your~~ fat or thin or neat or sloppy. What kind of clothes you wear. (Maybe *you're* ~~your~~ not wearing clothes at all). *Even p*~~P~~eople who know you personally don't ~~even~~ know who you are *if you conceal your identity* with an invented screen name. 3

Because of this anonymity, we ~~We~~ can communicate freely without being prejudged because of 3
our appearance. For example, *a high school student can participate in a physics discussion group, and not be dismissed by professional physicists in the group just because of her age. An adult man can chat about music with teenagers, who might otherwise ignore or laugh at him.* 4

A woman I know posed as a man on ~~I participate in~~ a snowboarding forum *and received none of the hostile responses such as "What does a girl know?" that I got when I revealed my gender on the same forum.* ~~that has mostly men. I didn't realize what I was getting into when I used my full name as my screen name. Before long, I was often being shouted down with such insults~~ as ~~"What does a girl know?" and "Why don't you go back to knitting?" Then a nice man I had been exchanging messages with wrote me a private e-mail, and he turned out to be a she! This woman had been wiser than me and hidden her gender with her screen name. She hadn't received any of the hostile responses I had, just because no one knew she was a woman~~. 5

Granted, concealing or altering identities on the Internet can be a problem, as when adults pose as children to seduce or harm them. These well-publicized occurrences say a great deal about the need to monitor the use of the Internet by children, and being cautious about getting together with Internet correspondents. However, they do not undermine the value of ~~As this example shows, posing as people different from who they really are can enable~~ people *being able* to make themselves heard in situations where normally (in the real world) they would be shut out. 6

The Internet's anonymity has a flip side too. We cannot be prejudged 3
and ~~W~~*w* We *also* cannot prejudge others because of their appearance. Often in face-to-face interaction we assume we know things about people just because of the way they look. *People with athletic builds must be dumb. Heavy* 4 *people must be uninteresting. People in wheelchairs must be unapproachable or pathetic. Perhaps most significant, people of other races must have fixed and contrary views about family values, crime, affirmative action and all sorts of other issues as well.*

Assumptions *like these* prevent people from discovering their shared interests and concerns; ~~and this is particularly true where race is concerned~~. *But with* ~~T~~*t*he anonymity of the Internet, ~~makes~~ *such* physical barriers *to understanding are* irrelevant; ~~and only people's minds meet. Because of this, the Internet could create a world free of physical bias.~~

~~Logged on to the Internet we can become more tolerant of others.~~ ~~We can become a community~~.

A world free of physical bias is a long way off, but the more we 6, 7 *communicate with just our minds the more likely it is that our minds will find common ground. Logged on, we can become more accepted and accepting, more tolerated and tolerant. We can become a community.*

Work Cited 8

Kadi, M. "Welcome to Cyberbia." Utne Reader Mar.-Apr. 1995: 57-59.

EXERCISE 5
Analyzing a revised draft

Compare Ling's revised draft with her first draft on page 51. Based on the discussion of her intentions for revision (pp. 56–57), can you see the reasons for most of her changes? Where would you suggest further revisions, and why?

EXERCISE 6
Considering your past work: Revising

In the past, have you usually revised your drafts extensively? Do you think your writing would benefit from more revision of the sort described in this chapter? Why or why not? Many students who don't revise much explain that they lack the time. Is time a problem for you? Can you think of ways to resolve the problem?

EXERCISE 7
Collaborating on revising strategies

Either online or face to face, discuss with one or more classmates the difficulties you've had with revision, the strategies that have helped you revise, and the ways you've seen your writing improve with revision. What can you learn from your classmate(s) about the challenges and benefits of revision?

rev
3c

EXERCISE 8
Revising your own draft

Revise your own first draft from Exercise 4 (p. 52). Use the checklist for revision on page 56 as a guide. Concentrate on purpose, content, and organization, leaving smaller problems for the next draft.

3c Editing the revised draft

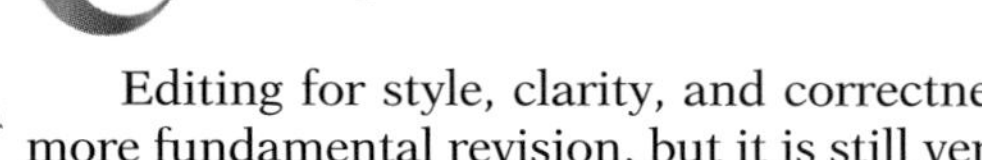

Editing for style, clarity, and correctness may come second to more fundamental revision, but it is still very important. A carefully developed essay will fall flat with readers if you overlook awkwardness and errors.

When you have revised your first draft, try the following approaches to editing:

Ways to find what needs editing

- Take a break, even fifteen or twenty minutes, to clear your head.
- If possible, work on a paper copy, even if you compose and revise on a computer. Most people find it much harder to spot errors on a computer screen than on paper. (Print your draft double-spaced so you have room for changes.)
- Read the draft *slowly,* and read what you *actually see.* Otherwise, you're likely to read what you intended to write but didn't.
- As you read the draft, imagine yourself encountering it for the first time, as a reader will.
- Have a friend or relative read your work. (If your native language is not English, you may find it especially helpful to have a native speaker read your revised drafts.) When you share your work in class, listen to the responses of your classmates or instructor. (See p. 66.)
- As when revising, read the draft aloud, preferably into a tape recorder, listening for awkward rhythms, repetitive sentence patterns, and missing or clumsy transitions.
- Learn from your own experience. Keep a record of the problems that others have pointed out in your writing. (See p. 69 for a suggested format.) When editing, check your work against this record.
- Don't rely on your word processor's spelling, grammar, and style checkers to find what needs editing. See the discussion of these checkers on page 62.

http://webster.commnet.edu/HP/pages/darling/grammar/composition/editing.htm Editing and proofreading tips, from the Guide to Grammar and Writing.

In your editing, work for clarity and a smooth movement among sentences and for correctness. Use the questions in the checklist below to guide your editing. (Page numbers indicate where you can look in the handbook for more information.) Note that the checklist may also serve as a guide if you are commenting on another writer's paper (see p. 66).

Checklist for editing

- **Clarity:** How well do words and sentences convey their intended meanings? Which if any words and sentences are confusing? Check the paper especially for these:

  Exact words (pp. 567–77)
  Parallelism (pp. 442–47)
  Clear modifiers (pp. 396–405)
  Clear reference of pronouns (pp. 381–87)
  Complete sentences (pp. 364–71)
  Sentences separated correctly (pp. 373–79)

- **Effectiveness:** How well do words and sentences engage and direct readers' attention? Where, if at all, does the writing seem wordy, choppy, or dull? Check the paper especially for these:

  Emphasis of main ideas (pp. 418–22)
  Smooth and informative transitions (pp. 88–90, 113–15)
  Variety in sentence length and structure (pp. 449–54)
  Appropriate words (pp. 559–66)
  Concise sentences (pp. 578–84)
  Consistent, appropriate tone (pp. 12–14)

- **Correctness:** How little or how much do surface errors interfere with clarity and effectiveness? Check the paper especially for these:

  Spelling (pp. 603–16)
  Pronoun forms (pp. 292–300)
  Verb forms, especially *-s* and *-ed* endings and correct forms of irregular verbs (pp. 301–08)
  Verb tenses, especially consistency (pp. 318–25, 391–92)
  Agreement between subjects and verbs, especially when words come between them or the subject is *each, everyone,* or a similar word (pp. 333–40)
  Agreement between pronouns and antecedents, especially when the antecedent contains *or* or the antecedent is *each, everyone, person,* or a similar word (pp. 340–45)
  Sentence fragments (pp. 364–71)
  Commas, especially with comma splices (pp. 375-78), with *and* or *but* (469), with introductory elements (471), with nonessential elements (473–77), and with series (479)
  Apostrophes in possessives but not plural nouns (*Dave's/witches,* pp. 501–03) and in contractions but not possessive personal pronouns (*it's/its,* pp. 504–05)

If you work on a computer, you can download the editing checklist from this book's Web site at *http://www.awlonline.com/littlebrown*. Save the list in a file, and duplicate it for each writing project. Then insert your answers to the questions along with notes on specific changes you need or want to make. Print the expanded list so it's handy while you edit. (See pp. 183–85 for more on word-processing functions.)

Editing on a computer presents distinct advantages and disadvantages, whether you edit on screen or work on printed copy and transfer corrections onto the computer:

- If you edit printed copy, the Find command can help you locate the passages to change on the computer copy.
- If you're aware of mistakes or stylistic problems that tend to crop up in your writing—certain misspellings, overuse of *there is,* wordy phrases such as *the fact that,* and so on—you can use the Find command to locate and correct them.
- Your word processor may have spelling, grammar, and style checkers that highlight misspellings or possible flaws such as very long sentences, mismatched subjects and verbs, or many uses of *to be* verbs. The checkers may point you toward areas of your work that need editing, but they are far from foolproof: the spelling checker can't distinguish a misuse of a correctly spelled word, such as *there* for *their,* and the grammar and style checker may misidentify errors and will ignore weaknesses it's not capable of spotting. If you use the checkers, do so only as a starting point. Read the draft yourself to locate problems in spelling, grammar, or style. (For more on working with checkers, see pp. 186–89.)
- The ease of editing on a computer can lead to overediting and steal the life from your prose. Resist any temptation to rewrite sentences over and over. (If your computer's grammar and style checker contributes to the temptation, consider turning it off.)
- Inserting or deleting text on a computer requires special care not to omit needed words or leave in unneeded words.
- A computer printout may look perfect just because it's clean. To make sure it's perfect, read the printout carefully. (See the suggestions on pp. 60 and 64.)

In response to the questions in the editing checklist and her own sense of clarity and effectiveness, Sara Ling edited the revised draft of her essay. The second paragraph appears on the facing page. One change Ling made throughout the essay shows up here: she resolved an inconsistency in references to *you, people,* and *we,* settling on a consistent *we.* In addition, Ling corrected several sentence fragments in the middle of the paragraph.

Edited draft (excerpt)

Writing on the Internet, ~~you~~ *we* can be as anonymous as ~~you~~ *we* like. Unless ~~you~~ *we* tell them, the people ~~you~~ *we* communicate with do not know ~~your~~ *our* age or gender or race~~.~~, ~~W~~*w*hether ~~you're~~ *we're* fat or thin or neat or sloppy~~.~~, *or* ~~W~~*w*hat kind of clothes ~~you~~ *we* wear~~.~~ (~~Maybe you're not~~ *if we're* wearing clothes at all). Even people who know ~~you~~ *us* personally don't know who ~~you~~ *we* are if ~~you~~ *we* conceal ~~your~~ *our* identit~~y~~*ies* with ~~an~~ invented screen name*s*.

EXERCISE 9
Considering your past work: Editing

How do you find what needs editing in your drafts? What kinds of changes do you make most often? Have you tried focusing on particular kinds of changes, such as correcting mistakes you made in previous writing? If your readers often comment on editing concerns in your work, what can you do to reduce such comments?

EXERCISE 10
Editing your own draft

Use the checklist for editing (p. 61) and your own sense of your essay's needs to edit the revised draft of your essay-in-progress.

3d Preparing and proofreading the final draft

After editing your essay, retype or print it once more for submission to your instructor. You may be required to use one of the following formats: MLA (pp. 215–18), Chicago (pp. 832–33), APA (pp. 855–58), or CBE (pp. 876–77). If no format is specified, consult the document-design guidelines in Chapter 9. If you've composed on a word processor, use the Print Preview function under the File menu to check for formatting problems that may not otherwise show up on your screen.

Be sure to proofread the final essay several times to spot and correct errors. To increase the accuracy of your proofreading, you may need to experiment with ways to keep yourself from relaxing into the rhythm and the content of your prose. The box on the next page gives a few tricks, including some used by professional proofreaders.

Sara Ling's final essay begins on the next page, typed in MLA format except for page breaks. Comments in the margins point out key features of the essay's content. (You can also view Ling's final draft and the marginal comments at this book's Web site: *http://www.awlonline.com/littlebrown.*)

Techniques for proofreading

- Read printed copy, even if you will eventually submit the paper electronically. Most people proofread more accurately when reading type on paper than when reading it on a computer screen. (At the same time, don't view the printed copy as necessarily error-free just because it's clean. Clean-looking copy may still harbor errors.)
- Read the paper aloud, very slowly, and distinctly pronounce exactly what you see.
- Place a ruler under each line as you read it.
- Read "against copy," comparing your final draft one sentence at a time against the edited draft you copied it from.
- Take steps to keep the content of your writing from distracting you while you proofread. Read the essay backward, end to beginning, examining each sentence as a separate unit. Or, taking advantage of a computer, isolate each paragraph from its context by printing it on a separate page. (Of course, reassemble the paragraphs before submitting the paper.)

Final draft

Sara Ling

Professor Nelson

English 120A

14 April 2000

The Internet: Fragmentation or Community? — *Descriptive title*

Introduction — We hear all sorts of predictions about how the Internet will enrich our individual lives and promote communication, tolerance, and thus community in our society. But are these promises realistic? *(1. Question to be addressed)* In her essay "Welcome to Cyberbia," M. Kadi argues that they are not. Instead, she maintains, the Internet will lead to more fragmentation, not community, because users merely seek out others with the same biases, concerns, and needs as their own. *(2. Summary of Kadi's essay)* The point is an interesting one, but Kadi seems to overlook that the Internet's uniquely anonymous form of interaction could actually build diversity into community by lowering the barriers of physical appearance in communication. *(3. Thesis statement)*

Explanation of Internet's anonymity — Writing on the Internet, we can be as anonymous as we like. Unless we tell them, the people we communicate with do not know our age or gender or race, whether we're fat or thin or neat or sloppy, or what kind of clothes we wear (if we're wearing clothes at all). Even people who know us personally don't know who we are if we conceal our identities with invented screen names.

First main point: We are not prejudged by others.

1. Examples

Because of this anonymity, we can communicate freely on the Internet without being prejudged because of our physical attributes. For example, a high school student can participate in a physics discussion group without fear of being dismissed by the group's professional physicists just because of her age. Similarly, an adult man can chat about music with teenagers who might otherwise ignore or laugh at him. A woman I know posed as a man on a snowboarding forum and received none of the hostile responses --such as "What does a girl know?"--that I got when I innocently revealed my gender on the same forum.

2. Qualification of first main point

Granted, concealing or altering identities on the Internet can be a problem, as when adults pose as children to seduce or harm them. These well-publicized occurrences say much about the need to monitor children's use of the Internet and be cautious about meeting Internet correspondents.

3. Conclusion of first main point

However, they do not undermine the value of being able to make ourselves heard in situations where normally (in the real world) we would be shut out.

Second main point: We cannot prejudge others.

1. Clarification of second main point

The Internet's anonymity has a flip side, too: just as we cannot be prejudged, so we cannot prejudge others because of their appearance. Often in face-to-face interaction, we assume we know things about people just because of the way they look.

2. Examples

People with athletic builds must be unintelligent. Heavy people must be uninteresting. People in wheelchairs must be unapproachable or pathetic. Perhaps most significant, people of other races must have fixed and contrary views about all kinds of issues, from family values to crime to affirmative action.

3. Effects

Assumptions like these prevent us from discovering the interests and concerns we share with people who merely look different.

4. Conclusion of second main point

But with the anonymity of the Internet, such physical barriers to understanding are irrelevant.

A world without physical bias may be an unreachable ideal, but the more we communicate with just our minds, the more likely it is that our minds will find common ground. Logged on, we can become more accepted and more accepting, more tolerated and more tolerant. We can become a community.

Conclusion, summarizing essay

Work Cited

Kadi, M. "Welcome to Cyberbia." Utne Reader Mar.-Apr. 1995: 57–59.

Work cited in MLA style (see p. 719)

EXERCISE 11
Proofreading

Proofread the following passage, using any of the techniques listed on page 64 to bring errors into the foreground. There are thirteen errors in the passage: missing and misspelled words, typographical errors, and the like. If you are in doubt about any spellings, consult a dictionary.

An envirnmental group, Natural Resources Defense Council, has estimated that 5,500 to 6,200 children who are preschool today may contract cancer during there lives becuase of the pesticides they consume in there food In addition, these children will be at greater risk for kidney damage, problems with immunity, and other serious imparments. The government bases it's pesticide-safety standards on adults, but childen consume many more the fruits and fruit products likely too contain pestcides.

EXERCISE 12
Preparing your final draft

Prepare the final draft of the essay you have been working on throughout Chapters 1–3. Proofread carefully and correct all errors before submitting your essay for review.

3e Giving and receiving comments

1 Working collaboratively

Almost all the writing you do in college will generate responses from an instructor. In courses that stress writing, you may submit early drafts as well as your final paper, and your readers may include your classmates as well as your instructor. Like Sara Ling's, such courses may feature **collaborative learning,** in which students work together on writing, from completing exercises to commenting on each other's work to producing whole papers. (At more and more schools this group work occurs over a computer network. See pp. 243–52.)

Whether you participate as a writer or as a writing "coach," collaboration can give you experience in reading written work and in reaching readers through writing. You may at first be anxious about criticizing others' work or sharing your own rough drafts, but you'll soon grow to appreciate the interaction and the confidence it gives you in your own reading and writing.

ESL In some cultures writers do not expect criticism from readers, or readers do not expect to respond critically to what they read. If critical responses are uncommon in your native culture, collaboration may at first be uncomfortable for you. Consider that many writers in English think of a draft or even a final paper as an exploration of ideas, and they are interested in their readers' questions and suggestions. Readers of English, in turn, often approach a text in a skeptical frame of mind. Their tactful questions and suggestions are usually considered appropriate.

2 Responding to the writing of others

If you are the reader of someone else's writing, keep the following principles in mind:

Commenting on others' writing

- Be sure you know what the writer is saying. If necessary, summarize the paper to understand its content. (See pp. 127–28.)
- Unless you have other instructions, address only your most significant concerns with the work. (Use the revision checklist on p. 56 as a guide to what is significant.) Remember that you are the reader, not the writer. Resist the temptation to edit sentences, add details, or otherwise assume responsibility for the paper.
- Be specific. If something confuses you, say *why*. If you disagree with a conclusion, say *why*.
- Be supportive as well as honest. Tell the writer what you like about the paper. Word comments positively: instead of *This paragraph doesn't interest me,* say *You have an interesting detail here that I almost missed.* Comment in a way that emphasizes the effect of the work on you, the reader: *This paragraph confuses me because. . . .* And avoid measuring the work against a set of external standards: *This essay is poorly organized. Your thesis statement is inadequate.*
- While reading, make your comments in writing, even if you will be delivering them in person later on. Then you'll be able to recall what you thought.

(continued)

http://www.gmu.edu/departments/writingcenter/handouts/eiphand.html
"A Guide to Gracious Criticism," from George Mason University.

Commenting on others' writing
(continued)

- If you are reading the paper on a computer, not on paper, then be sure to specify what part of the paper each of your comments relates to. When you review papers using e-mail, you can embed your comments directly into the paper. You can do the same when you review papers in word-processor files, or you may be able to use your word processor's Comment function to insert your comments as annotations on the paper. (See pp. 243–52 for more about collaborating on computers and pp. 183–85 and 190 for more about word-processing functions.)
- If you are responding on paper or online, not face to face with the writer, remember that the writer won't be able to ask for immediate clarification or infer additional information from your gestures, facial expressions, and tone of voice. In these situations, word your comments carefully to avoid misunderstandings.

3 Responding to comments on your own writing

When you *receive* the comments of others, whether your classmates or your instructor, you will get more out of the process if you follow the guidelines below:

Benefiting from comments on your writing

- Think of your readers as counselors or coaches who will help you see the virtues and flaws in your work and sharpen your awareness of readers' needs.
- Read or listen to comments closely.
- Make sure you know what the critic is saying. If you need more information, ask for it, or consult the appropriate section of this handbook. (See "Preface for Students: Using This Book," p. v, for a guide to the handbook.)
- Don't become defensive. Letting comments offend you will only erect a barrier to improvement in your writing. As one writing teacher advises, "Leave your ego at the door."
- When comments seem appropriate, revise your work in response to them, whether or not you are required to do so. You will learn more from actually revising than from just thinking about it.
- Though you should be open to suggestions, you are the final authority on your paper. You are free to decline advice when you think it is inappropriate.
- Keep track of both the strengths and the weaknesses others identify. Then in following assignments you can build on your successes and give special attention to problem areas.

As the last item in the preceding box indicates, you'll gain the most from collaboration if you carry your learning from one assignment into the next. To keep track of things to work on, try a chart like the one below, with a vertical column for each assignment (or draft) and a horizontal row for each weakness. The handbook section is noted for each problem, and check marks indicate how often the problem occurs in each essay. The chart also provides a convenient place to keep track of words you misspell so that you can master their spellings.

	Assignment		
Weaknesses	**1**	**2**	**3**
not enough details for readers (1d)	✓	✓	✓
unity—wanders away from thesis (2c)	✓		
parallelism (25)	✓✓	✓	✓
agreement (15a)	✓		✓
comma splice (18)	✓✓	✓	✓
misspellings	among deceive	rebel seize	omission cruelty

3f Preparing a writing portfolio

Your writing teacher may ask you to assemble samples of your writing into a portfolio, or folder, once or more during the course. Such a portfolio gives you a chance to consider all your writing over a period and showcase your best work.

Teachers' requirements for portfolios vary. For instance, some teachers ask students to choose their five or so best papers and to submit final drafts only. Others ask for final papers illustrating certain kinds of writing—say, one narrative, one critique, one argument, one research paper, and so on. Still others ask for notes and

http://www.nau.edu/~comp/Portfolio_System.html Information about developing a writing portfolio, intended for students at Northern Arizona University but useful for others as well.

http://www.cwrl.utexas.edu/~syverson/olr/portfolios.html Creating an online writing portfolio, from the University of Texas.

drafts along with selected papers. If your class is using online writing tools, your work may be archived as part of the course site and you may be asked to submit your portfolio electronically.

Just as teachers' requirements differ, so do their purposes. But most are looking for a range of writing that demonstrates your progress and strengths as a writer. You, in turn, see how you have advanced from one assignment to the next, as you've had time for new knowledge to sink in and time for practice. Teachers often allow students to revise papers before placing them in the portfolio, even if the papers have already been submitted earlier. In that case, every paper in the portfolio can benefit from all your learning.

An assignment to assemble a writing portfolio will probably also provide guidelines for what to include, how the portfolio will be evaluated, and how (or whether) it will be weighted for a grade. Be sure you understand the purpose of the portfolio and who will read it. For instance, if your composition teacher will be the only reader and her guidelines urge you to show evidence of progress, you might include a paper that took big risks but never entirely succeeded. In contrast, if a committee of teachers will read your work and the guidelines urge you to demonstrate your competence as a writer, you might include only papers that did succeed.

Unless the guidelines specify otherwise, provide error-free copies of your final drafts, label all your samples with your name, and assemble them all in a folder. Add a cover letter or memo that lists the samples, explains why you've included each one, and evaluates your progress as a writer. The self-evaluation involved should be a learning experience for you and will help your teacher assess your development as a writer.

EXERCISE 13
Analyzing an essay

Carefully read the essay below by Johanna Abrams. (Abrams's earlier work on this essay appears on pp. 24–25 and 38–39.) Answer the following questions about the essay:

1. What is Abrams's purpose?
2. Who do you think constitutes Abrams's intended audience? What role does she seem to be assuming? What does the tone reveal about her attitude toward the topic?
3. How well does the thesis statement convey Abrams's purpose and attitude? What assertion does the thesis statement make? How specific is the statement? How well does it preview Abrams's ideas and organization?
4. What organization does Abrams use? Is it clear throughout the essay?
5. What details, examples, and reasons does Abrams use to support her ideas? Where is supporting evidence skimpy?

6. How successful is Abrams in making you care about the topic and her views of it?

(For a computer exercise on Abrams's paper, see p. 191. You can view and download the paper at the Web site for this book: *http://www.awlonline.com/littlebrown.*)

Working in the Barnyard

Until two months ago I thought summer jobs occupied time and helped pay the next year's tuition but otherwise provided no useful training. Then I took a temporary job in a large government agency. Two months there taught me the very valuable lesson that the hierarchy of supervisor to employee should be respected.

Last May I was hired by the personnel department of the agency to fill in for vacationing workers in the mail room. I had seven coworkers and a boss, Mrs. King. Our job was to sort the huge morning and afternoon mail shipments into four hundred slots, one for every employee in the agency. Then we delivered the sorted mail out of grocery carts that we wheeled from office to office along assigned corridors, picking up outgoing mail as we went along. Each mail delivery took an entire half-day to sort and deliver.

My troubles began almost as soon as I arrived. Hundreds of pieces of mail were dumped on a shallow table against a wall of mail slots. I was horrified to see that the slots were labeled not with people's names but with their initials—whereas the incoming letters, of course, contained full names. Without thinking, I asked why this was a good idea, only to receive a sharp glance from Mrs. King. So I repeated the question. This time Mrs. King told me not to question what I didn't understand. It was the first of many such exchanges, and I hadn't been on the job a half-hour.

I mastered the initials and the sorting and delivery procedures after about a week. But the longer I worked at the job, the more I saw how inefficient all the procedures were, from delivery routes to times for coffee breaks. When I asked Mrs. King about the procedures, however, she always reacted the same way: it was none of my business.

I pestered Mrs. King more and more over the next seven weeks, but my efforts were fruitless, even counterproductive. Mrs. King began calling me snide names. Then she began picking on my work and singling me out for reprimands, even though I did my best and worked faster than most of the others.

Two months after I had started work, the personnel manager called me in and fired me. I objected, of course, calling up all the deficiencies I had seen in Mrs. King and her systems. The manager interrupted to ask if I had ever heard of the barnyard pecking order: the top chicken pecks on the one below it, the second pecks on the third, and so on all the way down the line to the lowliest chicken, whose life is a constant misery. Mrs. King, the manager said, was that lowliest chicken at the bottom of the pecking order in the agency's management. With little education, she had spent her entire adult life building up her small domain, and she had to protect it from everyone, especially the people who worked for her. The arbitrariness of her systems was an assertion of her power, for no one should doubt for a moment that she ruled her roost.

I had a month before school began again to think about my adventure. At first it irritated me that I should be humiliated while Mrs. King continued on as before. But eventually I saw how arrogant, and how unsympathetic, my behavior had been. In my next job, I'll learn the pecking order before I become a crusader, *if* I do.

—Johanna Abrams

CHAPTER 4

Writing and Revising Paragraphs

A **paragraph** is a group of related sentences set off by a beginning indention or, sometimes, by extra space. For you and your readers, paragraphs provide breathers from long stretches of text and indicate key changes in the development of your thesis. They help to organize and clarify ideas.

In the body of your essay, you may use paragraphs for any of these purposes:

- To introduce one of the main points supporting your essay's central idea (its thesis) and to develop the point with examples, facts, or other supporting evidence. (See pp. 30–34 for a discussion of an essay's thesis.)
- Within a group of paragraphs centering on one main point, to introduce and develop a key example or other important evidence.
- To shift approach—for instance, from pros to cons, from problem to solution, from questions to answers.
- To mark movement in a sequence, such as from one reason or step to another.

In addition, you will use paragraphs for special purposes:

- To introduce or to conclude an essay. (See pp. 106 and 109.)
- Occasionally, to give strong emphasis to an important point or mark a significant transition from one point to another. (See p. 111.)
- In dialogue, to indicate that a new person has begun speaking. (See p. 112.)

The following paragraph illustrates simply how an effective body paragraph works to help both writer and reader. The thesis of the essay in which this paragraph appears is that a Texas chili championship gives undue attention to an unpleasant food.

http://www.clearcf.uvic.ca/writersguide/Pages/paragraphsTOC.html
Developing and organizing paragraphs, from the University of Victoria.

¶ un 4

> Some people really like chili, apparently, but nobody can agree how the stuff should be made. C. V. Wood, twice winner at Terlingua, uses flank steak, pork chops, chicken, and green chilis. My friend Hughes Rudd of CBS News, who imported five hundred pounds of chili powder into Russia as a condition of accepting employment as Moscow correspondent, favors coarse-ground beef. Isadore Bleckman, the cameraman I must live with on the road, insists upon one-inch cubes of stew beef and puts garlic in his chili, an Illinois affectation. An Indian of my acquaintance, Mr. Fulton Batisse, who eats chili for breakfast when he can, uses buffalo meat and plays an Indian drum while it's cooking. I ask you.
>
> —CHARLES KURALT, *Dateline America*

General statement relating to thesis: announces topic of paragraph

Four specific examples, all providing evidence for general statement

While you are drafting, conscious attention to the requirements of the paragraph may sometimes help pull ideas out of you or help you forge relationships. But don't expect effective paragraphs like Kuralt's to flow from your fingertips while you are grappling with what you want to say. Instead, use the following checklist to guide your revision of paragraphs so that they work to your and your readers' advantage:

Checklist for revising paragraphs

- Is the paragraph **unified?** Does it adhere to one general idea that is either stated in a **topic sentence** or otherwise apparent? (See opposite.)
- Is the paragraph **coherent?** Do the sentences follow a clear sequence (p. 82)? Are the sentences linked as needed by parallelism (p. 86), repetition or restatement (p. 86), pronouns (p. 87), consistency (p. 87), and transitional expressions (p. 88)?
- Is the paragraph **developed?** Is the general idea of the paragraph well supported with specific evidence such as details, facts, examples, and reasons? (See p. 93.)

On the World Wide Web, the paragraphing conventions described here do not always apply. Web readers sometimes skim text instead of reading word for word, and they are accustomed to embedded links that may take them from the paragraph to another page. Writing for the Web, you still want to unify your paragraphs around a central idea and connect sentences with coherence devices such as restatement and transitional expressions. But you may want to write shorter paragraphs than you would in printed documents, leaving some development to linked pages. And you may want to place embedded links near the ends of paragraphs so that readers who pursue the links don't miss important information. (For more on composing for the Web, see pp. 224–42.)

ESL Not all languages share the conventions of English paragraphs. In some languages, for instance, writing moves differently from English—not from left to right, but from right to left or down rows from top to bottom. Even in languages that move as English does, writers may not use paragraphs at all. Or they may use paragraphs but not state the central ideas or provide transitional expressions to show readers how sentences relate. If your native language is not English and you have difficulty with paragraphs, don't worry about paragraphing during drafting. Instead, during a separate step of revision, divide your text into parts that develop your main points. Mark those parts with indentions.

4a Maintaining paragraph unity

Readers generally expect a paragraph to explore one idea. They will be alert for that idea and will patiently follow its development. In other words, they will seek and appreciate paragraph **unity,** clear identification and clear elaboration of one idea and of that idea only.

In an essay the thesis statement often asserts the main idea as a commitment to readers (see p. 30). In a paragraph a **topic sentence** often alerts readers to the essence of the paragraph by asserting the central idea and expressing the writer's attitude toward it. In a brief essay each body paragraph will likely treat one main point supporting the essay's thesis statement; the topic sentences simply elaborate on parts of the thesis. In longer essays paragraphs tend to work in groups, each group treating one main point. Then the topic sentences will tie into that main point, and all the points together will support the thesis.

1 Focusing on the central idea

Like the thesis sentence, the topic sentence is a commitment to readers, and the rest of the paragraph delivers on that commitment. Look again at Kuralt's paragraph on chili (opposite page):

http://webster.commnet.edu/HP/pages/darling/grammar/paragraphs.htm
Building paragraphs using topic sentences, from the Guide to Grammar and Writing.

the opening statement conveys the author's promise that he will describe various ways to make chili, and the following sentences keep the promise. But what if Kuralt had written this paragraph instead?

> Some people really like chili, apparently, but nobody can agree how the stuff should be made. [Topic sentence: general statement] C. V. Wood, twice winner at Terlingua, uses flank steak, pork chops, chicken, and green chilis. My friend Hughes Rudd, who imported five hundred pounds of chili powder into Russia as a condition of accepting employment as Moscow correspondent, favors coarse-ground beef. [Two examples supporting statement] He had some trouble finding the beef in Moscow, though. He sometimes had to scour all the markets and wait in long lines. For any American used to overstocked supermarkets and department stores, Russia can be quite a shock. [Digression]

By wandering off from chili ingredients to consumer deprivation in Russia, the paragraph fails to deliver on the commitment of its topic sentence.

You should expect digressions while you are drafting: if you allow yourself to explore ideas, as you should, then of course every paragraph will not be tightly woven, perfectly unified. But spare your readers the challenge and frustration of repeatedly shifting focus to follow your rough explorations: revise each paragraph so that it develops a single idea.

While revising your paragraphs for unity, you may want to highlight the central idea of each paragraph to be sure it's stated and to focus on it. On paper, you can bracket or circle the idea. On a computer, you can underline or boldface the idea. Just be sure to remove the highlighting before printing the final draft.

2 Placing the topic sentence

The topic sentence of a paragraph and its supporting details may be arranged variously, depending on how you want to direct readers' attention and how complex your central idea is. In the most common arrangements, the topic sentence comes at the beginning of the paragraph, comes at the end, or is not stated at all but is nonetheless apparent. The advantages of each approach are described below. If you write on a computer, you can easily experiment with different positions by moving the topic sentence around (or deleting it) to see the effect. (The sentence will probably take some editing to work smoothly into various positions.)

Topic sentence at the beginning

When the topic sentence appears first in a paragraph, it can help you select the details that follow. For readers, the topic-first model establishes an initial context in which all the supporting details can be understood. Look again at Kuralt's paragraph on page 74 to see how easily we readers relate each detail or example back to the point made in the first sentence.

The topic-first model is common not only in expository paragraphs, such as Kuralt's, but also in argument paragraphs, such as the one following:

> It is a misunderstanding of the American retail store to think we go there necessarily to buy. Some of us shop. There's a difference. Shopping has many purposes, the least interesting of which is to acquire new articles. We shop to cheer ourselves up. We shop to practice decision-making. We shop to be useful and productive members of our class and society. We shop to remind ourselves how much is available to us. We shop to remind ourselves how much is to be striven for. We shop to assert our superiority to the material objects that spread themselves before us.
>
> —PHYLLIS ROSE, "Shopping and Other Spiritual Adventures"

Topic sentence: statement of misconception

Correction of misconception

Topic sentence at the end

In some paragraphs the central idea may be stated at the end, after supporting sentences have made a case for the general statement. Since this model leads the reader to a conclusion by presenting all the evidence first, it can prove effective in argument. And because the point of the paragraph is withheld until the end, this model can be dramatic in exposition too, as illustrated by the following example from an essay about William Tecumseh Sherman, a Union general during the US Civil War:

> Sherman is considered by some to be the inventor of "total war": the first general in human history to carry the logic of war to its ultimate extreme, the first to scorch the earth, the first to consciously demoralize the hostile civilian population in order to subdue its army, the first to wreck an economy in order to starve its soldiers. He has been called our first "merchant of terror" and seen as the spiritual father of our Vietnam War concepts of "search and destroy," "pacification," "strategic hamlets," and "free-fire

Information supporting and building to topic sentence

> zones." As such, he remains a cardboard figure of our history: a monstrous arch-villain to unreconstructed Southerners, and an embarrassment to Northerners. [Topic sentence]
>
> —Adapted from JAMES RESTON, JR., "You Cannot Refine It"

Expressing the central idea at the end of the paragraph does not eliminate the need to unify the paragraph. The idea in the topic sentence must still govern the selection of all the preceding details.

Central idea not stated

Occasionally, a paragraph's central idea will be stated in the previous paragraph or will be so obvious that it need not be stated at all. The following is from an essay on the actor Humphrey Bogart:

> Usually he wore the trench coat unbuttoned, just tied with the belt, and a slouch hat, rarely tilted. Sometimes it was a captain's cap and a yachting jacket. Almost always his trousers were held up by a cowboy belt. You know the kind: one an Easterner waiting for a plane out of Phoenix buys just as a joke and then takes a liking to. Occasionally, he'd hitch up his slacks with it, and he often jabbed his thumbs behind it, his hands ready for a fight or a dame. [Details adding up to the unstated idea that Bogart's character could be seen in his clothing]
>
> —PETER BOGDANOVICH, "Bogie in Excelsis"

Paragraphs in descriptive writing (like the one above) and in narrative writing (relating a sequence of events) often lack stated topic sentences. But a paragraph without a topic sentence still should have a central idea, and its details should develop that idea.

EXERCISE 1
Finding the central idea

What is the central idea of each paragraph below? In what sentence or sentences is it expressed?

1. Today many black Americans enjoy a measure of economic se- 1
curity beyond any we have known in the history of black America.
But if they remain in a nasty blue funk, it's because their very exis- 2
tence seems an affront to the swelling ranks of the poor. Nor have 3
black intellectuals ever quite made peace with the concept of the
black bourgeoisie, a group that is typically seen as devoid of cultural authenticity, doomed to mimicry and pallid assimilation. I 4
once gave a talk before an audience of black academics and educators, in the course of which I referred to black middle-class culture.
Afterward, one of the academics in the audience, deeply affronted, 5
had a question for me. "Professor Gates," he asked rhetorically, his 6

voice dripping with sarcasm, "what *is* black middle-class culture?"
I suggested that if he really wanted to know, he need only look 7
around the room. But perhaps I should just have handed him a 8
mirror: for just as nothing is more American than anti-American-
ism, nothing is more characteristic of the black bourgeoisie than
the sense of shame and denial that the identity inspires.

—HENRY LOUIS GATES, JR., "Two Nations . . . Both Black"

2. Though they do not know why the humpback whale sings, 1
scientists do know something about the song itself. They have 2
measured the length of a whale's song: from a few minutes to
over half an hour. They have recorded and studied the variety 3
and complex arrangements of low moans, high squeaks, and slid-
ing squeals that make up the song. And they have learned that 4
each whale sings in its own unique pattern.

—JANET LIEBER (student), "Whales' Songs"

EXERCISE 2
Revising a paragraph for unity

The following paragraph contains ideas or details that do not support its central idea. Identify the topic sentence in the paragraph and delete the unrelated material.

In the southern part of the state, some people still live much as they did a century ago. They use coal- or wood-burning stoves for heating and cooking. Their homes do not have electricity or indoor bathrooms or running water. The towns they live in don't receive adequate funding from the state and federal governments, so the schools are poor and in bad shape. Beside most homes there is a garden where fresh vegetables are gathered for canning. Small pastures nearby support livestock, including cattle, pigs, horses, and chickens. Most of the people have cars or trucks, but the vehicles are old and beat-up from traveling on unpaved roads.

EXERCISE 3
Considering your past work: Paragraph unity

For a continuing exercise in this chapter, choose a paper you've written in the past year. Examine the body paragraphs for unity. Do they have clear topic sentences? If not, are the paragraphs' central ideas still clear? Are the paragraphs unified around their central ideas? Should any details be deleted for unity? Should other, more relevant details be added in their stead?

EXERCISE 4
Collaborating on paragraph unity

Either online or face to face, discuss with at least one classmate the challenges of creating unified paragraphs. While drafting, for example, do you have difficulty sticking with a central idea? While revising, do you have difficulty locating digressions or cutting unrelated sentences that took a lot of effort to write? What strategies can each participant contribute to help meet the challenges?

¶ coh
4b

EXERCISE 5
Writing a unified paragraph

Develop the following topic sentence into a unified paragraph by using the relevant information in the statements below it. Delete each statement that does not relate directly to the topic, and then rewrite and combine sentences as appropriate. Place the topic sentence in the position that seems most effective to you.

Topic sentence

Mozart's accomplishments in music seem remarkable even today.

Supporting information

Wolfgang Amadeus Mozart was born in 1756 in Salzburg, Austria.
He began composing music at the age of five.
He lived most of his life in Salzburg and Vienna.
His first concert tour of Europe was at the age of six.
On his first tour he played harpsichord, organ, and violin.
He published numerous compositions before reaching adolescence.
He married in 1782.
Mozart and his wife were both poor managers of money.
They were plagued by debts.
Mozart composed over six hundred musical compositions.
His most notable works are his operas, symphonies, quartets, and piano concertos.
He died at the age of thirty-five.

EXERCISE 6
Turning topic sentences into unified paragraphs

Develop three of the following topic sentences into detailed and unified paragraphs.

1. Men and women are different in at least one important respect.
2. The best Web search engine is [*name*].
3. Fans of country music [or rock music, classical music, jazz] come in [*number*] varieties.
4. Professional sports have [or have not] been helped by extending the regular season with championship play-offs.
5. Working for good grades can interfere with learning.

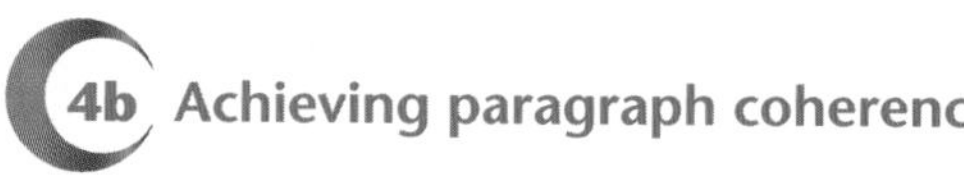

4b Achieving paragraph coherence

A paragraph is unified if it holds together—if all its details and examples support the central idea. A paragraph is **coherent** if readers can see *how* the paragraph holds together—how the sentences relate to each other—without having to stop and reread. The following box summarizes how to make a paragraph coherent so that it clarifies relationships:

Ways to achieve paragraph coherence

- Organize effectively (p. 82).
- Use parallel structures (p. 86).
- Repeat or restate words and word groups (p. 86).
- Use pronouns (p. 87).
- Be consistent in nouns, pronouns, and verbs (p. 87).
- Use transitional expressions (p. 88).

Incoherence gives readers the feeling of being yanked around, as the following example shows:

> The ancient Egyptians were masters of preserving dead people's bodies by making mummies of them. Mummies several thousand years old have been discovered nearly intact. The skin, hair, teeth, finger- and toenails, and facial features of the mummies were evident. It is possible to diagnose the diseases they suffered in life, such as smallpox, arthritis, and nutritional deficiencies. The process was remarkably effective. Sometimes apparent were the fatal afflictions of the dead people: a middle-aged king died from a blow on the head, and polio killed a child king. Mummification consisted of removing the internal organs, applying natural preservatives inside and out, and then wrapping the body in layers of bandages.

Topic sentence

Sentences related to topic sentence but disconnected from each other

The paragraph as it was actually written appears on the next page. It is much clearer because the writer arranged information differently and also built links into his sentences so that they would flow smoothly:

- After stating the central idea in a topic sentence, the writer moves to two more specific explanations and illustrates the second with four sentences of examples.
- Circled words repeat or restate key terms or concepts.
- Boxed words link sentences and clarify relationships.
- Underlined phrases are in parallel grammatical form to reflect their parallel content.

Strategies and devices for achieving paragraph coherence:

http://owl.english.purdue.edu/Files/100.html From the Purdue Online Writing Lab.

http://webster.commnet.edu/HP/pages/darling/grammar/transitions.htm From the Guide to Grammar and Writing.

> The ancient Egyptians were masters of preserving dead people's bodies by making mummies of them. Basically, mummification consisted of removing the internal organs, applying natural preservatives inside and out, and then wrapping the body in layers of bandages. And the process was remarkably effective. Indeed, mummies several thousand years old have been discovered nearly intact. Their skin, hair, teeth, finger- and toenails, and facial features are still evident. Their diseases in life, such as smallpox, arthritis, and nutritional deficiencies, are still diagnosable. Even their fatal afflictions are still apparent: a middle-aged king died from a blow on the head; a child king died from polio.
>
> —MITCHELL ROSENBAUM (student), "Lost Arts of the Egyptians"

Topic Sentence

Explanation 1: what mummification is

Explanation 2: why the Egyptians were masters

Specific examples of explanation 2

Though some of the connections in this paragraph were added in revision, the writer attended to them while drafting as well. Not only superficial coherence but also an underlying clarity of relationships can be achieved by tying each sentence to the one before—generalizing from it, clarifying it, qualifying it, adding to it, illustrating it. Each sentence in a paragraph creates an expectation of some sort in the mind of the reader, a question such as "How was a mummy made?" or "How intact are the mummies?" or "What's another example?" When you recognize these expectations and try to fulfill them, readers are likely to understand relationships without struggle.

1 Organizing the paragraph

The paragraphs on mummies illustrate an essential element of coherence: information must be arranged in an order that readers can follow easily and that corresponds to their expectations. The common organizations for paragraphs correspond to those for entire essays (see pp. 42–45): by space, by time, and for emphasis. (In addition, the patterns of development also suggest certain arrangements. See pp. 95–104.)

If you want to try rearranging a paragraph to achieve different emphases, you can easily do so on a computer by moving sentences around. To evaluate the versions, however, you need to edit each one so that the sentences flow smoothly, attending to parallelism, repetition, transitions, and the other techniques discussed in this section.

Organizing by space or time

A paragraph organized **spatially** focuses readers' attention on one point and scans a person, object, or scene from that point. The movement usually parallels the way people actually look at things, from top to bottom, from side to side, from near to far. Virginia Woolf follows the last pattern in this paragraph:

> The sun struck straight upon the house, making the white walls glare between the dark windows. Their panes, woven thickly with green branches, held circles of impenetrable darkness. Sharp-edged wedges of light lay upon the window-sill and showed inside the room plates with blue rings, cups with curved handles, the bulge of a great bowl, the criss-cross pattern in the rug, and the formidable corners and lines of cabinets and bookcases. Behind their conglomeration hung a zone of shadow in which might be a further shape to be disencumbered of shadow or still denser depths of darkness.
>
> —Virginia Woolf, *The Waves*

Description moving from outside (closer) to inside (farther)

Unstated central idea: sunlight barely penetrated the house's secrets.

Another familiar way of organizing the elements of a paragraph is **chronologically**—that is, in order of their occurrence in time. In a chronological paragraph, as in experience, the earliest events come first, followed by more recent ones.

> Nor can a tree live without soil. A hurricane-born mangrove island may bring its own soil to the sea. But other mangrove trees make their own soil—and their own islands—from scratch. These are the ones which interest me. The seeds germinate in the fruit on the tree. The germinated embryo can drop anywhere—say, onto a dab of floating muck. The heavy root end sinks; a leafy plumule unfurls. The tiny seedling, afloat, is on its way. Soon aerial roots shooting out in all directions trap debris. The sapling's networks twine, the interstices narrow, and water calms in the lee. Bacteria thrive on organic broth; amphipods swarm. These creatures grow and die at the tree's wet feet. The soil thickens, accumulating rainwater, leaf rot, seashells, and guano; the island spreads.
>
> —Annie Dillard, "Sojourner"

Topic sentence

Details in order of their occurrence

Organizing for emphasis

Some organizational schemes are imposed on paragraphs to achieve a certain emphasis. The most common is the **general-to-specific** scheme, in which the topic sentence generally comes first and then the following sentences become increasingly specific. The paragraph on mummies (p. 82) illustrates this organization: each sentence is either more specific than the one before it or at the same level of generality. Here is another illustration:

> Perhaps the simplest fact about sleep is that individual needs for it vary widely. Most adults sleep between seven and nine hours, but occasionally people turn up who need twelve hours or so, while some rare types can get by on three or four. Rarest of all are those legendary types who require almost no sleep at all; respected researchers have recently studied three such people. One of them—a healthy, happy woman in her seventies—sleeps about an hour every two or three days. The other two are men in early middle age, who get by on a few minutes a night. One of them complains about the daily fifteen minutes or so he's forced to "waste" in sleeping.
>
> —Lawrence A. Mayer, "The Confounding Enemy of Sleep"

Topic sentence

Supporting examples, increasingly specific

In the less common **specific-to-general** organization, the elements of the paragraph build to a general conclusion:

> It's disconcerting that so many college women, when asked how their children will be cared for if they themselves work, refer with vague confidence to "the day care center" as though there were some great amorphous kiddie watcher out there that the state provides. But such places, adequately funded, well run, and available to all, are still scarce in this country, particularly for middle-class women. And figures show that when she takes time off for family-connected reasons (births, child care), a woman's chances for career advancement plummet. In a job market that's steadily tightening and getting more competitive, these obstacles bode the kind of danger ahead that can shatter not only professions, but egos. A hard reality is that there's not much more support for our daughters who have family-plus-career goals than there was for us; there's simply a great deal more self and societal pressure.
>
> —Judith Wax, *Starting in the Middle*

Common belief

Actual situation

General conclusion: topic sentence

As its name implies, the **problem-solution** arrangement introduces a problem and then proposes or explains a solution. This paragraph explains how to gain from Internet newsgroups despite their limitations:

> Even when you do find a newsgroup with apparently useful material, you have no assurance of a correspondent's authority because of e-mail's inherent anonymity. Many people don't cite their credentials. Besides, anyone can pose as an expert. The best information you can get initially is apt to be a reference to something of which you were not aware but can then investigate for yourself. Internet newsgroups can be valuable for that alone. I have been directed to software-problem solutions, owners of out-of-print books, and important people who know nothing about communicating through electronic communities. It is best to start with the assumption that you are conversing with peers, people who know things that you don't, while you probably know things that they don't. Gradually, by trading information, you develop some virtual relationships and can assess the relative validity of your sources. Meanwhile, you will probably have learned a few things along the way.
>
> —Adapted from John A. Butler, *Cybersearch*

Topic sentence and clarification: statement of the problem

Solution to the problem

When your details vary in significance, you can arrange them in a **climactic** order, from least to most important or dramatic:

> Nature has put many strange tongues into the heads of her creatures. There is the frog's tongue, rooted at the front of the mouth so it can be protruded an extra distance for nabbing prey. There is the gecko lizard's tongue, so long and agile that the lizard uses it to wash its eyes. But the ultimate lingual whopper has been achieved in the anteater. The anteater's head, long as it is, is not long enough to contain the tremendous tongue which licks deep into anthills. Its tongue is not rooted in the mouth or throat: it is fastened to the breastbone.
>
> —Alan Devoe, "Nature's Utmost"

Topic sentence

Least dramatic example

Most dramatic example

In other organizations, you can arrange details according to how you think readers are likely to understand them. In discussing the virtues of public television, for instance, you might proceed from **most familiar to least familiar,** from a well-known program your readers have probably seen to less well-known programs they may not have seen. Or in defending the right of government employees to strike, you might arrange your reasons from **simplest to most complex,** from the employees' need to be able to redress grievances to more subtle consequences for relations between employers and employees.

2 Using parallel structures

Another way to achieve coherence, although not necessarily in every paragraph, is through **parallelism**—the use of similar grammatical structures for similar elements of meaning within a sentence or among sentences. (See Chapter 25 for a detailed discussion of parallelism.) Parallel structures help tie together the last three sentences in the paragraph on mummies (p. 82). In the following paragraph, underlining highlights the parallel structures linking sentences. Aphra Behn (lived 1640–89) was the first Englishwoman to write professionally.

> In addition to her busy career as a writer, Aphra Behn also found time to briefly marry and spend a little while in debtor's prison. She found time to take up a career as a spy for the English in their war against the Dutch. She made the long and difficult voyage to Suriname [in South America] and became involved in a slave rebellion there. She plunged into political debate at Will's Coffee House and defended her position from the stage of the Drury Lane Theater. She actively argued for women's rights to be educated and to marry whom they pleased, or not at all. She defied the seventeenth-century dictum that ladies must be "modest" and wrote freely about sex. —Angeline Goreau, "Aphra Behn"

3 Repeating or restating words and word groups

Repeating or restating key words or word groups is an important means of achieving paragraph coherence and of reminding your readers what the topic is. In the next example, notice how the circled words tie the sentences together and stress the important ideas of the paragraph:

> Having listened to both Chinese and English, I also tend to be suspicious of any comparisons between the two languages. Typically, one language—that of the person doing the comparing—is often used as the standard, the benchmark for a logical form of expression. And so the language being compared is always in danger of being judged deficient or superfluous, simplistic or unnecessarily complex, melodious or cacophonous. English speakers point out that Chinese is extremely difficult because it relies on variations in

> tone barely discernible to the human ear. By the same token, Chinese speakers tell me English is extremely difficult because it is inconsistent, a language of too many broken rules, of Mickey Mice and Donald Ducks. —AMY TAN, "The Language of Discretion"

Note Though planned repetition can be effective, careless or excessive repetition weakens prose (see p. 581).

4 Using pronouns

Pronouns, such as *she, he, it, they,* and *who,* refer to and function as nouns (see p. 292). Thus pronouns naturally help relate sentences to one another. In the following paragraph the pronouns and the nouns they refer to are circled:

> After dark, on the warrenlike streets of Brooklyn where I live, I often see women who fear the worst from me. They seem to have set their faces on neutral, and with their purse straps strung across their chests bandolier-style, they forge ahead as though bracing themselves against being tackled. I understand, of course, that the danger they perceive is not a hallucination. Women are particularly vulnerable to street violence, and young black males are drastically overrepresented among the perpetrators of that violence. Yet these truths are no solace against the kind of alienation that comes of being ever the suspect, a fearsome entity with whom pedestrians avoid making eye contact.
>
> —BRENT STAPLES, "Black Men and Public Space"

5 Being consistent

Being consistent is the most subtle way to achieve paragraph coherence because readers are aware of consistency only when it is absent. Consistency (or the lack of it) occurs primarily in the tense of verbs and the number and person of nouns and pronouns (see Chapter 20). Although some shifts will be necessary because of meaning, inappropriate shifts, as in the following passages, will interfere with a reader's ability to follow the development of ideas:

Shifts in tense

In the Hopi religion, water is the driving force. Since the Hopi lived in the Arizona desert, they needed water urgently for drinking, cooking, and irrigating crops. Their complex beliefs are focused in part on gaining the assistance of supernatural forces in obtaining water. Many of the Hopi kachinas, or spirit essences, were directly concerned with clouds, rain, and snow.

Shifts in number

Kachinas represent spiritually the things and events of the real world, such as cumulus clouds, mischief, cornmeal, and even death. A kachina is not worshipped as a god but regarded as an interested friend. They visit the Hopi from December through July in the form of men who dress in kachina costumes and perform dances and other rituals.

Shifts in person

Unlike the man, the Hopi woman does not keep contact with kachinas through costumes and dancing. Instead, one receives a tihu, or small effigy, of a kachina from the man impersonating the kachina. You are more likely to receive a tihu as a girl approaching marriage, though a child or older woman sometimes receives one, too.

The grammar checker on a word processor cannot help you locate shifts in tense, number, or person among sentences. As noted before, shifts are sometimes necessary (as when tenses change to reflect actual differences in time), and even a passage with needless shifts may still consist of sentences that are grammatically correct (as all the sentences are in the preceding examples). The only way to achieve consistency in your writing is to review it yourself. (See pp. 188–89 for more on grammar checkers.)

6 Using transitional expressions

Specific words and word groups, called **transitional expressions,** can connect sentences whose relationships may not be instantly clear to readers. Notice the difference in these two versions of the same paragraph:

> Medical science has succeeded in identifying the hundreds of viruses that can cause the common cold. It has discovered the most effective means of prevention. One person transmits the cold viruses to another most often by hand. An infected person covers his mouth to cough. He picks up the telephone. His daughter picks up the telephone. She rubs her eyes. She has a cold. It spreads. To avoid colds, people should wash their hands often and keep their hands away from their faces.

Paragraph is choppy and hard to follow

http://www.unc.edu/depts/wcweb/handouts/transitions.html The functions of transitions, from the University of North Carolina.

http://www.wisc.edu/writetest/Handbook/Transitions.html Transitional expressions, from the University of Wisconsin.

> Medical science has thus succeeded in identifying the hundreds of viruses that can cause the common cold. It has also discovered the most effective means of prevention. One person transmits the cold viruses to another most often by hand. For instance, an infected person covers his mouth to cough. Then he picks up the telephone. Half an hour later, his daughter picks up the same telephone. Immediately afterward, she rubs her eyes. Within a few days, she, too, has a cold. And thus it spreads. To avoid colds, therefore, people should wash their hands often and keep their hands away from their faces.
>
> —Kathleen LaFrank (student), "Colds: Myth and Science"

Transitional expressions (boxed) remove choppiness and spell out relationships

To see where transitional expressions might be needed in your paragraphs, examine the movement from each sentence to the next. (On a computer or on paper, you can highlight the transitional expressions already present and check the sentences without them.) Abrupt changes are most likely to need a transition: a shift from cause to effect, a contradiction, a contrast. But you can also smooth and clarify other kinds of transitions, such as those in the headings of the following box. (You can smooth and clarify transitions *between* paragraphs, too. See pp. 112 and 113–15.)

Transitional expressions

To add or show sequence

again, also, and, and then, besides, equally important, finally, first, further, furthermore, in addition, in the first place, last, moreover, next, second, still, too

To compare

also, in the same way, likewise, similarly

To contrast

although, and yet, but, but at the same time, despite, even so, even though, for all that, however, in contrast, in spite of, nevertheless, notwithstanding, on the contrary, on the other hand, regardless, still, though, yet

(continued)

Transitional expressions
(continued)

To give examples or intensify

after all, an illustration of, even, for example, for instance, indeed, in fact, it is true, of course, specifically, that is, to illustrate, truly

To indicate place

above, adjacent to, below, elsewhere, farther on, here, near, nearby, on the other side, opposite to, there, to the east, to the left

To indicate time

after a while, afterward, as long as, as soon as, at last, at length, at that time, before, earlier, formerly, immediately, in the meantime, in the past, lately, later, meanwhile, now, presently, shortly, simultaneously, since, so far, soon, subsequently, then, thereafter, until, when

To repeat, summarize, or conclude

all in all, altogether, as has been said, in brief, in conclusion, in other words, in particular, in short, in simpler terms, in summary, on the whole, that is, therefore, to put it differently, to summarize

To show cause or effect

accordingly, as a result, because, consequently, for this purpose, hence, otherwise, since, then, therefore, thereupon, thus, to this end, with this object

---

Note Draw carefully on this list of transitional expressions because the ones in each group are not interchangeable. For instance, *besides, finally,* and *second* may all be used to add information, but each has its own distinct meaning.

ESL If transitional expressions are not common in your native language, you may be tempted to compensate when writing in English by adding them to the beginnings of most sentences. But such explicit transitions aren't needed everywhere, and in fact too many can be intrusive and awkward. When inserting transitional expressions, consider the reader's need for a signal: often the connection from sentence to sentence is already clear from the context, or it can be made clear by relating the content of sentences more closely (see p. 86–87). When you do need transitional expressions, try varying their positions in your sentences, as shown in the sample paragraph on the preceding page.

Punctuating transitional expressions

A transitional expression is usually set off by a comma or commas from the rest of the sentence:

Immediately afterward, she rubs her eyes. Within a few days, she, too, has a cold.

See page 475 for more on this convention and its exceptions.

7 Combining devices to achieve coherence

The devices we have examined for achieving coherence rarely appear in isolation in effective paragraphs. As any example in this chapter shows, writers usually combine sensible organization, parallelism, repetition, pronouns, consistency, and transitional expressions to help readers follow the development of ideas. And the devices also figure, naturally, in the whole essay (see pp. 114–15 for an example of paragraphs linked in an essay).

EXERCISE 7
Analyzing paragraphs for coherence

Study the paragraphs by Janet Lieber (p. 79), Hillary Begas (p. 95), and Freeman Dyson (p. 97) for the authors' use of various devices to achieve coherence. Look especially for organization, parallel structures and ideas, repetition and restatement, pronouns, and transitional expressions.

EXERCISE 8
Arranging sentences coherently

After the topic sentence (sentence 1), the sentences in the student paragraph below have been deliberately scrambled to make the paragraph incoherent. Using the topic sentence and other clues as guides, rearrange the sentences in the paragraph to form a well-organized, coherent unit.

We hear complaints about the Postal Service all the time, 1
but we should not forget what it does *right*. The total volume of 2
mail delivered by the Postal Service each year makes up almost
half the total delivered in all the world. Its 70,000 employees han- 3
dle 140,000,000,000 pieces of mail each year. And when was the 4
last time they failed to deliver yours? In fact, on any given day 5
the Postal Service delivers almost as much mail as the rest of the
world combined. That huge number means over 2,000,000 pieces 6
per employee and over 560 pieces per man, woman, and child in
the country.

EXERCISE 9
Eliminating inconsistencies

The following paragraph is incoherent because of inconsistencies in person, number, or tense. Identify the inconsistencies and revise the paragraph to give it coherence. (For further exercises in eliminating inconsistencies, see pp. 391, 392–93, and 394–95.)

The Hopi tihu, or kachina effigy, is often called a "doll," but its owner, usually a girl or woman, does not regard them as a plaything. Instead, you treated them as a valued possession and hung them out of the way on a wall. For its owner the tihu represents a connection with the kachina's spirit. They are considered part of the kachina, carrying a portion of the kachina's power.

EXERCISE 10
Using transitional expressions

Transitional expressions have been removed from the following paragraph at the numbered blanks. Fill in each blank with an appropriate transitional expression (1) to contrast, (2) to intensify, and (3) to show effect. Consult the list on pages 89–90 if necessary.

All over the country, people are swimming, jogging, weightlifting, dancing, walking, playing tennis—doing anything to keep fit. ___(1)___ this school has consistently refused to construct and equip a fitness center. The school has ___(2)___ refused to open existing athletic facilities to all students, not just those playing organized sports. ___(3)___ students have no place to exercise except in their rooms and on dangerous public roads.

EXERCISE 11
Considering your past work: Paragraph coherence

Continuing from Exercise 3 (p. 79), examine the body paragraphs of your essay to see how coherent they are and how their coherence could be improved. Do the paragraphs have a clear organization? Do you use parallelism, repetition and restatement, pronouns, and transitional expressions to signal relationships? Are the paragraphs consistent in person, number, and tense? Revise two or three paragraphs in ways you think will improve their coherence.

EXERCISE 12
Collaborating on paragraph coherence

Either online or face to face, discuss with at least one classmate the advantages you as readers see in paragraph coherence. (For a starting point, you may want to use the unrevised and revised paragraphs on mummies given on pp. 81–82.) Then consider the challenges of creating coherent paragraphs. While drafting, for instance, do you have difficulty controlling organization or building in coherence devices such as restatement or transitional expressions? While revising, do you have difficulty rearranging material or rewriting sentences that took a lot of effort to draft? What strategies can each participant contribute to help meet the challenges?

EXERCISE 13
Writing a coherent paragraph

Write a coherent paragraph from the following information, combining and rewriting sentences as necessary. First, begin the paragraph with the topic sentence given and arrange the supporting sentences in a climactic order. Then combine and rewrite the supporting sentences, helping the reader see connections by introducing parallelism, repetition and restatement, pronouns, consistency, and transitional expressions.

Topic sentence

Hypnosis is far superior to drugs for relieving tension.

Supporting information

Hypnosis has none of the dangerous side effects of the drugs that relieve tension.
Tension-relieving drugs can cause weight loss or gain, illness, or even death.
Hypnosis is nonaddicting.
Most of the drugs that relieve tension do foster addiction.
Tension-relieving drugs are expensive.
Hypnosis is inexpensive even for people who have not mastered self-hypnosis.

EXERCISE 14
Turning topic sentences into coherent paragraphs

Develop three of the following topic sentences into coherent paragraphs. Organize your information by space, by time, or for emphasis, as seems most appropriate. Use parallelism, repetition and restatement, pronouns, consistency, and transitional expressions to link sentences.

1. The most interesting character in the book [or movie] was ________.
2. Of all my courses, ________ is the one that I think will serve me best throughout life.
3. Although we in the United States face many problems, the one we should concentrate on solving first is ________.
4. The most dramatic building in town is the ________.
5. Children should not have to worry about the future.

4c Developing the paragraph

In an essay that's understandable and interesting to readers, you will provide plenty of solid information to support your general statements. You work that information into the essay through the paragraph, as you build up each point relating to the thesis.

A paragraph may be unified and coherent but still be inadequate if you skimp on details. Take this example:

> Despite complaints from viewers, television commercials aren't getting any more realistic. Their makers still present idealized people in unreal situations. And the advertisers also persist in showing a version of male-

General statements needing examples to be convincing

> female relationships that can't exist in more than two households. What do the advertisers know about us, or about how we see ourselves, that makes them continue to plunge millions of dollars into these kinds of commercials?

This paragraph lacks **development,** completeness. It does not provide enough information for us to evaluate or even care about the writer's assertions.

1 Using specific information

If they are sound, the general statements you make in any writing will be based on what you have experienced, observed, read, and thought. Readers will assume as much and will expect you to provide the evidence for your statements—sensory details, facts, statistics, examples, quotations, reasons. Whatever helps you form your views you need, in turn, to share with readers.

Here is the actual version of the preceding sample paragraph. With examples, the paragraph is interesting and convincing.

> Despite complaints from viewers, television commercials aren't getting any more realistic. Their makers still present idealized people in unreal situations. Friendly shopkeepers stock only their favorite brand of toothpaste or coffee or soup. A mother cleans and buffs her kitchen floor to a mirror finish so her baby can play on it. A rosy-cheeked pregnant woman uses two babies, two packaged diapers neatly dissected, and two ink blotters to demonstrate one diaper's superior absorbency to her equally rosy-cheeked and pregnant friend. The advertisers also persist in showing a version of male-female relationships that can't exist in more than two households. The wife panics because a meddlesome neighbor points out that her husband's shirt is dirty. Or she fears for her marriage because her finicky husband doesn't like her coffee. What do the advertisers know about us, or about how we see ourselves, that makes them continue to plunge millions of dollars into these kinds of commercials?
>
> —Kelly Phelps (student), "Television Advertising"

Examples supporting general statements about idealized people and false relationships

If your readers often comment that your writing needs more specifics, you should focus on that improvement in your revisions. Try listing the general statements of each paragraph on lines by themselves with space underneath. Then use one of the discovery techniques discussed on pages 19–29 (freewriting, brainstorming, and so on) to find the details to support each sentence. Write these into your draft.  If you write on a computer, you can do this revision directly on your draft. First create a duplicate of your draft (see pp. 183–84), and then, working on the copy, separate the sentences and explore their support. Rewrite the details into sentences, reassemble the paragraph, and edit it for coherence.

2 Using a pattern of development

If you have difficulty developing an idea or shaping your information, then try using one of the patterns of development. (They correspond to the patterns of essay development discussed on pp. 26–28.) Ask yourself a series of questions about an idea.

How did it happen? (Narration)

Narration retells a significant sequence of events, usually in the order of their occurrence (that is, chronologically):

> Jill's story is typical for "recruits" to religious cults. She was very lonely in college and appreciated the attention of the nice young men and women who lived in a house near campus. They persuaded her to share their meals and then to move in with them. Between intense bombardments of "love," they deprived her of sleep and sometimes threatened to throw her out. Jill became increasingly confused and dependent, losing touch with any reality besides the one in the group. She dropped out of school and refused to see or communicate with her family. Before long she, too, was preying on lonely college students.
>
> —Hillary Begas (student), "The Love Bombers"

Important events in chronological order

As this paragraph illustrates, a narrator is concerned not just with the sequence of events but also with their consequence, their importance to the whole. Thus a narrative rarely corresponds to real time; instead, it collapses transitional or background events and focuses on events of particular interest. In addition, writers sometimes rearrange events, as when they simulate the workings of memory by flashing back to an earlier time.

http://www.clearcf.uvic.ca/writersguide/Pages/paragraphsTOC.html
Developing and organizing paragraphs with the patterns of development, from the University of Victoria.

How does it look, sound, feel, smell, taste? (Description)

Description details the sensory qualities of a person, place, thing, or feeling. You use concrete and specific words to convey a dominant mood, to illustrate an idea, or to achieve some other purpose. Some description is **subjective:** the writer filters the subject through his or her biases and emotions. In the subjective description by Virginia Woolf on page 83, the *glare* of the walls, the *impenetrable darkness,* the *bulge of a great bowl,* and the *formidable corners and lines* all indicate the author's feelings about what she describes.

In contrast to subjective description, journalists and scientists often favor description that is **objective,** conveying the subject without bias or emotion:

> The two toddlers, both boys, sat together for half an hour in a ten-foot-square room with yellow walls (one with a two-way mirror for observation) and a brown carpet. The room was unfurnished except for two small chairs and about two dozen toys. The boys' interaction was generally tense. They often struggled physically and verbally over several toys, especially a large red beach ball and a small wooden fire engine. The larger of the two boys often pushed the smaller away or pried his hands from the desired object. This larger boy never spoke, but he did make grunting sounds when he was engaging the other. In turn, the smaller boy twice uttered piercing screams of "No!" and once shouted "Stop that!" When he was left alone, he hummed and muttered to himself.
>
> —Ray Mattison (student), "Case Study: Play Patterns of Toddlers"

Objective description: specific record of sensory data without interpretation

What are examples of it or reasons for it? (Illustration or support)

Some ideas can be developed simply by **illustration or support**—supplying detailed examples or reasons. The writer of the paragraph on television commercials (p. 94) developed her idea with several specific examples of each general statement. You can also supply a single extended example:

> The language problem that I was attacking loomed larger and larger as I began to learn more. When I would describe in English certain concepts and objects enmeshed in Korean emotion and imagination, I became slowly aware of nuances, of differences between two languages even in simple expression. The remark "Kim entered the house" seems to be simple enough, yet, unless a

Topic sentence (assertion to be illustrated)

> reader has a clear visual image of a Korean house, his understanding of the sentence is not complete. When a Korean says he is "in the house," he may be in his courtyard, or on his porch, or in his small room! If I wanted to give a specific picture of entering the house in the Western sense, I had to say "room" instead of house—sometimes. I say "sometimes" because many Koreans entertain their guests on their porches and still are considered to be hospitable, and in the Korean sense, going into the "room" may be a more intimate act than it would be in the English sense. Such problems!
>
> —Kim Yong Ik, "A Book-Writing Venture"

Single detailed example

Sometimes you can develop a paragraph by providing your reasons for stating a general idea:

> There are three reasons, quite apart from scientific considerations, that mankind needs to travel in space. The first reason is the need for garbage disposal: we need to transfer industrial processes into space, so that the earth may remain a green and pleasant place for our grandchildren to live in. The second reason is the need to escape material impoverishment: the resources of this planet are finite, and we shall not forgo forever the abundant solar energy and minerals and living space that are spread out all around us. The third reason is our spiritual need for an open frontier: the ultimate purpose of space travel is to bring to humanity not only scientific discoveries and an occasional spectacular show on television but a real expansion of our spirit.
>
> —Freeman Dyson, "Disturbing the Universe"

Topic sentence

Three reasons arranged in order of increasing drama and importance

What is it? What does it encompass, and what does it exclude? (Definition)

A **definition** says what something is and is not, specifying the characteristics that distinguish the subject from the other members of its class. You can easily define concrete, noncontroversial terms in a single sentence: *A knife is a cutting instrument* (its class) *with a sharp blade set in a handle* (the characteristics that set it off from, say, scissors or a razor blade). But defining a complicated or controversial topic often requires extended explanation, and you may need to devote a whole paragraph or even an essay to it. Such a definition may provide examples to identify the subject's characteristics. It may also involve other methods of development discussed here, such as classification or comparison and contrast.

The following definition of the word *quality* comes from an essay asserting that "quality in product and effort has become a vanishing element of current civilization":

> In the hope of possibly reducing the hail of censure which is certain to greet this essay (I am thinking of going to Alaska or possibly Patagonia in the week it is published), let me say that quality, as I understand it, means investment of the best skill and effort possible to produce the finest and most admirable result possible. Its presence or absence in some degree characterizes every man-made object, service, skilled or unskilled labor—laying bricks, painting a picture, ironing shirts, practicing medicine, shoemaking, scholarship, writing a book. You do it well or you do it half-well. Materials are sound and durable or they are sleazy; method is painstaking or whatever is easiest. Quality is achieving or reaching for the highest standard as against being satisfied with the sloppy or fraudulent. It is honesty of purpose as against catering to cheap or sensational sentiment. It does not allow compromise with the second-rate.
>
> —Barbara Tuchman, "The Decline of Quality"

General definition

Activities in which quality may figure

Contrast between quality and nonquality

What are its parts or characteristics? (Division or analysis)

Division and **analysis** both involve separating something into its elements, the better to understand it. Here is a simple example:

> A typical daily newspaper compresses considerable information into the top of the first page, above the headlines. The most prominent feature of this space, the newspaper's name, is called the *logo* or *nameplate*. Under the logo and set off by rules is a line of small type called the *folio line,* which contains the date of the issue, the volume and issue numbers, copyright information, and the price. To the right of the logo is a block of small type called a *weather ear,* a summary of the day's forecast. And above the logo is a *skyline,* a kind of advertisement in which the paper's editors highlight a special feature of the issue.
>
> —Kansha Stone (student), "Anatomy of a Paper"

The subject being divided

Elements of the subject, arranged spatially

Generally, analysis goes beyond simply identifying elements. Often used as a synonym for *critical thinking,* analysis also involves interpreting the elements' meaning, significance, and relationships.

You identify and interpret elements according to your particular interest in the subject. (See pp. 118–36 for more on critical thinking and analysis.)

The following paragraph comes from an essay about soap operas. The analytical focus of the whole essay is the way soap operas provide viewers with a sense of community missing from their own lives. The paragraph itself has a narrower focus related to the broader one.

> The surface realism of the soap opera conjures up an illusion of "liveness." The domestic settings and easygoing rhythms encourage the viewer to believe that the drama, however ridiculous, is simply an extension of daily life. The conversation is so slow that some have called it "radio with pictures." (Advertisers have always assumed that busy housewives would listen, rather than watch.) Conversation is casual and colloquial, as though one were eavesdropping on neighbors. There is plenty of time to "read" the character's face; close-ups establish intimacy. The sets are comfortably familiar: well-lit interiors of living rooms, restaurants, offices, and hospitals. Daytime soaps have little of the glamour of their prime-time relations. The viewer easily imagines that the conversation is taking place in real time.
>
> —Ruth Rosen, "Search for Yesterday"

Topic and focus: how "liveness" seems an extension of daily life

Elements:
Slow conversation

Casual conversation

Intimate close-ups
Familiar sets

Absence of glamour
Appearance of real time

What groups or categories can it be sorted into? (Classification)

Classification involves sorting many things into groups based on their similarities. Using the pattern, we scan a large group composed of many members that share at least one characteristic—office workers, say—and we assign the members to smaller groups on the basis of some principle—salary, perhaps, or dependence on computers. Here is an example:

> In my experience, the parents who hire daytime sitters for their school-age children tend to fall into one of three groups. The first group includes parents who work and want someone to be at home when the children return from school. These parents are looking for an extension of themselves, someone who will give the care they would give if they were at home. The second group includes parents who may be home all day themselves but are too disorganized or too frazzled by their children's demands to handle child care alone.

Topic sentence

Three groups:
Alike in one way (all hire sitters)
No overlap in groups (each has a different attitude)

They are looking for an organizer and helpmate. The third and final group includes parents who do not want to be bothered by their children, whether they are home all day or not. Unlike the parents in the first two groups, who care for their children whenever and however they can, these parents are looking for a permanent substitute for themselves.

Classes arranged in order of increasing drama

—NANCY WHITTLE (student), "Modern Parenting"

How is it like, or different from, other things? (Comparison and contrast)

Asking about similarities and differences leads to **comparison and contrast:** comparison focuses on similarities, whereas contrast focuses on differences. The two may be used separately or together to develop an idea or to relate two or more things. Commonly, comparisons are organized in one of two ways. In the first, **subject by subject,** the two subjects are discussed separately, one at a time:

Consider the differences also in the behavior of rock and classical music audiences. At a rock concert, the audience members yell, whistle, sing along, and stamp their feet. They may even stand during the entire performance. The better the music, the more active they'll be. At a classical concert, in contrast, the better the performance, the more *still* the audience is. Members of the classical audience are so highly disciplined that they refrain from even clearing their throats or coughing. No matter what effect the powerful music has on their intellects and feelings, they sit on their hands.

Subjects: rock and classical audiences

Rock audience

Classical audience

—TONY NAHM (student), "Rock and Roll Is Here to Stay"

In the second comparative organization, **point by point,** the two subjects are discussed side by side and matched feature for feature:

The first electronic computer, ENIAC, went into operation just over fifty years ago, yet the differences between it and today's home computer are enormous. ENIAC was enormous itself, consisting of forty panels, each two feet wide and four feet deep. Today's PC or Macintosh, by contrast, can fit easily on one's desk or even lap. ENIAC had to be configured by hand, with its programmers taking up to two days to reset switches and cables. Today, the average home user can change

Subjects: ENIAC and home computer

Size: ENIAC, home computer

Ease of programming: ENIAC, home computer

programs in an instant. And for all its size and inconvenience, ENIAC was also slow. In its time, its operating speed of 100,000 pulses per second seemed amazingly fast. However, today's home machine can operate at 1 billion pulses per second or faster.

Speed: ENIAC, home computer

—Shirley Kajiwara (student),
"The Computers We Deserve"

The following examples show the two organizing schemes in outline form. The one on the left corresponds to the point-by-point paragraph about computers. The one on the right uses the same information but reorganizes it to cover the two subjects separately, first one, then the other.

Point by point

I. Size
  A. ENIAC
  B. Home computer
II. Ease of programming
  A. ENIAC
  B. Home computer
III. Speed
  A. ENIAC
  B. Home computer

Subject by subject

I. ENIAC
  A. Size
  B. Ease of programming
  C. Speed
II. Home computer
  A. Size
  B. Ease of programming
  C. Speed

Is it comparable to something that is in a different class but more familiar to readers? (Analogy)

Whereas we draw comparisons and contrasts between elements in the same general class (audiences, computers), we link elements in different classes with a special kind of comparison called **analogy.** Most often in analogy we illuminate or explain an unfamiliar, abstract class of things with a familiar and concrete class of things:

We might eventually obtain some sort of bedrock understanding of cosmic structure, but we will never understand the universe in detail; it is just too big and varied for that. If we possessed an atlas of our galaxy that devoted but a single page to each star system in the Milky Way (so that the sun and all its planets were crammed on one page), that atlas would run to more than ten million volumes of ten thousand pages each. It would take a library the size of Harvard's to house the atlas, and merely to flip through it, at the rate of a page per second, would require over ten thousand years.

Abstract subject: the universe, specifically the Milky Way

Concrete subject: an atlas

—Timothy Ferris,
Coming of Age in the Milky Way

Why did it happen, or what results did it have? (Cause-and-effect analysis)

When you use analysis to explain why something happened or what is likely to happen, then you are determining causes and effects. **Cause-and-effect analysis** is especially useful in writing about social, economic, or political events or problems. In the next paragraph the author looks at the causes of Japanese collectivism, which he elsewhere contrasts with American individualism:

> The *shinkansen* or "bullet train" speeds across the rural areas of Japan giving a quick view of cluster after cluster of farmhouses surrounded by rice paddies. This particular pattern did not develop purely by chance, but as a consequence of the technology peculiar to the growing of rice, the staple of the Japanese diet. The growing of rice requires the construction and maintenance of an irrigation system, something that takes many hands to build. More importantly, the planting and the harvesting of rice can only be done efficiently with the cooperation of twenty or more people. The "bottom line" is that a single family working alone cannot produce enough rice to survive, but a dozen families working together can produce a surplus. Thus the Japanese have had to develop the capacity to work together in harmony, no matter what the forces of disagreement or social disintegration, in order to survive.
>
> —William Ouchi, *Theory Z: How American Business Can Meet the Japanese Challenge*

Effect: pattern of Japanese farming

Causes: Japanese dependence on rice, which requires collective effort

Effect: working in harmony

Cause-and-effect paragraphs tend to focus either on causes, as Ouchi's does, or on effects, as this paragraph does:

> At each step, with every graduation from one level of education to the next, the refrain from bystanders was strangely the same: "Your parents must be so proud of you." I suppose that my parents were proud, although I suspect, too, that they felt more than pride alone as they watched me advance through my education. They seemed to know that my education was separating us from one another, making it difficult to resume familiar intimacies. Mixed with the instincts of parental pride, a certain hurt also communicated itself—too private ever to be adequately expressed in words, but real nonetheless.
>
> —Richard Rodriguez, "Going Home Again"

Cause: education

Effects:
Pride
Separation
Loss of intimacies
Hurt

How does one do it, or how does it work? (Process analysis)

When you analyze how to do something or how something works, you explain the steps in a **process.** Paragraphs developed by process analysis are usually organized chronologically, as the steps in the process occur. Some process analyses tell the reader how to do a task:

> As a car owner, you waste money when you pay a mechanic to change the engine oil. [Process: changing oil] The job is not difficult, even if you know little about cars. All you need is a wrench to remove the drain plug, a large, flat pan to collect the draining oil, plastic bottles to dispose of the used oil, and fresh oil. [Equipment needed] First, warm up the car's engine so that the oil will flow more easily. When the engine is warm, shut it off and remove its oil-filler cap (the owner's manual shows where this cap is). Then locate the drain plug under the engine (again consulting the owner's manual for its location) and place the flat pan under the plug. Remove the plug with the wrench, letting the oil flow into the pan. When the oil stops flowing, replace the plug and, at the engine's filler hole, add the amount and kind of fresh oil specified by the owner's manual. Pour the used oil into the plastic bottles and take it to a waste-oil collector, which any garage mechanic can recommend. [Steps in process]
>
> —ANTHONY ANDREAS (student), "Do-It-Yourself Car Care"

Other process analyses explain how processes are done or how they work in nature. Annie Dillard's paragraph on mangrove islands (p. 83) is one example. Here is another:

> What used to be called "laying on of hands" is now practiced seriously by nurses and doctors. [Process: therapeutic touch] Studies have shown that therapeutic touch, as it is now known, can aid relaxation and ease pain, two effects that may in turn cause healing. [Benefits] A "healer" must first concentrate on helping the patient. Then, hands held a few inches from the patient's body, the healer moves from head to foot. Healers claim that they can detect energy disturbances in the patient that indicate tension, pain, or sickness. With further hand movements, the healer tries to redirect the energy. [Steps in process] Patients report feeling heat from the healer's hands, perhaps indicating an energy transfer between healer and patient. [How process works]
>
> —LISA KUKLINSKI (student), "Old Ways to Noninvasive Medicine"

Diagrams, photographs, and other figures can do much to clarify process analyses. See pages 208–12 for guidelines on creating and clearly labeling figures.

Combining patterns of development

Whatever pattern you choose as the basis for developing a paragraph, other patterns may also prove helpful. Combined patterns have appeared often in this section: Dyson analyzes causes and effects in presenting reasons (p. 97); Tuchman uses contrast to define *quality* (p. 98); Nahm uses description to compare (p. 100); Ouchi uses process analysis to explain causes (p. 102).

As you will see on pages 113–15, the paragraphs within an essay inevitably will be developed with a variety of patterns, even when one controlling pattern develops and structures the entire essay.

3 Checking length

The average paragraph contains between 100 and 150 words, or between four and eight sentences. The actual length of a paragraph depends on the complexity of its topic, the role it plays in developing the thesis of the essay, and its position in the essay. Nevertheless, very short paragraphs are often inadequately developed; they may leave readers with a sense of incompleteness. And very long paragraphs often contain irrelevant details or develop two or more topics; readers may have difficulty following, sorting out, or remembering ideas.

When you are revising your essay, reread the paragraphs that seem very long or very short, checking them especially for unity and adequate development. If the paragraph wanders, cut everything from it that does not support your main idea (such as sentences that you might begin with *By the way*). If it is underdeveloped, supply the specific details, examples, or reasons needed, or try one of the methods of development we have discussed here.

EXERCISE 15
Analyzing paragraph development

Examine the paragraphs by Henry Louis Gates, Jr. (p. 78–79) and Judith Wax (p. 84) to discover how the authors achieve paragraph development. What pattern or patterns of development does each author use? Where does each author support general statements with specific evidence?

EXERCISE 16
Analyzing and revising skimpy paragraphs

The following paragraphs are not well developed. Analyze them, looking especially for general statements that lack support or leave questions in your mind. Then rewrite one into a well-developed paragraph, supplying your own concrete details or examples.

1. One big difference between successful and unsuccessful teachers is the quality of communication. A successful teacher is sensitive to students' needs and excited by the course subject. In contrast, an unsuccessful teacher seems uninterested in students and bored by the subject.

2. Gestures are one of our most important means of communication. We use them instead of speech. We use them to supplement the words we speak. And we use them to communicate some feelings or meanings that words cannot adequately express.

3. I've discovered that a word processor can do much—but not everything—to help me improve my writing. I can easily make changes and try out different versions of a paper. But I still must do the hard work of revising.

EXERCISE 17
Considering your past work: Paragraph development

Continuing from Exercises 3 (p. 79) and 11 (p. 92), examine the development of the body paragraphs in your writing. Where does specific information seem adequate to support your general statements? Where does support seem skimpy? Revise the paragraphs as necessary to make your ideas clearer and more interesting. It may help you to pose the questions on pages 95–103. (You can download these questions from this book's Web site at *http://www.awlonline.com/littlebrown.*)

EXERCISE 18
Writing with the patterns of development

Write at least three unified, coherent, and well-developed paragraphs, each one developed with a different pattern. Draw on the topics provided here, or choose your own topics.

1. *Narration*
   An experience of public speaking
   A disappointment
   Leaving home
   Waking up
2. *Description (objective or subjective)*
   Your room
   A crowded or deserted place
   A food
   An intimidating person
3. *Illustration or support*
   Why study
   Having a headache
   The best sports event
   Usefulness (or uselessness) of a self-help book
4. *Definition*
   Humor
   An adult
   Fear
   Authority
5. *Division or analysis*
   A television news show
   A barn
   A site on the World Wide Web
   A piece of music
6. *Classification*
   Factions in a campus controversy
   Styles of playing poker

Types of Web sites
Kinds of teachers

7. *Comparison and contrast*
   Surfing the Web and watching TV
   AM and FM radio announcers
   High school and college football
   Movies on TV and in a theater
8. *Analogy*
   Paying taxes and giving blood
   The US Constitution and a building's foundation
   Graduating from high school and being released from prison
9. *Cause-and-effect analysis*
   Connection between tension and anger
   Causes of failing a course
   Connection between credit cards and debt
   Causes of a serious accident
10. *Process analysis*
    Preparing for a job interview
    Setting up an e-mail account
    Protecting your home from burglars
    Making a jump shot

4d Writing special kinds of paragraphs

Several kinds of paragraphs do not always follow the guidelines for unity, coherence, development, and length because they serve special functions. These are the essay introduction, the essay conclusion, the transitional or emphatic paragraph, and the paragraph of spoken dialogue.

1 Opening an essay

Most of your essays will open with a paragraph that draws readers from their world into your world. A good opening paragraph usually satisfies several requirements:

- It focuses readers' attention on your subject and arouses their curiosity about what you have to say.
- It specifies what your topic is and implies your attitude.
- Often it provides your thesis statement.
- It is concise and sincere.

The box on the facing page provides a range of options for achieving these goals.

Note If you are composing on the World Wide Web, you'll want to consider the expectations of Web readers. Your opening page may take the place of a conventional introduction, providing concise text indicating your site's subject and purpose and an

http://webster.commnet.edu/HP/pages/darling/grammar/intros.htm
Functions of and strategies for introductions, from the Guide to Grammar and Writing.

Some strategies for opening paragraphs

- Ask a question.
- Relate an incident.
- Use a vivid quotation.
- Offer a surprising statistic or other fact.
- State an opinion related to your thesis.
- Outline the argument your thesis refutes.
- Provide background.
- Create a visual image that represents your subject.
- Make a historical comparison or contrast.
- Outline a problem or dilemma.
- Define a word central to your subject.
- In some business or technical writing, summarize your paper.

overview of its contents, often in the form of a menu or links to other pages. (See pp. 224–42 for more on composing for the Web.)

ESL The requirements and options for essay introductions may not be what you are used to if your native language is not English. In other cultures, readers may seek familiarity or reassurance from an author's introduction, or they may prefer an indirect approach to the subject. In English, however, writers and readers prefer originality and concise, direct expression.

The funnel introduction

One reliably effective introduction forms a kind of funnel: it starts generally with a statement or question about the subject, clarifies or narrows the subject in one or more sentences, and then, in the thesis statement, asserts the central idea of the essay (see pp. 30–34). Here are two examples:

> We Americans are a clean people. We bathe or shower regularly and spend billions of dollars each year on soaps and deodorants to wash away or disguise our dirt and odor. [Subject related to reader's experience] Yet cleanliness is a relatively recent habit with us. [Narrowing of subject: bridge to thesis statement] From the time of the Puritans until the turn of the twentieth century, bathing in the United States was rare and sometimes even illegal. [Thesis statement]
>
> —Amanda Harris (student), "The Cleaning of America"

> Can your home or office computer make you sterile? Can it strike you blind or dumb? The answer is: probably not. [Subject related to reader's experience] Nevertheless, reports of side effects relating to computer use should be examined, especially in the area of birth defects, eye complaints, and postural difficulties. Although little conclusive evidence [Clarification of subject: bridge to thesis statement]

exists to establish a causal link between computer use and problems of this sort, the circumstantial evidence can be disturbing. — Thesis statement
—THOMAS HARTMANN, "How Dangerous Is Your Computer?"

Other effective introductions

Several other types of introduction can be equally effective, though they are sometimes harder to invent and control. You can begin with a quotation that leads into the thesis statement:

> "It is difficult to speak adequately or justly of London," wrote Henry James in 1881. "It is not a pleasant place; it is not agreeable, or cheerful, or easy, or exempt from reproach. It is only magnificent." Were he alive today, James, a connoisseur of cities, might easily say the same thing about New York or Paris or Tokyo, for the great city is one of the paradoxes of history. In countless different ways, it has almost always been an unpleasant, disagreeable, cheerless, uneasy and reproachful place; in the end, it can only be described as magnificent.
> —*Time*

You can relate an incident or convey a visual image that sets the stage for the thesis:

> Canada is pink. I knew that from the map I owned when I was six. On it, New York was green and brown, which was true as far as I could see, so there was no reason to distrust the map maker's portrayal of Canada. When my parents took me across the border and we entered the immigration booth, I looked excitedly for the pink earth. Slowly it dawned on me; this foreign, "different" place was not so different. I discovered that the world in my head and the world at my feet were not the same.
> —ROBERT ORNSTEIN, *Human Nature*

You can open with a startling question or opinion:

> Caesar was right. Thin people need watching. I've been watching them for most of my adult life, and I don't like what I see. When these narrow fellows spring at me, I quiver to my toes. Thin people come in all personalities, most of them menacing. You've got your "together" thin person, your mechanical thin person, your condescending thin person, your tsk-tsk thin person. All of them are dangerous. —SUZANNE BRITT, "That Lean and Hungry Look"

When some background to the essay is useful, you can begin with a historical comparison or contrast:

> Throughout the first half of this century, the American Medical Association, the largest and most powerful medical organization in the world, battled relentlessly to rid the country of quack potions and cure-alls; and it is the AMA that is generally credited with being the single most powerful force behind the enactment of

> the early pure food and drug laws. Today, however, medicine's guardian seems to have done a complete about-face and become one of the pharmaceutical industry's staunchest allies—often at the public's peril and expense.
>
> —MAC JEFFERY, "Does Rx Spell Rip-off?"

An effective introductory paragraph need not be long, as the following opener shows:

> I've often wondered what goes into a hot dog. Now I know and I wish I didn't. —WILLIAM ZINSSER, *The Lunacy Boom*

Ineffective introductions

When writing and revising an introductory paragraph, avoid the following approaches that are likely to bore readers or make them question your sincerity or control:

Openings to avoid

- Don't reach back too far with vague generalities or truths, such as those beginning "Throughout human history . . ." or "In today's world. . . ." You may have needed a warm-up paragraph to start drafting, but your readers can do without it.
- Don't start with "The purpose of this essay is . . . ," "In this essay I will . . . ," or any similar flat announcement of your intention or topic.
- Don't refer to the title of the essay in the first sentence—for example, "This is my favorite activity" or "This is a big problem."
- Don't start with "According to Webster . . ." or a similar phrase leading to a dictionary definition. A definition can be an effective springboard to an essay, but this kind of lead-in has become dull with overuse.
- Don't apologize for your opinion or for inadequate knowledge with "I'm not sure if I'm right, but I think . . . ," "I don't know much about this, but . . . ," or a similar line.

---

2 Closing an essay

Unless you are writing for the World Wide Web (see the next page), most of your compositions will end with a closing statement or conclusion, a signal to readers that you have not simply stopped writing but have actually finished. The conclusion completes an es-

http://leo.stcloudstate.edu/acadwrite/conclude.html Tips and examples for writing successful conclusions, from Saint Cloud State University.

say, bringing it to a climax while assuring readers that they have understood your intention.

Note Compositions for the Web usually do not provide the kind of closure featured in essays. In fact, you'll need to ensure that your Web pages don't dead-end, leaving the reader stranded without options for moving backward or forward through your material. (For more on Web composition, see pp. 224–42.)

An essay conclusion may consist of a single sentence or a group of sentences, usually set off in a separate paragraph. The conclusion may take one or more of the approaches below:

Some strategies for closing paragraphs

- Strike a note of hope or despair
- Give a symbolic or powerful fact or other detail.
- Give an especially compelling example.
- Create a visual image that represents your subject.
- Use a quotation.
- Recommend a course of action.
- Summarize the paper.
- Echo the approach of the introduction.
- Restate your thesis and reflect on its implications.

The following paragraph concludes the essay on bathing habits whose introduction is on page 107:

> Thus changed attitudes and advances in plumbing finally freed us to bathe whenever [Summary] we want. Perhaps partly to make up for our ancestors' bad habits, we have transformed that freedom into a national obsession. [Link between past and today]
>
> —Amanda Harris (student), "The Cleaning of America"

Maxine Hong Kingston uses a different technique—a vivid image—to conclude an essay on her aunt, a suicide by drowning:

> My aunt haunts me—her ghost drawn to me because now, after fifty years of neglect, I alone devote pages of paper to her, though not origamied into houses and clothes. I do not think she always means me well. I am telling on her, and she was a spite suicide, drowning herself in the drinking water. [Summary] The Chinese are always very frightened of the drowned one, whose weeping ghost, wet hair hanging and skin bloated, waits silently by the water to pull down a substitute. [Image]
>
> —Maxine Hong Kingston, "No Name Woman"

In the next paragraph the author concludes an essay on environmental protection with a call for action:

> Until we get the answers, I think we had better keep on building power plants and growing food with the help of fertilizers and such insect-controlling chemicals as we now have. The risks are well known, thanks to the environmentalists. If they had not created a widespread public awareness of the ecological crisis, we wouldn't stand a chance. But such awareness by itself is not enough. Flaming manifestos and prophecies of doom are no longer much help, and a search for scapegoats can only make matters worse. The time for sensations and manifestos is about over. Now we need rigorous analysis, united effort and very hard work.
>
> —PETER F. DRUCKER, "How Best to Protect the Environment"

Summary and opinion

Call for action

The preceding three paragraphs illustrate ways of avoiding several pitfalls of conclusions:

Closings to avoid

- Don't simply restate your introduction—statement of subject, thesis sentence, and all. Presumably the paragraphs in the body of your essay have contributed something to the opening statements, and it's that something you want to capture in your conclusion.
- Don't start off in a new direction, with a subject different from the one your essay has been about. If you arrive at a new idea, this may be a signal to start fresh with that idea as your thesis.
- Don't conclude more than you reasonably can from the evidence you have presented. If your essay is about your frustrating experience trying to clear a parking ticket, you cannot reasonably conclude that *all* local police forces are tied up in red tape.
- Don't apologize for your essay or otherwise cast doubt on it. Don't say, "Even though I'm no expert," or "This may not be convincing, but I believe it's true," or anything similar. Rather, to win your readers' confidence, display confidence.

3 Using short emphatic or transitional paragraphs

A short emphatic paragraph can give unusual stress to an important idea, in effect asking the reader to pause and consider before moving on.

> In short, all those who might have taken responsibility ducked it, and catastrophe was inevitable.

A transitional paragraph, because it is longer than a word or phrase and set off by itself, moves a discussion from one point to another more slowly or more completely than does a single transitional expression or even a transitional sentence attached to a larger paragraph.

> These, then, are the causes of the current contraction in hospital facilities. But how does this contraction affect the medical costs of the government, private insurers, and individuals?
>
> So the debates were noisy and emotion-packed. But what did they accomplish? Historians have identified at least three direct results.

Use transitional paragraphs only to shift readers' attention when your essay makes a significant turn. A paragraph like the following one betrays a writer who is stalling:

> Now that we have examined these facts, we can look at some others that are equally central to an examination of this important issue.

4 Writing dialogue

When recording a conversation between two or more people, start a new paragraph for each person's speech. The paragraphing establishes for the reader the point at which one speaker stops talking and another begins.

> The dark shape was indistinguishable. But once I'd flooded him with light, there he stood, blinking.
>
> "Well," he said eventually, "you're a sight for sore eyes. Should I stand here or are you going to let me in?"
>
> "Come in," I said. And in he came.
>
> —Louise Erdrich, *The Beet Queen*

Though dialogue appears most often in fictional writing (the source of the preceding example), it may occasionally freshen or enliven narrative or expository essays. (For guidance in using quotation marks and other punctuation in passages of dialogue, see pp. 482–84 and 511–12.)

EXERCISE 19

Analyzing an introduction and conclusion

Analyze the introductory and concluding paragraphs in the first and final drafts of the student essay in Chapter 3, pages 51 and 64–66. (Both drafts are also online at this book's Web site: *http://www.awlonline.com/littlebrown.*) What is wrong with the first-draft paragraphs? Why are the final-draft paragraphs better? Could they be improved still further?

EXERCISE 20
Considering your past work: Introductions and conclusions

Examine the opening and closing paragraphs of the essay you've been analyzing in Exercises 3, 11, and 17. Do the paragraphs fulfill the requirements and avoid the pitfalls outlined on pages 106–11? Revise them as needed for clarity, conciseness, focus, and interest.

EXERCISE 21
Collaborating on introductions and conclusions

Either online or face to face, discuss with at least one classmate the challenges of creating effective introductions and conclusions for your essays. Do you have more difficulties with introductions or with conclusions, and why? What strategies can each participant contribute to help meet the challenges?

4e Linking paragraphs in the essay

Your paragraphs do not stand alone: each one is a key unit of a larger piece of writing. Though you may draft paragraphs or groups of paragraphs almost as mini-essays, you will eventually need to stitch them together into a unified, coherent, well-developed whole. The techniques parallel those for linking sentences in paragraphs:

- Make sure each paragraph contributes to your thesis.
- You will probably use varied patterns of development for individual paragraphs, even when the whole essay is developed and structured by some other pattern. Just be sure to follow through on your overall pattern.
- Arrange the paragraphs in a clear, logical order. See pages 35–46 for advice on essay organization.
- Create links between paragraphs. Use repetition and restatement to stress and connect key terms, and use transitional expressions and transitional sentences to indicate sequence, direction, contrast, and other relationships.

- When composing for the World Wide Web, you need to think a little differently about transitions. For each page of your site, the opening screen serves as a transition from other pages that readers may have visited: What information will they already have? What new information will they need at this point? Your goal is to make the transition from page to page as smooth as possible. (See pp. 224–42 for more on Web compositions.)

The following essay illustrates the way effective paragraphs can build an effective essay. The overall pattern of development is analysis. The overall organization is climactic. Sentences and paragraphs are linked by repetition, restatement, and pronouns (circled words); transitional expressions (boxed words); parallelism (underlined); and transitional sentences (noted in marginal comments).

A Picture of Hyperactivity

A hyperactive committee member can contribute to efficiency. A hyperactive salesperson can contribute to profits. When a child is hyperactive, though, people—even parents—may wish he had never been born. A collage of those who must cope with hyperactivity in children is a dark picture of frustration, anger, and loss. — Thesis statement

The first part of the collage is the doctors. — Transitional topic sentence In their terminology the word *hyperactivity* is short for H-LD, a hyperkinesis-learning disability syndrome. They apply the word to children who are "abnormally or excessively busy." But doctors do not fully understand the problem and thus differ over how to treat it. For example, some recommend a special diet; others, behavior-modifying drugs; and still others, who do not consider hyperactivity to be a medical problem, a psychiatrist for the entire family. The result is a merry-go-round of tests, confusion, and frustration for the parents and the child.

Paragraph developed by definition, example, and cause-and-effect analysis

As the parent of a hyperactive child, I can say what the word *hyperactivity* means to the parents who form the second part of the collage. — Transitional topic sentence It means worry that is deep and enduring. It means despair that is a companion on dark and sleepless nights. It means fear that is heart twisting and constant, for the hyperactive child is most destructive toward himself. It means a mixture of frustration, guilt, and anger. And finally, since there are

Paragraph developed by definition and cause-and-effect analysis times when that anger goes out of control and the child is in danger from the parent, it means self-loathing.

The weight of hyperactivity, however, rests not on the doctors or the parents but on the child. For him is reserved the final and darkest part of the collage because he is most affected. From early childhood he is dragged from doctor to doctor, is attached to strange and frightening machines, and is tested or discussed by physicians, parents, neighbors, teachers, peers. His playmates dislike him because of his temper and his unwillingness to follow rules. Even his pets fear and mistrust him because he treats them erratically, often hurting them without meaning to. As time goes on, he sees his parents more and more often in tears and anger, and he knows that he is the cause. He is highly intelligent but he does poorly when he enters school because of his short attention span. He is fond of sports and games, but he never joins the other children on the playground because he has an uncontrollable temper and poor coordination. By the time he reaches age seven or eight, he is obsessed with one thought: "Mama," my son asks me repeatedly, "why do I have to be hyperactive?"

Transitional sentence

Topic sentence

Paragraph developed by narration and cause-and-effect analysis

At last the collage is completed, and it is dark and somber. *Hyperactivity,* as applied to children, is a word with uncertain, unattractive, and bitter associations. But the picture does have a bright spot, for inside every hyperactive child is a loving, trustful, calm person waiting to be recognized.

Transitional sentence

—Linda Devereaux (student)

EXERCISE 22
Analyzing paragraphs in essays

Analyze the ways in which paragraphs combine in the two student essays in Chapter 3, pages 64 and 71. (Both essays are also online at this book's Web site: *http://www.awlonline.com/littlebrown.*) With what techniques does each writer link paragraphs to the thesis statement and to each other? Where, if at all, does the writer seem to stray from the thesis or fail to show how paragraphs relate to it? How would you revise the essays to solve any problems they exhibit?

EXERCISE 23
Considering your past work: Paragraphs in the essay

Examine the overall effect of the essay you've been analyzing in Exercises 3, 11, 17, and 20. Do all the paragraphs relate to your thesis? Are they arranged clearly and logically? How do repetition and restatement, transitional expressions, or transitional sentences connect the paragraphs? Can you see ways to improve the essay's unity, coherence, and development?

PART II

Critical Thinking, Reading, and Writing

CHAPTER 5

Taking a Critical Perspective

Throughout college and beyond, you will be expected to think, read, and write critically. **Critical** here means "skeptical," "exacting," "creative." When you operate critically, you question, test, and build on what others say and what you yourself think. The word *critical* does not mean "negative" in this context. It comes from Greek words meaning "to separate" and "to discern": a critical thinker, reader, or writer separates a subject into its parts, discerns how the parts work together and how the subject relates to other subjects, and (often) judges the subject's quality and value.

You already operate critically every day of your life, as when you probe a friendship ("What did she mean by that?") or when you discuss a movie you just saw ("Don't you think the bad guy was too obvious?"). Such questioning helps you figure out why things happen to you or what your experiences mean.

This chapter introduces more formal methods for thinking and reading critically (opposite) and writing critically (p. 137). Learning and applying these methods will both engage you in and prepare you for school courses, career, and life in a democratic society:

- Operating critically improves your ability to learn and to perform as a student and a worker. Your teachers and employers in every field, from the arts to social work to zoology, will expect you to assess what you read and hear and to make a good case for your own ideas.
- Operating critically helps you understand your own actions and ideas, weigh them against opposing views, and persuasively articulate your reasoning and motivations.
- Your very independence and freedom depend on your ability to think, read, and write critically. An open democracy allows as much play for stupid and false claims as for sound ones, and the claims that seem sound often conflict with each other. Whether you are watching the evening news, reading an adver-

http://www.criticalthinking.org/K12/k12class/strat/stratall.nclk An extensive list of strategies for critical thinking and writing, from the Foundation for Critical Thinking.

tisement, or voting in an election, critical thinking empowers you to decide for yourself what's useful, fair, and wise—and what's not.

There's no denying that critical thinking, reading, and writing require discipline and hard work. Besides channeling your curiosity, paying attention, and probing, you will often need to consult experts, interpreting and evaluating their ideas. Such an approach also requires a healthy tolerance for doubt or uncertainty—that feeling you may have when the old rules don't seem to apply or when a change is frightening but still attractive. Out of uncertainty, though, comes creativity—the capacity to organize and generate knowledge, to explain, resolve, illuminate, play. Compared to passive, rote learning, creative work is more involving, more productive, and more enjoyable.

5a Thinking and reading critically

You can think critically about almost anything: an argument you overhear on a bus, a new CD by your favorite solo musician, a software program, your roommate's ideas about baseball, even a dog-food commercial. By "separating" and "discerning" any of these, you would be able to understand it better, see its relations to other events or things, and evaluate it.

Of course, in college much of your critical thinking will focus on written texts (a short story, a journal article, an Internet posting, a site on the World Wide Web) or on visual objects (a photograph, a chart, a film). Like all subjects worthy of critical consideration, such works operate on at least three levels: (1) what the creator actually says or shows, (2) what the creator does not say or show but builds into the work (intentionally or not), and (3) what you think. Discovering each level of the work, even if it is visual, involves a number of reading techniques that are discussed in this chapter and summarized in the box on the next page.

The techniques of critical reading are not steps in a firm sequence. You will not use all of them for all the reading you do. On some occasions, even when a close, critical reading is required, you may simply lack the time to preview, read, and reread. (But if your reading time is continually squeezed by your schedule, you may need to rethink your schedule.) On other occasions your reason for reading (your purpose) will determine which techniques you use.

http://www.colostate.edu/Depts/WritingCenter/references/reading/critread/page1.htm Extensive guidance on reading critically, from Colorado State University.

Techniques of critical reading

For reading a work of literature, which requires a somewhat different approach, see pp. 791–95.

- **Writing:** making notes on your reading throughout the process (below)
- **Previewing:** getting background; skimming (p. 122)
- **Reading:** interacting with and absorbing the text (p. 122)
- **Summarizing:** distilling and understanding content (p. 127)
- **Forming your critical response** (p. 129)

  Analyzing: separating into parts
  Interpreting: inferring meaning and assumptions
  Synthesizing: reassembling parts; making connections
  Evaluating: judging quality and value

Even a work like *People* magazine is open to different methods of reading for different purposes:

Purpose	Learn some gossip while filling time in the dentist's office.
Kind of reading	Quick, uncritical
Purpose	Examine *People* as an artifact of our popular culture that reflects and perhaps even molds contemporary values.
Kind of reading	Close, critical

Course assignments, too, differ in their requirements. A book report may require writing, previewing, reading, and summarizing but not intense critical reading. An evaluation of a journal article, in contrast, requires all the techniques listed above.

ESL The idea of reading critically may require you to make some adjustments if readers in your native culture tend to seek understanding or agreement more than engagement from what they read. As noted above, readers of English use texts for all kinds of reasons, including pleasure, reinforcement, information, and many others. But they also read skeptically, critically, to see the author's motives, test their own ideas, and arrive at new knowledge.

1 Writing while reading

There are two good reasons to write while you read: to record information and ideas for future use, and to get more out of the work. The first is discussed in detail as part of research writing (see pp. 619–20). The second has more to do with critical reading.

Critical reading is *active* reading. You interact with the work, getting involved with it, bringing to it *your* experiences, ideas, and questions. When you use a pen or pencil or keyboard while reading, you create writing in response to writing. In this way you "translate" the work into your own words and reconstruct it for yourself.

Many readers keep a **reading journal,** a notebook or computer file in which they regularly work out questions and thoughts about what they read. One technique for keeping such a journal is to divide a page or computer screen into two vertical columns, the left side for the work itself, such as summary and questions, and the right side for what the work makes you think, such as agreements or doubts based on your own experiences, comparisons with other works, and ideas for writing. A two-column journal can encourage you to go beyond summarizing what you read to interacting critically with it because the blank right column will beckon you to respond. See page 125 for an example of this technique. And see pages 19–21 for more on journal keeping.

If you don't keep a regular reading journal, you can still benefit from writing while reading in other ways:

- If you're reading a printed work that you own, you may opt to write directly on the pages as you read them (see p. 124).
- If you don't own the material, make your notes on a separate sheet or a photocopy or in a computer file.
- If you're reading a page on the World Wide Web or another online source, you have several options: you can print out a copy of the material and annotate that; you can open your word processor at the same time and make notes in the word-processing document; you can copy and paste the material into a word-processing document and use the word processor's Comment function to annotate the source (see p. 190); or you can compose electronic mail while you're reading and then send it to yourself. You may also want to download (or save) the online material to a diskette or hard drive. Then you can import it into your word processor to comment on it, and you will not risk losing the material if, as often happens, it changes on the Internet or disappears entirely.

Note Whenever you download a document or take notes separately from the text you're reading, be sure to record all necessary information about the text's location so that you can find it again and cite it fully if you use it. (See p. 629 for a list of information to record.) Online sources sometimes restrict downloading, so check

http://www.gmu.edu/departments/writingcenter/handouts/puller.html
Tips on keeping a reading journal, from George Mason University.

the source's copyright notice to see whether any restrictions apply. See pages 690–92 for more on copying and acknowledging online sources.

2 Previewing the material

When you're reading a work of literature, such as a story or a poem, it's often best just to plunge right in (see p. 791). But for critical reading of other works, it's worthwhile to form some expectations and even some preliminary questions before you start reading word for word. The preview will make your reading more informed and fruitful.

One way to preview is to **skim,** looking for clues about content, author, and how you will interact with the work. Not the same as idly turning pages or scrolling through screens, skimming is a focused, concentrated activity in which you seek information. Use the questions below as a guide. In your journal write down any impressions that you may want to return to later.

Questions for previewing

- **Length:** Is the material brief enough to read in one sitting, or do you need more time? To gauge the length of an online source such as a Web site, study any menus for an indication of the source's complexity. Then scroll through a couple of pages and follow a couple of links to estimate the overall length.
- **Facts of publication:** Does the date of publication suggest currency or datedness? Does the publisher or publication specialize in a particular kind of material—scholarly articles, say, or popular books? For a Web source, who or what sponsors the site: an individual? a nonprofit organization? an academic institution? a corporation? a government body? (See pp. 630–31 on locating the authors of online sources and p. 197 on reading electronic addresses.)
- **Content cues:** What do the title, summary or abstract, headings, illustrations, and other features tell you? What questions do they raise in your mind?
- **Author:** What does the biographical information tell you about the author's publications, interests, biases, and reputation in the field? For an online message, which may be posted by an unfamiliar or anonymous author, what can you gather about the author from his or her words? If possible, trace unfamiliar authors to learn more about them. (See p. 670.)
- **Yourself:** Do you anticipate particular difficulties with the content? What biases of your own may influence your response to the text—for instance, anxiety, curiosity, boredom, or an outlook similar or opposed to that of the author?

3 Reading

Reading is itself more than a one-step process. Your primary goal is to understand the first level on which the text operates—what the author actually says.

First reading

The first time through new material, read as steadily and smoothly as possible, trying to get the gist of what the author is saying and a sense of his or her tone.

- To help your concentration, read in a quiet place away from distractions such as music or talking.
- Give yourself time. Rushing yourself or worrying about something else you have to do will prevent you from grasping what you read.
- Try to enjoy the work. Seek connections between it and what you already know. Appreciate new information, interesting relationships, forceful writing, humor, good examples.
- Make notes sparingly during this reading. Mark major stumbling blocks—such as a paragraph you don't understand—so that you can try to resolve them before rereading.
- If you're browsing a Web site with multiple pages and links to other sites, use the Bookmarks or Favorites function of your Web browser to mark interesting pages and links so that you can return to them. Then, when reading pages, proceed steadily without taking frequent or extensive notes, reserving that work for the next reading.

ESL On your first reading, don't stop and look up every unfamiliar word. You will lose more in concentration than you gain in understanding. Instead, try to guess the meanings of words from their contexts (see p. 600), or circle unfamiliar words and look them up later.

Rereadings

After the first reading, plan on at least one other. This time read *slowly.* Your main concern should be to grasp the content and how it is constructed. That means rereading a paragraph if you didn't get the point, or looking up key words in a dictionary, or following more links at a Web site.

http://www.ucc.vt.edu/stdysk/essays.html A guide for reading academic essays, from Virginia Polytechnic Institute and State University.

Use your pen, pencil, or keyboard freely to annotate the text or make separate notes:

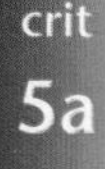

- If you can't write directly on the material (because you don't own it or it's online), make separate notes as suggested on page 121.
- If you can write directly on the material, use any system of annotations that works for you—perhaps "?" in the margin next to passages you don't understand, circles around unfamiliar words, underlining or brackets for main points, "*" for passages you agree with, "!" for those you find startling, "So what?" for those you can't see the point of.

- If you're reading an online source that you can download into your word processor, highlight text you have questions or comments on, and insert your annotations either using bold or italic type or using your word processor's Comment function (see p. 190).

Following are examples of active reading from a student, Charlene Robinson. She was responding to Thomas Sowell's "Student Loans," an essay beginning on the next page. First Robinson annotated a photocopy of the essay (the first four paragraphs appear below):

> The first lesson of economics is scarcity: There is never enough of anything to fully satisfy all those who want it.
>
> The first lesson of politics is to disregard the first lesson of economics. When politicians discover some group that is being vocal about not having as much as they want, the "solution" is to give them more. Where do politicians get this "more"? They rob Peter to pay Paul.
>
> After a while, of course, they discover that Peter doesn't have enough. Bursting with compassion, politicians rush to the rescue. Needless to say, they do not admit that robbing Peter to pay Paul was a dumb idea in the first place. On the contrary, they now rob Tom, Dick, and Harry to help Peter.
>
> The latest chapter in this long-running saga is that politicians have now suddenly discovered that many college students graduate heavily in debt. To politicians it follows, as the night follows the day, that the government should come to their rescue with the taxpayers' money.

Basic contradiction between economics and politics

biblical reference?

ironic and dismissive language

politicians = fools? or irresponsible?

After reading the text, Robinson wrote about it in the journal she kept on her computer. She divided the journal into two columns, one each for the text and her responses. Here is the portion pertaining to the paragraphs above:

Text	**Responses**
Economics teaches lessons (1), and politics (politicians) and economics are at odds	Is economics truer or more reliable than politics? More scientific?
Politicians don't accept econ. limits--always trying to satisfy "vocal" voters by giving them what they want (2)	Politicians do spend a lot of our money. Is that what they're elected to do, or do they go too far?
"Robbing Peter to pay Paul" (2)--from the Bible (the Apostles)?	
Politicians support student loan program with taxpayer funds bec. of "vocal" voters (2-4): another ex. of not accepting econ. limits	I support the loan program, too. Are politicians being irresponsible when they do? (Dismissive language underlined on copy.)

You should try to answer the questions about meaning that you raise in your annotations and your journal, and that may take another reading or some digging in other sources, such as dictionaries and encyclopedias. Recording in your journal what you think the author means will help you build an understanding of the text, and a focused attempt to summarize will help even more (see p. 127). Such efforts will resolve any confusion you feel, or they will give you the confidence to say that your confusion is the fault of the author, not the reader.

EXERCISE 1
Reading

Reprinted below is an essay by Thomas Sowell on the federal government's student-loan program. A respected conservative economist, Sowell is also a newspaper columnist and the author of many books on economics, politics, and education. This essay appeared in Sowell's collection *Is Reality Optional?*

Read this essay at least twice, until you think you understand what the author is saying. Either on these pages or separately, note your questions and reactions in writing. Look up any words you don't know, and try to arrive at answers to your questions. (It may help to discuss the selection with classmates.)

Student Loans

The first lesson of economics is scarcity: There is never enough of anything to fully satisfy all those who want it. 1

The first lesson of politics is to disregard the first lesson of economics. When politicians discover some group that is being vocal about not having as much as they want, the "solution" is to give them more. Where do politicians get this "more"? They rob Peter to pay Paul. 2

After a while, of course, they discover that Peter doesn't 3
have enough. Bursting with compassion, politicians rush to the rescue. Needless to say, they do not admit that robbing Peter to pay Paul was a dumb idea in the first place. On the contrary, they now rob Tom, Dick, and Harry to help Peter.

The latest chapter in this long-running saga is that politi- 4
cians have now suddenly discovered that many college students graduate heavily in debt. To politicians it follows, as the night follows the day, that the government should come to their rescue with the taxpayers' money.

How big is this crushing burden of college students' debt 5
that we hear so much about from politicians and media deep thinkers? For those students who graduate from public colleges owing money, the debt averages a little under $7,000. For those who graduate from private colleges owing money, the average debt is a little under $9,000.

Buying a very modestly priced automobile involves more 6
debt than that. And a car loan has to be paid off faster than the ten years that college graduates get to repay their student loans. Moreover, you have to keep buying cars every several years, while one college education lasts a lifetime.

College graduates of course earn higher incomes than other 7
people. Why, then, should we panic at the thought that they have to repay loans for the education which gave them their opportunities? Even graduates with relatively modest incomes pay less than 10 percent of their annual salary on the loan the first year—with declining percentages in future years, as their pay increases.

Political hysteria and media hype may focus on the low-in- 8
come student with a huge debt. That is where you get your heart-rending stories—even if they are not at all typical. In reality, the soaring student loans of the past decade have resulted from allowing high-income people to borrow under government programs.

Before 1978, college loans were available through govern- 9
ment programs only to students whose family income was below some cut-off level. That cut-off level was about double the national average income, but at least it kept out the Rockefellers and the Vanderbilts. But, in an era of "compassion," Congress took off even those limits.

That opened the floodgates. No matter how rich you were, 10
it still paid to borrow money through the government at low interest rates. The money you had set aside for your children's education could be invested somewhere else, at higher interest rates. Then, when the student loan became due, parents could pay it off with the money they had set aside—pocketing the difference in interest rates.

To politicians and the media, however, the rapidly growing 11
loans showed what a great "need" there was. The fact that many students welshed when time came to repay their loans showed how "crushing" their burden of debt must be. In reality, those who welsh typically have smaller loans, but have dropped out of college before finishing. People who are irresponsible in one way are often irresponsible in other ways.

No small amount of the deterioration of college standards 12
has been due to the increasingly easy availability of college to
people who are not very serious about getting an education. College is not a bad place to hang out for a few years, if you have
nothing better to do, and if someone else is paying for it. Its
costs are staggering, but the taxpayers carry much of that burden, not only for state universities and city colleges, but also to
an increasing extent even for "private" institutions.

Numerous government subsidies and loan programs make 13
it possible for many people to use vast amounts of society's resources at low cost to themselves. Whether in money terms or in
real terms, federal aid to higher education has increased several
hundred percent since 1970. That has enabled colleges to raise
their tuition by leaps and bounds and enabled professors to be
paid more and more for doing less and less teaching.

Naturally all these beneficiaries are going to create hype 14
and hysteria to keep more of the taxpayers' money coming in.
But we would be fools to keep on writing blank checks for them.

When you weigh the cost of things, in economics that's 15
called "trade-offs." In politics, it's called "mean-spirited." Apparently, if we just took a different attitude, scarcity would go away.

—Thomas Sowell

4 Summarizing

Before you can see what is beneath the surface of a text and figure out what you think of it, you need to understand exactly what the author is actually saying. A good way to master the content of a text and see its strengths and weaknesses is to **summarize** it: distill it to its main points, in your own words.

Some assignments call for brief summaries, as when you summarize the plot in a critical essay about a novel (p. 806). Summary is also an essential tool in research papers and other writing that draws on sources (p. 679). Here, though, we're concerned with summarizing for yourself—for your own enlightenment.

A summary should state in as few words as possible the main ideas of a passage. When you need to summarize a few paragraphs or a brief article, your summary should not exceed one-fifth the length of the original. For longer works, such as chapters of books or whole books, your summary should be quite a bit shorter in proportion to the original. A procedure for drafting a summary appears in the box on the next page. (You've seen the beginning of this process in Charlene Robinson's journal on p. 125.)

http://www.english.uiuc.edu/cws/wworkshop/summaries.htm A guide to writing summaries, from the University of Illinois at Urbana-Champaign.

Writing a summary

- Look up words or concepts you don't know so that you understand the author's sentences and how they relate to one another.
- Work through the text to identify its sections—single paragraphs or groups of paragraphs focused on a single topic, related pages or links in a Web site. To understand how parts of a work relate to one another, try drawing a tree diagram or creating an outline (pp. 37–41). Both tools work well for straight text; the tree diagram may work better for nonlinear material such as a Web site.
- Write a one- or two-sentence summary of each section you identify. Focus on the main point of the section, omitting examples, facts, and other supporting evidence.
- Write a sentence or two stating the author's central idea.
- Write a full paragraph (or more, if needed) that begins with the central idea and supports it with the sentences that summarize sections of the work. The paragraph should concisely and accurately state the thrust of the entire work.
- *Use your own words.* By writing, you re-create the meaning of the work in a way that makes sense for you.

Summarizing even a single paragraph can be tricky. Here is one attempt to summarize paragraphs 1–4 of Thomas Sowell's "Student Loans" (pp. 125–26):

Draft summary As much as politicians would like to satisfy voters by giving them everything they ask for, the government cannot afford a student loan program.

This sentence "misreads" the four paragraphs because it asserts that the government cannot afford student loans. Sowell's point is more complicated than that. This accurate summary captures it:

Revised summary As their support of the government's student loan program illustrates, politicians ignore the economic reality that using resources to benefit one group (students in debt) involves taking the resources from another group (taxpayers).

Note When you write a summary, using your own words will ensure that you avoid plagiarism. Even when the summary is in your own words, if you use it in something written for others you must cite the source of the ideas. See pages 686–92.

EXERCISE 2
Summarizing

Start where the preceding summary of Thomas Sowell's essay ends (at paragraph 5) to summarize the entire essay. Your summary, in your own words, should not exceed one paragraph. (For additional exercises in summarizing, see pp. 685–86.)

5 Forming your critical response

Once you've grasped the content of what you're reading—what the author says—then you can turn to understanding what the author does not say outright but suggests or implies or even lets slip. At this stage you are concerned with the purpose or intention of the author and with how he or she carries it out. Depending on what you are reading and why, you may examine evidence, organization, attitude, use of language, and other elements of the text.

Critical thinking and reading consist of four operations: analyzing, interpreting, synthesizing, and (often) evaluating. Although we'll look at them one by one, these operations interrelate and overlap. Indeed, the first three are often combined under the general label *analysis,* and evaluation is sometimes taken for granted as a result of the process.

In the following pages, we use three quite different examples to show how critical reading can work: *People* magazine, Sowell's "Student Loans," and a Web site.

Analyzing

Analysis is the separation of something into its parts or elements, the better to understand it. To see these elements in what you are reading, begin with a question that reflects your purpose in analyzing the text: why you are curious about it or what you're trying to make out of it. This question will serve as a kind of lens that highlights some features and not others. Here, for example, are some questions you might ask about *People* magazine, listed along with the elements of the magazine that each question highlights:

Question for analysis	Elements
Does *People* challenge or perpetuate stereotypes?	Stereotypes: Explicit and implicit stereotypes or challenges in the magazine
Does the magazine offer positive role models for its readers?	Role models: Text and photographs presenting positive or negative role models
Does the magazine's editorial material (articles and accompanying photographs) encourage readers to consume goods and entertainment?	Encouragement of consumption: References to goods and entertainment, focus on consumers, equation of consumption with happiness or success

http://www.users.drew.edu/~sjamieso/Synthesis.htm A guide to analysis and synthesis, from Drew University.

As these examples show, a question for analysis concentrates your attention on relevant features and eliminates irrelevant features. To answer the question about *People*'s encouragement of consumption, you would focus on items that feature consumption and the products consumed: photographs of designer clothes and celebrities' well-appointed homes, articles on the authors of best-selling books and the stars of new movies. At the same time, you would skip over items that have little or no relevance to consumption, such as uplifting stories about families or the physically challenged.

Analyzing Thomas Sowell's "Student Loans" (pp. 125–27), you might ask what Sowell's attitude is toward politicians. That question would lead you to examine Sowell's references to politicians—the content of what he says, his words, his tone. Or you might ask how Sowell supports his assertions about the loan program's costs or recipients. Then you would focus on evidence, such as statistics and examples.

The screen shot below shows the opening page of a Web site that promises relief from student-loan debt. Analyzing this page, you might ask what kind of organization the Federated Loan Consolidation Corporation is or what its intentions are. Answering either ques-

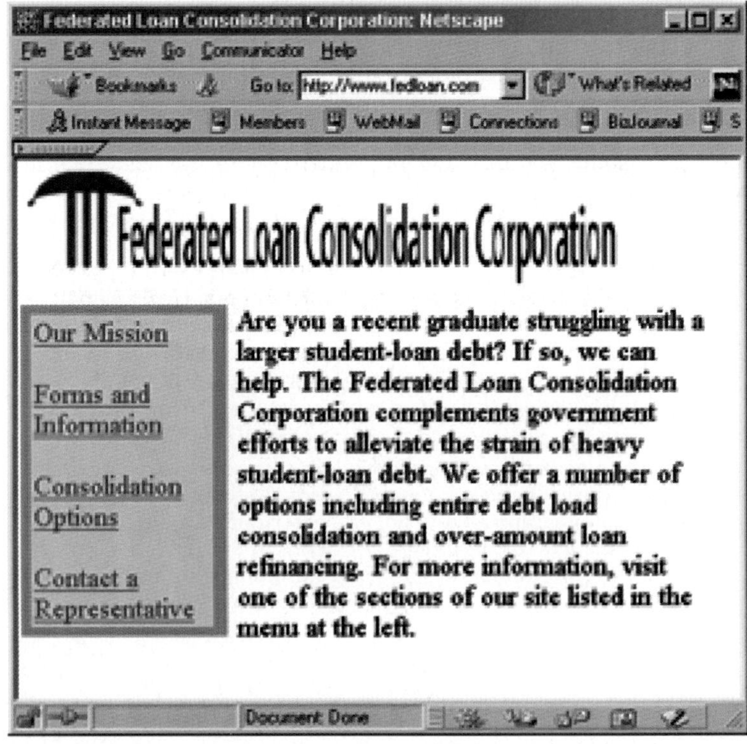

tion, you would examine the address of the site (in the field at the top of the page), the organization's name, the paragraph of text, and the design of the page—its use of type, color, and decorative elements.

A difference in the kinds of questions asked is a key distinction among academic disciplines. A sociologist neatly outlined three disciplines' approaches to poverty:

> Political science does a wonderful job looking at poverty as a policy issue. Economics does an equally wonderful job looking at it from an income-distribution perspective. But sociology asks how people in poverty live and what they aspire to.

Even within disciplines, approaches may differ. The sociologist quoted above may focus on how people in poverty live, but another might be more interested in the effects of poverty on cities or the changes in the poor population over the last fifty years. (See Chapters 48–52 for more on the disciplines' analytical questions.)

Interpreting

Identifying the elements of something is of course only the beginning: you also need to interpret the meaning or significance of the elements and of the whole. Interpretation usually requires you to infer the author's **assumptions,** opinions or beliefs about what is or what could or should be. (**Infer** means to draw a conclusion based on evidence.)

The word *assumption* here has a more specific meaning than it does in everyday usage, where it may stand for expectation ("I assume you'll pay"), speculation ("It was a mere assumption"), or error ("The report was riddled with assumptions"). Defined more strictly as what a person *supposes* to be true, assumptions are unavoidable. We all adhere to certain values and beliefs; we all form opinions. We live our lives by such assumptions.

Though pervasive, assumptions are not always stated outright. Speakers and writers may judge that their audience already understands and accepts their assumptions; they may not even be aware of their assumptions; or they may deliberately refrain from stating their assumptions for fear that the audience will disagree. That is why your job as a critical thinker is to interpret what the assumptions are.

Like an author deciding what to say in an article, the publishers of *People* magazine make assumptions that guide their selection of content for the magazine. One set of assumptions, perhaps the most important, concerns what readers want to see: as a for-profit enterprise, the magazine naturally aims to maintain and even expand its readership (currently about 3.5 million each week). If your analysis of the magazine's editorial material reveals that much of it features consumer products, you might infer the following:

Reasonable The publishers of *People* assume that the magazine's readers are consumers who want to see and hear about goods and entertainment.

Nowhere in *People* will you find a statement of this assumption, but the evidence implies it.

crit 5a

Similarly, Thomas Sowell's "Student Loans" (pp. 125–27) is based on certain assumptions, some obvious, some not so obvious. If you were analyzing Sowell's attitude toward politicians, as suggested earlier, you would focus on his statements about them. Sowell says that they "disregard the first lesson of economics" (paragraph 2), which implies that they ignore important principles (knowing that Sowell is an economist himself makes this a reasonable assumption on your part). Sowell also says that politicians "rob Peter to pay Paul," are "[b]ursting with compassion," do not admit to a "dumb idea," are characters in a "long-running saga," and arrive at the solution of spending taxes "as the night follows the day"—that is, inevitably (paragraphs 2–4). From these statements and others, you can infer the following:

Reasonable Sowell assumes that politicians become compassionate when a cause is loud and popular, not necessarily just, and they act irresponsibly by trying to solve the problem with other people's (taxpayers') money.

Interpreting the screen shot on page 130 to discover the nature of the Federated Loan Consolidation Corporation, you would look at the site's address, where *com* indicates that the organization is a commercial entity. (See p. 670 for more on interpreting electronic addresses.) Yet you might also notice that the site does not resemble other corporate sites, which typically have flashier designs incorporating more images, color, and boxes, among other elements. Instead, the site's look is rather plain—the sort of design you might expect from a government site. The prominent *Federated* in the organization's name and *complements government efforts* in the text reinforce the appearance of a government connection. These findings might lead you to infer the following:

Reasonable The Federated Loan Consolidation Corporation assumes that its readers (potential customers) will be more willing to explore its refinancing options if they believe that it is a reliable organization somehow affiliated with the government.

Interpreting assumptions in this way gives you greater insight into an author's intentions. But it's crucial that inferences fit the evidence of the text, as those above about *People,* Sowell's essay, and the Web site do. Sometimes it's tempting to read too much into the text, as in the next examples:

Guidelines for analysis, interpretation, and synthesis

- What is the purpose of your reading?
- What questions do you have about the work? Which question interests you the most or opens up the most possibilities? What elements does the question highlight for examination? What elements can be ignored as a result?
- How do you interpret the meaning and significance of the elements, both individually and in relation to the whole work? What are your assumptions about the work? What do you infer about the author's assumptions?
- What patterns can you see in (or synthesize from) the elements? How do the elements relate? How does this whole work relate to other works?
- What do you conclude about the work? What does this conclusion add to the work?

Faulty *People's* publishers deliberately skew the magazine's editorial material to promote products on which they receive kickbacks. [The inference is far-fetched, even absurd. It would be reasonable only if there were hard evidence of kickbacks.]

Faulty Sowell thinks that politicians should not be entrusted with running the country. [The inference misreads Sowell. Although he does not outline a solution for politicians' irresponsibility, there's no evidence that he would overhaul our democratic political system.]

Faulty The Federated Loan Consolidation Corporation illegitimately claims that it is a government-sponsored agency in order to exploit graduates with heavy student-loan debt. [The inference takes an unwarranted leap. The site does not claim government affiliation or sanction, and it contains no evidence of exploitation.]

Faulty inferences like those above are often based on the reader's *own* assumptions about the text or its subject. When thinking and reading critically, you need to look hard at *your* ideas, too.

Synthesizing

If you stopped at analysis and interpretation, critical thinking and reading might leave you with a pile of elements and possible meanings but no vision of the whole. With **synthesis** you make connections among parts *or* among wholes. You create a new whole by drawing conclusions about relationships and implications.

The following conclusion pulls together the analysis of *People* magazine's editorial content (p. 130) and the interpretation of the publisher's assumptions about readers (p. 132):

Conclusion *People* magazine appeals to its readers' urge to consume by displaying, discussing, and glamorizing consumer goods.

The statement below about Thomas Sowell's essay "Student Loans" connects his assumptions about politicians (p. 132) to a larger idea also implied by the essay:

Conclusion Sowell's view that politicians are irresponsible with taxpayers' money reflects his overall opinion that the laws of economics, not politics, should drive government.

The next statement draws on elements of the Federated Loan Consolidation Corporation Web site (p. 130) and the inference about the company's understanding of its readers (p. 132):

Conclusion The Federated Loan Consolidation Corporation uses its name, a mention of the government, and a restrained design to appeal to potential customers who may be wary of commercial lending operations.

You can also synthesize your critical readings of a number of sources, again drawing your own conclusions:

Conclusion In *People, Us, Vanity Fair,* and other magazines aimed at consumers, the line between advertising and editorial material is sometimes almost invisible.

(Synthesizing several sources is important in research writing. See pp. 673–74.)

To create your own links between experiences, ideas, and entire sources, it helps (again) to write while reading and thinking. The active reading recommended earlier (p. 124) is the place to start, as you note your questions and opinions about the text. You can also create connections with a combination of writing and drawing: start with your notes, or write your ideas out fresh, and draw connections between related thoughts with lines and arrows.  (On a computer you can underline or boldface related ideas or use the Comment function to signal connections. See also p. 190.) You want to open up your thinking, so experiment freely.

With synthesis, you create something different from what you started with. To the supermarket shopper reading *People* while standing in line, the magazine may be entertaining and inconsequential. To you—after a critical reading in which you analyze, interpret, and synthesize—the magazine is (at least in part) a significant vehicle of our consumer culture. The difference depends entirely on the critical reading.

Evaluating

Many critical reading and writing assignments end at analysis, interpretation, and synthesis: you explain your understanding of what the author says and doesn't say. Only if you are expected to **evaluate** the work will you state and defend the judgments you've made about its quality and its significance. You'll inevitably form such judgments while reading the work: "What a striking series of images," or "That just isn't enough evidence." In evaluating, you collect your judgments, determine that they are generally applicable and are themselves not trivial, and turn them into assertions: "The poet creates fresh, intensely vivid images"; "The author does not summon the evidence to support his case." And you support these statements with citations from the text.

Evaluation takes a certain amount of confidence. You may think that you lack the expertise to cast judgment on another's writing, especially if the text is difficult or the author well known. True, the more informed you are, the better a critical reader you are. But conscientious reading and analysis will give you the internal authority to judge a work *as it stands* and *as it seems to you,* against your own unique bundle of experiences, observations, and attitudes.

The box below gives questions that can help you evaluate many kinds of works. There's more on evaluation (including evaluation of online sources) on pages 667–72. For arguments and in academic

Guidelines for evaluation

- What are your reactions to the work? What in the work are you responding to?
- Is the work sound in its general idea? in its facts, examples, and other evidence?
- Has the author achieved his or her purpose? Is the purpose worthwhile?
- Does the author seem authoritative? trustworthy? sincere?
- Is the work unified, with all the parts pertaining to a central idea? Is it coherent, with the parts relating clearly to one another? If the material is from an online source such as a Web site, these ideals of unity and coherence might be given a backseat in favor of expansive and varied lines of thought connected to the site by links. Then ask what the purpose of the links is and whether they provide worthwhile insight into the subject.

- If the work includes color, graphics, or (online) sound or video, do these elements add meaning to the work or merely dress it up?
- What is the overall quality of the work? What is its value or significance in the larger scheme of things?
- Do you agree or disagree with the work? Can you support, refute, or extend it?

disciplines, you'll require additional, more specific criteria. See Chapters 6 and 48–52.

EXERCISE 3
Thinking critically

Following are some statements about the communications media. Use systematic critical thinking to understand not only what the statement says but why its author might have said it. As in the example, do your thinking in writing: the act of writing will help you think, and your notes will help you discuss your ideas with your classmates. (Additional exercises in critical reading appear on pp. 674–75.)

Example:

Statement: Every year sees the disappearance of more book publishers because the larger companies gobble up the smaller ones.

Analysis: Why did the author make this statement? Certain words reveal the author's purpose: *disappearance of more book publishers; because; larger companies gobble up smaller ones.*

Interpretation: More book publishers means others have disappeared. *Because* specifies cause. *Gobble up* implies consumption, predator to prey. Author's assumptions: Large publishers behave like predators. The predatory behavior of large companies causes the disappearance of small companies. The more publishing companies there are, the better.

Synthesis: The author objects to the predatory behavior of large publishing companies, which he or she holds responsible for eliminating small companies and reducing the total number of companies.

Evaluation: This biased statement against large publishers holds them responsible for the shrinking numbers of book publishers. But are the large companies solely responsible? And why is the shrinking necessarily bad?

1. Newspapers and newsmagazines are better news sources than television because they demand reading, not just viewing.
2. Radio call-in shows are the true democratic forum, giving voice to people of all persuasions.
3. Online communication threatens to undermine our ability to interact face to face.

EXERCISE 4
Reading an essay critically

Reread Thomas Sowell's "Student Loans" (pp. 125–27) in order to form your own critical response to it. Follow the guidelines for analysis, interpretation, synthesis, and evaluation in the boxes on pages 133 and 135. Focus on any elements suggested by your question about the text: possibilities are assumptions, evidence, organization, use of language, tone, authority, vision of education or students. Be sure to write while reading and thinking; your notes will help your analysis and enhance your creativity, and they will be essential for writing about the selection (Exercise 8, p. 140).

EXERCISE 5
Reading a magazine critically

Do your own critical reading of *People* or another magazine. What do you see beyond the obvious? What questions does your reading raise? Let the guidelines on pages 133 and 135 direct your response, and do your work in writing. (A writing suggestion based on this exercise appears on p. 140.)

EXERCISE 6
Reading a Web site critically

Use your Web browser to find the Web site of a corporation or other commercial organization with which you are familiar, such as the manufacturer of a car, television, computer, or other product you own; the bank where you have your account; or the online store where you buy books or music. Examine the site's layout, color, images, sound, video, and interactive features as well as the content of the text. What do the elements tell you about the site's purpose or purposes—for instance, does the site aim to sell something, to give advice, to provide services? What assumptions does it make about readers? How well do the elements achieve the site's purposes? Refer to the boxes on pages 133 and 135 for additional questions to consider, and do your thinking in writing. (A writing suggestion based on this exercise appears on p. 140.)

5b Writing critically

Like critical reading, critical writing is largely influenced by its purpose and by the discipline or profession in which it occurs. Thus the topic is covered more extensively in Chapters 7 (argument), 49 (literature), 50 (other humanities), 51 (social sciences), and 52 (natural and applied sciences). In this introduction, we'll look at some fundamentals and an illustration.

Remember that critical writing is *not* summarizing. You may write a summary to clarify for yourself what the author says (pp. 127–28), and you may briefly summarize a work in your own larger piece of writing. But your job in critical writing is not just to report what a text says; it is to transmit your analysis, interpretation, synthesis, and perhaps evaluation of the text.

http://www.its-ps.uni.edu:206/reineke/developi.htm Strategies for critical writing, from the University of Northern Iowa.

The following essay by Charlene Robinson, a student, is a response to Thomas Sowell's "Student Loans." Robinson arrived at her response through the process of critical reading outlined in this chapter and then by gathering and organizing her ideas, developing her own central idea (or thesis) about Sowell's text, and drafting and revising until she believed she had supported her central idea. Robinson does not assume that her readers see the same things in Sowell's essay or share her views, so she offers evidence of Sowell's ideas in the form of direct quotations, summaries, and paraphrases (restatements in her own words). (See pp. 678–83 for more on these techniques.) Robinson then documents these borrowings from Sowell using the style of the Modern Language Association (MLA): the numbers in parentheses are page numbers in the book containing Sowell's essay, listed at the end as a "work cited." (See Chapter 46 for more on MLA style.)

Weighing the Costs

In his essay "Student Loans," the economist Thomas Sowell challenges the US government's student-loan program for several reasons: a scarce resource (taxpayers' money) goes to many undeserving students, a high number of recipients fail to repay their loans, and the easy availability of money has led to both lower academic standards and higher college tuitions. Sowell wants his readers to "weigh the costs of things" (133) in order to see, as he does, that the loan program should not receive so much government funding. But does he provide the evidence of cost and other problems to lead the reader to agree with him? The answer is no, because hard evidence is less common than debatable and unsupported assumptions about students, scarcity, and the value of education.

Introduction:
1. Summary of Sowell's essay
2. Robinson's critical question
3. Thesis statement

Sowell's portrait of student-loan recipients is questionable. It is based on averages, some statistical and some not, but averages are often deceptive. For example, Sowell cites college graduates' low average debt of $7,000 to $9,000 (131) without acknowledging the fact that many students' debt is much higher or giving the full range of statistics. Similarly, Sowell dismisses "heart-rending stories" of "the low-income student with a huge debt" as "not at all typical" (132), yet he invents his own exaggerated version of the typical loan recipient: an affluent slacker ("Rockefellers" and "Vanderbilts") for whom college is a place to "hang out for a few years" sponging off the government, while his or her parents clear a profit from making use of the

First main point
Evidence for first point:
1. Paraphrases and quotations from Sowell's text (with source citations in MLA style)

loan program (132). While such students (and parents) may well exist, are they really typical? Sowell does not offer any data one way or the other—for instance, how many loan recipients come from each income group, what percentage of loan funds go to each group, how many loan recipients receive significant help from their parents, and how many receive none.

2. Sowell's omissions

Another set of assumptions in the essay has to do with "scarcity": "There is never enough of anything to fully satisfy all those who want it," Sowell says (131). This statement appeals to readers' common sense, but does the "lesson" of scarcity necessarily apply to the student-loan program? Sowell omits many important figures needed to prove that the nation's resources are too scarce to support the program, such as the total cost of the program, its percentage of the total education budget and the total federal budget, and its cost compared to the cost of defense, Medicare, and other expensive programs. Moreover, Sowell does not mention the interest paid by loan recipients, even though the interest must offset some of the costs of running the program and covering unpaid loans.

Transition to second main point

Second point

Evidence for second point: Sowell's omissions

The most fundamental and most debatable assumption underlying Sowell's essay is that higher education is a kind of commodity that not everyone is entitled to. In order to diminish the importance of graduates' average debt from education loans, Sowell claims that a car loan will probably be higher (131). This comparison between education and an automobile implies that the two are somehow equal as products and that an affordable higher education is no more a right than a new car is. Sowell also condemns the "irresponsible" students who drop out of school and "the increasingly easy availability of college to people who are not very serious about getting an education" (132). But he overlooks the value of encouraging education, including education of those who don't finish college or who aren't scholars. For many in the United States, education has a greater value than that of a mere commodity like a car. And even from an economic perspective such as Sowell's, the cost to society of an uneducated public needs to be taken into account.

Third main point

Evidence for third point: paraphrases and quotations of Sowell's text (with source citations in MLA style)

Sowell writes with conviction, and his concerns are valid: high taxes, waste, unfairness, declining educational standards, obtrusive government. However, the essay's flaws make it unlikely that Sowell could convince readers who do not al-

Conclusion:

1. Acknowledgment of Sowell's concerns

ready agree with him. He does not support his portrait of the typical loan recipient, he fails to demonstrate a lack of resources for the loan program, and he neglects the special nature of education compared to other services and products. Sowell may have the evidence to back up his assumptions, but by omitting it he himself does not truly weigh the costs of the loan program.

2. Summary of three main points

3. Return to theme of introduction: weighing costs

Work Cited

Sowell, Thomas. "Student Loans." Is Reality Optional? and Other Essays. Stanford: Hoover, 1993. 131–33.

Reference to complete source for Sowell's essay (in MLA style)

—Charlene Robinson

EXERCISE 7
Responding to critical writing

Read Charlene Robinson's essay carefully. (You can read and respond to the essay on your computer by downloading it from this book's Web site at *http://www.awlonline.com/littlebrown.*) What is Robinson's critical question about Sowell's essay? How does it relate to her thesis statement? What assumptions does she identify in Sowell's essay? What conclusions does she reach about the essay? Do you think her response is accurate and fair? Is it perceptive? Does Robinson provide enough evidence from Sowell's essay to convince you of her points? Does she miss anything you would have mentioned? Write your responses in a brief essay.

EXERCISE 8
Writing critically about an essay

Write an essay based on your own critical reading of Thomas Sowell's essay (Exercise 4, pp. 136–37). Your critique may be entirely different from Charlene Robinson's, or you may have developed some of the same points. If there are similarities, they should be expressed and supported in your own way, in the context of your own approach.

EXERCISE 9
Writing critically about a magazine

Write an essay based on your critical response to *People* magazine or another magazine (Exercise 5, p. 137). Follow the guidelines on pages 137–38 for developing and organizing your essay.

EXERCISE 10
Writing critically about a Web site

Write an essay based on your critical response to a commercial Web site (Exercise 6, p. 137). Be sure to use specific examples of the site's elements to support your ideas about the site. Follow the guidelines on pages 137–38 for developing and organizing your essay.

CHAPTER 6

Reading Arguments Critically

Argument is writing that attempts to open readers' minds to an opinion, change readers' own opinions, or move readers to action. A good argument is neither a cold exercise in logic nor an attempt to beat others into submission. It is a work of negotiation and problem solving in which both writer and reader search for the knowledge that will create common ground between them.

Of course, not all arguments are "good." Whether deliberately or not, some are unclear, incomplete, misleading, or downright false. The negotiation fails; the problem remains unsolved. This chapter will help you recognize good arguments when you read them, and the following chapter will help you write good arguments when you need to.

ESL The ways of reading and writing arguments described in this chapter and the next may be initially uncomfortable to you if your native culture approaches such writing differently. In some cultures, for example, a writer is expected to begin indirectly, to avoid asserting his or her opinion outright, to rely for evidence on appeals to tradition, or to establish a compromise rather than argue a position. Readers and writers of English, as these chapters explain, look or aim for a well-articulated opinion, evidence gathered from many sources, and a direct and concise argument for the opinion.

6a Recognizing the elements of argument

Few arguments are an easy read. Most demand the attentive critical reading discussed in the previous chapter. (If you haven't read pp. 119–36, you should do so before continuing.) As a reader of

http://www.unc.edu/depts/wcweb/handouts/argument.html An introduction to the nature of argument and its key role in academic writing, from the University of North Carolina.

http://commhum.mccneb.edu/argument/summary.htm A tutorial for reading arguments critically, from Metropolitan Community College.

http://www.eslplanet.com/teachertools/argueweb/frntpage.htm A guide to reading and writing arguments, from the ESL Planet.

Questions for critically reading an argument

- What **claims** does the writer make? (below and opposite)
- What kind and quality of **evidence** does the writer provide to support the claims? (below and p. 146)
- What **assumptions** underlie the argument, connecting evidence to claims? (below and p. 150)
- What is the writer's **tone?** How does the writer use **language?** (p. 151)
- Is the writer **reasonable?** (p. 152)
- Is the argument logical? Has the writer committed any **fallacies?** (p. 155)
- Are you convinced? Why or why not?

argument, your purpose will almost always be the same: you'll want to know whether you should be convinced by the argument. This purpose focuses your attention on the elements that make an argument convincing, or not.

In a scheme adapted from the work of the British philosopher Stephen Toulmin, an argument has three main elements:

- **Claims:** positive statements that require support. In an argument the central claim is stated outright as the **thesis** (see p. 30); it is what the argument is about. For instance:

  The college needs a new chemistry laboratory to replace the existing outdated lab.

  Several minor claims, such as that the present equipment is inadequate, will contribute to the central assertion.

- **Evidence:** the facts, examples, expert opinions, and other information that support the claims. (Toulmin calls evidence *data* or *grounds,* terms that indicate both its specificity and its work as an argument's foundation.) Evidence to support the preceding claim might include the following:

  The present lab's age
  An inventory of equipment
  The testimony of chemistry professors

  Like the claims, the evidence is always stated outright.

- **Assumptions:** the writer's underlying (and often unstated) beliefs, opinions, principles, or inferences that tie the evidence to the claims. (Toulmin calls these assumptions *warrants:* they justify making the claims on the basis of the evidence provided.) For instance, the following assumption might connect the evidence of professors' testimony with the claim that a new lab is needed:

> Chemistry professors are the most capable of evaluating the present lab's quality.

In the following pages, we'll examine each of these elements along with several others: tone and language, reasonableness, and common errors in reasoning. The student paper in the previous chapter, Charlene Robinson's "Weighing the Costs" (pp. 138–40), provides a good example of critically reading an argument for its claims, evidence, and assumptions.

Note Online arguments often differ considerably from conventional written arguments and may require different ways of reading and evaluating. A Web site, for instance, may partly support claims with links to other pages or sites rather than directly in the main document itself. And online discussions tend to build arguments gradually from the give and take of the participants, so that no one contribution is definitive. In reading such arguments, you may have to do more work than with conventional arguments to put opinions in context and locate the backbone of claims, evidence, and assumptions.

6b Testing claims

The claims or assertions in an argument carry specific burdens: they should state arguable opinions, and they should define their terms.

1 Distinguishing facts, opinions, beliefs, and prejudices

Most statements we hear, read, or make in speaking and writing are claims of fact, opinion, belief, or prejudice. In an argument the acceptability of a claim depends partly on which of these categories it falls into.

Note When reading arguments that appear online, you should be especially vigilant for claims of belief or prejudice that pose as considered opinions. Anyone with a computer and an Internet connection can post anything on the Internet, without passing it through an editorial screening like that undergone by books and articles in journals and magazines. The filtering of such material is entirely up to the reader.

http://www.cod.edu/dept/KiesDan/engl_102/factuall.htm Information on claims, from the College of DuPage.

Facts

A **fact** is verifiable—that is, one can determine whether it is true. It may involve numbers or dates:

> World War II ended in 1945.
> The football field is 100 yards long.

The numbers may be implied:

> The earth is closer to the sun than Saturn is.
> The cost of medical care is rising.

Or the fact may involve no numbers at all:

> The city council adjourned without taking a vote.
> The President vetoed the bill.

Facts provide crucial evidence for the claims of an argument, and as evidence they may be problematic because they can be misinterpreted or distorted (see pp. 148–49). But they are ultimately verifiable, so they do not make worthwhile arguments by themselves.

Opinions

An **opinion** is a judgment *based* on facts, an honest attempt to draw a reasonable conclusion from evidence. For example:

> Mandatory drug testing in workplaces is essential to increase employees' productivity.
>
> Mandatory drug testing in workplaces does not substantially increase employees' productivity.
>
> Mandatory drug testing in workplaces violates constitutional freedoms.

All three of these opinions share certain features:

- They express viewpoints based on an interpretation of facts.
- They are arguable. Indeed, they argue with each other, though each writer had access to the same facts.
- They are potentially changeable. With more evidence the writers might alter their opinions partly or wholly.

The main claim, or thesis, of an argument is always an opinion. Other, more specific claims of opinion generally form the backbone of the argument supporting the thesis. By themselves, however, opinions do not make arguments. As a critical reader, you must satisfy yourself that the writer has specified the evidence for the opinions and that the assumptions linking claims and evidence are clear and believable.

Beliefs

An opinion is not the same as a **belief,** a conviction based on cultural or personal faith, morality, or values:

Abortion is legalized murder.

Capital punishment is legalized murder.

The primary goal of government should be to provide equality of opportunity for all.

Such statements are often called opinions because they express viewpoints, but they are not based on facts and other evidence. Since they cannot be disproved by facts or even contested on the basis of facts, they cannot serve as the central claim of an argument. Statements of belief do figure in argument, however: they can serve as a kind of evidence, and they often form the assumptions linking claims and evidence. See pages 147 and 151.

Prejudices

One kind of assertion that has no place in argument is a prejudice, an opinion based on insufficient or unexamined evidence:

Women are bad drivers.
Fat people are jolly.
Teenagers are irresponsible.

Unlike a belief, a prejudice is testable: it can be contested and disproved on the basis of facts. Very often, however, we form prejudices or accept them from others—parents, friends, the communications media—without questioning their meaning or testing their truth. Writers who display prejudice do not deserve the confidence and agreement of readers. Readers who accept prejudice are not thinking critically.

2 Looking for defined terms

In any argument, but especially in arguments about abstract ideas, clear and consistent definition of terms is essential. In the following claim, the writer is not clear about what she means by the crucial term *justice:*

Over the past few decades, justice has deteriorated so badly that it almost does not exist anymore.

The word *justice* is **abstract:** it does not refer to anything specific or concrete and in fact has varied meanings. (The seven definitions in *The American Heritage Dictionary* include "the principle of moral rightness" and "the administration and procedure of law.") When the writer specifies her meaning, her assertion is much clearer:

If by *justice* we mean treating people fairly, punishing those who commit crimes, and protecting the victims of those crimes, then justice has deteriorated badly over the past few decades.

Writers who use highly abstract words such as *justice, equality, success,* and *maturity* have a responsibility to define them. If the word is important to the argument, such a definition may take an entire paragraph. As a reader you have the obligation to evaluate the writer's definitions before you accept his or her assertions. (See pp. 97–98 for more on definition and a paragraph defining the abstract word *quality*.)

6c Weighing evidence

In argument, evidence demonstrates the validity of the writer's claims. If the evidence is inadequate or questionable, the claims are at best doubtful.

1 Recognizing kinds of evidence

Writers draw on several kinds of evidence to support their claims:

Evidence for argument

- **Facts:** verifiable statements
- **Statistics:** facts expressed in numbers
- **Examples:** specific cases
- **Expert opinions:** the judgments of authorities
- **Appeals to readers' beliefs or needs**

Facts

Facts are statements whose truth can be verified by observation or research (see p. 144):

Poland is slightly smaller than New Mexico.
Insanity is grounds for divorce in a majority of the states.

Facts employing numbers are **statistics:**

Of those polled, 62 percent stated a preference for a flat tax.

In 1997 there were 1,216,318 men and women in the US armed forces.

The average American household consists of 2.64 persons.

Examples

Examples are specific instances of the point being made, including historical precedents and personal experiences. The passage that follows uses a personal narrative as partial support for the claim in the first sentence.

http://www.cod.edu/dept/KiesDan/engl_102/evidence.htm Discussion of evidence, from the College of DuPage.

> Besides broadening students' knowledge, required courses can also introduce students to possible careers that they otherwise would have known nothing about. Somewhat reluctantly, I enrolled in a psychology course to satisfy the requirement for work in social science. But what I learned in the course about human behavior has led me to consider becoming a clinical psychologist instead of an engineer.

Expert opinions

Expert opinions are the judgments formed by authorities on the basis of their own examination of the facts. In the following passage the writer cites the opinion of an expert to support the claim in the first sentence:

> Despite the fact that affirmative action places some individuals at a disadvantage, it remains necessary to right the wrongs inflicted historically on whole groups of people. Howard Glickstein, a past director of the US Commission on Civil Rights, maintains that "it simply is not possible to achieve equality and fairness" unless the previous grounds for discrimination (such as sex, race, and national origin) are now considered as grounds for admission to schools and jobs (26).

As this passage illustrates, a citation of expert opinion should always refer the reader to the source, here indicated by the page number in parentheses, "(26)." Such a citation is also generally accompanied by a reference to the expert's credentials. See pages 697 and 698–99.

ESL In some cultures a person with high standing in government, society, or organized religion may be considered an authority on many different subjects. For native English speakers, authority tends to derive from study, learning, and experience: the more knowledge a person can demonstrate about a subject, the more authority he or she has.

Appeals to beliefs or needs

An **appeal to beliefs or needs** asks readers to accept an assertion in part because they already accept it as true without evidence or because it coincides with their needs. Each of the following examples combines such an appeal (second sentence) with a summary of factual evidence (first sentence).

> Thus the chemistry laboratory is outdated in its equipment. In addition, its shabby, antiquated appearance shames the school, making it seem a second-rate institution. [Appeals to readers' belief that their school is or should be first-rate.]

> That police foot patrollers reduce crime has already been demonstrated. Such officers might also restore our sense that our neighborhoods are orderly, stable places. [Appeals to readers' need for order and stability.]

(For more on beliefs, see pp. 144–45. For more on appeals to emotion, see pp. 171–72.)

2 Judging the reliability of evidence

arg 6c

To support claims and convince readers, evidence must be reliable. The tests of reliability for appeals to readers' beliefs and needs are specific to the situation: whether they are appropriate for the argument and correctly gauge how readers actually feel (see p. 172). With the other kinds of evidence, the standards are more general, applying to any argument.

Note If you are reading an argument that cites online sources (and their addresses) for its evidence, you can easily use your Web browser to track down the sources and see for yourself how reliable the evidence is. Just be aware that online materials often change and sometimes disappear entirely.

Accuracy

Accurate evidence is true:

- It is drawn from trustworthy sources.
- It is quoted exactly.
- It is presented with the original meaning undistorted.

In an essay favoring gun control, a writer should not rely exclusively on procontrol sources, which are undoubtedly biased. Instead, the writer should also cite anticontrol sources (representing the opposite bias) and neutral sources (attempting to be unbiased). If the writer quotes an expert, the quotation should present the expert's true meaning, not just a few words that happen to support the writer's argument. (As a reader you may have difficulty judging the accuracy of quotations if you are not familiar with the expert's opinions.)

Not just opinions but also facts and examples may be misinterpreted or distorted. Suppose you were reading an argument for extending a three-year-old law allowing the police to stop vehicles randomly as a means of apprehending drunk drivers. If the author cited statistics showing that the number of drunk-driving accidents dropped in the first two years of the law but failed to note that the number rose back to the previous level in the third year, then the

---

Criteria for weighing evidence

- Is it **accurate:** trustworthy, exact, undistorted?
- Is it **relevant:** authoritative, pertinent, current?
- Is it **representative:** true to context?
- Is it **adequate:** plentiful, specific?

---

evidence would be distorted and thus inaccurate. You or any reader would be justified in questioning the entire argument, no matter how accurate the rest seemed.

Relevance

Relevant evidence pertains to the argument:

- It comes from sources with authority on the subject.
- It relates directly to the point the writer is making.
- It is current.

In an argument against a method of hazardous-waste disposal, a writer should not offer his aunt's opinion as evidence unless she is an authority on the subject and her expertise is up to date. If she is an authority on Method A and not Method B, the writer should not use her opinion as evidence against Method B. Similarly, the writer's own experience of living near a hazardous-waste site may be relevant evidence *if* it pertains to his thesis. His authority in this case is that of a close observer and a citizen. (See also p. 157 on the fallacy of false authority.)

Representativeness

Representative evidence is true to its context:

- It reflects the full range of the sample from which it is said to be drawn.
- It does not overrepresent any element of the sample.

In an essay arguing that dormitories should stay open during school holidays, a writer might say that "the majority of the school's students favor leaving the dormitories open." But that writer would mislead you and other readers if the claim were based only on a poll of her roommates and dormitory neighbors. A few dormitory residents could not be said to represent the entire student body, particularly the nonresident students. To be representative, the poll would have to take in many more students in proportions that reflect the numbers of resident and nonresident students on campus.

Adequacy

Adequate evidence is sufficient:

- It is plentiful enough to support the writer's assertions.
- It is specific enough to support the writer's assertions.

A writer arguing against animal abuse cannot hope to win over readers solely with statements about her personal experiences and claims of her opinions. Her experience may indeed be relevant evidence if, say, she has worked with animals or witnessed animal abuse. And her opinions are indeed important to the argument, to let readers know what she thinks. But even together these are not adequate evidence: they cannot substitute entirely for facts, nonpersonal examples, and the opinions of experts to demonstrate abuse and describe the scope of the problem.

6d Discovering assumptions

Assumptions connect evidence to claims: they are the opinions or beliefs that explain why a particular piece of evidence is relevant to a particular claim. As noted in the preceding chapter on critical thinking (pp. 131–32), assumptions are not flaws in arguments but necessities: we all acquire beliefs and opinions that shape our view of the world. Here are some examples that you, or people you know, may hold:

Criminals should be punished.
Hard work is virtuous.
Teachers' salaries are too low.

Assumptions are inevitable in argument, but they aren't neutral. For one thing, an assumption can weaken an argument. Say that a writer claims that real estate development should be prevented in your town. As evidence for this claim, the writer offers facts about past developments that have replaced older buildings. But the evidence is relevant to the claim only if you accept the writer's extreme assumptions that old buildings are always worthy and new development is always bad.

In such a case, the writer's bias may not even be stated. Hence a second problem: in arguments both sound and unsound, assumptions are not always explicit. Here, for example, is a summary of a reasonable argument. What is the unstated assumption?

Claim

The town should create a plan to manage building preservation and new development.

Evidence

Examples of how such plans work; expert opinions on how and why both preservation and development are needed.

In this instance the assumption is that neither uncontrolled development nor zero development is healthy for the town. If you can accept this assumption, you should be able to accept the writer's claim (though you might still disagree over particulars).

http://www.cod.edu/dept/KiesDan/engl_102/assume.htm An examination of stated and unstated assumptions in arguments, from the College of DuPage.

Here are some tips for dealing with assumptions:

Guidelines for analyzing assumptions

- What are the assumptions underlying the argument? How does the writer connect claims with evidence?
- Are the assumptions believable? Do they express your values? Do they seem true in your experience?
- Are the assumptions consistent with each other? Is the argument's foundation solid, not slippery?

6e Watching language, hearing tone

Tone is the expression of the writer's attitudes toward himself or herself, toward the subject, and toward the reader (see pp. 12–14 for a discussion). Tone can tell you quite a bit about the writer's intentions, biases, and trustworthiness. For example:

> Some women cite personal growth as a reason for pursuing careers while raising children. Of course, they are equally concerned with the personal growth of the children they relegate to "child-care specialists" while they work.

In the second sentence this writer is being **ironic,** saying one thing while meaning another. The word *relegate* and the quotation marks with *child-care specialists* betray the writer's belief that working mothers may selfishly neglect their children for their own needs. Irony can sometimes be effective in argument, but here it marks the author as insincere in dealing with the complex issues of working parents and child care.

When reading arguments, you should be alert for the author's language. Look for words that **connote,** or suggest, certain attitudes and evoke certain responses in readers. (Notice your own responses to these word pairs with related meanings but different connotations: *daring/foolhardy, dislike/detest, glad/joyous, angry/rabid, freedom/license.*) Connotative language is no failure in argument; indeed, the strongest arguments use it skillfully to appeal to readers' hearts as well as their minds (see pp. 171–72). But be suspicious if the language runs counter to the substance of the argument.

Look also for evasive words. **Euphemisms,** such as *attack of a partly sexual nature* for "rape" or *peace-keeping force* for a warmaking army, are supposedly inoffensive substitutes for words that may frighten or offend readers (see pp. 562–63). In argument, though, they are sometimes used to hide or twist the truth. An honest, forthright arguer will avoid them.

Finally, watch carefully for sexist, racist, and other biased language that reveals deep ignorance or, worse, entrenched prejudice on the part of the writer. Obvious examples are *broad* for woman and *fag* for homosexual. (See pp. 563–66 for more on such language.)

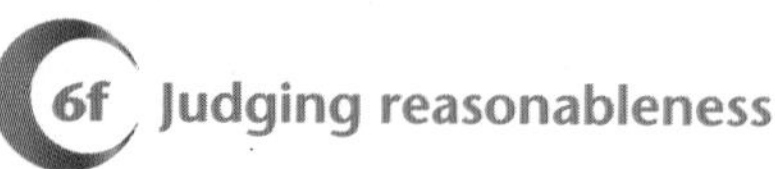

6f Judging reasonableness

The **reasonableness** of an argument is the sense you get as a reader that the author is fair and sincere. The reasonable writer does not conceal or distort facts, hide prejudices, mask belief as opinion, manipulate you with language, or resort to any of dozens of devices used unconsciously by those who don't know better and deliberately by those who do.

Reasonableness involves all the elements of argument examined so far: claims, evidence, assumptions, and language. In addition, the fair, sincere argument always avoids so-called fallacies (covered in the next section), and it acknowledges the opposition.

Judging whether a writer deals adequately with his or her opposition is a fairly simple matter for the reader of argument. By definition, an arguable issue has more than one side. Even if you have no preconceptions about a subject, you will know that another side exists. If the writer pretends otherwise, or dismisses the opposition too quickly, you are justified in questioning the honesty and fairness of the argument. (For the more complicated business of *writing* an acknowledgment of oppositing views, see pp. 173–74.)

EXERCISE 1
Reading arguments critically

Following are two brief arguments. Though not directly opposed, the two arguments do represent different stances on environmental issues. Read each argument critically, following the process outlined in the previous chapter (pp. 119–37) and answering the questions in the box on page 142 (questions about claims, evidence, assumptions, and the other elements of argument). Develop your responses in writing so that you can refer to them for later exercises and class discussion.

The Environmental Crisis Is Not Our Fault

I am as responsible as most eco-citizens: I bike everywhere; I don't own a car; I recycle newspapers, bottles, cans, and plastics; I have a vegetable garden in the summer; I buy organic products; and I put all vegetable waste into my backyard compost bin, probably the only one in all of Greenwich Village. But I don't at the same time believe that I am saving the planet, or in fact doing anything of much consequence about the various eco-crises around us. What's more, I don't even believe that if "all of us" as individuals started doing the same it would make any but the slightest difference. 1

Leave aside ozone depletion and rain forest destruction—those are patently corporate crimes that no individual actions can remedy to any degree. Take, instead, energy consumption in this country. In the most recent figures, residential consumption was 7.2 percent of the total, commercial 5.5 percent, and industrial 23.3 percent; of the remainder, 27.8 percent was transportation (about one-third of it by private car) and 36.3 percent was electric generation (about one-third for residential use). Individual energy use, in sum, was something like 28 percent of total consumption. Although you and I cutting down on energy consumption would have some small effect (and should be done), it is surely the energy consumption of industry and other large institutions such as government and agribusiness that needs to be addressed first. And it is industry and government that must be forced to explain what their consumption is for, what is produced by it, how necessary it is, and how it can be drastically reduced. 2

The point is that the ecological crisis is essentially beyond "our" control, as citizens or householders or consumers or even voters. It is not something that can be halted by recycling or double-pane insulation. It is the inevitable by-product of our modern industrial civilization, dominated by capitalist production and consumption and serviced and protected by various institutions of government, federal to local. It cannot possibly be altered or reversed by simple individual actions, even by the actions of the millions who take part in Earth Day—even if they all go home and fix their refrigerators and from then on walk to work. Nothing less than a drastic overhaul of this civilization and an abandonment of its ingrained gods—progress, growth, exploitation, technology, materialism, anthropocentricity, and power—will do anything substantial to halt our path to environmental destruction, and it's hard to see how life-style solutions will have an effect on that. 3

What I find truly pernicious about such solutions is that they get people thinking they are actually making a difference and doing their part to halt the destruction of the earth: "There, I've taken all the bottles to the recycling center and used my string bag at the grocery store; I guess that'll take care of global warming." It is the kind of thing that diverts people from the hard truths and hard choices and hard actions, from the recognition that they have to take on the larger forces of society—corporate and governmental—where true power, and true destructiveness, lie. 4

And to the argument that, well, you have to start somewhere to raise people's consciousness, I would reply that this individualistic approach does not in fact raise consciousness. It does not move people beyond their old familiar liberal perceptions of the world, it does nothing to challenge the belief in technofix or write-your-Congressperson solutions, and it does not begin to provide them with the new vocabulary and modes of thought necessary for a true change of consciousness. We need, for example, to think of recycling centers not as the answer to 5 our waste problems, but as a confession that the system of packaging and production in this society is out of control. Recycling centers are like hospitals; they are the institutions at the end of the cycle that take care of problems that would never exist if ecological criteria had operated at the beginning of the cycle. Until we have those kinds of understandings, we will not do anything with consciousness except reinforce it with the same misguided ideas that created the crisis.

—Kirkpatrick Sale

Myths We Wouldn't Miss

There are tall tales and legends. There are fables and apocryphal stories. And there are myths—a number of which we would like to see disappear. Here are some myths that would not be missed: 1

Myth: Offshore drilling would be an ecological disaster. 2

Truth is, there hasn't been a serious spill in US waters resulting from offshore drilling operations in more than thirty years—and even that one, in Santa Barbara Channel in 1969, caused no permanent damage to the environment. 3

This is why we always have such a problem with the reasoning of those who call for moratoriums or outright bans on such activity while the nation continues to import foreign oil. The fact is, oil industry offshore drilling operations cause less pollution than urban runoff, atmospheric phenomena, municipal discharges or natural seeps. 4

Why this nation would choose *not* to drill for oil and *not* to provide the jobs, profits and taxes such activity would mean for the American economy when there are no better alternatives is a mystery we hope puzzles others as much as it does us. 5

Myth: America is a profligate waster of energy. 6

The myth makers like to throw around numbers that read like this: with only 5 percent of the world's population, the US uses about 25 percent of the world's energy. But ours is a big country—three thousand miles from one ocean to the next. Transportation accounts for more than 60 percent of US oil use. We could probably cut down if we moved everybody into one corner of the country, but where is the waste? 7

It certainly isn't the automobiles that are inefficient. They are twice as efficient as the ones we used thirty years ago. If American drivers use more gasoline than their counterparts in Europe and Japan, it may just have something to do with the country's size. 8

In fact, proof of the country's size may be in our economic output—and may also hold a clue as to why we use the energy we do. Despite having only 5 percent of the world's population, America may indeed use 25 percent of the world's energy. However, according to the latest statistics, we also produce about 25 percent of the world's goods and services. Again, where's the waste? 9

MYTH: Conservation is *the answer* to America's energy prob- 10
lems.

No doubt about it, we all need to be careful of the amount 11
of energy we use. But as long as this nation's economy needs to grow, we are going to need energy to fuel that growth.

For the foreseeable future, there are no viable alternatives to 12
petroleum as the major source of energy, especially for transportation fuels. Let's face it. Over the past thirty years we *have* learned to conserve—in our factories, our homes, our cars. We probably can—and should—do more. But conservation and new exploration should not be mutually exclusive, because even without an increase in energy consumption, we are using up domestic reserves of oil and gas and must replace them. For the good of the economy, those reserves should be replaced with new domestic production, to the extent economically possible. Otherwise, the only solutions would be additional imports or no growth. And stifling growth would be a gross disservice to the people for whom such growth would provide the opportunity for a better life.

Simply put, America is going to need more energy for all its 13
people.

And that is no myth. 14

—Oil corporation advertisement

6g Recognizing fallacies

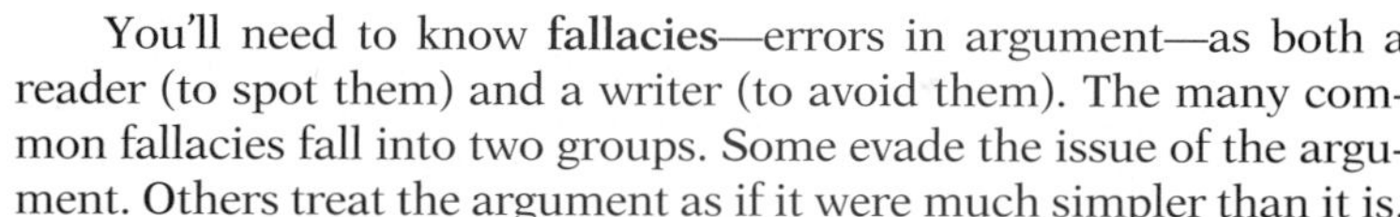

You'll need to know **fallacies**—errors in argument—as both a reader (to spot them) and a writer (to avoid them). The many common fallacies fall into two groups. Some evade the issue of the argument. Others treat the argument as if it were much simpler than it is.

1 Recognizing evasions

The central claim of an argument defines an issue or question: Should real estate development be controlled? Should drug testing be mandatory in the workplace? An effective argument faces the central issue squarely with relevant opinions, beliefs, and evidence. An ineffective argument dodges the issue.

Begging the question

A writer **begs the question** by treating an opinion that is open to question as if it were already proved or disproved. (In essence, the writer begs readers to accept his or her ideas from the start.)

http://www1.ca.nizkor.org/features/fallacies/index.html A comprehensive list, with examples, of common fallacies, from the Nizkor Project.

Checklist of fallacies

Evasions

- **Begging the question:** treating an opinion that is open to question as if it were already proved or disproved.
- **Non sequitur** ("it does not follow"): drawing a conclusion from irrelevant evidence.
- **Red herring:** introducing an irrelevant issue to distract readers.
- **False authority:** citing as expert opinion the views of a person who is not an expert.
- **Inappropriate appeals:**

  Appealing to readers' fear or pity.

  Snob appeal: appealing to readers' wish to be like those who are more intelligent, famous, rich, and so on.

  Bandwagon: appealing to readers' wish to be part of the group.

  Flattery: appealing to readers' intelligence, taste, and so on.

  Argument ad populum ("to the people"): appealing to readers' general values, such as patriotism or love of family.

  Argument ad hominem ("to the man"): attacking the opponent rather than the opponent's argument.

Oversimplifications

- **Hasty generalization (jumping to a conclusion):** asserting an opinion based on too little evidence.
- **Sweeping generalization:** asserting an opinion as applying to all instances when it may apply to some, or to none. **Absolute statements** and **stereotypes** are variations.
- **Reductive fallacy:** generally, oversimplifying causes and effects.
- **Post hoc fallacy:** assuming that *A* caused *B* because *A* preceded *B*.
- **Either/or fallacy (false dilemma):** reducing a complicated question to two alternatives.
- **False analogy:** exaggerating the similarities in an analogy or ignoring key differences.

> The college library's expenses should be reduced by cutting subscriptions to useless periodicals. [Begged questions: Are some of the library's periodicals useless? Useless to whom?]
>
> The fact is that the welfare system is too corrupt to be reformed. [Begged questions: How corrupt is the welfare system? Does corruption, even if extensive, put the system beyond reform?]

Non sequitur

A **non sequitur** occurs when no logical relation exists between two or more connected ideas. In Latin *non sequitur* means "it does not follow." In the sentences below, the second thought does not follow from the first:

If high school English were easier, fewer students would have trouble with the college English requirement. [Presumably, if high school English were easier, students would have *more* trouble.]

Kathleen Newsome has my vote for mayor because she has the best-run campaign organization. [Shouldn't one's vote be based on the candidate's qualities, not the campaign organization's?]

Red herring

A **red herring** is literally a kind of fish that might be drawn across a path to distract a bloodhound from a scent it's following. In argument, a red herring is an irrelevant issue intended to distract readers from the relevant issues. The writer changes the subject rather than pursue the argument.

A campus speech code is essential to protect students, who already have enough problems coping with rising tuition. [Tuition costs and speech codes are different subjects. What protections do students need that a speech code will provide?]

Instead of developing a campus speech code that will infringe on students' First Amendment rights, administrators should be figuring out how to prevent another tuition increase. [Again, tuition costs and speech codes are different subjects. How would the code infringe on rights?]

False authority

Arguments often cite as evidence the opinions of people who are experts on the subject (see p. 147). But writers use **false authority** when they cite as an expert someone whose expertise is doubtful or nonexistent.

Jason Bing, a recognized expert in corporate finance, maintains that pharmaceutical companies do not test their products thoroughly enough. [Bing's expertise in corporate finance bears no apparent relation to the testing of pharmaceuticals.]

According to Helen Liebowitz, the Food and Drug Administration has approved sixty dangerous drugs in the last two years alone. [Who is Helen Liebowitz? On what authority does she make this claim?]

Inappropriate appeals

Appeals to readers' emotions are common in effective arguments. But such appeals must be relevant and must supplement rather than substitute for facts, examples, and other evidence.

Writers sometimes ignore the question with **appeals to readers' fear or pity.**

By electing Susan Clark to the city council, you will prevent the city's economic collapse. [Trades on people's fears. Can Clark single-handedly prevent economic collapse?]

She should not have to pay taxes because she is an aged widow with no friends or relatives. [Appeals to people's pity. Should age and loneliness, rather than income, determine a person's tax obligation?]

Sometimes writers ignore the question by appealing to readers' sense of what other people believe or do. One approach is **snob appeal,** inviting readers to accept an assertion in order to be identified with others they admire.

As any literate person knows, James Joyce is the best twentieth-century novelist. [But what qualities of Joyce's writing make him a superior novelist?]

Michael Jordan banks at Big City, and so should you. [A celebrity's endorsement of course does not automatically guarantee the worth of a product, a service, an idea, or anything else.]

A similar tactic invites readers to accept an assertion because everybody else does. This is the **bandwagon approach.**

As everyone knows, marijuana use leads to heroin addiction. [What is the evidence?]

Yet another diversion involves **flattery** of readers, in a way inviting them to join in a conspiracy.

We all understand campus problems well enough to see the disadvantages of such a backward policy. [What are the disadvantages of the policy?]

The **argument ad populum** ("argument to the people") asks readers to accept a conclusion based on shared values or even prejudices and nothing else.

Any truly patriotic American will support the President's action. [But why is the action worth taking?]

One final and very common kind of inappropriate emotional appeal addresses *not* the pros and cons of the issue itself but the real or imagined negative qualities of the people who hold the opposing view. This kind of argument is called **ad hominem,** Latin for "to the man."

One of the scientists has been treated for emotional problems, so his pessimism about nuclear waste merits no attention. [Do the scientist's previous emotional problems invalidate his current views?]

2 Recognizing oversimplifications

To **oversimplify** is to conceal or ignore complexities in a vain attempt to create a neater, more convincing argument than reality allows.

Hasty generalization

A **hasty generalization,** also called **jumping to a conclusion,** is a claim based on too little evidence or on evidence that is unrepresentative. (See also p. 149.)

> It is disturbing that several of the youths who shot up schools were users of violent video games. Obviously, these games can breed violence, and they should be banned. [A few cases do not establish the relation between the games and violent behavior. Most youths who play violent video games do not behave violently.]
>
> From the way it handled this complaint, we can assume that the consumer protection office has little intention of protecting consumers. [One experience with the office does not demonstrate its intention or overall performance.]

Sweeping generalization

Whereas a hasty generalization comes from inadequate evidence, a **sweeping generalization** probably is not supportable at all. One kind of sweeping generalization is the **absolute statement** involving words such as *all, always, never,* and *no one* that allow no exceptions. Rarely can evidence support such terms. Moderate words such as *some, sometimes, rarely,* and *few* are more reasonable.

Another common sweeping generalization is the **stereotype,** a conventional and oversimplified characterization of a group of people.

> People who live in cities are unfriendly.
> Californians are fad-crazy.
> Women are emotional.
> Men can't express their feelings.

(See also pp. 563–66 on sexist and other biased language.)

Reductive fallacy

The **reductive fallacy** oversimplifies (or reduces) the relation between causes and their effects. The fallacy (sometimes called **oversimplification**) often involves linking two events as if one caused the other directly, whereas the causes may be more complex or the relation may not exist at all. For example:

> Poverty causes crime. [If so, then why do people who are not poor commit crimes? And why aren't all poor people criminals?]
>
> The better a school's athletic facilities are, the worse its academic programs are. [The sentence assumes a direct cause-and-effect link between athletics and scholarship.]

Post hoc fallacy

Related to the reductive fallacy is the assumption that because *A* preceded *B,* then *A* must have caused *B.* This fallacy is called in

Latin *post hoc, ergo propter hoc,* meaning "after this, therefore because of this," or the **post hoc fallacy** for short.

> In the two months since he took office, Mayor Holcomb has allowed crime in the city to increase 2 percent. [The increase in crime is probably attributable to conditions existing before Holcomb took office.]
>
> The town council erred in permitting the adult bookstore to open, for shortly afterward two women were assaulted. [It cannot be assumed without evidence that the women's assailants visited or were influenced by the bookstore.]

Either/or fallacy

In the **either/or fallacy** (also called **false dilemma**), the writer assumes that a complicated question has only two answers, one good and one bad, both bad, or both good.

> City police officers are either brutal or corrupt. [Most city police officers are neither.]
>
> Either we permit mandatory drug testing in the workplace or productivity will continue to decline. [Productivity is not necessarily dependent on drug testing.]

False analogy

An **analogy** is a comparison between two essentially unlike things for the purpose of definition or illustration. (See also p. 101.) In arguing by analogy, a writer draws a likeness between things on the basis of a single shared feature and then extends the likeness to other features. For instance, the "war on drugs" equates a battle against a foe with a program to eradicate (or at least reduce) sales and use of illegal drugs. Both involve an enemy, a strategy of overpowering the enemy, a desired goal, officials in uniform, and other similarities.

Analogy can only illustrate a point, never prove it: just because things are similar in one respect, they are not *necessarily* alike in other respects. In the fallacy called **false analogy,** the writer assumes such a complete likeness. Here is the analogy of the war on drugs taken to its false extreme:

> To win the war on drugs, we must wage more of a military-style operation. Prisoners of war are locked up without the benefit of a trial by jury, and drug dealers should be, too. Soldiers shoot their enemy on sight, and officials who encounter big drug operations should, too. Military traitors may be executed, and corrupt law enforcers could be, too.

EXERCISE 2
Analyzing advertisements

Leaf through a magazine or watch commercial television for half an hour, looking for advertisements that attempt to sell a product not on the basis of its worth but by snob appeal, flattery, or other inappropriate appeals to emotions. Be prepared to discuss the advertisers' techniques.

EXERCISE 3
Identifying and revising fallacies

Identify at least one fallacy illustrated by each of the following sentences. Then revise the sentence to make it more reasonable.

1. A successful marriage demands a maturity that no one under twenty-five possesses.
2. Students' persistent complaints about the grading system prove that it is unfair.
3. The United States got involved in World War II because the Japanese bombed Pearl Harbor.
4. People watch television because they are too lazy to talk or read or because they want mindless escape from their lives.
5. Racial tension is bound to occur when people with different backgrounds are forced to live side by side.

EXERCISE 4
Identifying fallacies in arguments

Analyze the two arguments on pages 152–55 for fallacies. To what extent do any fallacies weaken either argument? Explain.

EXERCISE 5
Identifying fallacies online

Use a Web browser to reach the online conversations at RemarQ (*http://www.remarq.com/*). Find a conversation about drug testing in the workplace, environmental pollution, violence in the media, or any other subject that interests you and that is debatable. Read through the arguments made in the conversation, noting the fallacies you see. List the fallacious statements as well as the types of fallacies they illustrate, keeping in mind that a given statement may illustrate more than a single type.

CHAPTER 7

Writing an Argument

In composing an argument, you try to illuminate an issue or solve a problem by finding the common ground between you and others who will read your work. Using critical thinking, you develop and test your own ideas. Using a variety of techniques, you engage readers in an attempt to narrow the distance between your views and theirs.

Note Much of what's involved in reading arguments applies to writing arguments, too. Thus you will want to read the preceding chapter before this one. The chapter will also be more helpful if you have already read Chapter 5 on taking a critical perspective and Chapters 1–3 on the writing process.

7a Finding a topic

An argument topic must be arguable—that is, reasonable people will disagree over it and be able to support their positions with evidence. This sentence implies the *do*s and *don't*s listed in the box opposite. If you feel uncertain about finding a topic for argument, try some of the techniques listed on page 19 for discovering ideas.

Although an argument made via a Web site may differ in structure from a conventional argument (see p. 143), the Web argument must still have a focused, debatable topic. If reasonable people won't disagree over the topic, you won't have an argument at all.

ESL The guidelines for an argument topic may make you uncomfortable if your native language is something other than English and you're not accustomed to the kinds of arguments discussed here. One way to find a topic for argument is to read a newspaper every day for at least a week, looking for issues that involve or interest

http://www.powa.org/argufrms.htm Extensive guidance on writing arguments, from Paradigm Online Writing Assistant.

http://www.colostate.edu/Depts/WritingCenter/references/processes/topic/pop9c.htm Guidance on selecting a topic for an argument, from Colorado State University.

Tests for an argument topic

A good topic:

- Concerns a matter of opinion—a conclusion drawn from evidence (see p. 144).
- Can be disputed: others might take a different position.
- *Will* be disputed: it is controversial.
- Is something you care about and know about or want to research.
- Is narrow enough to argue in the space and time available (see pp. 7–9).

A bad topic:

- Cannot be disputed because it concerns a fact, such as the distance to Saturn or the functions of the human liver.
- Cannot be disputed because it concerns a personal preference or belief, such as a liking for a certain vacation spot or a moral commitment to vegetarianism.
- *Will not* be disputed because few if any disagree over it—the virtues of a secure home, for instance.

you. Following the development of the issues in articles, editorials, and letters to the editor will give you a sense of how controversial they are, what the positions are, and what your position might be.

EXERCISE 1
Finding a topic for argument

Analyze each topic below to determine whether it is appropriate for argument. (Refer to the box above if you need help.) Explain your reasoning in each case.

1. Granting of athletic scholarships
2. Care of automobile tires
3. Censoring the Web sites of hate groups
4. History of the town park
5. Housing for the homeless
6. Billboards in urban residential areas or in rural areas
7. Animal testing for cosmetics research
8. Cats versus dogs as pets
9. Ten steps in recycling wastepaper
10. Benefits of being a parent

7b Conceiving a thesis

Once you have a topic, you may also have a thesis, or you may need to do some research and writing to find your angle. The **thesis** is the main idea of your paper (see pp. 30–34). In an argument the

thesis statement makes the claim that you want your readers to accept or act on. Here are two thesis statements on the same subject:

> The new room fees are unjustified given the condition of the dormitories.
>
> The administration should postpone the new room fees at least until conditions in the dormitories are improved.

Your thesis statement must satisfy the same requirements as the topic (see the box on the previous page). But it must also specify the basis for your claim. In both thesis statements above, the basis for protesting the room fees is that the dormitories are in poor condition.

Note that the writer of either of these arguments must clarify the definition of *conditions(s)* if the argument is to be clear and reasonable. Always take pains to define abstract and general terms that are central to your argument, preferably in or just after the thesis statement. (See pp. 145–46.)

EXERCISE 2
Conceiving a thesis statement

For each topic in Exercise 1 that you deemed arguable, draft a tentative thesis statement that specifies the basis for an argument. If you prefer, choose five arguable topics of your own and draft a thesis statement for each one. One thesis statement should interest you enough to develop into a complete argument in later exercises.

7c Analyzing your purpose and your audience

Your purpose in argument is, broadly, to engage readers in order to convince them of your position or persuade them to act. But arguments have more specific purposes as well, such as the following:

To strengthen the commitment of existing supporters
To win new supporters from the undecided or uninformed
To get the opposition to reconsider
To inspire supporters to act
To deter the undecided from acting

http://www.powa.org/argufrms.htm Information about creating a thesis statement for an argument, from Paradigm Online Writing Assistant.

http://www.colostate.edu/Depts/WritingCenter/references/documents/argument/page5.htm Guidance on considering audience for arguments, from Colorado State University.

It's no accident that each of these purposes characterizes the audience (*existing supporters, the undecided,* and so on). In argument even more than in other kinds of writing, achieving your purpose depends on the response of your readers, so you need a sense of who they are and where they stand. The "Questions About Audience" on page 11 can help you identify readers' knowledge, beliefs, and other pertinent information. (You can download the questions from this book's Web site: *http://www.awlonline.com/littlebrown.*) In addition, you need to know how readers stand on your topic—not only whether they agree or disagree generally, but also which specific assertions they will find more or less convincing.

Your purpose can help you fill in this information. If you decide to address supporters or opponents, you essentially select readers with certain inclinations and ignore other readers who may tune in. If you decide to win new supporters from those who are undecided on your topic, you'll have to imagine skeptical readers who will be convinced only by an argument that is detailed, logical, and fair. Like you when you read an argument critically, these skeptical readers seek to be reasoned with, not manipulated into a position or hammered over the head.

EXERCISE 3
Analyzing purpose and audience

Specify a purpose and likely audience for the thesis statement you chose to develop in Exercise 2. What do purpose and audience suggest about the way you should develop the argument?

7d Using reason

As a reader of argument, you seek evidence for the writer's claims and clear reasoning about the relationship of evidence to claims. As a writer of argument, you seek to provide what the reader needs in a way that furthers your case.

The thesis of your argument is a conclusion you reach by reasoning about evidence. Two common processes of reasoning are induction and deduction—methods of thinking that you use all the time even if you don't know their names. You can think of induction and deduction as two different ways of moving among claims, evi-

http://www.sjsu.edu/depts/itl/graphics/induc/ind-ded.html#intro Information and tutorials on inductive and deductive reasoning, from San Jose State University.

dence, and assumptions—the elements of argument derived from Stephen Toulmin's work and discussed on pages 142–50.

1 Reasoning inductively

When you're about to buy a used car, you consult friends, relatives, and consumer guides before deciding what kind of car to buy. Using **inductive reasoning**, you make specific observations about cars (your evidence) and you induce, or infer, a **generalization** (or claim) that Model X is the most reliable. Writing a paper on the effectiveness of print advertising, you might also use inductive reasoning:

First analyze statistics on advertising in print and in other media (evidence).
Then read comments by advertisers and publishers (more evidence).
Finally, form a conclusion that print is the most cost-effective advertising medium (generalization).

This reasoning builds from the evidence to the claim, with assumptions connecting evidence to claim.

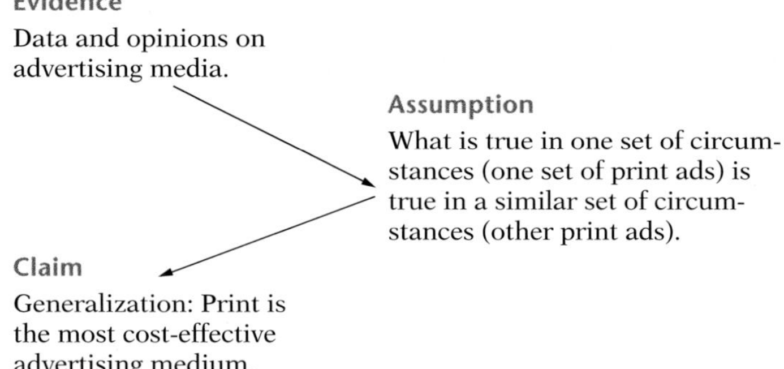
Evidence
Data and opinions on advertising media.
Assumption
What is true in one set of circumstances (one set of print ads) is true in a similar set of circumstances (other print ads).
Claim
Generalization: Print is the most cost-effective advertising medium.

With induction, you predict something about the unknown based on what you know: you create new knowledge out of old.

The more evidence you accumulate, the more probable it is that your generalization is true. Note, however, that absolute certainty is not possible. At some point you must *assume* that your evidence justifies your generalization, for yourself and your readers. Most errors in inductive reasoning involve oversimplifying either the evidence or the generalization. See pages 155–60 on fallacies.

2 Reasoning deductively

You use **deductive reasoning** when you proceed from your generalization that Model X is the most reliable used car to your own specific circumstances (you want to buy a used car) to the conclusion (or claim) that you should buy a Model X car. Like induction, deduction uses the elements of argument—claims, evidence, and assumptions—but differently. The following diagram corresponds to the one for induction on the facing page, picking up the example of print advertising:

Assumption

A fact, a principle, a belief, or (as here) a generalization from induction: Print is the most cost-effective advertising medium.

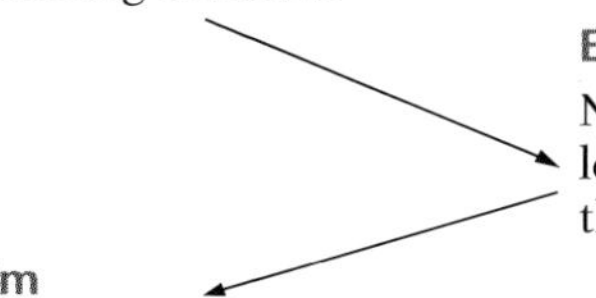

Evidence

New information: Companies on lean budgets should advertise in the most cost-effective medium.

Claim

Conclusion: Companies on lean budgets should advertise in print.

With deduction, you apply old information to new.

The conventional way of displaying a deductive argument is in a **syllogism.** If you want the school administration to postpone new room fees for one dormitory, your deductive argument might be expressed in this syllogism:

> *Premise:* The administration should not raise fees on dorm rooms in poor condition. [A generalization, fact, principle, or belief that you assume to be true.]
> *Premise:* The rooms in Polk Hall are in poor condition. [New information: a specific case of the first premise.]
> *Conclusion:* The administration should not raise fees on the rooms in Polk Hall.

As long as the premises of a syllogism are true, the conclusion derives logically and certainly from them.

The force of deductive reasoning depends on the reliability of the premises and the care taken to apply them in drawing conclusions. The reasoning process is **valid** if the premises lead logically to the conclusion. It is **true** if the premises are believable. Sometimes the reasoning is true but *not* valid:

> *Premise:* The administration should not raise fees on dorm rooms in bad condition.
> *Premise:* Tyler Hall is a dormitory.
> *Conclusion:* The administration should not raise fees on the rooms in Tyler Hall.

Both premises may be true, but the first does not *necessarily* apply to the second, so the conclusion is invalid.

Tests for inductive and deductive reasoning

Induction

- Have you stated your evidence clearly?
- Is your evidence complete enough and good enough to justify your claim? What is the assumption that connects evidence and claim? Is it believable?
- Have you avoided fallacies? (See p. 155.)

Deduction

- What are the premises leading to your conclusion? Look especially for unstated premises.
- What does the first premise assume? Is the assumption believable?
- Does the first premise necessarily apply to the second premise?
- Is the second premise believable?
- Have you avoided fallacies? (See p. 155.)

Sometimes, too, the reasoning is valid but *not* true:

> *Premise:* All college administrations are indifferent to students' needs.
> *Premise:* The administration of Central State is a college administration.
> *Conclusion:* The administration of Central State is indifferent to students' needs.

This syllogism is valid but useless: the first premise is an untrue assumption, so the entire argument is untrue. Invalid and untrue syllogisms underlie many of the fallacies discussed on pages 155–60.

A particular hazard of deductive reasoning is the **unstated premise:** the basic assumption linking evidence and conclusion is not stated but implied. Here the unstated premise is believable and the argument is reasonable:

> Ms. Stein has worked with drug addicts for fifteen years, so she knows a great deal about their problems. [Unstated premise: Anyone who has worked fifteen years with drug addicts knows about their problems.]

But when the unstated premise is wrong or unfounded, the argument is false. For example:

> Since Jane Lightbow is a senator, she must receive money illegally from lobbyists. [Unstated premise: All senators receive money illegally from lobbyists.]

To avoid such false conclusions, you may be tempted to make your claims sound more reasonable. But even a conclusion that sounds reasonable must be supportable. For instance, changing *must* to *might* modifies the unstated assumption about Senator Lightbow:

> Since Jane Lightbow is a senator, she might receive money illegally from lobbyists. [Unstated premise: *Some* senators receive money illegally from lobbyists.]

But it does not necessarily follow that Senator Lightbow is one of the "some." The sentence, though logical, is not truly reasonable unless evidence demonstrates that Senator Lightbow should be linked with illegal activities.

EXERCISE 4
Reasoning inductively

Study the facts below and then evaluate each of the numbered conclusions following them. Which of the generalizations are reasonable given the evidence, and which are not? Why?

In 1997–98 each American household viewed an average of 49 hours and 16 minutes of television weekly.

Each individual viewed an average of 30 hours and 39 minutes per week.

Those viewing the most television per week (43 hours and 20 minutes) were women over age 55.

Those viewing the least television per week (22 hours and 24 minutes) were children ages 6 to 11.

Households earning under $30,000 a year watched an average of 53 hours and 26 minutes a week.

Households earning more than $60,000 a year watched an average of 47 hours and 51 minutes a week.

1. Households with incomes under $30,000 tend to watch more television than average.
2. Women watch more television than men.
3. Nonaffluent people watch less television than affluent people.
4. Women over age 55 tend to watch more television than average.
5. Children watch less television than critics generally assume.

EXERCISE 5
Reasoning deductively

Convert each of the following statements into a syllogism. (You may have to state unstated assumptions.) Use the syllogism to evaluate both the validity and the truth of the statement.

Example:

DiSantis is a banker, so he does not care about the poor.

Premise: Bankers do not care about the poor.
Premise: DiSantis is a banker.
Conclusion: DiSantis does not care about the poor.

The statement is untrue because the first premise is untrue.

1. The mayor opposed pollution controls when he was president of a manufacturing company, so he may not support new controls or vigorously enforce existing ones.
2. Information on corporate Web sites is unreliable because the sites are sponsored by for-profit entities.
3. Schroeder is a good artist because she trained at Parsons, like many other good artists.
4. Wealthy athletes who use their resources to help others deserve our particular appreciation.
5. Jimson is sexist because she has hired only one woman.

7e Using evidence

Whether your argument is reasonable or not depends heavily on the evidence you marshal to support it. The kinds of evidence and the criteria for evaluating evidence are discussed in detail on pages 146–50. How to find evidence is discussed under research writing on pages 633–65. How to evaluate sources of evidence, including online sources, is discussed under research writing on pages 667-72.

The kind and quantity of evidence you use should be determined by your purpose, your topic, and the needs of your audience. Some arguments, such as a plea for volunteer help in a soup kitchen, will rely most heavily on examples (including perhaps a narrative of your own experience) and on appeals to readers' beliefs. Other arguments, such as a proposal for mandatory side air bags in cars, will rely much more on statistics and expert opinions. Most arguments, including these, will mingle facts, examples, expert opinions, and appeals to readers' beliefs and needs (see also pp. 146–48).

In using evidence for argument, you'll need to be especially wary of certain traps that carelessness or zeal can lure you into. These are listed in the following box:

Responsible use of evidence

- **Don't distort.** You mislead readers when you twist evidence to suit your argument—for instance, when you claim that crime in your city occurs five times more often than it did in 1955, without mentioning that the population is also seven times larger.

http://www.colostate.edu/Depts/WritingCenter/references/documents/argument/pop28c.htm Information about using evidence in arguments, from Colorado State University.

- **Don't stack the deck.** Ignoring damning evidence is like cheating at cards. You must deal forthrightly with the opposition (see p. 173).
- **Don't exaggerate.** Watch your language. Don't try to manipulate readers by characterizing your own evidence as *pure* and *rock-solid* and the opposition's as *ridiculous* and *half-baked.* Make the evidence speak for itself.
- **Don't oversimplify.** Avoid forcing the evidence to support more than it can. (See also p. 158.)
- **Don't misquote.** When you cite experts, quote them accurately and fairly.

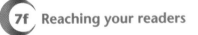

EXERCISE 6
Using reason and evidence in your argument

Develop the structure and evidence for the argument you began in Exercises 2 and 3 (pp. 164 and 165). (You may want to begin drafting at this stage.) Is your argument mainly inductive or mainly deductive? Use the box on page 168 to test the reasoning of the argument. Use the boxes on page 148 and above to test your evidence.

7f Reaching your readers

To reach your readers in argument, you appeal directly to their reason and emotions, you present yourself as someone worth heeding, and you account for views opposing your own.

1 Appealing to readers

In forming convictions about arguable issues, we generally interpret the factual evidence through the filter of our values, beliefs, tastes, desires, and feelings. You may object to placing the new town dump in a particular wooded area because the facts suggest that the site is not large enough and that prevailing winds will blow odors back through the town. But you may also have fond memories of playing in the wooded area as a child, feelings that color your interpretation of the facts and strengthen your conviction that the dump should be placed elsewhere. Your conviction is partly rational, because it is based on evidence, and partly emotional, because it is also based on feelings.

http://www.cod.edu/dept/KiesDan/engl_102/evidence.htm Guidance on rational, emotional, and ethical appeals, from the College of DuPage.

Rational and emotional appeals

In most arguments you will combine **rational appeals** to readers' capacities for reasoning logically between evidence and claim with **emotional appeals** to readers' beliefs and feelings. The following passages, all arguing the same view on the same subject, illustrate how either a primarily rational or a primarily emotional appeal may be weaker than an approach that uses both:

Rational appeal

Advertising should show more physically challenged people. The millions of disabled Americans have considerable buying power, yet so far advertisers have made no attempt to tap that power. [Appeals to the logic of financial gain.]

Emotional appeal

Advertising should show more physically challenged people. By keeping the physically challenged out of the mainstream depicted in ads, advertisers encourage widespread prejudice against disability, prejudice that frightens and demeans those who hold it. [Appeals to the sense of fairness, open-mindedness.]

Rational and emotional appeals

Advertising should show more physically challenged people. The millions of disabled Americans have considerable buying power, yet so far advertisers have made no attempt to tap that power. Further, by keeping the physically challenged out of the mainstream depicted in ads, advertisers encourage widespread prejudice against disability, prejudice that frightens and demeans those who hold it.

The third passage, in combining both kinds of appeal, gives readers both rational and emotional bases for agreeing with the writer.

For an emotional appeal to be successful, it must be appropriate for the audience and the argument:

- It must not misjudge readers' actual feelings.
- It must not raise emotional issues that are irrelevant to the claims and the evidence. (See pp. 157–58 for a discussion of specific inappropriate appeals, such as bandwagon.)

One further caution: When you compose an argument for the World Wide Web, you may be tempted to use images, video, or sound to reinforce your claims. Multimedia elements can have a strong emotional appeal, to be sure. But in argument you have a particular responsibility to ensure that such elements are relevant to your claims and to explain their relevance in your text.

Ethical appeal

A third kind of approach to readers, the **ethical appeal,** is the sense you give of being a competent, fair, trustworthy person. A sound argument backed by ample evidence—a rational appeal—will convince readers of your knowledge and reasonableness. (So will your acknowledging the opposition. See below.) Appropriate emotional appeals will demonstrate that you share readers' beliefs and needs. An argument that is concisely written and correct in grammar, spelling, and other matters will underscore your competence. In addition, a sincere and even tone will assure readers that you are a balanced person who wants to reason with them.

A sincere and even tone need not exclude language with emotional appeal—words such as *frightens* and *demeans* at the end of the third example opposite. But avoid certain forms of expression that will mark you as unfair:

- Insulting words such as *idiotic* or *fascist.*
- Biased language such as *fags* or *broads.* (See pp. 563–66.)
- Sarcasm—for instance, using the sentence *What a brilliant idea* to indicate contempt for the idea and its originator.
- Exclamation points! They'll make you sound shrill!

See also page 151 on tone.

2 Answering opposing views

A good test of your fairness in argument is how you handle possible objections. Assuming your thesis is indeed arguable, then others can marshal their own evidence to support a different view or views. You need to find out what these other views are and what the support is for them. Then, in your argument, you need to take these views on, refute those you can, grant the validity of others, and demonstrate why, despite their validity, the opposing views are less compelling than your own.

The student who wrote the following paragraph first stated an opposing view, then conceded its partial validity, and finally demonstrated its irrelevance:

> The athletic director argues against reducing university support for athletic programs on the grounds that they make money that goes toward academic programs. It is true that here at Springfield the surpluses from the football and basketball programs have gone into the general university fund, and some of that money may have made it into academic departments (the fund's accounting methods make it impossible to say for sure). But the athletic director misses

http://www.eslplanet.com/teachertools/argueweb/bothsds.htm An in-depth tutorial exploring opposing views in arguments, from ESL Planet. Though prepared for nonnative English speakers, the tutorial is valuable for native speakers as well.

the point. The problem is not that the athletic programs might cost more than they take in but that they demand too much to begin with. For an institution that hopes to become first-rate academically, too many facilities, too much money, too much energy, and too many people are tied up in the effort to produce championship sports teams.

Before or while you draft your essay, list for yourself all the opposing views you can think of. You'll find them in your research, by talking to friends and classmates, and by critically thinking about your own ideas. (On a computer or on paper, you can annotate the claims in your draft with opposing arguments for each one.)

To deal with opposing views, figure out which ones you can refute (do more research if necessary), and prepare to concede those views you can't refute. It's not a mark of weakness or failure to admit that the opposition has a point or two. Indeed, by showing yourself to be honest and fair, you strengthen your ethical appeal and thus your entire argument.

EXERCISE 7
Identifying appeals

Identify each passage below as primarily a rational appeal or primarily an emotional appeal. Which passages make a strong ethical appeal as well?

1. Web surfing may contribute to the global tendency toward breadth rather than depth of knowledge. Using those most essential of skills—pointing and clicking—our brightest minds may now never encounter, much less read, the works of Plato, Shakespeare, and Darwin.
2. Thus the data collected by these researchers indicate that a mandatory sentence for illegal possession of handguns may lead to reduction in handgun purchases.
3. Most broadcasters worry that further government regulation of television programming could breed censorship—certainly, an undesirable outcome. Yet most broadcasters also accept that children's television is a fair target for regulation.
4. Anyone who cherishes life in all its diversity could not help being appalled by the mistreatment of laboratory animals. The so-called scientists who run the labs are misguided.
5. Many experts in constitutional law have warned that the rule violates the right to free speech. Yet other experts have viewed the rule, however regretfully, as necessary for the good of the community as a whole.

EXERCISE 8
Reaching your readers

Continuing your argument-in-progress from Exercise 6 (p. 171), analyze whether your claims are rational or emotional and whether the mix is appropriate for your audience and argument. Analyze your ethical appeal, too, considering whether it can be strengthened. Then make a list of possible opposing views. Think freely at first, not stopping to censor views that seem far-fetched or irrational. When your list is complete, decide which views must be taken seriously and why, and develop a response to each one.

7g Organizing your argument

All arguments include the same parts:

- The introduction establishes the significance of the subject and provides background. The introduction generally includes the thesis statement. However, if you think your readers may have difficulty accepting your thesis statement before they see at least some support for it, then it may come later in the paper. (See pp. 106–09 for more on introductions.)
- The body states claims relating to the thesis and, in one or more paragraphs, develops each claim with clearly relevant evidence. See below for more on organizing the body.
- The response to opposing views details those views and either demonstrates your argument's greater strengths or concedes the opponents' points. See below for more on organizing this response.
- The conclusion restates the thesis, summarizes the argument, and makes a final appeal to readers. (See pp. 109–11 for more on conclusions.)

The structure of the body and the response to opposing views depend on your subject, purpose, audience, and form of reasoning. The box on the next page shows several possible arrangements. You may want to experiment with these possibilities—for instance, trying out your strongest claims first or last in the body, stating claims outright or letting the evidence build to them, answering the opposition near the beginning or near the end or claim by claim. You can do this experimentation on paper, of course, but it's easier on a computer. Try rearranging your outline as described on page 36. Or try rearranging your draft (work with a copy) by cutting and pasting parts of it for different emphases.

http://www.colostate.edu/Depts/WritingCenter/references/documents/argument/page60.htm Information on organizing arguments, from Colorado State University.

arg 7h

Organizing an argument's body and response to opposing views

The traditional scheme
Claim 1 and evidence
Claim 2 and evidence
Claim X and evidence
Response to opposing views

The problem-solution scheme
The problem: claims and evidence
The solution: claims and evidence
Response to opposing views

Variations on the traditional scheme

Use a variation if you believe your readers will reject your argument without an early or intermittent response to opposing views.

Response to opposing views
Claim 1 and evidence
Claim 2 and evidence
Claim X and evidence

Claim 1 and evidence
Response to opposing views
Claim 2 and evidence
Response to opposing views
Claim X and evidence
Response to opposing views

EXERCISE 9
Organizing your argument

Continuing from Exercise 8 (pp. 174–75), develop a structure for your argument. Consider especially how you will introduce it, how you will arrange your claims, where you will place your responses to opposing views, and how you will conclude.

7h Revising your argument

When you revise your argument, do it in at least two stages—revising underlying meaning and structure, and editing more superficial elements. The checklists on pages 56 and 61 can be a guide. Supplement them with the checklist opposite, which encourages you to think critically about your own argument.

EXERCISE 10
Writing and revising your argument

Draft and revise the argument you have developed in the exercises in this chapter. Use the revision checklists on page 61 and opposite to review your work.

http://owl.english.purdue.edu/Files/132/8-revise.html Revising papers, with examples and links to additional resources, from the Purdue Online Writing Lab.

Checklist for revising an argument

- What is your thesis? In what ways is it an arguable claim (p. 163)?
- Where have you provided the evidence readers need (pp. 146 and 170)? Where have you considered readers' probable beliefs and values (p. 164)?
- Does your thesis derive from induction, deduction, or both (p. 165)? If induction, where have you related the evidence to your generalization? If deduction, is your syllogism both true and valid? Have you avoided fallacies in reasoning (p. 155)?
- Where, if at all, is your evidence not accurate, relevant, representative, and adequate (p. 148)? (Answer this question from the point of view of a neutral or even a skeptical reader.)
- Where do you make rational appeals or emotional appeals (p. 171)? Are both appropriate for your audience? What is your ethical appeal (p. 172)?
- Where have you answered opposing arguments (p. 173)? (Again, consider the neutral or skeptical reader.)
- How clear and effective is your organization (p. 175)?

7i Examining a sample argument

The following essay by Lee Morrison, a student, illustrates the principles discussed in this chapter. As you read the essay, notice especially the structure, the relation of claims and supporting evidence, the kinds of appeals Morrison makes, and the ways he responds to opposing views.

Share the Ride

Introduction: identification of problem

Every year we encounter more bad news about the environment, and a good portion of it is due to the private automobile. Respected scientists warn that carbon dioxide emissions, such as those from cars, may produce disastrous global warming. Soot, sulfur, and other automobile emissions are contributing to reduced air quality almost everywhere. The oil that powers cars comes from rapidly depleting reserves, leading to an unhappy choice between imports of foreign oil and exploration, such as offshore drilling, that threatens the environment.

In its own way Beverly Community College contributes to the problem. Campus parking lots are filled with about 1800 cars every weekday, so that means 3600 trips a day are made to and from campus. If just a third of the solo drivers shared rides with one another, the total trips to and from campus would be reduced by at least 600. It is time for the BCC community to make a difficult move toward an organized car-pooling system that would achieve this modest goal.

Thesis statement: proposal for a solution

The first step in getting car-pools going is to form a task force of administrators, faculty, and students to devise a workable system. School records would be used to connect people who live near each other and would be willing to car-pool. With administration backing, the task force would initiate a school-wide campaign of meetings, rallies, posters, and other public relations efforts to overcome resistance to car-pooling, answer questions, and win converts. The administration would assign staff to help with records and to keep the system current each term, since schedules and the student population change. As soon as administrators thought it was feasible, they could give a big boost to the system by creating monetary incentives to car-pool. Students who participate in car-pooling could receive a tuition rebate—say, $100 a term for full-time students. Faculty and staff could receive equivalent bonuses. In addition, parking fees could be instituted to discourage driving to school.

Explanation of the proposed solution

The most obvious advantage of this proposal is that it would reduce car trips and thus reduce needless use of oil and pollution of the air. If the average length of a trip to or from BCC is 10 miles (a conservative number) and the average car gets 30 miles to the gallon (a generous number), then it takes only 3 trips to burn a gallon of gasoline. Saving just 600 trips a day would keep 200 gallons of gasoline in the pumps. The effects on air pollution can be seen in the example of carbon dioxide. Burning a single gallon of gasoline produces 20 pounds of carbon dioxide (New York Times 1999 Almanac 766), so a daily savings of 600 BCC trips would reduce carbon dioxide emissions by 4000 pounds.

Support for the proposal: first advantage

The unused gasoline would also save money for participants. If a full-time student drove half as often as now, the gasoline savings would be about $30 a term, plus the savings in wear and tear on the car. If the school instituted a $100 tuition rebate, the cash savings would rise to $130 a term. If the school instituted a parking fee of, say, $1 a day, the cash savings would rise to more than $160 a term. (All figures assume that car-pools consist of two people who share driving and expenses equally.)

Support for the proposal: second advantage

Support for the proposal: third advantage

There are more abstract advantages, too. Individual freedom is a cherished right in our society, but it has no meaning outside the community. Like recycling and other environmental efforts, car-pooling would ask the individual to make a sacrifice on behalf of the community. Car-poolers would be actively participating in something larger than themselves, instead of just furthering their own self-interest.

Probable opposing view and response

Members of the BCC administration may point out that the proposed program asks for sacrifice from the school as well. They may object that rebates or bonuses and the costs of running the program are not feasible given the school's tight budget. True, $100 rebates or bonuses for an estimated 600 participants would cost $60,000 a term, and administrative time would also cost something. But considerable money could be raised by instituting a dollar parking fee, which could produce as much as $1500 a day, nearly $100,000 a term, in revenue. Furthermore, sponsoring a car-pooling system is no more than many corporations do that encourage their employees to take public transportation by contributing to their monthly passes. Businesses, schools, and other institutions that require their people to assemble in one place should help reduce the environmental cost of commuting.

Probable opposing view and response

Of course, it is the cost of commuters' convenience that will probably make or break the program. Students and faculty may have to arrive at school earlier than they want or leave later because of their car-pools. While considerable, this inconvenience could over time be turned to an advantage if car-poolers learned to use their extra on-campus time wisely to prepare for classes (work they would have to do at home anyway). In addition, this inconvenience might seem worthwhile in exchange for helping the environment and the concrete rewards of a rebate or bonus and savings on parking.

Probable opposing view

It is no small flaw in the proposal that not all commuters would be able to participate in the program, even if they wanted to. The fact is that many part-time faculty and students have schedules that are too complicated or erratic to permit car-pooling. Many teachers and students must make intermediate stops between their homes and BCC, such as for work. These commuters would not have access to the rebates or bonuses and still would be subject to the parking fee.

This unfairness is regrettable but, for now, unavoidable; we have to start somewhere. A change away from single-passenger cars to car-pools is like all other significant changes we must make on behalf of the environment. The shift in consciousness and responsibility will be halting and prolonged, and the costs and benefits will not always be distributed equally. One thing we can be sure of, however, is that the shift will not occur at all if we don't take the difficult first steps.

Response to probable opposing view

Conclusion

Work Cited

The New York Times 1999 Almanac. Ed. John W. Wright. New York: Penguin, 1998.

—Lee Morrison

EXERCISE 11

Critically reading an argument

Analyze the construction and effectiveness of the preceding essay by answering the following questions. (Morrison's essay and these questions are also available for downloading at this book's Web site: *http://www.awlonline.com/littlebrown.*)

1. Where does Morrison make claims related to his thesis statement, and where does he provide statistics or other evidence to support the claims?
2. Where does Morrison appeal primarily to reason, and where does he appeal primarily to emotion? What specific beliefs, values, and desires of readers does he appeal to?
3. How would you characterize Morrison's ethical appeal?
4. What objections to his plan does Morrison anticipate? How does he respond to each one?
5. How effective do you find this argument? To what extent do you agree with Morrison about the problems identified in his introduction? To what extent does he convince you that his plan is desirable and workable and would address those problems? Does he fail to anticipate any major objections to his plan?
6. Write a critical evaluation of "Share the Ride." First summarize Morrison's views. Then respond to those views by answering the questions posed in item 5 above.

PART III

Using Computers Critically

CHAPTER 8

Becoming Computer Literate

Knowing how to operate computers and communicate electronically is essential these days for most students and in most professions. Yet becoming computer literate involves much more than simply learning about computers and their software. Just as important, it involves learning to be a critical producer and consumer of electronic information.

This and the following three chapters treat computer work that is especially relevant to writers: using a word processor, electronic mail, the World Wide Web, and other computer resources (this chapter); designing documents (Chapter 9); composing for the Web (Chapter 10); and collaborating online (Chapter 11). The chapters introduce essential computer skills, some of which you may already know; but they also show how you can apply the skills critically to achieve your purpose in writing.

Note The examples in these chapters illustrate functions and concepts that are common to most computer systems and software. However, the system or software that you use may rely on slightly different terms and operations. If you need assistance, use the Help menu built into most software programs, consult your instructor, or see the technology advisers at your school.

8a Writing and revising with a word processor

Computers have a great advantage for writers: word-processing programs, even the simplest, make it easy to revise and edit. Removing the drudgery of having to cut pages apart or retype whole pages, the word processor frees you to make mistakes, to try differ-

http://microsoft.com/education/tutorial/classroom/ Word-processing tutorials for use in and out of the classroom, from Microsoft.

http://www.corel.com/support/options/tips.htm Tips and tricks for the word processor WordPerfect and other programs, from Corel.

http://help.unc.edu/documentation/ Computer support, from the University of North Carolina.

ent forms of expression, to experiment with organization. Many tips for using a word processor appear in Chapters 1–3 opposite the marginal computer symbol. Here, you'll find more advice for using files, altering text, and formatting documents.

1 Working with files

On many word processors you create, save, and open documents using the File menu: click New to create a new document, Save to save the document as a file, and Open to read a saved document. To organize files, you can store one or more related documents in a folder. You may be familiar with these basic operations already. However, by going beyond the basics you can try out revisions and make comments on a draft while keeping the original intact. The following screen shots and explanations (keyed to each other by number) show how you can work with different versions of a paper by saving files under different names.

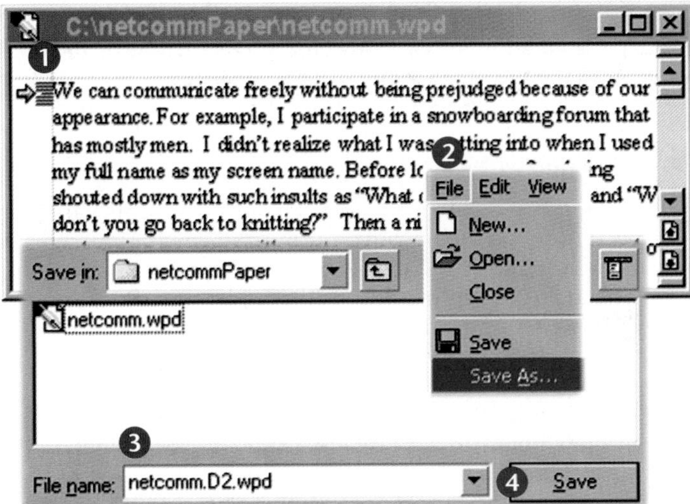

1. Save the original draft with a file name you'll be able to recognize later. The illustrated document's name is *netcomm.wpd.* Place the file in a folder of its own—you'll add later versions to the same folder. The folder name for the illustrated document is *netcommPaper.*

http://www.wcu.edu/ccenter_inf/CatOnline/Basics File-saving and other computer tips, from Western Carolina University.

2. Create a duplicate version of the original by selecting Save As from the File menu.
3. Give the duplicate a new file name. Use a simple system for naming files—for instance, adding *D2* to the original name for the second draft, *D3* for the third draft, and so on.
4. Save the new version. The original remains intact.

Besides creating duplicates to retrieve ideas and track the development of your papers, you can also save the same file with alternative names when you need to match the file-naming conventions of a class—for instance, renaming *netcomm* as *Assignment 1.* In addition, creating duplicates of files makes it easy to provide comments on others' documents (see p. 250).

Note Two precautions can prevent significant loss of work if the computer malfunctions:

- Save your work every five to ten minutes. Most word processors have an Auto Save function that will save your work automatically as you type, at the interval you specify. Still, get in the habit of saving manually whenever you make major changes.
- After doing any major work on a project, create a backup version of the file on a second drive or diskette.

2 Working with text

Working flexibly with the text of your documents can open up your writing process, allowing you to draft, revise, and edit more fluidly and productively. This benefit goes beyond the simple ability to rewrite small bits of material without retyping. By adding, highlighting, copying, and cutting whole passages, you can do the essential work of revision, such as filling in details, reorganizing, and focusing. (See pp. 52–59 for more on revision.)

The screen shots opposite and the following numbered explanations show how you can use a word processor's functions to revise your papers. These are basic functions, to be sure, but together with duplicating and managing files they can become writing skills that help you create effective papers.

1. Word processors allow you to draw attention to portions of your document by selecting and highlighting text. You might use this function to emphasize a topic sentence while you consider the organization of a paragraph or to flag aspects of your writing that require extra attention. Highlighting is also essential for copying, cutting, and pasting text, as described below.
2. Cut a highlighted passage by selecting Cut from the Edit menu. (You can also use toolbar and keyboard shortcuts for cutting and for copying and pasting.) The computer retains the mate-

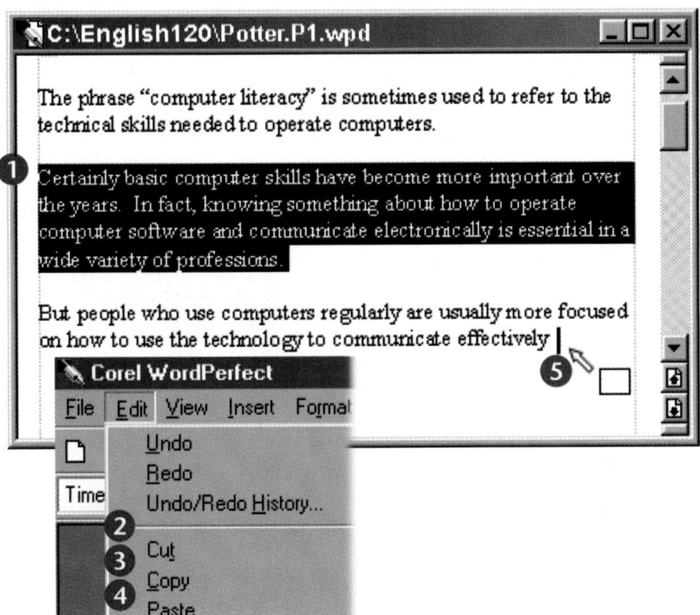

rial in its memory but removes the passage from the document. If you want to use the passage elsewhere, you can paste it into a different spot in the document or into another file (see below). If you don't have an immediate use for the passage, you can paste it in a scrap file that holds deleted ideas and information you may someday need.

3. Copy a highlighted passage by selecting Copy from the Edit menu. Copying leaves the original passage intact but creates a duplicate for you to paste elsewhere. With copying, you can try out new arrangements of material without disturbing the first one. You can also move information between documents—for instance, copying the notes for a project from one file into a draft in another file.
4. Paste text you have cut or copied by placing your cursor where you want the information to go and selecting Paste from the Edit menu. Pasting is useful for moving information within and between documents.
5. Dragging text is a little trickier, but it's faster than the separate operations of cutting or copying and then pasting. Click on the selected text with your mouse, and then, while holding down the mouse button, move the text where you want it to go. In the screen shot above, the small square on the bottom right indicates that text is being dragged to this location.

3 Formatting documents

A few essential word-processor functions will help you format many of your academic papers. For more on using these functions on your word processor, consult its Help menu. For more on document design, see the following chapter.

- Set margins by selecting Page Setup in the File menu. Page Setup also controls paper size, paper source, the orientation of the page, and other features.
- Unless you also plan to use headers or footers (see below), add page numbers by selecting Page Numbers in the Format or Insert menu.
- Add your name, the paper title, the date, or other information as headers (tops of pages) or footers (bottoms of pages) by selecting Headers and Footers in the View or Insert menu. You can add page numbers at the same time.
- Use the Format menu to create bulleted or numbered lists (select Bullets and Numbering) or to create text in more than one column (select Columns).
- Use the Insert menu for many functions, such as creating a new page (select Break or New Page), adding an illustration to a document (select Graphics or Picture), or adding footnotes or endnotes to a document (select Footnote/Endnote).
- Preview the way your printed document will look by selecting Print Preview from the File menu.

8b Working with spelling checkers and other writing tools

Most word processors include a Tools menu with functions such as a spelling checker, a grammar checker, a thesaurus, and a program for tracking revisions. However, these tools will help you only if you approach them critically. Used uncritically, they can cause you considerable problems.

Note The first two tools discussed below—spelling checkers and grammar and style checkers—can usually be set to flag possible errors as you type them. But many writers find this function distracting when they are trying to generate ideas or do in-depth revision. If you are attending too much to the flagged problems in your writing, use the Tools menu to turn off the checker. You can instruct the computer to check for errors when you are ready to do so.

1 Using a spelling checker

Your word processor's spelling checker can be a great ally: it will flag words that are spelled incorrectly and usually suggest alternative spellings that resemble what you've typed. However, this ally also has the potential to undermine you because of its limitations:

- The checker flags all words that don't match entries in its dictionary. Thus it may flag a word that you've spelled correctly just because it doesn't recognize the word.
- In providing a list of alternative spellings for your word, the checker may highlight the one it considers most likely to be correct. You need to verify that this alternative is actually what you intend before selecting it. Keep in mind, too, that the checker's list may not provide a correct alternative at all. Consult an online or printed dictionary when you aren't sure of the checker's recommendations (see Chapter 39).
- Most important, a spelling checker will not flag words that appear in its dictionary but are misused by you. Five such errors appear in the text of the screen shot below, all unrecognized by the spelling checker: *sale* for *sail, there* for *their, ships* for *ship's, sales* for *sails,* and *it's* for *its.*

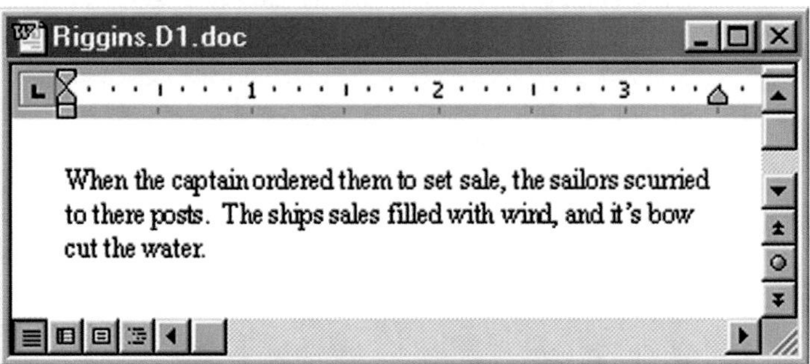

The following jingle has circulated widely as a warning about spelling checkers (we found it in the *Bulletin of the Missouri Council of Teachers of Mathematics*). The jingle contains thirteen misspellings that a spelling checker did not catch. Can you spot them?

I have a spelling checker,
It came with my PC;
It plainly marks four my revue
Mistakes I cannot sea.
I've run this poem threw it,
I'm sure your please too no.
Its letter perfect in it's weigh,
My checker tolled me sew.

You can supplement a spelling checker by maintaining a file of your frequent misspellings and selecting Find under the Edit menu to check for them. But in the end *the only way to rid your papers of spelling errors is to proofread your papers yourself.* See page 64 for proofreading tips. And see Chapter 41 for more advice on spelling.

2 Using a grammar and style checker

Word processors' grammar and style checkers can flag incorrect grammar or punctuation and wordy or awkward sentences. However, these programs can call your attention only to passages that *may* be faulty. They miss many errors because they are not yet capable of analyzing language in all its complexity (for instance, they can't accurately distinguish a word's part of speech when there are different possibilities, as *light* can be a noun, a verb, or an adjective). And they often question passages that don't need editing, such as an appropriate passive verb or a deliberate and emphatic use of repetition.

In the screen shot below, the checker has flagged a direct repetition of *light* in the first sentence but left unflagged the other intrusive repetitions of the word. And the checker has flagged the entire second sentence because it is long, but in fact the sentence is grammatically correct and clear.

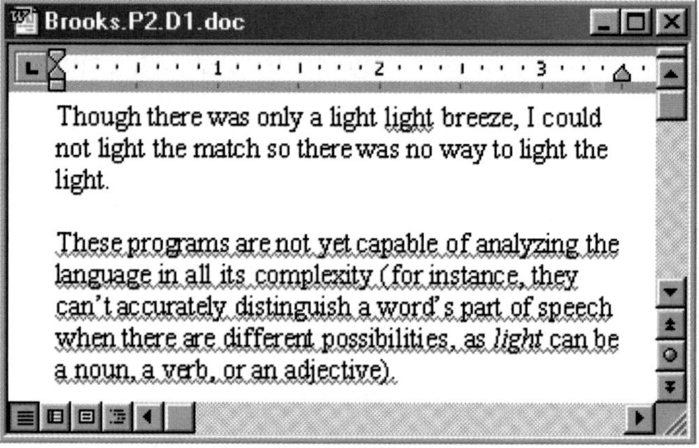
Brooks.P2.D1.doc
Though there was only a light light breeze, I could not light the match so there was no way to light the light.
These programs are not yet capable of analyzing the language in all its complexity (for instance, they can't accurately distinguish a word's part of speech when there are different possibilities, as *light* can be a noun, a verb, or an adjective).

You can customize your grammar and style checker to suit your needs and habits as a writer. With the checkers on most word processors, for instance, you can select Options under the Tools menu and then specify certain features to look for, such as possessives and plurals, subject-verb agreement, commonly confused words, passive voice, and clichés. If you have little problem with agreement, you can instruct the checker to ignore that error. But if you often use the passive voice or mistakenly add apostrophes to plural nouns, you can set the checker to find possible problems.

Style checkers can also be set to correspond to the level of writing you intend, such as formal, standard, and informal. The checker will then flag passages it deems inappropriate for the specified level—for instance, contractions in formal writing or long sentences in informal writing. For the screen shot above, the setting was

"Standard"; when it was changed to "Formal," the checker did not flag the second sentence.

As with a spelling checker, so with a grammar or style checker: it will not do your editing for you. Each time it questions something, you must determine whether a change is needed at all and what change will be most effective, and you must read your papers carefully on your own to find any errors the program missed.

3 Using other word-processing tools

Word processors either come with or are compatible with a number of optional programs. These programs, too, can both help and hurt your writing depending on how critically you use them.

- *Thesaurus programs* help with word choices by responding to your word with a display of several synonyms (words that have similar meanings). A single keystroke allows you to replace your word with a displayed word. Thesaurus programs are limited because they display only some synonyms, not all, and even a narrow list may contain words that do not suit your meaning. Neither an electronic nor a printed thesaurus will be any help if it leads you to misuse words whose meanings you don't know. Before you use a word suggested by a thesaurus, always check its meaning in a dictionary. (See pp. 569 and 589 for more on thesauruses.)
- *Invention or discovery programs* help you develop a topic by prompting you with a structured set of questions or by providing creative analogies that help you think imaginatively. These programs can help you get started, develop new insights, and conceive a purpose for your writing. But they can also be limited because many employ all-purpose prompts. Use such programs critically, thinking of additional ways that you can explore the elements of your topic.
- *Outlining programs* help you organize your work by providing automatic indentions, easy resequencing, and other features. However, some writers consider these programs straitjackets because they allow little leeway in outline structure. To experiment with whether an outlining program can help you, select Outline or Bullets and Numbering/Outline from the Insert or Format menu of your word processor.
- *Graphics programs* allow you to create charts and graphs or images to be inserted into your documents. You can also use the programs to resize and crop images that you wish to add to your documents. (See pp. 208–09 for more on these programs.)
- *Documentation programs* help you format your source citations in many disciplines' styles. (See p. 699 for more on these programs.)

4 Commenting on documents and tracking changes

Your word processor may provide two additional functions that can significantly affect the way you write: adding comments and tracking changes.

Commenting on documents

If your instructor asks you to provide feedback on your classmates' papers or you want to annotate your own work, the Comment function of your word processor will prove invaluable. In most word processors you can add comments to a document by selecting Comment from the Insert menu and then composing your commentary. An icon or highlight in the text will indicate that a comment has been added, and readers can view the commentary by selecting the icon or highlighted item. In the following screen shot, clicking on the highlighted phrase at the bottom of the document has produced the pop-up comment you see.

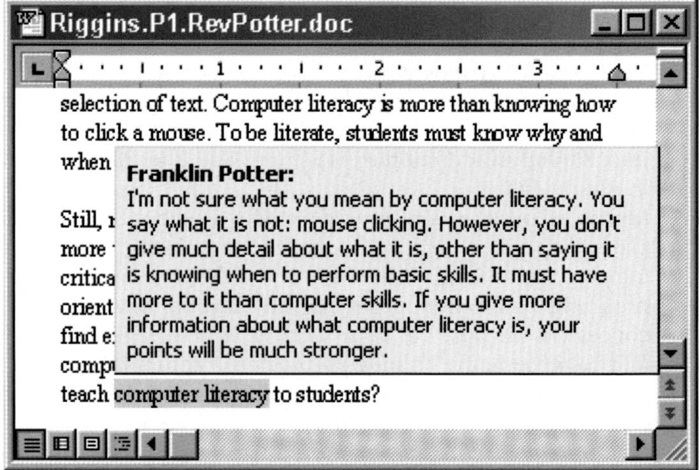

Riggins.P1.RevPotter.doc
selection of text. Computer literacy is more than knowing how
to click a mouse. To be literate, students must know why and
when
Franklin Potter:
I'm not sure what you mean by computer literacy. You
say what it is not: mouse clicking. However, you don't
give much detail about what it is, other than saying it
is knowing when to perform basic skills. It must have
more to it than computer skills. If you give more
information about what computer literacy is, your
points will be much stronger.
teach computer literacy to students?

To use a word processor's Comment function, it's smart to work with multiple versions of documents, as discussed on pages 183–84. A good strategy is to open the document you wish to comment on, rename and resave the file so that you leave the original intact, and then add comments on the new duplicate. See pages 66–69 for tips on reviewing others' writing and 243–52 for more about collaboration using computers. Your instructor may also have specific instructions.

Tracking changes

A word processor can also track the revisions you make in a document, usually with an option found under the Tools or File menu. In the screen shot below, the revisions are in blue: deleted copy crossed out and added copy underlined.

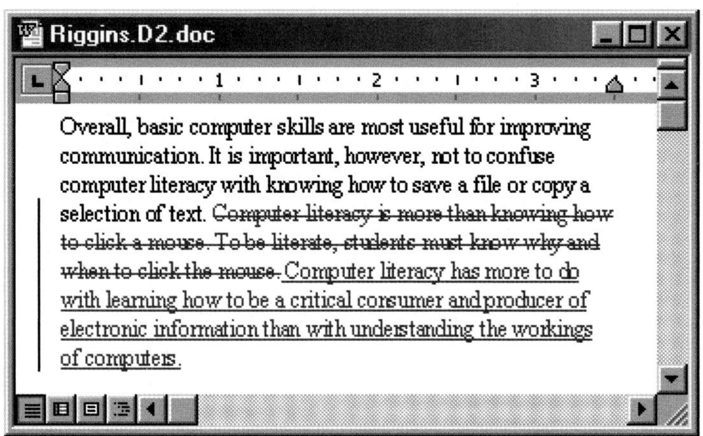

Tracking changes may encourage you to revise more freely because you can always revert to your original text. It also allows you to weigh the effectiveness of your changes because you can see the two versions side by side (you can then easily accept or reject changes). And it gives you a way to evaluate the kinds of changes you are making. For instance, if during revision you see only minor surface alterations (word substitutions and the like), then you might consider whether and where to make more fundamental changes.

EXERCISE 1
Commenting on a document

Download a copy of the essay "Working in the Barnyard" and the related reading questions from this book's Web site at *http://www.awlonline.com/littlebrown.* Open the document in your word processor. Then use the word processor's Comment function to add your own questions and suggestions for revision. Arrange with a classmate to exchange the files containing the essay and your comments. What did your classmate notice that you didn't, and vice versa? What revisions seem most needed in the essay, and why?

EXERCISE 2
Tracking changes as you revise

Experiment with a word processor's Track Changes or Document Review function as you revise one of your papers. When you have finished revising, consider the scope and effectiveness of your changes. Are they substantial, not just surface alterations in wording? Do they improve the paper as you intended? Are there places where new text is less effective than the original or where some combination of new and old would be most effective?

8c Using electronic mail

If you work on a computer, you'll probably be using electronic mail, or e-mail, for a host of reasons, from conversing with friends to conducting serious research. This section covers e-mail basics: composing and sending messages, responding to messages, and observing Internet etiquette. For more on using e-mail to interact with the other students in a course, see pages 243–46. For more on using e-mail as a research tool, see page 659.

Note The e-mail program you use will probably differ from the one illustrated in the screen shots here, and the ways of accessing e-mail also vary. If you aren't sure how to use e-mail on your school's computer system, ask your instructor or one of the school's technology advisers.

1 Composing and sending messages

The screen shot opposite illustrates the essential features of an e-mail message. (The numbers below correspond to those in the screen shot.)

1. Enter the e-mail address of the person you are contacting in the To or Recipient field. Type the address exactly: an incorrect letter will send the message astray.
2. Give the message a subject heading that describes its content.
3. Include in the Cc field the e-mail addresses of others to whom you want to send copies of the message. In the screen shot opposite, the author was asking for feedback on a group project, and he sent his message to the other members of his group, too.
4. You can attach a file—such as a document from your word processor—to be sent with the e-mail message to all the message's recipients. When you tell it to attach a file, your e-mail program will prompt you to select the appropriate one from

http://www.learnthenet.com/english/section/e-mail.html Guidelines on e-mail messages, addresses, attachments, and more, from Learn the Net.

http://www.webfoot.com/advice/e-mail.top.html The nature of e-mail and strategies for composing messages, from *A Beginner's Guide to Effective E-Mail.*

Two directories of e-mail addresses that may help you locate someone online:

http://www.bigfoot.com/
http://people.yahoo.com/

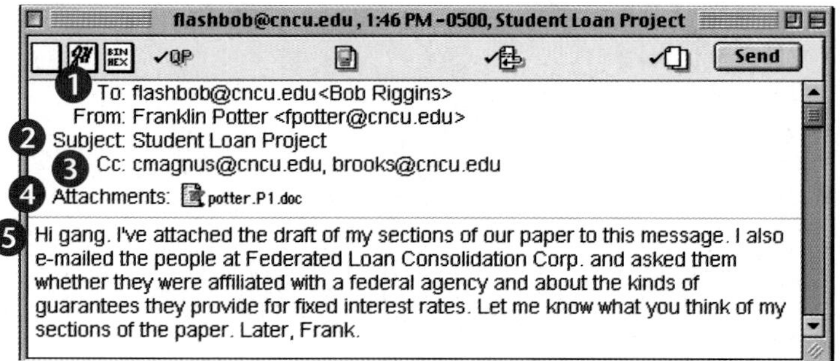

your computer's hard drive or a diskette. When sent, the file will then be downloaded and stored on the recipients' e-mail servers or personal computers. Note, however, that attachments are not always readable because of incompatible file formats or translation problems. If you and your partners use different word processors (such as WordPerfect and Microsoft Word), you may not be able to read each other's files. And documents sent over the Internet are sometimes encoded in special formats (such as MIME) that may need to be decoded at the recipients' end. You can usually solve the problem of incompatible word processors by saving the files in a generic format such as rich text format (RTF). To learn how to decode attachments, consult with your school's technology advisers.

flashbob@cncu.edu, 1:46 PM -0500, Student Loan Project
Send
1 To: flashbob@cncu.edu<Bob Riggins>
From: Franklin Potter <fpotter@cncu.edu>
2 Subject: Student Loan Project
3 Cc: cmagnus@cncu.edu, brooks@cncu.edu
4 Attachments: potter.P1.doc
5 Hi gang. I've attached the draft of my sections of our paper to this message. I also e-mailed the people at Federated Loan Consolidation Corp. and asked them whether they were affiliated with a federal agency and about the kinds of guarantees they provide for fixed interest rates. Let me know what you think of my sections of the paper. Later, Frank.

5. Compose a suitable message that is concise and relevant to your recipients' concerns. Adjust the formality of your message to your writing situation: for instance, you might use slang and be casual about spelling and grammar in a quick reply to a friend, but you'd want to be more formal (and scrupulously correct) in addressing a potential employer. In the message shown in the screen shot above, the writer knows the recipients well and yet has serious information to convey to them, so he writes informally and yet states his points carefully. (See p. 196 for more on composing e-mail messages.)

Note Only some e-mail programs allow underlining, italics, and boldface. Even if you can use such highlighting, you should assume that your recipients will not be able to see it in your messages. For alternatives, use underscores to indicate _underlining_ or asterisks to provide *emphasis*.

2 Responding to messages

To respond to an e-mail message, use the Reply or Respond feature of your e-mail program. The essentials of a response are illustrated in the screen shot on the next page.

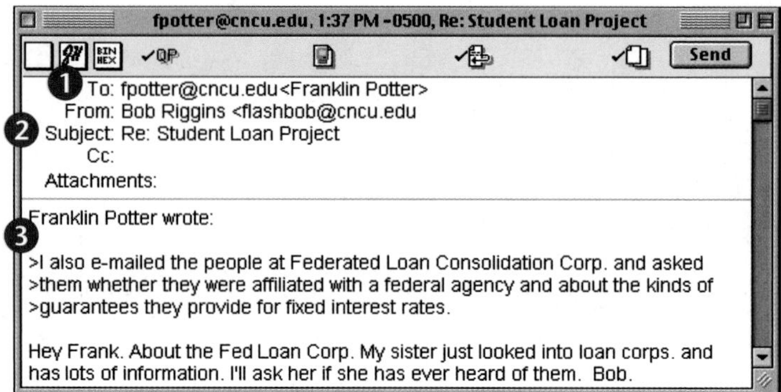

1. Check that the response addresses the appropriate person or people. Using the Reply or Respond feature generally prompts the e-mail program to provide a message screen with the original sender's address inserted in the To field, your address inserted in the From field, and the original copy recipients' addresses inserted in the Cc field. In the illustration above, the author, Bob Riggins, was passing information directly to the original author, Franklin Potter; Riggins did not want to bother the other group members, so he omitted their names from the Cc field. (See opposite for more on addressing responses.)
2. Check that the reply still has an appropriate subject heading. Most e-mail programs label a response with the same subject heading as the original, preceded by *Re:* (from Latin, meaning "In reference to"). If your response indeed continues the same subject, then *Re:* indicates as much. However, if you raise a new issue, you should rewrite the subject heading to say so.
3. Use quoted material from earlier messages critically. Most e-mail programs can copy the original message into your response, setting off the quoted material with angle brackets (>) or some other device. By weaving your replies into the quoted material, you can respond to the author point by point, as you would in conversation. However, delete from the original anything you are not responding to so that your recipient can focus on what you have to say without wading through his or her own words. (In the screen shot above, Riggins selected only the part of Potter's message that he wanted to comment on, deleting the rest.)

EXERCISE 3
Finding an address and sending a message

At one of the Web sites given on page 192, search for the e-mail address of someone you know—a favorite teacher, a relative, a special person from your past. Open your e-mail program, address a message to this person, and then compose and send a simple message. Be sure to give your message an appropriate subject heading.

EXERCISE 4
Exchanging e-mail messages

Exchange e-mail messages with at least two classmates. First, make sure you have each other's correct e-mail addresses. After opening your e-mail program, address a message to one of the classmates and address a copy of the message to the other classmate in the Cc field. Compose a brief message setting down your expectations and concerns about the course you're taking together. When you receive the others' messages, respond to them.

EXERCISE 5
Sending an e-mail attachment

Use your word processor to compose a paragraph or two discussing your best and worst experiences as a writer. Name the file, and save it on a diskette or drive on your computer. Then open your e-mail program, address a message to a classmate who is also completing this exercise, add an appropriate subject heading, and attach the saved file. Send the message and file. When you receive your partner's message and file, open and read the attachment.

3 Observing netiquette

To communicate effectively online, you'll need to abide by some rules of behavior and simple courtesies. You won't always see others observing this **netiquette,** or Internet etiquette, but you will see that those who do observe it receive the more thoughtful and considerate replies.

Addressing messages

- Consider that your recipient's list of incoming mail may be extensive—some people receive dozens of messages a day. Give your message a subject heading that accurately describes its content so that your reader knows what priority to assign it.
- With a few keystrokes, you can broadcast a message to many recipients at once—all the students in a course, say, or all the participants in a discussion group. Occasionally, you may indeed

http://www.netsquirrel.com/roadmap96/map07.html The *do*s and *don't*s of netiquette, especially flaming, from Roadmap's netiquette page.

http://www.fau.edu/netiquette/net/index.html A guide to netiquette, from Florida Atlantic University.

have a worthwhile idea or important information that everyone on the list will want to know. But flooding whole lists with irrelevant messages—called **spamming**—is rude and irritating.

- Avoid sending frivolous messages to all the members of a group. Instead of dashing off "I agree" and distributing the two-word message widely, put some time into composing a thoughtful response and send it only to those who will be interested.

Composing messages

- Remember that the messages you receive represent individuals. Don't say or do anything that you wouldn't say or do face to face.
- In the body of your message, address your reader(s) by name if possible and sign off with your own name and information on how to contact you. Your own name is especially important if your e-mail address does not spell it out.
- Take the time to read and revise your message before sending it, looking for ways to condense and clarify your ideas and moderate your tone. Use short paragraphs with blank lines between them. For long messages—which recipients can review only one screen at a time—a tight structure, a clear forecast of the content, and a clear division into parts (using headings if necessary) not only improve effectiveness but also show courtesy. Proofread all but the most informal messages for errors in grammar, punctuation, and spelling.
- Pay careful attention to tone in online messages. Refrain from **flaming,** or attacking, correspondents. Don't use all-capital letters, which SHOUT. And use irony or sarcasm only cautiously: in the absence of facial expressions, they can lead to misunderstandings. To indicate irony and emotions, you can use **emoticons,** such as the smiley :-). These sideways faces made up of punctuation can easily be overused, though, and should not substitute for thoughtfully worded opinions.
- Avoid saying anything in e-mail that you would not say in a printed document such as a letter or memo. E-mail can usually be retrieved from the server, and in business and academic settings it may well be retrieved in disputes over contracts, grades, and other matters.

Reading and responding to messages

- Be a forgiving reader. Avoid nitpicking over spelling or other surface errors. And because attitudes are sometimes difficult to convey, give authors an initial benefit of the doubt: a writer

http://wwws.enterprise.net/fortknox/emoticon/smiley.html A list of emoticons, from Emoticon Limited.

who at first seems hostile may simply have tried too hard to be concise; a writer who at first seems unserious may simply have failed at injecting humor into a worthwhile message.

- When you respond to a message by copying it into your own message, delete all but the *relevant* parts of the original. (See also p. 194.)
- You may want to forward a message you've received to someone else, but do so only if you know that the author of the message won't mind.
- Avoid participating in flame "wars," overheated dialogues that contribute little or no information or understanding. If a war breaks out in a discussion, ignore it: don't rush to defend someone who is being attacked, and don't respond even if you are under attack yourself.

8d Going places on the Web

A large part of computer literacy is using the World Wide Web efficiently, productively, and critically. This section explains the basics of Web addresses and directs you to resources on a range of Web activities.

1 Using Web addresses

Every file on the Web has a unique location, called a **uniform resource locator,** or **URL.** A URL has three parts and a fixed form: *protocol://domain/path.* Here is a translation of the address *http://www.nyu.edu/urban/leaders.html:*

- The Internet uses specific standards or **protocols** to transfer files. Most Web files are transferred using the hypertext transfer protocol (HTTP); its abbreviation appears in small letters at the beginning of a URL, followed by a colon and two slashes.
- Immediately after the two slashes, the **domain** names the computer, or **server,** that houses the document you seek. Each server has a unique name, usually referring to the organization that owns it. In *www.nyu.edu,* for instance, *nyu* stands for New York University and *edu* indicates an educational institution. (Domain names can be useful in evaluating Internet sources. See p. 670.)
- The **path** specifies the location and name of the document you seek. For instance, */urban/leaders.html* identifies a directory (*urban*) and a file inside it (*leaders.html*).

Note *A URL must be typed exactly as you find it:* same capitals and small letters, same punctuation, same spacing. Even a tiny error will keep you from reaching your destination.

To reach a Web site and its files, you need a program called a **browser:** Netscape Communicator and Microsoft Internet Explorer are the most common, and one of them is probably in use at your school. Enter the URL in the browser's Address or Location field, as shown below.

8e

2 Consulting Web resources

Both in this book and on the Web itself, you can find resources that will help you become a proficient Web user:

- Information about the workings and possibilities of the Internet appears on many Web sites, including those given at the bottom of the page.
- Information about composing for the Web, with links to helpful Web sites, appears in Chapter 10.
- Information about conducting research on the Web, including using search engines and evaluating Web sources, appears on pages 652–58 and 667–72.
- Web sites for specific disciplines appear on pages 801 (literature), 821–22 (history, art, and other humanities), 839–40 (social sciences), and 867–69 (natural and applied sciences).
- Documentation models for electronic sources appear on pages 730–38 (MLA style), 828–30 (Chicago style), 851–53 (APA style), 875–76 (CBE style), and 881–91 (Columbia online style).

8e Developing other computer skills

Besides word processing, electronic mail, and the Web, computers offer other means of sharing information and ideas. The resources listed opposite, both in this book and on the Web, can help you extend your skills as an online communicator.

Information about using the Internet:

http://www.learnthenet.com/english/section/intbas.html From Learn the Net.

http://www.pbs.org/uti From the Public Broadcasting Service.

http://www.newbie.net/CyberCourse From Newbie Net.

- Discussion groups—Internet spaces organized around specific topics—can be quite useful to writers who know how to tap into the expertise they offer and avoid their pitfalls. For information on discussion groups, see pages 659–61.
- Many discussions on the Internet take place instantaneously, like telephone conversations. These real-time, or **synchronous,** exchanges can be useful for exploring topics and for collaboration. For more on real-time interaction, see pages 250–51 and consult the Web site *http://www.du.org/cybercomp.html.*
- Many college classes now rely on online learning programs, sometimes called **courseware,** that use the Web to involve students in online discussion and to promote collaboration. For more on online collaboration, see Chapter 11.

CHAPTER 9

Designing Documents

Imaginehowharditwouldbetoreadandwriteiftextlookedlikethis. To make reading and writing easier, we place a space between words. This convention and many others—such as page margins, page numbers, and paragraph breaks—have evolved over time to help writers communicate clearly with readers.

This chapter looks at the principles and elements of design that can help you present your documents effectively. The examples range from a flyer to a report, and a separate section covers academic papers (see p. 215). For information on designing documents specifically for business, see Chapter 56. For information on designing for the World Wide Web, see Chapter 10.

9a Considering principles of design

Most of the principles of design respond to the ways we read. White space, for instance, relieves our eyes and helps to lead us through a document. Groupings or lists help to show relationships. Type sizes, images, and color add variety and help to emphasize important elements.

The flyer on the facing page illustrates some of these principles. An advertisement intended both to attract attention and to convey information, the flyer is at first glance visually appealing, but it also effectively organizes information and directs our attention:

- The white space and arrangement create a familiar zigzag movement: information flows down and across from left to right, left to right.

http://www.graphic-design.com. General design resources, from the Internet Design and Publishing Center.

http://desktopPublishing.com Links to design information, templates, and images, from DesktopPublishing.com.

http://www.pomona.edu/visual-lit/intro/intro.html Conceptual discussion of shape, color, scale, and visual elements, from the On-Line Visual Literacy Project.

VA Literacy Volunteers

ANNUAL
AWARDS
DINNER

Friday Night
February 25th
7:30-9:30
Suite 42
Springfield
VA Hospital

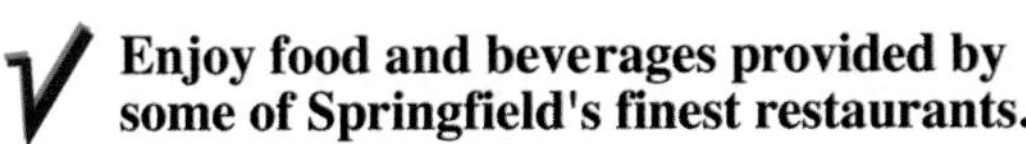

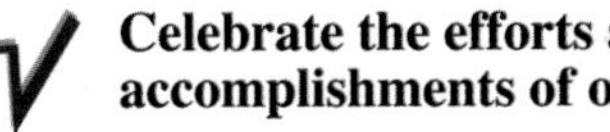

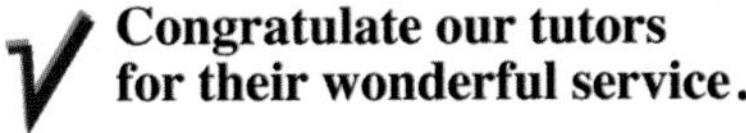

For information, contact VA Literacy Volunteers at (962) 555-9191.

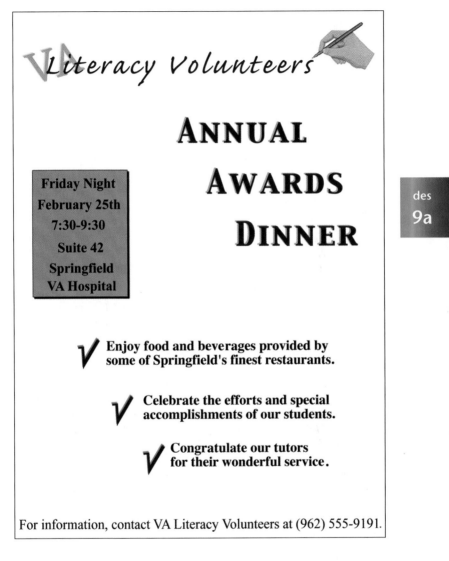

- Color and a box emphasize crucial information about the event being advertised.
- The event's activities are set off in a list with colored check marks and are surrounded with generous space.

The flyer looks simple, but it achieves its purpose through careful attention to the flow and emphasis of information.

As you begin to design your own documents, think about your purpose, the expectations of your readers, and how readers will

Principles of document design

- **Create flow** to conduct the reader through the document.
- **Space elements** to give the reader's eye a rest and to focus the reader's attention.
- **Group related elements** in lists or under similar headings.
- **Emphasize important elements.**
- **Standardize elements** to match appearance with content and to minimize variations.

move through your document. Also consider the general principles of design discussed below, noting how they overlap and support each other.

Creating flow

Many of the other design principles work in concert with the larger goal of conducting the reader through a document by establishing flow, a pattern for the eye to follow. In some documents, such as reports, flow may be achieved mainly with headings, lists, and illustrations (see pp. 218–19). In other documents, such as the flyer on the previous page, flow will come from the arrangement and spacing of information as well as from headings.

Spacing

The white space on a page eases crowding and focuses readers' attention. On an otherwise full page, just the space indicating paragraphs (an indention or a line of extra space) gives readers a break and reassures them that ideas are divided into manageable chunks. (See p. 104 on paragraph length.)

In papers, reports, and other formal documents, spacing appears mainly in paragraph breaks, in margins, and around headings and lists. In publicity documents, such as flyers and brochures, spacing is usually more generous between elements and helps boxes, headings, and the like pop off the page.

Grouping

Grouping information shows relationships visually, reinforcing the sense of the text itself. Here in this discussion, we group the various principles of design under visually identical headings to emphasize them and their similar importance. In the flyer on the previous page, a list set off with check marks itemizes the activities planned for the advertised event. The list covers *all* the activities and *only* the activities: details of date, time, and place, for instance, appear elsewhere on the page. Thinking of likely groups as you write can help you organize your material so that it makes sense to you and your readers.

Emphasizing

Part of a critical reader's task is to analyze and interpret the meaning of a document, and design helps the reader by stressing what's important. Type fonts and sizes, headings, indentions, color, boxes, white space—all of these establish hierarchies of information, so that the reader almost instinctively grasps what is crucial, what is less so, and what is merely supplementary. In this book, for example, the importance of headings is clear from their size and the presence or absence of decorative elements (the circle around 9b below and the diamond on the next page); and boxes like the one opposite clearly mark summaries and other key information. As you design a document, considering where and how to emphasize elements can actually help you determine your document's priorities.

Standardizing

As we read a document, the design of its elements quickly creates expectations in us. We assume, for instance, that headings in the same size and color signal information of the same importance or that a list contains items of parallel content. Just as the design creates expectations, so it should fulfill them, treating similar elements similarly. Anticipating design standards as you write a document can help you develop a consistent approach to its elements.

Standardizing also creates clear, uncluttered documents. Even if they are used consistently, too many variations in type fonts and sizes, colors, indentions, and the like overwhelm readers as they try to determine the significance of the parts. Most formal documents, such as papers and reports, need no more than a single type font for text and headings, with type size and highlighting (such as CAPITAL LETTERS, **boldface,** or *italics*) distinguishing the levels of headings. Publicity documents, such as flyers and brochures, generally employ more variation to arrest readers' attention. The flyer on page 201, for example, uses three type fonts: one for the organization's name, another for the event's title, and a third for everything else. Variations in the third font distinguish the box, the list, and the information along the bottom.

9b Using the elements of design

Applying the preceding design principles involves seven main elements of document design: print quality, margins, and text (next page); lists and headings (p. 207); tables, figures, and images (p. 208);

and color (p. 212). You won't use all these elements for every project, however, and in many writing situations you will be required to follow a prescribed format (see pp. 215–18 on academic papers and pp. 902–15 on business writing).

Note Your word processor may provide wizards or templates for many kinds of documents, such as letters, memos, reports, agendas, résumés, and brochures. **Wizards** guide you through setting up and writing complicated documents. **Templates** are preset forms to which you add your own text, headings, and other elements. Wizards and templates can be helpful, but not if they lead you to create cookie-cutter documents no matter what the writing situation. Always keep in mind that a document should be appropriate for your subject, audience, and purpose.

1 Print quality

The cartridge on your printer should be fresh enough to produce a dark impression. A printer that forms characters out of tiny dots may be acceptable for your academic papers, but make sure the tails on letters such as *j*, *p*, and *y* fall below the line of type, as they do here. For documents that are complex or that will be distributed to the public, use an inkjet or laser printer, which creates characters more like the ones you see here. If you require color, varied type fonts, or illustrations and your printer is not up to the job, you may be able to use more advanced equipment in your school's computer lab.

2 Margins

Margins at the top, bottom, and sides of a page help to prevent the pages from overwhelming readers with unpleasant crowding. Most academic and business documents use a minimum one-inch margin on all sides (see also p. 217). Publicity documents, such as the flyer on page 201, often use narrower margins, compensating with white space between elements. For setting margins on a word processor, see page 186.

3 Text

A document must be readable. You can make text readable by attending to line spacing, type fonts and sizes, highlighting, word spacing, and line breaks.

Line spacing

Most academic documents are double-spaced, with an initial indention for paragraphs, while most business documents are single-spaced, with an extra line of space between paragraphs. Double or triple spacing sets off headings in both. Publicity documents, such as flyers and brochures, tend to use more line spacing to separate and group distinct parts of the content.

Type fonts and sizes

The readability of text also derives from the type fonts (or faces) and their sizes. For academic and business documents, choose a type size of 10 or 12 points, as in these samples:

10-point Courier	10-point Times New Roman
12-point Courier	12-point Times New Roman

For text, generally use a font with **serifs**—the small lines finishing the letters in the samples above and in the font you're reading now. **Sans serif** fonts (*sans* means "without" in French) include this one found on many word processors:

10-point Arial
12-point Arial

Though fine for headings, sans serif type can be more difficult than serif type to read in extended text.

Your word processor probably offers many decorative fonts as well:

10-POINT COPPERPLATE	10-point Tekton
10-POINT DECOTURA	10-point Ruzicka Freehand
10-POINT STENCIL	10-point Park Avenue
10-point Lucinda Sans	10-POINT TRAJAN

Such fonts often appear in publicity documents like the flyer on page 201, where they can attract attention, create motion, and reinforce a theme. (In publicity documents, too, font sizes are often much larger than 10 or 12 points, even for passages of text.) In academic and business writing, however, decorative fonts are inappropriate: letter forms should be conventional and regular.

Note The point size of a type font is often an unreliable guide to its actual size, as the decorative fonts above illustrate: all the samples are 10 points, but they vary considerably. Before you use a font, print out a sample to be sure it is the size you want.

Highlighting

Within a document's text, underlined, *italic,* **boldface,** or even color type can emphasize key words or sentences. Underlining is most common in academic writing situations, where instructors

http://www.fontsite.com Information about typography and fonts, from the FontSite.

often prefer it to italics, especially for titles in source citations. Italics are more common in business writing and publicity documents. Both academic and business writing sometimes use boldface to give strong emphasis—for instance, to a term being defined—and publicity documents often rely extensively on boldface to draw the reader's eye. Neither academic nor business writing generally uses color within passages of text. In publicity documents, however, color may be effective if the color is dark enough to be readable. (See p. 212 for more on color in document design.)

No matter what your writing situation, use highlighting selectively to complement your meaning, not merely to decorate your work. Many readers consider type embellishments to be distracting.

Word spacing

In most writing situations, follow these guidelines for spacing within and between words:

- Leave one space between words.
- Leave one space after all punctuation, with these exceptions:

Dash (two hyphens or the so-called em-dash on a computer)	book--its	book—its
Hyphen	one-half	
Apostrophe within a word	book's	
Two or more adjacent marks	book.")	
Opening quotation mark, parenthesis, or bracket	("book	[book

- Generally, leave one space before and after an ellipsis mark (see p. 527). The example below left shows MLA style for an ellipsis mark, with brackets on either side closed up to the following or preceding period. The example below right shows the style for most other disciplines.

MLA	**Other disciplines**
book [. . .] in	book . . . in

Line breaks

Your word processor will generally insert appropriate breaks between lines of continuous text: it will not, for instance, automatically begin a line with a comma or period, and it will not end a line with an opening parenthesis or bracket. However, you will have to prevent it from breaking a two-hyphen dash or a three-dot ellipsis mark by spacing to push the beginning of each mark to the next line.

When you instruct it to do so (usually under the Tools menu), your word processor will also automatically hyphenate words to prevent very short lines. If you must decide yourself where to break words, follow the guidelines in Chapter 37.

4 Lists

Lists give visual reinforcement to the relations between like items—for example, the steps in a process or the elements of a proposal. A list is easier to read than a paragraph and adds white space to the page.

When wording a list, work for parallelism among items—for instance, all complete sentences or all phrases (see also p. 445). Set the list with space above and below and with numbering or bullets (centered dots or other devices, used in the list below about headings). Most word processors can format a numbered or bulleted list automatically (see p. 186).

5 Headings

Headings are signposts: they direct the reader's attention by focusing the eye on a document's most significant content.

Academic papers and business documents

You won't always need headings in academic papers and business documents: a three-page paper or a one-page letter, for instance, probably will not require signposts. But in many longer documents, headings are useful to break the text into discrete parts, create emphasis, and orient the reader. See the example on page 219.

When you use headings in academic and business writing, follow these guidelines:

- Use one, two, or three levels of headings depending on the needs of your material and the length of your document. Some level of heading every two or so pages will help keep readers on track.
- Create an outline of your document in order to plan where headings should go. Reserve the first level of heading for the main points (and sections). Use a second and perhaps a third level of heading to mark subsections of supporting information.
- Keep headings as short as possible while making them specific about the material that follows.
- Word headings consistently—for instance, all questions (*What Is the Scientific Method?*), all phrases with *-ing* words (*Understanding the Scientific Method*), or all phrases with nouns (*The Scientific Method*).
- Indicate the relative importance of headings with type size, positioning, and highlighting, such as capital letters, underlining, or boldface, as in the following examples.

FIRST-LEVEL HEADING

Second-Level Heading

Third-Level Heading

First-Level Heading

Second-Level Heading

Third-Level Heading

Generally, you can use the same type font and size for headings as for the text. For variety you may want to increase the heading size a bit and try a sans serif font like that in the second set of examples above. Avoid very decorative fonts like those shown on page 205.

- Don't break a page immediately after a heading. Push the heading to the next page.

Note Document format in psychology and some other social sciences requires a particular treatment of headings. See pages 856–57.

Publicity documents

In publicity documents, headings not only direct but capture the reader's attention, and they work with white space and other elements to organize the flow of information. Some of the preceding guidelines for academic and business writing apply to publicity documents, too: headings should be as short as possible, and their relative importance should be clear. But publicity headings are usually in a font different from and considerably larger than the document's text, they may use decorative fonts that reinforce the document's message, and they often use color. See pages 201, 221, and 223 for examples.

6 Tables, figures, and images

Tables, figures, and images can often make a point for you more efficiently than words can. Tables present data. Figures (such as graphs and charts) usually recast data in visual form. Images (such as diagrams, drawings, photographs, and clip art) can explain processes, represent what something looks like, add emphasis, or convey a theme.

Note Many computer programs can help you create tables, graphs, charts, and other illustrations. Your word processor may in-

http://www.colostate.edu/Depts/WritingCenter/references/graphics.htm
In-depth information about using tables, figures, and images, from Colorado State University.

clude such a program. However, if you use many illustrations in your writing, you may want to learn a spreadsheet program such as Excel or Quattro (for graphs and charts) or a graphics program such as Photoshop, CorelDraw, FreeHand, or Canvas (for images). Your word processor may also include files of clip art, and the World Wide Web can be an excellent resource for photographs and other images. (See also pp. 233–34.)

Illustrations and the writing situation

Academic and many business documents tend to use tables, figures, and images differently from publicity documents. In the latter, illustrations are generally intended to attract readers' attention, enliven the piece, or emphasize a point, and they may not be linked directly to the document's text. In academic and business writing, however, illustrations directly reinforce and amplify the text. Follow these guidelines when using tables, figures, or images in academic and most business writing:

- Focus on a purpose for your illustration—a reason for including it and a point you want it to make. Otherwise, readers may find it irrelevant or confusing.
- Provide a source note whenever the data or the entire illustration is someone else's independent material (see p. 686). Each discipline has a slightly different style for such source notes: those in the table and figures on pages 210–11 reflect the style of the social sciences. See also Chapters 46 and 50–52.
- Number figures and images together, and label them as figures: Figure 1, Figure 2, and so on. Number and label tables separately from figures: Table 1, Table 2, and so on.
- Refer to each illustration (for instance, "See Figure 2") at the point(s) in the text where readers will benefit by consulting it.
- Unless your document includes many illustrations, place each one on a page by itself immediately after the page that refers to it.

Note Many businesses and academic disciplines have preferred styles for illustrations that differ from those given here. When in doubt about how to prepare and place tables and figures, ask your instructor or supervisor.

Tables

Tables usually summarize raw data, displaying the data concisely and clearly:

- Above the table, provide a self-explanatory title. Readers should see what the table shows without having to refer to the body of your document.

- Provide self-explanatory headings for horizontal rows and vertical columns. Use abbreviations only if you are certain readers will understand them.
- Lay out rows and columns for maximum clarity. In the sample below, for instance, lines divide the table into parts, headings align with their data, and numbers align vertically down columns.

Table 1

Computers, Telephones, and Televisions per 1000 People (1998)

Location	Computers	Telephones	Televisions
Worldwide	41	156	184
United States	429	966	916
Europe	108	521	429
Japan	131	651	632
Former Soviet republics	18	148	347

Note: From 12th Annual Computer Industry Almanac (p. 47), by K. P. Juliussen and E. Juliussen, 1999, Incline Village, NV: Computer Industry Almanac.

Figures

Figures represent data graphically. They include the three kinds presented on the facing page: pie charts (showing percentages making up a whole), bar graphs (showing comparative data), and line graphs (showing change).

- Below the figure, provide a self-explanatory caption or legend. Readers should see what the figure shows without having to refer to the body of your document.
- Provide self-explanatory labels for all parts of the figure.
- Draw the figure to reflect its purpose and the visual effect you want it to have. For instance, shortening the horizontal date axis in Figure 3 opposite emphasizes the dramatic upward movement of the line over time.
- When preparing a graph, generally make the width greater than the height. All graphs should have a zero point so that the values are clear.

Photographs, clip art, and other images

Images can either add substance to a document or simply enliven it. In a psychology paper, for instance, a photograph may illustrate a key experiment, while in a brochure a photograph may add

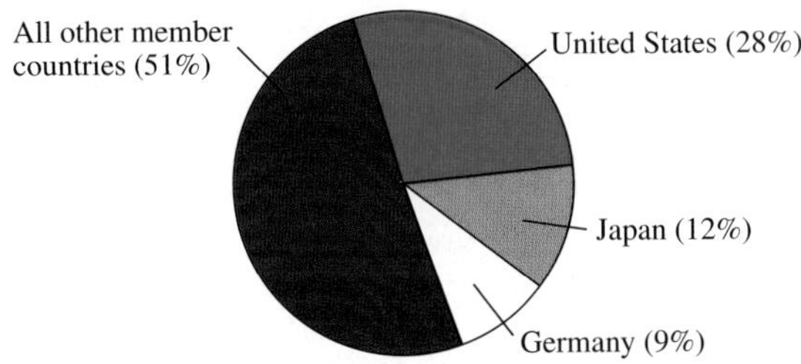

Figure 1. Member countries' assessments to United Nations budget of $1.1 billion in 1994. From "The U.N. at 50," by R. Mylan, 1995, October 18, Newsweek, p. 17.

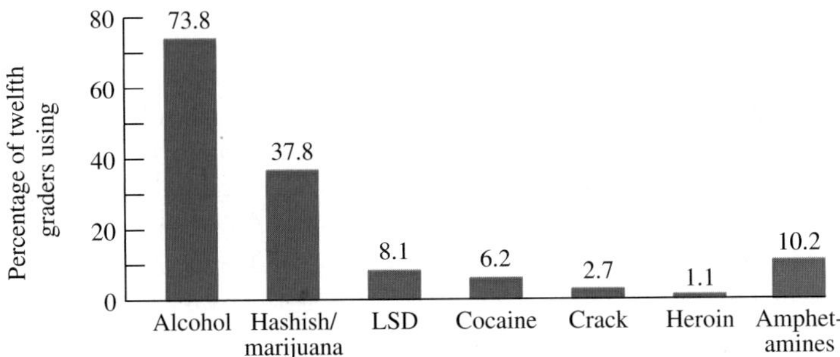

Figure 2. Use of alcohol, compared with other drugs, among twelfth graders (1999). Data from Monitoring the Future Survey Results on Drug Use, 1975–1999, 2000, Rockville, MD: National Institute on Drug Abuse.

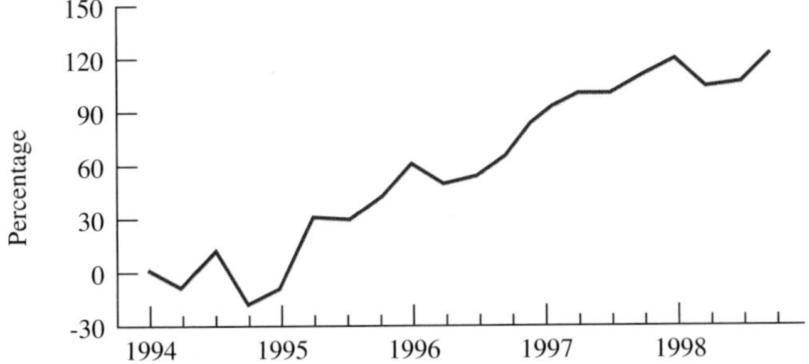

Figure 3. Five-year cumulative return for equities in Standard & Poor's 500 Index, 1994–1998.

the visual interest of, say, people working together or a cityscape. In academic and most business documents, images may include not only photographs but also diagrams and drawings. They are not

sufficient by themselves to represent your ideas: you need to consider carefully how they relate and add to your text, you need to explain their significance, and you need to label, number, and caption them (see p. 209).

One kind of image rarely appears in academic and business writing: **clip art,** icons and drawings such as the writing hand used in the flyer on page 201. Many word processors provide files of clip art, and they are also available from CD-ROMs and Web sites (see the box below for Web sources). But be selective in using these resources: clip art is mostly decorative (which is why it seldom appears in academic and business documents), and an overdecorated document is not only cluttered but unemphatic. In a publicity document, use only clip art that is relevant to your theme and content, directing readers' attention to elements you want to stress.

Note When using an image prepared by someone else—for instance, a photograph downloaded from the Web or an item of clip art from a CD-ROM—you must verify that the source permits reproduction of the image before you use it. In most documents but especially academic papers, you must also cite the source of any borrowed image. See pages 690–92 on copyright issues with Internet sources.

7 Color

With a color printer, many word processors and most desktop publishers can produce documents that use color for bullets, headings, borders, boxes, illustrations, and other elements. Publicity documents generally use color, whereas academic and business documents consisting only of text and headings may not need color. (Ask your instructor or supervisor for his or her preferences.) If you do use color, follow these guidelines:

- Employ color to clarify and highlight your content. Too much color or too many colors on a page will distract rather than focus readers' attention.

http://graphicdesign.miningco.com/arts/vadesign/graphicdesign/ A comprehensive resource for images, including tutorials, online design schools, and clip art, from About.com.

http://www.ecofuture.org/ecofuture/htmlgraf.html A clearinghouse for graphics, including tutorials, clip art, and Web images, from the Web Developer.

http://www.freegraphics.com/ A collection of free images, especially clip art, from Free Graphics.

http://www.poynter.org/vjold/DTC/pegie.html Four case studies exploring the use of color in document design, from the Virtual Seminar.

- If you use color for type, make sure the type is readable. For text, where type is likely to be relatively small, use only dark colors. For headings, lighter colors may be readable if the type is large and boldfaced.
- Stick to the same color for all headings at the same level (for instance, red for primary headings, black for secondary headings).
- For bullets, box backgrounds, lines, and other nontext elements, color can be used more decoratively to enliven the page. Still, stick to no more than a few colors to keep pages clean.
- For illustrations, use color to distinguish the segments of charts, the lines of graphs, and the parts of diagrams. Use only as many colors as you need to make your illustration clear.

8 Samples of effective and ineffective design

The two samples on the next page show the same document with very different designs. (The document content is adapted from eMarketer, a business information provider on the Web.) Even at a glance, you can see that the top sample is less inviting and readable than the bottom one. The following list highlights some of the differences contributing to this impression:

Top document (ineffective)	Bottom document (effective)
1. Does not use a distinctive type font to emphasize the title. Runs title and subtitle together and does not distinguish them.	1. Emphasizes the title with a distinctive font, a larger size, and boldface. Clearly distinguishes title and subtitle.
2. Crowds the page with minimal margins.	2. Provides adequate margins.
3. Does not separate paragraphs with white space.	3. Separates paragraphs with white space.
4. Buries statistics in the second paragraph.	4. Groups statistics into a bulleted list set off with space.
5. Presents the figure undynamically, flat on.	5. Presents the figure dynamically, tilted to emphasize the most significant segments of the chart.
6. Leaves large white space around the figure, contrasting with the tight space elsewhere and overemphasizing the figure.	6. Fills the white space that would surround the figure with the text pertaining to the figure.
7. Does not key or caption the figure to explain what its values represent, burying this information in the text.	7. Keys and captions the figure to explain what its values represent, using a distinctive type font.

Ineffective

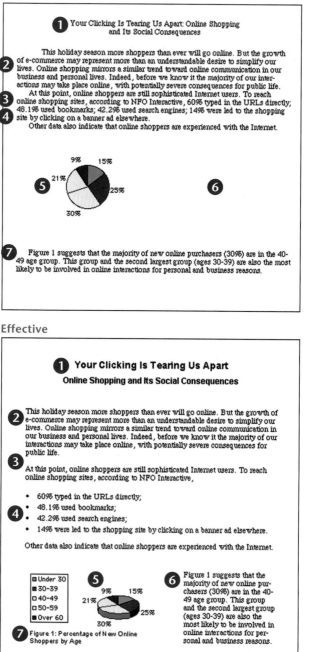

1 Your Clicking Is Tearing Us Apart: Online Shopping and Its Social Consequences

2 This holiday season more shoppers than ever will go online. But the growth of e-commerce may represent more than an understandable desire to simplify our lives. Online shopping mirrors a similar trend toward online communication in our business and personal lives. Indeed, before we know it the majority of our interactions may take place online, with potentially severe consequences for public life.

3 At this point, online shoppers are still sophisticated Internet users. To reach online shopping sites, according to NFO Interactive, 60% typed in the URLs directly; 48.1% used bookmarks; 42.2% used search engines; 14% were led to the shopping 4 site by clicking on a banner ad elsewhere.

Other data also indicate that online shoppers are experienced with the Internet.

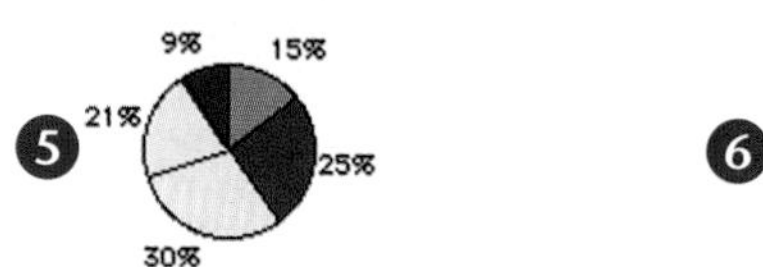

7 Figure 1 suggests that the majority of new online purchasers (30%) are in the 40-49 age group. This group and the second largest group (ages 30-39) are also the most likely to be involved in online interactions for personal and business reasons.

Effective

1 **Your Clicking Is Tearing Us Apart**

Online Shopping and Its Social Consequences

2 This holiday season more shoppers than ever will go online. But the growth of e-commerce may represent more than an understandable desire to simplify our lives. Online shopping mirrors a similar trend toward online communication in our business and personal lives. Indeed, before we know it the majority of our interactions may take place online, with potentially severe consequences for public life.

3

At this point, online shoppers are still sophisticated Internet users. To reach online shopping sites, according to NFO Interactive,

4

- 60% typed in the URLs directly;
- 48.1% used bookmarks;
- 42.2% used search engines;
- 14% were led to the shopping site by clicking on a banner ad elsewhere.

Other data also indicate that online shoppers are experienced with the Internet.

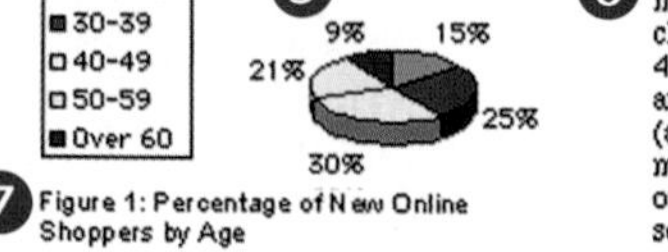

7 Figure 1: Percentage of New Online Shoppers by Age

6 Figure 1 suggests that the majority of new online purchasers (30%) are in the 40-49 age group. This group and the second largest group (ages 30-39) are also the most likely to be involved in online interactions for personal and business reasons.

EXERCISE
Redesigning a paper

Save a duplicate copy of a recent paper or one you are currently working on. Then format the duplicate using appropriate elements of design, such as type fonts, lists, and headings. (For a new paper, be sure your instructor will accept your new design.) When you have finished the redesign, share the work with your instructor.

9c Designing academic papers

Academic documents are typically text-heavy: design principles such as flow, grouping, and emphasis come more from the logic and evidence in the words than from elements such as varied type fonts, large spaces, or color. Still, academic documents do employ design elements, even if we don't always see them that way: for instance, page numbers keep the reader on track, margins ease crowding, and paragraph indentions separate ideas.

The relatively simple academic format described here is adapted from the *MLA Handbook for Writers of Research Papers,* the style guide for English, foreign languages, and some other disciplines. Most of these guidelines are standard, but your instructor may request that you follow different conventions in some matters or supplement these guidelines with those of other disciplines, as described elsewhere in this book:

- For history, art history, philosophy, and some other humanities,

Checklist for preparing a paper in MLA format

- Have you used sturdy white paper measuring 8½″ × 11″?
- Have you used only one side of each page?
- Is the type readable?
- Is everything double-spaced?
- Do your name, the instructor's name, the course title, and the date appear on the first page?
- Is your paper titled and the title centered?
- Are the margins at least one inch on all sides?
- Are all the pages numbered consecutively in the upper right, starting with page 1 for the first text page? Does your last name appear before each page number?
- If you have used sources, have you cited them in your text and attached a list of works cited?
- Have you proofread the paper and corrected all errors?
- Are the pages of your paper clipped, stapled, folded, or bound, as requested by your instructor?

see pages 832–33 on the Chicago format, derived from *The Chicago Manual of Style* and the student guide adapted from it, Kate L. Turabian's *Manual for Writers of Term Papers, Theses, and Dissertations*.

- For psychology and other social sciences, see pages 855–58 on the *Publication Manual of the American Psychological Association.*
- For the natural and applied sciences and mathematics, see pages 876–77 on *Scientific Style and Format,* the guide of the Council of Biology Editors.

Note For the special formats of source citations and a list of works cited or references, see pages 710–42 (MLA style), 822–31 (Chicago style), 841–55 (APA style), 869–76 (CBE style), or 881–91 (Columbia online style).

First page of paper with no title page

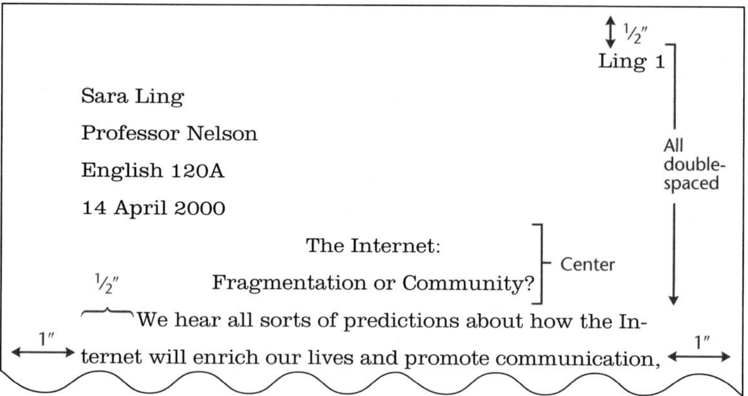

A later page of the paper

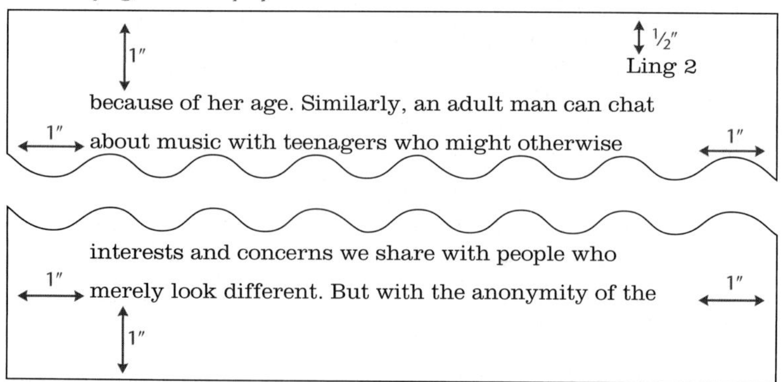

1 Paper, type, and margins

Use 8½″ × 11″ white bond paper of at least sixteen-pound weight, and use the same type of paper throughout a project. Print on only one side of each sheet. If your printer uses fanfold paper, remove the rows of holes along the sides and separate the pages at the folds before submitting the paper.

Select a standard serif font such as Courier or Times New Roman (see p. 205). Generally, you can use the same font for any headings, designed and spaced as shown on page 208.

Provide minimum one-inch margins on all sides of each page (see the illustration on the facing page). If you will be submitting your paper in a binder, provide a larger margin on the left so that the binding does not obscure any type. An uneven right margin is almost always acceptable in academic documents and is preferable if an even (or justified) margin sometimes leaves wide spaces between words.

Note If your instructor accepts handwritten papers, use white paper with lines spaced about one-quarter to three-eighths inch apart, use black or blue ink, and provide one-inch margins all around. Make your handwriting as uniform and legible as possible by, for instance, dotting every *i*, clearly distinguishing capital and small letters, and spacing consistently between words and sentences.

2 Title and identification

The *MLA Handbook* does not require a title page for a paper. If your instructor asks you to supply a title page, see the illustration and instructions on pages 746–47. Otherwise, follow the sample on the facing page, providing your name and the date, plus any other information requested by your instructor, on the first text page. Place this identification an inch from the top of the page, aligned with the left margin and double-spaced. Double-space again, and center the title. Don't underline the title or place quotation marks around it, and capitalize the words in the title according to guidelines on page 535. Double-space the lines of the title and between the title and the first line of text.

3 Paging

Begin numbering your paper on the first text page, and number consecutively through the end. Use Arabic numerals (1, 2, 3), and do not add periods, parentheses, hyphens, or the abbreviation "p." However, place your last name before the page number in case the pages become separated after you submit your paper (see the sample on the facing page). Align the page number with the right margin, and position it about half an inch from the top of the page, at least two lines above the first line of text.

9d Designing reports, newsletters, and brochures

You can use the design principles and elements discussed on pages 200–14 to good effect in long and complex reports and in documents such as flyers, newsletters, and brochures. A sample flyer appears on page 201, with discussion of its design. Here we illustrate parts of a report, a newsletter, and a brochure, with comments on the facing pages that highlight some of their most important design features.

A report

Reports are text-heavy documents, sometimes lengthy, that convey information such as the results of research. They usually contain tables or figures and may contain images as well. They may employ color. Other key design elements include headings (often in varied fonts) and lists.

The page shown here opens a business report intended to outline a problem and propose a solution. In keeping with a formal business-writing situation, the document is single-spaced (with double spacing between paragraphs and around the list), and the overall appearance is restrained. Color appears only in headings and the figure. The document uses two type fonts, one for the text and headings and one for the figure. Headings clearly delineate the structure of the page: first a summary, then an outline of the problem, and then a discussion of the solution. The figure is visually pleasing and clear, with a caption and labels that explain its content. A bulleted list emphasizes the group of alternative solutions.

Note In many academic disciplines and business organizations, reports have specific formatting requirements: in psychology, for instance, a report should include an abstract (see pp. 855–58). If you are unsure about the formatting requirements for your reports, ask your instructor or supervisor.

Canada Geese at ABC Institute: An Environmental Problem

Summary

The flock of Canada geese on and around ABC Institute's grounds has grown dramatically in recent years. What was once a source of pleasure for institute employees and others using the grounds has become a nuisance and an environmental problem. This report reviews the problem, considers the options for reducing the flock, and proposes as a solution the cooperation of ABC Institute, the municipalities around Taylor Lake, and the US Fish and Wildlife Service to reduce the flock by humane means.

The Problem

Canada geese began living at Taylor Lake, adjacent to ABC Institute, when they were relocated there in 1980 by the state game department. As a nonmigratory flock, the geese are present year-round, with the highest population each year occurring in fall, winter, and early spring, after the young have fledged.

des 9d

In recent years the flock of geese at Taylor Lake has grown dramatically. The Audubon Society's annual Christmas bird census shows a thirty-fold increase from the 37 geese counted in 1982 to the 1125 counted in 1998 (see Figure 1).

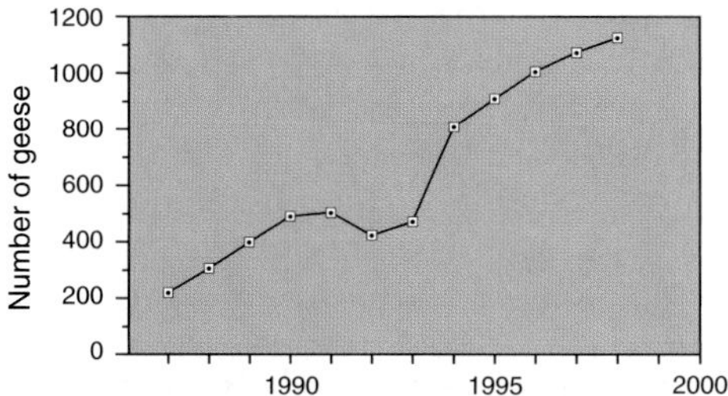

Figure 1. Goose population of Taylor Lake, 1987–1998.

The principal environmental problem caused by the geese is pollution of grass and water by defecation. During high-population months, geese droppings cover the ABC Institute's grounds as well as the park's athletic fields and picnicking areas. The runoff from these droppings into Taylor Lake has substantially affected the quality of the lake's water, so that local authorities have twice (1997 and 1998) issued warnings against swimming.

The Solution

Several possible solutions to the goose overpopulation and resulting environmental problems are *not viable alternatives:*

- Harass the geese with dogs and audiovisual effects (light and noise) so that the geese choose to leave. This solution is inhumane to the geese and unpleasant for human neighbors.
- Feed the geese a chemical that will weaken the shells of their eggs and thus reduce growth of the flock. This solution is inhumane to the geese and also impractical, because geese are long-lived.
- Kill adult geese. This solution is, obviously, inhumane to the geese.

The most appropriate and humane solution is to thin the goose population by trapping and removing many geese (perhaps 600) to areas less populated by humans, such as wildlife preserves and wilderness areas. Though costly (see figures below), this solution would be efficient and harmless to the geese, provided that sizable netted enclosures are used for traps. [Discussion of solution continues, followed by "Recommendations."]

A newsletter

Newsletters provide channels of communication for the members of organizations such as corporations, special-interest or professional groups, or charitable foundations.

Newsletters generally rely on columns, which create more room for text and headings and allow variations in the length and emphasis of sections. (See p. 204 on using templates and wizards, which can be very helpful for newsletters.) Within the columnar format, careful spacing and varied type fonts and sizes help readers skim for highlights and also read whole articles. In addition, boxes and lists often group and emphasize information; color often highlights headings, lines, and other features; and images often emphasize or decorate. With all these elements in play, standardizing can be difficult: similar elements should be treated similarly, and the overall appearance should be eye-catching but not so cluttered that it confuses the reader.

The page shown here comes from a newsletter that is designed to engage, motivate, and inform volunteer tutors who work with military veterans. To suit its purpose, the newsletter is lively in appearance, using extra-large type for title and headings, devices such as lines and borders to separate sections, and color to catch readers' eyes and focus their attention. The most important article on the page, the report on the awards dinner, spreads across two columns. A colored box in the first column provides information readers can use to work through the rest of the document. And a bulleted list (with decorative bullets) highlights and groups related items.

VA Literacy Volunteers

Springfield Veterans Administration Hospital SPRING 2000

From the director

Can you help us? With more and more learners in the VA's literacy program, we need more and more tutors. You may know people who would be interested in participating in the program, if only they knew about it.

Those of you who have been tutoring VA patients in reading and writing know both the great need you fulfill and the great benefits you bring to your students. New tutors need no special skills (we'll provide the training), only patience and an interest in helping others.

We've scheduled an orientation meeting for Friday, June 6, at 6:30 PM. Please come and bring a friend who is willing to contribute a couple of hours a week to our work.

Thanks,
Nancy Thomas

IN THIS ISSUE

AWARDS FOR STUDENTS AND TUTORS AT ANNUAL DINNER

The annual SVAH literacy awards dinner on February 25 was a great success. George Bello obtained food and beverage contributions from area restaurants and suppliers, and the students decorated the dining room on the theme of books and reading. In all, eighty-six people attended.

The highlight of the night was the awards ceremony. Ten students, recommended by their tutors, received certificates recognizing their efforts and special accomplishments in learning to read and write:

Ramon Berva
Edward Byar
David Dunbar
Tony Garnier
Chris Giugni
Akili Haynes
Pat Laird
Jim Livingston
Paul Obeid
B.J. Resnansky

In addition, nine tutors received certificates commemorating five years of service at SVAH:

Anita Crumpton
Felix Cruz-Rivera
Bette Eigen
Kelly Bortoluzzi
Harriotte Henderson
Andy Obiso
Carla Puente
Robert Smith
Sara Villante

Congratulations to all!

New Guidelines on PTSD

Most of us are working with veterans who have been diagnosed with post-traumatic stress disorder. Because this disorder is often complicated by alcoholism, depression, anxiety, and other problems, the National Center for PTSD has issued some guidelines for helping PTSD patients in a way that reduces their stress:

- The hospital must know your tutoring schedule, and you need to sign in and out before and after each tutoring session.
- Cancellations are stressful for patients. Stick to your schedule.
- To protect patients' privacy, meet them only in designated visiting and tutoring areas, never in their rooms.
- Treat patients with dignity and respect, even when (as sometimes happens) they grow frustrated and angry. Seek help from a nurse or orderly if you need it.

A brochure

Brochures advertise and inform: they are usually targeted to a specific audience, such as visitors to a historic site or potential clients for a business, and their designs convey both an attractive and a readable message. Brochures almost always use color and varied type fonts, and they often contain images and lists. They are often printed in three columns on both sides of a single sheet of paper, which is then folded in thirds. The result is three panels, each with an inner and an outer face, for six pages total.

Perhaps the most difficult challenge in brochure design is formatting the panels. Do some initial planning by folding a sheet of paper in thirds from top to bottom, turning the folded paper sideways, and sketching ideas and copy on each panel. When you have a plan, you can implement it on your computer by orienting a document horizontally on the screen and dividing the page into a column for each panel. Your word processor may include a brochure template (see p. 204), or you may have access to a desktop publishing program that provides several templates and makes it easy to arrange elements on a page.

As you format the panels, imagine readers looking at the final product. With a three-panel, two-sided brochure, readers see the cover first, then lift it to reveal two inside panels. Most readers will look first to the right, so your most immediate message should go there. The inside left then reinforces and elaborates on that message. The reinforcement is important because the inside left panel remains visible as readers continue to examine the brochure. On the innermost two panels you can put the details—information on your organization's accomplishments, the people involved, how readers can reach you, and so on. The outside middle panel (the back cover when the brochure is folded) usually resembles an envelope, with a return address in the upper left and the rest blank for a recipient's address and postage.

The sample here shows the cover and inside left panel of a brochure for the literacy group whose newsletter appears on the previous page. The cover's very simple layout and extensive white space draw readers to the group's name. Spaced out below, in smaller type, is a brief description of the group; and at the bottom, in still smaller type, is its affiliation. In contrast to the cover, the inside left panel contains more type, using headings to highlight its two parts and a list to outline and emphasize the group's activities. (The right panel facing this one included less text, briefly defining the problem of illiteracy among veterans and summarizing the group's approach to solving the problem.)

VA Literacy Volunteers

Dedicated to helping military veterans achieve literacy

Springfield Veterans Administration Hospital

Our Mission 

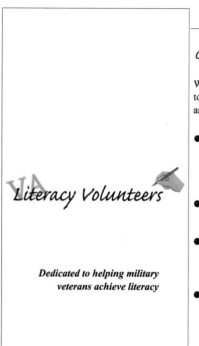

We organize and empower volunteers to help military veterans achieve literacy and to prepare them for lifelong learning.

- We provide workshops and formal lessons for veterans wishing to develop their reading and writing skills.
- We train volunteers to tutor veterans one on one.
- We maintain outreach programs to provide access to literacy training for all veterans.
- We create literacy resources and share them with others who promote literacy for veterans.

Our Volunteers 

The heart of the VA Literacy program is our volunteers. Their goodwill and generosity allow us to reach out to those who have served our country.

CHAPTER 10

Composing for the Web

You may be an experienced user of the World Wide Web—conducting research, purchasing books or CDs, or just surfing for entertainment. But you can use the Web for your own writing, too—creating a site to be shared by your family or friends, a resource for a group you belong to, even projects for your courses.

This chapter provides advice for composing Web pages. It notes some key differences between Web compositions and printed documents (below); discusses some content and design issues with Web compositions (pp. 227–34), building on the previous chapter's discussion of document design; and, finally, explains the basics of HTML editors, the software used to create Web compositions (pp. 235–42).

10a Distinguishing Web compositions from printed documents

A Web site is often called a **hypertext** because it provides more options for navigation than a traditional printed document does. We generally read printed documents **linearly**—that is, straight through from first page to last. Reference aids such as tables of contents, indexes, and cross-references can help us find material out of the linear order, but the text and any illustrations are usually intended to be read in sequence.

http://www.webcom.com/webcom/html Resources for Web publishing, including guides and links to other sources, from WebCom.

http://www.sun.com/styleguide/tables/Welcome.html A guide to Web style, from Sun Microsystems.

http://developer.netscape.com Information about Web building and design using Netscape software, from Netscape.

http://msdn.microsoft.com/workshop/default.asp Information about Web building and design using Internet Explorer software, from Microsoft.

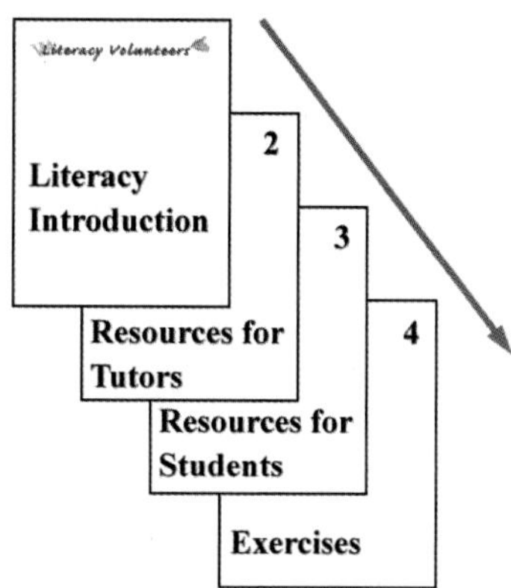

In contrast, a hypertext such as a Web site is intended to be examined in the order readers choose as they follow electronic links among the pages of the site and often to related sites.

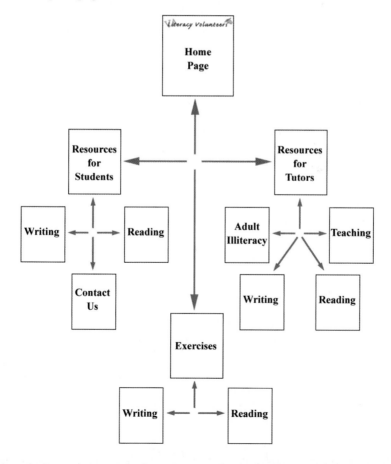

Literacy Volunteers

Home Page

Resources for Students

Resources for Tutors

Writing

Reading

Adult Illiteracy

Teaching

Contact Us

Writing

Reading

Exercises

Writing

Reading

The preceding illustration shows the structure of a fairly simple Web site: readers can move in any direction signaled by arrows or back to the home page with a single click of the mouse.

The main disadvantage of a hypertext is that it can disorient readers as they explore the various links. As discussed in the next section, a Web site requires careful planning of the links between pages and thoughtful cues to help readers keep track of their location in the site.

Several other differences between a Web composition and a printed document also deserve close attention:

- In a Web composition, each screen is a unit of meaning, somewhat comparable to related paragraphs in a printed document. The screen space is limited, so Web authors must carefully consider how to deploy text and any visual elements so that the meaning is clear, the emphasis appropriate, and the screen uncluttered.
- Web compositions can include not only tables, figures, and images (which printed documents may also have) but also video (such as animation or film clips) and audio (such as music or excerpts from speeches). Graphics, photographs, sound, and other multimedia elements can contribute substantially to the text of a composition *if* they are integrated with it, not merely used as embellishments. The elements can take a long time for the reader to download and may not be accessible to all readers, so they should be worthwhile and should be accompanied by alternative text descriptions. See pages 232–34 for more on multimedia.
- It's easy to incorporate material from other sources into a Web site, but you have the same obligation to cite your sources as you do in a printed document (see pp. 686–90). Further, your Web site is a form of publication, like a magazine or a book. Unless the material you are using explicitly allows copying without permission, you may need to seek the copyright holder's permission, just as print publishers do. (See pp. 690–92 for more on copyright.)

EXERCISE 1
Comparing printed documents and Web compositions

Either online or face to face, work with a partner or a small group of classmates to compare the strengths and weaknesses of printed documents and Web compositions. Consider ease of access, readability, flexibility, stability, visual appeal, organization, and any other features you can think of. When your team has compiled a list of differences and similarities, discuss your findings with the rest of the class.

10b Writing and designing for the Web

When you create a composition for the Web, it will likely fall into one of two categories: pages such as class papers that resemble printed documents in being linear and text-heavy and that call for familiar ways of writing and reading; or "native" hypertext documents that you build from scratch, which call for screen-oriented writing and reading. The two kinds of compositions require different approaches.

1 Composing text for the Web

If an instructor asks you to post a paper to a Web site, you can compose it on your word processor and then use the Save As HTML function available on most word processors to translate it into a Web page. (See pp. 235–42 for more on HTML.) After translating the paper, your word processor should allow you to modify some elements of the page, or you can open the translated document in an HTML editor. Before posting the page to the Web, you should consider design features that will make the document more accessible to Web readers. (These concerns apply to any text-heavy Web page.)

- Use a simple white or cream-colored background for your pages. It is more difficult to read text on a computer screen than on paper, and bright or dark background colors compound the problem. If you do use a nonwhite background, set the text color to contrast sharply with the background so that readers don't have to work to make out the text.
- Use standard type fonts for text (see p. 205), and use a type size that will be readable on various systems. With standard fonts, a size of at least 12 points should ensure that pages are readable on most systems.
- Web pages automatically run text the full width of the screen unless you give other instructions. To make reading easier, increase the margins so that lines run no more than seventy to eighty characters (including spaces). You may have to use tables (see p. 237) to create margins and columns that will shorten lines.

http://webreference.com/authoring/design/tutorials/html A Web design collection with links to numerous resources, from Webreference.

http://home.netscape.com/computing/webbuilding/studio/issue19980827.html Advice from Web authors on writing text for the Web, from Netscape.

- Use headings as signposts to direct readers through documents that require scrolling through several screens. The more screens readers must scroll through in a document, the more likely they are to lose their sense of its overall organization.

2 Creating original Web sites

When you create an original Web site, you need to be aware that Web readers generally alternate between skimming pages for highlights and focusing intently on sections of text. To facilitate this kind of reading, you'll want to consider the guidelines above for handling text and also your site's structure and content, flow, and ease of navigation. For information on using an HTML editor to create Web pages, see pages 235–42.

Structure and content

Your site's organization should be easy to grasp so that it does not disorient readers:

- Sketch possible site plans before getting started. (See p. 225 for an example.) Your aim is to develop a sense of the major components of your project and to create a logical space for each component. As you conceive the organization of your site, consider how menus on the site's pages can provide overviews of the organization as well as direct access to the pages (see pp. 230–31).
- Treat the first few sentences on any page as a crucial get-acquainted space for you and your readers. In this opening, try to hook readers with an interesting question or a central concern, and help to orient them by clarifying the relation of this page to the others on the site.
- As you create links within your own site or to other sites on the Web, indicate what's at the other locations. Instead of just *Click here,* for instance, say *Click here for writing exercises* or *Further information about snowboarding.* When you provide a list of links to related sites, annotate each one with information about its contents.
- Distill your text so that it includes only essential information. Of course, concise prose is essential in any writing situation, but Web readers expect to scan text quickly and, in any event, have difficulty following long text passages on a computer screen. (See pp. 578–84 for advice on writing concisely.)

http://www.w3.org/Provider/Style/Structure.html Advice on structuring Web compositions, from the WWW Consortium.

Flow

Beginning Web authors sometimes start at the top of the page and then add element upon element until information proceeds down the screen much as it would in a printed document. However, by thinking about how information will flow on a page, you can take better advantage of the Web's visual nature.

The screen shot below shows part of the opening page of the site mapped on page 225. Though simple in content and design, the page illustrates how the arrangement of elements can invite readers in and direct their attention. A large banner headline contains the sponsoring organization's logo. The opening text is set in a readable font, is written to engage readers' interest, and is broken into short paragraphs. A text box to the right adds variety to the page and provides a menu of the site so that readers can quickly move to the information they seek.

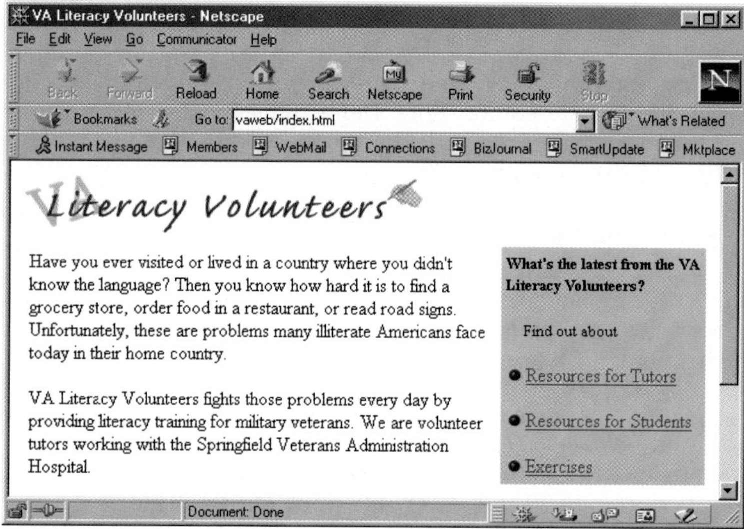

To achieve flow on your Web pages, follow these guidelines:

- Standardize elements of your design to create expectations in readers and to fulfill those expectations. For instance, develop a

http://www.gettingstarted.net/ Beginning, intermediate, and advanced design advice, from Project Cool.

http://www.hotwired.com/webmonkey/ Advanced design advice, from *Wired* magazine.

uniform style for the main headings of pages, for headings within pages, and for menus. (For more on standardizing, see p. 203.)

- Make scanning easy for readers. Focus them on crucial text by adding space around it. Use icons and other images to emphasize text. (See also pp. 232–33.) Add headings to break up text and to highlight content. Use lists to reinforce the parallel importance of items. (See pp. 203–13 for more on all these design elements.)
- Position boxes, illustrations, and other elements to help conduct readers through a page. Such elements can align in the center or on the left or right of the page. (You can use tables for more flexibility in placing elements. See pp. 237–38.) Use space around the elements to keep them from interfering with text and to highlight them. (See pp. 238–39 for more on inserting illustrations.)

Note If you know that your readers are using recent Web browsers (such as versions 4.0 and higher of Netscape Communicator and Microsoft Internet Explorer), you can use so-called style-sheet elements to control flow. Unlike tables and simple images, style sheets can be set precisely, allowing you to place material exactly where you want it on the page.

Ease of navigation

A Web site of more than a couple of pages requires a menu on every page so that readers can navigate the site. Like the table of contents in a book, a menu lists the features of the site, giving its plan at a glance. By clicking on any item in the list, readers can go directly to a page that interests them. The screen shot on page 229 shows a text menu, but you can also use icons like those in the illustration opposite. (Always supplement icons with verbal descriptions of the links to be sure readers understand where each link leads.)

Using a table (see p. 237), you can embed a menu at the top, side, or bottom of a page. Menus at the top or side are best on short pages because they will not scroll off the screen as readers move down the page. On longer pages, menus at the bottom prevent readers from dead-ending—that is, reaching a point where they can't easily move forward or backward. You can also use a combination of menus—for instance, one near the top of a page and another at the bottom.

http://www.w3.org/Style Advice on using style sheets, from the WWW Consortium.

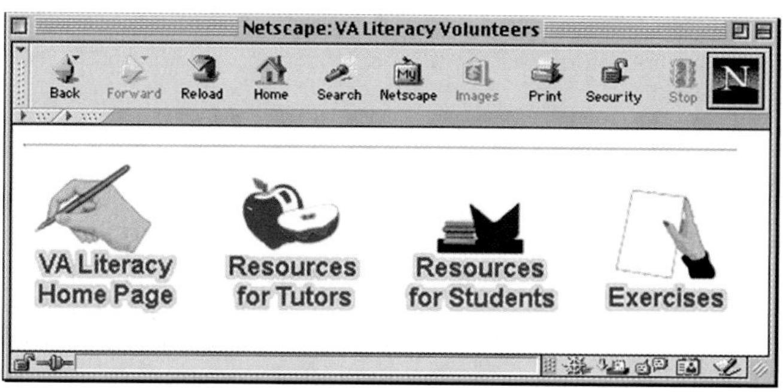

A more complicated approach is to divide a page into separate **frames,** or windows, and to place a menu within one frame. Menus within frames add stability to complex sites because they remain at the same spot on the screen no matter where readers go in the site. Most Web browsers support frames, but a few do not. Frames can also cause other problems—for instance, they sometimes prevent readers from printing or saving pages on a Web site.

In designing a menu, keep it simple: many different type fonts and colors will overwhelm readers instead of orienting them. And make the menus look the same from one page to the next so that readers recognize them easily.

EXERCISE 2
Mapping a Web site

As the first step in creating a Web site, use paper and a pencil to sketch possible Web structures for a project you have recently completed or one you are currently working on. (You can use boxes to represent pages, as in the illustration on page 225.) Consider what the site's home page should cover, how many pages you'll need and what they should cover, and how you will link the pages. Use the plan you like best as the basis for creating the site in Exercise 3, below, and Exercise 4, page 241.

EXERCISE 3
Examining and creating menus

Explore various Web sites for examples of navigation menus at the tops, bottoms, and sides of pages and in frames. Compare the examples you find, considering how clear the menus are and how their placement influences your movement through the site. Sketch

http://www.utoronto.ca/webdocs/HTMLdocs/NewHTML/frame.html
Information about using frames for organizing Web sites, from the University of Toronto.

possible menu designs for the Web project you began in the previous exercise. Where will you place your menu, and why? What will it contain?

3 Using images

The Web makes it easy to incorporate visual elements such as lines, circles, icons, graphs, drawings, photographs, and artwork. Exploring the Web, you'll see that site designers have taken advantage of these capabilities—so much so that Web readers often expect at least some visual enhancement of text.

Several guidelines can help you use images effectively in your Web compositions:

- Visual elements should supplement or replace text, highlight important features, and direct the flow of information. Don't use them for their own sake, as mere decoration.
- Make the size of your files a central concern so that readers don't have to wait forever for your site to download. As a rule, don't use images with a file size of more than thirty kilobytes (30k). The Web supports two standard image formats: GIF is best for images that are black and white or just a few colors, and JPEG is best for color photographs.
- If you are using lines or other icons, choose a limited number to speed downloading and to help readers make sense of your design.
- A graphics program can reduce the size of images and thus the time it takes to download them. If you are using photographs or other images with large files, consider reducing them to thumbnail size on a single page and linking the thumbnails to larger reproductions on other pages or sites. Readers can download the page with the smaller thumbnail images and then activate the links to download any images they wish to see larger.
- Compose descriptions of images that relate them to your text. Don't ask the elements to convey your meaning by themselves.
- Provide alternative descriptions of images to give a sense of them to readers with disabilities or readers whose Web browsers can't display them.

http://webreference.com/authoring/graphics/ Links to resources for using Web graphics, from Webreference.

http://www.zdnet.com/devhead/filters/0,9429,2133231,00.html Articles and links to resources for creating Web graphics, from ZDNet.

http://websitegarage.netscape.com/O=wsg/turbocharge/gif_lube/index.html An online assistant that will check and improve the graphics on Web pages, from Netscape.

- Observe any copyright restrictions on the use of images (see p. 690).

4 Using video and sound

Video and sound files can provide information that is simply unavailable in printed documents. For instance, as part of a film review you could place a short clip from the film on your Web page and then provide a close reading of the clip. Or as part of a project on a controversial issue you could provide links to sound files containing political speeches. You may be able to link directly to a video or sound file with your HTML editor, or you can learn more about embedding these elements into your pages at one of the Web sites listed below.

The advantages of video and sound in Web compositions are offset by their many complications:

- You and your readers need the right computer equipment. Readers' systems must have programs that can read video and sound files.
- The files are generally so large that readers using modems may not bother to wait for them to download. A so-called streaming program reduces the download time substantially, but preparing files for the program requires considerable experience.
- Most video and sound files on the Web are copyrighted, so you'll probably need to seek the permission of the copyright holder before using multimedia that you have downloaded from another site. (See also p. 690.)

Before you incorporate multimedia elements into your Web compositions, make certain that they have a legitimate purpose. They should add essential information that can't be provided in any other medium, and they should be well integrated with the rest of your composition.

5 Finding sources for images, video, and sound

To use multimedia elements in a Web composition, you can create your own or obtain them from other sources. Most advanced

http://www.builder.com/Graphics/Video/ss03.html Advice on adding video to a Web page, from Builder.Com.

http://www.developer.com/journal/techfocus/011298_sound.html Advice on adding sound to a Web page, from developer.com.

http://www.hotwired.com/webmonkey/multimedia/index.html Articles and resources for Web multimedia, from *Wired* magazine.

word processors include graphics programs with which you can draw charts, graphs, diagrams, and logos; and many computers come with a simple painting or drawing program. More sophisticated graphics programs are available, too, such as Photoshop, CorelDraw, FreeHand, or Canvas. Any graphics program requires learning and practice to be used efficiently, but the investment pays off in professional-looking illustrations.

You can also incorporate your own artwork, photographs, video clips, and sound recordings into Web compositions. You'll need additional equipment: a scanner for art and photographs and multimedia capture equipment for video and sound. You'll also need some specialized software. You may be able to find the right machines and get advice at your campus computer lab, or consult the Web sites listed below.

CD-ROMs and especially the Web itself provide vast collections of icons, drawings, photographs, video, and sound. Sometimes these resources are not restricted by copyright. When they are restricted, you will have to obtain the copyright holders' permission (see p. 690), but this obligation should not deter you from taking advantage of the offerings. In addition to thc sites listed below, those listed on page 212 can provide images. And almost every Internet directory offers graphics collections (see p. 653 for more on Internet directories).

You can download images from the Web by placing your cursor over the image and holding down the mouse button (on a Macintosh) or holding down the right mouse button (on a PC). A dialogue box appearing on your screen will offer a Save option that allows you to save the file on your own computer.

Downloading sound and video can be trickier. Sometimes you can retrieve sound and video as you do images, but you may need to save the file using the application that opens it. Whichever option you use, be sure that you have enough space on your hard drive or a diskette to hold the file. Many sound and video files will not fit on a diskette.

http://www.zdnet.com/swlib/graphics/graphics_tools.html Links to graphics programs and other utilities, from ZDNet.

http://dir.altavista.com/Computers/Graphics/Web_Graphics.shtml Links to image editors and graphics resources by category, from AltaVista.

http://webreference.com/multimedia Links to audio, video, and other Web multimedia, from Webreference.

http://www.projectcool.com/developer/gzone/02-getting/getting.html Information on finding graphics, including scanning, from Project Cool.

10c Using HTML

Most Web pages are created using hypertext markup language, or HTML, and an HTML editor. The HTML editing program inserts command codes into your document that achieve the effects you want when the material appears on the Web.

1 Working with HTML editors

The screen shots below show a passage composed on an HTML editor (top) and the codes inserted by the editor (bottom).

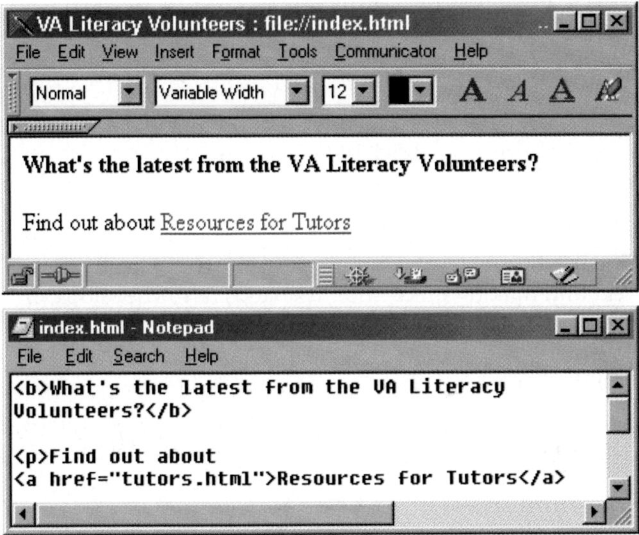

From the user's point of view, most HTML editors work much like word processors, with similar options for sizing, formatting, and highlighting copy and with a display that shows what you will see in the final version. Indeed, you can compose a Web page without bothering at all about the behind-the-scenes HTML coding. As you gain experience with Web building, however, you may want to

http://www.utoronto.ca/webdocs/HTMLdocs/NewHTML/htmlindex.html An introduction to HTML, with instructions and examples of HTML codes, from the University of Toronto.

http://developer.netscape/com/docs/manuals/htmlguid/index.htm A comprehensive source for HTML codes, from Netscape.

create more sophisticated pages by editing the codes themselves, using the HTML editor or a basic text editor such as Notepad or SimpleText. If you see something on the Web that you'd like to imitate, you can probably view its HTML coding by selecting Source or Page Source from the View menu of your Web browser.

There are many HTML editors on the market. Four with advanced features are FrontPage, PageMill, HomePage, and Dreamweaver. But your computer may already have a good HTML editor if it is fairly new or includes a popular Web browser: Composer comes with Netscape Communicator, and FrontPage Express comes with Microsoft Internet Explorer. Students can also download either of these editors for free from the sites given below. In addition, several of the other Web sites listed below offer free or low-cost HTML editors for downloading.

Note The examples in the following sections illustrate basic Web building with Netscape's Composer. If you use a different HTML editor, the steps may be somewhat different. Consult your editor's Help menu, your instructor, or your school's technology advisers any time you need assistance.

2 Working with text and creating links

The screen shots on the facing page illustrate the process of entering text and making links—the first steps in the development of a Web page that we'll follow throughout the next pages. The circled numbers in the screen shots point to some of the operations described in the list following.

http://www.netscape.com/download The download site for Netscape products, including Communicator and its Composer.

http://www.microsoft.com/downloads The download site for Microsoft products, including Internet Explorer and its FrontPage Express.

http://www.filemine.com/showDig?id=34 Reviews of HTML editors and selected editors for downloading, from TechWeb.

http://www.zdnet.com/products/content/pcmg/1702/262056.html Reviews of HTML editors, from ZDNet.

http://www.utoronto.ca/webdocs/HTMLdocs/tools_home.html HTML editors and other utilities, from the University of Toronto.

Two sites with information about creating links:

http://www.stars.com/Authoring/HTML/Tutorial/day_two_index.html From the Web Developer's Virtual Library.

http://www.ncsa.uiuc.edu/General/Internet/WWW/HTMLPrimerP2.html#LI2 From the National Center for Supercomputing Applications.

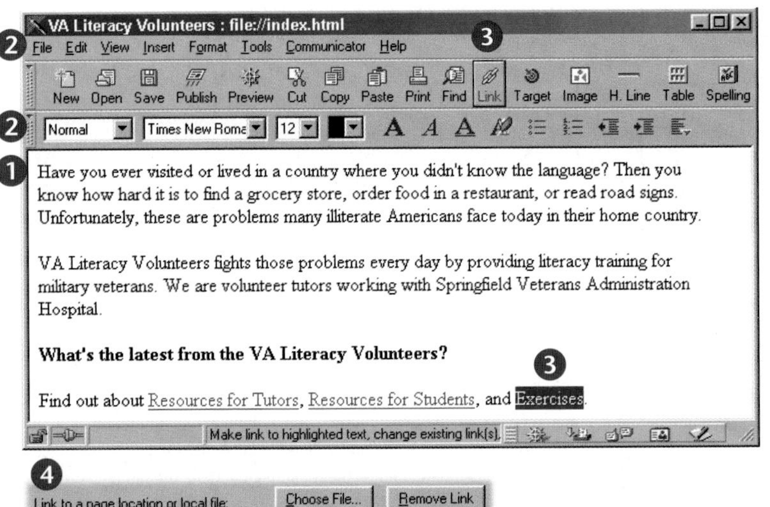

1. Create and edit text simply by entering it in the main composition window, as you would with a word processor.
2. Change the type fonts and colors, margins, backgrounds, and other elements by clicking on the drop-down menus across the top of the screen.
3. To create a link to another page on your site or another site, first select a section of text that readers will click on to activate the link, and then select the Link command from the toolbar buttons along the top of the screen.
4. To complete the link, enter the name of the file you are linking to (as in the screen shot) or the URL of another site on the Web. If you aren't sure of the name of the file you want to link to, select Choose File or Browse to locate it.

You can also create links to be activated when readers click on images or icons. First click once on the image to select it. Then, as you would with a passage of text, select the Link command and in the dialogue box enter the linked file name or URL.

3 Inserting tables

Tables provide an efficient means of adding variety, interest, and emphasis to pages without overloading them with images. Using tables, you can divide the page into segments, or cells, that may be arranged, colored, filled with illustrations, set off with borders, or otherwise varied to add interest and emphasis. In the following screen shot, the text on the left and the menu on the right are separate tables.

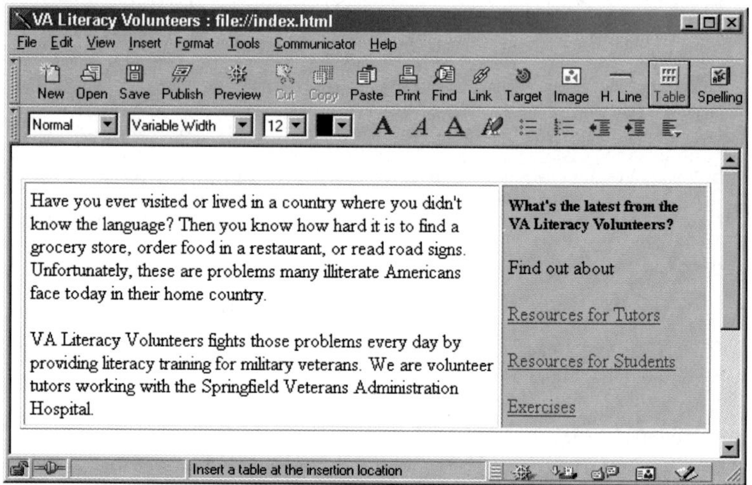

To create a table, place your cursor at the beginning of a new line where you want the table to appear on your page. Then use the Table toolbar button or select the Table command from the program's menus. Either option allows you to configure the table by adjusting its width and length, the number of rows and columns, the style of borders, the color, and other elements. If you have typed the table material beforehand, then you can cut it from the text and paste in into the table. Alternatively, you can create a blank table first and then add your material to it.

4 Inserting images

Like tables, images can enliven your pages and stress important elements. (See also pp. 232–33.) Adding the logo of the VA Literacy Volunteers to the top of the organization's first page involves the following steps, keyed by number to the screen shots opposite.

1. Begin by placing your cursor where you want the image to appear on your page.

http://home.netscape.com/assist/net_sites/tables.html Information on creating tables, from Netscape.

http://www.stars.com/Authoring/HTML/Tables/ Information on creating tables, from the Web Developer's Virtual Library.

http://www.aphids.com/susan/imres/refs.html Information on working with images, from the Image Help Site.

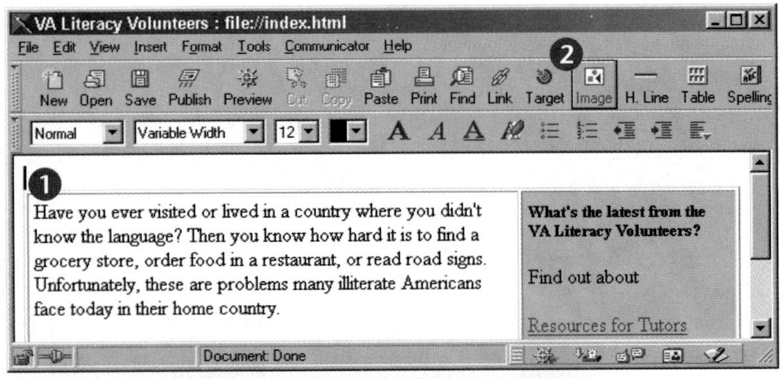

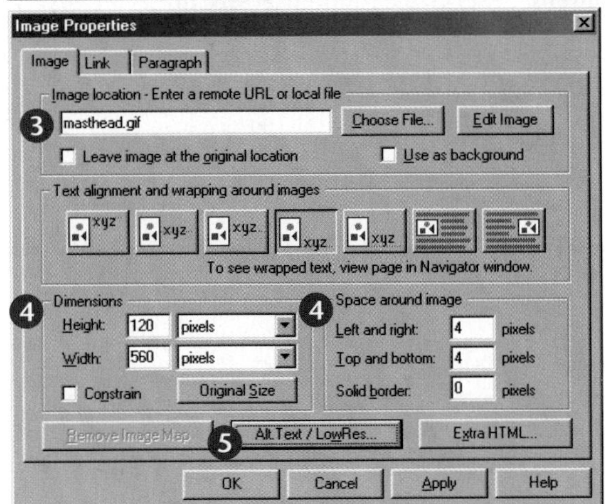

2. Select the Image command from the toolbar or from the program's menus (often under Insert).
3. Enter the name of the image file in the dialogue box that appears, or use the Choose File or Browse option to locate the file on your computer.
4. Using the dialogue box, adjust the height and width of the image, the vertical or horizontal space around it, and its border. Additional options allow you to control the relative placement of text and image—centering the image, for instance, or wrapping text around it.
5. Add an alternative description of the image for those who won't be able to see it because of disability or a limited browser.

5 Naming and working with files

When creating Web pages, you'll want to name and organize your files so that you can keep track of them and so that the Web

server to which you upload your site can recognize them. The screen shot below shows a folder containing some of the files for the VA Literacy Volunteers site. The circled numbers highlight conventions described in the list following.

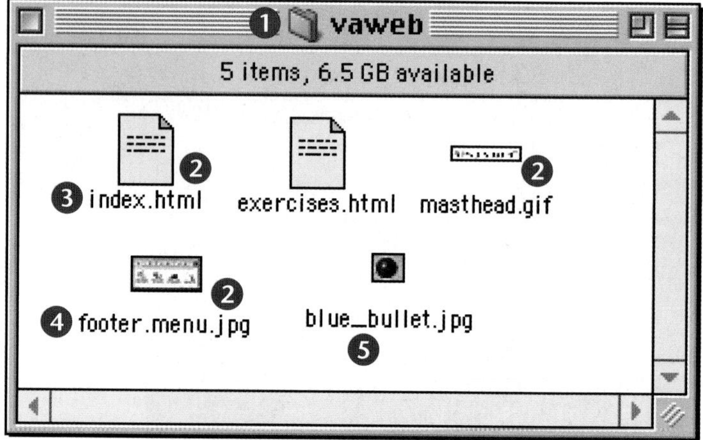

1. Keep all the files for a given project in a separate folder or directory on a diskette or hard drive. For complicated projects you may need several folders.
2. Use the proper extensions on all your file names. All the images listed in the illustrated folder end with the *.gif* or *.jpg* extension, indicating that they are GIF or JPEG images. All the HTML files end with the *.html* extension. (If you are using an older PC, you may need to use *.htm* instead.)
3. Generally, name the opening page of your site *index.html:* by default, Web browsers look for a file with this name, so it simplifies the eventual URL of your site.
4. Give your files simple and standardized names, and use those names accurately while creating your pages. The file names in the screen shot are all short and yet clearly describe the file contents, and they all use small letters. Any errors in using these names—such as inserting capital letters or adding asterisks, dollar signs, or other strange characters—would cause problems in moving the site to the server (see p. 242).
5. Don't use spaces in file names, because they can be translated by the server as unknown characters. Instead of a space, use a period or an underscore, as in the screen shot.

http://gettingstarted.net/basics/structure/02b-directories.html Guidelines for naming and organizing files, from gettingstarted.net.

EXERCISE 4
Creating a Web site

Building on the site map and navigation menu that you created in Exercises 2 and 3 (p. 231), create the Web site for your project. Compose the initial page, and save it with the name *index.html* in a project folder. Compose subsequent pages, and make links between them. Incorporate the navigation menu into each of the pages. Add appropriate images and other design elements as you refine each page of the site. When you're finished, ask classmates, your instructor, or your school's technology advisers for revision suggestions. Post the revised site to the Web, following the guidelines in the next section.

EXERCISE 5
Creating a personal Web page

Design a personal Web page—perhaps a site for family and friends that demonstrates your interests and activities or a site for potential employers that includes your résumé. (See pp. 909–12 on creating a résumé.) Compose the page with your purpose and audience in mind, using text, links, design elements, images, video, or sound as appropriate for your writing situation. Seek the advice of classmates, your instructor, or your school's technology advisers if you need help along the way or to test the final version. Then post the revised site on the Web, following the guidelines in the next section.

6 Uploading and troubleshooting files

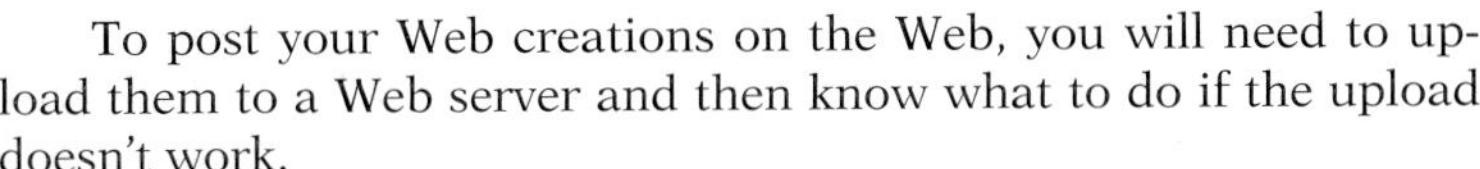

To post your Web creations on the Web, you will need to upload them to a Web server and then know what to do if the upload doesn't work.

You may be able to compose for the Web without seeking help, but for uploading, at least the first time, you almost certainly will have to consult with the server's or your school's technology advisers. Sometimes an HTML program can upload files. Usually, though, you will have to become familiar with an additional program that handles file transfer protocol (FTP), which moves files between computers.

Even when you have dutifully sought technical assistance and followed instructions, you are likely to find initial problems with the uploaded site, such as links that don't work or images that don't show up. To solve these problems, you will need to check your files,

Information on uploading and troubleshooting files:

http://help.unc.edu/cgi-bin/getdocs?docnumber=iid13 From the University of North Carolina.

http://www.ncsa.uiuc.edu/General/Internet/www/HTMLPrimerP3.html#TR From the National Center for Supercomputing Applications.

make the necessary changes in them, and then upload them again. Here are some troubleshooting strategies:

- *Did you upload all your files to the Web server?* If you uploaded your HTML files but left your images behind on your diskette or hard drive, the images will not appear on the Web.
- *Were any file names altered during the upload?* If you are using an FTP program, you can view the contents of your Web directory and use simple commands to correct file names.
- *Are your files named correctly?* Most problems with uploads come from improper file names, such as those that include spaces or that lack extensions. (See p. 240 on naming files.) Sometimes misnamed files will work fine on your computer but not on the Web server.

- *Do you need to make any changes in your HTML documents?* Double-check the names used to create your links and images in the HTML composition to be sure they correspond exactly with your file names. Any differences—typos, added or omitted capital letters, incorrect punctuation—will prevent your files from working on the server. Generally, you can perform this check by highlighting the nonworking link or image and then selecting the Link or Image command again to view the name.
- *Are you looking at the latest version of your pages?* Changes you make in your files may not appear on your Web browser until you use the Reload or Refresh command that asks the browser to display the latest version.
- *Can someone help?* If you can't locate the problem or you can't figure out how to solve it, seek assistance from a classmate, your instructor, or your school's technology advisers. Sometimes fresh eyes can spot something you overlooked, or experienced eyes can pinpoint an obscure error.

CHAPTER 11

Collaborating Online

Writing often involves collaboration with others as much as it does solitary work. Indeed, businesses and teachers often expect writers to collaborate on generating ideas and producing and revising drafts. (See also p. 66.) In this chapter we look at both the opportunities for and the methods of collaboration using computers: using electronic mail (below), using Web class tools (p. 246), and using Internet applications (p. 252). Although the chapter deals mainly with collaboration among the classmates in a course, much of the information applies also to business-writing activities and to collaborating on the Internet at large. (For guidelines on using computer collaboration specifically for research, see Chapter 43.)

Collaborating online to produce writing generally involves three activities: the collaborators form a bond that will enable them to work together productively; among themselves, they develop procedures and standards of behavior that they can refer to as they work together; and, of course, they perform the work of writing, sometimes individually, sometimes in concert. To become an effective online collaborator, you'll need to participate in all three activities and discern when each is (and is not) called for.

11a Collaborating using electronic mail

Many instructors integrate e-mail collaboration into their courses, encouraging students to use it for exchanging and commenting on drafts of projects and also for discussing class readings, ideas for writing, and other topics. Collaborating by e-mail requires

http://bestpractice.net/FMPro?-db=null.fp3&-format=/CLHE/CLHE.htm&-view Collaborative learning strategies from the Cooperative Learning Homepage, intended for teachers but useful for students wishing to know more about collaboration.

http://www.pbs.org/uti/guide/email.html Basic information about using e-mail, with links to many resources, from the Public Broadcasting System.

following e-mail conventions (described on pp. 192–97) and understanding how to use e-mail to accomplish specific tasks. Your instructor may provide instructions in addition to those below for the activities in his or her course.

1 Working on drafts

If you use e-mail to exchange and comment on drafts, following a few guidelines can help the work proceed smoothly and productively:

- If your e-mail program allows it, create a group address entry (sometimes called a nickname) containing all the e-mail addresses of your collaboration group. You can then send a message to all of your collaborators by using the group address. (See the Help menu of your e-mail program.)
- Set your e-mail program to store copies of outgoing and incoming messages. Then you'll be able to retrieve past messages when you need to recall information or track the development of a project.
- Your instructor may suggest how often you should check incoming e-mail or how quickly you should respond to messages. If not, then work with your group or partner to establish a procedure: for instance, checking messages every day, responding immediately to urgent messages, and responding to other messages within one or two days.
- To share drafts and comments by e-mail, you can copy and paste text into your e-mail messages or send word-processor files as attachments. (See pp. 192–93). Your group may need to experiment a bit to see which option works better, and you can then agree on procedures.
- Most e-mail programs provide only basic editing and highlighting tools. Thus if your group decides to share drafts and comments by e-mail (instead of using attachments), you should agree on a convention for embedding comments into a draft so that you can respond to specific parts of the draft. For instance, you could decide to break the lines of the draft to insert bracketed comments. You could also insert comments in all-capital letters, but such copy is difficult to read and can be interpreted as overly insistent.
- If your group shares files as attachments, you can use a word processor's Comment function to embed your questions and suggestions into drafts (see p. 190).
- When you are responding to others' drafts, especially early drafts, concentrate on deep issues such as thesis, purpose, audience, organization, and support for the thesis. (See p. 56 for a

revision checklist that can guide your reading.) Since it's often difficult to take in an entire paper when you're reading it one screen at a time, consider printing out the draft for review. Hold comments on style, grammar, punctuation, and other surface matters until you're reviewing late drafts, if indeed you are expected to comment on them at all.

2 Participating in class discussions

In addition to exchanging drafts and comments by e-mail, you can use a class e-mail discussion list (often called a **listserv**) to enter into conversations with classmates for gathering information, generating and testing ideas for assignments, or responding to readings. Once you subscribe to the class list (your instructor will tell you how), you will receive other list members' messages in your incoming e-mail. Messages addressing the same topic form a **thread.** Your message may start a new thread or may join a thread already in progress, as does the example below.

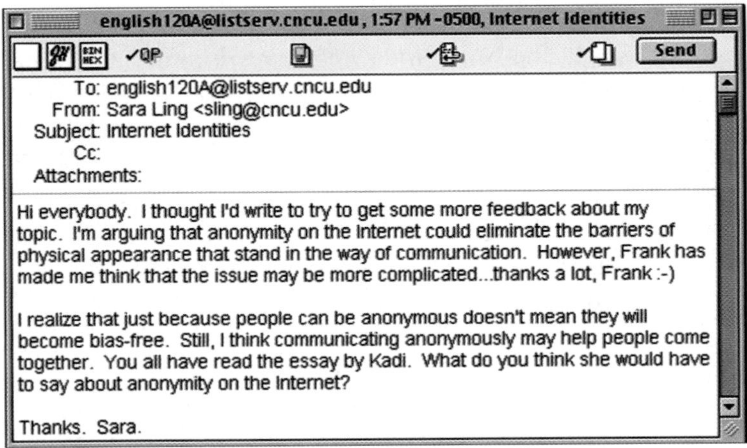
english120A@listserv.cncu.edu, 1:57 PM -0500, Internet Identities

Send

To: english120A@listserv.cncu.edu
From: Sara Ling <sling@cncu.edu>
Subject: Internet Identities
Cc:
Attachments:

Hi everybody. I thought I'd write to try to get some more feedback about my topic. I'm arguing that anonymity on the Internet could eliminate the barriers of physical appearance that stand in the way of communication. However, Frank has made me think that the issue may be more complicated...thanks a lot, Frank :-)

I realize that just because people can be anonymous doesn't mean they will become bias-free. Still, I think communicating anonymously may help people come together. You all have read the essay by Kadi. What do you think she would have to say about anonymity on the Internet?

Thanks. Sara.

When participating in an e-mail discussion list, consider these guidelines:

- Your discussion list will need to establish a code of conduct for participation—for instance, what topics will be appropriate, how frequently postings are required, and how formal or informal the conversations should be. (For more about e-mail

http://www.webcom.com/impulse/list.html Information on and resources for using e-mail discussion lists, from the Impulse Research Group.

etiquette, see p. 195.) Your instructor may offer suggestions, or the group may make such a code the topic of an early exchange.

- The class e-mail list is a public space. It can be easy (and embarrassing) to send a message that you intended for one person to the entire class instead. Always double-check the addresses on your messages before sending them.
- Participating in a discussion list can serve social as well as academic purposes, helping to cement the list's members into a cohesive group. Messages that do not contribute information or ideas for class work may still be worthwhile if they give the members a social foundation for collaborating. However, such messages should not overwhelm the threads devoted to writing. To keep the conversation on track, your instructor may ask list members to submit messages for checking or grading. But you and your classmates can take it upon yourselves to channel the conversation productively.

11b Collaborating using Web class tools

Increasingly, the World Wide Web serves as a medium for online collaboration among students in a course. Your class may have access to a Web site where you can check assignments, find resources, post messages, and share files, among other activities. Such a Web site can be the primary work space for the class, requiring the same investment that you would bring to class meetings.

The Web site for a course may be one that your instructor has created or may be part of a commercial **courseware** package such as BlackBoard, WebCT, FirstClass, TopClass, and Web Course in a Box. (Daedalus Online, available with this book, is another such package.) Both kinds of Web sites are likely to provide similar options for collaboration. Instructor-made sites are more likely to be open to the public, and courseware sites are more likely to be limited to class members only and to require a password for participation.

Note If you are engaged in distance learning, taking a course at a location remote from your school's campus, a class Web site may be the only medium for meeting with your instructor and fellow students and for submitting your work. If you are not already skilled at navigating and using Web resources, consult the sites

http://www.learnthenet.com/english/section/www.html Information and resources on using the Web, from Learn the Net.

http://illinois.online.uillinois.edu/model/StudentProfile.htm Students' self-evaluations and other information about working successfully online, from the Illinois Online Network.

given at the bottom of the facing page. Be prepared also to take the initiative with class activities. Your instructor may communicate frequently by e-mail, but you still will be responsible for tapping regularly into class resources, responding promptly to messages, and completing assignments on deadline.

1 Getting started

Your instructor will give you an address for reaching your class Web site. (For information on using Web addresses, see p. 197.) If the site is not password protected, you can simply enter its address in a Web browser to reach the site. However, many Web collaboration spaces require that you enter an account name and password.

Using class Web tools requires a variety of skills, but often the biggest problem that students encounter is simply forgetting their account name and password. Your account name and password may be predetermined by the system, or you may be able to choose them. Either way, you need to remember them. Write them down if you have a secure place to do so, or else etch them in your memory.

Once you have reached your class site, the opening page will probably provide introductory information and a menu listing the available tools. Of the many possible tools, the most common and useful are discussed below: forums, file sharing, chat functions, whiteboards, e-mail, and group spaces.

2 Holding discussions using Web forums

Sometimes called message or discussion forums, Web forums permit members of a class to engage in online conversations. As with e-mail discussion lists, participants send messages that other participants can later read and respond to, building threads of messages on related topics. The screen shots on the next page show the index of messages for one such thread, the message starting it, a first response, and a response to both previous messages.

Like e-mail discussions, discussions on Web forums evolve over time. Any message in a thread is merely part of a larger conversation. And whereas participants in face-to-face discussions respond spontaneously to what others say, forum participants can pause to digest a message and compose a thoughtful response.

Also like e-mail discussions, forum discussions tend to be more productive when the participants agree to a code of conduct (see pp. 245–46). Some messages may do little more than help the participants get to know each other personally, but keep in mind that the forum's main purpose is to exchange and refine ideas for writing. To encourage participants to achieve this purpose, your instructor may check or assign messages and may grade them.

⊟ Internet Identity	Ling, Sara	02-Nov-1999
Re: Internet Identity	Riggins, Bob	02-Nov-1999
Re: Internet Identity	Potter, Franklin	02-Nov-1999

Author: Ling, Sara <sling@cncu.edu>
Subject: Internet Identity

Hi everyone. I'm hoping you can give me some advice about my topic and maybe share some of your experiences. I disagree with Kadi's argument that the Internet will lead to more fragmentation, not community. On the snowboarding forum that I sometimes participate in, I received a lot of hostile responses when I logged on as a woman. But another member of the group wrote to tell me that when she logged on as a man, she was welcomed into the group. It made me realize that the anonymity of the Internet could be used to bring people together, not split them apart.

Have any of you had similar experiences when you've been online? Do you think that anonymity can bring people together?

Author: Riggins, Bob <flashbob@cncu.edu>
Subject: Re: Internet Identity

I had a similar experience when I tried to post a question to a newsgroup. I logged on with my e-mail account as my name, "flashbob." Nobody responded to my question at all. I think part of it was because the name I used was so playful that nobody took me seriously. You may be on to something, Sara.

Author: Potter, Franklin <fpotter@cncu.edu>
Subject: Re: Internet Identity

I think you and Bob both have a point about the names used on the Internet having a lot to do with how people relate. But I'm not sure that your experience totally challenges what Kadi is saying. When I've been online, I've found that people who are a lot alike tend to hang out and encourage each other. Even if the other woman on the snowboarding forum was able to change her identity, she still ended up confiding in you. I guess I would just be careful about claiming that anonymity will automatically bring different kinds of people together. Hope this helps. Frank.

Your instructor may also ask you to use a Web forum to review your classmates' drafts. If your forum can attach word-processor files to messages, you can exchange files and use your word processor's Comment function to convey your questions and suggestions (see p. 190). If the forum can't attach files, then you can copy and paste a paper into a message and add your comments to the paper's text.

3 Sharing files

One convenience of most Web class tools is their file-sharing capabilities, which allow you, your classmates, and your instructor

to exchange drafts, finished papers, and comments with just a few mouse clicks.

The two screen shots below show how file sharing works on one Web class tool. In the first, the student Bob Riggins has selected *Potter.P1.revRiggins.doc* from his own files and then clicked Open to upload, or send, the file to the shared Web space. In the second shot, the file appears last in a "DropBox" that lists the files uploaded to the group's file-sharing space. Other students can then select a file from this list and click on Save Link As to download and save it on their computers. The names of the functions and the options may be different in the Web tool your class uses, but the operations are generally the same. Consult your instructor if you need help.

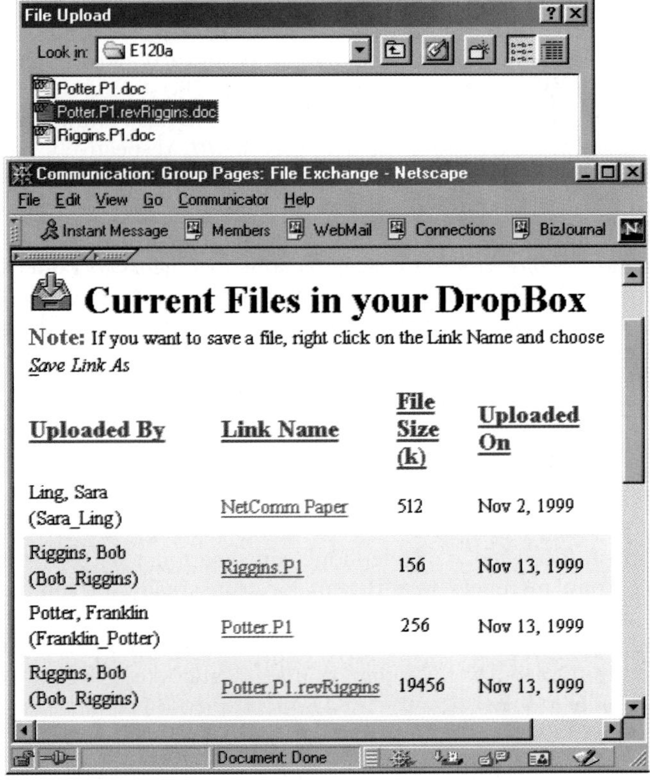

http://www.lib.rochester.edu/multimed/intro.htm Information on file formats, uploading, and downloading, from the University of Rochester.

You can find out more about managing, sharing, and commenting on files on pages 183–84, 190, and 192–93. Sharing files through a common Web space tends to reduce the challenges, but two are likely to come up:

- If you and your classmates work on different word-processing programs—or even different versions of the same program—you may be able to download one another's files but not open and work on them. In that case you should experiment with saving files in standard formats, such as rich text format (RTF), before sharing them.
- Passing files back and forth in a shared space increases the potential for confusion and lost work. For instance, some programs simply overwrite (and thus erase) an older file when a user uploads a new file with exactly the same name. To clarify who wrote what and preserve all past work, most Web-based courses use conventions for naming shared files. The second screen shot on the previous page shows that Bob Riggins and Franklin Potter named their files *Riggins.P1* and *Potter.P1,* respectively, including both the authors' last names and the assignment (*P1* is paper number 1). (Sara Ling, in contrast, named her file *NetComm Paper,* indicating neither her name nor the paper number.) For his review of Potter's draft, Riggins adds *revRiggins* to Potter's file name, ensuring that Riggins's comments won't overwrite Potter's original or be overwritten in turn by others' reviews of the same draft. If your instructor does not set conventions for naming files, develop a workable system with your classmates.

4 Using chat functions and whiteboards

Many class Web tools also permit collaboration that occurs not over time, with messages accumulating, but immediately in real time, as in face-to-face or telephone conversations. With chat functions, group members in different locations read electronic messages simultaneously. With so-called whiteboards, group members in different locations share an online drawing board that allows them simultaneously to exchange images and sketch visual ideas with drawing tools.

When collaborating via chat functions and whiteboards, your group will be more productive if you all follow a few guidelines:

- Chat functions and whiteboards can be the electronic equivalent of the student union or a busy hallway outside a classroom,

http://www2.famvid.com/i101/chat.html Information about chat on the Internet, including jargon guides, software, and etiquette, from Internet 101.

providing opportunities for class members to share personal ideas and information and to solidify the group. Eventually, however, social interaction must give way to accomplishing specific course goals. The group should agree on conventions that will help members make the most effective use of the medium—for instance, deciding on an agenda ahead of time or early in the session, or selecting a moderator to keep exchanges on track.

- Simultaneous collaboration is often fast-paced, and you may have trouble keeping up with everything that appears on the screen. Instead of struggling to grasp every contribution, try concentrating on a thread, or common topic, that strikes your interest.
- Because of its pace, online chat rarely allows lengthy consideration and articulation of messages. Thus the chat space may be better suited to brainstorming topics and exchanging impressions than to working out ideas in detail.
- You will be interacting spontaneously when you use whiteboards or chat functions. Write or draw as quickly and fluidly as possible. When chatting, don't worry about producing perfect prose.
- Like most electronic communication, simultaneous collaboration can become heated. Remember the standards of conduct expected from you and your classmates, and remind yourself that even someone who is upsetting or irritating you is, like you, an individual deserving of respect.
- Save transcripts of simultaneous collaborations so that you can refer to them later. (If you are unsure how to save transcripts, ask your instructor.)

5 Using e-mail and group spaces

Many Web class tools include two other communication features: e-mail and group spaces.

- With e-mail you may be able to send messages to individuals, to a group of classmates, or to the class as a whole. Unlike Web forums, e-mail can be used to make direct contact with particular classmates or group members. (See pp. 192–97 and 243–46 for more on using e-mail.)
- A group space provides private Web tools that a collaborative group can use apart from the rest of the class. (The screen shots on p. 248 come from a group space with just three participants.) If your course's Web tool provides group spaces, they will probably include file-sharing functions and may include a discussion forum and a chat function as well. You and your working partners can establish your own conventions and ex-

pectations for file sharing and discussion, knowing that the space is essentially your own.

11c Collaborating using Internet applications

Although most online activity occurs via e-mail or over the Web, the larger Internet offers additional options for collaborating with others.

- Meeting programs, such as Microsoft's NetMeeting, allow groups to chat, use whiteboards, hold video conferences, share applications, and even work together on the same document. For instance, you and a classmate might meet to discuss or edit a draft or to demonstrate some function of your word processor.
- Like the chat functions discussed on pages 250–51, Internet relay chat (IRC) programs and instant-messaging systems allow you and others to exchange messages in real time. Instant-messaging systems, such as Instant Messenger from Netscape and America Online, are simpler than IRC programs to use. You and a partner can agree to log on at a specified time and then, say, pose questions and comments about a draft.
- Virtual environments are spaces where people can meet to exchange ideas and collaborate on projects. Most of these spaces are called MUDs or MOOs and are created with text descriptions. For instance, a user accessing a MOO might see a description of a virtual campus and of a classroom or office where students can meet for discussion.

Besides those listed above, you can also use the discussion groups covered under research sources on pages 659–61. Any of these tools requires start-up time as you learn to use the system and develop conventions for effective collaboration. For more information, consult the Web sites given below, your instructor, or the technology advisers at your school.

http://www.microsoft.com/windows/netmeeting/ Instructions and resources for NetMeeting, from Microsoft.

http://home.netscape.com/aim Information and resources for instant messaging, from Netscape and America Online.

http://www.cservice.undernet.org/ Beginners' information about IRC options, from Undernet.

http://moo.du.org/cybercomp.html Information about using MOOs and MUDs for writing, from Composition in Cyberspace.

PART IV

Grammatical Sentences

CHAPTER 12

Understanding Sentence Grammar

Grammar describes how language works. Following the rules of standard English grammar is what allows you to communicate with others across barriers of personality, region, class, or ethnic origin. If you are a native English speaker, you follow these rules mostly unconsciously. But when you're trying to improve your ability to communicate, it can help to make the rules conscious and learn the language used to describe them.

Grammar tells a lot about a sentence, even if you don't know the meanings of all the words:

The rumfrums prattly biggled the pooba.

You don't know what this sentence means, but you can infer that some things called *rumfrums* did something to a *pooba.* They *biggled* it, whatever that means, in a *prattly* way. Two grammatical cues, especially, tell you that this sentence is like *The students easily passed the test:*

- Word forms. The ending *-s* means more than one *rumfrum.* The ending *-ed* means that *biggled* is an action that happened in the past. The ending *-ly* means that *prattly* probably describes *how* the rumfrums biggled.

http://webserver.maclab.comp.uvic.ca/writersguide/Pages/GrammarToc.html An online grammar glossary, from the University of Victoria.

http://webster.commnet.edu/HP/pages/darling/original.htm Comprehensive grammar information and exercises, from the Guide to Grammar and Writing.

http://www.english.uiuc.edu/cws/wworkshop/grammarmenu.htm Extensive coverage of the elements of grammar, from the University of Illinois at Urbana-Champaign.

http://www.aitech.ac.jp/~iteslj/quizzes/grammar.html Online grammar exercises for ESL writers, from the *Internet TESL Journal.*

http://www.clta.on.ca/grammmar.htm Resources and grammar exercises for ESL writers, from the Centre for Language Training and Assessment.

- Word order. *Rumfrums biggled pooba* resembles a common sequence in English: something (*rumfrums*) performed some action (*biggled*) to or on something else (*pooba*). Since *prattly* comes right before the action, it probably describes the action.

This chapter explains how such structures work and shows how practicing with them can help you communicate more effectively.

Note Computerized grammar and style checkers can both offer assistance and cause problems as you compose correct sentences. Look for the cautions and tips for using such checkers in this and the next five parts of this book. For more information about grammar and style checkers, see page 188.

12a Understanding the basic sentence

The **sentence** is the basic unit of thought. Its grammar consists of words with specific forms and functions arranged in specific ways.

1 Identifying subjects and predicates

Most sentences make statements. First they name something; then they make an assertion about or describe an action involving that something. These two sentence parts are the **subject** and the **predicate:**

Subject	Predicate
Art	can be controversial.
It	has caused disputes in Congress and in artists' studios.
Its meaning and value to society	are often the focus of debate.

ESL The subject of an English sentence may be a noun (*art*) or a pronoun that refers to a noun (*it*), but not both: *Art* [not *Art it*] *can be controversial.* See page 408.

2 Identifying the basic words: Nouns and verbs

The following five simple sentences consist almost entirely of two quite different kinds of words:

Subject	Predicate
The earth	trembled.
The earthquake	destroyed the city.
The result	was chaos.
The government	sent the city aid.
The citizens	considered the earthquake a disaster.

The parts of speech

Nouns name persons, places, things, ideas, or qualities: *Roosevelt, girl, Kip River, coastline, Koran, table, strife, happiness.* (See below.)

Pronouns usually substitute for nouns and function as nouns: *I, you, he, she, it, we, they, myself, this, that, who, which, everyone.* (See p. 258.)

Verbs express actions, occurrences, or states of being: *run, bunt, inflate, become, be.* (See the facing page.)

Adjectives describe or modify nouns or pronouns: *gentle, small, helpful.* (See p. 263.)

Adverbs describe or modify verbs, adjectives, other adverbs, or whole groups of words: *gently, helpfully, almost, really, someday.* (See p. 263.)

Prepositions relate nouns or pronouns to other words in a sentence: *about, at, down, for, of, with.* (See p. 266.)

Conjunctions link words, phrases, and clauses. **Coordinating conjunctions** and **correlative conjunctions** link words, phrases, or clauses of equal importance: *and, but, or, nor; both . . . and, not only . . . but also, either . . . or.* (See p. 282.) **Subordinating conjunctions** introduce subordinate clauses and link them to main clauses: *although, because, if, whenever.* (See p. 276.)

Interjections express feeling or command attention, either alone or in a sentence: *hey, oh, darn, wow.*

The words in the subject position name things, such as *earth, earthquake,* and *government.* In contrast, the words in the predicate position express states or actions, such as *trembled, destroyed,* and *sent.*

These two groups of words work in different ways. *Citizen* can become *citizens,* but not *citizened. Destroyed* can become *destroys,* but not *destroyeds.* Grammar reflects such differences by identifying the **parts of speech** or **word classes** shown in the box above. Except for *the* and *a,* which simply point to and help identify the words after them, the five sentences about the earthquake consist entirely of nouns and verbs.

Nouns

Meaning

Nouns name. They may name a person (*Rosie O'Donnell, Jesse Jackson, astronaut*), a thing (*chair, book, Mt. Rainier*), a quality

http://www.uottawa.ca/academic/arts/writcent/hypergrammar/partsp.html Information and exercises covering the parts of speech, from the University of Ottawa.

(*pain, mystery, simplicity*), a place (*city, Washington, ocean, Red Sea*), or an idea (*reality, peace, success*).

Form

Most nouns form the **possessive** to indicate ownership or source. Singular nouns usually add an apostrophe plus *-s* (*Auden's poems*); plural nouns usually add just an apostrophe (*citizens' rights*).

Nouns also change form to distinguish between singular (one) and plural (more than one). Most nouns add *-s* or *-es* for the plural: *earthquake, earthquakes; city, cities*. Some nouns have irregular plurals: *woman, women; child, children*.

ESL Some useful rules for forming noun plurals appear on pages 609–10. The irregular plurals must be memorized. Note that some nouns (noncount nouns) do not form plurals in English—for instance, *equality, anger, oxygen, equipment.* (See pp. 356–57.)

Nouns with *the, a,* and *an*

Nouns are often preceded by *the* or *a* (*an* before a vowel sound: *an apple*). These words are usually called **articles** or **determiners** and always indicate that a noun follows.

ESL See pages 356–58 for the rules governing the use of *the, a/an,* or no article at all before a noun.

gr 12a

Verbs

Meaning

Verbs express an action (*bring, change, grow*), an occurrence (*become, happen*), or a state of being (*be, seem*).

Form

Most verbs can be recognized by two changes in form:

- To indicate a difference between present and past time, most verbs add *-d* or *-ed* to the form listed in the dictionary: *They play today. They played yesterday.* Some verbs indicate past time irregularly: *eat, ate; begin, began* (see p. 303).
- When their subjects are singular nouns or some singular pronouns, all present-time verbs except *be* and *have* add *-s* or *-es* to the dictionary form: *The bear escapes. It runs. The woman begins. She sings.* The *-s* forms of *be* and *have* are *is* and *has.*

(See Chapter 14, pp. 301–17, for more on verb forms.)

Helping verbs

Certain forms of all verbs can combine with other words such as *do, have, can, might, will,* and *must.* These other words are called **helping verbs** or **auxiliary verbs.** In verb phrases such as *could run, will be running,* and *has escaped,* they help to convey time and other attributes. (See Chapter 14, pp. 303, 308–12.)

A note on form and function

In different sentences an English word may serve different functions, take correspondingly different forms, and belong to different word classes. For example:

> The government sent the city aid. [*Aid* functions as a noun.]
> Governments aid citizens. [*Aid* functions as a verb.]

Because words can function in different ways, we must always determine how a particular word works in a sentence before we can identify what part of speech it is. **The *function* of a word in a sentence always determines its part of speech in that sentence.**

Pronouns

Most **pronouns** substitute for nouns and function in sentences as nouns do. In the following sentence all three pronouns—*who, they, their*—refer to *nurses:*

> Some nurses who have families prefer the night shift because they have more time with their children.

The most common pronouns are the **personal pronouns** (*I, you, he, she, it, we, they*) and the **relative pronouns** (*who, whoever, which, that*). Most of these change form to indicate their function in the sentence—for instance, *He called me. I called him back.* (See Chapter 13 for a discussion of these form changes.)

EXERCISE 1
Identifying subjects and predicates

Identify the subject and the predicate of each sentence below. Then use each sentence as a model to create a sentence of your own.

Example:

An important scientist spoke at commencement.

subject predicate
An important scientist | spoke at commencement.
The hungry family ate at the diner.

1. The leaves fell.
2. October ends soon.
3. The orchard owners made apple cider.
4. They examined each apple carefully before using it.
5. Over a hundred people will buy cider at the roadside stand.

EXERCISE 2
Identifying nouns, verbs, and pronouns

In the following sentences identify all words functioning as nouns with *N,* all words functioning as verbs with *V,* and all pronouns with *P.*

Example:

We took the tour through the museum.

P V N N
We took the tour through the museum.

1. The trees died.
2. They caught a disease.
3. The disease was a fungus.
4. It ruined a grove that was treasured.
5. Our great-grandfather planted the grove in the last century.

EXERCISE 3
Using nouns and verbs

Identify each of the following words as a noun, as a verb, or as both. Then create sentences of your own, using each word in each possible function.

Example:

fly

Noun and verb.

The fly sat on the meat loaf. [Noun.] The planes fly low. [Verb.]

1. wish
2. tie
3. swing
4. mail
5. spend
6. label
7. door
8. company
9. whistle
10. glue

3 Forming sentence patterns with nouns and verbs

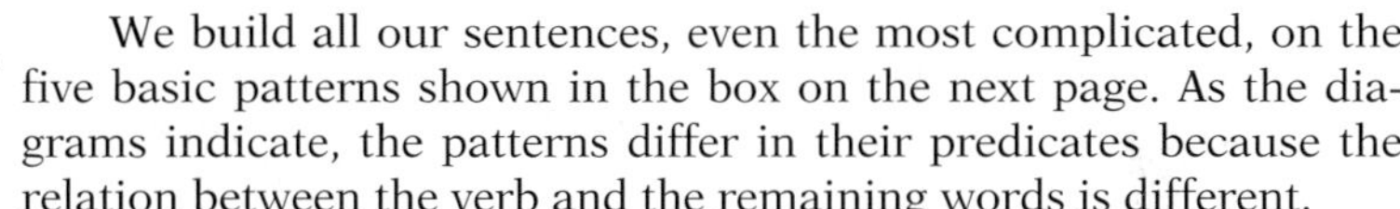

We build all our sentences, even the most complicated, on the five basic patterns shown in the box on the next page. As the diagrams indicate, the patterns differ in their predicates because the relation between the verb and the remaining words is different.

ESL The word order in English sentences may not correspond to word order in the sentences of your native language. English, for instance, strongly prefers subject first, then verb, then any other words, whereas some other languages prefer the verb first. The main exceptions to the word patterns discussed below appear on pages 286–88. See also pages 396–405 on positioning modifiers in sentences.

Pattern 1: The earth trembled.

In the simplest pattern the predicate consists only of the verb. Verbs in this pattern do not require following words to complete

http://webster.commnet.edu/HP/pages/darling/grammar/diagrams/one_pager1.htm Examples of basic sentence patterns, from the Guide to Grammar and Writing.

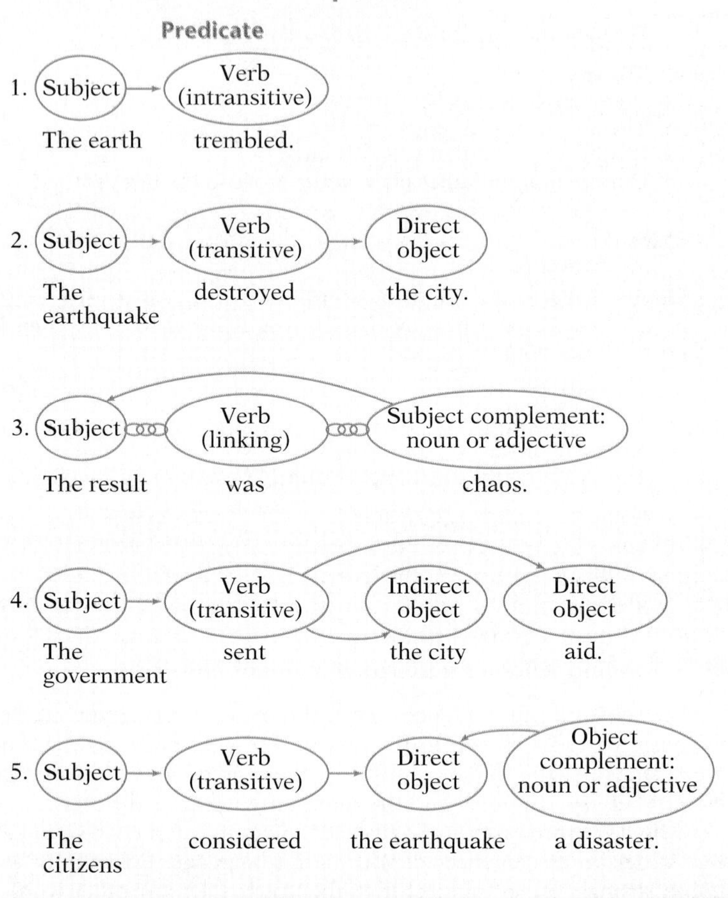

their meaning and thus are called **intransitive** (from Latin words meaning "not passing over").

Subject	Predicate *Intransitive verb*
The earth	trembled.
Mosquitoes	buzz.
The hospital	may close.

Pattern 2: The earthquake destroyed the city.

In pattern 2 the predicate consists of a verb followed by a noun that identifies who or what receives the action of the verb. This noun is a **direct object.** Verbs that require direct objects to complete their meaning are called **transitive** ("passing over"): the verb transfers the action from subject to object.

Subject	Predicate *Transitive verb*	*Direct object*
The earthquake	destroyed	the city.
The people	wanted	peace.
Education	opens	doors.

ESL The distinction between transitive verbs and intransitive verbs like those in pattern 1 is important because only transitive verbs can be used in the passive voice (*The city was destroyed*). (See p. 287.) Your dictionary says whether a verb is transitive or intransitive. Some verbs (*begin, learn, read, write,* and others) are both.

Pattern 3: The result was chaos.

In pattern 3 the predicate also consists of a verb followed by a noun, but here the noun renames or describes the subject. We could write the sentence *The result = chaos.* The verb serving as an equal sign is a **linking verb** because it links the subject and the following description. The linking verbs include *be, seem, appear, become, grow, remain, stay, prove, feel, look, smell, sound,* and *taste.* The word that describes the subject is called a **subject complement** (it complements, or completes, the subject).

Subject	Predicate *Linking verb*	*Subject complement*
The result	was	chaos.
The trees	are	elms.
The man	became	an accountant.

Subject complements in this sentence pattern may also be adjectives, words such as *tall* and *hopeful* (see p. 263):

Subject	Predicate *Linking verb*	*Subject complement*
The result	was	chaotic.
Rents	are	high.
The apartments	seem	expensive.

Pattern 4: The government sent the city aid.

In pattern 4 the predicate consists of a verb followed by two nouns. The second noun, *aid,* is a direct object (see pattern 2). But the first noun, *city,* is an **indirect object,** identifying to or for whom the action of the verb is performed. The direct object and indirect object refer to different things, people, or places.

Subject	Predicate		
	Transitive verb	*Indirect object*	*Direct object*
The government	sent	the city	aid.
Businesses	gave	the museum	money.
One company	offered	its employees	bonuses.

A number of verbs can take indirect objects, including those above and *allow, bring, buy, deny, find, get, leave, make, pay, read, sell, show, teach,* and *write.*

ESL With some verbs expressing action done to or for someone, the indirect object must be turned into a phrase beginning with *to* or *for.* These verbs include *admit, announce, demonstrate, explain, introduce, mention, prove, recommend, say,* and *suggest.* The *to* or *for* phrase then falls after the direct object.

Faulty The manual explains workers the new procedure.

Revised The manual explains the new procedure to workers.

Pattern 5: The citizens considered the earthquake a disaster.

In pattern 5 the predicate again consists of a verb followed by two nouns. But in this pattern the first noun is a direct object and the second noun renames or describes it. Here the second noun is an **object complement** (it complements, or completes, the object):

Subject	Predicate		
	Transitive verb	*Direct object*	*Object complement*
The citizens	considered	the earthquake	a disaster.
The class	elected	Joan O'Day	president.
Reporters	declared	her	the winner.

Just as a subject complement (pattern 3) renames or describes a subject, so an object complement renames or describes a direct object. Like a subject complement, an object complement may be a noun or an adjective, as below:

Subject	Predicate		
	Transitive verb	*Direct object*	*Object complement*
The citizens	considered	the earthquake	disastrous.
The results	proved	Sweeney	wrong.
Success	makes	some people	nervous.

EXERCISE 4
Identifying sentence patterns

In the following sentences, identify each verb as intransitive, transitive, or linking. Then identify each direct object (DO), indirect object (IO), subject complement (SC), and object complement (OC).

Example:

Children give their parents both headaches and pleasures.
Give is a transitive verb.

IO (parents), DO (headaches), DO (pleasures)

Children give their parents both headaches and pleasures.

1. Many people find New Orleans exciting.
2. Tourists flock there each year.
3. Usually they visit the French Quarter first.
4. The Quarter's old buildings are magnificent.
5. In the Quarter, artists sell tourists their paintings.

EXERCISE 5
Creating sentences

Create sentences by using each of the following verbs in the pattern indicated. (For the meanings of the abbreviations, see the directions for Exercise 4.) You may want to change the form of the verb.

Example:

give (S-V-IO-DO)
Sam gave his brother a birthday card.

1. laugh (S-V)
2. elect (S-V-DO-OC)
3. steal (S-V-DO)
4. catch (S-V-DO)
5. bring (S-V-IO-DO)
6. seem (S-V-SC)
7. call (S-V-DO-OC)
8. become (S-V-SC)
9. buy (S-V-IO-DO)
10. study (S-V)

12b Expanding the basic sentence with single words

Most of the sentences we read, write, or speak are more complex and also more informative and interesting than those examined so far. Most sentences contain one or more of the following: (1) modifying words (discussed here); (2) word groups, called phrases and clauses (p. 266); and (3) combinations of two or more words or word groups of the same kind (p. 282).

1 Using adjectives and adverbs

The simplest expansion of sentences occurs when we add modifying words to describe or limit the nouns and verbs. Modifying words add details:

Recently, the earth trembled.

http://owl.english.purdue.edu/Files/81.html Information on adjectives and adverbs, including examples and exercises, from the Purdue Online Writing Lab.

The earthquake nearly destroyed the old city.
The immediate result was chaos.
The federal government soon sent the city aid.
The grant was a very generous one but disappeared too quickly.

The underlined words represent two different parts of speech:

- **Adjectives** describe or modify nouns and pronouns. They specify which one, what quality, or how many.

old city — adjective noun
generous one — adjective pronoun
two pears — adjective noun

- **Adverbs** describe or modify verbs, adjectives, other adverbs, and whole groups of words. They specify when, where, how, and to what extent.

nearly destroyed — adverb verb
too quickly — adverb adverb
very generous — adverb adjective
Unfortunately, taxes will rise. — adverb, word group

An *-ly* ending often signals an adverb, but not always: *friendly* is an adjective; *never, not,* and *always* are adverbs. The only way to tell whether a word is an adjective or an adverb is to determine what it modifies.

Adjectives and adverbs appear in three forms:

- The **positive** form is the basic form, the one listed in the dictionary: *good, green, angry; badly, quickly, angrily.*
- The **comparative** form indicates a greater degree of the quality named by the word: *better, greener, angrier; worse, more quickly, more angrily.*
- The **superlative** form indicates the greatest degree of the quality named: *best, greenest, angriest; worst, most quickly, most angrily.*

(For further discussion of these forms, see p. 352.)

2 Using other words as modifiers

Nouns and special forms of verbs may sometimes serve as modifiers of other nouns. In combinations such as *office buildings, Thanksgiving prayer,* and *shock hazard,* the first noun modifies the second. In combinations such as *singing birds, corrected papers,* and *broken finger,* the first word is a verb form modifying the following noun. (These modifying verb forms are discussed in more detail on pp. 269–71.) Again, the part of speech to which we assign a word always depends on its function in a sentence.

EXERCISE 6
Identifying and using adjectives and adverbs

Identify the adjectives and adverbs in the following sentences. Then use each sentence as a model for creating a sentence of your own.

Example:

The red barn sat uncomfortably among modern buildings.

adjective adverb adjective
The red barn sat uncomfortably among modern buildings.
The little girl complained loudly to her busy mother.

1. The icy rain created glassy patches on the roads.
2. Happily, children played in the slippery streets.
3. Fortunately, no cars ventured out.
4. Wise parents stayed indoors where they could be warm and dry.
5. The dogs slept soundly near the warm radiators.

EXERCISE 7
Using verb forms as modifiers

Use each of the following verb forms to modify a noun in a sentence of your own.

Example:

smoking
Only a smoking cigar remained.

1. scrambled
2. twitching
3. rambling
4. typed
5. painted
6. written
7. charging
8. ripened
9. known
10. driven

EXERCISE 8
Sentence combining: Single-word modifiers

To practice expanding the basic sentence patterns with single-word modifiers, combine each group of sentences below into one sentence. You will have to delete and rearrange words.

Example:

New Orleans offers tourists food. New Orleans offers food proudly. The food is delicious.

New Orleans proudly offers tourists delicious food.

1. The turn of the century ushered in technology and materials. The century was the twentieth. The technology was improved. The materials were new.
2. A skeleton made the construction of skyscrapers possible. The skeleton was sturdy. It was made of steel.
3. By 1913 the Woolworth Building, with its ornaments, stood 760 feet (55 stories). The building was towering. The ornaments were Gothic.

4. At 1450 feet the Sears Tower in Chicago doubles the height of the Woolworth Building. The doubling is now. The Woolworth height is puny. The puniness is relative.
5. Skyscrapers would not have been practical if Elisha Graves Otis had not built the elevator in 1857. It was the first elevator. The elevator was safe. It served passengers.

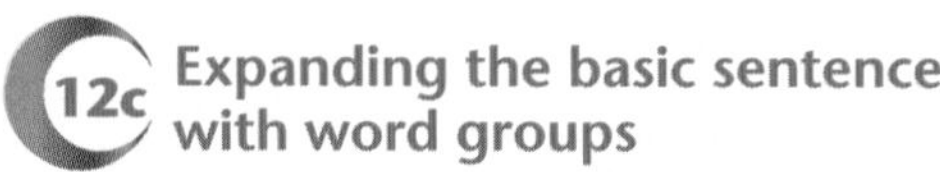

12c Expanding the basic sentence with word groups

Most sentences we read or write contain whole word groups that serve as nouns and modifiers. Such word groups enable us to combine several bits of information into one sentence and to make the relations among them clear, as in this sentence:

> subject (skaters) — verb (sought) — object (safety)
>
> When the ice cracked, the skaters, fearing an accident, sought safety at the lake's edge.

Attached to *skaters sought safety,* the skeleton of this sentence, are three groups of words that add related information: *When the ice cracked, fearing an accident,* and *at the lake's edge.* These constructions are phrases and clauses:

- A **phrase** is a group of related words that lacks either a subject or a predicate or both: *fearing an accident, at the lake's edge.*
- A **clause** contains both a subject and a predicate: *When the ice cracked* and *the skaters sought safety* are both clauses, though only the second can stand alone as a sentence.

1 Using prepositional phrases

Prepositions are connecting words. Unlike nouns, verbs, and modifiers, which may change form, prepositions never change form. As the box opposite shows, many prepositions signal relationships of time or space; others signal relationships such as addition, comparison or contrast, cause or effect, concession, condition, opposition, possession, and source. Notice that some prepositions consist of more than one word.

Note Some of the prepositions listed as signaling time or space also serve other functions and could be listed in the third column as

http://webster.commnet.edu/HP/pages/darling/grammar/prepositions.htm
Discussion and examples of prepositions and prepositional phrases, from the Guide to Grammar and Writing.

Common prepositions

Time or space (position or direction)		Other relationships (addition, comparison, etc.)
about	into	according to
above	near	as
across	next to	as for
after	off	aside from
against	on	because of
along	onto	concerning
along with	on top of	despite
among	out	except
around	out of	except for
at	outside	excepting
before	over	in addition to
behind	past	in spite of
below	since	instead of
beneath	through	like
beside	throughout	of
between	till	on account of
beyond	to	regarding
by	toward	regardless of
down	under	unlike
during	underneath	with
for	until	without
from	up	
in	upon	
inside	within	
inside of		

well. *By,* for instance, may signal time (*by tomorrow*) and source (*by William Faulkner*).

A preposition connects a noun or pronoun to another word in the sentence: *Robins nest in trees.* The noun or pronoun so connected (*trees*) is the **object of the preposition.** The preposition plus its object and any modifiers is a **prepositional phrase:**

Preposition	Object
on	the surface
with	great satisfaction
upon	entering the room
from	where you are standing
except for	ten employees

Prepositions normally come before their objects. But in speech and informal writing the preposition sometimes comes after its object: *What do you want to see him about?*

Prepositional phrases function as adjectives (modifying nouns) or as adverbs (modifying verbs, adjectives, or other adverbs). As modifiers, they add details that make sentences clearer and more interesting for readers.

> Life on a raft was an opportunity for adventure.
> (adjective phrase: on a raft; adjective phrase: for adventure)
>
> Huck Finn rode the raft by choice.
> (adverb phrase: by choice)

ESL The meanings and idiomatic uses of English prepositions can be difficult to master; most must be memorized or looked up in a dictionary (a list of ESL dictionaries appears on p. 587). See pages 316–17 for the uses of prepositions in two-word verbs such as *look after* and pages 572–73 for the uses of prepositions in idioms.

Punctuating prepositional phrases

gr 12c

Since a prepositional phrase lacks a subject and a predicate, it should not be punctuated as a complete sentence. If it is, the result is a **sentence fragment** (Chapter 17):

> **Fragment** Toward the sun.

The phrase must be attached to another group of words containing both a subject and a predicate:

> **Revised** The plane turned toward the sun.

A prepositional phrase that introduces a sentence is set off with punctuation, usually a comma, unless it is short (see p. 471):

> According to the newspaper and other sources, the governor has reluctantly decided to veto the bill.
>
> In 1865 the Civil War finally ended.

A prepositional phrase that interrupts or concludes a sentence is *not* set off with punctuation when it is essential to the meaning of the word or words it modifies (see p. 473):

> The announcement of a tuition increase surprised no one.
>
> Students expected new fees for the coming year.

When an interrupting or concluding prepositional phrase is *not* essential to meaning, but merely adds information to the sentence, then it *is* set off with punctuation, usually a comma or commas (see p. 473):

> The governor, according to the newspaper and other sources, has reluctantly decided to veto the bill.

As all the preceding examples illustrate, a preposition and its object are not separated by a comma.

EXERCISE 9
Identifying prepositional phrases

Identify the prepositional phrases in the following passage. Indicate whether each phrase functions as an adjective or as an adverb, and name the word that the phrase modifies.

Example:

After an hour I finally arrived at the home of my professor.

adverb — adverb — adjective
After an hour I finally arrived at the home of my professor.

The woman in blue socks ran from the police officer on horseback. She darted down Bates Street and then into the bus depot. At the depot the police officer dismounted from his horse and searched for the woman. The entrance to the depot and the interior were filled with travelers, however, and in the crowd he lost sight of the woman. She, meanwhile, had boarded a bus on the other side of the depot and was riding across town.

EXERCISE 10
Sentence combining: Prepositional phrases

To practice writing sentences with prepositional phrases, combine each group of sentences below into one sentence that includes one or two prepositional phrases. You will have to add, delete, and rearrange words. Some items have more than one possible answer.

Example:

I will start working. The new job will pay the minimum wage.
I will start working at a new job for the minimum wage.

1. The slow loris protects itself well. Its habitat is Southeast Asia. It possesses a poisonous chemical.
2. To frighten predators, the loris exudes the chemical. The chemical comes from a gland. The gland is on the loris's upper arm.
3. The loris's chemical is highly toxic. The chemical is not like a skunk's spray. Even small quantities of the chemical are toxic.
4. A tiny dose can affect a human. The dose would get in the mouth. The human would be sent into shock.
5. Predators probably can sense the toxin. They detect it at a distance. They use their nasal organs.

2 Using verbals and verbal phrases

Verbals are special verb forms such as *smoking* or *hidden* or *to win* that can function as nouns (*smoking is dangerous*) or as modifiers (*the hidden money, the urge to win*).

http://webster.commnet.edu/HP/pages/darling/grammar/verbs.htm#verbal Discussion of verbals, from the Guide to Grammar and Writing.

http://owl.english.purdue.edu/Files/5.html Information and exercises covering verbals, from the Purdue Online Writing Lab.

Note A verbal *cannot* stand alone as the complete verb in the predicate of a sentence. For example, *The man smoking* and *The money hidden* are not sentences but sentence fragments (see p. 365). Any verbal must combine with a helping verb to serve as the predicate of a sentence: *The man was smoking. The money is hidden.*

Because verbals cannot serve alone as sentence predicates, they are sometimes called **nonfinite verbs** (in essence, they are "unfinished"). **Finite verbs,** in contrast, can make an assertion or express a state of being without a helping verb (they are "finished"). Either of two tests can distinguish finite and nonfinite verbs.

Tests for finite and nonfinite verbs (verbals)

Test 1 Does the word require a change in form when a third-person subject changes from singular to plural?

Yes Finite verb: *It sings. They sing.*

No Nonfinite verb (verbal): *bird singing, birds singing*

Test 2 Does the word require a change in form to show the difference in present, past, and future?

Yes Finite verb: *It sings. It sang. It will sing.*

No Nonfinite verb (verbal): *The bird singing is/was/will be a robin.*

There are three kinds of verbals: participles, gerunds, and infinitives.

Participles

All verbs have two participle forms, a present and a past. The **present participle** consists of the dictionary form of the verb plus the ending *-ing: beginning, completing, hiding*. The **past participle** of most verbs consists of the dictionary form plus *-d* or *-ed: believed, completed.* Some common verbs have an irregular past participle: *begun, hidden.* (See pp. 303–06.)

Both present and past participles function as adjectives to modify nouns and pronouns:

Shopping malls sometimes frustrate shoppers.

Shoppers may feel trapped.

ESL For verbs expressing feeling, the present and past participles have different meanings: *It was a boring lecture. The bored students slept.* See page 355.

Gerunds

Gerund is the name given to the *-ing* form of the verb when it serves as a noun:

> subject
> Strolling through stores can exhaust the hardiest shopper.
>
> object
> Many children learn to hate shopping.

Present participles and gerunds can be distinguished *only* by their function in a sentence. If the *-ing* form functions as an adjective (*a teaching degree*), it is a present participle. If the *-ing* form functions as a noun (*Teaching is difficult*), it is a gerund.

ESL Always use a gerund rather than any other verb form as the object of a preposition: *Diners are prohibited from smoking.* See also the ESL note below.

Infinitives

The **infinitive** is the *to* form of the verb, the dictionary form preceded by the infinitive marker *to: to begin, to hide, to run.* Infinitives may function as adjectives, nouns, or adverbs:

> The question to answer is why shoppers endure mall fatigue.
> adjective
>
> The solution for mall fatigue is to leave.
> noun
>
> Still, shoppers find it difficult to quit.
> adverb

ESL Infinitives and gerunds may follow some verbs and not others and may differ in meaning after a verb: *The singer stopped to sing. The singer stopped singing.* (See pp. 313–15.)

Verbal phrases

Participles, gerunds, and infinitives—like other forms of verbs—may take subjects, objects, or complements, and they may be modified by adverbs. The verbal and all the words immediately related to it make up a **verbal phrase.** With verbal phrases, we can create concise sentences packed with information.

Like participles, **participial phrases** always serve as adjectives, modifying nouns or pronouns:

> Buying things, most shoppers feel themselves in control.
>
> They make selections determined by personal taste.

Gerund phrases, like gerunds, always serve as nouns:

subject

Shopping for clothing and other items satisfies personal needs.

object of preposition

Malls are good at creating such needs.

Infinitive phrases may serve as nouns, adverbs, or adjectives:

sentence subject — subject complement

To design a mall is to create an artificial environment.

noun phrase — noun phrase

Malls are designed to make shoppers feel safe.

adverb phrase

The environment supports the impulse to shop for oneself.

adjective phrase

Note When an infinitive or infinitive phrase serves as a noun after verbs such as *hear, let, help, make, see,* and *watch,* the infinitive marker *to* is omitted: *We all heard her tell* [not *to tell*] *the story.*

gr 12c

Punctuating verbals and verbal phrases

Verbal phrases punctuated as complete sentences are sentence fragments (Chapter 17). A complete sentence must contain a subject and a finite verb (p. 270):

Fragment Treating the patients kindly.

Revised She treats the patients kindly.

A verbal or verbal phrase serving as a modifier is almost always set off with a comma when it introduces a sentence (see p. 471):

To pay tuition, some students work at two jobs.

A modifying verbal or verbal phrase that interrupts or concludes a sentence is *not* set off with punctuation when it is essential to the meaning of the word or words it modifies (see p. 473):

Jobs paying well are hard to find.

When an interrupting or concluding verbal modifier is *not* essential to meaning, but merely adds information to the sentence, it *is* set off with punctuation, usually a comma or commas (see p. 473):

One good job, paying twelve dollars an hour, was filled in fifteen minutes.

EXERCISE 11
Identifying verbals and verbal phrases

The following sentences contain participles, gerunds, and infinitives as well as participial, gerund, and infinitive phrases. First identify each verbal or verbal phrase. Then indicate whether it is used as an adjective, an adverb, or a noun.

Example:

Laughing, the talk-show host prodded her guest to talk.

adjective adverb
Laughing, the talk-show host prodded her guest to talk.

1. Written in 1850 by Nathaniel Hawthorne, *The Scarlet Letter* tells the story of Hester Prynne.
2. Shunned by the community, Hester endures her loneliness.
3. Hester is humble enough to withstand her Puritan neighbors' cutting remarks.
4. Despite the cruel treatment, the determined young woman refuses to leave her home.
5. By living a life of patience and unselfishness, Hester eventually becomes the community's angel.

EXERCISE 12
Sentence combining: Verbals and verbal phrases

To practice writing sentences with verbals and verbal phrases, combine each pair of sentences below into one sentence. You will have to add, delete, change, and rearrange words. Each item has more than one possible answer.

Example:

My father took pleasure in mean pranks. For instance, he hid the neighbor's cat.

My father took pleasure in mean pranks such as hiding the neighbor's cat.

1. Air pollution is a health problem. It affects millions of Americans.
2. The air has been polluted mainly by industries and automobiles. It contains toxic chemicals.
3. Environmentalists pressure politicians. They think politicians should pass stricter laws.
4. Many politicians waver. They are not necessarily against environmentalism.
5. The problems are too complex. They cannot be solved easily.

3 Using absolute phrases

Absolute phrases consist of a noun or pronoun and a participle, plus any modifiers:

absolute phrase
Many ethnic groups, their own place established, are making way for new arrivals.

http://webster.commnet.edu/HP/pages/darling/grammar/phrases.htm#absolute Discussion and examples of absolute phrases, from the Guide to Grammar and Writing.

absolute phrase — absolute phrase

Their native lands left behind, an uncertain future looming, immigrants face many obstacles.

These phrases are called *absolute* (from a Latin word meaning "free") because they have no specific grammatical connection to a noun, verb, or any other word in the rest of the sentence. Instead, they modify the entire rest of the sentence, adding information or clarifying meaning.

Notice that absolute phrases, unlike participial phrases, always contain a subject. Compare the following:

participial phrase

For many immigrants learning English, the language introduces American culture.

absolute phrase

The immigrants having learned English, their opportunities widen.

We often omit the participle from an absolute phrase when it is some form of *be,* such as *being* or *having been:*

Two languages [being] at hand, bilingual citizens in fact have many cultural and occupational advantages.

gr 12c

Punctuating absolute phrases

Absolute phrases are always set off from the rest of the sentence with punctuation, usually a comma or commas (see also p. 478):

Their future more secure, these citizens will make room for new arrivals.

These citizens, their future more secure, will make room for new arrivals.

EXERCISE 13
Sentence combining: Absolute phrases

To practice writing sentences with absolute phrases, combine each pair of sentences below into one sentence that contains an absolute phrase. You will have to add, delete, change, and rearrange words.

Example:

The flower's petals wilted. It looked pathetic.
Its petals wilted, the flower looked pathetic.

1. Her husband died in office. Lindy Boggs was elected to his seat as a representative from Louisiana.
2. Representative Barbara Jordan spoke at the national Democratic convention. Her voice thundered through the auditorium.

3. A vacancy had occurred. Sandra Day O'Connor was appointed the first female Supreme Court justice.
4. Geraldine Ferraro's face beamed. She enjoyed the crowd's cheers after her nomination for Vice President.
5. The election was won. Susan Molinari was a US representative from New York.

4 Using subordinate clauses

A **clause** is any group of words that contains both a subject and a predicate. There are two kinds of clauses, and the distinction between them is important:

- A **main** or **independent clause** makes a complete statement and can stand alone as a sentence: *The sky darkened.*
- A **subordinate** or **dependent clause** is just like a main clause *except* that it begins with a subordinating word: *when the sky darkened; whoever calls.* The subordinating word reduces the clause to a single part of speech: an adjective, an adverb, or a noun. Because it only modifies or names something, a subordinate clause cannot stand alone as a sentence (see the discussion of punctuation on p. 278). (The word *subordinate* means "secondary" or "controlled by another." It comes from the Latin *sub,* "under," and *ordo,* "order.")

The following examples show the differences between main and subordinate clauses:

[main clause] [main clause]
The school teaches parents. It is unusual.

[subordinate clause] [main clause]
Because the school teaches parents, it is unusual.

[main clause] [main clause]
Some parents avoid their children's schools. They are often illiterate.

[main clause]
Parents who are illiterate often avoid their children's schools.
[subordinate clause: who are illiterate]

Two kinds of subordinating words introduce subordinate clauses: subordinating conjunctions and relative pronouns.

Information on clauses:

http://webster.commnet.edu/HP/pages/darling/grammar/clauses.htm
From the Guide to Grammar and Writing.

http://www.uottawa.ca/academic/arts/writcent/hypergrammar/bldcls.html#clause From the University of Ottawa.

Subordinating conjunctions

Subordinating conjunctions, like prepositions, never change form in any way. In the following box they are arranged by the relationships they signal. (Some fit in more than one group.)

Common subordinating conjunctions

Cause or effect	Condition	Comparison or contrast	Space or time
as	even if	as	after
because	if	as if	as long as
in order that	if only	as though	before
since	provided	rather than	now that
so that	since	than	once
	unless	whereas	since
Concession	when	whether	till
although	whenever	while	until
as if	whether		when
even if		**Purpose**	whenever
even though		in order that	where
though		so that	wherever
		that	while

ESL Subordinating conjunctions convey their meaning without help from other function words, such as the coordinating conjunctions *and, but, for,* or *so* (p. 282).

Faulty Even though the parents are illiterate, but their children may read well. [*Even though* and *but* have the same meaning, so both are not needed.]

Revised Even though the parents are illiterate, their children may read well.

Relative pronouns

Unlike subordinating conjunctions, **relative pronouns** usually act as subjects or objects in their own clauses, and two of them (*who* and *whoever*) change form accordingly (see p. 293).

Information on subordinating conjunctions:

http://www.uottawa.ca/academic/arts/writcent/hypergrammar/conjunct.html From the University of Ottawa.

http://webster.commnet.edu/HP/pages/darling/grammar/conjunctions.htm#subordinating_conjunctions From the Guide to Grammar and Writing.

Relative pronouns

which	what	who (whose, whom)
that	whatever	whoever (whomever)

Subordinate clauses

Subordinate clauses function as adjectives, adverbs, or nouns.

Adjective clauses

Adjective clauses modify nouns and pronouns, providing necessary or helpful information about them. They usually begin with the relative pronoun *who, whom, whose, which,* or *that,* although a few adjective clauses begin with *when* or *where* (standing for *in which, on which,* or *at which*). The pronoun is the subject or object of the clause it begins. The clause ordinarily falls immediately after the noun or pronoun it modifies:

Parents who are illiterate often have bad memories of school.

Schools that involve parents are more successful with children.

One school, which is open year-round, helps parents learn to read.

The school is in a city where the illiteracy rate is high.

Adverb clauses

Like adverbs, **adverb clauses** modify verbs, adjectives, other adverbs, and whole groups of words. They usually tell how, why, when, where, under what conditions, or with what result. They always begin with subordinating conjunctions.

The school began teaching parents when adult illiteracy gained national attention.

At first the program was not as successful as its founders had hoped.

Because it was directed at people who could not read, advertising had to be inventive.

An adverb clause can often be moved around in a sentence with no loss of clarity. Compare the preceding example and this one:

Advertising had to be inventive because it was directed at people who could not read.

gr
12c

Noun clauses

Noun clauses function as subjects, objects, and complements in sentences. They begin with *that, what, whatever, who, whom, whoever, whomever, when, where, whether, why,* or *how.* Unlike adjective and adverb clauses, noun clauses *replace* a word (a noun) within a clause; therefore, they can be difficult to identify.

> sentence subject
> Whether the program would succeed depended on door-to-door advertising.
>
> direct object
> Teachers explained in person how the program would work.
>
> sentence subject
> Whoever seemed slightly interested was invited to an open meeting.
>
> object of preposition
> A few parents were anxious about what their children would think.

Elliptical clauses

A subordinate clause that is grammatically incomplete but clear in meaning is an **elliptical clause** (*ellipsis* means "omission"). The meaning of the clause is clear because the missing element can be supplied from the context. Most often the elements omitted are the relative pronouns *that, which,* and *whom* from adjective clauses or the predicate from the second part of a comparison.

> The parents knew their children could read better than they [could read].
>
> Skepticism and fear were among the feelings [that] the parents voiced.
>
> Though [they were] often reluctant at first, about a third of the parents attended the meeting.

Punctuating subordinate clauses

Subordinate clauses punctuated as complete sentences are sentence fragments (Chapter 17). Though a subordinate clause contains a subject and a predicate and thus resembles a complete sentence, it also begins with a subordinating word that makes it into an adjective, adverb, or noun. A single part of speech cannot stand alone as a complete sentence.

Fragment	Because a door was ajar.
Revised	A door was ajar.
Revised	The secret leaked because a door was ajar.

A subordinate clause serving as an adverb is almost always set off with a comma when it introduces a sentence (see p. 471):

> Although the project was almost completed, it lost its funding.

A modifying subordinate clause that interrupts or concludes a main clause is *not* set off with punctuation when it is essential to the meaning of the word or words it modifies (see p. 473):

> The woman who directed the project lost her job.
>
> The project lost its funding because it was not completed on time.

When an interrupting or concluding subordinate clause is *not* essential to meaning, but merely adds information to the sentence, it *is* set off with punctuation, usually a comma or commas (see p. 473):

> The project lost its funding, although it was almost completed.
>
> The director, who holds a Ph.D., sought new funding.

EXERCISE 14
Identifying subordinate clauses

Identify the subordinate clauses in the following sentences. Then indicate whether each is used as an adjective, an adverb, or a noun. If the clause is a noun, indicate what function it performs in the sentence.

> *Example:*
>
> The article explained how one could build an underground house.
>
> noun
>
> The article explained how one could build an underground house. [Object of *explained.*]

1. Scientists who want to catch the slightest signals from space use extremely sensitive receivers.
2. Even though they have had to fight for funding, these scientists have persisted in their research.
3. The research is called SETI, which stands for Search for Extraterrestrial Intelligence.
4. The theory is that intelligent beings in space are trying to get in touch with us.
5. The challenge is to guess what frequency these beings would use to send signals.

EXERCISE 15
Sentence combining: Subordinate clauses

To practice writing sentences with subordinate clauses, combine each pair of main clauses below into one sentence. Use either subordinating conjunctions or relative pronouns as appropriate, referring to the lists on pages 276 and 277 if necessary. You will have to add, delete, and rearrange words. Each item has more than one possible answer.

> *Example:*
>
> She did not have her tire irons with her. She could not change her bicycle tire.

Because she did not have her tire irons with her, she could not change her bicycle tire.

1. Moviegoers expect something. Movie sequels should be as exciting as the original films.
2. A few sequels are good films. Most are poor imitations of the originals.
3. A sequel to a blockbuster film arrives in the theater. Crowds quickly line up to see it.
4. Viewers pay to see the same villains and heroes. They remember these characters fondly.
5. Afterward, viewers often grumble about filmmakers. The filmmakers rehash tired plots and characters.

5 Using appositives

An **appositive** is usually a noun that renames another noun nearby, most often the noun just before the appositive. (The word *appositive* derives from a Latin word that means "placed near to" or "applied to.") An appositive phrase includes modifiers as well.

> Bizen ware, a dark stoneware, has been produced in Japan since the fourteenth century.

> The name Bizen comes from the location of the kilns used to fire the pottery.

All appositives can replace the words they refer to: *A dark stoneware has been produced in Japan.*

Appositives are often introduced by words and phrases such as *or, that is, such as, for example,* and *in other words:*

> Bizen ware is used in the Japanese tea ceremony, that is, the Zen Buddhist observance that links meditation and art.

Appositives are economical alternatives to adjective clauses containing a form of *be:*

> Bizen ware, [which is] a dark stoneware, has been produced in Japan since the fourteenth century.

Although most appositives are nouns that rename other nouns, they may also be and rename other parts of speech, such as the verb *thrown* in the sentence below:

> The pottery is thrown, or formed on a potter's wheel.

http://owl.english.purdue.edu/Files/71.html Information and exercises on appositives, from the Purdue Online Writing Lab.

Punctuating appositives

Appositives punctuated as complete sentences are sentence fragments (see Chapter 17). To correct such fragments, you can usually connect the appositive to the main clause containing the word referred to:

Fragment An exceedingly tall man with narrow shoulders.

Revised He stood next to a basketball player, an exceedingly tall man with narrow shoulders.

An appositive is *not* set off with punctuation when it is essential to the meaning of the word it refers to (see p. 475):

The verb *howl* comes from the Old English verb *houlen*.

When an appositive is *not* essential to the meaning of the word it refers to, it *is* set off with punctuation, usually a comma or commas (see p. 475):

An aged elm, the tree was struck by lightning.
The tree, an aged elm, was struck by lightning.
Lightning struck the tree, an aged elm.

A nonessential appositive is sometimes set off with a dash or dashes, especially when it contains commas (see p. 523):

Three people—Will, Carolyn, and Tom—object to the new procedure.

A concluding appositive is sometimes set off with a colon (see p. 520):

Two principles guide the judge's decisions: justice and mercy.

EXERCISE 16
Sentence combining: Appositives

To practice writing sentences with appositives, combine each pair of sentences into one sentence that contains an appositive. You will have to delete and rearrange words. Some items have more than one possible answer.

Example:

The largest land animal is the elephant. The elephant is also one of the most intelligent animals.

The largest land animal, the elephant, is also one of the most intelligent animals.

1. Some people perform amazing feats when they are very young. These people are geniuses from birth.
2. John Stuart Mill was a British philosopher. He had written a history of Rome by age seven.
3. Two great artists began their work at age four. They were Paul Klee and Gustav Mahler.

4. Mahler was a Bohemian composer of intensely emotional works. He was also the child of a brutal father.
5. Paul Klee was a Swiss painter. As a child he was frightened by his own drawings of devils.

12d Compounding words, phrases, and clauses

A **compound construction** combines words that are closely related and equally important. It makes writing clearer and more economical because it pulls together linked information.

> Headaches can be controlled by biofeedback. Heart rate can be controlled by biofeedback.
>
> compound subject
>
> Headaches and heart rate can be controlled by biofeedback.

> Without medication, biofeedback cures headaches. It steadies heart rate. It lowers blood pressure. It relaxes muscles.
>
> compound predicate
>
> Without medication, biofeedback cures headaches, steadies heart rate, lowers blood pressure, and relaxes muscles.

1 Using coordinating conjunctions and correlative conjunctions

Two kinds of words create compound constructions: coordinating and correlative conjunctions. **Coordinating conjunctions** are few and do not change form. In the following box the relationship that each conjunction signals appears in parentheses:

Coordinating conjunctions

and (*addition*)	nor (*alternative*)	for (*cause*)	yet (*contrast*)
but (*contrast*)	or (*alternative*)	so (*effect*)	

To remember the coordinating conjunctions, use the word *fanboys: for, and, nor, but, or, yet, so.*

The coordinating conjunctions *and, but, nor,* and *or* always connect words or word groups of the same kind—that is, two or more

http://webster.commnet.edu/HP/pages/darling/grammar/conjunctions.htm
Discussion of using conjunctions to combine parts of sentences, from the Guide to Grammar and Writing.

nouns, verbs, adjectives, adverbs, phrases, subordinate clauses, or main clauses:

> Biofeedback or simple relaxation can relieve headaches.
> Biofeedback is effective but costly.
> Relaxation also works well, and it is inexpensive.
> Relaxation is effective yet inexpensive.

The conjunctions *for* and *so* connect only main clauses. *For* indicates cause; *so* indicates effect.

> Biofeedback can be costly, for the training involves technical equipment and specialists.
>
> Relaxation can be difficult to learn alone, so some people do seek help from specialists.

Some coordinating conjunctions pair up with other words to form **correlative conjunctions.** In the following box the relationship each conjunction signals appears in parentheses:

Common correlative conjunctions

both . . . and (*addition*)
not only . . . but also (*addition*)
not . . . but (*substitution*)
either . . . or (*alternative*)
neither . . . nor (*negation*)
whether . . . or (*alternative*)
as . . . as (*comparison*)

> Both biofeedback and relaxation can relieve headaches.
>
> The techniques require neither psychotherapy nor medication.
>
> The headache sufferer learns not only to recognize the causes of headaches but also to control those causes.

Punctuating compounded words, phrases, and clauses

Two words, phrases, or subordinate clauses that are connected by a coordinating conjunction are *not* separated by a comma (see p. 486):

> The library needs renovation and rebuilding.
>
> The work will begin after the spring term ends but before the fall term begins.

When two *main* clauses are joined into one sentence with a coordinating conjunction, a comma precedes the conjunction (see p. 469):

> The project will be lengthy, and everyone will suffer some inconvenience.

When two main clauses are joined *without* a coordinating conjunction, they must be separated with a semicolon to avoid the error called a comma splice (see p. 491):

> The work cannot be delayed; it's already overdue.

In a series of three or more items, commas separate the items, with *and* usually preceding the last item (see p. 479):

> The renovated library will feature new study carrels, new shelving, and a larger reference section.

Semicolons sometimes separate the items in a series if they are long or contain commas (see p. 496).

A comma also separates two or more adjectives when they modify a noun equally and are not joined by a coordinating conjunction (see p. 480):

> Cracked, crumbling walls will be repaired.

The comma does *not* separate adjectives when the one nearer the noun is more closely related to it in meaning (see p. 480):

> New reading lounges will replace the old ones.

2 Using conjunctive adverbs

One other kind of connecting word, called a **conjunctive adverb,** relates only main clauses, not words, phrases, or subordinate clauses. In the following box the conjunctive adverbs are arranged by the relationships they signal:

Common conjunctive adverbs

Addition	Comparison or contrast	Cause or effect
also	however	accordingly
besides	in comparison	as a result
further	in contrast	consequently
furthermore	instead	hence
in addition	likewise	similarly
incidentally	nevertheless	therefore
moreover	nonetheless	thus
	otherwise	
Emphasis		**Time**
certainly		finally
indeed		meanwhile
in fact		next
still		now
undoubtedly		then
		thereafter

It's important to distinguish between conjunctive adverbs and conjunctions (coordinating and subordinating) because they demand different punctuation (see the discussion below). Conjunctive adverbs are *adverbs:* they describe the relation of ideas in two clauses, and, like most adverbs, they can move around in their clause:

> Relaxation techniques have improved; however, few people know them.
>
> Relaxation techniques have improved; few people know them, however.

In contrast, conjunctions bind two clauses into a single grammatical unit, and they cannot be moved:

> Although few people know them, relaxation techniques have improved. [The subordinating conjunction can't be moved: *Few people know them although, relaxation techniques have improved.*]
>
> Relaxation techniques have improved, but few people know them. [The coordinating conjunction can't be moved: *Relaxation techniques have improved, few people know them but.*]

gr 12d

Note Some connecting words have more than one use. *After, before, until,* and some other words may be either prepositions or subordinating conjunctions. Some prepositions, such as *behind, in,* and *outside,* can serve also as adverbs, as in *He trailed behind.* And some conjunctive adverbs, particularly *however,* may also serve simply as adverbs in sentences such as *However much it costs, we must have it.* Again, the part of speech of a word depends on its function in a sentence.

Punctuating sentences containing conjunctive adverbs

Because the two main clauses related by a conjunctive adverb remain independent units, they must be separated by a semicolon (see p. 494). If they are separated by a comma, the result is a comma splice (Chapter 18):

Comma splice	Interest rates rose, therefore, real estate prices declined.
Revised	Interest rates rose**;** therefore, real estate prices declined.

A conjunctive adverb is almost always set off from its clause with a comma or commas (see p. 475):

> The decline was small**;** however**,** some investors were badly hurt.
> The decline was small**;** some investors**,** however**,** were badly hurt.

EXERCISE 17
Sentence combining: Compound constructions

To practice compounding words, phrases, and clauses, combine each pair of sentences below into one sentence that is as short as possible without altering meaning. Use an appropriate connecting word of the type specified in parentheses, referring to the lists on pages 282, 283, and 284 as necessary. You will have to add, delete, and rearrange words, and you may have to change or add punctuation.

Example:

The encyclopedia had some information. It was not detailed enough. (*Conjunctive adverb.*)

The encyclopedia had some information; however, it was not detailed enough.

1. All too often people assume that old age is not a productive time. Many people in their nineties have had great achievements. (*Conjunctive adverb.*)
2. In his nineties the philosopher Bertrand Russell spoke vigorously for international peace. He spoke for nuclear disarmament. (*Correlative conjunction.*)
3. Grandma Moses did not retire to an easy chair. She began painting at age seventy-six and was still going at one hundred. (*Conjunctive adverb.*)
4. The British general George Higginson published his memoirs after he was ninety. The British archaeologist Margaret Murray published her memoirs after she was ninety. (*Coordinating conjunction.*)
5. The architect Frank Lloyd Wright designed his first building at age twenty. He designed his last building at age ninety. (*Coordinating conjunction.*)

gr 12e

12e Changing the usual order of the sentence

So far, all the examples of basic sentence grammar have been similar: the subject of the sentence comes first, naming the performer of the predicate's action, and the predicate comes second. This arrangement of subject and predicate describes most sentences that occur in writing, but four other kinds of sentences alter the basic pattern.

1 Forming questions

The following are the most common ways of forming questions from statements. Remember to end a question with a question mark (p. 464).

- Move the verb or a part of it to the beginning of the question. The verb may be a form of *be:*

The rate is high.	Is the rate high?
We are going now.	Are we going now?

Or the verb may consist of a helping verb and a main verb. Then move the helping verb—or the first helping verb if there's more than one—to the front of the question:

Rates can rise.	Can rates rise?
Rates have been rising.	Have rates been rising?

Questions formed this way can be answered *yes* or *no*.

- If the verb consists of only one word and is not a form of *be,* start the question with a form of *do* and use the plain form of the verb. (These questions can also be answered *yes* or *no*.)

Interest rates rose.	Did interest rates rise?

- Add a question word—*how, what, who, when, where, which, why*—to the beginning of a yes-or-no question. Such a question requires an explanatory answer.

Did rates rise today?	Why did rates rise today?
Is the rate high?	Why is the rate high?
Can rates rise?	How can rates rise?

- Add *who, what,* or *which* to the beginning of a question as the subject. Then the subject-verb order remains the same as in a statement.

Something is the answer.	What is the answer?
Someone can answer.	Who can answer?

2 Forming commands

We construct commands very simply: we merely delete the subject of the sentence, *you:*

Think of options.	Eat your spinach.
Watch the news.	Leave me alone.

3 Writing passive sentences

When the subject of a sentence performs the action of the verb, the verb is in the **active voice:**

subject / active verb / object
Kyong wrote the paper.

We can change the form of the verb and make the object into the subject. The verb in this new sentence is in the **passive voice** because the subject *receives* the action:

subject / passive verb
The paper was written by Kyong.

Only transitive verbs (verbs that take objects) can be expressed in the passive voice. The passive verb consists of a form of *be* plus the past participle of the main verb (*paper was written, absences were excused*). The actual actor (the person performing the action of the verb) may be expressed in a prepositional phrase (as in the example above: *by Kyong*) or may be omitted entirely if it is unknown or unimportant: *The house was flooded.*

(For more on formation of the passive voice, see Chapter 14, pp. 329–31. Also see p. 331 on overuse of the passive voice.)

4 Writing sentences with postponed subjects

The subject follows the predicate in two sentence patterns that are not questions, commands, or passive sentences. In one pattern the normal word order is reversed for emphasis:

Henry comes here. [Normal order.]
Here comes Henry. [Reversed order.]

This pattern occurs most often when the normal order is subject–intransitive verb–adverb. Then the adverb moves to the front of the sentence while subject and predicate reverse order.

A second kind of sentence with a postponed subject begins with either *it* or *there,* as in the following:

verb — subject
There will be eighteen people attending the meeting.

verb — subject
It was surprising that Marinetti was nominated.

The words *there* and *it* in such sentences are **expletives.** Their only function is to postpone the sentence subject. Expletive sentences do have their uses (see p. 583), but they can be unemphatic because they add words and delay the sentence subject. Usually, the normal subject-predicate order is more effective: *Eighteen people will attend the meeting. Marinetti's nomination was surprising.*

ESL When you use an expletive construction, be careful to include *there* or *it.* Only commands and some questions can begin with verbs (see pp. 286–87).

Faulty No one predicted the nomination. Were no polls showing Marinetti ahead.

Revised No one predicted the nomination. There were no polls showing Marinetti ahead.

EXERCISE 18
Forming questions and commands

Form a question and a command from the following noun and verb pairs.

Example:

wood, split
Did you split all this wood?
Split the wood for our fire.

1. water, boil
2. music, stop
3. table, set
4. dice, roll
5. telephone, use

EXERCISE 19
Rewriting passives and expletives

Rewrite each passive sentence below as active, and rewrite each expletive construction to restore normal subject-predicate order. (For additional exercises with the passive voice and with expletives, see pp. 332 and 584.)

1. The screenplay for *Born on the Fourth of July* was cowritten by Ron Kovic.
2. The film was directed by Oliver Stone.
3. Tom Cruise was nominated for an Oscar by the Academy of Motion Picture Arts and Sciences.
4. It is possible that Tom Cruise will never have a better role.
5. There are few such roles available to actors.

12f Classifying sentences

We describe and classify sentences in two different ways: by function (statement, question, command, exclamation, and so on) or by structure. Four basic sentence structures are possible: simple, compound, complex, and compound-complex.

1 Writing simple sentences

A **simple sentence** consists of a single main clause and no subordinate clause:

main clause
Last summer was unusually hot.

main clause
The summer made many farmers leave the area for good or reduced them to bare existence.

http://www.uottawa.ca/academic/arts/writcent/hypergrammar/bldsent.html Discussion of forms and classes of sentences, from the University of Ottawa.

2 Writing compound sentences

A **compound sentence** consists of two or more main clauses and no subordinate clause. The clauses may be joined by a coordinating conjunction and a comma, by a semicolon alone, or by a conjunctive adverb and a semicolon.

main clause / main clause
Last July was hot, but August was even hotter.

main clause / main clause
The hot sun scorched the earth; the lack of rain killed many crops.

3 Writing complex sentences

A **complex sentence** contains one main clause and one or more subordinate clauses:

main clause / subordinate clause
Rain finally came, although many had left the area by then.

main clause / subordinate clause / subordinate clause
Those who remained were able to start anew because the government came to their aid.

Notice that length does not determine whether a sentence is complex or simple; both kinds can be short or long.

4 Writing compound-complex sentences

A **compound-complex sentence** has the characteristics of both the compound sentence (two or more main clauses) and the complex sentence (at least one subordinate clause):

subordinate clause / main clause / main clause
Even though government aid finally came, many people had already been reduced to poverty, and others had been forced to move.

EXERCISE 20
Identifying sentence structures

Mark the main clauses and subordinate clauses in the following sentences. Identify each sentence as simple, compound, complex, or compound-complex.

Example:

The police began patrolling more often when crime in the neighborhood increased.

main clause / subordinate clause
Complex: The police began patrolling more often when crime in the neighborhood increased.

1. Joseph Pulitzer endowed the Pulitzer Prizes.
2. Pulitzer, incidentally, was the publisher of the New York newspaper *The World.*
3. Although the first prizes were for journalism and letters only, Pulitzers are now awarded in music and other areas.
4. For example, Berke Breathed won for his *Bloom County* comic strip, and Roger Reynolds won for his musical composition *Whispers Out of Time.*
5. Although only one prize is usually awarded in each category, in 1989 Taylor Branch's *Parting the Waters* won a history prize, and it shared the honor with James M. McPherson's *Battle Cry of Freedom.*

EXERCISE 21
Sentence combining: Sentence structures

Combine each set of simple sentences below to produce the kind of sentence specified in parentheses. You will have to add, delete, change, and rearrange words.

Example:

The traffic passed the house. It never stopped. (*Complex.*)
The traffic that passed the house never stopped.

1. Recycling takes time. It reduces garbage in landfills. (*Compound.*)
2. People begin to recycle. They generate much less trash. (*Complex.*)
3. White tissues and paper towels biodegrade more easily than dyed ones. People still buy dyed papers. (*Complex.*)
4. The cans are aluminum. They bring recyclers good money. (*Simple.*)
5. Environmentalists have hope. Perhaps more communities will recycle newspaper and glass. Many citizens refuse to participate. (*Compound-complex.*)

CHAPTER 13

Case of Nouns and Pronouns

Case is the form of a noun or pronoun that shows the reader how it functions in a sentence—that is, whether it functions as a subject, as an object, or in some other way. As shown in the box on the facing page, only *I, we, he, she, they,* and *who* change form for each case. Thus these pronouns are the focus of this chapter.

The **subjective case** generally indicates that the word is a subject or a subject complement. (See pp. 255 and 261.)

> subject
> She and Novick discussed the proposal.
>
> subject
> The proposal ignores many who need help.
>
> subject complement
> The disgruntled planners were she and Novick.

The **objective case** generally indicates that the word is the object of a verb or preposition. (See pp. 260–61, 261–62, and 267.)

> object of verb
> The proposal disappointed her and Novick.
>
> object of verb / object of verb
> A colleague whom they respected let them down.
>
> object of preposition
> Their opinion of him suffered.

The **possessive case** generally indicates ownership or source:

> Her counterproposal is in preparation.
> Theirs is the more defensible position.
> The problem is not his.

Information on noun and pronoun case:

http://www.english.uiuc.edu/cws/wworkshop/case.htm From the University of Illinois at Urbana-Champaign.

http://owl.english.purdue.edu/Files/80.html From the Purdue Online Writing Lab.

http://www.clta.on.ca/gram06.htm For ESL writers, from the Centre for Language Training and Assessment.

Case forms of nouns and pronouns

	Subjective	Objective	Possessive
Nouns	boy	boy	boy's
	Jessie	Jessie	Jessie's
Personal pronouns			
Singular			
1st person	I	me	my, mine
2nd person	you	you	your, yours
3rd person	he	him	his
	she	her	her, hers
	it	it	its
Plural			
1st person	we	us	our, ours
2nd person	you	you	your, yours
3rd person	they	them	their, theirs
Relative and interrogative pronouns			
	who	whom	whose
	whoever	whomever	—
	which, that, what	which, that, what	—
Indefinite pronouns			
	everybody	everybody	everybody's

Do not use an apostrophe to form the possessive of personal pronouns: *yours* (not *your's*); *theirs* (not *their's*). (See p. 504. See also p. 500 for the possessive forms of nouns, which do use apostrophes.)

Note Computerized grammar and style checkers have difficulty with noun and pronoun cases: they may flag as incorrect many appropriate uses of nouns and pronouns and yet miss others that are incorrect. Carefully consider any flagged noun or pronoun, and review your sentences on your own as well, deciding for yourself which are correct.

13a Use the subjective case for compound subjects and for subject complements.

In compound subjects use the same pronoun form you would use if the pronoun stood alone as a subject:

subject
She and Novick will persist.

subject
The others may lend their support when she and Novick get a hearing.

A test for case forms in compound constructions

1. Identify a compound construction (one connected by *and, but, or, nor*).

   [He, Him] and [I, me] won the prize.
   The prize went to [he, him] and [I, me].

2. Write a separate sentence for each part of the compound.

   [He, Him] won the prize. [I, Me] won the prize.
   The prize went to [he, him]. The prize went to [I, me].

3. Choose the pronouns that sound correct.

   He won the prize. I won the prize. [Subjective.]
   The prize went to him. The prize went to me. [Objective.]

4. Put the separate sentences back together.

   He and I won the prize.
   The prize went to him and me.

If you are in doubt about the correct form, try the test in the box above.

After a linking verb, such as a form of *be,* a pronoun renaming the subject (a subject complement) should be in the subjective case:

> subject complement
> The ones who care most are she and Novick.
>
> subject complement
> It was they whom the mayor appointed.

If this construction sounds stilted to you, use the more natural order: *She and Novick are the ones who care most. The mayor appointed them.*

13b Use the objective case for compound objects.

In compound objects use the same pronoun form you would use if the pronoun stood alone as an object:

> direct object
> The mayor nominated Zhu and him.
>
> indirect object
> The mayor gave Zhu and him awards.
>
> object of preposition
> Credit goes equally to them and the mayor.

If you are in doubt about the correct form, try the test in the box above.

EXERCISE 1
Choosing between subjective and objective pronouns

From the pairs in brackets, select the appropriate subjective or objective pronoun(s) for each of the following sentences.

Example:

"Between you and [I, me]," the seller said, "this deal is a steal."
"Between you and me," the seller said, "this deal is a steal."

1. Jody and [I, me] had been hunting for jobs.
2. The best employees at our old company were [she, her] and [I, me], so [we, us] expected to find jobs quickly.
3. Between [she, her] and [I, me] the job search had lasted two months, and still it had barely begun.
4. Slowly, [she, her] and [I, me] stopped sharing leads.
5. It was obvious that Jody and [I, me] could not be as friendly as [we, us] had been.

13c Use the appropriate case when the plural pronoun *we* or *us* occurs with a noun.

Whether to use *we* or *us* with a noun depends on the use of the noun:

object of preposition
Freezing weather is welcomed by us skaters.

subject
We skaters welcome freezing weather.

13d In appositives the case of a pronoun depends on the function of the word described or identified.

object of verb / appositive identifies object
The class elected two representatives, DeShawn and me.

subject / appositive identifies subject
Two representatives, DeShawn and I, were elected.

If you are in doubt about case in an appositive, try the sentence without the word the appositive identifies: *The class elected DeShawn and me; DeShawn and I were elected.*

http://www.uottawa.ca/academic/arts/writcent/hypergrammar/prntrcky.html Discussion of pronouns in appositives and other tricky situations, from the University of Ottawa.

EXERCISE 2
Choosing between subjective and objective pronouns

From the pairs in brackets, select the appropriate subjective or objective pronoun for each of the following sentences.

Example:
Convincing [we, us] veterans to vote yes will be difficult.
Convincing us veterans to vote yes will be difficult.

1. Obtaining enough protein is important to [we, us] vegetarians.
2. Instead of obtaining protein from meat, [we, us] vegetarians get our protein from other sources.
3. Jeff claims to know only two vegetarians, Helena and [he, him], who avoid all animal products, including milk.
4. Some of [we, us] vegetarians eat fish, which is a good source of protein.
5. [We, Us] vegetarians in my family, my parents and [I, me], drink milk and eat fish.

13e The case of a pronoun after *than* or *as* in a comparison depends on the meaning.

When a pronoun follows *than* or *as* in a comparison, the case of the pronoun indicates what words may have been omitted. When the pronoun is subjective, it must serve as the subject of an omitted verb:

subject
Some critics like Glass more than he [does].

When the pronoun is objective, it must serve as the object of an omitted verb:

object
Some critics like Glass more than [they like] him.

13f Use the objective case for pronouns that are subjects or objects of infinitives.

subject of infinitive
The school asked him to speak.

object of infinitive
Students chose to invite him.

13g The case of the pronoun *who* depends on its function in its clause.

To choose between *who* and *whom, whoever* and *whomever,* you need to figure out whether the word is a subject or an object.

1 At the beginning of questions use *who* for a subject and *whom* for an object.

subject → Who wrote the policy? object ← Whom does it affect?

To help find the correct case of *who* in a question, try the test in the following box:

A test for *who* versus *whom* in questions

1. Pose the question.

   [Who, Whom] makes that decision?
   [Who, Whom] does one ask?

2. Answer the question, using a personal pronoun. Choose the pronoun that sounds correct, and note its case.

   [She, Her] makes that decision. She makes that decision. [Subjective.]

   One asks [she, her]. One asks her. [Objective.]

3. Use the same case (*who* or *whom*) in the question.

   Who makes that decision? [Subjective.]
   Whom does one ask? [Objective.]

Note In speech the subjective case *who* is commonly used whenever it is the first word of a question, regardless of whether it is a subject or an object. But formal writing requires a distinction between the forms:

Spoken Who should we credit?

Written Whom should we credit? (object)

http://webster.commnet.edu/HP/pages/darling/grammar/pronouns.htm#who Information about *who* versus *whom,* from the Guide to Grammar and Writing.

2 In subordinate clauses use *who* and *whoever* for all subjects, *whom* and *whomever* for all objects.

The case of a pronoun in a subordinate clause depends on its function in the clause, regardless of whether the clause itself functions as a subject, an object, or a modifier:

> subject
> Credit whoever wrote the policy.
>
> object
> Research should reveal whom to credit.

If you have trouble determining which form to choose, try the test in the following box:

A test for *who* versus *whom* in subordinate clauses

1. Locate the subordinate clause.

   Few people know [who, whom] they should ask.
   They are unsure [who, whom] makes the decision.

2. Rewrite the subordinate clause as a separate sentence, substituting a personal pronoun for *who, whom.* Choose the pronoun that sounds correct, and note its case.

   They should ask [she, her]. They should ask her. [Objective.]
   [She, her] makes the decision. She makes the decision. [Subjective.]

3. Use the same case (*who* or *whom*) in the subordinate clause.

   Few people know whom they should ask. [Objective.]
   They are unsure who makes the decision. [Subjective.]

Note Don't let expressions such as *I think* and *she says* confuse you when they come between the subject *who* and its verb:

> subject
> He is the one who the polls say will win.

To choose between *who* and *whom* in such constructions, delete the interrupting phrase: *He is the one who will win.*

EXERCISE 3
Choosing between *who* and *whom*

From the pairs in brackets, select the appropriate form of the pronoun in each of the following sentences.

Example:
My mother asked me [who, whom] I was going out with.
My mother asked me whom I was going out with.

ca 13g

1. The school administrators suspended Jurgen, [who, whom] they suspected of setting the fire.
2. Jurgen had been complaining to other custodians, [who, whom] reported him.
3. He constantly complained of unfair treatment from [whoever, whomever] happened to be passing in the halls, including pupils.
4. "[Who, Whom] here has heard Mr. Jurgen's complaints?" the police asked.
5. "[Who, Whom] did he complain most about?"

EXERCISE 4
Sentence combining: *Who* versus *whom*

Combine each pair of sentences below into one sentence that contains a clause beginning with *who* or *whom.* Be sure to use the appropriate case form. You will have to add, delete, and rearrange words. Each item may have more than one possible answer.

Example:

David is the candidate. We think David deserves to win.
David is the candidate who we think deserves to win.

1. Some children have undetected hearing problems. These children may do poorly in school.
2. They may not hear important instructions and information from teachers. Teachers may speak softly.
3. Classmates may not be audible. The teacher calls on those classmates.
4. Some hearing-impaired children may work harder to overcome their handicap. These children get a lot of encouragement at home.
5. Some hearing-impaired children may take refuge in fantasy friends. They can rely on these friends not to criticize or laugh.

Ordinarily, use a possessive pronoun or noun immediately before a gerund.

A **gerund** is the *-ing* form of a verb (*running, sleeping*) used as a noun (p. 271). Like nouns, gerunds are commonly preceded by possessive nouns and pronouns: *our vote* (noun), *our voting* (gerund).

The coach disapproved of their lifting weights.

The coach's disapproving was a surprise.

A noun or pronoun before an *-ing* verb form is not always possessive. Sometimes the *-ing* form will be a present participle modifying the preceding word:

Everyone had noticed him weightlifting. [Emphasis on *him.*]
objective pronoun — participle

Everyone had noticed his weightlifting. [Emphasis on the activity.]
possessive pronoun — gerund

Note that a gerund usually is not preceded by the possessive when the possessive would create an awkward construction:

Awkward	A rumor spread about everybody's on the team wanting to quit.
Less awkward	A rumor spread about everybody on the team wanting to quit.
Better	A rumor spread that everybody on the team wanted to quit.

EXERCISE 5
Revising: Case

Revise all inappropriate case forms in the following paragraph, and explain the function of each case form.

Written four thousand years ago, *The Epic of Gilgamesh* tells of the friendship of Gilgamesh and Enkidu. Gilgamesh was a bored king who his people thought was too harsh. Then he met Enkidu, a wild man whom had lived with the animals in the mountains. Immediately, him and Gilgamesh wrestled to see whom was more powerful. After hours of struggle, Enkidu admitted that Gilgamesh was stronger than him. Now the friends needed adventures worthy of the two strongest men on earth. Gilgamesh said, "Between you and I, mighty deeds will be accomplished, and our fame will be everlasting." Among their acts, Enkidu and him defeated a giant bull, Humbaba, and cut down the bull's cedar forests. Them bringing back cedar logs to Gilgamesh's treeless land won great praise from the people. When Enkidu died, Gilgamesh mourned his death, realizing that no one had been a better friend than him. When Gilgamesh himself died many years later, his people raised a monument praising Enkidu and he for their friendship and their mighty deeds of courage.

Note See page 362 for an exercise involving case along with other aspects of grammar.

CHAPTER 14

Verbs

The verb is the most complicated part of speech in English, changing form to express a wide range of information.

VERB FORMS

All verbs except *be* have five basic forms. The first three are the verb's **principal parts.**

- The **plain form** is the dictionary form of the verb. When the subject is a plural noun or the pronoun *I, we, you,* or *they,* the plain form indicates action that occurs in the present, occurs habitually, or is generally true.

  A few artists live in town today.
  They hold classes downtown.

- The **past-tense form** indicates that the action of the verb occurred before now. It usually adds *-d* or *-ed* to the plain form, although for some irregular verbs it forms in other ways (see p. 303).

  Many artists lived in town before this year.
  They held classes downtown. [Irregular verb.]

- The **past participle** is usually the same as the past-tense form, except in most irregular verbs. It combines with forms of *have* or *be* (*has climbed, was created*), or by itself it modifies nouns and pronouns (*the sliced apples*).

  Artists have lived in town for decades.
  They have held classes downtown. [Irregular verb.]

Information on verbs:

http://webster.commnet.edu/HP/pages/darling/grammar/verbs.htm From the Guide to Grammar and Writing.

http://www.uottawa.ca/academic/arts/writcent/hypergrammar/useverb.html From the University of Ottawa.

- The **present participle** adds *-ing* to the verb's plain form. It combines with forms of *be* (*is buying*), modifies nouns and pronouns (*the boiling water*), or functions as a noun (*Running exhausts me*).

  A few artists are living in town today.
  They are holding classes downtown.

- The **-*s* form** ends in *-s* or *-es.* When the subject is a singular noun, a pronoun such as *everyone,* or the personal pronoun *he, she,* or *it,* the *-s* form indicates action that occurs in the present, occurs habitually, or is generally true.

  The artist lives in town today.
  She holds classes downtown.

The verb *be* has eight forms rather than the five forms of most other verbs:

Plain form	be		
Present participle	being		
Past participle	been		
	I	*he, she, it*	*we, you, they*
Present tense	am	is	are
Past tense	was	was	were

Terms used to describe verbs

Tense

The time of the verb's action—for instance, present (*kick*), past (*kicked*), future (*will kick*). (See p. 318.)

Mood

The attitude of the verb's speaker or writer—the difference, for example, in *I kick the ball, Kick the ball,* and *I suggest that you kick the ball.* (See p. 327.)

Voice

The distinction between the **active,** in which the subject performs the verb's action (*I kick the ball*), and the **passive,** in which the subject is acted upon (*The ball is kicked by me*). (See p. 329.)

Person

The verb form that reflects whether the subject is speaking (*I/we kick the ball*), spoken to (*You kick the ball*), or spoken about (*She kicks the ball*). (See p. 334.)

Number

The verb form that reflects whether the subject is singular (*The girl kicks the ball*) or plural (*Girls kick the ball*). (See p. 334.)

Helping verbs

Helping verbs, also called **auxiliary verbs,** combine with some verb forms to indicate time and other kinds of meaning, as in *can run, was sleeping, had been eaten.* These combinations are **verb phrases.** Since the plain form, present participle, or past participle in any verb phrase always carries the principal meaning, it is sometimes called the **main verb.**

Verb phrase	
Helping	***Main***
Artists can	train others to draw.
The techniques have	changed little.

These are the most common helping verbs:

be able to	had better	must	used to
be supposed to	have to	ought to	will
can	may	shall	would
could	might	should	

Forms of *be:* be, am, is, are, was, were, been, being
Forms of *have:* have, has, had, having
Forms of *do:* do, does, did

See pages 308–13 for more on helping verbs.

14a Use the correct form of regular and irregular verbs.

Most verbs are regular; that is, they form their past tense and past participle by adding *-d* or *-ed* to the plain form.

Plain form	Past tense	Past participle
live	lived	lived
act	acted	acted

Since the past tense and past participle are created in the same way, the forms of regular verbs do not often cause problems in speech and writing (but see p. 307).

About two hundred English verbs are **irregular;** that is, they form their past tense and past participle in some irregular way.

http://www.uottawa.ca/academic/arts/writcent/hypergrammar/auxvb.html Information on helping verbs, from the University of Ottawa.

http://webster.commnet.edu/HP/pages/darling/grammar/verbs.htm#irregular Discussion, quizzes, and links on irregular verbs, from the Guide to Grammar and Writing.

Plain form	Past tense	Past participle
begin	began	begun
break	broke	broken
sleep	slept	slept

Check a dictionary under the plain form if you have any doubt about a verb's principal parts. If no other forms are listed, the verb is regular: both the past tense and the past participle add *-d* or *-ed* to the plain form. If the verb is irregular, the dictionary will list the plain form, the past tense, and the past participle in that order (*go, went, gone*). If the dictionary gives only two forms (as in *think, thought*), then the past tense and the past participle are the same.

The following list includes the most common irregular verbs. (When two forms are possible, as in *dived* and *dove,* both are included.)

Principal parts of common irregular verbs

Plain form	Past tense	Past participle
arise	arose	arisen
become	became	become
begin	began	begun
bid	bid	bid
bite	bit	bitten, bit
blow	blew	blown
break	broke	broken
bring	brought	brought
burst	burst	burst
buy	bought	bought
catch	caught	caught
choose	chose	chosen
come	came	come
cut	cut	cut
dive	dived, dove	dived
do	did	done
draw	drew	drawn
dream	dreamed, dreamt	dreamed, dreamt
drink	drank	drunk
drive	drove	driven
eat	ate	eaten
fall	fell	fallen
find	found	found
flee	fled	fled
fly	flew	flown
forget	forgot	forgotten, forgot
freeze	froze	frozen
get	got	got, gotten

Plain form	Past tense	Past participle
give	gave	given
go	went	gone
grow	grew	grown
hang (suspend)	hung	hung
hang (execute)	hanged	hanged
hear	heard	heard
hide	hid	hidden
hold	held	held
keep	kept	kept
know	knew	known
lay	laid	laid
lead	led	led
leave	left	left
lend	lent	lent
let	let	let
lie	lay	lain
lose	lost	lost
pay	paid	paid
prove	proved	proved, proven
ride	rode	ridden
ring	rang	rung
rise	rose	risen
run	ran	run
say	said	said
see	saw	seen
set	set	set
shake	shook	shaken
shrink	shrank, shrunk	shrunk, shrunken
sing	sang, sung	sung
sink	sank, sunk	sunk
sit	sat	sat
slide	slid	slid
speak	spoke	spoken
spring	sprang, sprung	sprung
stand	stood	stood
steal	stole	stolen
swim	swam	swum
swing	swung	swung
take	took	taken
tear	tore	torn
throw	threw	thrown
wear	wore	worn
write	wrote	written

Note Computerized grammar and style checkers may flag incorrect forms of irregular verbs, but they may also fail to do so. When in doubt about the forms of irregular verbs, refer to the list above, consult a dictionary, or consult the additional lists at the Web site given on page 303.

EXERCISE 1
Using irregular verbs

For each irregular verb in brackets, give either the past tense or the past participle, as appropriate, and identify the form you used.

Example:

Though we had [hide] the cash box, it was [steal].

Though we had hidden the cash box, it was stolen. [Two past participles.]

1. The world population has [grow] by two-thirds of a billion people in less than a decade.
2. Recently it [break] the 6 billion mark.
3. Experts have [draw] pictures of a crowded future.
4. They predict that the world population may have [slide] up to as much as 10 billion by the year 2050.
5. Though the food supply [rise] in the last decade, the share to each person [fall].

14b Distinguish between *sit* and *set, lie* and *lay,* and *rise* and *raise.*

The forms of *sit* and *set, lie* and *lay,* and *rise* and *raise* are easy to confuse:

Plain form	Past tense	Past participle
sit	sat	sat
set	set	set
lie	lay	lain
lay	laid	laid
rise	rose	risen
raise	raised	raised

In each of these confusing pairs, one verb is **intransitive** (it does not take an object) and one is **transitive** (it does take an object). (See pp. 259–61 for more on this distinction.)

Intransitive

The patients lie in their beds. [*Lie* means "recline" and takes no object.]

Visitors sit with them. [*Sit* means "be seated" or "be located" and takes no object.]

Patients' temperatures rise. [*Rise* means "increase" or "get up" and takes no object.]

Transitive

Orderlies lay the dinner trays on tables. [*Lay* means "place" and takes an object, here *trays.*]

Orderlies set the trays down. [*Set* means "place" and takes an object, here *trays.*]

Nursing aides raise the shades. [*Raise* means "lift" or "bring up" and takes an object, here *shades.*]

EXERCISE 2
Distinguishing *sit/set, lie/lay, rise/raise*

Choose the correct verb from the pair given in brackets. Then supply the past tense or past participle, as appropriate.

Example:

After I washed all the windows, I [lie, lay] down the squeegee and then I [sit, set] the table.

After I washed all the windows, I laid down the squeegee and then I set the table.

1. Yesterday afternoon the child [lie, lay] down for a nap.
2. The child has been [rise, raise] by her grandparents.
3. Most days her grandfather has [sit, set] with her, reading her stories.
4. She has [rise, raise] at dawn most mornings.
5. Her toys were [lie, lay] out on the floor.

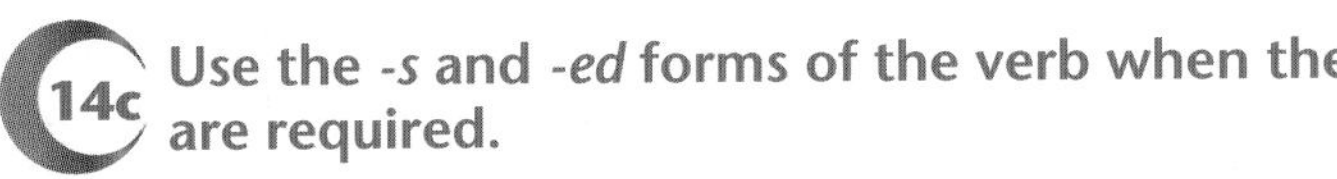

14c Use the *-s* and *-ed* forms of the verb when they are required.

Speakers of some English dialects and nonnative speakers of English sometimes omit verb endings required by standard English. The *-s* form of a verb is required when *both* of these situations hold:

- The subject is a singular noun (*boy*), an indefinite pronoun (*everyone*), or *he, she,* or *it.*
- The verb's action occurs in the present.

The letter asks [not ask] for a quick response.
Delay is [not be] costly.

Watch especially for the *-s* forms *has, does,* and *doesn't* (for *does not*).

The company has [not have] delayed responding.
It doesn't [not don't] have the needed data.
The contract does [not do] depend on the response.

Another ending sometimes omitted is *-d* or *-ed,* as in *we bagged* or *used cars.* The ending is particularly easy to omit if it isn't pronounced clearly in speech, as in *asked, discussed, mixed, supposed, walked,* and *used.* Use the ending for a regular verb in *any* of these situations:

- The verb's action occurred in the past:

  The company asked [not ask] for more time.

- The verb form functions as a modifier:

  The data concerned [not concern] should be retrievable.

- The verb form combines with a form of *be* or *have:*

  The company is supposed [not suppose] to be the best.
  It has developed [not develop] an excellent reputation.

Note Computerized grammar and style checkers will flag many omitted *-s* and *-ed* endings from verbs, such as in *he ask* or *was ask.* But they will miss many omissions, too. You'll need to proofread your papers carefully on your own to catch missing endings.

ESL Some languages do not require endings equivalent to the *-s* or *-ed* in English. If English is not your native language and you find you omit one or both of these endings, you may need to edit your drafts just for them.

EXERCISE 3
Using *-s* and *-ed* verb endings

Supply the correct form of each verb in brackets. Be careful to include *-s* and *-ed* (or *-d*) endings where they are needed for standard English.

A teacher sometimes [ask] too much of a student. In high school I was once [punish] for being sick. I had [miss] some school, and I [realize] that I would fail a test unless I had a chance to make up the classwork. I [discuss] the problem with the teacher, but he said I was [suppose] to make up the work while I was sick. At that I [walk] out of the class. I [receive] a failing grade then, but it did not change my attitude. Today I still balk when a teacher [make] unreasonable demands or [expect] miracles.

14d Use helping verbs with main verbs appropriately.

Helping verbs combine with some verb forms to form verb phrases (see p. 303).

http://webster.commnet.edu/HP/pages/darling/grammar/auxiliary.htm
Information and quizzes covering helping verbs, from the Guide to Grammar and Writing.

Note Computerized grammar and style checkers often spot omitted helping verbs and incorrect main verbs with helping verbs, but sometimes they do not. A checker flagged *Many been fortunate, She working,* and *Her ideas are grow more complex* but overlooked other examples on the following pages, such as *The conference will be occurred.* Careful proofreading is the only insurance against missing helping verbs and incorrect main verbs.

1 Use helping verbs when they are required.

Some English dialects omit helping verbs required by standard English. In the sentences below, the underlined helping verbs are essential:

> Archaeologists are conducting fieldwork all over the world. [Not Archaeologists conducting. . . .]
>
> Many have been fortunate in their discoveries. [Not Many been. . . .]
>
> Some could be real-life Indiana Joneses. [Not Some be. . . .]

In every example above, omitting the helping verb would create an incomplete sentence, or **sentence fragment** (see Chapter 17). In a complete sentence, some part of the verb (helping or main) must be capable of changing form to show changes in time: *I run, I ran; you are running, you were running* (see p. 365). But a present participle (*conducting*), an irregular past participle (*been*), and the infinitive *be* cannot change form in this way. They need helping verbs (which can change) to work as sentence verbs.

2 Combine helping verbs and main verbs appropriately for your meaning. ESL

Helping verbs and main verbs combine into verb phrases in specific ways.

Note The main verb in a verb phrase (the one carrying the main meaning) does not change to show a change in subject or time: *she has sung, you had sung.* Only the helping verb may change, as in these examples.

Form of *be* + present participle

The **progressive tenses** indicate action in progress (see p. 320). Create them with *be, am, is, are, was, were,* or *been* followed by the main verb's present participle:

> She is working on a new book.

http://www.hut.fi/u/rvilmi/LangHelp/Grammar/modalverbs.html
Exercises and links to resources on helping verbs for ESL writers, from the Grammar Help page.

Be and *been* require additional helping verbs to form the progressive tenses:

can	might	should	be working	have	been working
could	must	will		has	
may	shall	would		had	

When forming the progressive tenses, be sure to use the *-ing* form of the main verb:

Faulty Her ideas are grow more complex. She is developed a new approach to ethics.

Revised Her ideas are growing more complex. She is developing a new approach to ethics.

Form of *be* + past participle

The **passive voice** of the verb indicates that the subject *receives* the action of the verb (see p. 329). Create the passive voice with *be, am, is, are, was, were, being,* or *been* followed by the main verb's past participle:

Her latest book was completed in four months.

Be, being, and *been* require additional helping verbs to form the passive voice:

have	been completed	am	was	being completed
has		is	were	
had		are		

will be completed

Be sure to use the main verb's past participle for the passive voice:

Faulty Her next book will be publish soon.

Revised Her next book will be published soon.

Note Use only transitive verbs to form the passive voice:

Faulty A philosophy conference will be occurred in the same week. [*Occur* is not a transitive verb.]

Revised A philosophy conference will occur in the same week.

See pages 330–31 for advice on when to use and when to avoid the passive voice.

Forms of *have*

Four forms of *have* serve as helping verbs: *have, has, had, having.* One of these forms plus the main verb's past participle creates one of the **perfect tenses,** those expressing action completed before another specific time or action (see p. 320):

Some students have complained about the laboratory.
Others had complained before.

Will and other helping verbs sometimes accompany forms of *have* in the perfect tenses:

Several more students will have complained by the end of the week.

Forms of *do*

Do, does, and *did* have three uses as helping verbs, always with the plain form of the main verb:

- To pose a question: *How did the trial end?*
- To emphasize the main verb: *It did end eventually.*
- To negate the main verb, along with *not* or *never: The judge did not withdraw.*

Be sure to use the main verb's plain form with any form of *do:*

Faulty The judge did remained in court.

Revised The judge did remain in court.

Modals

The modal helping verbs include *can, could, may,* and *might,* along with several two- and three-word combinations, such as *have to* and *be able to.* (See p. 303 for a list of modals.)

Modals convey various meanings, with these being most common:

- **Ability:** *can, could, be able to*

  The equipment can detect small vibrations. [Present.]

  The equipment could detect small vibrations. [Past.]

  The equipment is able to detect small vibrations. [Present. Past: was able to. Future: will be able to.]

- **Possibility:** *could, may, might, could/may/might have* + past participle

  The equipment could fail. [Present.]
  The equipment may fail. [Present or future.]
  The equipment might fail. [Present or future.]
  The equipment may have failed. [Past.]

- **Necessity or obligation:** *must, have to, be supposed to*

  The lab must purchase a backup. [Present or future.]

  The lab has to purchase a backup. [Present or future. Past: had to.]

  The lab will have to purchase a backup. [Future.]

  The lab is supposed to purchase a backup. [Present. Past: was supposed to.]

- **Permission:** *may, can, could*

  The lab may spend the money. [Present or future.]

  The lab can spend the money. [Present or future.]

  The lab could spend the money. [Present or future, more tentative.]

  The school then announced that the lab could spend the money. [Past.]

- **Intention:** *will, shall, would*

  The lab will spend the money. [Future.]

  Shall we offer advice? [Future. Use *shall* for questions requesting opinion or consent.]

  We knew we would offer advice. [Past.]

- **Request:** *could, can, would*

  Could [or can or would] you please obtain a bid? [Present or future.]

- **Advisability:** *should, had better, ought to, should have* + past participle

  You should obtain three bids. [Present or future.]
  You had better obtain three bids. [Present or future.]
  You ought to obtain three bids. [Present or future.]
  You should have obtained three bids. [Past.]

- **Past habit:** *would, used to*

  In years past we would obtain five bids.
  We used to obtain five bids.

The following conventions govern the combination of modals and main verbs shown in the examples:

- One-word modals do not change form to show a change in subject: *I could run, she could run.* Most two- and three-word modals do change form, like other helping verbs: *I have to run, she has to run.*
- Modals can sometimes indicate past, present, or future time, occasionally with a word change (*can* to *could,* for instance) or with a form change in a two- or three-word modal (such as *is/was able to*).
- For present or future time, modals are used with the plain form of the main verb: *he can go, I might drive, I will be able to drive.* For past time, some modals change spelling (especially *can* to *could*), and others add *have* before the past participle of the main verb: *might have driven.*
- Don't use *to* between a one-word modal and the main verb: *can drive,* not *can to drive.* (Most of the two- and three-word modals do include *to: ought to drive.*)
- Don't use two one-word modals together: *I will be able to drive,* not *I will can drive.*

EXERCISE 4
Using helping verbs

Add helping verbs in the following sentences where they are needed for standard English.

1. Each year thousands of new readers been discovering Agatha Christie's mysteries.
2. The books written by a prim woman who had worked as a nurse during World War I.
3. Christie never expected that her play *The Mousetrap* be performed for decades.
4. During her life Christie always complaining about movie versions of her stories.
5. Readers of her stories been delighted to be baffled by her.

EXERCISE 5
Revising: Helping verbs plus main verbs ESL

Revise the following sentences so that helping verbs and main verbs are used correctly. Circle the number of any sentence that is already correct.

> *Example:*
>
> The college testing service has test as many as five hundred students at one time.
>
> The college testing service has tested as many as five hundred students at one time.

1. A report from the Bureau of the Census has confirm a widening gap between rich and poor.
2. As suspected, the percentage of people below the poverty level did increased over the last decade.
3. More than 17 percent of the population is make 5 percent of all the income.
4. About 1 percent of the population will keeping an average of $500,000 apiece after taxes.
5. The other 99 percent all together may retain about $300,000.

14e Use a gerund or an infinitive after a verb as appropriate. ESL

A **gerund** is the *-ing* form of a verb used as a noun (*opening*). An **infinitive** is the plain form of a verb preceded by *to* (*to open*). (See p. 271 for more on these forms.)

Gerunds and infinitives may follow certain verbs but not others. And sometimes the use of a gerund or infinitive with the same verb changes the meaning of the verb.

http://www.geocities.com/Athens/Olympus/7583/gerinflist.html An extensive list of verbs with gerunds and infinitives, from Grammar When You Need It.

Note Computerized grammar and style checkers will spot some errors in matching gerunds or infinitives with verbs, but they will miss others. Use the lists given here and an ESL dictionary (see p. 587) to determine for yourself whether an infinitive or a gerund is appropriate.

Either gerund or infinitive

A gerund or an infinitive may follow these verbs with no significant difference in meaning:

begin	hate	love
can't bear	hesitate	prefer
can't stand	intend	start
continue	like	

The pump began working.
The pump began to work.

Meaning change with gerund or infinitive

With four verbs, a gerund has quite a different meaning from an infinitive:

forget	stop
remember	try

The engineer stopped eating. [He no longer ate.]
The engineer stopped to eat. [He stopped in order to eat.]

Gerund, not infinitive

Do not use an infinitive after these verbs:

admit	discuss	mind	recollect
adore	dislike	miss	resent
appreciate	enjoy	postpone	resist
avoid	escape	practice	risk
consider	finish	put off	suggest
deny	imagine	quit	tolerate
detest	keep	recall	understand

Faulty He finished to eat lunch.

Revised He finished eating lunch.

Infinitive, not gerund

Do not use a gerund after these verbs:

agree	decide	mean	refuse
ask	expect	offer	say
assent	have	plan	wait
beg	hope	pretend	want
claim	manage	promise	wish

Faulty He decided checking the pump.
Revised He decided to check the pump.

Noun or pronoun + infinitive

Some verbs may be followed by an infinitive alone or by a noun or pronoun and an infinitive. The presence of a noun or pronoun changes the meaning.

ask	dare	need	wish
beg	expect	promise	would like
choose	help	want	

He expected to watch.
He expected his workers to watch.

Some verbs *must* be followed by a noun or pronoun before an infinitive:

admonish	encourage	oblige	require
advise	forbid	order	teach
allow	force	permit	tell
cause	hire	persuade	train
challenge	instruct	remind	urge
command	invite	request	warn
convince			

He instructed his workers to watch.

Do not use *to* before the infinitive when it follows one of these verbs and a noun or pronoun:

feel	make ("force")
have	see
hear	watch
let	

He let his workers learn by observation.

vb 14e

EXERCISE 6
Revising: Verbs plus gerunds or infinitives ESL

Revise the following sentences so that gerunds or infinitives are used correctly with verbs. Circle the number preceding any sentence that is already correct.

Example:
A politician cannot avoid to alienate some voters.
A politician cannot avoid alienating some voters.

1. A program called HELP Wanted tries to make citizens to take action on behalf of American competitiveness.
2. Officials working on this program hope improving education for work.

3. American businesses find that their workers need learning to read.
4. In the next ten years the United States expects facing a shortage of 350,000 scientists.
5. HELP Wanted suggests creating a media campaign.

14f Use the appropriate particles with two-word verbs. ESL

Some verbs consist of two words: the verb itself and a **particle,** a preposition or adverb that affects the meaning of the verb. For example:

Look up the answer. [Research the answer.]
Look over the answer. [Examine the answer.]

The meanings of these two-word verbs are often quite different from the meanings of the individual words that make them up. (There are some three-word verbs, too, such as *put up with* and *run out of.*) An ESL dictionary, such as those listed on page 587, will define two-word verbs for you. It will also tell you whether the verbs may be separated in a sentence, as explained below. Computerized grammar and style checkers will recognize few if any misuses of two-word verbs. You'll need to proofread on your own to catch and correct errors.

Note Many two-word verbs are more common in speech than in more formal academic or business writing. For formal writing, consider using *research* instead of *look up, examine* or *inspect* instead of *look over.*

Inseparable two-word verbs

Verbs and particles that may not be separated by any other words include the following:

call on	go out with	run across	stay away
catch on	go over	run into	stay up
come across	grow up	run out of	take care of
get along	keep on	speak up	turn out
get up	look for	speak with	turn up at
give in	look into	stand up	work for
go on	play around		

Faulty Children grow quickly up.

Revised Children grow up quickly.

Separable two-word verbs

Most two-word verbs that take direct objects may be separated by the object:

Parents help out their children.
Parents help their children out.

If the direct object is a pronoun, the pronoun *must* separate the verb from the particle:

Faulty Parents help out them.

Revised Parents help them out.

The separable two-word verbs include the following:

bring up	give back	make up	throw out
call off	hand in	point out	try on
call up	hand out	put away	try out
drop off	help out	put back	turn down
fill out	leave out	put off	turn on
fill up	look over	take out	wrap up
give away	look up	take over	

EXERCISE 7
Revising: Verbs plus particles ESL

Identify any two- or three-word verbs in the sentences below, and indicate whether each is separable (S) or inseparable (I). Then fill the blank with the correct option for placing nouns or pronouns with verbs and particles. Consult an ESL dictionary if necessary.

Example:

Hollywood producers never seem to come up with entirely new plots, but they also never _____ to present the old ones.

a. run out of new ways
b. run new ways out of
c. Either a or b

Hollywood producers never seem to come up with (I) entirely new plots, but they also never (a) run out of new ways to present the old ones.

1. American movies treat everything from going out with someone to making up an ethnic identity, but few people _____.

   a. look into their significance
   b. look their significance into
   c. Either a or b

2. While some viewers stay away from topical films, others _____ simply because a movie has sparked debate.

   a. turn up at the theater
   b. turn at the theater up
   c. Either a or b

3. Some movies aroused such strong responses that theaters were obliged to _____.

   a. throw out rowdy spectators
   b. throw rowdy spectators out
   c. Either a or b

vb 14f

4. Filmmakers have always been eager to _____ to the public.
   a. point out their influence
   b. point their influence out
   c. Either a or b

5. Everyone agrees that filmmakers will _____, if only because it can fill up theaters.
   a. keep on creating controversy
   b. keep creating controversy on
   c. Either a or b

TENSE

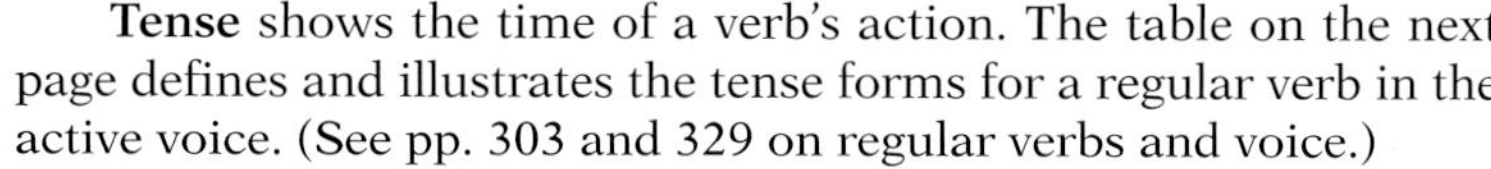

Tense shows the time of a verb's action. The table on the next page defines and illustrates the tense forms for a regular verb in the active voice. (See pp. 303 and 329 on regular verbs and voice.)

Note Computerized grammar and style checkers can provide little help with incorrect verb tenses and tense sequences because correctness is usually dependent on meaning. Proofread carefully yourself to catch errors in tense or tense sequence.

t 14g

14g Use the appropriate tense to express your meaning.

Many errors in verb tense are actually errors in verb form like those discussed earlier. Still, the present tense, the perfect tenses, and the progressive tenses can cause problems.

1 Observe the special uses of the present tense.

Most academic and business writing uses the past tense (*the rebellion occurred*), but the present tense has several distinctive uses:

Action occurring now

She understands the problem.
We define the problem differently.

Information and exercises on verb tenses:

http://owl.english.purdue.edu/Files/72.html From the Purdue Online Writing Lab.

http://webster.commnet.edu/HP/pages/darling/grammar/verbs.htm#tense From the Guide to Grammar and Writing.

http://www.hut.fi/u/rvilmi/LangHelp/Grammar/verbs.html For ESL writers, from the Grammar Help page.

Tenses of a regular verb (active voice)

Present Action that is occurring now, occurs habitually, or is generally true

Simple present Plain form or *-s* form

I walk.
You/we/they walk.
He/she/it walks.

Present progressive *Am, is,* or *are* plus *-ing* form

I am walking.
You/we/they are walking.
He/she/it is walking.

Past Action that occurred before now

Simple past Past-tense form (*-d* or *-ed*)

I/he/she/it walked.
You/we/they walked.

Past progressive *Was* or *were* plus *-ing* form

I/he/she/it was walking.
You/we/they were walking.

Future Action that will occur in the future

Simple future Plain form plus *will*

I/you/he/she/it/we/they will walk.

Future progressive *Will be* plus *-ing* form

I/you/he/she/it/we/they will be walking.

Present perfect Action that began in the past and is linked to the present

Present perfect *Have* or *has* plus past participle (*-d* or *-ed*)

I/you/we/they have walked.
He/she/it has walked.

Present perfect progressive *Have been* or *has been* plus *-ing* form

I/you/we/they have been walking.
He/she/it has been walking.

Past perfect Action that was completed before another past action

Past perfect *Had* plus past participle (*-d* or *-ed*)

I/you/he/she/it/we/they had walked.

Past perfect progressive *Had been* plus *-ing* form

I/you/he/she/it/we/they had been walking.

Future perfect Action that will be completed before another future action

Future perfect *Will have* plus past participle (*-d* or *-ed*)

I/you/he/she/it/we/they will have walked.

Future perfect progressive *Will have been* plus *-ing* form

I/you/he/she/it/we/they will have been walking.

Habitual or recurring action

Banks regularly undergo audits.
The audits monitor the banks' activities.

A general truth

The mills of the gods grind slowly.
The earth is round.

Discussion of literature, film, and so on (see also p. 800)

Huckleberry Finn has adventures we all envy.
In that article the author examines several causes of crime.

Future time

Next week we draft a new budget.
Funding ends in less than a year.

(In the last two examples, time is really indicated by *Next week* and *in less than a year.*)

2 Observe the uses of the perfect tenses.

The perfect tenses generally indicate action completed before another specific time or action. (The term *perfect* derives from the Latin *perfectus,* "completed.") The present perfect tense also indicates action begun in the past and continued into the present. The perfect tenses consist of a form of *have* plus the verb's past participle.

present perfect
The dancer has performed here only once. [The action is completed at the time of the statement.]

present perfect
Critics have written about the performance ever since. [The action began in the past and continues now.]

past perfect
The dancer had trained in Asia before his performance. [The action was completed before another past action.]

future perfect
He will have performed here again by next month. [The action begins now or in the future and will be completed by a specified time in the future.]

ESL With the present perfect tense, the words *since* and *for* are followed by different information. After *since,* give a specific point in time: *The United States has been a member of the United Nations since 1945.* After *for,* give a span of time: *The United States has been a member of the United Nations for over half a century.*

3 Observe the uses of the progressive tenses. **ESL**

The progressive tenses indicate continuing (therefore progressive) action. They consist of a form of *be* plus the verb's *-ing* form (present participle). (The words *be* and *been* must be combined with other helping verbs. See p. 310.)

> present progressive
> The economy is improving.
>
> past progressive
> Last year the economy was stagnating.
>
> future progressive
> Economists will be watching for signs of growth.
>
> present perfect progressive
> The government has been expecting an upturn.
>
> past perfect progressive
> Various indicators had been suggesting improvement.
>
> future perfect progressive
> By the end of this month, investors will have been pushing the markets up for half a year.

Note Verbs that express unchanging states (especially mental states) rather than physical actions do not usually appear in the progressive tenses. These verbs include *adore, appear, believe, belong, care, doubt, hate, have, hear, imagine, know, like, love, mean, need, own, prefer, realize, remember, see, sound, taste, think, understand,* and *want.*

Faulty	She is wanting to study ethics.
Revised	She wants to study ethics.

14h Use the appropriate sequence of verb tenses.

The term **sequence of tenses** refers to the relation between the verb tense in a main clause and the verb tense in a subordinate clause or phrase. The tenses need not be identical as long as they reflect changes in actual or relative time. For example, the verbs in the following sentence are in clear sequence:

> Ramon's father arrived in the United States thirty years ago, after he had married, and now Ramon has decided that he will return to his father's homeland.

The difficulties with tense sequence are discussed below. (For a discussion of tense shifts—changes *not* required by meaning—see pp. 391–92.)

1 Use the appropriate tense sequence with infinitives.

The tense of an infinitive is determined by the tense of the verb in the predicate. The **present infinitive** is the verb's plain form preceded by *to* (see p. 271). It indicates action *at the same time* as or *later* than that of the verb:

verb: present / infinitive: present

The researcher expects to see change.

verb: present perfect / infinitive: present

She would have liked to see [not to have seen] change before now.

The verb's **perfect infinitive** consists of *to have* followed by the past participle, as in *to have talked, to have won.* It indicates action *earlier* than that of the verb:

verb: present / infinitive: perfect

Other researchers would like [not would have liked] to have seen change as well.

verb: present / infinitive: perfect

They judge the data to have been interpreted correctly.

2 Use the appropriate tense sequence with participles.

The tense of a participle is determined by the tense of the verb in the predicate. The present participle shows action occurring *at the same time* as that of the verb:

participle: present / verb: past perfect

Testing a large group, the researcher had posed multiple-choice questions.

The past participle and the present perfect participle show action occurring *earlier* than that of the verb:

participle: past / verb: past

Prepared by earlier failures, she knew not to ask open questions.

participle: present perfect / verb: past

Having tested many people, she understood the process.

3 Use the appropriate tense sequence with the past or past perfect tense.

When the verb in the main clause is in the past or past perfect tense, the verb in the subordinate clause must also be past or past perfect:

main clause: past / subordinate clause: past

The researchers discovered that people varied widely in their knowledge of public events.

main clause: past / subordinate clause: past perfect

The variation occurred because respondents had been born in different decades.

main clause: past perfect / subordinate clause: past

None of them had been born when Warren G. Harding was President.

Exception Always use the present tense for a general truth, such as *The earth is round:*

main clause: past — subordinate clause: present

Most understood that popular Presidents are not necessarily good Presidents.

4 Use the appropriate tense sequence in conditional sentences. ESL

A **conditional sentence** states a factual relation between cause and effect, makes a prediction, or speculates about what might happen. Such a sentence usually consists of a subordinate clause beginning with *if, when,* or *unless* along with a main clause stating the result. The three kinds of conditional sentences use distinctive verbs.

Factual relation

For statements that something always or usually happens whenever something else happens, use the present tense in both clauses:

subordinate clause: present — main clause: present

When a voter casts a ballot, he or she has complete privacy.

If the linked events occurred in the past, use the past tense in both clauses:

subordinate clause: past — main clause: past

When voters registered in some states, they had to pay a poll tax.

Prediction

For a prediction, generally use the present tense in the subordinate clause and the future tense in the main clause:

subordinate clause: present — main clause: future

Unless citizens regain faith in politics, they will not vote.

Sometimes the verb in the main clause consists of *may, can, should,* or *might* plus the verb's plain form: *If citizens regain faith, they may vote.*

Speculation

Speculations are mainly of two kinds, each with its own verb pattern. For events that are possible in the present, though unlikely, use the past tense in the subordinate clause and *would, could,* or *might* plus the verb's plain form in the main clause:

subordinate clause: past — main clause: *would* + verb

If voters had more confidence, they would vote more often.

Use *were* instead of *was* when the subject is *I, he, she, it,* or a singular noun. (See p. 328 for more on this distinctive verb form.)

subordinate clause: past — main clause: *would* + verb

If the voter were more confident, he or she would vote more often.

For events that are impossible in the present, that are contrary to fact, use the same forms as above (including the distinctive *were* when applicable):

subordinate clause: past — main clause: *might* + verb

If Lincoln were alive, he might inspire confidence.

For events that were impossible in the past, use the past perfect tense in the subordinate clause and *would, could,* or *might* plus the present perfect tense in the main clause:

subordinate clause: past perfect — main clause: *might* + present perfect

If Lincoln had lived past the Civil War, he might have helped stabilize the country.

5 Use the appropriate tense sequence with indirect quotations. ESL

An **indirect quotation** reports what someone said or wrote but not in the exact words and not in quotation marks: *Lincoln said that events had controlled him* (quotation: "Events have controlled me"). An indirect quotation generally appears in a subordinate clause (underlined above), with certain conventions governing verb tense in most cases.

When the verb in the main clause is in the present tense, the verb in the indirect quotation (subordinate clause) is in the same tense as the original quotation:

main clause: present — indirect quotation: present

Haworth says that Lincoln is our noblest national hero. [Quotation: "Lincoln is our noblest national hero."]

main clause: present — indirect quotation: past

He says that Lincoln was a complicated person. [Quotation: "Lincoln was a complicated person."]

When the verb in the main clause is in the past tense, the verb in the indirect quotation usually changes tense from the original quotation. Present tense changes to past tense.

main clause: past — indirect quotation: past

An assistant to Lincoln said that the President was always generous. [Quotation: "The President is always generous."]

Past tense and present tense change to past perfect tense. (Past perfect tense does not change.)

> main clause: past — indirect quotation: past perfect
>
> Lincoln said that events had controlled him. [Quotation: "Events have controlled me."]

When the direct quotation states a general truth or reports a situation that is still true, the verb in the indirect quotation remains in the present tense regardless of the verb in the main clause:

> main clause: past — indirect quotation: present
>
> Lincoln said that right makes might. [Quotation: "Right makes might."]

Note As several of these examples show, an indirect quotation differs in at least two additional ways from the original quotation:

- The indirect quotation is usually preceded by *that.*
- The indirect quotation changes pronouns, especially from forms of *I* or *we* to forms of *he, she,* or *they.*

EXERCISE 8
Adjusting tense sequence: Past or past perfect tense

The tenses in each sentence below are in correct sequence. Change the tense of one verb as instructed. Then change the tense of infinitives, participles, and other verbs to restore correct sequence. Some items have more than one possible answer.

Example:

Delgado will call when he reaches his destination. (*Change will call to called.*)

Delgado called when he reached [or had reached] his destination.

1. Diaries that Adolf Hitler is supposed to have written have surfaced in Germany. (*Change have surfaced to had surfaced.*)
2. Many people believe that the diaries are authentic because a well-known historian has declared them so. (*Change believe to believed.*)
3. However, the historian's evaluation has been questioned by other authorities, who call the diaries forgeries. (*Change has been questioned to was questioned.*)
4. They claim, among other things, that the paper is not old enough to have been used by Hitler. (*Change claim to claimed.*)
5. Eventually, the doubters will win the debate because they have the best evidence. (*Change will win to won.*)

EXERCISE 9
Revising: Tense sequence with conditional sentences ESL

Supply the appropriate tense for each verb in brackets below.

Example:

If Babe Ruth or Jim Thorpe [be] athletes today, they [remind] us that even sports heroes must contend with a harsh reality.

If Babe Ruth or Jim Thorpe were athletes today, they might [or could or would] remind us that even sports heroes must contend with a harsh reality.

1. When an athlete [turn] professional, he or she commits to a grueling regimen of mental and physical training.
2. If athletes [be] less committed, they [disappoint] teammates, fans, and themselves.
3. If professional athletes [be] very lucky, they may play until age forty.
4. Unless an athlete achieves celebrity status, he or she [have] few employment choices after retirement.
5. If professional sports [be] less risky, athletes [have] longer careers and more choices after retirement.

EXERCISE 10
Using verb tenses in indirect quotations ESL

Each passage below comes from the British essayist Charles Lamb (1775–1834). Indirectly quote each passage in a sentence of your own, beginning with the words given in parentheses.

Example:

"The greatest pleasure I know is to do a good action by stealth and to have it found out by accident." (*Charles Lamb said that. . . .*)

Charles Lamb said that the greatest pleasure he knew was to do a good action by stealth and to have it found out by accident.

1. "Coleridge holds that a man cannot have a pure mind who refuses apple-dumplings." (*Lamb cited Coleridge's observation that. . . .*)
2. "The human species, according to the best theory I can form of it, is composed of two distinct races, the men who borrow, and the men who lend." (*Lamb wrote that. . . .*)
3. "Nothing puzzles me more than time and space; and yet nothing troubles me less, as I never think about them." (*He muses that. . . .*)
4. "When I am not walking, I am reading; I cannot sit and think." (*He admitted that. . . .*)
5. "Sentimentally I am disposed to harmony. But organically I am incapable of a tune." (*He confesses that. . . .*)

MOOD

Mood in grammar is a verb form that indicates the writer's or speaker's attitude toward what he or she is saying. The **indicative mood** states a fact or opinion or asks a question:

> The theater needs help. [Opinion.]
> The ceiling is falling in. [Fact.]
> Will you contribute to the theater? [Question.]

The **imperative mood** expresses a command or gives a direction. It omits the subject of the sentence, *you:*

> Help the theater. [Command.]
> Send contributions to the theater. [Direction.]

The **subjunctive mood** expresses a suggestion, a requirement, or a desire, or it states a condition that is contrary to fact (that is, imaginary or hypothetical). The subjunctive mood uses distinctive verb forms.

- **Suggestion or requirement:** plain form with all subjects.

  The manager asked that he donate money. [Suggestion.]
  Rules require that every donation be mailed. [Requirement.]

- **Desire or present condition contrary to fact:** past tense; for *be,* the past tense *were.*

  We wish that the theater had more money. [Desire.]

  It would be in better shape if it were better funded. [Present condition contrary to fact.]

- **Past condition contrary to fact:** past perfect.

  The theater could have been better funded if it had been better managed.

With conditions contrary to fact, the verb in the main clause also expresses the imaginary or hypothetical with the helping verb *could* or *would,* as in the last two sample sentences above.

(For a discussion of keeping mood consistent within and among sentences, see p. 392.)

Information on verb moods:
http://webster.commnet.edu/HP/pages/darling/grammar/verbs.htm#mood From the Guide to Grammar and Writing.

http://www.uottawa.ca/academic/arts/writcent/hypergrammar/moods.html From the University of Ottawa.

14i Use the subjunctive verb forms appropriately.

Contemporary English uses distinctive subjunctive verb forms in only a few constructions and idioms. (For the sequence of tenses in many subjunctive sentences, see pp. 323–24.)

Note Computerized grammar and style checkers may spot some errors in the subjunctive mood, but they may miss others. Instead of relying on checkers to find and correct problems, proofread your work looking for appropriate uses of subjunctive verbs.

1 Use the subjunctive in contrary-to-fact clauses beginning with *if* or expressing desire.

If the theater were saved, the town would benefit.
We all wish the theater were not so decrepit.
I wish I were able to donate money.

Note The indicative form *was* (*We all wish the theater was not so decrepit*) is common in speech and in some informal writing, but the subjunctive *were* is usual in formal English.

Not all clauses beginning with *if* express conditions contrary to fact. In the sentence *If Joe is out of town, he hasn't heard the news,* the verb *is* is correct because the clause refers to a condition presumed to exist.

2 Use *would* or *could* only in the main clause of a conditional statement.

The helping verb *would* or *could* appears in the main clause of a sentence expressing a condition contrary to fact. The helping verb does not appear in the subordinate clause beginning with *if:*

Not Many people would have helped if they would have known.
But Many people would have helped if they had known.

3 Use the subjunctive in *that* clauses following verbs that demand, request, or recommend.

Verbs such as *ask, demand, insist, mandate, require, recommend, request, require, suggest,* and *urge* indicate demand or suggestion. They often precede subordinate clauses beginning with *that* and containing the substance of the demand or suggestion. The verb in such a *that* clause should be in the subjunctive mood:

The board urged that everyone contribute.
The members insisted that they themselves be donors.
They suggested that each donate both time and money.

Note These constructions have widely used alternative forms that do not require the subjunctive, such as *The board urged everyone to contribute* or *The members insisted on donating.*

4 Use the subjunctive in some set phrases and idioms.

Several English expressions commonly use the subjunctive. For example:

Come rain or come shine.
Be that as it may.
The people be damned.

EXERCISE 11
Revising: Subjunctive mood

Revise the following sentences with appropriate subjunctive verb forms.

Example:
I would help the old man if I was able to reach him.
I would help the old man if I were able to reach him.

1. If John Hawkins would have known of the dangerous side effects of smoking tobacco, would he have introduced the dried plant to England in 1565?
2. Hawkins noted that if a Florida Indian was to travel for several days, he would have smoked tobacco to satisfy his hunger and thirst.
3. Early tobacco growers feared that their product would not gain acceptance unless it was perceived as healthful.
4. To prevent fires, in 1646 the General Court of Massachusetts passed a law requiring that a colonist smoked tobacco only if he was five miles from any town.
5. To prevent decadence, in 1647 Connecticut passed a law mandating that one's smoking of tobacco was limited to once a day in one's own home.

VOICE

The **voice** of a verb tells whether the subject of the sentence performs the action (**active voice**) or is acted upon (**passive voice**).

Information on passive and active voice:

http://webster.commnet.edu/HP/pages/darling/grammar/verbs.htm#passive From the Guide to Grammar and Writing.

http://lc.byuh.edu/cnn_n/Prev_gram.html#Actives For ESL students, from Brigham Young University in Hawaii.

Active and passive voice

Active voice The subject acts.

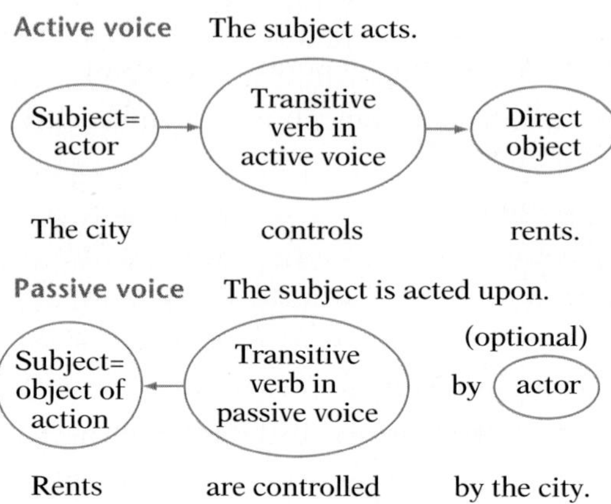

In the passive voice, the actual actor may be named in a prepositional phrase (such as *by the city*) or may be omitted.

ESL A passive verb always consists of a form of *be* plus the past participle of the main verb: *rents are controlled*. Other helping verbs must also be used with *be, being,* and *been: rents have been controlled*. Only a transitive verb (one that takes an object) may be used in the passive voice. (See p. 310.)

Converting active to passive

To change a transitive verb from active to passive voice, convert either an indirect object or a direct object into the subject of the sentence, and use the passive verb form:

	subject	transitive verb	indirect object	direct object
Active	The city	gives	tenants	leases.
	new subject	passive verb	direct object	
Passive	Tenants	are given	leases.	
	new subject	passive verb	indirect object	old subject
	Leases	are given	tenants	by the city.

Converting passive to active

To change a passive verb to active, name the verb's actor as subject, use an active verb form, and convert the old subject into an object:

	subject	passive verb	
Passive	Tenants	are protected	by leases.
	new subject	active verb	old subject = object
Active	Leases	protect	tenants.

14j Generally, prefer the active voice. Use the passive voice when the actor is unknown or unimportant.

Because the passive omits or de-emphasizes the actor (the performer of the verb's action), it can deprive writing of vigor and is often vague or confusing. The active voice is usually stronger, clearer, and more forthright.

Weak passive The Internet is used for research by many scholars, and its expansion to the general public has been criticized by some.

Strong active Many scholars use the Internet for research, and some have criticized its expansion to the general public.

The passive voice is useful in two situations: when the actor is unknown and when the actor is unimportant or less important than the object of the action.

> The Internet was established in 1969 by the US Department of Defense. The network has now been extended internationally to governments, foundations, corporations, educational institutions, and private individuals. [In the first sentence the writer wishes to stress the Internet rather than the Department of Defense. In the second sentence the actor is unknown or too complicated to name.]

> After the solution had been cooled to 10°C, the acid was added. [The person who cooled and added, perhaps the writer, is less important than the facts that the solution was cooled and acid was added. Passive sentences are common in scientific writing. See page 865.]

Except in such situations, however, you should prefer the active voice in your writing.

Note Most computerized grammar and style checkers can be set to spot the passive voice. But they will then flag every instance, both appropriate (such as when the actor is unknown) and ineffective. And they will flag as passive some unobjectionable phrases that are actually a form of *be* plus a verb form serving as an adjective, such as the underlined words in this sentence: *We were delighted*. You'll need to decide for yourself whether flagged phrases really are passive and whether they are appropriate for your meaning.

EXERCISE 12
Converting between active and passive voices

To practice using the two voices of the verb, convert the following sentences from active to passive or from passive to active. (In converting from passive to active, you may have to add a subject for the new sentence.) Which version of each sentence seems more effective, and why? (For additional exercises with the passive voice, see pp. 289 and 427.)

Example:

The aspiring actor was discovered in a nightclub.
A talent scout discovered the aspiring actor in a nightclub.

1. When the Eiffel Tower was built in 1889, it was thought by the French to be ugly.
2. At that time many people still resisted industrial technology.
3. The tower's naked steel construction epitomized this technology.
4. Beautiful ornament was expected to grace fine buildings.
5. Further, the tower could not even be called a building because it had no solid walls.

EXERCISE 13
Revising: Verb forms, tense, mood

Circle all the verbs and verbals in the following paragraph and correct their form, tense, or mood if necessary.

For centuries the natives of Melanesia, a group of islands laying northeast of Australia, have practice an unusual religion. It began in the eighteenth century when European explorers first have visited the islands. The natives were fascinated by the rich goods or "cargo" possessed by the explorers. They saw the wealth as treasures of the gods, and cargo cults eventually had arised among them. Over the centuries some Melanesians turned to Christianity in the belief that the white man's religion will bring them the white man's treasures. During World War II, US soldiers, having arrived by boat and airplane to have occupied some of the islands, introduced new and even more wonderful cargo. Even today some leaders of the cargo cults insist that the airplane is worship as a vehicle of the Melanesians' future salvation.

Note See page 362 for an exercise involving verbs along with other aspects of grammar.

CHAPTER 15

Agreement

Agreement helps readers understand the relations between elements in a sentence. Subjects and verbs agree in number and person:

> More Japanese Americans (subject) live (verb) in Hawaii and California than elsewhere.

> Daniel Inouye (subject) was (verb) the first Japanese American in Congress.

Pronouns and their **antecedents**—the words they refer to—agree in person, number, and gender:

> Inouye (antecedent) makes his (pronoun) home in Hawaii.

> Hawaiians (antecedent) value his work for them (pronoun).

15a Make subjects and verbs agree in number.

Most subject-verb agreement problems arise when endings are omitted from subjects or verbs or when the relation between sentence parts is uncertain.

http://www.clearcf.uvic.ca/writersguide/Pages/Agreement.html#Subject/Verb Discussion of both verb and pronoun agreement, from the University of Victoria.

Information on subject-verb agreement:

http://webster.commnet.edu/HP/pages/darling/grammar/sv_agr.htm From the Guide to Grammar and Writing.

http://owl.english.purdue.edu/Files/73.html From the Purdue Online Writing Lab.

http://www.wisc.edu/writetest/Handbook/SubjectVerb.html From the University of Wisconsin at Madison.

Person and number in subject-verb agreement

	Number	
Person	***Singular***	***Plural***
First	I eat.	We eat.
Second	You eat.	You eat.
Third	He/she/it eats. The bird eats.	They eat. Birds eat.

Note Computerized grammar and style checkers will look for problems with subject-verb agreement. Most checkers also allow you to customize settings so that you can turn off other options and look just for agreement problems (see p. 188). However, a checker may mistakenly flag correct agreement and may then suggest "corrections" that are wrong. In addition, a checker may fail to spot actual errors. Do not automatically accept a checker's pointers, and proofread your work carefully on your own.

1 The *-s* and *-es* endings work differently for nouns and verbs.

An *-s* or *-es* ending does opposite things to nouns and verbs: it usually makes a noun *plural,* but it always makes a present-tense verb *singular.* Thus if the subject noun is plural, it will end in *-s* or *-es* and the verb will not. If the subject is singular, it will not end in *-s* and the verb will.

Singular	**Plural**
The boy plays.	The boys play.
The bird soars.	The birds soar.

The only exceptions to these rules involve the nouns that form irregular plurals, such as *child/children, woman/women.* The irregular plural still requires a plural verb: The *children* play.

Writers often omit *-s* and *-es* endings from nouns or verbs because they are not pronounced clearly in speech (as in *asks* and *lists*) or because they are not used regularly in some English dialects. However, the endings are required in standard English:

Nonstandard	The voter resist change.
Standard	The voter resists change.

Remember that the verb *be* is irregular: it changes spelling for singular and plural in both present and past tense.

Summary of subject-verb agreement

- Basic subject-verb agreement (p. 334):

Singular	**Plural**
The kite flies.	The kites fly.

- Words between subject and verb (p. 336):

  The kite with two tails flies badly. The tails of the kite compete.

- Subjects joined by *and* (p. 336):

  The kite and the bird are almost indistinguishable.

- Subjects joined by *or* or *nor* (p. 337):

  The kite or the bird dives. Kites or birds fill the sky.

- Indefinite pronouns as subjects (p. 337):

  No one knows. All the spectators wonder.

- Collective nouns as subjects (p. 338):

  A flock appears. The flock disperse.

- Inverted word order (p. 339):

  Is the kite or the bird blue? Are the kite and the bird both blue?

- Linking verbs (p. 339):

  The kite is a flier and a dipper.

- *Who, which, that* as subjects (p. 339):

  The kite that flies longest wins. Kites that fall lose.

- Subjects with plural form and singular meaning (p. 340):

  Aeronautics plays a role in kite flying.

- Titles and words named as words (p. 340):

  Kite Dynamics is one title. *Vectors* is a key word.

agr
15a

Present tense

he, she, it, singular nouns	is	all plurals	are

Past tense

he, she, it, singular nouns	was	all plurals	were

ESL Most noncount nouns—those that do not form plurals—take singular verbs: *That information is helpful.* (See p. 338 on collective nouns.)

Note In a verb phrase (main verb plus helping verb), the helping verb sometimes reflects the number of the subject and sometimes does not: *The car does run. The cars do run. The car/cars will run.* The main verb (*run*) does not change in any way.

2 Subject and verb should agree even when other words come between them.

When the subject and verb are interrupted by other words, make sure the verb agrees with the subject:

> A catalog of courses and requirements often baffles [not baffle] students.

> The requirements stated in the catalog are [not is] unclear.

Note Phrases beginning with *as well as, together with, along with,* and *in addition to* do not change the number of the subject:

> The president, as well as the deans, has [not have] agreed to revise the catalog.

If you really mean *and* in such a sentence, use it. Then the subject is compound, and the verb should be plural: *The president and the deans have agreed to revise the catalog.*

3 Subjects joined by *and* usually take plural verbs.

Two or more subjects joined by *and* usually take a plural verb, whether one or all of the subjects are singular:

> Frost and Roethke were contemporaries.

> Frost, Roethke, Stevens, and Pound are among the great American poets.

Exceptions When the parts of the subject form a single idea or refer to a single person or thing, they take a singular verb:

> Avocado and bean sprouts is a California sandwich.

When a compound subject is preceded by the adjective *each* or *every,* the verb is usually singular:

> Each man, woman, and child has a right to be heard.

But a compound subject *followed* by *each* takes a plural verb:

> The man and the woman each have different problems.

4 When parts of a subject are joined by *or* or *nor*, the verb agrees with the nearer part.

When all parts of a subject joined by *or* or *nor* are singular, the verb is singular; when all parts are plural, the verb is plural.

Either the painter or the carpenter knows the cost.

The cabinets or the bookcases are too costly.

When one part of the subject is singular and the other plural, avoid awkwardness by placing the plural part closer to the verb so that the verb is plural:

Awkward Neither the owners nor the contractor agrees.

Revised Neither the contractor nor the owners agree.

When the subject consists of nouns and pronouns of different person requiring different verb forms, the verb agrees with the nearer part of the subject. Reword if this construction is awkward:

Awkward Either Juarez or I am responsible.

Revised Either Juarez is responsible, or I am.

5 With an indefinite pronoun, use a singular or plural verb as appropriate.

An **indefinite pronoun** is one that does not refer to a specific person or thing. Most indefinite pronouns take a singular verb, but some take a plural verb and some take a singular *or* a plural verb.

Common indefinite pronouns

Singular			Singular or plural	Plural
anybody	everyone	no one	all	both
anyone	everything	nothing	any	few
anything	much	one	more	many
each	neither	somebody	most	several
either	nobody	someone	some	
everybody	none	something		

The singular indefinite pronouns refer to a single unspecified person or thing, and they take a singular verb:

Something smells. Neither is right.

The plural indefinite pronouns refer to more than one unspecified thing, and they take a plural verb:

Both are correct. Several were invited.

The other indefinite pronouns take a singular or a plural verb depending on whether the word they refer to is singular or plural. The word may be stated in the sentence:

All of the money is reserved for emergencies.

All of the funds are reserved for emergencies.

Or the word may be implied:

All are planning to attend. [*All* implies "all the people."]

All is lost. [*All* implies "everything."]

ESL See page 359 for the distinction between *few* ("not many") and *a few* ("some").

6 Collective nouns take singular or plural verbs depending on meaning.

A **collective noun** has singular form but names a group of individuals or things—for example, *army, audience, committee, crowd, family, group, team.* As a subject, a collective noun may take a singular or plural verb, depending on the context. When the group acts as one unit, use a singular verb:

The group agrees that action is necessary.

But when considering the group's members as individuals who act separately, use the plural form of the verb:

The old group have gone their separate ways.

The collective noun *number* may be singular or plural. Preceded by *a,* it is plural; preceded by *the,* it is singular.

A number of people are in debt.

The number of people in debt is very large.

ESL Some noncount nouns (nouns that don't form plurals) are collective nouns because they name groups: for instance, *furniture, clothing, mail.* These noncount nouns usually take singular verbs:

Mail arrives daily. But some of these nouns take plural verbs, including *clergy, military, people, police,* and any collective noun that comes from an adjective, such as *the poor, the rich, the young, the elderly.* If you mean one representative of the group, use a singular noun such as *police officer* or *poor person.*

7 The verb agrees with the subject even when the normal word order is inverted.

Inverted subject-verb order occurs mainly in questions and in constructions beginning with *there* or *it* and a form of *be:*

> Is voting a right or a privilege?
>
> Are a right and a privilege the same thing?
>
> There are differences between them.

In constructions beginning with *there,* you may use *is* before a compound subject when the first element in the subject is singular:

> There is much work to do and little time to do it.

Word order may sometimes be inverted for emphasis. The verb still agrees with its subject:

> From the mountains comes an eerie, shimmering light.

8 A linking verb agrees with its subject, not the subject complement.

A linking verb such as *is* or *are* should agree with its subject, usually the first element in the sentence, not with the noun or pronoun serving as a subject complement (see p. 261):

> The child's sole support is her court-appointed guardians.
>
> Her court-appointed guardians are the child's sole support.

9 *Who, which,* and *that* take verbs that agree with their antecedents.

When used as subjects, *who, which,* and *that* refer to another word in the sentence, called the **antecedent.** The verb agrees with the antecedent:

> Mayor Garber ought to listen to the people who work for her.
>
> Bardini is the only aide who has her ear.

agr
15a

Agreement problems often occur with relative pronouns when the sentence includes *one of the* or *the only one of the:*

> Bardini is one of the aides who work unpaid. [Of the aides who work unpaid, Bardini is one.]

> Bardini is the only one of the aides who knows the community. [Of the aides, only one, Bardini, knows the community.]

ESL In phrases like those above beginning with *one of the,* be sure the noun is plural: *Bardini is one of the aides* [not aide] *who work unpaid.*

10 Nouns with plural form but singular meaning take singular verbs.

Some nouns with plural form (that is, ending in *-s*) are usually regarded as singular in meaning. They include *athletics, economics, linguistics, mathematics, measles, mumps, news, physics, politics,* and *statistics,* as well as place names such as *Athens, Wales,* and *United States.*

> After so long a wait, the news has to be good.

> Statistics is required of psychology majors.

A few of these words take plural verbs only when they describe individual items rather than whole bodies of activity or knowledge: *The statistics prove him wrong.*

Measurements and figures ending in *-s* may also be singular when the quantity they refer to is a unit:

> Three years is a long time to wait.

> Three-fourths of the library consists of reference books.

11 Titles and words named as words take singular verbs.

When your sentence subject is the name of a corporation, the title of a work (such as a book), or a word you are defining or describing, the verb should be singular even if the name, title, or word is plural:

> Hakada Associates is a new firm.

> *Dream Days* remains a favorite book.

> *Folks* is a down-home word for *people.*

EXERCISE 1
Revising: Subject-verb agreement

Revise the verbs in the following sentences as needed to make subjects and verbs agree in number. If the sentence is already correct as given, circle the number preceding it.

Example:

Each of the job applicants type sixty words per minute.
Each of the job applicants types sixty words per minute.

1. Weinstein & Associates are a consulting firm that try to make businesspeople laugh.
2. Statistics from recent research suggests that humor relieves stress.
3. Reduced stress in businesses in turn reduce illness and absenteeism.
4. Reduced stress can also reduce friction within an employee group, which then work more productively.
5. In special conferences held by one consultant, each of the participants practice making the others laugh.
6. One consultant to many companies suggest cultivating office humor with practical jokes such as a rubber fish in the water cooler.
7. When employees or their manager regularly post cartoons on the bulletin board, office spirit usually picks up.
8. When someone who has seemed too easily distracted is entrusted with updating the cartoons, his or her concentration often improves.
9. In the face of levity, the former sourpuss becomes one of those who hides bad temper.
10. Every one of the consultants caution, however, that humor has no place in life-affecting corporate situations such as employee layoffs.

agr 15b

15b Make pronouns and their antecedents agree in person, number, and gender.

The **antecedent** of a pronoun is the noun or other pronoun to which the pronoun refers:

Homeowners fret over their tax bills.
antecedent — pronoun

Its constant increases make the tax bill a dreaded document.
pronoun — antecedent

Information on pronoun-antecedent agreement:

http://webster.commnet.edu/HP/pages/darling/grammar/pronouns.htm From the Guide to Grammar and Writing.

http://owl.english.purdue.edu/Files/79.html From the Purdue Online Writing Lab.

Since a pronoun derives its meaning from its antecedent, the two must agree in person, number, and gender.

Person, number, and gender in pronoun-antecedent agreement

	Number	
Person	***Singular***	***Plural***
First	*I*	*we*
Second	*you*	*you*
Third	*he, she, it,* indefinite pronouns, singular nouns	*they,* plural nouns
Gender		
Masculine	*he,* nouns naming males	
Feminine	*she,* nouns naming females	
Neuter	*it,* all other nouns	

Note Computerized grammar and style checkers cannot help you with agreement between pronoun and antecedent. You'll need to check for errors on your own.

ESL The gender of a pronoun should match its antecedent, not a noun that the pronoun may modify: *Sara Young invited her* [not *his*] *son to join the company's staff.* Also, nouns in English have only neuter gender unless they specifically refer to males or females. Thus nouns such as *book, table, sun,* and *earth* take the pronoun *it.*

1 Antecedents joined by *and* usually take plural pronouns.

Two or more antecedents joined by *and* usually take a plural pronoun, whether one or all of the antecedents are singular:

Mr. Bartos and I cannot settle our dispute.

The dean and my adviser have offered their help.

Exceptions When the compound antecedent refers to a single idea, person, or thing, then the pronoun is singular:

My friend and adviser offered her help.

When the compound antecedent follows *each* or *every,* the pronoun is singular:

Every girl and woman took her seat.

Summary of pronoun-antecedent agreement

- Basic pronoun-antecedent agreement:

  Old Faithful spews its columns of water, each of them over 115 feet high.

- Antecedents joined by *and* (opposite):

  Old Faithful and Giant are geysers known for their height.

- Antecedents joined by *or* or *nor* (below):

  Either Giant or Giantess ejects its column the highest.

- Indefinite words as antecedents (below):

  Each of the geysers has its own personality. Each person who visits has his or her memories.

- Collective nouns as antecedents (p. 345):

  A crowd amuses itself watching Old Faithful. The crowd go their separate ways.

2 When parts of an antecedent are joined by *or* or *nor,* the pronoun agrees with the nearer part.

When the parts of an antecedent are connected by *or* or *nor,* the pronoun should agree with the part closer to it:

Tenants or owners must present their grievances.

Either the tenant or the owner will have her way.

When one subject is plural and the other singular, the sentence will be awkward unless you put the plural one second:

Awkward Neither the tenants nor the owner has yet made her case.

Revised Neither the owner nor the tenants have yet made their case.

3 With an indefinite word as antecedent, use a singular or plural pronoun as appropriate.

Indefinite words do not refer to any specific person or thing. They include **indefinite pronouns** such as *anyone, everybody, no one, one, somebody* (see p. 337 for a longer list). They also include **generic nouns,** or singular nouns that refer to typical members of a group, as in *The individual has rights* or *The job requires a person with computer skills.*

The pronoun referring to a singular generic noun should always be singular: *The wolf nurses its young.* The pronoun referring to an indefinite pronoun should be singular or plural depending on the meaning of the indefinite pronoun. Four indefinite pronouns—*both, few, many, several*—are always plural in meaning and are referred to with plural pronouns:

Few realize how their athletic facilities have changed.

Five indefinite pronouns—*all, any, more, most, some*—may be singular or plural depending on the word to which they refer:

Few women athletes had changing spaces, so most had to change in their rooms.

Most of the changing space was dismal, its color a drab olive green.

All other indefinite words—nouns and pronouns—are singular and take singular pronouns:

Now everyone on the women's teams has her own locker.

Each of the men still has his own locker.

Most agreement problems arise with the singular indefinite words. We often use these words to mean something like "many" or "all" rather than "one" and then refer to them with plural pronouns, as in *Everyone has their own locker* or *A person can padlock their locker.* Often, too, we mean indefinite words to include both masculine and feminine genders and thus resort to *they* instead of the **generic *he***—the masculine pronoun referring to both genders, as in *Everyone has his own locker.* (For more on the generic *he,* which many readers view as sexist, see p. 565.) To achieve agreement in such cases, you have several options:

Ways to correct agreement with indefinite words

- Change the indefinite word to a plural, and use a plural pronoun to match:

  Athletes deserve their privacy.

  All athletes are entitled to their own lockers. [Notice that *locker* also changes to *lockers.*]

- Rewrite the sentence to omit the pronoun:

  The athlete deserves privacy.
  Everyone is entitled to a locker.

- Use *he or she* (*him or her, his or her*) to refer to the indefinite word:

  The athlete deserves his or her privacy.

  However, used more than once in several sentences, *he or she* quickly becomes awkward. (Many readers do not accept the alternative *he/she.*) In most cases, using the plural or omitting the pronoun will not only correct agreement problems but create more readable sentences.

---

4 Collective noun antecedents take singular or plural pronouns depending on meaning.

Collective nouns such as *army, committee, family, group,* and *team* have singular form but may be referred to by singular or plural pronouns, depending on the meaning intended. When the group acts as a unit, the pronoun is singular:

The committee voted to disband itself.

When the members of the group act separately, the pronoun is plural:

The old group have gone their separate ways.

In the last example, note that the verb and pronoun are consistent in number (see also p. 390).

Inconsistent The old group has gone their separate ways.

Consistent The old group have gone their separate ways.

ESL Collective nouns that are noncount nouns (they don't form plurals) usually take singular pronouns: *The mail sits in its own basket.* A few noncount nouns take plural pronouns, including *clergy, military, people, police, the rich,* and *the poor: The police support their unions.* (See also pp. 338–39.)

agr 15b

EXERCISE 2
Revising: Pronoun-antecedent agreement

Revise the following sentences so that pronouns and their antecedents agree in person and number. Some items have more than one possible answer. Try to avoid the generic *he* (see the previous page). If you change the subject of a sentence, be sure to change verbs as necessary for agreement. If the sentence is already correct as given, circle the number preceding it.

Example:
Each of the Boudreaus' children brought their laundry home at Thanksgiving.

All of the Boudreaus' children brought their laundry home at Thanksgiving. *Or:* Each of the Boudreaus' children brought laundry home at Thanksgiving. *Or:* Each of the Boudreaus' children brought his or her laundry home at Thanksgiving.

1. Each girl raised in a Mexican American family in the Rio Grande Valley of Texas hopes that one day they will be given a *quinceañera* party for their fifteenth birthday.
2. Such celebrations are very expensive because it entails a religious service followed by a huge party.
3. A girl's immediate family, unless they are wealthy, cannot afford the party by themselves.
4. Her parents will ask each close friend or relative if they can help with the preparations.
5. Surrounded by her family and attended by her friends and their escorts, the *quinceañera* is introduced as a young woman eligible for fashionable Mexican American society.

EXERCISE 3
Adjusting for agreement

In the sentences below, subjects agree with verbs and pronouns agree with antecedents. Make the change specified in parentheses after each sentence, and then revise the sentence as necessary to maintain agreement. Some items have more than one possible answer.

Example:

The student attends weekly conferences with her teacher. (*Change The student to Students.*)

Students attend weekly conferences with their teacher.

1. A biologist wishes to introduce captive red wolves into the Smoky Mountains in order to increase the wild population of this endangered species. (*Change A biologist to Biologists.*)
2. When freed, the wolf naturally has no fear of humans and thus is in danger of being shot. (*Change wolf to wolves.*)
3. The first experiment to release the wolves was a failure. (*Change experiment to experiments.*)
4. Now researchers pen the wolf puppy in the wooded area that will eventually be its territory. (*Change puppy to puppies.*)
5. The wolf has little contact with people, even its own keeper, during the year of its captivity. (*Change wolf to wolves.*)

EXERCISE 4
Revising: Agreement

Revise the sentences in the following paragraphs to correct errors in agreement between subjects and verbs or between pronouns and their antecedents. Try to avoid the generic *he* (see p. 344).

The writers Richard Rodriguez and Maxine Hong Kingston, despite their differences, shares one characteristic: their parents was immigrants to California. A frequent theme of their writings are the difficulties of growing up with two languages and two cultures.

A child whose first language is not English is often ridiculed because they cannot communicate "properly." Rodriguez learned Spanish at home, but at school everyone expected him to use their language, English. He remembers his childish embarrassment because of his parents' poor English. College and graduate school, which usually expands one's knowledge, widened the gap between Rodriguez and his Latino culture. His essays suggests that he lost a part of himself, a loss that continue to bother him.

Kingston spoke Chinese at home and also learned her first English at school. She sometimes write of these experiences, but more often she write to recover and preserve her Chinese culture. *The Woman Warrior,* which offer a blend of autobiography, family history, and mythic tales, describe the struggle of Kingston's female relatives. *China Men* focus on Kingston's male ancestors; each one traveled to Hawaii or California to make money for their wife back in China. Kingston's work, like Rodriguez's essays, reflect the tension and confusion that the child of immigrants often feel when they try to blend two cultures.

Note See page 362 for an exercise involving agreement along with other aspects of grammar.

CHAPTER 16

Adjectives and Adverbs

Adjectives and adverbs are modifiers that describe, restrict, or otherwise qualify the words to which they relate.

Functions of adjectives and adverbs

Adjectives modify nouns:	serious student
pronouns:	ordinary one
Adverbs modify verbs:	warmly greet
adjectives:	only three people
adverbs:	quite seriously
phrases:	nearly to the edge of the cliff
clauses:	just when we arrived
sentences:	Fortunately, she is employed.

Many of the most common adjectives are familiar one-syllable words such as *bad, strange, large,* and *wrong.* Many others are formed by adding endings such as *-al, -able, -ful, -less, -ish, -ive,* and *-y* to nouns or verbs: *optional, fashionable, beautiful, fruitless, selfish, expressive, dreamy.*

Most adverbs are formed by adding *-ly* to adjectives: *badly, strangely, largely, beautifully.* But note that we cannot depend on *-ly*

http://owl.english.purdue.edu/Files/81.html A comparison of adjectives and adverbs, from the Purdue Online Writing Center.

http://www.english.uiuc.edu/cws/wworkshop/adjectivedef.htm Information on adjectives, from the University of Illinois at Urbana-Champaign.

http://webster.commnet.edu/HP/pages/darling/grammar/adjectives.htm In-depth information and quizzes on adjectives, from the Guide to Grammar and Writing.

http://webster.commnet.edu/HP/pages/darling/grammar/adverbs.htm In-depth information and quizzes on adverbs, from the Guide to Grammar and Writing.

to identify adverbs, since some adjectives also end in *-ly* (*fatherly, lonely*) and since some common adverbs do not end in *-ly* (*always, here, not, now, often, there*). Thus the only sure way to distinguish between adjectives and adverbs is to determine what they modify.

Note Computerized grammar and style checkers will spot few problems with misused adjectives and adverbs. For instance, a checker flagged none of the errors in Exercise 1 on page 351. You'll need to proofread your work on your own to find errors in adjectives and adverbs.

ESL In English an adjective does not change along with the noun it modifies to show plural number: *white* [not *whites*] *shoes, square* [not *squares*] *spaces.* Only nouns form plurals.

16a Use adjectives only to modify nouns and pronouns.

Adjectives modify only nouns and pronouns. Using adjectives instead of adverbs to modify verbs, adverbs, or other adjectives is nonstandard:

Nonstandard The groups view family values different.

Standard The groups view family values differently.

The adjectives *good* and *bad* often appear where standard English requires the adverbs *well* and *badly:*

Nonstandard Educating children good is everyone's focus.

Standard Educating children well is everyone's focus.

Nonstandard Some children suffer bad.

Standard Some children suffer badly.

ESL To negate a verb or an adjective, use the adverb *not:*

They are not learning. They are not stupid.

To negate a noun, use the adjective *no:*

No child should fail to read.

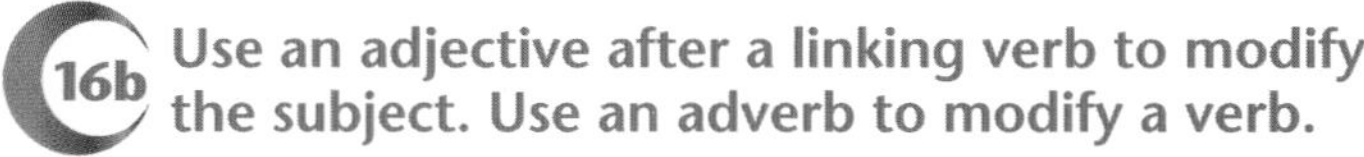

16b Use an adjective after a linking verb to modify the subject. Use an adverb to modify a verb.

A **linking verb** is one that links, or connects, a subject and its complement: *They are golfers. He is lucky.* (See also p. 261.) Linking verbs are forms of *be,* the verbs associated with our five senses (*look, sound, smell, feel, taste*), and a few others (*appear, seem, become, grow, turn, prove, remain, stay*).

Some of these verbs may or may not be linking, depending on their meaning in the sentence. When the word after the verb modifies the subject, the verb is linking and the word should be an adjective: *He feels strong*. When the word modifies the verb, however, it should be an adverb: *He feels strongly about that.*

Two word pairs are especially troublesome in this context. One is *bad* and *badly:*

The weather grew bad. [grew: linking verb; bad: adjective]

She felt bad. [felt: linking verb; bad: adjective]

Flowers grow badly in such soil. [grow: verb; badly: adverb]

The other pair is *good* and *well. Good* serves only as an adjective. *Well* may serve as an adverb with a host of meanings or as an adjective meaning only "fit" or "healthy."

Decker trained well. [trained: verb; well: adverb]

She felt well. [felt: linking verb; well: adjective]

Her health was good. [was: linking verb; good: adjective]

16c After a direct object, use an adjective to modify the object and an adverb to modify the verb.

After a direct object, an adjective modifies the object, whereas an adverb modifies the verb of the sentence. (See pp. 260–61 for more on direct objects.)

Campus politics made Mungo angry. [angry: adjective]

Mungo repeated the words angrily. [angrily: adverb]

You can test whether a modifier should be an adjective or an adverb by trying to separate it from the direct object. If you can separate it, it should be an adverb: *Mungo angrily repeated the words.* If you cannot separate it, it is probably an adjective.

> The instructor considered the student's work thorough. [The adjective can be moved in front of *work* (*student's thorough work*), but it cannot be separated from *work.*]
>
> The instructor considered the student's work thoroughly. [The adverb can be separated from *work.* Compare *The instructor thoroughly considered the student's work.*]

16d When an adverb has a short form and an *-ly* form, distinguish carefully between the forms.

Some adverbs have two forms, one with an *-ly* ending and one without. These include the following:

cheap, cheaply	quick, quickly
high, highly	sharp, sharply
late, lately	slow, slowly
loud, loudly	wrong, wrongly
near, nearly	

With some of these pairs the choice of form is a matter of idiom, for the two forms have developed entirely separate meanings:

He went late.
Winter is drawing near.

Lately he has been eating more.
Winter is nearly here.

In other pairs the long and short forms have the same meaning. However, the short forms generally occur in informal speech and writing. The *-ly* forms are preferable in formal writing:

Informal Drive slow.

Formal The funeral procession moved slowly through the village.

ad 16d

EXERCISE 1
Revising: Adjectives and adverbs

Revise the following sentences so that adjectives and adverbs are used appropriately. If any sentence is already correct as given, circle the number preceding it.

Example:
The announcer warned that traffic was moving very slow.
The announcer warned that traffic was moving very slowly.

1. King George III of England declared Samuel Johnson suitably for a pension.
2. Johnson was taken serious as a critic and dictionary maker.
3. Thinking about his meeting with the king, Johnson felt proudly.
4. Johnson was relieved that he had not behaved badly in the king's presence.
5. After living cheap for over twenty years, Johnson finally had enough money from the pension to eat and dress good.

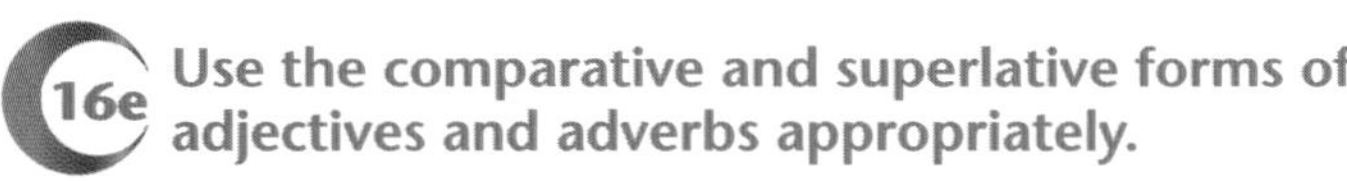

16e Use the comparative and superlative forms of adjectives and adverbs appropriately.

Adjectives and adverbs can show degrees of quality or amount with the endings *-er* and *-est* or with the words *more* and *most* or *less* and *least.* Most modifiers have three forms:

	Adjectives	**Adverbs**
Positive The basic form listed in the dictionary	red awful	soon quickly
Comparative A greater or lesser degree of the quality named	redder more/less awful	sooner more/less quickly
Superlative The greatest or least degree of the quality named	reddest most/least awful	soonest most/least quickly

If sound alone does not tell you whether to use *-er/-est* or *more/most,* consult a dictionary. If the endings can be used, the dictionary will list them. Otherwise, use *more* or *most.*

1 Use the correct forms of irregular adjectives and adverbs.

The irregular modifiers change the spelling of their positive form to show comparative and superlative degrees:

Degrees of irregular adjectives and adverbs

Positive	**Comparative**	**Superlative**
Adjectives		
good	better	best
bad	worse	worst
little	littler, less	littlest, least
many some much	more	most
Adverbs		
well	better	best
badly	worse	worst

Information on comparatives and superlatives:

http://www.edunet.com/english/grammar/adjectiv.html#comparison From Online English Grammar.

http://www.english.uiuc.edu/cws/wworkshop/comparatives.htm From the University of Illinois at Urbana-Champaign.

2 Use either *-er/-est* or *more/most,* not both.

A double comparative or double superlative combines the *-er* or *-est* ending with the word *more* or *most.* It is redundant.

Chang was the wisest [not most wisest] person in town.
He was smarter [not more smarter] than anyone else.

3 Use the comparative for comparing two things and the superlative for comparing three or more things.

It is the shorter of her two books. [Comparative.]
The Yearling is the most popular of the six books. [Superlative.]

In conversation the superlative form is often used to compare only two things: *When two people argue, the angriest one is usually wrong.* But the distinction between the forms should be observed in writing.

4 Use comparative or superlative forms only for modifiers that can logically be compared.

Some adjectives and adverbs cannot logically be compared—for instance, *perfect, unique, dead, impossible, infinite.* These absolute words can be preceded by adverbs like *nearly* and *almost* that mean "approaching," but they cannot logically be modified by *more* or *most* (as in *most perfect*). This distinction is sometimes ignored in speech, but it should always be made in writing:

Not He was the most unique teacher we had.
But He was a unique teacher.

EXERCISE 2
Using comparatives and superlatives

Write the comparative and superlative forms of each adjective or adverb below. Then use all three forms in your own sentences.

Example:
heavy: heavier (comparative), heaviest (superlative)
The barbells were too heavy for me. The magician's trunk was heavier than I expected. Joe Clark was the heaviest person on the team.

1. badly
2. steady
3. good
4. well
5. understanding

EXERCISE 3
Revising: Comparatives and superlatives

Revise the sentences below so that the comparative and superlative forms of adjectives and adverbs are appropriate for formal usage. Circle the number preceding any sentence that is already correct.

Example:

Attending classes full time and working at two jobs was the most impossible thing I ever did.

Attending classes full time and working at two jobs was impossible [or the hardest thing I ever did].

1. Charlotte was the older of the three Brontë sisters, all of whom were novelists.
2. Some readers think Emily Brontë's *Wuthering Heights* is the most saddest novel they have ever read.
3. Of the other two sisters, Charlotte and Anne, Charlotte was probably the more talented.
4. Critics still argue about whether Charlotte or Emily wrote more better.
5. Certainly this family of women novelists was the most unique.

16f Watch for double negatives.

ad 16g

In a **double negative** two negative words such as *no, none, neither, barely, hardly,* or *scarcely* cancel each other out. Some double negatives are intentional: for instance, *She was not unhappy* indicates with understatement that she was indeed happy. But most double negatives say the opposite of what is intended: *Jenny did not feel nothing* asserts that Jenny felt other than nothing, or something. For the opposite meaning, one of the negatives must be eliminated or changed to a positive: *She felt nothing* or *She did not feel anything.*

Faulty The IRS cannot hardly audit all tax returns. None of its audits never touch many cheaters.

Revised The IRS cannot audit all tax returns. Its audits never touch many cheaters.

16g Use nouns sparingly as modifiers.

We often use one noun to modify another. For example:

child care flood control security guard

Such phrases can be both clear and concise, but overuse of noun modifiers can lead to flat, even senseless, writing. To avoid awkwardness or confusion, observe two principles. First, prefer possessives or adjectives as modifiers.

http://webster.commnet.edu/HP/pages/darling/grammar/confusion.htm#double_negatives Guidance on avoiding double negatives, from the Guide to Grammar and Writing.

Not	A student takes the state medical board exams to become a dentist technician.
But	A student takes the state medical board's exams to become a dental technician.

Second, use only short nouns as modifiers and use them only in two- or three-word sequences:

Confusing	Minimex maintains a plant employee relations improvement program.
Revised	Minimex maintains a program for improving relations among plant employees.

16h Distinguish between present and past participles as adjectives. ESL

Both present participles and past participles may serve as adjectives: *a burning building, a burned building.* As in the examples, the two participles usually differ in the time they indicate.

But some present and past participles—those derived from verbs expressing feeling—can have altogether different meanings. The present participle refers to something that causes the feeling: *That was a frightening storm.* The past participle refers to something that experiences the feeling: *They quieted the frightened horses.*

The following participles are among those likely to be confused:

amazing/amazed
amusing/amused
annoying/annoyed
astonishing/astonished
boring/bored
confusing/confused
depressing/depressed
embarrassing/embarrassed
exciting/excited
exhausting/exhausted
fascinating/fascinated
frightening/frightened
frustrating/frustrated
interesting/interested
pleasing/pleased
satisfying/satisfied
shocking/shocked
surprising/surprised
tiring/tired
worrying/worried

EXERCISE 4
Revising: Present and past participles ESL

Revise the adjectives in the following sentences as needed to distinguish between present and past participles. If the sentence is already correct as given, circle the number preceding it.

http://www.aitech.ac.jp/~iteslj/quizzes/fb012-ld.html An online quiz covering the use of participles as adjectives, from the *Internet TESL Journal.*

Example:

The subject was embarrassed to many people.
The subject was embarrassing to many people.

1. Several critics found Alice Walker's *The Color Purple* to be a fascinated book.
2. One confused critic wished that Walker had deleted the scenes set in Africa.
3. Another critic argued that although the book contained many depressed episodes, the overall impact was excited.
4. Since other readers found the book annoyed, this critic pointed out its many surprised qualities.
5. In the end most critics agreed that the book was a satisfied novel.

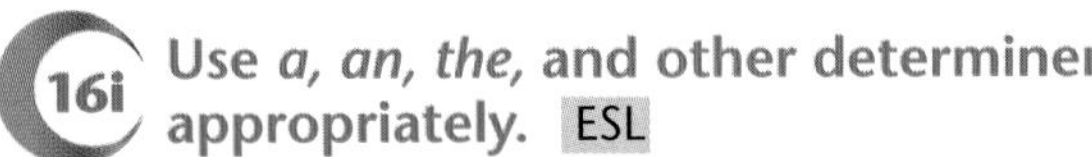

16i Use *a, an, the,* and other determiners appropriately. ESL

Determiners are special kinds of adjectives that mark nouns because they always precede nouns. Some common determiners are *a, an,* and *the* (called **articles**) and *my, their, whose, this, these, those, one, some,* and *any.* They convey information to readers—for instance, by specifying who owns what, which one of two is meant, or whether a subject is familiar or unfamiliar.

Native speakers of English can rely on their intuition when using determiners, but nonnative speakers often have difficulty with them because many other languages use them quite differently or not at all. In English the use of determiners depends on the context they appear in and the kind of noun they precede:

- A **proper noun** names a particular person, place, or thing and begins with a capital letter: *February, Joe Allen, Red River.* Most proper nouns are not preceded by determiners.
- A **count noun** names something that is countable in English and can form a plural: *girl/girls, apple/apples, child/children.* A singular count noun is always preceded by a determiner; a plural count noun sometimes is.
- A **noncount noun** names something not usually considered countable in English, and so it does not form a plural. A noncount noun is sometimes preceded by a determiner. Here is a sample of noncount nouns, sorted into groups by meaning:

Information on using articles and other determiners:

http://webster.commnet.edu/HP/pages/darling/grammar/determiners/determiners.htm From the Guide to Grammar and Writing.

http://www.aitech.ac.jp/~iteslj/quizzes/grammar.html#ART From the *Internet TESL Journal.*

Abstractions: confidence, democracy, education, equality, evidence, health, information, intelligence, knowledge, luxury, peace, pollution, research, success, supervision, truth, wealth, work

Food and drink: bread, candy, cereal, flour, meat, milk, salt, water, wine

Emotions: anger, courage, happiness, hate, joy, love, respect, satisfaction

Natural events and substances: air, blood, dirt, gasoline, gold, hair, heat, ice, oil, oxygen, rain, silver, smoke, weather, wood

Groups: clergy, clothing, equipment, furniture, garbage, jewelry, junk, legislation, machinery, mail, military, money, police, vocabulary

Fields of study: architecture, accounting, biology, business, chemistry, engineering, literature, psychology, science

An ESL dictionary will tell you whether a noun is a count noun, a noncount noun, or both. (See p. 587 for recommended dictionaries.)

Note Many nouns can be both count and noncount nouns:

> The library has a room for readers. [*Room* is a count noun meaning "walled area."]
>
> The library has room for reading. [*Room* is a noncount noun meaning "space."]

Partly because the same noun may fall into different groups, computerized grammar and style checkers are unreliable guides to missing or misused articles and other determiners. For instance, a checker flagged the omitted *a* before *Scientist* in *Scientist developed new processes,* did not flag the omitted *a* before *new* in *A scientist developed new process,* and mistakenly flagged the correctly omitted article *the* before *Vegetation* in *Vegetation suffers from drought.* To correct omitted or misused articles, you'll need to proofread carefully on your own.

1 Use *a, an,* and *the* where they are required.

With singular count nouns

A or *an* precedes a singular count noun when the reader does not already know its identity, usually because you have not mentioned it before:

> A scientist in our chemistry department developed a process to strengthen metals. [*Scientist* and *process* are being introduced for the first time.]

The precedes a singular count noun that has a specific identity for the reader, usually because (1) you have mentioned it before, (2) you identify it immediately before or after you state it, (3) it is unique (the only one in existence), or (4) it refers to an institution or facility that is shared by a community:

A scientist in our chemistry department developed a process to strengthen metals. The scientist patented the process. [*Scientist* and *process* were identified in the preceding sentence.]

The most productive laboratory is the research center in the chemistry department. [*Most productive* identifies *laboratory*. *In the chemistry department* identifies *research center*. And *chemistry department* is a shared facility.]

The sun rises in the east. [*Sun* and *east* are unique.]

Many men and women aspire to the presidency. [*Presidency* is a shared institution.]

The fax machine has changed business communication. [*Fax machine* is a shared facility.]

The is not used before a singular noun that names a general category:

Sherman said that war is hell. [*War* names a general category.]
The war in Croatia left many dead. [*War* names a specific war.]

With plural count nouns

A or *an* never precedes a plural noun. *The* does not precede a plural noun that names a general category. *The* does precede a plural noun that names specific representatives of a category.

Men and women are different. [*Men* and *women* name general categories.]

The women formed a team. [*Women* refers to specific people.]

With noncount nouns

A or *an* never precedes a noncount noun. *The* does precede a noncount noun when it names specific representatives of a general category:

Vegetation suffers from drought. [*Vegetation* names a general category.]

The vegetation in the park withered or died. [*Vegetation* refers to specific plants.]

With proper nouns

A or *an* never precedes a proper noun. *The* generally does not precede a proper noun:

Garcia lives in Boulder.

There are exceptions, however. For instance, we generally use *the* before plural proper nouns (*the Murphys, the Boston Celtics*) and the names of groups and organizations (*the Department of Justice, the Sierra Club*), ships (*the Lusitania*), oceans (*the Pacific*), mountain ranges (*the Alps*), regions (*the Middle East*), rivers (*the Mississippi*), and some countries (*the United States, the Sudan*).

2 Use other determiners appropriately.

The uses of English determiners besides articles also depend on context and kind of noun. The following determiners may be used as indicated with singular count nouns, plural count nouns, or noncount nouns.

With any kind of noun (singular count, plural count, noncount)

my, our, your, his, her, its, their, possessive nouns (*boy's, boys'*)
whose, which(ever), what(ever)
some, any, the other
no

Their account is overdrawn. [Singular count.]
Their funds are low. [Plural count.]
Their money is running out. [Noncount.]

Only with singular nouns (count and noncount)

this, that

This account has some money. [Count.]
That information may help. [Noncount.]

Only with noncount nouns and plural count nouns

most, enough, other, such, all, all of the, a lot of

Most money is needed elsewhere. [Noncount.]
Most funds are committed. [Plural count.]

Only with singular count nouns

one, every, each, either, neither, another

One car must be sold. [Singular count.]

Only with plural count nouns

these, those
both, many, few, a few, fewer, fewest, several
two, three, and so forth

Two cars are unnecessary. [Plural count.]

Note *Few* means "not many" or "not enough." *A few* means "some" or "a small but sufficient quantity."

Few committee members came to the meeting.
A few members can keep the committee going.

Do not use *much* with a plural count noun:

Many [not much] members want to help.

Only with noncount nouns

much, more, little, a little, less, least, a large amount of

Less luxury is in order. [Noncount.]

Note *Little* means "not many" or "not enough." *A little* means "some" or "a small but sufficient quantity."

> Little time remains before the conference.
> The members need a little help from their colleagues.

Do not use *many* with a noncount noun:

> Much [not many] work remains.

EXERCISE 5
Revising: Articles ESL

For each blank below, indicate whether *a, an, the,* or no article should be inserted.

From ___ native American Indians who migrated from ___ Asia 20,000 years ago to ___ new arrivals who now come by ___ planes, ___ United States is ___ nation of foreigners. It is ___ country of immigrants who are all living under ___ single flag.

Back in ___ seventeenth and eighteenth centuries, at least 75 percent of the population came from ___ England. However, between 1820 and 1975 more than 38 million immigrants came to this country from elsewhere in ___ Europe. Many children of ___ immigrants were self-conscious and denied their heritage; many even refused to learn ___ native language of their parents and grandparents. They tried to "Americanize" themselves. The so-called Melting Pot theory of ___ social change stressed ___ importance of blending everyone together into ___ kind of stew. Each nationality would contribute its own flavor, but ___ final stew would be something called "American."

This Melting Pot theory was never completely successful. In the last half of the twentieth century, ___ ethnic revival changed ___ metaphor. Many people now see ___ American society as ___ mosaic. Americans are once again proud of their heritage, and ___ ethnic differences make ___ mosaic colorful and interesting.

EXERCISE 6
Revising: Adjectives and adverbs

Revise the following paragraph so that it conforms to formal usage of adjectives and adverbs.

Americans often argue about which professional sport is better: basketball, football, or baseball. Basketball fans contend that their sport offers more action because the players are constant running and shooting. Because it is played indoors in relative small arenas, basketball allows fans to be more closer to the action than the other sports do. Fans point to how graceful the players fly through the air to the hoop. Football fanatics say they don't hardly stop yelling once the game begins. They cheer when their team executes a real complicated play good. They roar more louder when the defense stops the opponents in a goal-line stand. They yell loudest when a fullback crashes in for a score. In contrast, the supporters of baseball believe that it might be the most perfect sport. It combines the one-on-one duel of pitcher and batter struggling valiant with the tight teamwork of double and triple plays. Because the game is played slow and careful, fans can analyze and discuss the manager's strategy. Besides, they don't never know when they might catch a foul ball as a souvenir. However, no matter what the sport, all fans feel happily only when their team wins!

Note See the next page for an exercise involving adjectives and adverbs along with other aspects of grammar.

EXERCISE ON CHAPTERS 13–16
Revising: Grammatical sentences

The paragraphs below contain errors in pronoun case, verb forms, subject-verb agreement, pronoun-antecedent agreement, and the forms of adjectives and adverbs. Revise the paragraphs to correct the errors.

Occasionally, musicians become "crossover artists" whom can perform good in more than one field of music. For example, Wynton and Branford Marsalis was train in jazz by their father, the great pianist Ellis Marsalis. Both of the sons has became successful classical artists. Branford's saxophone captures the richness of pieces by Ravel and Stravinsky. Wynton's albums of classical trumpet music from the Baroque period has brung him many awards. Still, if he was to choose which kind of music he likes best, Wynton would probable choose jazz. In contrast to the Marsalises, Yo-Yo Ma and Jean-Pierre Rampal growed up studying classical music. Then in the 1980s they was invited by Claude Bolling, a French pianist, to record Bolling's jazz compositions. In fact, Rampal's flute blended with Bolling's music so good that the two men have did three albums.

gr

Such crossovers are often more harder for vocalists. Each type of music has their own style and feel that is hard to learn. For example, Luciano Pavarotti and Kiri te Kanawa, two great opera performers, have sang popular music and folk songs in concerts and on albums. On each occasion, their technique was the most perfect, yet each sounded as if he was simply trying to sing proper. It is even more difficulter for pop or country vocalists to sing opera, as Linda Ronstadt and Gary Morris founded when they appear in *La Bohème*. Each of them have a clear, pure voice, but a few critics said that him and her lacked the vocal power necessary for opera. However, Bobby McFerrin been successful singing both pop and classical pieces. He won a Grammy award for his song "Don't Worry, Be Happy." But he is equal able to sing classical pieces *a cappella* (without musical accompaniment). His voice's remarkable range and clarity allows him to imitate many musical instruments.

No matter how successful, all of these musicians has shown great courage by performing in a new field. They are willing to test and stretch their talents, and each of we music fans benefit.

PART V

Clear Sentences

CHAPTER 17

Sentence Fragments

A **sentence fragment** is part of a sentence that is set off as if it were a whole sentence by an initial capital letter and a final period or other end punctuation. Although writers occasionally use fragments deliberately and effectively (see p. 371), readers perceive most fragments as serious errors because, expecting complete sentences, they find partial sentences distracting or confusing. (Before reading further, you may find it helpful to review pp. 255–62 and 275–78 on sentences and clauses.)

Complete sentence versus sentence fragment

A **complete sentence** or **main clause**

- contains a subject and a verb (*The wind blows*)
- and is not a subordinate clause (beginning with a word such as *because* or *who*).

A **sentence fragment**

- lacks a verb (*The wind blowing*)
- or lacks a subject (*And blows*)
- or is a subordinate clause not attached to a complete sentence (*Because the wind blows*).

Information and exercises on sentence fragments:

http://webster.commnet.edu/HP/pages/darling/grammar/fragments.htm From the Guide to Grammar and Writing.

http://owl.english.purdue.edu/Files/67.html From the Purdue Online Writing Lab.

http://www.english.uiuc.edu/cws/wworkshop/grammar/fragments.htm From the University of Illinois at Urbana-Champaign.

http://www.clearcf.uvic.ca/writersguide/Pages/SentFrags.html From the University of Victoria.

http://webnz.com/checkers/GramSentFrag.html For ESL writers, from Superteach.

Note Computerized grammar and style checkers can spot many but not all sentence fragments. For instance, a checker flagged *The network growing* as a fragment but failed to flag *Thousands of new sites on the Web.* Repair any fragments that your checker does find, but proofread your work yourself to ensure that it's fragment-free.

17a Test your sentences for completeness, and revise any fragments.

The following three tests will help you determine whether a word group punctuated as a sentence is actually a complete sentence. If the word group does not pass *all three* tests, it is a fragment and needs to be revised.

Tests for sentence fragments

A sentence is complete only when it passes *all three* tests:

1. Find the verb.
2. Find the subject.
3. Make sure the clause is not subordinate.

frag 17a

Test 1: Find the verb.

Look for a verb in the group of words. If you do not have one, the word group is a fragment:

Fragment Thousands of new sites on the World Wide Web. [Compare a complete sentence: *Thousands of new sites have appeared on the World Wide Web.*]

Any verb form you find must be a **finite verb,** one that changes form as indicated below. A verbal does not change; it cannot serve as a sentence verb without the aid of a helping verb.

	Finite verbs in complete sentences	Verbals in sentence fragments
Singular	The network grows.	The network growing.
Plural	Networks grow.	Networks growing.
Present	The network grows.	The network growing.
Past	The network grew.	
Future	The network will grow.	

ESL Some languages allow forms of *be* to be omitted as helping verbs or linking verbs. But English requires stating forms of *be:*

Fragments The network growing. It already larger than its developers anticipated. [Compare complete sentences: *The network is growing. It is already larger than its developers anticipated.*]

Test 2: Find the subject.

If you find a finite verb, look for its subject by asking who or what performs the action or makes the assertion of the verb. The subject of the sentence will usually come before the verb. If there is no subject, the word group is probably a fragment:

Fragment And has enormous popular appeal. [Compare a complete sentence: *And the Web has enormous popular appeal.*]

In one kind of complete sentence, a command, the subject *you* is understood: [*You*] *Experiment with the Web.*

ESL Some languages allow the omission of the sentence subject, especially when it is a pronoun. But in English, except in commands, the subject is always stated:

Fragments Web commerce is expanding dramatically. Is threatening traditional stores. [Compare a complete sentence: *It is threatening traditional stores.*]

frag
17a

Test 3: Make sure the clause is not subordinate.

A subordinate clause usually begins with a subordinating word:

Subordinating conjunctions			Relative pronouns	
after	once	until	that	who/whom
although	since	when	which	whoever/whomever
as	than	where		whose
because	that	whereas		
if	unless	while		

(See p. 276 for a longer list of subordinating conjunctions.)

Subordinate clauses serve as parts of sentences (nouns or modifiers), not as whole sentences:

Fragment When the government devised the Internet. [Compare a complete sentence: *The government devised the Internet.* Or: *When the government devised the Internet, no expansive computer network existed.*]

Fragment The reason that the government devised the Internet. [This fragment is a noun (*reason*) plus its modifier (*that . . . Internet*). Compare a complete sentence: *The reason that the government devised the Internet was to* *provide secure links among departments and defense contractors.*]

Note Questions beginning with *how, what, when, where, which, who, whom, whose,* and *why* are not sentence fragments: *Who was responsible? When did it happen?*

Revising sentence fragments

Almost all sentence fragments can be corrected in one of two ways, the choice depending on the importance of the information in the fragment:

Revision of sentence fragments

- Rewrite the fragment as a complete sentence.
- Combine the fragment with the appropriate main clause.

Rewriting the fragment as a complete sentence gives the information in the fragment the same importance as that in other complete sentences:

Fragment A recent addition to the Internet is the World Wide Web. Which allows users to move easily between sites.

Revised A recent addition to the Internet is the World Wide Web. It allows users to move easily between sites.

Two main clauses may be separated by a semicolon instead of a period (see p. 491).

The second method of correcting a fragment, combining it with a main clause, subordinates the information in the fragment to the information in the main clause:

Fragment The Web is easy to use. Loaded with links and graphics.

Revised The Web, loaded with links and graphics, is easy to use.

In this example, commas separate the inserted phrase from the rest of the sentence because the phrase is not essential to the meaning of any word in the main clause but simply adds information (see p. 473). When a phrase or subordinate clause *is* essential to the meaning of a word in the main clause, a comma or commas do *not* separate the two elements:

Fragment With the links, users can move to other Web sites. That they want to consult.

Revised With the links, users can move to other Web sites that they want to consult.

Sometimes a fragment may be combined with the main clause using a colon or a dash (see pp. 519 and 522, respectively):

Fragment	The Web connects sites from all over the Internet. Different databases, different software, different machines.
Revised	The Web connects sites from all over the Internet: different databases, different software, different machines.
Fragment	The Internet and now the Web are a boon to researchers. A vast and accessible library.
Revised	The Internet and now the Web are a boon to researchers—a vast and accessible library.

EXERCISE 1
Identifying and revising sentence fragments

Apply the tests for completeness to each of the following word groups. If a word group is a complete sentence, circle the number preceding it. If it is a sentence fragment, revise it in two ways: by making it a complete sentence, and by combining it with a main clause written from the information given in other items.

Example:

And could not find his money.

The word group has a verb (*could . . . find*) but no subject.

Revised into a complete sentence: And he could not find his money.

Combined with a new main clause: He was lost and could not find his money.

1. In an interesting article about vandalism against works of art.
2. The motives of the vandals varying widely.
3. Those who harm artwork are usually angry.
4. But not necessarily at the artist or the owner.
5. For instance, a man who hammered at Michelangelo's *Pietà*.
6. And knocked off the Virgin Mary's nose.
7. Because he was angry at the Roman Catholic Church.
8. Which knew nothing of his grievance.
9. Although many damaged works can be repaired.
10. Usually even the most skillful repairs are forever visible.

frag 17b

17b A subordinate clause is not a complete sentence.

Subordinate clauses contain both subjects and verbs, but they always begin with a subordinating conjunction (*although, if,* and so on) or a relative pronoun (*who, which, that*). (See p. 275.) Subordinate clauses serve as nouns or modifiers, but they cannot stand alone as complete sentences.

To correct a subordinate clause set off as a sentence, combine it with the main clause or remove or change the subordinating word to create a main clause:

Fragment	Many pine trees bear large cones. Which appear in August.
Revised	Many pine trees bear large cones, which appear in August.
Revised	Many pine trees bear large cones. They appear in August.

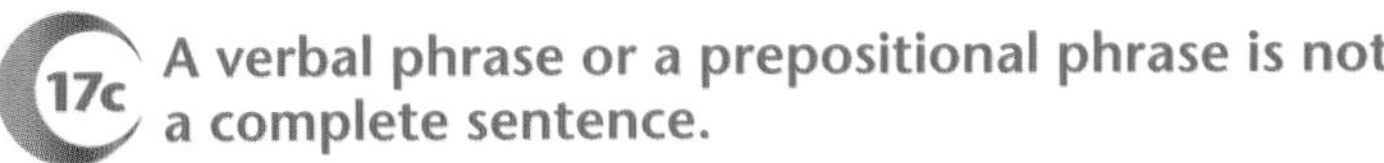

17c A verbal phrase or a prepositional phrase is not a complete sentence.

A **verbal phrase** consists of an infinitive (*to choose*), a past participle (*chosen*), or a present participle or gerund (*choosing*) together with any objects and modifiers it may have (see p. 269). A verbal phrase is a noun or modifier and cannot serve as the verb in a complete sentence:

Fragment	For many of the elderly, their house is their only asset. Offering some security but no income.
Revised	For many of the elderly, their house is their only asset, offering some security but no income.
Revised	For many of the elderly, their house is their only asset. It offers some security but no income.

frag 17c

A **prepositional phrase** is a modifier consisting of a preposition (such as *in, on, to,* and *with*) together with its object and any modifiers (see p. 266). A prepositional phrase cannot stand alone as a complete sentence:

Fragment	In a squeeze between a valuable asset and little income. Eventually many elderly people sell their homes.
Revised	In a squeeze between a valuable asset and little income, eventually many elderly people sell their homes.
Revised	Many elderly people are in a squeeze between a valuable asset and little income. Eventually they may sell their homes.

ESL Some prepositions consist of two or three words: *as well as, along with, in addition to, on top of,* and others. Don't let prepositions of more than one word mislead you into writing sentence fragments:

Fragment In today's retirement communities, the elderly may have health care, housekeeping, and new friends. As well as financial security.

Revised In today's retirement communities, the elderly may have health care, housekeeping, and new friends, as well as financial security.

17d Any word group lacking a subject or a verb or both is not a complete sentence.

We often follow a noun with a modifier. No matter how long the noun and its modifier are, they cannot stand alone as a sentence:

Fragments People waving flags and cheering. Lined the streets for the parade.

Revised People waving flags and cheering lined the streets for the parade.

Fragment Veterans who fought in Vietnam. They are finally being honored.

Revised Veterans who fought in Vietnam are finally being honored.

Appositives are nouns, or nouns and their modifiers, that rename or describe other nouns (see p. 280). They cannot stand alone as sentences:

Fragment When I was a child, my favorite adult was an old uncle. A retired sea captain who always told me long stories of wild adventures in faraway places.

Revised When I was a child, my favorite adult was an old uncle, a retired sea captain who always told me long stories of wild adventures in faraway places.

Compound predicates are predicates made up of two or more verbs and their objects, if any (see p. 282). A verb or its object cannot stand alone as a sentence:

Fragment Uncle Marlon drew out his tales. And embellished them.

Revised Uncle Marlon drew out his tales and embellished them.

Fragment He described characters he had met. And storms at sea.

Revised He described characters he had met and storms at sea.

Note Beginning a sentence with a coordinating conjunction such as *and* or *but* can lead to a sentence fragment. Check every sentence you begin with a coordinating conjunction to be sure it is complete.

EXERCISE 2
Revising: Sentence fragments

Correct any sentence fragment below either by combining it with a main clause or by making it a main clause. If an item contains no sentence fragment, circle the number preceding it.

Example:

Jujitsu is good for self-protection. Because it enables one to overcome an opponent without the use of weapons.

Jujitsu is good for self-protection because it enables one to overcome an opponent without the use of weapons.

1. Human beings who perfume themselves. They are not much different from other animals.
2. Animals as varied as insects and dogs release *pheromones.* Chemicals that signal other animals.
3. Human beings have a diminished sense of smell. And do not consciously detect most of their own species' pheromones.
4. The human substitute for pheromones may be perfumes. Especially musk and other fragrances derived from animal oils.
5. Some sources say that humans began using perfume to cover up the smell of burning flesh. During sacrifices to the gods.
6. Perfumes became religious offerings in their own right. Being expensive to make, they were highly prized.
7. The earliest historical documents from the Middle East record the use of fragrances. Not only in religious ceremonies but on the body.
8. In the nineteenth century chemists began synthesizing perfume oils. Which previously could be made only from natural sources.
9. The most popular animal oil for perfume today is musk. Although some people dislike its heavy, sweet odor.
10. Synthetic musk oil would help conserve a certain species of deer. Whose gland is the source of musk.

Be aware of the acceptable uses of incomplete sentences.

A few word groups lacking the usual subject-predicate combination are not sentence fragments because they conform to the expectations of most readers. They include exclamations (*Oh no!*);

questions and answers (*Where next? To Kansas.*); and commands (*Move along. Shut the window.*). Another kind of incomplete sentence, occurring in special situations, is the transitional phrase (*So much for the causes, now for the results. One final point.*).

Experienced writers sometimes use sentence fragments when they want to achieve a special effect. Such fragments appear more in informal than in formal writing. Unless you are experienced and thoroughly secure in your own writing, you should avoid all fragments and concentrate on writing clear, well-formed sentences.

EXERCISE 3
Revising: Sentence fragments

Revise the following paragraph to eliminate sentence fragments by combining them with main clauses or rewriting them as main clauses.

Baby red-eared slider turtles are brightly colored. With bold patterns on their yellowish undershells. Which serve as a warning to predators. The bright colors of skunks and other animals. They signal that the animals will spray nasty chemicals. In contrast, the turtle's colors warn largemouth bass. That the baby turtle will actively defend itself. When a bass gulps down a turtle. The feisty baby claws and bites. Forcing the bass to spit it out. To avoid a similar painful experience. The bass will avoid other baby red-eared slider turtles. The turtle loses its bright colors as it grows too big. For a bass's afternoon snack.

Note See page 416 for an exercise involving sentence fragments along with comma splices, fused sentences, and other sentence errors.

CHAPTER 18

Comma Splices and Fused Sentences

A sentence or main clause contains at least a subject and a predicate, which together express a complete thought (see p. 255). We can separate two consecutive main clauses in one of four ways:

- With a period:

  The ship was huge**.** Its mast stood eighty feet high.

- With a semicolon:

  The ship was huge**;** its mast stood eighty feet high.

- With a comma preceding a coordinating conjunction that joins the clauses and specifies the relation between them:

  The ship was huge**,** <u>and</u> its mast stood eighty feet high.

- Occasionally with a colon when the second clause explains the first (see pp. 519–20):

  The ship was huge**:** its mast stood eighty feet high.

The period, semicolon, or colon alone or the comma plus coordinating conjunction signals readers that one main clause (complete thought) is ending and another is beginning.

Two problems in punctuating main clauses deprive readers of this signal and often force them to reread for sense. One is the **comma splice,** in which the clauses are joined (or spliced) *only* with a comma.

Comma splice
The ship was huge, its mast stood eighty feet high.

The other problem is the **fused sentence,** in which no punctuation or coordinating conjunction appears between the clauses.

Information on comma splices and fused sentences:

http://webster.commnet.edu/HP/pages/darling/grammar/runons.htm
From the Guide to Grammar and Writing.

http://www.english.uiuc.edu/cws/wworkshop/grammar/runons.htm
From the University of Illinois at Urbana-Champaign.

Fused sentence

The ship was huge its mast stood eighty feet high.

Exception Experienced writers sometimes use a comma without a coordinating conjunction between very brief main clauses that are grammatically parallel:

He's not a person, he's a monster.

However, many readers view such punctuation as incorrect. Unless you are certain that your readers will not object to the comma in a sentence like this one, separate the clauses with periods or semicolons, as described in this chapter.

Note Computerized grammar and style checkers can detect many comma splices, but they will not recognize every fused sentence and may flag errors in sentences that are complex but actually correct. Verify that revision is actually needed on any flagged sentence, and read your work carefully on your own to be sure it is correct.

ESL An English sentence may not include more than one main clause unless the clauses are separated by a comma and a coordinating conjunction or by a semicolon. If your native language does not have such a rule or has accustomed you to writing long sentences, you may need to edit your English writing especially for comma splices and fused sentences.

18

Situations that may produce comma splices and fused sentences

- The first clause is negative; the second, positive:

  Splice Petric is not a nurse, she is a doctor.
  Revised Petric is not a nurse; she is a doctor.

- The second clause amplifies or illustrates the first:

  Fused She did well in college her average was 3.9.
  Revised She did well in college: her average was 3.9.

- The second clause contains a conjunctive adverb or other transitional expression, such as *however* or *for example* (see p. 377):

  Splice She had intended to become a biologist, however, medicine seemed more exciting.
  Revised She had intended to become a biologist; however, medicine seemed more exciting.

- The subject of the second clause repeats or refers to the subject of the first clause:

  Fused Petric is an internist she practices in Topeka.
  Revised Petric is an internist. She practices in Topeka.

- Splicing or fusing is an attempt to link related ideas or to smooth choppy sentences:

  Splice She is very committed to her work, she devotes almost all her time to patient care.

  Revised Because she is very committed to her work, she devotes almost all her time to patient care.

  Revised She is so committed to her work that she devotes almost all her time to patient care.

- Words identifying the speaker divide a quotation between two complete sentences. (See p. 482 for the punctuation to use in this case.)

  Splice "Medicine is a human frontier," Petric says, "The boundaries are unknown."

  Revised "Medicine is a human frontier," Petric says. "The boundaries are unknown."

COMMA SPLICES

18a Separate two main clauses with a comma *only* when they are joined by a coordinating conjunction.

A comma cannot separate main clauses unless they are linked by a coordinating conjunction (*and, but, or, nor, for, so, yet*). Readers expect the same main clause to continue after a comma alone. When they find themselves reading a second main clause before they realize they have finished the first, they may have to reread.

You have several options for revising comma splices.

Making separate sentences

Revising a comma splice by making separate sentences from the main clauses will always be correct. The period is not only correct but preferable when the ideas expressed in the two main clauses are only loosely related:

Comma splice Chemistry has contributed much to our understanding of foods, many foods such as wheat and beans can be produced in the laboratory.

Revised Chemistry has contributed much to our understanding of foods. Many foods such as wheat and beans can be produced in the laboratory.

http://www.odu.edu/~wts/csplice.htm Discussion of comma splices, from Old Dominion University.

Revision of comma splices and fused sentences

- Underline the main clauses in your draft.
- When two main clauses fall in the same sentence, check the connection between them.
- If nothing falls between the clauses or only a comma does, revise in one of the following ways, depending on the relation you want to establish between the clauses. (See the text discussion for examples.)

  Make the clauses into separate sentences.
  Insert a comma followed by *and, but,* or another coordinating conjunction. Or, if the comma is already present, insert just the coordinating conjunction.
  Insert a semicolon between clauses.
  Subordinate one clause to the other.

ESL Making separate sentences may be the best option if you are used to writing very long sentences in your native language and often write comma splices in English.

Inserting a coordinating conjunction

When the ideas in the main clauses are closely related and equally important, you may correct a comma splice by inserting the appropriate coordinating conjunction immediately after the comma to join the clauses:

Comma splice	Some laboratory-grown foods taste good, they are nutritious.
Revised	Some laboratory-grown foods taste good**,** and they are nutritious.

Using a semicolon

If the relation between the ideas expressed in the main clauses is very close and obvious without a conjunction, you can separate the clauses with a semicolon. (See also opposite.)

Comma splice	Good taste is rare in laboratory-grown vegetables, they are usually bland.
Revised	Good taste is rare in laboratory-grown vegetables**;** they are usually bland.

Subordinating one clause

When the idea in one clause is more important than that in the other, you can express the less important idea in a phrase or a subordinate clause. (See p. 276 for a list of subordinating conjunctions and pp. 434–36 for more on subordination.) Subordination is often more effective than forming separate sentences because it defines the relation between ideas more precisely:

Comma splice	The vitamins are adequate, the flavor is deficient.
Revised	The vitamins are adequate. The flavor is deficient. [Both ideas receive equal weight.]
Improved	Even though the vitamins are adequate, the flavor is deficient. [Emphasis on the second idea.]

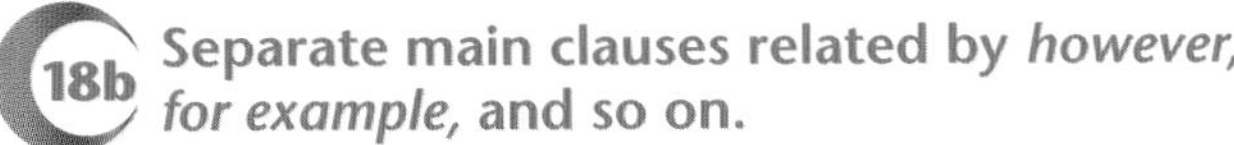

18b Separate main clauses related by *however, for example,* and so on.

Two kinds of words that are not conjunctions describe how one main clause relates to another:

- **Conjunctive adverbs,** such as *consequently, finally, hence, however, indeed, therefore,* or *thus.* (See p. 284 for a longer list.)
- Other **transitional expressions,** such as *even so, for example, in fact, of course, to the right,* and *to this end.* (See pp. 89–90 for a longer list.)

When two clauses are related by a conjunctive adverb or a transitional expression, they must be separated by a period or by a semicolon. The adverb or expression is also generally set off by a comma or commas (see pp. 475–76):

Comma splice	Most Americans refuse to give up unhealthful habits, consequently our medical costs are higher than those of many other countries.
Revised	Most Americans refuse to give up unhealthful habits. Consequently, our medical costs are higher than those of many other countries.
Revised	Most Americans refuse to give up unhealthful habits; consequently, our medical costs are higher than those of many other countries.

Conjunctive adverbs and transitional expressions are different from coordinating conjunctions (*and, but,* and so on) and subordinating conjunctions (*although, because,* and so on):

- Unlike conjunctions, conjunctive adverbs and transitional expressions do not join two clauses into a grammatical unit but merely describe the way two clauses relate in meaning.

http://www.wisc.edu/writing/Handbook/Semicolons.html Guidance on using semicolons, from the University of Wisconsin at Madison.

- Thus, unlike conjunctions, conjunctive adverbs and transitional expressions can be moved from one place to another in a clause (see also p. 285). No matter where in the clause an adverb or expression falls, though, the clause must be separated from another main clause by a period or semicolon.

Comma splice

The increased time devoted to watching television is not the only cause of the decline in reading ability, however, it is one of the important causes.

Period

The increased time devoted to watching television is not the only cause of the decline in reading ability. However, it is one of the important causes.

Semicolon

The increased time devoted to watching television is not the only cause of the decline in reading ability; however, it is one of the important causes.

The increased time devoted to watching television is not the only cause of the decline in reading ability; it is, however, one of the important causes.

EXERCISE 1
Identifying and revising comma splices

Correct each comma splice below in *two* of the ways described on pages 375–77. If an item contains no comma splice, circle the number preceding it.

Example:

Carolyn still had a headache, she could not get the child-proof cap off the aspirin bottle.

Carolyn still had a headache because she could not get the child-proof cap off the aspirin bottle. [Subordination.]

Carolyn still had a headache, for she could not get the child-proof cap off the aspirin bottle. [Coordinating conjunction.]

1. Money has a long history, it goes back at least as far as the earliest records.
2. Many of the earliest records concern financial transactions, indeed, early history must often be inferred from commercial activity.
3. Every known society has had a system of money, though the objects serving as money have varied widely.
4. Sometimes the objects have had real value, in modern times, however, their value has been more abstract.
5. Cattle, fermented beverages, and rare shells have served as money, each one had actual value for the society.

FUSED SENTENCES

18c Combine two main clauses only with an appropriate conjunction or punctuation mark between them.

When two main clauses are joined without a word to connect them or a punctuation mark to separate them, the result is a **fused sentence.** Fused sentences can rarely be understood on first reading, and they are never acceptable in standard written English.

Fused Our foreign policy is not well defined it confuses many countries.

Fused sentences may be corrected in the same ways as comma splices. See pages 375–77.

Separate sentences
Our foreign policy is not well defined. It confuses many countries.

Comma and coordinating conjunction
Our foreign policy is not well defined, and it confuses many countries.

Semicolon
Our foreign policy is not well defined; it confuses many countries.

Subordinating conjunction
Because our foreign policy is not well defined, it confuses many countries.

fs
18c

EXERCISE 2
Identifying and revising fused sentences

Revise each of the fused sentences below in *two* of the four ways shown above.

Example:
Tim was shy he usually refused invitations.
Tim was shy, so he usually refused invitations.
Tim was shy; he usually refused invitations.

1. Throughout history money and religion were closely linked there was little distinction between government and religion.

http://owl.english.purdue.edu/Files/11.html Information on fused sentences, with links to further resources, from the Purdue Online Writing Lab.

2. The head of state and the religious leader were often the same person all power rested in one ruler.
3. These powerful leaders decided what objects would serve as money their backing encouraged public faith in the money.
4. Coins were minted of precious metals the religious overtones of money were then strengthened.
5. People already believed the precious metals to be divine their use in money intensified its allure.

EXERCISE 3
Sentence combining: Comma splices and fused sentences

Combine each pair of sentences below into one sentence without creating a comma splice or fused sentence. Combine sentences by (1) supplying a comma and coordinating conjunction, (2) supplying a semicolon, or (3) subordinating one clause to the other. You will have to add, delete, or change words as well as punctuation.

> *Example:*
>
> The sun sank lower in the sky. The colors gradually faded.
>
> As the sun sank lower in the sky, the colors gradually faded. [The first clause is subordinated to the second.]

1. The exact origin of paper money is unknown. It has not survived as coins, shells, and other durable objects have.
2. Perhaps goldsmiths were also bankers. Thus they held the gold of their wealthy customers.
3. The goldsmiths probably gave customers receipts for their gold. These receipts were then used in trade.
4. The goldsmiths were something like modern-day bankers. Their receipts were something like modern-day money.
5. The goldsmiths became even more like modern-day bankers. They began issuing receipts for more gold than they actually held in their vaults.

EXERCISE 4
Revising: Comma splices and fused sentences

Identify and revise the comma splices and fused sentences in the following paragraph.

All those parents who urged their children to eat broccoli were right, the vegetable really is healthful. Broccoli contains sulforaphane, moreover, this mustard oil can be found in kale and Brussels sprouts. Sulforaphane causes the body to make an enzyme that attacks carcinogens, these substances cause cancer. The enzyme speeds up the work of the kidneys then they can flush harmful chemicals out of the body. Other vegetables have similar benefits however, green, leafy vegetables like broccoli are the most efficient. Thus, wise people will eat their broccoli it could save their lives.

Note See page 416 for an exercise involving comma splices and fused sentences along with other sentence errors.

CHAPTER 19

Pronoun Reference

A **pronoun** such as *it* or *they* derives its meaning from its **antecedent,** the noun it substitutes for. Therefore, a pronoun must refer clearly and unmistakably to its antecedent in order for the meaning to be clear. A sentence such as *Jim told Mark he was not invited* is not clear because the reader does not know whether *he* refers to Jim or to Mark.

One way to make pronoun reference clear is to ensure that the pronoun and antecedent agree in person, number, and gender (see p. 341). The other way is to ensure that the pronoun refers unambiguously to a single, close, specific antecedent.

Note Computerized grammar and style checkers are not sophisticated enough to recognize unclear pronoun reference. For instance, a checker did not spot any of the problems in Exercise 2 on page 387. You must proofread your work to spot unclear pronoun reference.

ESL A pronoun does need a clear antecedent nearby, but don't use both a pronoun and its antecedent as the subject of the same sentence or clause: *Jim* [not *Jim he*] *told Mark to go alone.* (See also pp. 408–09.)

19a Make a pronoun refer clearly to one antecedent.

When either of two nouns can be a pronoun's antecedent, the reference will not be clear:

Confusing Emily Dickinson is sometimes compared with Jane Austen, but she was quite different.

Information on pronoun reference:

http://www.uottawa.ca/academic/arts/writcent/hypergrammar/pronref.html From the University of Ottawa.

http://webster.commnet.edu/HP/pages/darling/grammar/pronouns.htm From the Guide to Grammar and Writing.

Principal causes of unclear pronoun reference

- More than one possible antecedent (previous page and below):

Confusing To keep birds from eating seeds, soak them in blue food coloring.

Clear To keep birds from eating seeds, soak the seeds in blue food coloring.

- Antecedent too far away (opposite):

Confusing Employees should consult with their supervisor who require personal time.

Clear Employees who require personal time should consult with their supervisor.

- Antecedent only implied (p. 384):

Confusing Many children begin reading on their own by watching television, but this should be discounted in government policy.

Clear Many children begin reading on their own by watching television, but such self-instruction should be discounted in government policy.

See also pages 385–87.

ref
19a

Revise such a sentence in one of two ways:

- Replace the pronoun with the appropriate noun:

Clear Emily Dickinson is sometimes compared with Jane Austen, but Dickinson [or Austen] was quite different.

- Avoid repetition by rewriting the sentence. If you use the pronoun, make sure it has only one possible antecedent:

Clear Despite occasional comparison, Emily Dickinson and Jane Austen were quite different.

Clear Though sometimes compared with her, Emily Dickinson was quite different from Jane Austen.

Sentences that report what someone said, using verbs such as *said* or *told,* often require direct rather than indirect quotation:

Confusing Juliet Noble told Ann Torre that she was mistaken.

Clear Juliet Noble told Ann Torre, "I am mistaken."

Clear Juliet Noble told Ann Torre, "You are mistaken."

Note Avoid the awkward device of using a pronoun followed by the appropriate noun in parentheses, as in the following example:

Weak Noble should apologize to Torre, and she (Noble) should notify the press.

Improved Noble should apologize to Torre and notify the press.

19b Place a pronoun close enough to its antecedent to ensure clarity.

A clause beginning *who, which,* or *that* generally should fall immediately after the word to which it refers:

Confusing Jody found a dress in the attic that her aunt had worn.

Clear In the attic Jody found a dress that her aunt had worn.

Even when only one word could possibly serve as the antecedent of a pronoun, the relationship between the two may still be unclear if they are widely separated:

Confusing Jane Austen had little formal education but was well educated at home. Far from living an isolated life in the English countryside, the Austens were a large family with a wide circle of friends who provided entertainment and cultural enrichment. They also provided material for her stories.

Clear Jane Austen had little formal education but was well educated at home. Far from living an isolated life in the English countryside, the Austens were a large family with a wide circle of friends who provided entertainment and cultural enrichment. They also provided material for Jane Austen's stories.

The confusing separation of pronoun and antecedent is most likely to occur in long sentences and, as illustrated above, in adjacent sentences within a paragraph.

EXERCISE 1
Revising: Ambiguous and remote pronoun reference

Rewrite the following sentences to eliminate unclear pronoun reference. If you use a pronoun in your revision, be sure that it refers to only one antecedent and that it falls close enough to its antecedent to ensure clarity.

Example:

Saul found an old gun in the rotting shed that was just as his grandfather had left it.

In the rotting shed Saul found an old gun that was just as his grandfather had left it.

1. There is a difference between the heroes of the twentieth century and the heroes of earlier times: they have flaws in their characters.
2. Sports fans still admire Pete Rose, Babe Ruth, and Joe Namath even though they could not be perfect.
3. Fans liked Rose for having his young son serve as batboy when he was in Cincinnati.
4. Rose's reputation as a gambler and tax evader may overshadow his reputation as a ball player, but it will survive.
5. Rose amassed an unequaled record as a hitter, using his bat to do things no one else has ever done. It stands even though Rose has been banned from baseball.

19c Make a pronoun refer to a specific antecedent, not an implied one.

A pronoun should refer to a specific noun or other pronoun. The reader can only guess at the meaning of a pronoun when its antecedent is implied by the context, not stated outright.

1 Use *this, that, which,* and *it* cautiously.

The most common kind of implied reference occurs when the pronoun *this, that, which,* or *it* refers to a whole idea or situation described in the preceding clause, sentence, or even paragraph. Such reference, often called **broad reference,** is acceptable only when the pronoun refers clearly to the entire preceding clause. In the following sentence, *which* could not possibly refer to anything but the whole preceding clause:

I can be kind and civil to people, which is more than you can.
—George Bernard Shaw

But if a pronoun might confuse a reader, you should avoid using it or provide an appropriate noun:

Confusing The faculty agreed on changing the requirements, but it took time.

Clear The faculty agreed on changing the requirements, but the agreement took time.

Clear The faculty agreed on changing the requirements, but the change took time.

Confusing The British knew little of the American countryside, and they had no experience with the colonists' guerrilla tactics. This gave the colonists an advantage.

Clear The British knew little of the American countryside, and they had no experience with the colonists' guerrilla tactics. This ignorance and inexperience gave the colonists an advantage.

2 Implied nouns are not clear antecedents.

A noun may be implied in some other word or phrase, such as an adjective (*happiness* implied in *happy*), a verb (*driver* implied in *drive*), or a possessive (*mother* implied in *mother's*). But a pronoun cannot refer clearly to an implied noun, only to a specific, stated one:

Confusing Cohen's report brought her a lawsuit.

Clear Cohen was sued over her report.

Confusing Her reports on psychological development generally go unnoticed outside it.

Clear Her reports on psychological development generally go unnoticed outside the field.

3 Titles of papers are not clear antecedents.

The title of a paper is entirely separate from the paper itself, so a pronoun should not be used in the opening sentence of a paper to refer to the title:

Title How to Row a Boat

Not This is not as easy as it looks.

But Rowing a boat is not as easy as it looks.

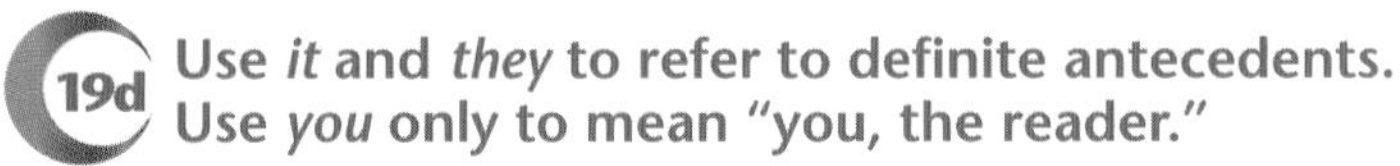

19d Use *it* and *they* to refer to definite antecedents. Use *you* only to mean "you, the reader."

In conversation we commonly use expressions such as *It says in the paper* or *In Texas they say*. But such indefinite use of *it* and *they* is inappropriate in writing. The constructions are not only unclear but wordy:

Confusing In Chapter 4 of this book, it describes the early flights of the Wright brothers.

Clear Chapter 4 of this book describes the early flights of the Wright brothers.

Confusing In the average television drama, they present a false picture of life.

Clear The average television drama presents a false picture of life.

In all but very formal writing, *you* is acceptable when the meaning is clearly "you, the reader." But the context must be appropriate for such a meaning:

Inappropriate In the fourteenth century you had to struggle simply to survive.

Revised In the fourteenth century one [or a person] had to struggle simply to survive.

19e Use the pronoun *it* only one way in a sentence.

We use *it* idiomatically in expressions such as *It is raining.* We use *it* to postpone the subject in sentences such as *It is true that more jobs are available to women today.* And we use *it* as a personal pronoun in sentences such as *Joan wanted the book, but she couldn't find it.* All these uses are standard, but two of them in the same passage can confuse the reader:

Confusing It is true that the Constitution sets limits, but it is also flexible.

Clear The Constitution does set limits, but it is also flexible.

19f Use *who, which,* and *that* for appropriate antecedents.

The relative pronouns *who, which,* and *that* commonly refer to persons, animals, or things. *Who* refers most often to persons but may also refer to animals that have names:

Dorothy is the girl who visits Oz.
Her dog, Toto, who accompanies her, gives her courage.

Which refers to animals and things:

The Orinoco River, which is 1,600 miles long, flows through Venezuela into the Atlantic Ocean.

That refers to animals and things and occasionally to persons when they are collective or anonymous:

> The rocket that failed cost millions.
> Infants that walk need constant tending.

(See also p. 475 for the use of *which* and *that* in nonessential and essential clauses.)

The possessive *whose* generally refers to people but may refer to animals and things to avoid awkward and wordy *of which* constructions:

> The book whose binding broke was rare. [Compare *The book of which the binding broke was rare.*]

EXERCISE 2
Revising: Indefinite and inappropriate pronoun reference

Many of the pronouns in the following sentences do not refer to specific, appropriate antecedents. Revise the sentences as necessary to make them clear.

Example:

In Grand Teton National Park, they have moose, elk, and trumpeter swans.

Moose, elk, and trumpeter swans live in Grand Teton National Park.

1. "Life begins at forty" is a cliché many people live by, and this may well be true.
2. When she was forty, Pearl Buck's novel *The Good Earth* won the Pulitzer Prize.
3. Buck was a novelist which wrote primarily about China.
4. In *The Good Earth* you have to struggle, but fortitude is rewarded.
5. Buck received much critical praise and earned over $7 million, but she was very modest about it.
6. Kenneth Kaunda, past president of Zambia, was elected to it in 1964, at age forty.
7. When Catherine I became empress of Russia at age forty, they feared more than loved her.
8. At forty, Paul Revere made his famous ride to warn American revolutionary leaders that the British were going to arrest them. This gave the colonists time to prepare for battle.
9. In the British House of Commons they did not welcome forty-year-old Nancy Astor as the first female member when she entered in 1919.
10. In AD 610 Muhammad, age forty, began to have a series of visions that became the foundation of the Muslim faith. Since then, millions of people have become one.

EXERCISE 3
Revising: Pronoun reference

Revise the following paragraph so that each pronoun refers clearly to a single specific and appropriate antecedent.

In Charlotte Brontë's *Jane Eyre,* she is a shy young woman that takes a job as governess. Her employer is a rude, brooding man named Rochester. He lives in a mysterious mansion on the English moors, which contributes an eerie quality to Jane's experience. Eerier still are the fires, strange noises, and other unexplained happenings in the house; but Rochester refuses to discuss this. Eventually, they fall in love. On the day they are to be married, however, she learns that he has a wife hidden in the house. She is hopelessly insane and violent and must be guarded at all times, which explains his strange behavior. Heartbroken, Jane leaves the moors, and many years pass before they are reunited.

Note See page 416 for an exercise involving unclear pronoun reference along with sentence fragments, comma splices, and other sentence errors.

CHAPTER 20

Shifts

Inconsistencies in grammatical elements will confuse your readers and distort your meaning. In the following passage from a first draft, the underlining highlights confusing inconsistencies in verbs and subjects:

First draft

A bank commonly owes more to its customers than is held in reserve. They kept enough assets to meet reasonable withdrawals, but panicked customers may demand all their deposits. Then demands will exceed supplies, and banks failed. These days, a person's losses are not likely to be great because the government insures your deposits.

Revised

A bank commonly owes more to its customers than it holds in reserve. It keeps enough assets to meet reasonable withdrawals, but panicked customers may demand all their deposits. Then demands will exceed supplies, and the bank will fail. These days, the losses of customers are not likely to be great because the government insures their deposits.

Holds to match *owes*

Singular *It* and present tense *keeps* to match *bank . . . owes*

Singular *bank* to match *bank;* future tense to match *will exceed*

Plural *customers* to match *customers*

Their to match *customers*

Shifts like those in the first draft are likely to occur while you are trying to piece together meaning during drafting. But you should straighten out your sentences during revision.

Information and exercises on shifts:

http://owl.english.purdue.edu/Files/72.html From the Purdue Online Writing Lab.

http://webster.commnet.edu/HP/pages/darling/grammar/consistency.htm From the Guide to Grammar and Writing.

Note Computerized grammar and style checkers are not sophisticated enough to recognize most shifts in sentences. Proofread your work on your own, looking carefully for inconsistencies.

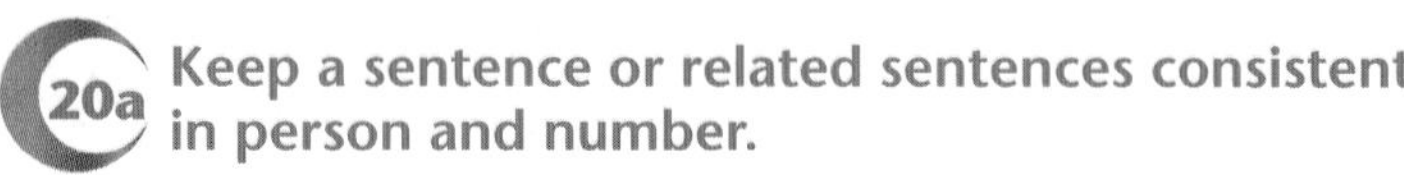

20a Keep a sentence or related sentences consistent in person and number.

Person in grammar refers to the distinction among the person talking (first person), the person spoken to (second person), and the person, object, or concept being talked about (third person). **Number** refers to the distinction between one (singular) and more than one (plural).

Shifts in person

Most shifts in person occur because we can refer to people in general, including our readers, either in the third person (*a person, one; people, they*) or in the second person (*you*):

> People should not drive when they have been drinking.
> One should not drive when he or she has been drinking.
> You should not drive when you have been drinking.

Although any one of these possibilities is acceptable in an appropriate context, a mixture of them is inconsistent:

Inconsistent	If a person works hard, you can accomplish a great deal.
Revised	If you work hard, you can accomplish a great deal.
Revised	If a person works hard, he or she can accomplish a great deal.
Better	If people work hard, they can accomplish a great deal.

Shifts in number

Inconsistency in number occurs most often between a pronoun and its antecedent (see p. 341):

Inconsistent	If a student does not understand a problem, they should consult the instructor.
Revised	If a student does not understand a problem, he or she should consult the instructor.
Better	If students do not understand a problem, they should consult the instructor.
Or	A student who does not understand a problem should consult the instructor.

Note Generic nouns and most indefinite pronouns take singular pronouns with a definite gender: *he, she,* or *it.* When we use a generic noun like *student* or *person* or an indefinite pronoun like *everyone* or *each,* we often mean to include both males and females. To indicate this meaning, use *he or she* rather than *he* (as in the first of the preceding revisions) or, better still, rewrite in the plural or rewrite to avoid the pronoun (as in the second and third of the revisions). See pages 344–45 for more discussion and examples.

Inconsistency in number can also occur between other words (usually nouns) that relate to each other in meaning.

Inconsistent All the boys have a good reputation.

Revised All the boys have good reputations.

The consistency in the revised sentence is called **logical agreement** because the nouns are consistent (the *boys* have *reputations,* not a single *reputation*).

EXERCISE 1
Revising: Shifts in person and number

Revise the following sentences to make them consistent in person and number.

Example:

A plumber will fix burst pipes, but they won't repair waterlogged appliances.

Plumbers will fix burst pipes, but they won't repair waterlogged appliances.

1. When a taxpayer is waiting to receive a tax refund from the Internal Revenue Service, you begin to notice what time the mail carrier arrives.
2. If the taxpayer does not receive a refund check within six weeks of filing a return, they may not have followed the rules of the IRS.
3. If a taxpayer does not include a Social Security number on a return, you will have to wait for a refund.
4. When taxpayers do not file their return early, they will not get a refund quickly.
5. If one makes errors on the tax form, they might even be audited, thereby delaying a refund even longer.

shift 20b

20b Keep a sentence or related sentences consistent in tense and mood.

Shifts in tense

Within a sentence or from one sentence to another, certain changes in tense may be required to indicate changes in actual or relative time (see p. 321). For example:

Ramon will graduate from college thirty-one years after his father arrived in the United States.

But changes that are not required by meaning distract readers. Unnecessary shifts between past and present in passages narrating a series of events are particularly confusing:

Inconsistent Immediately after Booth shot Lincoln, Major Rathbone threw himself upon the assassin. But Booth pulls a knife and plunges it into the major's arm.

Revised Immediately after Booth shot Lincoln, Major Rathbone threw himself upon the assassin. But Booth pulled a knife and plunged it into the major's arm.

Use the present tense consistently to describe what an author has written, including the action in literature or a film:

Inconsistent The main character in the novel suffers psychologically because he has a clubfoot, but he eventually triumphed over his disability.

Revised The main character in the novel suffers psychologically because he has a clubfoot, but he eventually triumphs over his disability.

Shifts in mood

Shifts in the mood of verbs occur most frequently in directions when the writer moves between the imperative mood (*Unplug the appliance*) and the indicative mood (*You should unplug the appliance*). (See p. 327.) Directions are usually clearer and more concise in the imperative, as long as its use is consistent:

Inconsistent Cook the mixture slowly, and you should stir it until the sugar is dissolved.

Revised Cook the mixture slowly, and stir it until the sugar is dissolved.

EXERCISE 2
Revising: Shifts in tense and mood

Revise the following sentences to make them consistent in tense and mood.

Example:

Lynn ran to first, rounded the base, and keeps running until she slides into second.

Lynn ran to first, rounded the base, and kept running until she slid into second.

1. When your cholesterol count is too high, adjusting your diet and exercise level reduced it.
2. After you lowered your cholesterol rate, you decrease the chances of heart attack and stroke.

3. First eliminate saturated fats from your diet; then you should consume more whole grains and raw vegetables.
4. To avoid saturated fats, substitute turkey and chicken for beef, and you should use cholesterol-free salad dressing and cooking oil.
5. A regular program of aerobic exercise, such as walking or swimming, improves your cholesterol rate and made you feel much healthier.

20c Keep a sentence or related sentences consistent in subject and voice.

When a verb is in the **active voice,** the subject names the actor: *Linda passed the peas.* When a verb is in the **passive voice,** the subject names the receiver of the action: *The peas were passed* [*by Linda*]. (See pp. 329–31.)

A shift in voice may sometimes help focus the reader's attention on a single subject, as in *The candidate campaigned vigorously and was nominated on the first ballot.* However, most shifts in voice also involve shifts in subject. They are unnecessary and confusing.

Inconsistent Internet newsgroups cover an enormous range of topics for discussion. Forums for meeting people with like interests are provided in these groups.

Revised Internet newsgroups cover an enormous range of topics for discussion and provide forums for meeting people with like interests.

EXERCISE 3
Revising: Shifts in subject and voice

Make the following sentences consistent in subject and voice.

Example:

At the reunion they ate hot dogs and volleyball was played.
At the reunion they ate hot dogs and played volleyball.

1. If students learn how to study efficiently, much better grades will be made on tests.
2. Conscientious students begin to prepare for tests immediately after the first class is attended.
3. Before each class all reading assignments are completed, and the students outline the material and answer any study questions.
4. In class they listen carefully and good notes are taken.
5. Questions are asked by the students when they do not understand the professor.

Keep a quotation or a question consistently direct or indirect.

Direct quotations or questions report the exact words of a quotation or question:

> "I am the greatest," bragged Muhammad Ali.
> In his day few people asked, "Is he right?"

Indirect quotations or questions report that someone said or asked something, but not in the exact words:

> Muhammad Ali bragged that he was the greatest.
> In his day few people asked whether he was right.

Shifts between direct and indirect quotations or questions are difficult to follow, especially when, as in the first example below, the direct quotation does not appear in quotation marks:

Shift in quotation	Kapek reported that the rats avoided the maze and as of this writing, none responds to conditioning.
Revised (indirect)	Kapek reported that the rats avoided the maze and that as of his writing none responded to conditioning.
Revised (direct)	Kapek reported, "The rats avoid the maze. As of this writing, none responds to conditioning."
Shift in question	The reader wonders whether the experiment failed or did it perhaps succeed?
Revised (indirect)	The reader wonders whether the experiment failed or whether it perhaps succeeded.
Revised (direct)	Did the experiment fail? Or did it perhaps succeed?

For more on quotations, see pages 324–25 (tense and other changes in indirect quotations), 482–84 (commas with signal phrases such as *she said*), 508–13 (quotation marks), and 693–97 (integrating quotations into your writing). For more on questions, see page 464 (punctuation and word order).

shift 20d

EXERCISE 4
Revising: Shifts in direct and indirect quotations and questions

Revise each of the following sentences twice, once to make it consistently direct, once to make it consistently indirect. (You will have to guess at the exact wording of direct quotations and questions that are now stated indirectly.)

Example:

We all wonder what the next decade will bring and will we thrive or not?

Direct: What will the next decade bring? Will we thrive or not?

Indirect: We all wonder what the next decade will bring and whether we will thrive or not.

1. One anthropologist says that the functions of marriage have changed and "nowhere more dramatically than in industrialized cultures."
2. The question even arises of whether siblings may marry and would the union be immoral?
3. The author points out, "Sibling marriage is still illegal everywhere in the United States" and that people are still prosecuted under the law.
4. She says that incest could be considered a universal taboo and "the questions asked about the taboo vary widely."
5. Some ask is the taboo a way of protecting the family or whether it may be instinctive.

EXERCISE 5
Revising: Shifts

Revise the following paragraph to eliminate unnecessary shifts in person, number, tense, mood, and voice.

Driving in snow need not be dangerous if you practice a few rules. First, one should avoid fast starts, which prevent the wheels from gaining traction and may result in the car's getting stuck. Second, drive more slowly than usual, and you should pay attention to the feel of the car: if the steering seemed unusually loose or the wheels did not seem to be grabbing the road, slow down. Third, avoid fast stops, which lead to skids. One should be alert for other cars and intersections that may necessitate that the brakes be applied suddenly. If you need to slow down, the car's momentum can be reduced by downshifting as well as by applying the brakes. When braking, press the pedal to the floor only if you have antilock brakes; otherwise, the pedal should be pumped in short bursts. If you feel the car skidding, the brakes should be released and the wheel should be turned into the direction of the skid, and then the brakes should be pressed or pumped again. If one repeated these motions, the skid would be stopped and the speed of the car would be reduced.

Note See page 416 for an exercise involving shifts along with sentence fragments, comma splices, and other sentence errors.

CHAPTER 21

Misplaced and Dangling Modifiers

In reading a sentence in English, we depend principally on the arrangement of the words to tell us how they are related. In writing, we may create confusion if we fail to connect modifiers to the words they modify.

Note Computerized grammar and style checkers do not recognize many problems with modifiers. For instance, a checker failed to flag the misplaced modifiers in *Gasoline high prices affect usually car sales* or the dangling modifier in *The vandalism was visible passing the building.* Proofread your work on your own to find and correct problems with modifiers.

MISPLACED MODIFIERS

A modifier is **misplaced** if readers can't easily relate it to the word it modifies. Misplaced modifiers may be awkward, confusing, or even unintentionally funny.

21a Place modifiers where they will clearly modify the words intended.

Readers tend to link a modifying word, phrase, or clause to the nearest word it could modify: *I saw a man in a green hat.* Thus the writer must place the phrase so that it clearly modifies the intended word and not some other.

Information on modifiers:

http://webster.commnet.edu/HP/pages/darling/grammar/modifiers.htm From the Guide to Grammar and Writing.

http://www.uottawa.ca/academic/arts/writcent/hypergrammar/modifier.html From the University of Ottawa.

http://www.english.uiuc.edu/cws/wworkshop/misplacedmod.htm From the University of Illinois at Urbana-Champaign.

Confusing He served steak to the men on paper plates.

Revised He served the men steak on paper plates.

Confusing Many dogs are killed by automobiles and trucks roaming unleashed.

Revised Many dogs roaming unleashed are killed by automobiles and trucks.

Confusing This is the only chocolate chip cookie in a bag that tastes like Mom's. [Actual advertisement.]

Revised This is the only bagged [or packaged] chocolate chip cookie that tastes like Mom's.

EXERCISE 1
Revising: Misplaced phrases and clauses

Revise the following sentences so that phrases and clauses clearly modify the appropriate words.

Example:
I came to enjoy flying over time.
Over time I came to enjoy flying.

1. Women have contributed much to knowledge and culture of great value.
2. Emma Willard founded the Troy Female Seminary, the first institution to provide a college-level education for women in 1821.
3. Sixteen years later Mary Lyon founded Mount Holyoke Female Seminary, the first true women's college with directors and a campus who would sustain the college even after Lyon's death.
4. *Una* was the first US newspaper, which was founded by Pauline Wright Davis in 1853, that was dedicated to gaining women's rights.
5. Mitchell's Comet was discovered in 1847, which was named for Maria Mitchell.

21b Place limiting modifiers carefully.

Limiting modifiers include *almost, even, exactly, hardly, just, merely, nearly, only, scarcely,* and *simply*. They modify the expressions that immediately follow them, as these uses of *just* show:

Just the manuscript was discovered by an archaeologist.
The manuscript was just discovered by an archaeologist.
The manuscript was discovered just by an archaeologist.

In speech several limiting modifiers frequently occur before the verb, regardless of the words they are intended to modify. In writing, however, these modifiers should fall immediately before the word or word group they modify to avoid any ambiguity:

Unclear He only discovered this manuscript on his last dig.

Revised He discovered only this manuscript on his last dig.

Revised He discovered this manuscript only on his last dig.

EXERCISE 2
Using limiting modifiers

Use each of the following limiting modifiers in two versions of the same sentence.

Example:
only
He is the only one I like. He is the one only I like.

1. almost
2. even
3. hardly
4. simply
5. nearly

21c Make each modifier refer to only one grammatical element.

A modifier can modify only *one* element in a sentence—the subject, the verb, or some other element. A **squinting modifier** seems confusingly to refer to either of two words:

Squinting Snipers who fired on the soldiers often escaped capture.

Clear Snipers who often fired on the soldiers escaped capture.

Clear Snipers who fired on the soldiers escaped capture often.

When an adverb modifies an entire main clause, as in the last example, it can usually be moved to the beginning of the sentence: *Often, snipers who fired on the soldiers escaped capture.*

EXERCISE 3
Revising: Squinting modifiers

Revise each sentence twice so that the squinting modifier applies clearly first to one element and then to the other.

Example:

The work that he hoped would satisfy him completely frustrated him.

The work that he hoped would completely satisfy him frustrated him.

The work that he hoped would satisfy him frustrated him completely.

1. People who sunbathe often can damage their skin.
2. Sunbathers who apply a sunscreen frequently block some of the sun's harmful ultraviolet rays.
3. Men and women who lie out in the sun often have leathery, dry skin.
4. Doctors tell sunbathers when they are older they risk skin cancer.
5. People who stay out of the sun usually will have better skin and fewer chances of skin cancer.

21d Keep subjects, verbs, and objects together.

English sentences tend to move from subject to verb to object. The movement is so familiar that modifiers between these elements can be awkward.

A subject and verb may be separated by an adjective that modifies the subject: *Kuwait, which has a population of 1.3 million, is a rich nation.* But an adverb of more than a word usually stops the flow of the sentence:

Awkward Kuwait (subject), after the Gulf War ended in 1991 (adverb), began (verb) returning to normal.

Revised After the Gulf War ended in 1991 (adverb), Kuwait (subject) began (verb) returning to normal.

A modifier between a verb and its direct object is always awkward:

Awkward The war had damaged (verb) badly (adverb) many (object) of Kuwait's oil fields.

Revised The war had badly damaged (verb; badly = adverb) many (object) of Kuwait's oil fields.

See the next page on inserting single-word adverbs between parts of a verb phrase, as in the revision above.

mm 21d

21e Keep parts of infinitives or verb phrases together.

An **infinitive** consists of the marker *to* plus the plain form of a verb: *to produce, to enjoy.* The two parts of the infinitive are widely regarded as a grammatical unit that should not be split:

Awkward The weather service expected temperatures to not rise. [infinitive: to … rise]

Revised The weather service expected temperatures not to rise. [infinitive: to rise]

A split infinitive may sometimes be natural and preferable, though it may still bother some readers:

Several US industries expect to more than triple their use of robots. [infinitive: to … triple]

Here the split infinitive is more economical than the alternatives, such as *Several US industries expect to increase their use of robots by more than three times.*

A **verb phrase** consists of a helping verb plus a main verb, as in *will call, was going, had been writing* (see p. 303). We regularly insert single-word adverbs after the helping verb in a verb phrase (or the first helping verb if more than one): *Scientists have lately been using spacecraft to study the sun.* But when longer adverbs interrupt verb phrases, the result is almost always awkward.

Awkward The spacecraft *Ulysses* will after traveling near the sun report on the sun's energy fields. [helping verb: will; adverb: after traveling near the sun; main verb: report]

Revised After traveling near the sun, the spacecraft *Ulysses* will report on the sun's energy fields. [adverb: After traveling near the sun; verb phrase: will report]

ESL In a question, place a one-word adverb after the first helping verb and the subject:

Will spacecraft ever be able to leave the solar system? [helping verb: Will; subject: spacecraft; adverb: ever; rest of verb phrase: be able]

EXERCISE 4
Revising: Separated sentence parts

Revise the following sentences to connect separated parts (subject-predicate, verb-object, verb phrase, infinitive).

Example:

Most children have by the time they are seven lost a tooth.
By the time they are seven, most children have lost a tooth.

1. Myra Bradwell founded in 1868 the *Chicago Legal News.*
2. Bradwell was later denied, although she had qualified, admission to the Illinois Bar Association.
3. In an attempt to finally gain admission to the bar, she carried the case to the Supreme Court, but the justices decided against her.
4. Bradwell was determined that no other woman would, if she were qualified, be denied entrance to a profession.
5. The Illinois legislature finally passed, in response to Bradwell's persuasion, a bill ensuring that no one on the basis of gender would be restricted from a profession.

21f Position adverbs with care. ESL

Most adverbs may fall in several places in a sentence, as long as they clearly modify the intended word (21b, 21c) and do not separate sentence parts awkwardly (21d, 21e). A few adverbs are subject to additional conventions as well.

Adverbs of frequency

Adverbs of frequency include *always, never, often, rarely, seldom, sometimes,* and *usually.* They appear at the beginning of a sentence, before a one-word verb, or after the helping verb in a verb phrase:

Awkward Robots have put sometimes humans out of work. [verb phrase: have put; adverb: sometimes]

Revised Robots have sometimes put humans out of work. [helping verb: have; adverb: sometimes; main verb: put]

Revised Sometimes robots have put humans out of work. [adverb: Sometimes; verb phrase: have put]

Adverbs of frequency always follow the verb *be:*

Awkward Robots often are helpful to workers. [adverb: often; verb: are]

Revised Robots are often helpful to workers. [verb: are; adverb: often]

Adverbs of degree

Adverbs of degree include *absolutely, almost, certainly, completely, especially, extremely, hardly,* and *only.* They fall just before the word modified (an adjective, another adverb, sometimes a verb):

Awkward Robots have been useful especially in making cars. [adjective: useful; adverb: especially]

Revised Robots have been especially useful in making cars. [adverb: especially; adjective: useful]

http://members.home.net/englishzone/grammar/advcls1.html Exercise on adverb order, from English-Zone.Com.

Adverbs of manner

Adverbs of manner include *badly, beautifully, openly, sweetly, tightly, well,* and others that describe how something is done. They usually fall after the verb:

Awkward Robots <u>smoothly</u> [adverb] work [verb] on assembly lines.

Revised Robots work [verb] <u>smoothly</u> [adverb] on assembly lines.

The adverb *not*

When the adverb *not* modifies a verb, place it after the helping verb (or the first helping verb if more than one):

Awkward Robots do [helping verb] think [main verb] <u>not</u>.

Revised Robots do [helping verb] <u>not</u> think [main verb].

Place *not* after a form of *be: Robots are <u>not</u> thinkers.*

When *not* modifies another adverb or an adjective, place it before the other modifier: *Robots are <u>not</u> sleek machines.*

21g Arrange adjectives appropriately. ESL

English follows distinctive rules for arranging two or three adjectives before a noun. (A string of more than three adjectives before a noun is rare.) The order depends on the meaning of the adjectives, as indicated in the following table:

Determiner	Opinion	Size or shape	Age	Color	Origin	Material	Noun used as adjective	Noun
many			new				state	laws
	striking			green	Thai			birds
a	fine				German			camera
this		square				wooden		table
all			recent				business	reports
the				blue		litmus		paper

http://members.home.net/englishzone/grammar/adjs.html Information and exercises on adjective order, from English-Zone.Com.

See page 480 for guidelines on punctuating two or more adjectives before a noun.

EXERCISE 5
Revising: Placement of adverbs and adjectives ESL

Revise the sentences below to correct the positions of adverbs or adjectives. If a sentence is already correct as given, circle the number preceding it.

Example:
Gasoline high prices affect usually car sales.
High gasoline prices usually affect car sales.

1. Some years ago Detroit cars often were praised.
2. Luxury large cars especially were prized.
3. Then a serious oil shortage led drivers to value small foreign cars that got good mileage.
4. Now with gasoline ample supplies, consumers are returning to American large cars.
5. However, the large cars not are luxury sedans but vans and sport-utility vehicles.

DANGLING MODIFIERS

21h Relate dangling modifiers to their sentences.

A **dangling modifier** does not sensibly modify anything in its sentence:

Dangling Passing the building, the vandalism became visible. [The modifying phrase seems to describe *vandalism,* but vandalism does not pass buildings. Who was passing the building? Who saw the vandalism?]

Dangling modifiers usually introduce sentences, contain a verb form, and imply but do not name a subject: in the preceding example, the implied subject is the someone or something passing the building. Readers assume that this implied subject is the same as the subject of the sentence (*vandalism* in the example). When it is not, the modifier "dangles" unconnected to the rest of the sentence.

Information on dangling modifiers:

http://www.english.uiuc.edu/cws/wworkshop/danglingmods.htm From the University of Illinois at Urbana-Champaign.

http://owl.english.purdue.edu/Files/24.html From the Purdue Online Writing Lab.

Certain modifiers are most likely to dangle:

- Participial phrases:

Dangling Passing the building, the vandalism became visible.

Revised As we passed the building, the vandalism became visible.

- Infinitive phrases:

Dangling To understand the causes, vandalism has been extensively investigated.

Revised To understand the causes, researchers have extensively investigated vandalism.

- Prepositional phrases in which the object of the preposition is a gerund:

Dangling After studying the problem, vandals are now thought to share certain characteristics.

Revised After studying the problem, researchers think that vandals share certain characteristics.

- Elliptical clauses in which the subject and perhaps the verb are omitted:

Dangling When destructive, researchers have learned that vandals are more likely to be in groups.

Revised When vandals are destructive, researchers have learned, they are more likely to be in groups.

Dangling modifiers are especially likely when the verb in the main clause is in the **passive voice** instead of the **active voice**—that is, when the verb expresses what is *done to* the subject instead of what the subject *does* (see pp. 329–31). The passive voice appears in the second and third examples above: *vandalism has been investigated; vandals are thought.* The revisions recast the verbs and subjects as active: *researchers have investigated; researchers think.*

Note that a modifier may be dangling even when the sentence elsewhere contains a word the modifier might seem to describe, such as *vandals* below:

Dangling When destructive, researchers have learned that vandals are more likely to be in groups.

In addition, a dangling modifier may fall at the end of a sentence:

Dangling The vandalism was visible passing the building.

Revising dangling modifiers

Revise most dangling modifiers in one of two ways, depending on what you want to emphasize in the sentence.

Identifying and revising dangling modifiers

- If the modifier lacks a subject of its own (e.g., *when in diapers*), identify what it describes.
- Verify that what the modifier describes is in fact the subject of the main clause. If it is not, the modifier is probably dangling.
- Revise a dangling modifier (*a*) by recasting it with a subject of its own or (*b*) by changing the subject of the main clause.

Dangling When in diapers, my mother remarried. (modifier: When in diapers; subject: my mother)

Revision *a* When I was in diapers, my mother remarried.

Revision *b* When in diapers, I attended my mother's second wedding.

- Change the subject of the main clause to a word the modifier properly describes:

Dangling To express themselves, graffiti decorate walls.

Revised To express themselves, some youths decorate walls with graffiti.

- Rewrite the dangling modifier as a complete clause with its own stated subject and verb:

Revised Because some youths need to express themselves, graffiti decorate walls.

dm 21h

EXERCISE 6
Revising: Dangling modifiers

Revise the following sentences to eliminate any dangling modifiers. Each item has more than one possible answer.

Example:

Driving north, the vegetation became increasingly sparse.

Driving north, we noticed that the vegetation became increasingly sparse.

As we drove north, the vegetation became increasingly sparse.

1. After accomplishing many deeds of valor, Andrew Jackson's fame led to his election to the presidency in 1828 and 1832.
2. By the age of fourteen, both of Jackson's parents had died.
3. To aid the American Revolution, service as a mounted courier was chosen by Jackson.
4. Though not well educated, a successful career as a lawyer and judge proved Jackson's ability.
5. Winning many military battles, the American public believed in Jackson's leadership.

EXERCISE 7
Sentence combining: Placing modifiers

Combine each pair of sentences below into a single sentence by rewriting one as a modifier. Make sure the modifier applies clearly to the appropriate word. You will have to add, delete, and rearrange words, and you may find that more than one answer is possible in each case.

Example:

Bob demanded a hearing from the faculty. Bob wanted to appeal the decision.

Wanting to appeal the decision, Bob demanded a hearing from the faculty.

1. Evening falls in the Central American rain forests. The tungara frogs begin their croaking chorus.
2. Male tungara frogs croak loudly at night. The "songs" they sing are designed to attract female frogs.
3. But predators also hear the croaking. They gather to feast on the frogs.
4. The predators are lured by their croaking dinners. The predators include bullfrogs, snakes, bats, and opossums.
5. The frogs hope to mate. Their nightly chorus can result in death instead.

EXERCISE 8
Revising: Misplaced and dangling modifiers

Revise the following paragraph to eliminate any misplaced or dangling modifiers.

Central American tungara frogs silence several nights a week their mating croaks. When not croaking, the chance that the frogs will be eaten by predators is reduced. The frogs seem to fully believe in "safety in numbers." They more than likely will croak along with a large group rather than by themselves. By forgoing croaking on some nights, the frogs' behavior prevents the species from "croaking."

Note See page 416 for an exercise involving misplaced and dangling modifiers along with other sentence errors.

CHAPTER 22

Mixed and Incomplete Sentences

MIXED SENTENCES

A **mixed sentence** contains two or more parts that are incompatible—that is, the parts do not fit together. The misfit may be in grammar or in meaning.

Note Computerized grammar and style checkers are not sophisticated enough to recognize most mixed sentences. Proofread your own work carefully to locate and revise problem sentences.

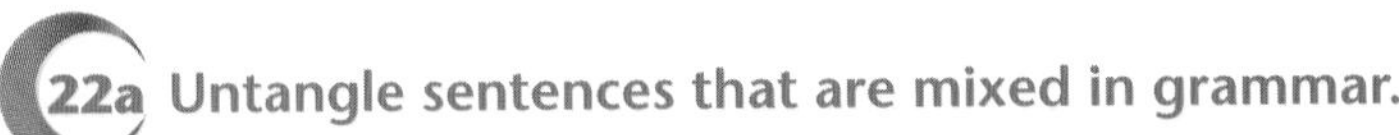

22a Untangle sentences that are mixed in grammar.

Sentences mixed in grammar combine two or more incompatible grammatical structures.

1 Make sure subject and verb fit together grammatically.

A mixed sentence may occur when you start a sentence with one plan and end it with another:

modifier (prepositional phrase) — verb
Mixed By paying more attention to impressions than facts leads us to misjudge others.

This mixed sentence makes a prepositional phrase work as the subject of *leads,* but prepositional phrases function as modifiers, not as nouns, and thus not as sentence subjects. (See p. 266.)

modifier (prepositional phrase) — subject + verb
Revised By paying more attention to impressions than facts, we misjudge others.

subject (gerund phrase) — verb
Revised Paying more attention to impressions than facts leads us to misjudge others.

Mixed sentences are especially likely on a word processor when you connect parts of two sentences or rewrite half a sentence but not the other half. Mixed sentences may also occur when you don't focus your sentences on the subject and verb so that these elements carry the principal meaning. (See p. 419.) If you need help identifying the subject and verb, see pages 255 and 257. Otherwise, the cure for grammatically mixed sentences is careful editing and proofreading.

Here are two more examples of mixed grammar:

modifier (adverb clause) — verb

Mixed Although he was seen with a convicted thief does not make him a thief.

subject (noun clause) — verb

Revised That he was seen with a convicted thief does not make him a thief.

modifier (adverb clause) — subject + verb

Revised Although he was seen with a convicted thief, he is not necessarily a thief.

subject — modifier (adjective clause)

Mixed The fact that someone may be considered guilty just for associating with someone guilty.

subject verb

Revised The fact is that someone may be considered guilty just for associating with someone guilty.

subject — verb

Revised Someone may be considered guilty just for associating with someone guilty.

mixed 22a

In some mixed sentences the grammar is so jumbled that the writer has little choice but to start over:

Mixed My long-range goal is through law school and government work I hope to help people deal with those problems we all deal with more effectively.

Possible My long-range goal is to go to law school and then work in government so that I can help people deal more effectively with problems we all face.

2 State parts of sentences, such as subjects, only once. ESL

In some languages other than English, certain parts of sentences may be repeated. These include the subject in any kind of clause or an object or adverb in an adjective clause. In English, however, these parts are stated only once in a clause.

Repetition of subject

You may be tempted to restate a subject as a pronoun before the verb. But the subject needs stating only once in its clause.

Faulty The liquid it reached a temperature of 180°F.
Revised The liquid reached a temperature of 180°F.

Faulty Gases in the liquid they escaped.
Revised Gases in the liquid escaped.

Faulty The supervisor of the lab she had just left.
Revised The supervisor of the lab had just left.

Repetition in an adjective clause

Adjective clauses begin with *who, whom, whose, which, that, where,* and *when* (see p. 277). The beginning word replaces another word: the subject (*He is the person who called*), an object of a verb or preposition (*He is the person whom I mentioned*), or a preposition and pronoun (*He knows the office where [in which] the conference will occur*).

Do not state the word being replaced in an adjective clause:

Faulty The technician whom the test depended on her was burned. [*Whom* should replace *her*.]

Revised The technician whom the test depended on was burned.

Adjective clauses beginning with *where* or *when* do not need an adverb such as *there* or *then:*

Faulty Gases escaped at a moment when the technician was unprepared then.

Revised Gases escaped at a moment when the technician was unprepared.

Note *Whom, which,* and similar words are sometimes omitted but are still understood by the reader. Thus the word being replaced should not be stated:

Faulty Accidents rarely happen to technicians the lab has trained them. [*Whom* is understood: *technicians whom the lab has trained.*]

Revised Accidents rarely happen to technicians the lab has trained.

22b Match subjects and predicates in meaning.

In a sentence with mixed meaning, the subject is said to be or do something it cannot logically be or do. Such a mixture is sometimes called **faulty predication** because the predicate conflicts with the subject.

Illogical equation with *be*

When a form of *be* connects a subject and a word that describes the subject (a complement), the subject and complement must be logically related:

Mixed A compromise between the city and the country would be the ideal place to live.

Revised A community that offered the best qualities of both city and country would be the ideal place to live.

Is when, is where

Definitions require nouns on both sides of *be*. Definition clauses beginning with *when* or *where* are common in speech but should be avoided in writing:

Mixed An examination is when you are tested on what you know.

Revised An examination is a test of what you know.

Reason is because

mixed
22b

The commonly heard construction *reason is because* is redundant since *because* means "for the reason that":

Mixed The reason the temple requests donations is because the school needs expansion.

Revised The reason the temple requests donations is that the school needs expansion.

Revised The temple requests donations because the school needs expansion.

Other mixed meanings

Mismatched subjects and predicates are not confined to sentences with *be:*

Mixed The use of emission controls was created to reduce air pollution.

Revised Emission controls were created to reduce air pollution.

Mixed The area of financial mismanagement poses a threat to small businesses.

Revised Financial mismanagement poses a threat to small businesses.

EXERCISE 1
Revising: Sentences mixed in grammar or meaning

Revise the following sentences so that their parts fit together both in grammar and in meaning. Each item has more than one possible answer.

Example:

When they found out how expensive pianos are is why they were discouraged.

They were discouraged because they found out how expensive pianos are.

When they found out how expensive pianos are, they were discouraged.

1. A hurricane is when the winds in a tropical depression rotate counterclockwise at more than seventy-four miles per hour.
2. Because hurricanes can destroy so many lives and so much property is why people fear them.
3. Through high winds, storm surge, floods, and tornadoes is how a hurricane can kill thousands of people.
4. Among the hurricanes in history, they have become less deadly since 1950.
5. The reason for the lower death rates is because improved communication systems and weather satellites warn people early enough to escape the hurricane.

EXERCISE 2
Revising: Repeated sentence parts ESL

Revise the following sentences to eliminate any unnecessary repetition of sentence parts.

Example:

Over 79 percent of Americans they have heard of global warming.

Over 79 percent of Americans have heard of global warming.

1. Global warming it is caused by the gradual erosion of the ozone layer that protects the earth from the sun.
2. Scientists who study this problem they say that the primary causes of erosion are the use of fossil fuels and the reduction of forests.
3. Many nonscientists they mistakenly believe that aerosol spray cans are the primary cause of erosion.
4. One scientist whom others respect him argues that Americans have effectively reduced their use of aerosol sprays.
5. He argues that we will stop global warming only when the public learns the real causes then.

INCOMPLETE SENTENCES

The most serious kind of incomplete sentence is the fragment (see Chapter 17). But sentences are also incomplete when they omit one or more words needed for clarity.

Note Computerized grammar and style checkers will not flag most kinds of incomplete sentences discussed in this section. Only your own careful proofreading can ensure that sentences are complete.

22c Omissions from compound constructions should be consistent with grammar or idiom.

In both speech and writing, we commonly omit words not necessary for meaning, such as those in brackets in the following examples. Notice that all the sentences contain compound constructions (see p. 282):

> By 2005 automobile-emission standards will be tougher, and by 2010 [automobile-emission standards will be] tougher still.
>
> Some cars will run on electricity and some [will run] on methane or another alternative fuel.
>
> Environmentalists have hopes for alternative fuels and [for] public transportation.

Such omissions are possible only when you omit words that are common to all the parts of a compound construction. When the parts differ in either grammar or idiom, all words must be included in all parts:

> One new car gets eighty miles per gallon of gasoline; some old cars get as little as five miles per gallon. [One verb is singular, the other plural.]
>
> Environmentalists were invited to submit proposals and were eager to do so. [Each *were* has a different grammatical function: the first is a helping verb; the second is a linking verb.]
>
> They believe in and work for fuel conservation. [Idiom requires different prepositions with *believe* and *work*.]

Notice that in the sentence *My brother and friend moved to Dallas,* the omission of *my* before *friend* indicates that *brother* and *friend* are the same person. If two different persons are meant, the modifier or article must be repeated: *My brother and my friend moved to Dallas.*

(See p. 573 for a list of English idioms with prepositions and pp. 442–46 for a discussion of grammatical parallelism.)

22d All comparisons should be complete and logical.

Comparisons make statements about the relation between two or more things, as in *Dogs are more intelligent than cats.*

1 State a comparison fully enough to ensure clarity.

A comparison must not omit words needed to clarify meaning:

Unclear Car makers worry about their industry more than environmentalists.

Clear Car makers worry about their industry more than environmentalists do.

Clear Car makers worry about their industry more than they worry about environmentalists.

2 The items being compared should in fact be comparable.

A comparison is logical only if it compares items that can sensibly be compared:

Illogical The cost of an electric car is greater than a gasoline-powered car. [Illogically compares a cost and a car.]

Revised The cost of an electric car is greater than the cost of [or that of] a gasoline-powered car.

3 Use *any* or *any other* appropriately in comparisons.

Comparing a person or thing with all others in the same group creates two units: (1) the individual person or thing and (2) all *other* persons or things in the group. The two units need to be distinguished:

Illogical Los Angeles is larger than any city in California. [Since Los Angeles is itself a city in California, the sentence seems to say that Los Angeles is larger than itself.]

Logical Los Angeles is larger than any other city in California.

Comparing a person or thing with the members of a *different* group assumes separate units to begin with. The two units do not need to be distinguished with *other:*

Illogical Los Angeles is larger than any other city in Canada. [The cities in Canada constitute a group to which Los Angeles does not belong.]

Logical Los Angeles is larger than any city in Canada.

4 Comparisons should state what is being compared.

Brand X gets clothes whiter. [Whiter than what?]
Brand Y is so much better. [Better than what?]

22e Include all needed prepositions, articles, and other words.

In haste or carelessness we sometimes omit small words such as articles and prepositions that are needed for clarity:

Incomplete Regular payroll deductions are a type painless savings. You hardly notice missing amounts, and after period of years the contributions can add a large total.

Revised Regular payroll deductions are a type of painless savings. You hardly notice the missing amounts, and after a period of years the contributions can add up to a large total.

Be careful not to omit *that* when the omission is confusing:

Incomplete The personnel director expects many employees will benefit from the plan. [*Many employees* seems to be the object of *expects.*]

Revised The personnel director expects that many employees will benefit from the plan.

Attentive proofreading is the best insurance against the kinds of omissions described in this section. *Proofread all your papers carefully.* See page 64 for tips.

ESL If your native language is not English, you may have difficulty knowing when to use the English articles *a, an,* and *the.* For guidelines on using articles, see pages 356–58.

EXERCISE 3
Revising: Incomplete sentences

Revise the following sentences so that they are complete, logical, and clear. Some items have more than one possible answer.

Example:

Our house is closer to the courthouse than the subway stop.

Our house is closer to the courthouse than it is to the subway stop.

Our house is closer to the courthouse than the subway stop is.

1. The first ice cream, eaten in China in about 2000 BC, was more lumpy than the modern era.

2. The Chinese made their ice cream of milk, spices, and overcooked rice and packed in snow to solidify.
3. In the fourteenth century ice milk and fruit ices appeared in Italy and the tables of the wealthy.
4. At her wedding in 1533 to the king of France, Catherine de Médicis offered more flavors of fruit ices than any hostess offered.
5. Modern sherbets resemble her ices; modern ice cream her soft dessert of thick, sweetened cream.

EXERCISE 4
Revising: Mixed and incomplete sentences

Revise the following paragraph to eliminate mixed or incomplete constructions.

The Hancock Tower in Boston is thin mirror-glass slab that rises almost eight hundred feet. When it was being constructed in the early 1970s was when its windows began cracking, and some fell crashing to the ground. In order to minimize risks is why the architects and owners replaced over a third the huge windows with plywood until the problem could be found and solved. With its plywood sheath, the building was homelier than any skyscraper, the butt of many jokes. Eventually, however, it was discovered that the reason the windows cracked was because joint between the double panes of glass was too rigid. The solution of thicker single-pane windows was installed, and the silly plywood building crystallized into reflective jewel.

Note See the next page for an exercise involving mixed and incomplete sentences along with sentence fragments, comma splices, and other sentence errors.

EXERCISE ON CHAPTERS 17–22
Revising: Clear sentences

Clarify meaning in the following paragraphs by revising sentence fragments, comma splices, fused sentences, problems with pronoun reference, awkward shifts, misplaced and dangling modifiers, and mixed and incomplete sentences. Most errors can be corrected in more than one way.

Many people who are physically challenged. They have accomplished much. Which proves that they are not "handicapped." Confined to wheelchairs, successful careers have been forged by Bob Sampson and Stephen Hawking. Despite Sampson's muscular dystrophy, he has earned a law degree he has also worked for United Airlines for more than thirty years. Stephen Hawking most famous for his book *A Brief History of Time.* Unable to speak, Hawking's voice synthesizer allows him to dictate his books and conduct public lectures. And teach mathematics classes at Cambridge University.

Franklin D. Roosevelt, Ann Adams, and Itzhak Perlman all refused let polio destroy their lives. Indeed, Roosevelt led the United States during two of the worst periods of its history as President. The Great Depression and World War II. Reassured by his strong, firm voice, Roosevelt inspired hope and determination in the American people. Ann Adams, who was talented in art before polio paralyzed her, knew she had to continue to be one. Having retrained herself to draw with a pencil grasped in her teeth. She produces sketches of children and pets. That were turned into greeting cards. The profits from the cards sustained her. Roosevelt and Adams were stricken with polio when they were adults; Itzhak Perlman when a child. He was unable to play sports, instead he studied the violin, now many think he is greater than any violinist in the world.

Like Perlman, many physically challenged individuals turn to the arts. Perhaps the reason is because the joy of artistic achievement compensates for other pleasures they cannot experience. Ray Charles, Stevie Wonder, José Feliciano, and Ronnie Milsap all express, through their music, their souls. Although unable to see physically, their music reveals truly how well they see. Hearing impairment struck Ludwig van Beethoven and Marlee Matlin it did not stop them from developing their talents. Already a successful composer, many of Beethoven's most powerful pieces were written after he became deaf. Similarly, Matlin has had excellent acting roles in movies, plays, and television programs, indeed she won an Oscar for *Children of a Lesser God.* She encourages others to develop their ability, and many hearing-impaired actors have been inspired by her.

PART VI

Effective Sentences

CHAPTER 23

Emphasizing Ideas

When you emphasize the main ideas in your sentences, you hold and channel readers' attention.

Note Many computerized grammar and style checkers can spot some problems with emphasis, such as nouns made from verbs, passive voice (see p. 331), wordy phrases (see p. 578), and long sentences that may also be flabby and unemphatic. However, the checkers cannot help you identify the important ideas in your sentences or whether those ideas receive appropriate emphasis.

Ways to emphasize ideas

- Use the subjects and verbs of sentences to state key actors and actions (opposite).
- Use the beginnings and endings of sentences to pace and stress information (p. 420).
- Arrange series items in order of increasing importance (p. 423).
- Use an occasional balanced sentence (p. 423).
- Carefully repeat key words and phrases (p. 425).
- Set off important ideas with punctuation (p. 425).
- Write concisely (p. 426).

Advice on achieving emphasis:

http://owl.english.purdue.edu/Files/89.html From the Purdue Online Writing Lab.

http://researchpaper.com/writing_center/89.html From Research-paper.com

http://www.rpi.edu/dept/llc/writecenter/web/text/proseman.html From Rensselaer Polytechnic Institute.

http://www.wisc.edu/writing/Handbook/ClearConciseSentences.html From the University of Wisconsin at Madison.

23a Using subjects and verbs effectively

The heart of every sentence is its subject, which usually names the actor, and its verb, which usually specifies the subject's action: *Children* [subject] *grow* [verb]. When these elements do not identify the sentence's key actor and action, readers must find that information elsewhere and the sentence may be wordy and unemphatic.

In the following sentences, the subjects and verbs are underlined:

Unemphatic The intention of the company was to expand its workforce. A proposal was also made to diversify the backgrounds and abilities of employees.

These sentences are unemphatic because their key ideas (the company's intending and deciding) do not appear in their subjects and verbs. Revised, the sentences are not only clearer but more concise:

Revised The company intended to expand its workforce. It also proposed to diversify the backgrounds and abilities of employees.

Several constructions can drain meaning from a sentence's subject and verb:

- Nouns made from verbs can obscure the key actions of sentences and add words. These nouns include *intention* (from *intend*), *proposal* (from *propose*), *decision* (from *decide*), *expectation* (from *expect*), *persistence* (from *persist*), *argument* (from *argue*), and *inclusion* (from *include*).

Unemphatic After the company made a decision to hire more disabled workers, its next step was the construction of wheelchair ramps and other facilities.

Revised After the company decided to hire more disabled workers, it next constructed wheelchair ramps and other facilities.

- Weak verbs, such as *made* and *was* in the unemphatic sentence above, tend to stall sentences just where they should be moving and often bury key actions:

Unemphatic The company is now the leader among businesses in complying with the 1990 Americans with Disabilities Act. Its officers make speeches on the act to business groups.

Revised The company now leads other businesses in complying with the 1990 Americans with Disabilities Act. Its officers speak on the act to business groups.

- Verbs in the passive voice state actions received by, not performed by, their subjects. Thus the passive de-emphasizes the true actor of the sentence, sometimes omitting it entirely. Generally, prefer the active voice, in which the subject performs the verb's action. (See also p. 331.)

Unemphatic The 1990 law is seen by most businesses as fair, but the costs of complying have sometimes been exaggerated.

Revised Most businesses see the 1990 law as fair, but some opponents have exaggerated the costs of complying.

EXERCISE 1
Revising: Emphasis of subjects and verbs

Rewrite the following sentences so that their subjects and verbs identify their key actors and actions.

Example:

The issue of students making a competition over grades is a reason why their focus on learning may be lost.

Students who compete over grades may lose their focus on learning.

1. The work of many heroes was crucial in helping to emancipate the slaves.
2. The contribution of Harriet Tubman, an escaped slave herself, included the guidance of hundreds of other slaves to freedom on the Underground Railroad.
3. A return to slavery was risked by Tubman or possibly death.
4. During the Civil War she was also a carrier of information from the South to the North.
5. After the war needy former slaves were helped by Tubman's raising of money for refuges.

23b Using sentence beginnings and endings

Readers automatically seek a writer's principal meaning in the main clause of a sentence—essentially, in the subject that names the actor and the verb that usually specifies the action (see p. 419). Thus you can help readers understand your intended meaning by controlling the information in your subjects and the relation of the main clause to any modifiers attached to it.

Old and new information

Generally, readers expect the beginning of a sentence to contain information that they already know or that you have already introduced. They then look to the sentence ending for new information. In the unemphatic passage below, the subjects of the second and third sentences both introduce new topics (underlined) while the old topics (the controversy and education) appear at the ends of the sentences:

Unemphatic Education almost means controversy these days, with rising costs and constant complaints about its inadequacies. But the value of schooling should not be obscured by the controversy. The single best means of economic advancement, despite its shortcomings, remains education.

In the more emphatic revision, the underlined old information begins each sentence and new information ends the sentence. The passage follows the pattern A→B. B→C. C→D.

Revised Education almost means controversy these days, with rising costs and constant complaints about its inadequacies. But the controversy should not obscure the value of schooling. Education remains, despite its shortcomings, the single best means of economic advancement.

Cumulative and periodic sentences

You can call attention to information by placing it first or last in a sentence, reserving the middle for incidentals:

Unemphatic Education remains the single best means of economic advancement, despite its shortcomings. [Emphasizes shortcomings.]

Revised Despite its shortcomings, education remains the single best means of economic advancement. [Emphasizes advancement more than shortcomings.]

Revised Education remains, despite its shortcomings, the single best means of economic advancement. [Deemphasizes shortcomings.]

Many sentences begin with the main clause and then add more modifiers to explain, amplify, or illustrate it. Such sentences are called **cumulative** (because they accumulate information as they proceed) or **loose** (because they are not tightly structured). They parallel the way we naturally think.

Cumulative Education has no equal in opening minds, instilling values, and creating opportunities.

Cumulative Most of the Great American Desert is made up of bare rock, rugged cliffs, mesas, canyons, mountains, separated from one another by broad flat basins covered with sunbaked mud and alkali, supporting a sparse and measured growth of sagebrush

> or creosote or saltbush, depending on location and elevation. —EDWARD ABBEY

The opposite kind of sentence, called **periodic,** saves the main clause until just before the end (the period) of the sentence. Everything before the main clause points toward it.

Periodic In opening minds, instilling values, and creating opportunities, education has no equal.

Periodic With people from all over the world—Korean grocers, Jamaican cricket players, Vietnamese fishers, Haitian cabdrivers, Chinese doctors—the American mosaic is continually changing.

The periodic sentence creates suspense for readers by reserving important information for the end. But readers should already have an idea of the sentence's subject—because it was discussed or introduced in the preceding sentence—so that they know what the opening modifiers describe. In a variation of the periodic sentence, you can name the subject at the beginning, follow it with a modifier, and then complete the main clause:

> Thirty-eight-year-old Dick Hayne, who works in jeans and loafers and likes to let a question cure in the air for a while before answering it, bears all the markings of what his generation used to call a laid-back kind of guy. —GEORGE RUSH

EXERCISE 2
Sentence combining: Beginnings and endings

Locate the main idea in each group of sentences below. Then combine each group into a single sentence that emphasizes that idea by placing it at the beginning or the end. For sentences 2–5, determine the position of the main idea by considering its relation to the previous sentences: if the main idea picks up a topic that's already been introduced, place it at the beginning; if it adds new information, place it at the end.

Example:
The storm blew roofs off buildings. It caused extensive damage. It knocked down many trees. It severed power lines.

Main idea at beginning: The storm caused extensive damage, blowing roofs off buildings, knocking down many trees, and severing power lines.

Main idea at end: Blowing roofs off buildings, knocking down many trees, and severing power lines, the storm caused extensive damage.

1. Pat Taylor strode into the room. The room was packed. He greeted students called "Taylor's Kids." He nodded to their parents and teachers.
2. This was a wealthy Louisiana oilman. He had promised his

"Kids" free college educations. He was determined to make higher education available to all qualified but disadvantaged students.

3. The students welcomed Taylor. Their voices joined in singing. They sang "You Are the Wind Beneath My Wings." Their faces beamed with hope. Their eyes flashed with self-confidence.
4. The students had thought a college education was beyond their dreams. It seemed too costly. It seemed too demanding.
5. Taylor had to ease the costs and the demands of getting to college. He created a bold plan. The plan consisted of scholarships, tutoring, and counseling.

23c Arranging parallel elements effectively

Series

With parallelism, you use similar grammatical structures for ideas linked by *and, but,* and similar words (see Chapter 25). In addition, you should arrange the parallel ideas in order of their importance:

Unemphatic The storm ripped the roofs off several buildings, killed ten people, and knocked down many trees in town. [Buries the most serious damage—deaths—in the middle.]

Emphatic The storm knocked down many trees in town, ripped the roofs off several buildings, and killed ten people. [Arranges items in order of increasing importance.]

You may want to use an unexpected item at the end of a series for humor or for another special effect:

> Early to bed and early to rise makes a man healthy, wealthy, and dead.
> —James Thurber

But be careful not to use such a series carelessly. The following series seems thoughtlessly random rather than intentionally humorous:

Unemphatic The painting has subdued tone, intense feeling, and a length of about three feet.

Emphatic The painting, about three feet long, has subdued tone and intense feeling.

Balanced sentences

A sentence is **balanced** when its clauses are parallel—that is, matched in grammatical structure (Chapter 25). Read the following examples aloud to hear their rhythm.

> The fickleness of the women I love is equalled only by the infernal constancy of the women who love me.
>
> —George Bernard Shaw

In a pure balanced sentence two main clauses are exactly parallel: they match item for item.

> Scratch a lover, and find a foe.
>
> —Dorothy Parker

But the term is commonly applied to sentences that are only approximately parallel or that have only some parallel parts:

> If thought corrupts language, language can also corrupt thought.
>
> —George Orwell

> As the traveler who has once been from home is wiser than he who has never left his own doorstep, so a knowledge of one other culture should sharpen our ability to scrutinize more steadily, to appreciate more lovingly, our own.
>
> —Margaret Mead

Balanced sentences are heavily emphatic but require thoughtful planning. When used carefully, they can be an especially effective way to alert readers to a strong contrast between two ideas.

EXERCISE 3

Revising: Series and balanced elements

Revise the following sentences so that elements in a series or balanced elements are arranged to give maximum emphasis to main ideas.

Example:

The campers were stranded without matches, without food or water, and without a tent.

The campers were stranded without matches, without a tent, and without food or water.

1. Remembering her days as a "conductor" on the Underground Railroad made Harriet Tubman proud, but she got angry when she remembered her years as a slave.
2. Tubman wanted freedom regardless of personal danger, whereas for her husband, John, personal safety was more important than freedom.
3. Tubman proved her fearlessness in many ways: she led hundreds of other slaves to freedom, she was a spy for the North during the Civil War, and she disobeyed John's order not to run away.
4. To conduct slaves north to freedom, Tubman risked being returned to slavery, being hanged for a huge reward, and being caught by Southern patrollers.
5. After the war Tubman worked tirelessly for civil rights and women's suffrage; raising money for homes for needy former slaves was something else she did.

23d Repeating ideas

Careless repetition often clutters and weakens sentences (see p. 581). But planned repetition of key words and phrases can be an effective means of emphasis. Such repetition often combines with parallelism. It may occur in a series of sentences within a paragraph (see p. 86). Or it may occur in a series of words, phrases, or clauses within a sentence, as in the following examples:

> There is something uneasy in the Los Angeles air this afternoon, some unnatural stillness, some tension.
>
> —JOAN DIDION

> We have the tools, all the tools—we are suffocating in tools—but we cannot find the actual wood to work or even the actual hand to work it.
>
> —ARCHIBALD MACLEISH

23e Separating ideas

When you save important information for the end of a sentence, you can emphasize it even more by setting it off from the rest of the sentence, as in the second example below:

> Mothers and housewives are the only workers who do not have regular time off, so they are the great vacationless class.

> Mothers and housewives are the only workers who do not have regular time off. They are the great vacationless class.
>
> —ANNE MORROW LINDBERGH

You can vary the degree of emphasis by varying the extent to which you separate one idea from the others. A semicolon provides more separation than a comma, and a period provides still more separation. Compare the following sentences:

> Most of the reading which is praised for itself is neither literary nor intellectual**,** but narcotic.

> Most of the reading which is praised for itself is neither literary nor intellectual**;** it is narcotic.

> Most of the reading which is praised for itself is neither literary nor intellectual**.** It is narcotic.
>
> —DONALD HALL

Sometimes a dash or a pair of dashes will isolate and thus emphasize a part of a statement (see also pp. 522–23):

> His schemes were always elaborate, ingenious, and exciting**—**and wholly impractical.

> Athletics**—**that is, winning athletics**—**has become a profitable university operation.

EXERCISE 4
Emphasizing with repetition or separation

Emphasize the main idea in each sentence or group of sentences below by following the instructions in parentheses: either combine sentences so that parallelism and repetition stress the main idea, or place the main idea in a separate sentence. Each item has more than one possible answer.

Example:

I try to listen to other people's opinions. When my mind is closed, I find that other opinions open it. And they can change my mind when it is wrong. (*Parallelism and repetition.*)

I try to listen to other people's opinions, for they can open my mind when it is closed and they can change my mind when it is wrong.

1. One of the few worthwhile habits is daily reading. One can read for information. One can read for entertainment. Reading can give one a broader view of the world. (*Parallelism and repetition.*)
2. Reading introduces new words. One encounters unfamiliar styles of expression through reading. (*Parallelism and repetition.*)
3. Students who read a great deal will more likely write vividly, coherently, and grammatically, for they will have learned from other authors. (*Separation.*)
4. Reading gives knowledge. One gets knowledge about other cultures. One will know about history and current events. One gains information about human nature. (*Parallelism and repetition.*)
5. As a result of reading, writers have more resources and more flexibility, and thus reading creates better writers. (*Separation.*)

23f Being concise

Conciseness—brevity of expression—aids emphasis no matter what the sentence structure. Unnecessary words detract from necessary words. They clutter sentences and obscure ideas.

Weak In my opinion the competition in the area of grades is distracting. It distracts many students from their goal, which is to obtain an education that is good. There seems to be a belief among a few students that grades are more important than what is measured by them.

Emphatic The competition for grades distracts many students from their goal of obtaining a good education. A few students seem to believe that grades are more important than what they measure.

Some techniques for tightening sentences appear earlier in this chapter (pp. 419–20). Because conciseness comes mainly from deleting unneeded words, these techniques are also covered, along with others, in Chapter 38 on choosing and using words (see p. 578).

Ways to achieve conciseness

- Make the subject and verb of each sentence identify its actor and action (pp. 419, 578):

  Avoid nouns made from verbs.
  Use strong verbs.
  Rewrite the passive voice as active.
- Cut or shorten empty words or phrases (p. 580):

  Shorten filler phrases, such as *by virtue of the fact that.*
  Cut all-purpose words, such as *area, factor.*
  Cut unneeded qualifiers, such as *in my opinion, for the most part.*
- Cut unnecessary repetition (p. 581).
- Reduce clauses to phrases and phrases to single words (p. 583).
- Avoid constructions beginning with *there is* or *it is* (p. 583).
- Combine sentences (p. 583).
- Cut or rewrite jargon (p. 584).

EXERCISE 5
Revising: Conciseness

Revise the following sentences to make them more emphatic by eliminating wordiness.

Example:

The problem in this particular situation is that we owe more money than we can afford under present circumstances.

The problem is that we owe more money than we can afford.

1. As far as I am concerned, customers who are dining out in restaurants in our country must be wary of suggestive selling, so to speak.
2. In suggestive selling, diners are asked by the waiter to buy additional menu selections in addition to what was ordered by them.
3. For each item on the menu, there is another food that will naturally complement it.
4. For example, customers will be presented with the question of whether they want to order french fries along with a sandwich or whether they want to order a salad with a steak dinner.
5. Due to the fact that customers often give in to suggestive selling, they often find that their restaurant meals are more costly than they had intended to pay.

EXERCISE 6
Revising: Emphasizing ideas

Drawing on the advice in this chapter, rewrite the following paragraph to emphasize main ideas and to de-emphasize less important information.

In preparing pasta, there is a requirement for common sense and imagination rather than for complicated recipes. The key to success in this area is fresh ingredients for the sauce and perfectly cooked pasta. The sauce may be made with just about any fresh fish, meat, cheese, herb, or vegetable. As for the pasta itself, it may be dried or fresh, although fresh pasta is usually more delicate and flavorful, as many experienced cooks find. Dried pasta is fine with zesty sauces; with light oil and cream sauces fresh pasta is the best choice. There is a difference in the cooking time for dried and fresh pasta, with dried pasta taking longer. It is important that the cook follow the package directions and that the pasta be tested before the cooking time is up. The pasta is done when the texture is neither tough nor mushy but *al dente,* or "firm to the bite," according to the Italians, who ought to know.

Note See page 458 for an exercise involving emphasis along with parallelism and other techniques for effective sentences.

CHAPTER 24

Using Coordination and Subordination

When clearly written, your sentences show the relations between ideas and stress the more important ideas over the lesser ones. Two techniques can help you achieve such clarity:

- **Coordination** shows that two or more elements in a sentence are equally important in meaning. You signal coordination with words such as *and, but,* and *or.*

  equally important
  Car and health insurance are modern necessities.

  equally important
  Car insurance is costly, but health insurance seems a luxury.

- **Subordination** shows that some elements in a sentence are less important than other elements for your meaning. Usually, the main idea appears in the main clause, and supporting information appears in single words, phrases, and subordinate clauses.

  less important (subordinate clause) | more important (main clause)
  Because accidents and thefts occur frequently, car insurance is costly.

  more important (main clause) | less important (phrase)
  The health-insurance industry is changing, for better or worse.

Note Computerized grammar and style checkers may spot errors in punctuating coordinated and subordinated elements, and they can flag long sentences that may contain excessive coordination or subordination. But otherwise they provide little help because they cannot recognize the relations among ideas in sentences. You'll need to weigh and clarify those relations yourself.

http://owl.english.purdue.edu/Files/113.html Advice on sentence revision, including using coordination and subordination, from the Purdue Online Writing Lab.

http://www.english.uiuc.edu/cws/wworkshop/conjunctdef.htm Information on coordinating and subordinating conjunctions, from the University of Illinois at Urbana-Champaign.

Ways to coordinate and subordinate information in sentences

Use **coordination** to relate ideas of equal importance (opposite):

- Link main clauses with a comma and a coordinating conjunction: *and, but, or, nor, for, so, yet* (p. 469).

  Independence Hall in Philadelphia is now restored, but fifty years ago it was in bad shape.

- Relate main clauses with a semicolon alone or a semicolon and a conjunctive adverb: *however, indeed, thus,* etc. (pp. 491, 494).

  The building was standing; however, it suffered from neglect.

- Within clauses, link words and phrases with a coordinating conjunction: *and, but, or, nor* (p. 282).

  The people and officials of the nation were indifferent to Independence Hall or took it for granted.

- Link main clauses, words, or phrases with a correlative conjunction: *both . . . and, not only . . . but also,* etc. (p. 283).

  People not only took the building for granted but also neglected it.

Use **subordination** to de-emphasize ideas (p. 434):

- Use a subordinate clause beginning with a subordinating conjunction: *although, because, if, whereas,* etc. (p. 275).

  Although some citizens had tried to rescue the building, they had not gained substantial public support.

- Use a subordinate clause beginning with a relative pronoun: *who, whoever, which, that* (p. 275).

  The first strong step was taken by the federal government, which made the building a national monument.

- Use a phrase (p. 266).

  Like most national monuments, Independence Hall is protected by the National Park Service. [Prepositional phrase.]

  Protecting many popular tourist sites, the service is a highly visible government agency. [Verbal phrase.]

- Use an appositive (p. 280).

  The National Park Service, a branch of the Department of Interior, also runs Yosemite and other wilderness parks.

- Use a modifying word.

  At the red brick Independence Hall, park rangers give guided tours and protect the irreplaceable building from vandalism.

24a Coordinating to relate equal ideas

By linking equally important information, you can emphasize the relations for readers. Compare the passages below:

String of simple sentences

We should not rely so heavily on oil. Coal and uranium are also overused. We have a substantial energy resource in the moving waters of our rivers. Smaller streams add to the total volume of water. The resource renews itself. Coal and oil are irreplaceable. Uranium is also irreplaceable. The cost of water does not increase much over time. The costs of coal, oil, and uranium rise dramatically.

Ideas coordinated

We should not rely so heavily on coal, oil, and uranium, for we have a substantial energy resource in the moving waters of our rivers and streams. Coal, oil, and uranium are irreplaceable and thus subject to dramatic cost increases; water, however, is self-renewing and more stable in cost.

The information in both passages is essentially the same, but the second is shorter and considerably easier to read and understand because it builds connections among coordinate ideas.

To link ideas, you can use coordinating conjunctions (*and, but, or, nor, for, so, yet*), correlative conjunctions (*both . . . and* and others), and conjunctive adverbs (*however, thus,* and others). These words signal certain relationships, such as addition (*and, both . . . and, moreover*) and contrast (*but, not . . . but, however*). See the full lists of these words on pages 282–84.

coord 24a

Punctuating coordinated words, phrases, and clauses

Most coordinated words, phrases, and subordinate clauses are not punctuated with commas (see p. 487). The exceptions are items in a series and coordinate adjectives:

We rely heavily on coal, oil, and uranium. [A series; see p. 479.]

Dirty, unhealthy air is one result. [Coordinate adjectives; see p. 480.]

In a sentence consisting of two main clauses, punctuation depends on whether a coordinating conjunction, a conjunctive adverb, or no connecting word links the clauses:

Oil is irreplaceable, but water is self-renewing. [See p. 469.]
Oil is irreplaceable; however, water is self-renewing. [See p. 494.]
Oil is irreplaceable; water is self-renewing. [See p. 491.]

1 Using coordination effectively

A string of coordinated elements—especially main clauses—creates the same effect as a string of simple sentences: it obscures the relative importance of ideas and details.

Excessive coordination The weeks leading up to the resignation of President Nixon were eventful, and the Supreme Court and the Congress closed in on him, and the Senate Judiciary Committee voted to begin impeachment proceedings, and finally the President resigned on August 9, 1974.

Such a passage needs editing to stress the important points (underlined below) and to de-emphasize the less important information:

Revised The weeks leading up to the resignation of President Nixon were eventful, as the Supreme Court and the Congress closed in on him and the Senate Judiciary Committee voted to begin impeachment proceedings. Finally, the President resigned on August 9, 1974.

2 Coordinating logically

Coordinated sentence elements should be logically equal and related, and the relation between them should be the one expressed by the connecting word. If either principle is violated, the result is **faulty coordination:**

Faulty John Stuart Mill was a nineteenth-century utilitarian, and he believed that actions should be judged by their usefulness or by the happiness they cause. [The two clauses are not separate and equal: the second expands on the first by explaining what a utilitarian such as Mill believed.]

Revised John Stuart Mill, a nineteenth-century utilitarian, believed that actions should be judged by their usefulness or by the happiness they cause.

Faulty Mill is recognized as a utilitarian, and he did not found the utilitarian school of philosophy. [The two clauses seem to contrast, requiring *but* or *yet* between them.]

Revised Mill is recognized as a utilitarian, but he did not found the utilitarian school of philosophy.

Sometimes faulty coordination occurs because the writer omits necessary information:

Faulty Jeremy Bentham founded the utilitarian school, and Mill was precocious. [The two clauses seem unrelated.]

Revised Jeremy Bentham founded the utilitarian school before Mill was born, and Mill joined at the precocious age of twenty.

EXERCISE 1
Sentence combining: Coordination

Combine sentences in the following passages to coordinate related ideas in the way that seems most effective to you. You will have to supply coordinating conjunctions or conjunctive adverbs and the appropriate punctuation.

1. Many chronic misspellers do not have the time to master spelling rules. They may not have the motivation. They may rely on dictionaries to catch misspellings. Most dictionaries list words under their correct spellings. One kind of dictionary is designed for chronic misspellers. It lists each word under its common *mis*spellings. It then provides the correct spelling. It also provides the definition.
2. Henry Hudson was an English explorer. He captained ships for the Dutch East India Company. On a voyage in 1610 he passed by Greenland. He sailed into a great bay in today's northern Canada. He thought he and his sailors could winter there. The cold was terrible. Food ran out. The sailors mutinied. The sailors cast Hudson adrift in a small boat. Eight others were also in the boat. Hudson and his companions perished.

EXERCISE 2
Revising: Excessive or faulty coordination

Revise the following sentences to eliminate excessive or faulty coordination. Relate ideas effectively by adding or subordinating information or by forming more than one sentence. Each item has more than one possible answer.

Example:

My dog barks, and I have to move out of my apartment.

Because my dog's barking disturbs my neighbors, I have to move out of my apartment.

1. Often soldiers admired their commanding officers, and they gave them nicknames, and these names frequently contained the word "old," but not all of the commanders were old.
2. General Thomas "Stonewall" Jackson was also called "Old Jack," and he was not yet forty years old.
3. Another Southern general in the Civil War was called "Old Pete," and his full name was James Longstreet.

4. The Union general Henry W. Halleck had a reputation as a good military strategist, and he was an expert on the work of a French military authority, Henri Jomini, and Halleck was called "Old Brains."
5. General William Henry Harrison won the Battle of Tippecanoe, and he received the nickname "Old Tippecanoe," and he used the name in his presidential campaign slogan "Tippecanoe and Tyler, Too," and he won the election in 1840, but he died of pneumonia a month after taking office.

24b Subordinating to distinguish main ideas

With **subordination** you use words or word groups to indicate that some elements in a sentence are less important than others. In the following sentence, it is difficult to tell what is most important:

Excessive coordination In recent years computer prices have dropped, and production costs have dropped more slowly, and computer manufacturers have had to contend with shrinking profits.

The following rewrite places the point of the sentence (shrinking profits) in the main clause and reduces the rest of the information to a subordinate clause (underlined):

Revised Because production costs have dropped more slowly than prices in recent years, computer manufacturers have had to contend with shrinking profits.

No rules can specify what information in a sentence you should make primary and what you should subordinate; the decision will depend on your meaning. But, in general, you should consider using subordinate structures for details of time, cause, condition, concession, purpose, and identification (size, location, and the like). You can subordinate information with the following structures:

- Subordinate clauses beginning with subordinating conjunctions (*because, when,* and others) or relative pronouns (mainly *who, which, that*). (See pp. 276–77 for full lists of these words.) Because subordinate clauses are longer and grammatically

http://www.rpi.edu/dept/llc/writecenter/web/text/prose1.html#9 Discussion of stating ideas clearly with subordination, from Rensselaer Polytechnic Institute.

http://webster.commnet.edu/HP/pages/darling/grammar/conjunctions.htm#subordinating_conjunctions Discussion of using subordinating conjunctions, from the Guide to Grammar and Writing.

more like main clauses than phrases or single words, they tend to place the greatest emphasis on subordinate information.

- Phrases, including appositives renaming nouns (*her son, a man named Carl*), prepositional phrases beginning with a preposition such as *in* or *on* (*in the book*), or verbal phrases beginning with a verb form such as *saving* or *to save*. (See pp. 280, 266, and 269, respectively, for more on these kinds of phrases.) Phrases give less weight than subordinate clauses but more than single words.
- Single words, such as adjectives and adverbs that modify other words. Single words give the least weight to subordinate information.

The following examples show how subordinate structures may convey various meanings with various weights. (Some appropriate subordinating conjunctions, relative pronouns, and prepositions for each meaning appear in parentheses.)

Space or time (*after, before, since, until, when, while; at, in, on, until*)

The mine explosion killed six workers. The owners adopted safety measures.

After the mine explosion killed six workers, the owners adopted safety measures. [Subordinate clause.]

After six deaths, the owners adopted safety measures. [Prepositional phrase.]

Cause or effect (*as, because, since, so that; because of, due to*)

Jones had been without work for six months. He was having trouble paying his bills.

Because Jones had been without work for six months, he was having trouble paying his bills. [Subordinate clause.]

Having been jobless for six months, Jones could not pay his bills. [Verbal phrase.]

Condition (*if, provided, since, unless, whenever; with, without*)

Forecasters predict a mild winter. Farmers hope for an early spring.

Whenever forecasters predict a mild winter, farmers hope for an early spring. [Subordinate clause.]

With forecasts for a mild winter, farmers hope for an early spring. [Prepositional phrase.]

Concession (*although, as if, even though, though; despite, except for, in spite of*)

The horse looked gentle. It proved hard to manage.

Although the horse looked gentle, it proved hard to manage. [Subordinate clause.]

The horse, a gentle-looking animal, proved hard to manage. [Appositive.]

The gentle-looking horse proved hard to manage. [Single word.]

Purpose (*in order that, so that, that; for, toward*)

Congress passed new immigration laws. Many Vietnamese refugees could enter the United States.

Congress passed new immigration laws so that many Vietnamese refugees could enter the United States. [Subordinate clause.]

Congress passed new immigration laws, permitting many Vietnamese refugees to enter the United States. [Verbal phrase.]

Identification (*that, when, where, which, who; by, from, of*)

Old barns are common in New England. They are often painted red.

Old barns, which are often painted red, are common in New England. [Subordinate clause.]

Old barns, often painted red, are common in New England. [Verbal phrase.]

Old red barns are common in New England. [Single word.]

Punctuating subordinate constructions

A modifying word, phrase, or clause that introduces a sentence is usually set off from the rest of the sentence with a comma (see p. 471):

Unfortunately, the bank failed.
In a little over six months, the bank became insolvent.
When the bank failed, many reporters investigated.

sub 24b

A modifier that interrupts or concludes a main clause is *not* set off with punctuation when it is essential to the meaning of a word or words in the clause (see p. 473):

One article about the bank failure won a prize.

The article that won the prize appeared in the local newspaper.

The reporter wrote the article because the bank failure affected many residents of the town.

When an interrupting or concluding modifier is *not* essential to meaning, but simply adds information to the sentence, it *is* set off with punctuation, usually a comma or commas (see p. 473):

The bank, over forty years old, never reopened after its doors were closed.

The bank managers, who were cleared of any wrongdoing, all found new jobs.

Some customers of the bank never recovered all their money, though most of them tried to do so.

Like a modifier, an appositive is set off with punctuation (usually a comma or commas) only when it is *not* essential to the meaning of the word it refers to (see p. 475):

> The bank, First City, was the oldest in town.
>
> The newspaper, the Chronicle, was one of several reporting the story.

A dash or dashes may also be used to set off a nonessential appositive, particularly when it contains commas (see p. 522). A concluding appositive is sometimes set off with a colon (see p. 520).

1 Subordinating logically

Use subordination only for the less important information in a sentence. **Faulty subordination** reverses the dependent relation the reader expects:

Faulty Ms. Angelo was in her first year of teaching, although she was a better instructor than others with many years of experience. [The sentence suggests that Angelo's inexperience is the main idea, whereas the writer intended to stress her skill *despite* her inexperience.]

Revised Although Ms. Angelo was in her first year of teaching, she was a better instructor than others with many years of experience.

2 Using subordination effectively

Subordination can do much to organize and emphasize information. But it loses that power when you try to cram too much loosely related detail into one long sentence:

Overloaded The boats that were moored at the dock when the hurricane, which was one of the worst in three decades, struck were ripped from their moorings, because the owners had not been adequately prepared, since the weather service had predicted the storm would blow out to sea, which storms do at this time of year.

Such sentences usually have more than one idea that deserves a main clause, so they are best revised by sorting their details into more than one sentence:

Revised Struck by one of the worst hurricanes in three decades, the boats at the dock were ripped from their moorings. The owners were unprepared because the weather service had said that storms at this time of year blow out to sea.

A common form of excessive subordination occurs when a string of adjective clauses begin with *which, who,* or *that,* as in the following:

Stringy The company opened a new plant outside Louisville, which is in Kentucky and which is on the Ohio River, which forms the border between Kentucky and Ohio.

To revise such sentences, recast some of the subordinate clauses as other kinds of modifying structures:

Revised The company opened a new plant outside Louisville, Kentucky, a city across the Ohio River from Ohio.

EXERCISE 3
Sentence combining: Subordination

Combine each of the following pairs of sentences twice, each time using one of the subordinate structures in parentheses to make a single sentence. You will have to add, delete, change, and rearrange words.

Example:

During the late eighteenth century, workers carried beverages in brightly colored bottles. The bottles had cork stoppers. (*Clause beginning that. Phrase beginning with.*)

During the late eighteenth century, workers carried beverages in brightly colored bottles that had cork stoppers.

During the late eighteenth century, workers carried beverages in brightly colored bottles with cork stoppers.

1. The bombardier beetle sees an enemy. It shoots out a jet of chemicals to protect itself. (*Clause beginning when. Phrase beginning seeing.*)
2. The beetle's spray is very potent. It consists of hot and irritating chemicals. (*Phrase beginning consisting. Phrase beginning of.*)
3. The spray's two chemicals are stored separately in the beetle's body and mixed in the spraying gland. The chemicals resemble a nerve-gas weapon. (*Phrase beginning stored. Clause beginning which.*)
4. The tip of the beetle's abdomen sprays the chemicals. The tip revolves like a turret on a World War II bomber. (*Phrase beginning revolving. Phrase beginning spraying.*)
5. The beetle defeats most of its enemies. It is still eaten by spiders and birds. (*Clause beginning although. Phrase beginning except.*)

EXERCISE 4
Revising: Subordination

Rewrite the following paragraph in the way you think most effective to subordinate the less important ideas to the more important ones. Use subordinate clauses, phrases, and single words as you think appropriate.

Many students today are no longer majoring in the liberal arts. I mean by "liberal arts" such subjects as history, English, and the social sciences. Students think a liberal arts degree will not help them get jobs. They are wrong. They may not get practical, job-related experience from the liberal arts, but they will get a broad education, and it will never again be available to them. Many employers look for more than a technical, professional education. They think such an education can make an employee's views too narrow. The employers want open-minded employees. They want employees to think about problems from many angles. The liberal arts curriculum instills such flexibility. The flexibility is vital to the health of our society.

EXERCISE 5
Revising: Faulty or excessive subordination

Revise the following sentences to eliminate faulty or excessive subordination. Correct faulty subordination by reversing main and subordinate structures. Correct excessive subordination by coordinating equal ideas or by making separate sentences.

Example:

Terrified to return home, he had driven his mother's car into a cornfield.

Having driven his mother's car into a cornfield, he was terrified to return home.

1. Genaro González is blessed with great writing talent, which means that several of his stories and his novel *Rainbow's End* have been published.
2. He loves to write, although he has also earned a doctorate in psychology.
3. His first story, which reflects his growing consciousness of his Aztec heritage and place in the world, is entitled "Un Hijo del Sol."
4. In 1990 González, who writes equally well in English and Spanish, received a large fellowship that enabled him to take a leave of absence from Pan American University, where he teaches psychology, so that he could write without worrying about an income.
5. González wrote the first version of "Un Hijo del Sol" while he was a sophomore at Pan American, which is in the Rio Grande valley of southern Texas, which González calls "el Valle" in the story.

sub
24c

24c Choosing clear connectors

Most connecting words signal specific and unambiguous relations; for instance, the coordinating conjunction *but* clearly indicates contrast, and the subordinating conjunction *because* clearly indicates cause. A few connectors, however, require careful use, either because they are ambiguous in many contexts or because they are often misused.

1 Using *as* and *while* clearly

The subordinating conjunction *as* can indicate several relations, including comparison and time:

Comparison Technicians work as rapidly as possible.

Time One shift starts as the other stops.

Avoid using *as* to indicate cause. It is unclear.

Unclear As the experiment was occurring, the laboratory was sealed. [Time or cause intended?]

Revised When the experiment was occurring, the laboratory was sealed. [Time.]

Revised Because the experiment was occurring, the laboratory was sealed. [Cause.]

The subordinating conjunction *while* can indicate either time or concession. Unless the context makes the meaning of *while* unmistakably clear, choose a more exact connector:

Unclear While technicians work in the next room, they cannot hear the noise. [Time or concession intended?]

Revised When technicians work in the next room, they cannot hear the noise. [Time.]

Revised Although technicians work in the next room, they cannot hear the noise. [Concession.]

Do not use *while* in place of *and* or *but:*

Faulty The technicians do not think a new study is necessary, while the institute insists on it.

Revised The technicians do not think a new study is necessary, but the institute insists on it.

2 Using *as* and *like* correctly

The use of *as* as a substitute for *whether* or *that* is considered nonstandard (it does not conform to spoken and written standard English):

Nonstandard They are not sure as the study succeeded.

Revised They are not sure whether [or that] the study succeeded.

Although the preposition *like* is often used as a conjunction in informal speech and in advertising (*Dirt-Away works like a soap should*), writing generally requires the conjunction *as, as if, as though,* or *that:*

Speech It seemed like it did succeed.

Writing It seemed as if [or as though or that] it did succeed.

EXERCISE 6
Revising: Coordination and subordination

The following paragraph consists entirely of simple sentences. Use coordination and subordination to combine sentences in the way you think most effective to emphasize main ideas.

Sir Walter Raleigh personified the Elizabethan Age. That was the period of Elizabeth I's rule of England. The period occurred in the last half of the sixteenth century. Raleigh was a courtier and poet. He was also an explorer and entrepreneur. Supposedly, he gained Queen Elizabeth's favor. He did this by throwing his cloak beneath her feet at the right moment. She was just about to step over a puddle. There is no evidence for this story. It does illustrate Raleigh's dramatic and dynamic personality. His energy drew others to him. He was one of Elizabeth's favorites. She supported him. She also dispensed favors to him. However, he lost his queen's goodwill. Without her permission he seduced one of her maids of honor. He eventually married the maid of honor. Elizabeth died. Then her successor imprisoned Raleigh in the Tower of London. Her successor was James I. Raleigh was charged falsely with treason. He was released after thirteen years. He was arrested again two years later on the old treason charges. At the age of sixty-six he was beheaded.

Note See page 458 for an exercise involving coordination and subordination along with parallelism and other techniques for effective sentences.

CHAPTER 25

Using Parallelism

Parallelism is a similarity of grammatical form between two or more elements.

The air is dirtied by || factories belching smoke
and || cars spewing exhaust.

Parallel structure reinforces and highlights a close relation between compound sentence elements, whether words, phrases, or clauses.

The principle underlying parallelism is that form should reflect meaning: since the parts of compound constructions have the same function and importance, they should have the same grammatical form.

Note Computerized grammar and style checkers cannot recognize faulty parallelism because they cannot recognize the relations among ideas. You will need to find and revise problems with parallelism on your own.

25a Using parallelism for coordinate elements

Use parallelism in all the situations illustrated in the box opposite.

Note Parallel elements match each other in structure, as in the example above, but they do not always match word for word:

The pioneers passed || through the town
and || into the vast, unpopulated desert.

Information on parallelism:

http://webster.commnet.edu/HP/pages/darling/grammar/parallelism.htm From the Guide to Grammar and Writing.

http://owl.english.purdue.edu/Files/68.html From the Purdue Online Writing Lab.

http://leo.stcloudstate.edu/grammar/parallelism.html From St. Cloud State University.

Patterns of parallelism

Use parallel structures for all coordinated elements.

- For elements connected by coordinating conjunctions (*and, but, or,* etc.) or correlative conjunctions (*both . . . and, neither . . . nor,* etc.) (this page):

  In 1988 a Greek cyclist, backed up by || engineers,
physiologists,
and || athletes,
broke the world's record for human flight
with neither || a boost
nor || a motor.

- For elements being compared or contrasted (p. 445):

  || Pedal power
rather than || horse power
propelled the plane.

- For lists, outlines, or headings (p. 445):

  The four-hour flight was successful because
|| (1) the cyclist was very fit,
|| (2) he flew a straight course over water,
and || (3) he kept the aircraft near the water's surface.

1 Using parallelism for elements linked by coordinating conjunctions

The coordinating conjunctions *and, but, or, nor,* and *yet* always signal a need for parallelism:

The industrial base was shifting and shrinking.

Politicians rarely acknowledged the problem or proposed alternatives.

Industrial workers were understandably disturbed that they were losing their jobs and that no one seemed to care.

If sentence elements linked by coordinating conjunctions are not parallel in structure, the resulting sentence will be awkward and distracting:

Nonparallel Three reasons why steel companies kept losing money were that their plants were inefficient, high labor costs, and foreign competition was increasing.

Revised Three reasons why steel companies kept losing money were inefficient plants, high labor costs, and increasing foreign competition.

All the words required by idiom or grammar must be stated in compound constructions (see also p. 412).

Nonparallel Given training, workers can acquire the skills and interest in other jobs. [*Skills* and *interest* require different prepositions, so both must be stated.]

Revised Given training, workers can acquire the skills for and interest in other jobs.

Often, the same word must be repeated to avoid confusion:

Confusing Thoreau stood up for his principles by not paying his taxes and spending a night in jail. [Did he spend a night in jail or not?]

Revised Thoreau stood up for his principles by not paying his taxes and by spending a night in jail.

Be sure that clauses beginning *who* or *which* are coordinated only with other *who* or *which* clauses, even when the pronoun is not repeated:

Nonparallel Thoreau was the nineteenth-century essayist who retired to the woods and he wrote about nature.

Revised Thoreau was the nineteenth-century essayist who retired to the woods and [who] wrote about nature.

2 Using parallelism for elements linked by correlative conjunctions

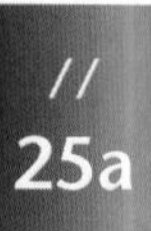

Correlative conjunctions are pairs of connectors. For example:

both . . . and	neither . . . nor	not only . . . but also
either . . . or	not . . . but	whether . . . or

// 25a

They stress equality and balance and thus emphasize the relation between elements, even long phrases and clauses. The elements should be parallel to confirm their relation:

> It is not a tax bill but a tax relief bill, providing relief not for the needy but for the greedy.
>
> —Franklin Delano Roosevelt

> At the end of the novel, Huck Finn both rejects society's values by turning down money and a home and affirms his own values by setting out for "the territory."

http://webster.commnet.edu/HP/pages/darling/grammar/conjunctions.htm#correlative_conjunctions Information on correlative conjunctions, from the Guide to Grammar and Writing.

Most errors in parallelism with correlative conjunctions occur when the element after the second connector does not match the element after the first connector:

Nonparallel Mark Twain refused either to ignore the moral blindness of his society or spare the reader's sensibilities. [*To* follows *either,* so it must also follow *or.*]

Revised Mark Twain refused either to ignore the moral blindness of his society or to spare the reader's sensibilities.

Nonparallel Huck Finn learns not only that human beings have an enormous capacity for folly but also enormous dignity. [The first element includes *that human beings have;* the second element does not.]

Revised Huck Finn learns that human beings have not only an enormous capacity for folly but also enormous dignity.

3 Using parallelism for elements being compared or contrasted

Elements being compared or contrasted should ordinarily be cast in the same grammatical form.

It is better to live rich than to die rich.

—Samuel Johnson

Weak The study found that most welfare recipients wanted to work rather than handouts.

Revised The study found that most welfare recipients wanted work rather than handouts.

Revised The study found that most welfare recipients wanted to work rather than to accept handouts.

4 Using parallelism for lists, outlines, or headings

The elements of a list or outline that divides a larger subject are coordinate and should be parallel in structure. Parallelism is essential in the headings that divide a paper into sections (see pp. 207–08) and in a formal topic outline (see pp. 40–41).

Faulty	**Improved**
Changes in Renaissance England	Changes in Renaissance England
1. Extension of trade routes	1. Extension of trade routes
2. Merchant class became more powerful	2. Increased power of the merchant class
3. The death of feudalism	3. Death of feudalism

4. Upsurging of the arts	4. Upsurge of the arts
5. The sciences were encouraged	5. Encouragement of the sciences
6. Religious quarrels began	6. Rise of religious quarrels

EXERCISE 1
Identifying parallel elements

Identify the parallel elements in the following sentences. How does parallelism contribute to the effectiveness of each sentence?

1. Eating an animal has not always been an automatic or an everyday affair; it has tended to be done on solemn occasions and for a special treat. —MARGARET VISSER
2. They [pioneer women] rolled out dough on the wagon seats, cooked with fires made out of buffalo chips, tended the sick, and marked the graves of their children, their husbands and each other. —ELLEN GOODMAN
3. The mornings are the pleasantest times in the apartment, exhaustion having set in, the sated mosquitoes at rest on ceiling and walls, sleeping it off, the room a swirl of tortured bedclothes and abandoned garments, the vines in their full leafiness filtering the hard light of day, the air conditioner silent at last, like the mosquitoes. —E. B. WHITE
4. Aging paints every action gray, lies heavy on every movement, imprisons every thought. —SHARON CURTIN

EXERCISE 2
Revising: Parallelism

Revise the following sentences to make coordinate, compared, or listed elements parallel in structure. Add or delete words or rephrase as necessary.

Example:

After emptying her bag, searching the apartment, and she called the library, Jennifer realized she had lost the book.

After emptying her bag, searching the apartment, and calling the library, Jennifer realized she had lost the book.

1. The ancient Greeks celebrated four athletic contests: the Olympic Games at Olympia, the Isthmian Games were held near Corinth, at Delphi the Pythian Games, and the Nemean Games were sponsored by the people of Cleonae.
2. Each day of the games consisted of either athletic events or holding ceremonies and sacrifices to the gods.
3. In the years between the games, competitors were taught wrestling, javelin throwing, and how to box.
4. Competitors participated in running sprints, spectacular chariot and horse races, and running long distances while wearing full armor.
5. The purpose of such events was developing physical strength,

demonstrating skill and endurance, and to sharpen the skills needed for war.

6. Events were held for both men and for boys.
7. At the Olympic Games the spectators cheered their favorites to victory, attended sacrifices to the gods, and they feasted on the meat not burned in offerings.
8. The athletes competed less to achieve great wealth than for gaining honor both for themselves and their cities.
9. Of course, exceptional athletes received financial support from patrons, poems and statues by admiring artists, and they even got lavish living quarters from their sponsoring cities.
10. With the medal counts and flag ceremonies, today's Olympians sometimes seem to be proving their countries' superiority more than to demonstrate individual talent.

25b Using parallelism to increase coherence

Effective parallelism will enable you to combine in a single, well-ordered sentence related ideas that you might have expressed in separate sentences. Compare the following three sentences with the original single sentence written by H. L. Mencken:

> Slang originates in the effort of ingenious individuals to make the language more pungent and picturesque. They increase the store of terse and striking words or widen the boundaries of metaphor. Thus a vocabulary for new shades and differences in meaning is provided by slang.

> Slang originates in the effort of ingenious individuals to make the language more pungent and picturesque—to increase the store of terse and striking words, to widen the boundaries of metaphor, and to provide a vocabulary for new shades and differences in meaning.
>
> —H. L. Mencken

Parallel structure works as well to emphasize the connections among related sentences in a paragraph.

> *Lewis Mumford stands* high in the company of this century's sages. A scholar of cosmic cultural reach and conspicuous public conscience, a distinguished critic of life, arts, and letters, an unequaled observer of cities and civilizations, *he is* secure in the modern pantheon of great men. *He is* also an enigma and an anachronism. A legend of epic proportions in intellectual and academic circles, *he is* surprisingly little known to the public.
>
> —Ada Louise Huxtable

Here, Huxtable tightly binds her sentences with two layers of paralelism: the subject-verb patterns of all four sentences (italic and underlined) and the appositives of the second and fourth sentences (underlined). (See p. 86 for another illustration of parallelism among sentences.)

// 25b

EXERCISE 3
Sentence combining: Parallelism

Combine each group of sentences below into one concise sentence in which parallel elements appear in parallel structures. You will have to add, delete, change, and rearrange words. Each item has more than one possible answer.

Example:

The new process works smoothly. It is efficient, too.
The new process works smoothly and efficiently.

1. People can develop post-traumatic stress disorder (PTSD). They develop it after experiencing a dangerous situation. They will also have felt fear for their survival.
2. The disorder can be triggered by a wide variety of events. Combat is a typical cause. Similarly, natural disasters can result in PTSD. Some people experience PTSD after a hostage situation.
3. PTSD can occur immediately after the stressful incident. Or it may not appear until many years later.
4. Sometimes people with PTSD will act irrationally. Moreover, they often become angry.
5. Other symptoms include dreaming that one is reliving the experience. They include hallucinating that one is back in the terrifying place. In another symptom one imagines that strangers are actually one's former torturers.

EXERCISE 4
Revising: Parallelism

Revise the following paragraph to create parallelism wherever it is required for grammar or for coherence.

The great white shark has an undeserved bad reputation. Many people consider the great white not only swift and powerful but also to be a cunning and cruel predator on humans. However, scientists claim that the great white attacks humans not by choice but as a result of chance. To a shark, our behavior in the water is similar to that of porpoises, seals, and sea lions—the shark's favorite foods. These sea mammals are both agile enough and can move fast enough to evade the shark. Thus the shark must attack with swiftness and noiselessly to surprise the prey and giving it little chance to escape. Humans become the shark's victims not because the shark has any preference or hatred of humans but because humans can neither outswim nor can they outmaneuver the shark. If the fish were truly a cruel human-eater, it would prolong the terror of its attacks, perhaps by circling or bumping into its intended victims before they were attacked.

Note See page 458 for an exercise involving parallelism along with other techniques for effective sentences.

CHAPTER 26

Achieving Variety

In a paragraph or an essay, each sentence stands in relation to those before and after it. To make sentences work together effectively, you need to vary their length, structure, and word order to reflect the importance and complexity of ideas. Variety sometimes takes care of itself, but you can practice established techniques for achieving varied sentences:

Ways to achieve variety among sentences

- Vary the length and structure of sentences so that important ideas stand out (p. 450).
- Vary the beginnings of sentences with modifiers, transitional words and expressions, and occasional expletive constructions (p. 452).
- Occasionally, invert the normal order of subject, verb, and object or complement (p. 455).
- Occasionally, use a command, question, or exclamation (p. 455).

A series of similar sentences will prove monotonous and ineffective, as this passage illustrates:

> Ulysses S. Grant and Robert E. Lee met on April 9, 1865. Their meeting place was the parlor of a modest house at Appomattox Court House, Virginia. They met to work out the terms for the sur-

Information on achieving sentence variety:

http://webster.commnet.edu/HP/pages/darling/grammar/sentences.htm From the Guide to Grammar and Writing.

http://owl.english.purdue.edu/Files/113.html From the Purdue Online Writing Lab.

http://www.esc.edu/htmlpages/writer/pandg/ways.htm From the State University of New York.

http://leo.stcloudstate.edu/style/sentencev.html From St. Cloud State University.

> render of Lee's Army of Northern Virginia. One great chapter of American life ended with their meeting, and another began. Grant and Lee were bringing the Civil War to its virtual finish. Other armies still had to surrender, and the fugitive Confederate government would struggle desperately and vainly. It would try to find some way to go on living with its chief support gone. Grant and Lee had signed the papers, however, and it was all over in effect.

These eight sentences are all between twelve and sixteen words long (counting initials and dates), they are about equally detailed, and they all begin with the subject. We get a sense of names, dates, and events but no immediate sense of how they relate or what is most important.

Now compare the preceding passage with the actual passage written by Bruce Catton. Here the four sentences range from eleven to fifty-five words, and only one sentence begins with its subject:

> When Ulysses S. Grant and Robert E. Lee met in the parlor of a modest house at Appomattox Court House, Virginia, on April 9, 1865, to work out the terms for the surrender of Lee's Army of Northern Virginia, a great chapter in American life came to a close, and a great new chapter began. [Suspenseful periodic sentence (p. 422) focuses attention on meeting. Details of place, time, and cause are in opening subordinate clause.]
>
> These men were bringing the Civil War to its virtual finish. [Short sentence sums up.] To be sure, other armies had yet to surrender, and for a few days the fugitive Confederate government would struggle desperately and vainly, trying to find some way to go on living now that its chief support was gone. [Cumulative sentence (p. 421) reflects lingering obstacles to peace.] But in effect it was all over when Grant and Lee signed the papers. [Short final sentence indicates futility of further struggle.]
>
> —BRUCE CATTON, "Grant and Lee"

var 26a

The rest of this chapter suggests how you can vary your sentences for the kind of interest and clarity achieved by Catton.

Note Some computerized grammar and style checkers will flag long sentences, and you can check for appropriate variety in a series of such sentences. But generally these programs cannot help you see where variety may be needed because they cannot recognize the relative importance and complexity of your ideas. To edit for variety, you need to listen to your sentences and determine whether they clarify your meaning.

26a Varying sentence length and structure

The sentences of a stylistically effective essay will vary most obviously in their length and the arrangement of main clauses and modifiers. The variation in length and structure makes writing both readable and clear.

1 Varying length

In most contemporary writing, sentences vary from about ten to about forty words, with an average of fifteen to twenty-five words.

If your sentences are all at one extreme or the other, your readers may have difficulty focusing on main ideas and seeing the relations among them:

- If most of your sentences contain thirty-five words or more, your main ideas may not stand out from the details that support them. Break some of the long sentences into shorter, simpler ones.
- If most of your sentences contain fewer than ten or fifteen words, all your ideas may seem equally important and the links between them may not be clear. Try combining them with coordination (p. 431) and subordination (p. 434) to show relationships and stress main ideas over supporting information.

2 Rewriting strings of brief and simple sentences

A series of brief and simple sentences is both monotonous and hard to understand because it forces the reader to sort out relations among ideas. If you find that you depend on brief, simple sentences, work to increase variety by combining some of them into longer units that emphasize and link important ideas while de-emphasizing incidental information. (See Chapter 24.)

The following examples show how a string of simple sentences can be revised into an effective piece of writing:

Monotonous The moon is now drifting away from the earth. It moves away at the rate of about one inch a year. This movement is lengthening our days. They increase a thousandth of a second every century. Forty-seven of our present days will someday make up a month. We might eventually lose the moon altogether. Such great planetary movement rightly concerns astronomers, but it need not worry us. The movement will take 50 million years.

Revised The moon is now drifting away from the earth <u>about one inch a year</u>. <u>At a thousandth of a second every century</u>, this movement is lengthening our days. Forty-seven of our present days will someday make up a month, <u>if we don't eventually lose the moon altogether</u>. Such great planetary movement rightly concerns astronomers, but it need not worry us. It will take 50 million years.

In the revision underlining indicates subordinate structures that were simple sentences in the original. With five sentences instead of the original eight, the revision emphasizes the moon's movement, our lengthening days, and the enormous span of time involved.

3 Rewriting strings of compound sentences

Because compound sentences are usually just simple sentences linked with conjunctions, a series of them will be as weak as a series of brief simple sentences, especially if the clauses of the compound sentences are all about the same length:

Monotonous Physical illness may involve more than the body, for the mind may also be affected. Disorientation is common among sick people, but they are often unaware of it. They may reason abnormally, or they may behave immaturely.

Revised Physical illness may involve the mind as well as the body. Though often unaware of it, sick people are commonly disoriented. They may reason abnormally or behave immaturely.

The first passage creates a seesaw effect. The revision, with some main clauses shortened or changed into modifiers (underlined), is both clearer and more emphatic. (See p. 432 for more on avoiding excessive coordination.)

EXERCISE 1
Revising: Varied sentence structures

Rewrite the following paragraph to increase variety so that important ideas receive greater emphasis than supporting information does. You will have to change some main clauses into modifiers and then combine and reposition the modifiers and the remaining main clauses.

Charlotte Perkins Gilman was a leading intellectual in the women's movement during the first decades of the twentieth century. She wrote *Women and Economics.* This book challenged Victorian assumptions about differences between the sexes, and it explored the economic roots of women's oppression. Gilman wrote little about gaining the vote for women, but many feminists were then preoccupied with this issue, and historians have since focused their analyses on this issue. As a result, Gilman's contribution to today's women's movement has often been overlooked.

26b Varying sentence beginnings

An English sentence often begins with its subject, which generally captures old information from a preceding sentence (see pp. 420–21):

The defendant's lawyer was determined to break the prosecution's witness. She relentlessly cross-examined the stubborn witness for a week.

However, an unbroken sequence of sentences beginning with the subject quickly becomes monotonous, as shown by the unvaried passage on Grant and Lee that opened this chapter (pp. 449–50). You can vary this subject-first pattern by adding modifiers or other elements before the subject.

Note The final arrangement of sentence elements should always depend on two concerns: the relation of a sentence to those preceding and following it and the emphasis required by your meaning.

Adverb modifiers

Adverbs modify verbs, adjectives, other adverbs, and whole clauses. They can often fall in a variety of spots in a sentence. Consider these different emphases:

For a week, the defendant's lawyer relentlessly cross-examined the stubborn witness.

Relentlessly, the defendant's lawyer cross-examined the stubborn witness for a week.

Relentlessly, for a week, the defendant's lawyer cross-examined the stubborn witness.

Notice that the last sentence, with both modifiers at the beginning, is periodic and thus highly emphatic (see p. 422).

ESL Placing certain adverb modifiers at the beginning of a sentence requires you to change the normal subject-verb order as well. The most common of these modifiers are negatives, including *seldom, rarely, in no case, not since,* and *not until.*

Faulty Seldom [adverb] a witness [subject] has held [verb phrase] the stand so long.

Revised Seldom [adverb] has [helping verb] a witness [subject] held [main verb] the stand so long.

Adjective modifiers

Adjectives, modifying nouns and pronouns, may include participles and participial phrases, as in *flying geese* or *money well spent* (see pp. 270–71). These modifiers may sometimes fall at the beginning of a sentence to postpone the subject:

The witness was exhausted from his testimony, and he did not cooperate.

Exhausted from his testimony, the witness did not cooperate.

Coordinating conjunctions and transitional expressions

When the relation between two successive sentences demands, you may begin the second with a connecting word or phrase: a coordinating conjunction such as *and* or *but* (p. 282) or a transitional expression such as *first, for instance, however,* or *therefore* (p. 89).

> The witness had expected to be dismissed after his first long day of cross-examination. But he was not.
>
> The price of clothes has risen astronomically in recent years. For example, a cheap cotton shirt that once cost $6 now costs $25.

Occasional expletive constructions

An expletive construction—*it* or *there* plus a form of *be*—may occasionally be useful to delay and thus emphasize the subject of the sentence:

> His judgment seems questionable, not his desire.
> It is his judgment that seems questionable, not his desire.

However, expletive constructions are more likely to flatten writing by adding extra words. You should use them rarely, only when you can justify doing so. (See also p. 583.)

EXERCISE 2
Revising: Varied sentence beginnings

Follow the instructions in parentheses to revise each group of sentences below: either create a single sentence that begins with an adverb or adjective modifier, or make one sentence begin with an appropriate connector.

> *Example:*
>
> The *Seabird* took first place. It moved quickly in the wind. (*One sentence with adjective modifier beginning* moving.)
>
> Moving quickly in the wind, the *Seabird* took first place.

1. Some people are champion procrastinators. They seldom complete their work on time. (*Two sentences with transitional expression.*)
2. Procrastinators may fear criticism. They may fear rejection. They will delay completing an assignment. (*One sentence with adverb modifier beginning* if.)
3. Procrastinators often desire to please a boss or a teacher. They fear failure so much that they cannot do the work. (*Two sentences with coordinating conjunction.*)
4. Procrastination seems a hopeless habit. It is conquerable. (*One sentence with adverb modifier beginning* although.)
5. Teachers or employers can be helpful. They can encourage procrastinators. They can give procrastinators the confidence to do good work on time. (*One sentence with adjective modifier beginning* helpfully encouraging.)

EXERCISE 3
Revising: Varied sentence beginnings

Revise the following paragraph to vary sentence beginnings by using each of the following at least once: an adverb modifier, an adjective modifier, a coordinating conjunction, and a transitional expression.

Scientists in Egypt dug up 40-million-year-old fossil bones. They had evidence of primitive whales. The whale ancestors are called mesonychids. They were small, furry land mammals with four legs. These limbs were complete with kneecaps, ankles, and little toes. Gigantic modern whales have tiny hind legs inside their bodies and flippers instead of front legs. Scientists are certain that these two very different creatures share the same family tree.

26c Inverting the normal word order

The word order of subject, verb, and object or complement is strongly fixed in English (see pp. 259–62). Thus an inverted sentence can be emphatic:

> Voters once had some faith in politicians, and they were fond of incumbents. But now all politicians, especially incumbents, voters seem to detest. [The object *all politicians* precedes the verb *detests*.]

Inverting the normal order of subject, verb, and complement can be useful in two successive sentences when the second expands on the first:

> Critics have not been kind to Presidents who have tried to apply the ways of private business to public affairs. Particularly explicit was the curt verdict of one critic of President Hoover: Mr. Hoover was never President of the United States; he was four years chairman of the board.
>
> —Adapted from EMMET JOHN HUGHES, "The Presidency vs. Jimmy Carter"

var 26d

Inverted sentences used without need are artificial. Avoid descriptive sentences such as *Up came Larry and down went Cindy's spirits.*

26d Mixing types of sentences

Most written sentences make statements. Occasionally, however, questions, commands, or exclamations may enhance variety.

Questions may set the direction of a paragraph, as in *What does a detective do?* or *How is the percentage of unemployed workers calculated?* More often, though, the questions used in exposition or argument do not require answers but simply emphasize ideas that readers can be expected to agree with. Such **rhetorical questions** are illustrated in the following passage:

> Another word that has ceased to have meaning due to overuse is *attractive. Attractive* has become verbal chaff. Who, by some stretch of language and imagination, cannot be described as attractive? And just what is it that attractive individuals are attracting?
>
> —Diane White

Commands occur frequently in an explanation of a process, particularly in directions, as this passage on freewriting illustrates:

> The idea is simply to write for ten minutes (later on, perhaps fifteen or twenty). Don't stop for anything. Go quickly, without rushing. Never stop to look back, to cross something out, to wonder how to spell something, to wonder what word or thought to use, or to think about what you are doing. —Peter Elbow

Notice that the authors of these examples use questions and commands to achieve some special purpose. Variety occurs because a particular sentence type is effective for the context, not because the writer set out to achieve variety for its own sake.

EXERCISE 4
Writing varied sentences

Imagine that you are writing an essay on a transportation problem at your school. Practice varying sentences by composing a sentence or passage to serve each purpose listed below.

1. Write a question that could open the essay.
2. Write a command that could open the essay.
3. Write an exclamation that could open the essay.
4. For the body of the essay, write an appropriately varied paragraph of at least five sentences, including at least one short and one long sentence beginning with the subject; at least one sentence beginning with an adverb modifier; at least one sentence beginning with a coordinating conjunction or transitional expression; and one rhetorical question or command.

EXERCISE 5
Analyzing variety

Examine the following paragraph for sentence variety. By analyzing your own response to each sentence, try to explain why the author wrote each short or long sentence, each cumulative or periodic sentence, each sentence beginning with its subject or beginning some other way, and each question.

That night in my rented room, while letting the hot water run over my can of pork and beans in the sink, I opened [H. L. Mencken's] *A Book of Prefaces* and began to read. I was jarred and shocked by the style, the clear, clean, sweeping sentences. Why did he write like that? And how did one write like that? I pictured the man as a raging demon, slashing with his pen, consumed with hate, denouncing everything American, extolling everything European or German, laughing at the weaknesses of people, mocking God, authority. What was this? I stood up, trying to realize what reality lay behind the meaning of the words. Yes, this man was fighting, fighting with words. He was using words as a weapon, using them as one would use a club. Could words be weapons? Well, yes, for here they were. Then, maybe, perhaps, I could use them as a weapon? No. It frightened me. I read on and what amazed me was not what he said, but how on earth anybody had the courage to say it.

—RICHARD WRIGHT, *Black Boy*

EXERCISE 6
Revising: Variety

The following paragraph consists entirely of simple sentences that begin with their subjects. As appropriate, use the techniques discussed in this chapter to vary sentences. Your goal is to make the paragraph more readable and make its important ideas stand out clearly. You will have to delete, add, change, and rearrange words.

The Italian volcano Vesuvius had been dormant for many years. It then exploded on August 24 in the year AD 79. The ash, pumice, and mud from the volcano buried two busy towns. Herculaneum is one. The more famous is Pompeii. Both towns lay undiscovered for many centuries. Herculaneum and Pompeii were discovered in 1709 and 1748, respectively. The excavation of Pompeii was the more systematic. It was the occasion for initiating modern methods of conservation and restoration. Herculaneum was simply looted of its most valuable finds. It was then left to disintegrate. Pompeii appears much as it did before the eruption. A luxurious house opens onto a lush central garden. An election poster decorates a wall. A dining table is set for breakfast.

Note See the next page for an exercise involving variety along with parallelism and other techniques for effective sentences.

EXERCISE ON CHAPTERS 23–26
Revising: Effective sentences

Revise the paragraphs below to emphasize main ideas, de-emphasize supporting information, and achieve a pleasing, clear variety in sentences. As appropriate, employ the techniques discussed in Chapters 23–26, such as using subjects and verbs appropriately, subordinating and coordinating, creating parallelism, and varying sentence beginnings. Edit the finished product for punctuation.

Modern Americans owe many debts to Native Americans. Several pleasures are among the debts. Native Americans originated two fine junk foods. They discovered popcorn. Potato chips were also one of their contributions.

The introduction of popcorn to the European settlers came from Native Americans. Massasoit provided popcorn at the first Thanksgiving feast. The Aztecs offered popcorn to the Spanish explorer Hernando Cortés. The Aztecs wore popcorn necklaces. So did the natives of the West Indies. There were three ways that the Native Americans popped the corn. First, they roasted an ear over fire. The ear was skewered on a stick. They ate only some of the popcorn. They ate the corn that fell outside the flames. Second, they scraped the corn off the cob. The kernels would be thrown into the fire. Of course, the fire had to be low. Then the popped kernels that did not fall into the fire were eaten. The third method was the most sophisticated. It involved a shallow pottery vessel. It contained sand. The vessel was heated. The sand soon got hot. Corn kernels were stirred in. They popped to the surface of the sand and were eaten.

A Native American chef was responsible for devising the crunchy potato chip. His name was George Crum. In 1853 Crum was cooking at Moon Lake Lodge. The lodge was in Saratoga Springs, New York. Complaints were sent in by a customer. The man thought Crum's french-fried potatoes were too thick. Crum tried a thinner batch. These were also unsuitable. Crum became frustrated. He deliberately made the potatoes thin and crisp. They could not be cut with a knife and fork. Crum's joke backfired. The customer raved about the potato chips. The chips were named Saratoga Chips. Soon they appeared on the lodge's menu. They also appeared throughout New England. Crum later opened his own restaurant. Of course, he offered potato chips.

Now all Americans munch popcorn in movies. They crunch potato chips at parties. They gorge on both when alone and bored. They can be grateful to Native Americans for these guilty pleasures.

eff

PART VII

Punctuation

Commas, semicolons, colons, dashes, parentheses

(For explanations, consult the pages in parentheses.)

Sentences with two main clauses

The bus stopped, but no one got off. (p. 469)
The bus stopped; no one got off. (p. 491)
The bus stopped; however, no one got off. (p. 494)
The mechanic replaced the battery, the distributor cap, and the starter; but still the car would not start. (p. 495)
Her duty was clear: she had to locate the problem. (p. 520)

Introductory elements

Modifiers (p. 471)

After the argument was over, we laughed at ourselves.
Racing over the plain, the gazelle escaped the lion.
To dance in the contest, he had to tape his knee.
Suddenly, the door flew open.
With 125 passengers aboard, the plane was half full.
In 1983 he won the Nobel Prize.

Absolute phrases (p. 478)

Its wing broken, the bird hopped around on the ground.

Interrupting and concluding elements

Nonessential modifiers (p. 473)

Jim's car, which barely runs, has been impounded.
We consulted the dean, who had promised to help us.
The boy, like his sister, wants to be a pilot.
They moved across the desert, shielding their eyes from the sun.
The men do not speak to each other, although they share a car.

Nonessential appositives

Bergen's daughter, Candice, became an actress. (p. 475)
The residents of three counties—Suffolk, Springfield, and Morrison—were urged to evacuate. (p. 522)
Father demanded one promise: that we not lie to him. (p. 520)

Essential modifiers (p. 475)

The car that hit mine was uninsured.
We consulted a teacher who had promised to help us.
The boy in the black hat is my cousin.
They were surprised to find the desert teeming with life.
The men do not speak to each other because they are feuding.

Essential appositives (p. 475)

Shaw's play *Saint Joan* was performed last year.
Their sons Tony, William, and Steve all chose military careers, leaving only Joe to run the family business.

Transitional or parenthetical expressions

We suspect, however, that he will not come. (p. 475)
Jan is respected by many people—including me. (p. 522)
George Balanchine (1904–83) was a brilliant choreographer. (p. 525)

Absolute phrases (p. 478)

The bird, its wing broken, hopped about on the ground.
The bird hopped about on the ground, its wing broken.

Phrases expressing contrast (p. 478)

The humidity, not just the heat, gives me headaches.
My headaches are caused by the humidity, not just the heat.

Concluding summaries and explanations

The movie opened to bad notices: the characters were judged shallow and unrealistic. (p. 520)
We dined on gumbo and jambalaya—a Cajun feast. (p. 523).

Items in a series

Three or more items

Chimpanzees, gorillas, orangutans, and gibbons are all apes. (p. 479)
The cities singled out for praise were Birmingham, Alabama; Lincoln, Nebraska; Austin, Texas; and Troy, New York. (p. 496)

Two or more adjectives before a noun (p. 480)

Dingy, smelly clothes decorated their room.
The luncheon consisted of one tiny watercress sandwich.

Introductory series (p. 523)

Appropriateness, accuracy, and necessity—these criteria should govern your selection of words.

Concluding series

Every word should be appropriate, accurate, and necessary. (p. 488)
Every word should meet three criteria: appropriateness, accuracy, and necessity. (p. 520)
Pay attention to your words—to their appropriateness, their accuracy, and their necessity. (p. 523)

p

CHAPTER 27

End Punctuation

End punctuation marks—the period, the question mark, and the exclamation point—signal the ends of sentences.

Note Do not rely on a computerized grammar and spelling checker to identify missing or misused end punctuation. Although a checker may flag missing question marks after direct questions or incorrect combinations of marks (such as a question mark and a period at the end of a sentence), it cannot do much else.

THE PERIOD

Use a period to end a statement, mild command, or indirect question.

Statements

These are exciting and trying times.
The airline went bankrupt.

Mild commands

Please do not smoke.
Think of the possibilities.

If you are unsure whether to use an exclamation point or a period after a command, use a period. The exclamation point should be used only rarely (see p. 465).

An **indirect question** reports what someone has asked but not in the form or exact words of the original.

Advice on periods, question marks, and exclamation points:

http://www.uottawa.ca/academic/arts/writcent/hypergrammar/endpunct.html From the University of Ottawa.

http://webster.commnet.edu/HP/pages/darling/grammar/marks.htm From the Guide to Grammar and Writing.

Indirect questions

Students sometimes wonder whether their teachers read the papers they write.

Abused children eventually stop asking why they are being punished.

ESL Unlike a direct question, an indirect question uses the wording and subject-verb order of a statement: *The reporter asked why the negotiations failed*, not *why did the negotiations fail.*

27b Use periods with many abbreviations.

Use periods with most abbreviations involving small letters:

p.	Mrs., Mr.	e.g.	Feb.
Ph.D.	Ms.	a.m., p.m.	ft.

Note that a period follows *Ms.*, even though it is not actually an abbreviation.

Many abbreviations of two or more words using all capital letters may be written with or without periods. Just be consistent.

BA or B.A.	US or U.S.	BC or B.C.	AM or A.M.

Omit periods from these abbreviations:

- The initials of a well-known person: *FDR, JFK.*
- The initials of an organization: *IBM, USMC.*
- A postal abbreviation: *NY, AVE.* (See also p. 906.)
- An **acronym,** a pronounceable word formed from initials: *UNESCO, VISTA.*

Note When an abbreviation falls at the end of a sentence, use only one period: *The school offers a Ph.D.*

See also pages 545–48 on uses of abbreviations in writing.

EXERCISE 1
Revising: Periods

Revise the following sentences so that periods are used correctly.

Example:

Several times I wrote to ask when my subscription ended?
Several times I wrote to ask when my subscription ended.

1. The instructor asked when Plato wrote *The Republic?*
2. Give the date within one century
3. The exact date is not known, but it is estimated at 370 B.C..
4. Dr Arn will lecture on Plato at 7:30 p.m..
5. The area of the lecture hall is only 1600 sq ft

. 27b

THE QUESTION MARK

27c Use a question mark after a direct question.

Direct questions

What is the difference between these two people?
Will economists ever really understand the economy?

After an indirect question, use a period: *The senator asked why the bill had passed.* (See p. 463.)

Questions in a series are each followed by a question mark:

The officer asked how many times the suspect had been arrested. Three times? Four times? More than that?

The use of capital letters for questions in a series is optional (see p. 535).

Note Question marks are never combined with other question marks, exclamation points, periods, or commas:

Faulty Readers ask, "What is the point?."
Revised Readers ask, "What is the point?"

27d Use a question mark within parentheses to indicate doubt about the correctness of a number or date.

The Greek philosopher Socrates was born in 470 (?) BC and died in 399 BC from drinking poison after having been condemned to death.

Note Don't use a question mark within parentheses to express sarcasm or irony. Express these attitudes through sentence structure and word choice. (See Chapters 23 and 38.)

Faulty Stern's friendliness (?) bothered Crane.
Revised Stern's insincerity bothered Crane.

EXERCISE 2
Revising: Question marks

Revise the following sentences so that question marks (along with other punctuation marks) are used correctly.

Example:
"When will it end?," cried the man dressed in rags.
"When will it end?" cried the man dressed in rags.

1. In Homer's *Odyssey,* Odysseus took seven years to travel from Troy to Ithaca. Or was it eight years. Or more?

2. Odysseus must have wondered whether he would ever make it home?
3. "What man are you and whence?," asks Odysseus's wife, Penelope.
4. Why does Penelope ask, "Where is your city? Your family?"?
5. Penelope does not recognize Odysseus and asks who this stranger is?

THE EXCLAMATION POINT

27e Use an exclamation point after an emphatic statement, interjection, or command.

No! We must not lose this election!
Come here immediately!

Follow mild interjections and commands with commas or periods, as appropriate:

No, the response was not terrific.
To prolong your car's life, change its oil regularly.

Note Exclamation points are never combined with other exclamation points, question marks, periods, or commas:

Faulty "This will not be endured!," he roared.

Revised "This will not be endured!" he roared.

27f Use exclamation points sparingly.

Don't express sarcasm, irony, or amazement with the exclamation point. Rely on sentence structure and word choice to express these attitudes. (See Chapters 23 and 38.)

Faulty After traveling 4.4 billion miles through space, *Voyager 2* was off-target by 21 miles (!).

Revised After traveling 4.4 billion miles through space, *Voyager 2* was off-target by a mere 21 miles.

Relying on the exclamation point for emphasis is like crying wolf: the mark loses its power to impress the reader. Frequent exclamation points can also make writing sound overemotional. In the following passage, the writer could have conveyed ideas more effectively by punctuating sentences with periods:

> Our city government is a mess! After just six months in office, the mayor has had to fire four city officials! In the same period the city councilors have done nothing but argue! And city services decline with each passing day!

EXERCISE 3
Revising: Exclamation points

Revise the following sentences so that exclamation points (along with other punctuation marks) are used correctly. If a sentence is punctuated correctly as given, circle the number preceding it.

Example:
"Well, now!," he said loudly.
"Well, now!" he said loudly.

1. As the firefighters moved their equipment into place, the police shouted, "Move back!".
2. A child's cries could be heard from above: "Help me. Help."
3. When the child was rescued, the crowd called "Hooray."
4. The rescue was the most exciting event of the day!
5. Let me tell you about it.

EXERCISE 4
Revising: End punctuation

Insert appropriate punctuation (periods, question marks, or exclamation points) where needed in the following paragraph.

When visitors first arrive in Hawaii, they often encounter an unexpected language barrier Standard English is the language of business and government, but many of the people speak Pidgin English Instead of an excited "Aloha" the visitors may be greeted with an excited Pidgin "Howzit" or asked if they know "how fo' find one good hotel" Many Hawaiians question whether Pidgin will hold children back because it prevents communication with the *haoles,* or Caucasians, who run businesses Yet many others feel that Pidgin is a last defense of ethnic diversity on the islands To those who want to make standard English the official language of the state, these Hawaiians may respond, "Just 'cause I speak Pidgin no mean I dumb" They may ask, "Why you no listen" or, in standard English, "Why don't you listen"

Note See page 532 for a punctuation exercise combining periods with other marks of punctuation.

CHAPTER 28

The Comma

Commas usually function within sentences to separate elements (see the box on the next page). Omitting needed commas or inserting needless ones can confuse the reader:

Comma needed	Though very tall Abraham Lincoln was not an overbearing man.
Revised	Though very tall, Abraham Lincoln was not an overbearing man.
Unneeded commas	The hectic pace of Beirut, broke suddenly into frightening chaos when the city became, the focus of civil war.
Revised	The hectic pace of Beirut broke suddenly into frightening chaos when the city became the focus of civil war.

Note Computerized grammar and style checkers will recognize only some comma errors, ignoring others. Revise any errors that your checker points out, but you'll have to proofread your work on your own to find and correct most errors.

Information, sometimes with exercises, on using the comma:

http://leo.stcloudstate.edu/punct/comma.html From St. Cloud State University.

http://webster.commnet.edu/HP/pages/darling/grammar/commas.htm From the Guide to Grammar and Writing.

http://owl.english.purdue.edu/Files/3.html From the Purdue Online Writing Lab.

http://www.esc.edu/htmlpages/writer/pandg/comma.htm From the State University of New York.

http://www.uottawa.ca/academic/arts/writcent/hypergrammar/comma.html From the University of Ottawa.

http://www.clearcf.uvic.ca/writersguide/Pages/GramPunc.html#comma From The University of Victoria.

Principal uses of the comma

- To separate main clauses linked by a coordinating conjunction (facing page):

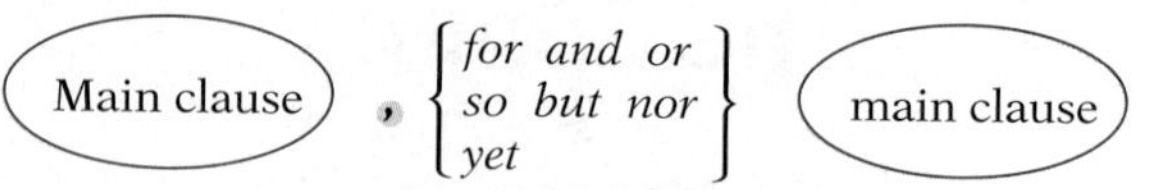

The building is finished, but it has no tenants.

- To set off most introductory elements (p. 471):

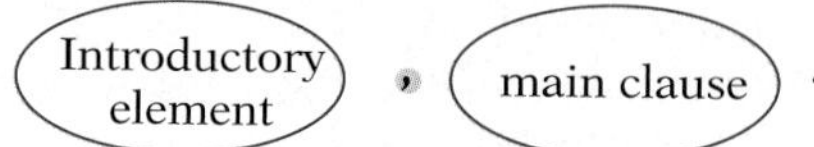

Unfortunately, the only tenant pulled out.

- To set off nonessential elements (p. 473):

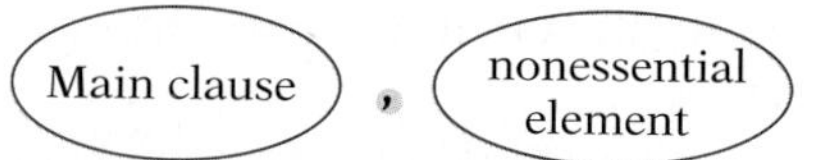

The empty building symbolizes a weak local economy, which affects everyone.

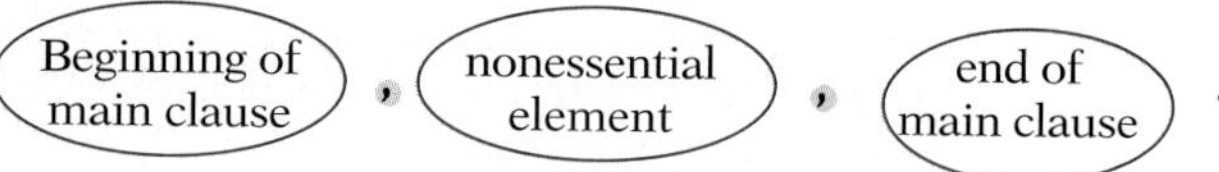

The primary cause, the decline of local industry, is not news.

- To separate items in a series (p. 479):

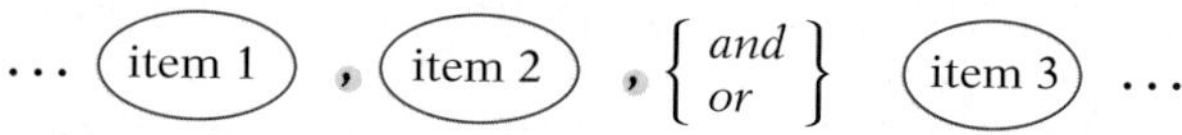

The city needs healthier businesses, new schools, and improved housing.

- To separate coordinate adjectives (p. 480):

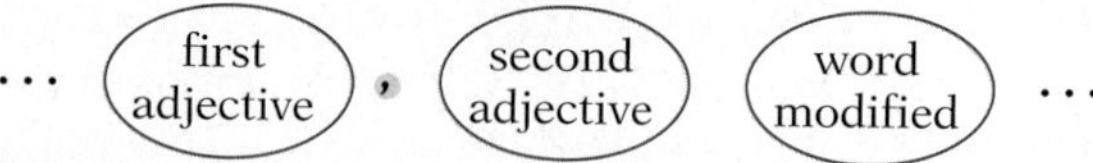

A tall, sleek skyscraper is not needed.

Other uses of the comma:

To set off absolute phrases (p. 478).
To set off phrases expressing contrast (p. 478).
To separate parts of dates, addresses, long numbers (p. 481).
To separate quotations and signal phrases (p. 482).
To prevent misreading (p. 485).

See also page 485 for when *not* to use the comma.

28a Use a comma before *and, but,* or another coordinating conjunction linking main clauses.

The coordinating conjunctions are *and, but, or, nor, for, so,* and *yet*. When these link words or phrases, do not use a comma: *Dugain plays and sings Irish and English folk songs.* However, *do* use a comma when a coordinating conjunction joins main clauses. A **main clause** has a subject and a predicate (but no subordinating word at the beginning) and makes a complete statement (see p. 275).

> Caffeine can keep coffee drinkers alert, and it may elevate their mood.
>
> Caffeine was once thought to be safe, but now researchers warn of harmful effects.
>
> Coffee drinkers may suffer sleeplessness, for the drug acts as a stimulant to the nervous system.

Note Do not add a comma *after* a coordinating conjunction between main clauses (see also p. 487):

> **Not** Caffeine increases the heart rate, and, it constricts blood vessels.
>
> **But** Caffeine increases the heart rate, and it constricts blood vessels.

Exceptions When the main clauses in a sentence are very long or grammatically complicated, or when they contain internal punctuation, a semicolon before the coordinating conjunction will clarify the division between clauses (see p. 495):

> Caffeine may increase alertness, elevate mood, and provide energy; but it may also cause irritability, anxiety, stomach pains, and other ills.

When main clauses are very short and closely related in meaning, you may omit the comma between them as long as the resulting sentence is clear:

> Caffeine helps but it also hurts.

If you are in doubt about whether to use a comma in such a sentence, use it. It will always be correct.

http://webster.commnet.edu/HP/pages/darling/grammar/conjunctions.htm#coordinating_conjunctions Advice on punctuation with coordinating conjunctions, from the Guide to Grammar and Writing.

EXERCISE 1
Punctuating linked main clauses

Insert a comma before each coordinating conjunction that links main clauses in the following sentences.

Example:

I would have attended the concert and the reception but I had to baby-sit for my niece.

I would have attended the concert and the reception, but I had to baby-sit for my niece.

1. Parents once automatically gave their children the father's surname but some no longer do.
2. Instead, they bestow the mother's name for they believe that the mother's importance should be recognized.
3. The child's surname may be just the mother's or it may link the mother's and the father's with a hyphen.
4. Sometimes the first and third children will have the mother's surname and the second child will have the father's.
5. Occasionally the mother and father combine parts of their names and a new hybrid surname is born.

EXERCISE 2
Sentence combining: Linked main clauses

Combine each group of sentences below into one sentence that contains only two main clauses connected by the coordinating conjunction in parentheses. Separate the main clauses with a comma. You will have to add, delete, and rearrange words.

Example:

The circus had come to town. The children wanted to see it. Their parents wanted to see it. (*and*)

The circus had come to town, and the children and their parents wanted to see it.

1. Parents were once legally required to bestow the father's surname on their children. These laws have been contested in court. They have been found invalid. (*but*)
2. Parents may now give their children any surname they choose. The arguments for bestowing the mother's surname are often strong. They are often convincing. (*and*)
3. Critics sometimes question the effects of unusual surnames on children. They wonder how confusing the new surnames will be. They wonder how fleeting the surnames will be. (*or*)
4. Children with surnames different from their parents' may suffer embarrassment. They may suffer identity problems. Giving children their father's surname is still very much the norm. (*for*)
5. Hyphenated names are awkward. They are also difficult to pass on. Some observers think they will die out in the next generation. Or they may die out before. (*so*)

28b Use a comma to set off most introductory elements.

An introductory element modifies a word or words in the main clause that follows. These elements are usually set off from the rest of the sentence with a comma:

Subordinate clause (p. 275)

Even when identical twins are raised apart, they grow up very like each other.

Because they are similar, such twins interest scientists.

Verbal or verbal phrase (p. 269)

Explaining the similarity, some researchers claim that one's genes are one's destiny.

Concerned, other researchers deny the claim.

Prepositional phrase (p. 266)

In a debate that has lasted centuries, scientists use identical twins to argue for or against genetic destiny.

Transitional or parenthetical expression (p. 89)

Of course, scientists can now look directly at the genes themselves.

The comma may be omitted after short introductory elements if its omission does not create confusion. (If you are in doubt, however, the comma is always correct.)

Clear	In a hundred years genetics may no longer be a mystery.
Confusing	Despite intensive research scientists still have more questions than answers.
Clear	Despite intensive research, scientists still have more questions than answers.

Note Take care to distinguish *-ing* words used as modifiers from *-ing* words used as subjects. The former almost always take a comma; the latter never do.

modifier — subject — verb

Studying identical twins, geneticists learn about inheritance.

subject — verb

Studying identical twins helps geneticists learn about inheritance.

http://www.odu.edu/~wts/cintro.htm Information on using commas with introductory elements, from Old Dominion University.

EXERCISE 3
Punctuating introductory elements

Insert commas where needed after introductory elements in the following sentences. If a sentence is punctuated correctly as given, circle the number preceding it.

Example:

After the new library opened the old one became a student union.

After the new library opened, the old one became a student union.

1. Moving in a fluid mass is typical of flocks of birds and schools of fish.
2. Because it is sudden and apparently well coordinated the movement of flocks and schools has seemed to be directed by a leader.
3. However new studies have discovered that flocks and schools are leaderless.
4. When each bird or fish senses a predator it follows individual rules for fleeing.
5. Multiplied over hundreds of individuals these responses look as if they have been choreographed.

EXERCISE 4
Sentence combining: Introductory elements

Combine each pair of sentences below into one sentence that begins with an introductory phrase or clause as specified in parentheses. Follow the introductory element with a comma. You will have to add, delete, change, and rearrange words.

Example:

The girl was humming to herself. She walked upstairs. (*Phrase beginning Humming.*)

Humming to herself, the girl walked upstairs.

1. Scientists have made an effort to explain the mysteries of flocks and schools. They have proposed bizarre magnetic fields and telepathy. (*Phrase beginning In.*)
2. Scientists developed computer models. They have abandoned earlier explanations. (*Clause beginning Since.*)
3. The movement of a flock or school starts with each individual. It is rapidly and perhaps automatically coordinated among individuals. (*Phrase beginning Starting.*)
4. One zoologist observes that human beings seek coherent patterns. He suggests that investigators saw purpose in the movement of flocks and schools where none existed. (*Phrase beginning Observing.*)
5. One may want to study the movement of flocks or schools. Then one must abandon a search for purpose or design. (*Phrase beginning To.*)

28c Use a comma or commas to set off nonessential elements.

Commas around part of a sentence often signal that the element is not essential to the meaning of the sentence:

Nonessential element

The company, which is located in Oklahoma, has a good reputation.

This **nonessential element** may modify or rename the word it refers to (*company* in the example), but it does not limit the word to a particular individual or group. (Because it does not restrict meaning, a nonessential element is also called a **nonrestrictive element.**) Nonessential elements are *not* essential, but punctuation *is.*

In contrast, an **essential** (or **restrictive**) element *does* limit the word it refers to:

Essential element

The company rewards employees who work hard.

In this example the underlined essential element cannot be omitted without leaving the meaning of *employees* too general. Because it is essential, such an element is *not* set off with commas. The element *is* essential, but punctuation is *not.*

Meaning and context

The same element in the same sentence may be essential or nonessential depending on your intended meaning and the context in which the sentence appears. For example, look at the second sentence in each passage below:

Essential

Not all the bands were equally well received, however. The band playing old music held the audience's attention. The other groups created much less excitement. [*Playing old music* identifies a particular band.]

Nonessential

A new band called Fats made its debut on Saturday night. The band, playing old music, held the audience's attention. If this performance is typical, the group has a bright future. [*Playing old music* adds information about a band already named.]

28c

Information on the comma with essential and nonessential elements:

http://www.wisc.edu/writing/Handbook/Commas.html From the University of Wisconsin at Madison.

http://www.odu.edu/~wts/cclause.htm From Old Dominion University.

A test for essential and nonessential elements

1. Identify the element.

   Hai Nguyen who emigrated from Vietnam lives in Denver.
   Those who emigrated with him live elsewhere.

2. Remove the element. Does the fundamental meaning of the sentence change?

   Hai Nguyen lives in Denver. **No.**
   Those live elsewhere. **Yes.** [Who are *Those?*]

3. If **no,** the element is *nonessential* and should be set off with punctuation.

   Hai Nguyen, who emigrated from Vietnam, lives in Denver.

   If **yes,** the element is *essential* and should *not* be set off with punctuation.

   Those who emigrated with him live elsewhere.

Punctuation of interrupting nonessential elements

When a nonessential element falls in the middle of a sentence, be sure to set it off with a pair of commas, one *before* and one *after* the element. Dashes or parentheses may also set off nonessential elements (see pp. 522 and 525).

1 Use a comma or commas to set off nonessential clauses and phrases.

Clauses and phrases serving as adjectives and adverbs may be either nonessential or essential. Only nonessential clauses and phrases are set off with punctuation. In the following examples the underlined clauses and phrases could be omitted without changing the meaning of the words they modify:

Nonessential

Elizabeth Blackwell was the first woman to graduate from an American medical school, in 1849.

She was a medical pioneer, helping to found the first medical college for women.

She taught at the school, which was affiliated with the New York Infirmary.

Blackwell, who published books and papers on medicine, practiced pediatrics and gynecology.

She moved to England in 1869, when she was forty-eight.

Note Most adverb clauses are essential because they describe conditions necessary to the main clause. They are set off by a comma only when they introduce sentences (see p. 471) and when they are truly nonessential, adding incidental information (as in the last of the preceding examples) or expressing a contrast beginning *although, even though, though, whereas,* and the like.

In the following sentences, the underlined elements limit the meaning of the words they modify. Removing the elements would leave the meaning too general.

Essential

The history of aspirin began with the ancient Greeks.

Physicians who sought to relieve their patients' pains recommended chewing willow bark.

Willow bark contains a chemical that is similar to aspirin.

Note Whereas both nonessential and essential clauses may begin with *which,* only essential clauses begin with *that.* Some writers prefer *that* exclusively for essential clauses and *which* exclusively for nonessential clauses. See the Glossary of Usage, page 940, for advice on the use of *that* and *which.*

2 Use a comma or commas to set off nonessential appositives.

An **appositive** is a noun or noun substitute that renames another noun just before it. (See p. 280.) Many appositives are nonessential; thus they are set off, usually with commas:

Nonessential

Toni Morrison's fifth novel, *Beloved,* won the Pulitzer Prize in 1988.

Morrison, a native of Ohio, won the Nobel Prize in 1993.

Take care *not* to set off essential appositives; like other essential elements, they limit or define the word to which they refer.

Essential

Morrison's novel *The Bluest Eye* is about an African American girl who longs for blue eyes.

The critic Michiko Kakutani says that Morrison's work "stands radiantly on its own as an American epic."

3 Use a comma or commas to set off transitional or parenthetical expressions.

Transitional expressions

Transitional expressions form links between ideas. They include conjunctive adverbs such as *however* and *moreover* as well as other words or phrases such as *for example* and *of course.* (See pp. 89–90 for a list of transitional words and phrases.) Transitional expressions are nonessential, so set them off with a comma or commas:

> American workers, for example, receive fewer holidays than European workers do.

When a transitional expression links main clauses, precede it with a semicolon and follow it with a comma. (See p. 494.)

> European workers often have long paid vacations; indeed, they may receive a full month.

Note The conjunctions *and* and *but,* sometimes used as transitional expressions, are not followed by commas (see p. 487). Nor are commas required after some transitional expressions that we read without pauses, such as *also, hence, next, now,* and *thus.* A few transitional expressions, notably *therefore* and *instead,* do not need commas when they fall inside or at the ends of clauses.

> American workers thus put in more work days. But the days themselves may bc shorter.

Parenthetical expressions

Parenthetical expressions provide comments, explanations, digressions, or other supplementary information not essential to meaning—for example, *fortunately, unfortunately, all things considered, to be frank, in other words.* Set parenthetical expressions off with commas:

> Few people would know, or even guess, the most celebrated holiday on earth.
>
> That holiday is, surprisingly, New Year's Day.

(Dashes and parentheses may also set off parenthetical expressions. See pp. 522 and 525, respectively.)

4 Use a comma or commas to set off *yes* and *no,* tag questions, words of direct address, and mild interjections.

Yes and *no*

Yes, the editorial did have a point.
No, that can never be.

Tag questions

Jones should be allowed to vote, should he not?
They don't stop to consider others, do they?

Direct address

Cody, please bring me the newspaper.
With all due respect, sir, I will not do that.

Mild interjections

Well, you will never know who did it.
Oh, they forgot all about the baby.

(You may want to use an exclamation point to set off a forceful interjection. See p. 465.)

EXERCISE 5
Punctuating essential and nonessential elements

Insert commas in the following sentences to set off nonessential elements, and delete any commas that incorrectly set off essential elements. If a sentence is correct as given, circle the number preceding it.

Example:

Our language has adopted the words, *garage* and *fanfare,* from the French.

Our language has adopted the words *garage* and *fanfare* from the French.

1. Italians insist that Marco Polo the thirteenth-century explorer did not import pasta from China.
2. Pasta which consists of flour and water and often egg existed in Italy long before Marco Polo left for his travels.
3. A historian who studied pasta places its origin in the Middle East in the fifth century.
4. Most Italians dispute this account although their evidence is shaky.
5. Wherever it originated, the Italians are now the undisputed masters, in making and cooking pasta.
6. Marcella Hazan, who has written several books on Italian cooking, insists that homemade and hand-rolled pasta is the best.
7. Most cooks must buy dried pasta lacking the time to make their own.
8. The finest pasta is made from semolina, a flour from hard durum wheat.
9. Pasta manufacturers choose hard durum wheat, because it makes firmer cooked pasta than common wheat does.
10. Pasta, made from common wheat, tends to get soggy in boiling water.

EXERCISE 6
Sentence combining: Essential and nonessential elements

Combine each pair of sentences below into one sentence that uses the element described in parentheses. Insert commas as appropriate. You will have to add, delete, change, and rearrange words. Some items have more than one possible answer.

> *Example:*
>
> Mr. Ward's oldest sister helped keep him alive. She was a nurse in the hospital. (*Nonessential clause beginning who.*)
>
> Mr. Ward's oldest sister, who was a nurse in the hospital, helped keep him alive.

1. American colonists first imported pasta from the English. The English had discovered it as tourists in Italy. (*Nonessential clause beginning who.*)
2. The English returned from their grand tours of Italy. They were called *macaronis* because of their fancy airs. (*Essential phrase beginning returning.*)
3. A hair style was also called *macaroni.* It had elaborate curls. (*Essential phrase beginning with.*)
4. The song "Yankee Doodle" refers to this hairdo. It reports that Yankee Doodle "stuck a feather in his cap and called it macaroni." (*Essential clause beginning when.*)
5. The song was actually intended to poke fun at unrefined American colonists. It was a creation of the English. (*Nonessential appositive beginning a creation.*)

28d Use a comma or commas to set off absolute phrases.

An **absolute phrase** modifies a whole main clause rather than any word in the clause, and it usually consists of at least a participle (such as *done* or *having torn*) and its subject (a noun or pronoun). (See p. 273.) Absolute phrases can occur at almost any point in the sentence, and they are always set off by a comma or commas:

> Domestic recycling having succeeded, the city now wants to extend the program to businesses.
>
> Many businesses, their profits already squeezed, resist recycling.

28e Use a comma or commas to set off phrases expressing contrast.

> The essay needs less wit, more pith.
> The substance, not the style, is important.
> Substance, unlike style, cannot be faked.

Note Writers often omit commas around contrasting phrases beginning with *but: A full but hazy moon shone down.*

EXERCISE 7
Punctuating absolute phrases and phrases of contrast

Insert commas in the following sentences to set off absolute phrases and phrases of contrast.

Example:

The recording contract was canceled the band having broken up.

The recording contract was canceled, the band having broken up.

1. Prices having risen rapidly the government debated a price freeze.
2. A price freeze unlike a rise in interest rates seemed a sure solution.
3. The President would have to persuade businesses to accept a price freeze his methods depending on their recalcitrance.
4. No doubt the President his advisers having urged it would first try a patriotic appeal.
5. The President not his advisers insisted on negotiations with businesses.

28f Use commas between items in a series and between coordinate adjectives.

1 Use commas between words, phrases, or clauses forming a series.

Place commas between all elements of a **series**—that is, three or more items of equal importance:

Anna Spingle married at the age of seventeen, had three children by twenty-one, and divorced at twenty-two.

She worked as a cook, a baby-sitter, and a crossing guard.

Though some writers omit the comma before the coordinating conjunction in a series (*Breakfast consisted of coffee, eggs and kippers*), the final comma is never wrong and it always helps the reader see the last two items as separate:

Confusing Spingle's new job involves typing, filing and answering correspondence.

Clear Spingle's new job involves typing, filing, and answering correspondence.

Exception When items in a series are long and grammatically complicated, they may be separated by semicolons. When the items contain commas, they must be separated by semicolons. (See p. 496.)

2 Use commas between two or more adjectives that equally modify the same word.

When two or more adjectives modify the same word equally, they are said to be **coordinate.** The adjectives may be separated either by *and* or by a comma:

> Spingle's scratched and dented car is an eyesore, but it gets her to work.
>
> She has dreams of a sleek, shiny car.

Adjectives are not coordinate—and should *not* be separated by commas—when the one nearer the noun is more closely related to the noun in meaning. In each of the next examples, the second adjective and the noun form a unit that is modified by the first adjective:

> Spingle's children work at various odd jobs.
> They all expect to go to a nearby community college.

See the box below for a test to use in punctuating adjectives.

Note Numbers are not coordinate with other adjectives:

Faulty Spingle has three, teenaged children.

Revised Spingle has three teenaged children.

Punctuating two or more adjectives

1. Identify the adjectives.

   She was a faithful sincere friend.
   They are dedicated medical students.

2. Can the adjectives be reversed without changing meaning?

   She was a sincere faithful friend. **Yes.**
   They are medical dedicated students. **No.**

3. Can the word *and* be inserted between the adjectives without changing meaning?

   She was a faithful and sincere friend. **Yes.**
   They are dedicated and medical students. **No.**

4. If **yes** to both questions, the adjectives are coordinate and should be separated by a comma.

   She was a faithful, sincere friend.

   If **no** to both questions, the adjectives are *not* coordinate and should *not* be separated by a comma.

   They are dedicated medical students.

Do not use a comma between the final adjective and the noun:

Faulty The children hope to avoid their mother's hard, poor, life.

Revised The children hope to avoid their mother's hard, poor life.

EXERCISE 8
Punctuating series and coordinate adjectives

Insert commas in the following sentences to separate coordinate adjectives or elements in series. Circle the number preceding each sentence whose punctuation is already correct.

Example:

Quiet by day, the club became a noisy smoky dive at night.
Quiet by day, the club became a noisy, smoky dive at night.

1. Shoes with high heels originated to protect feet from the mud garbage and animal waste in the streets.
2. The first known high heels worn strictly for fashion appeared in the sixteenth century.
3. The heels were worn by men and made of colorful silk brocades soft suedes or smooth leathers.
4. High-heeled shoes received a boost when the short powerful King Louis XIV of France began wearing them.
5. Eventually only wealthy fashionable French women wore high heels.

Use commas according to convention in dates, addresses, place names, and long numbers.

Use commas to separate most parts of dates, addresses, and place names: *June 20, 1950; 24 Fifth Avenue, Suite 601; Cairo, Illinois.* Within a sentence, any element preceded by a comma should be followed by a comma as well, as in the examples below:

Dates

July 4, 1776, was the day the Declaration of Independence was signed.

The bombing of Pearl Harbor on Sunday, December 7, 1941, prompted American entry into World War II.

Do not use commas between the parts of a date in inverted order: *Their anniversary on 15 December 1999 was their fiftieth.* You need not use commas in dates consisting of a month or season and a year: *For the United States the war began in December 1941 and ended in August 1945.*

Addresses and place names

Columbus, Ohio, is the state capital and the location of Ohio State University.

The population of Garden City, Long Island, New York, is 30,000.

Use the address 220 Cornell Road, Woodside, California 94062, for all correspondence.

As illustrated above, do not use a comma between a state and a zip code.

Long numbers

Use the comma to separate the figures in long numbers into groups of three, counting from the right. With numbers of four digits, the comma is optional.

A kilometer is 3,281 feet [*or* 3281 feet].

The new assembly plant cost $7,525,000 to design and build.

ESL Usage in American English differs from that in some other languages, which use a period, not a comma, to separate the figures in long numbers.

EXERCISE 9
Punctuating dates, addresses, place names, numbers

Insert commas as needed in the following sentences.

Example:
The house cost $27000 fifteen years ago.
The house cost $27,000 fifteen years ago.

1. The festival will hold a benefit dinner and performance on March 10 2002 in Asheville.
2. The organizers hope to raise more than $100000 from donations and ticket sales.
3. Performers are expected from as far away as Milan Italy and Kyoto Japan.
4. All inquiries sent to Mozart Festival PO Box 725 Asheville North Carolina 28803 will receive a quick response.
5. The deadline for ordering tickets by mail is Monday December 3 2001.

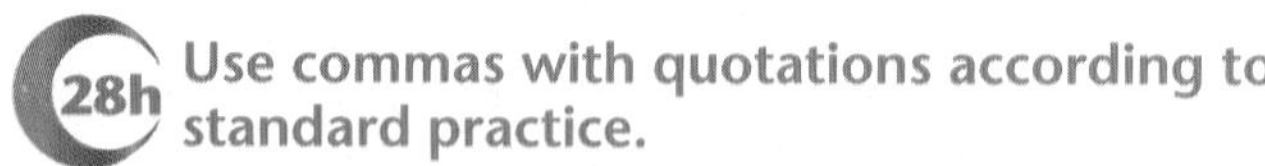

28h Use commas with quotations according to standard practice.

The words *he said, she replied,* and so on identify the source of a quotation. These **signal phrases** may come before, after, or in the middle of the quotation. A signal phrase must always be separated

http://www.odu.edu/~wts/cquote.htm Information on using commas with quotations, from Old Dominion University.

from the quotation by punctuation, usually a comma or commas. (See pp. 509–10 for a summary of this and other conventions regarding quotations.)

1 Ordinarily, use a comma with a signal phrase before or after a quotation.

Eleanor Roosevelt said, "You must do the thing you think you cannot do."

"Knowledge is power," wrote Francis Bacon.

Exceptions Do not use a comma when a signal phrase follows a quotation ending in an exclamation point or a question mark:

"Claude!" Mrs. Harrison called.
"Why must I come home?" he asked.

Do not use commas with a quotation introduced by *that* or with a quotation that is integrated into your sentence structure:

James Baldwin insists that "one must never, in one's life, accept . . . injustices as commonplace."

Baldwin thought that the violence of a riot "had been devised as a corrective" to his own violence.

Use a colon instead of a comma after a signal phrase that introduces a quotation when the signal phrase is actually a complete sentence and the quotation is very formal or longer than a sentence. (See also p. 521.)

The Bill of Rights is unambiguous: "Congress shall make no law respecting an establishment of religion, or prohibiting the free exercise thereof."

2 With an interrupted quotation, precede the signal phrase with a comma and follow it with the punctuation required by the quotation.

Quotation

"The shore has a dual nature, changing with the swing of the tides."

Signal phrase

"The shore has a dual nature," observes Rachel Carson, "changing with the swing of the tides." [The signal phrase interrupts the quotation at a comma and thus ends with a comma.]

Quotation

"However mean your life is, meet it and live it; do not shun it and call it hard names."

Signal phrase

"However mean your life is, meet it and live it," Thoreau advises in *Walden*; "do not shun it and call it hard names." [The signal phrase interrupts the quotation at a semicolon and thus ends with a semicolon.]

Quotation

"This is the faith with which I return to the South. With this new faith we will be able to hew out of the mountain of despair a stone of hope."

Signal phrase

"This is the faith with which I return to the South," Martin Luther King, Jr., proclaimed. "With this new faith we will be able to hew out of the mountain of despair a stone of hope." [The signal phrase interrupts the quotation at the end of a sentence and thus ends with a period.]

Note Using a comma instead of a semicolon or a period in the last two examples would result in the error called a comma splice: two main clauses separated only by a comma. (See pp. 375–77).

3 Place commas that follow quotations within quotation marks.

"Death is not the greatest loss in life," claims Norman Cousins.

"The greatest loss," Cousins says, "is what dies inside us while we live."

EXERCISE 10
Punctuating quotations

Insert commas or semicolons in the following sentences to correct punctuation with quotations. Circle the number preceding any sentence whose punctuation is already correct.

Example:

The shoplifter declared "I didn't steal anything."
The shoplifter declared, "I didn't steal anything."

1. The writer and writing teacher Peter Elbow proposes an "open-ended writing process" that "can change you, not just your words."
2. "I think of the open-ended writing process as a voyage in two stages" Elbow says.
3. "The sea voyage is a process of divergence, branching, proliferation, and confusion" Elbow continues "the coming to land is a process of convergence, pruning, centralizing, and clarifying."
4. "Keep up one session of writing long enough to get loosened up and tired" advises Elbow "long enough in fact to make a bit of a voyage."
5. "In coming to new land" Elbow says "you develop a new conception of what you are writing about."

28i Use commas to prevent misreading.

In some sentences words may run together in unintended and confusing ways unless a comma separates them:

Confusing	Soon after the business closed its doors.
Clear	Soon after, the business closed its doors.

EXERCISE 11
Punctuating to prevent misreading

Insert commas in the following sentences to prevent misreading.

Example:

To Laura Ann symbolized decadence.
To Laura, Ann symbolized decadence.

1. Though happy people still have moments of self-doubt.
2. In research subjects have reported themselves to be generally happy people.
3. Yet those who have described sufferings as well as joys.
4. Of fifty eight subjects reported bouts of serious depression.
5. For half the preceding year had included at least one personal crisis.

28j Use commas only where required.

Commas can make sentences choppy and even confusing if they are used more often than needed. The main misuses of commas are summarized in the box on page 487.

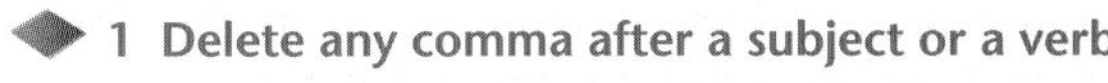

1 Delete any comma after a subject or a verb.

Commas interrupt the movement from subject to verb to object or complement (see pp. 259–62):

Faulty	The returning soldiers, received a warmer welcome than they expected. [Separation of subject and verb.]
Revised	The returning soldiers received a warmer welcome than they expected.
Faulty	They had chosen, to fight for their country. [Separation of verb *chosen* and object *to fight.*]
Revised	They had chosen to fight for their country.

http://www.odu.edu/~wts/csunnec.htm Information on unnecessary commas, from Old Dominion University.

Exception Use commas between subject, verb, and object or complement only when other words between these elements require punctuation:

> Americans, who are preoccupied with other sports, have not developed a strong interest in professional soccer. [Commas set off a nonessential clause.]

2 Delete any comma that separates a pair of words, phrases, or subordinate clauses joined by a coordinating conjunction.

When linking elements with *and, or,* or another coordinating conjunction, do not use a comma unless the elements are main clauses (see p. 469):

Faulty Banks could, and should help older people manage their money. [Compound helping verb.]

Revised Banks could and should help older people manage their money.

Faulty Older people need special assistance because they live on fixed incomes, and because they are not familiar with new accounts, and rates. [Compound subordinate clauses *because . . . because* and compound object of preposition *with.*]

Revised Older people need special assistance because they live on fixed incomes and because they are not familiar with new accounts and rates.

Faulty Banks, and community groups can assist the elderly, and eliminate the confusion they often feel. [Compound subject and compound predicate.]

Revised Banks and community groups can assist the elderly and eliminate the confusion they often feel.

3 Delete any comma after a conjunction.

no ^ 28j

The coordinating conjunctions (*and, but,* and so on) and the subordinating conjunctions (*although, because,* and so on) are not followed by commas:

Faulty Parents of adolescents notice increased conflict at puberty, and, they complain of bickering.

Revised Parents of adolescents notice increased conflict at puberty, and they complain of bickering.

Faulty Although, other primates leave the family at adolescence, humans do not.

Revised Although other primates leave the family at adolescence, humans do not.

Principal misuses of the comma

- Don't use a comma after a subject or verb (p. 485):

  Faulty Anyone with breathing problems, should not exercise during smog alerts.

  Revised Anyone with breathing problems should not exercise during smog alerts.

- Don't separate a pair of words, phrases, or subordinate clauses joined by *and, or,* or *nor* (facing page):

  Faulty Asthmatics are affected by ozone, and sulfur oxides.

  Revised Asthmatics are affected by ozone and sulfur oxides.

- Don't use a comma after *and, but, although, because,* or another conjunction (facing page):

  Faulty Smog is dangerous and, sometimes even fatal.

  Revised Smog is dangerous and sometimes even fatal.

- Don't set off essential elements (this page):

  Faulty Even people, who are healthy, should be careful.

  Revised Even people who are healthy should be careful.

- Don't set off a series (p. 488):

  Faulty Cars, factories, and even bakeries, contribute to smog.

  Revised Cars, factories, and even bakeries contribute to smog.

- Don't set off an indirect quotation or a single word that is an essential appositive (p. 488):

  Faulty Experts say, that the pollutant, ozone, is especially damaging.

  Revised Experts say that the pollutant ozone is especially damaging.

4 Delete any commas that set off essential elements.

Commas do not set off an essential element, which limits the meaning of the word it refers to (see p. 473):

Faulty Hawthorne's work, *The Scarlet Letter,* was the first major American novel. [The title is essential to distinguish the novel from the rest of Hawthorne's work.]

Revised Hawthorne's work *The Scarlet Letter* was the first major American novel.

Faulty	The symbols, that Hawthorne used, influenced other novelists. [The clause identifies which symbols were influential.]
Revised	The symbols that Hawthorne used influenced other novelists.

5 Delete any comma before or after a series unless a rule requires it.

Commas separate the items *within* a series (p. 479) but do not separate the series from the rest of the sentence:

Faulty	The skills of, hunting, herding, and agriculture, sustained the Native Americans.
Revised	The skills of hunting, herding, and agriculture sustained the Native Americans.

In the following sentence the commas before and after the series are appropriate because the series is a nonessential appositive (see p. 475):

> The four major television networks, ABC, CBS, Fox, and NBC, face fierce competition from the cable networks.

However, many writers prefer to use dashes rather than commas to set off series functioning as appositives (see pp. 522–23).

6 Delete any comma setting off an indirect quotation or a single word that is an essential appositive.

Indirect quotation

Faulty	The report concluded, that dieting could be more dangerous than overeating.
Revised	The report concluded that dieting could be more dangerous than overeating.

Quoted or italicized word

no ^, 28j

A quoted or italicized word is an essential appositive when it limits the word it refers to (see p. 475). Do not use commas around an essential appositive:

Faulty	James Joyce's story, "Araby," was assigned last year. [The commas imply wrongly that Joyce wrote only one story.]
Revised	James Joyce's story "Araby" was assigned last year.
Faulty	The word, *open,* can be either a verb or an adjective.
Revised	The word *open* can be either a verb or an adjective.

The following sentence requires commas because the quoted title is a nonessential appositive:

> Her only poem about death, "Mourning," was printed in *The New Yorker.*

EXERCISE 12
Revising: Needless or misused commas

Revise the following sentences to eliminate needless or misused commas. Circle the number preceding each sentence that is already punctuated correctly.

Example:

The portrait of the founder, that hung in the dining hall, was stolen by pranksters.

The portrait of the founder that hung in the dining hall was stolen by pranksters.

1. Nearly 32 million US residents, speak a first language other than English.
2. After English the languages most commonly spoken in the United States are, Spanish, French, and German.
3. Almost 75 percent of the people, who speak foreign languages, used the words, "good" or "very good," when judging their proficiency in English.
4. Recent immigrants, especially those speaking Spanish, Chinese, and Korean, tended to judge their English more harshly.
5. The states with the highest proportion of foreign language speakers, are New Mexico, and California.

EXERCISE 13
Revising: Commas

Insert commas in the following paragraphs wherever they are needed, and eliminate any misused or needless commas.

Ellis Island New York has reopened for business but now the customers are tourists not immigrants. This spot which lies in New York Harbor was the first American soil seen, or touched by many of the nation's immigrants. Though other places also served as ports of entry for foreigners none has the symbolic power of, Ellis Island. Between its opening in 1892 and its closing in 1954, over 20 million people about two-thirds of all immigrants were detained there before taking up their new lives in the United States. Ellis Island processed over 2000 newcomers a day when immigration was at its peak between 1900 and 1920.

As the end of a long voyage and the introduction to the New World Ellis Island must have left something to be desired. The "huddled masses" as the Statue of Liberty calls them indeed were huddled. New arrivals were herded about kept standing in lines for hours or days yelled at and abused. Assigned numbers they submitted their bodies to the pokings and proddings of the silent nurses and doctors, who were charged with ferreting out the slightest sign of sickness, disability or insanity. That test having been passed the immigrants faced interrogation by an official through an interpreter. Those, with names deemed inconveniently long or difficult to pronounce, often found themselves permanently labeled with abbreviations, of their names, or with the names, of their hometowns. But, millions survived the examination humiliation and confusion, to take the last short boat ride to New York City. For many of them and especially for their descendants Ellis Island eventually became not a nightmare but the place where life began.

Note See page 532 for a punctuation exercise combining commas with other marks of punctuation.

CHAPTER 29

The Semicolon

The semicolon separates equal and balanced sentence elements, usually main clauses (below through p. 495), sometimes items in series (p. 496).

Note Computerized grammar and style checkers can spot few errors in the use of semicolons and may suggest adding them incorrectly. To find semicolon errors, you'll need to proofread on your own.

29a Use a semicolon between main clauses not joined by *and, but,* or another coordinating conjunction.

Main clauses contain a subject and a predicate and do not begin with a subordinating word (see p. 275). When you join two main clauses in a sentence, you have two primary options for separating them:

- Insert a comma and a coordinating conjunction: *and, but, or, nor, for, so, yet.* (See p. 469.)

  The drug does little to relieve symptoms, and it can have side effects.

- Insert a semicolon:

  The side effects are not minor; some leave the patient quite ill.

Advice on the semicolon:

http://www.wisc.edu/writing/Handbook/Semicolons.html From the University of Wisconsin at Madison.

http://www.uottawa.ca/academic/arts/writcent/hypergrammar/semicoln.html From the University of Ottawa.

http://www.odu.edu/~wts/semicol.htm From Old Dominion University.

http://leo.stcloudstate.edu/punct/col-semi.html From St. Cloud State University.

http://owl.english.purdue.edu/Files/12.html From the Purdue Online Writing Lab.

Note If you do not link main clauses with a coordinating conjunction and you separate them only with a comma or with no punctuation at all, you will produce a comma splice or a fused sentence. (See Chapter 18.)

Exception Writers sometimes use a comma instead of a semicolon between very short and closely parallel main clauses:

> The poor live, the rich just exist.

But a semicolon is safer, and it is always correct.

Distinguishing the comma, the semicolon, and the colon

The **comma** chiefly separates both equal and unequal sentence elements.

- It separates main clauses when they are linked by a coordinating conjunction (p. 469):

  An airline once tried to boost sales by advertising the tense alertness of its crews, but nervous fliers did not want to hear about pilots' sweaty palms.

- It separates subordinate information that is part of or attached to a main clause, such as an introductory element or a nonessential modifier (pp. 471, 473):

  Although the airline campaign failed, many advertising agencies, including some clever ones, copied its underlying message.

The **semicolon** chiefly separates equal and balanced sentence elements. Often the first clause creates an expectation, and the second clause fulfills the expectation.

- It separates complementary main clauses that are *not* linked by a coordinating conjunction (p. 494):

  The airline campaign had highlighted only half the story; the other half was buried in the copy.

- It separates complementary main clauses that are related by a conjunctive adverb or other transitional expression (p. 495):

  The campaign should not have stressed the pilots' insecurity; instead, the campaign should have stressed the improved performance resulting from that insecurity.

The **colon** chiefly separates unequal sentence elements.

- It separates a main clause from a following explanation or summary, which may or may not be a main clause (p. 519):

  Many successful advertising campaigns have used this message: the anxious seller is harder working and smarter than the competitor.

EXERCISE 1
Punctuating between main clauses

Insert semicolons to separate main clauses in the following sentences.

Example:

One man at the auction bid prudently another spent his bank account.

One man at the auction bid prudently**;** another spent his bank account.

1. More and more musicians are playing computerized instruments more and more listeners are worrying about the future of acoustic instruments.
2. The computer is not the first new technology in music the pipe organ and saxophone were also technological breakthroughs in their day.
3. Musicians have always experimented with new technology audiences have always resisted the experiments.
4. Most computer musicians are not merely following the latest fad they are discovering new sounds and new ways to manipulate sound.
5. Few musicians have abandoned acoustic instruments most value acoustic sounds as much as electronic sounds.

EXERCISE 2
Sentence combining: Related main clauses

Combine each set of three sentences below into one sentence containing only two main clauses, and insert a semicolon between the clauses. You will have to add, delete, change, and rearrange words. Most items have more than one possible answer.

Example:

The painter Andrew Wyeth is widely admired. He is not universally admired. Some critics view his work as sentimental.

The painter Andrew Wyeth is widely but not universally admired**;** some critics view his work as sentimental.

1. Electronic instruments are prevalent in jazz. They are also prevalent in rock music. They are less common in classical music.
2. Jazz and rock change rapidly. They nourish experimentation. They nourish improvisation.
3. Traditional classical music does not change. Its notes and instrumentation were established by a composer. The composer was writing decades or centuries ago.
4. Contemporary classical music not only can draw on tradition. It also can respond to innovations. These are innovations such as jazz rhythms and electronic sounds.
5. Much contemporary electronic music is more than just one type of music. It is more than just jazz, rock, or classical. It is a fusion of all three.

29b Use a semicolon between main clauses related by *however, for example,* and so on.

Two kinds of words can relate main clauses: **conjunctive adverbs,** such as *consequently, hence, however, indeed,* and *thus* (see p. 284), and other **transitional expressions,** such as *even so, for example,* and *of course* (see pp. 89–90). When either of these connects two main clauses, the clauses should be separated by a semicolon:

> An American immigrant, Levi Strauss, invented blue jeans in the 1860s**;** eventually, his product clothed working men throughout the West.

The position of the semicolon between main clauses never changes, but the conjunctive adverb or transitional expression may move around within a clause. The adverb or expression is usually set off with a comma or commas (see pp. 475–76):

> Blue jeans have become fashionable all over the world**;** however**,** the American originators still wear more jeans than anyone else.
>
> Blue jeans have become fashionable all over the world**;** the American originators**,** however**,** still wear more jeans than anyone else.

Its mobility distinguishes a conjunctive adverb or transitional expression from other connecting words, such as coordinating and subordinating conjunctions. See page 285 on this distinction.

Note If you use a comma or no punctuation at all between main clauses connected by a conjunctive adverb or transitional expression, you will produce a comma splice or a fused sentence. (See Chapter 18.)

EXERCISE 3
Punctuating main clauses related by conjunctive adverbs or transitional expressions

Insert a semicolon in each sentence below to separate main clauses related by a conjunctive adverb or transitional expression, and insert a comma or commas where needed to set off the adverb or expression.

Example:

He knew that tickets for the concert would be scarce therefore he arrived at the box office hours before it opened.

He knew that tickets for the concert would be scarce**;** therefore**,** he arrived at the box office hours before it opened.

1. Music is a form of communication like language the basic elements however are not letters but notes.
2. Computers can process any information that can be represented numerically as a result they can process musical information.

3. A computer's ability to process music depends on what software it can run it must moreover be connected to a system that converts electrical vibration into sound.
4. Computers and their sound systems can produce many different sounds indeed the number of possible sounds is infinite.
5. The powerful music computers are very expensive therefore they are used only by professional musicians.

EXERCISE 4

Sentence combining: Main clauses related by conjunctive adverbs or transitional expressions

Combine each set of three sentences below into one sentence containing only two main clauses. Connect the clauses with the conjunctive adverb or transitional expression in parentheses, and separate them with a semicolon. (Be sure the adverbs and expressions are punctuated appropriately.) You will have to add, delete, change, and rearrange words. Each item has more than one possible answer.

Example:

The Albanians censored their news. We got little news from them. And what we got was unreliable. (*therefore*)

The Albanians censored their news**;** therefore**,** the little news we got from them was unreliable.

1. Most music computers are too expensive for the average consumer. Digital keyboard instruments can be inexpensive. They are widely available. (*however*)
2. Inside the keyboard is a small computer. The computer controls a sound synthesizer. The instrument can both process and produce music. (*consequently*)
3. The person playing the keyboard presses keys or manipulates other controls. The computer and synthesizer convert these signals. The signals are converted into vibrations and sounds. (*immediately*)
4. The inexpensive keyboards can perform only a few functions. To the novice computer musician, the range is exciting. The range includes drum rhythms and simulated instruments. (*still*)
5. Would-be musicians can orchestrate whole songs. They start from just the melody lines. They need never again play "Chopsticks." (*thus*)

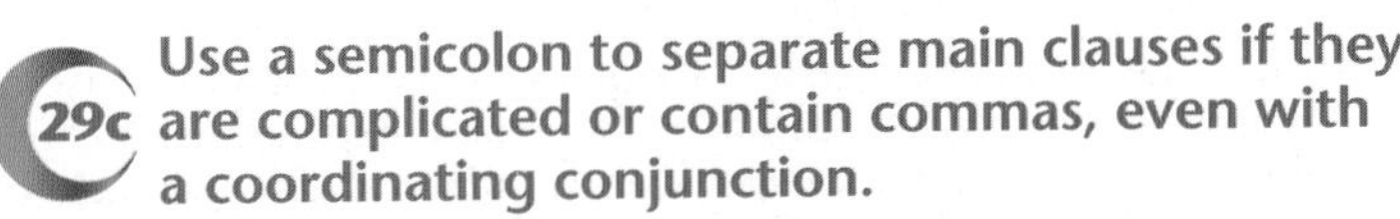

29c Use a semicolon to separate main clauses if they are complicated or contain commas, even with a coordinating conjunction.

We normally use a comma with a coordinating conjunction such as *and* or *but* between main clauses (see p. 469). But a semicolon makes a sentence easier to read when the main clauses contain commas or are grammatically complicated:

> By a conscious effort of the mind, we can stand aloof from actions and their consequences**;** and all things, good and bad, go by us like a torrent.
>
> —Henry David Thoreau

> I doubt if the texture of Southern life is any more grotesque than that of the rest of the nation, but it does seem evident that the Southern writer is particularly adept at recognizing the grotesque**;** and to recognize the grotesque, you have to have some notion of what is not grotesque and why.
>
> —Flannery O'Connor

29d Use semicolons to separate items in a series if they are long or contain commas.

We normally use commas to separate items in a series (see p. 479). But when the items are long or internally punctuated, semicolons help readers identify the items:

> The custody case involved Amy Dalton, the child**;** Ellen and Mark Dalton, the parents**;** and Ruth and Hal Blum, the grandparents.

> One may even reasonably advance the claim that the sort of communication that really counts, and is therefore embodied into permanent records, is primarily written**;** that "words fly away, but written messages endure," as the Latin saying put it two thousand years ago**;** and that there is no basic significance to at least fifty per cent of the oral interchange that goes on among all sorts of persons, high and low.
>
> —Mario Pei

EXERCISE 5

Punctuating long main clauses and series items

Substitute semicolons for commas in the following sentences to separate main clauses or series items that are long or contain commas.

Example:

After graduation he debated whether to settle in San Francisco, which was temperate but far from his parents, New York City, which was exciting but expensive, or Atlanta, which was close to home but already familiar.

After graduation he debated whether to settle in San Francisco, which was temperate but far from his parents**;** New York City, which was exciting but expensive**;** or Atlanta, which was close to home but already familiar.

1. The Indian subcontinent is separated from the rest of the world by clear barriers: the Bay of Bengal and the Arabian Sea to the east and west, respectively, the Indian Ocean to the south, and 1600 miles of mountain ranges to the north.

2. In the north of India are the world's highest mountains, the Himalayas, and farther south are fertile farmlands, unpopulated deserts, and rain forests.
3. India is a nation of ethnic and linguistic diversity, with numerous religions, including Hinduism, Islam, and Christianity, with distinct castes and ethnic groups, and with sixteen languages, including the official Hindi and the "associate official" English.
4. Between the seventeenth and nineteenth centuries, the British colonized most of India, taking control of government, the bureaucracy, and industry, and they assumed a social position above all Indians.
5. During British rule the Indians' own unresolved differences and their frustrations with the British erupted in violent incidents such as the Sepoy Mutiny, which began on February 26, 1857, and lasted two years, the Amritsar Massacre on April 13, 1919, and violence between Hindus and Muslims during World War II that resulted in the separation of Pakistan from India.

29e Use the semicolon only where required.

Semicolons do not separate unequal sentence elements and should not be overused.

1 Delete or replace any semicolon that separates a subordinate clause or a phrase from a main clause.

The semicolon does not separate subordinate clauses from main clauses or phrases from main clauses:

Faulty Pygmies are in danger of extinction; because of encroaching development.

Revised Pygmies are in danger of extinction because of encroaching development.

Faulty According to African authorities; only about 35,000 Pygmies exist today.

Revised According to African authorities, only about 35,000 Pygmies exist today.

Note Many readers regard a phrase or subordinate clause set off with a semicolon as a kind of sentence fragment. (See Chapter 17.)

2 Delete or replace any semicolon that introduces a series or explanation.

Colons and dashes, not semicolons, introduce series, explanations, and so forth. (See pp. 519–24.)

Faulty Teachers have heard all sorts of reasons why students do poorly; psychological problems, family illness, too much work, too little time.

Revised Teachers have heard all sorts of reasons why students do poorly: psychological problems, family illness, too much work, too little time.

Revised Teachers have heard all sorts of reasons why students do poorly—psychological problems, family illness, too much work, too little time.

3 Use the semicolon sparingly.

Use the semicolon only occasionally. Many semicolons in a passage, even when they are required by rule, often indicate repetitive sentence structure. To revise a passage with too many semicolons, you'll need to restructure your sentences, not just remove the semicolons. (See p. 449 for tips on varying sentences.)

Semicolon overused

The Make-a-Wish Foundation helps sick children; it grants the wishes of children who are terminally ill. The foundation learns of a child's wish; the information usually comes from parents, friends, or hospital staff; the wish may be for a special toy, perhaps, or a visit to Disneyland. The foundation grants some wishes with its own funds; for other wishes it appeals to those who have what the child desires.

Revised

The Make-a-Wish Foundation grants the wishes of children who are terminally ill. From parents, friends, or hospital staff, the foundation learns of a child's wish for a special toy, perhaps, or a visit to Disneyland. It grants some wishes with its own funds; for other wishes it appeals to those who have what the child desires.

EXERCISE 6
Revising: Misused or overused semicolons

Revise the following sentences to eliminate misused or overused semicolons, substituting other punctuation as appropriate.

Example:

The doctor gave everyone the same advice; get exercise.
The doctor gave everyone the same advice: get exercise.

1. The main religion in India is Hinduism; a way of life as well as a theology and philosophy.
2. Unlike Christianity and Judaism; Hinduism is a polytheistic religion; with deities numbering in the hundreds.
3. Hinduism is unlike many other religions; it allows its creeds and practices to vary widely from place to place and person to person. Other religions have churches; Hinduism does not.

Other religions have principal prophets and holy books; Hinduism does not. Other religions center on specially trained priests or other leaders; Hinduism promotes the individual as his or her own priest.

4. In Hindu belief there are four types of people; reflective, emotional, active, and experimental.
5. Each type of person has a different technique for realizing the true, immortal self; which has infinite existence, infinite knowledge, and infinite joy.

EXERCISE 7
Revising: Semicolons

Insert semicolons in the following paragraph wherever they are needed. Eliminate any misused or needless semicolons, substituting other punctuation as appropriate.

The set, sounds, and actors in the movie captured the essence of horror films. The set was ideal; dark, deserted streets, trees dipping their branches over the sidewalks, mist hugging the ground and creeping up to meet the trees, looming shadows of unlighted, turreted houses. The sounds, too, were appropriate, especially terrifying was the hard, hollow sound of footsteps echoing throughout the film. But the best feature of the movie was its actors; all of them tall, pale, and thin to the point of emaciation. With one exception, they were dressed uniformly in gray and had gray hair. The exception was an actress who dressed only in black; as if to set off her pale yellow, nearly white, long hair; the only color in the film. The glinting black eyes of another actor stole almost every scene, indeed, they were the source of all the film's mischief.

Note See page 532 for a punctuation exercise combining semicolons with other marks of punctuation.

CHAPTER 30

The Apostrophe

Unlike other punctuation marks, which separate words, the apostrophe (') appears as *part* of a word to indicate possession, the omission of one or more letters, or (in a few cases) plural number.

Note Computerized grammar and style checkers have mixed results in recognizing apostrophe errors. For instance, they generally flag missing apostrophes in contractions (as in *isnt*) but cannot distinguish between *its* and *it's, their* and *they're, your* and *you're, whose* and *who's*. The checkers can identify some apostrophe errors in possessives but will overlook others and may flag correct plurals. Instead of relying on your checker, try using your word processor's Search or Find function to hunt for all words you have ended in *-s*. Then check them to ensure that they correctly omit or include apostrophes and that needed apostrophes are correctly positioned.

30a Use the apostrophe to indicate the possessive case for nouns and indefinite pronouns.

The **possessive case** shows ownership or possession of one person or thing by another. Possession may be shown with an *of* phrase (*the hair of the dog*); or it may be shown with the addition of an apostrophe and, usually, an *-s* (*the dog's hair*).

Note Apostrophes are easy to misuse. For safety's sake, check your drafts with two aims.

Advice on using the apostrophe:

http://www.esc.edu/htmlpages/writer/pandg/apost.htm From the State University of New York.

http://owl.english.purdue.edu/Files/13.html From the Purdue Online Writing Center.

http://www.uottawa.ca/academic/arts/writcent/hypergrammar/apostrph.html From the University of Ottawa.

http://webster.commnet.edu/HP/pages/darling/grammar/marks.htm#apostrophe From the Guide to Grammar and Writing.

Uses and misuses of the apostrophe

Uses

Possessives of nouns and indefinite pronouns (p. 500)

Singular	**Plural**
Ms. Park**'s**	the Parks**'**
everyone**'s**	two weeks**'**
boy**'s**	boys**'**

Contractions (p. 504)

won**'**t	shouldn**'**t
they**'**re	it**'**s a girl

Optional: Plurals of abbreviations, dates, and words or characters named as words (p. 506)

MA**'**s or MAs	C**'**s or Cs
1960**'**s or 1960s	if**'**s or ifs

Misuses

Singular, not plural, possessives (p. 502)

Not	**But**
the Kim's car	the Kim**s'** car
boy's fathers	boy**s'** fathers

Plurals of nouns (p. 503)

Not	**But**
book's are	books are
candy's	cand**ie**s

Third-person singulars of verbs (p. 504)

Not	**But**
swim's	swims
go's	go**es**

Possessives of personal pronouns (p. 504)

Not	**But**
it's toes	its toes
her's	hers

- Make sure that every word ending in *-s* neither omits a needed apostrophe nor adds an unneeded one.
- Remember that the apostrophe or apostrophe-plus-*s* is an *addition.* Before this addition, always spell the name of the owner or owners without dropping or adding letters: *girls* becomes *girls',* not *girl's.*

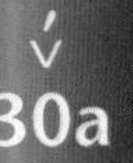

1 Add *-'s* to singular nouns and indefinite pronouns.

Bill Boughton**'s** skillful card tricks amaze children.

Anyone**'s** eyes would widen. [Indefinite pronoun.]

Most tricks will pique an adult**'s** curiosity, too.

Add *-'s* as well to singular nouns that end in *-s:*

Henry James**'s** novels reward the patient reader.

Los Angeles**'s** weather is mostly warm.

The business**'s** customers filed suit.

Exception We often do not pronounce the possessive *-s* of a few singular nouns ending in an *s* or *z* sound: names with more than one *s* sound (*Moses*), names that sound like plurals (*Rivers, Bridges*), and nouns followed by a word beginning in *s*. In these cases, many writers add only the apostrophe to show possession.

Moses**'** mother concealed him in the bulrushes.
Joan Rivers**'** jokes offend many people.
For conscience**'** sake she confessed her lie.

However, usage varies widely, and the final *-s* is not wrong with words like these (*Moses***'s**, *Rivers***'s**, *conscience***'s**).

2 Add *-'s* to plural nouns *not* ending in *-s*.

The bill establishes children**'s** rights.
Publicity grabbed the media**'s** attention.

3 Add only an apostrophe to plural nouns ending in *-s*.

Workers**'** incomes have not risen much over the past decade.
Many students benefit from several years**'** work after high school.
The Jameses**'** talents are extraordinary.

Note the difference in the possessives of singular and plural words ending in *-s*. The singular form usually takes *-s: James***'s**. The plural takes only the apostrophe: *Jameses***'**.

4 Add *-'s* only to the last word of compound words or word groups.

The council president**'s** address was a bore.
The brother-in-law**'s** business failed.
Taxes are always somebody else**'s** fault.

5 With two or more words, add *-'s* to one or both depending on meaning.

Individual possession

Zimbale**'s** and Mason**'s** comedy techniques are similar. [Each comedian has his own technique.]

Joint possession

The child recovered despite her mother and father**'s** neglect. [The mother and father were jointly neglectful.]

EXERCISE 1
Forming possessives

Form the possessive case of each word or word group in brackets.

√ 30a

Example:

The [men] blood pressures were higher than the [women].
The men**'s** blood pressures were higher than the women**'s**.

1. In the myths of the ancient Greeks, the [goddesses] roles vary widely.
2. [Demeter] responsibility is the fruitfulness of the earth.
3. [Athena] role is to guard the city of Athens.
4. [Artemis] function is to care for wild animals and small children.
5. [Athena and Artemis] father, Zeus, is the king of the gods.
6. Even a single [goddess] responsibilities are often varied.
7. Over several [centuries] time, Athena changes from a [mariner] goddess to the patron of crafts.
8. Athena is also concerned with fertility and with [children] well-being, since [Athens] strength depended on a large and healthy population.
9. Athena often changes into [birds] forms.
10. In [Homer] *Odyssey* she assumes a [sea eagle] form.
11. In ancient Athens the myths of Athena were part of [everyone] knowledge and life.
12. A cherished myth tells how Athena fights to retain possession of her [people] land when the god Poseidon wants it.
13. [Athena and Poseidon] skills are different, and each promises a special gift to the Athenians.
14. At the [contest] conclusion, Poseidon has given water and Athena has given an olive tree, for sustenance.
15. The other gods decide that the [Athenians] lives depend more on Athena than on Poseidon.

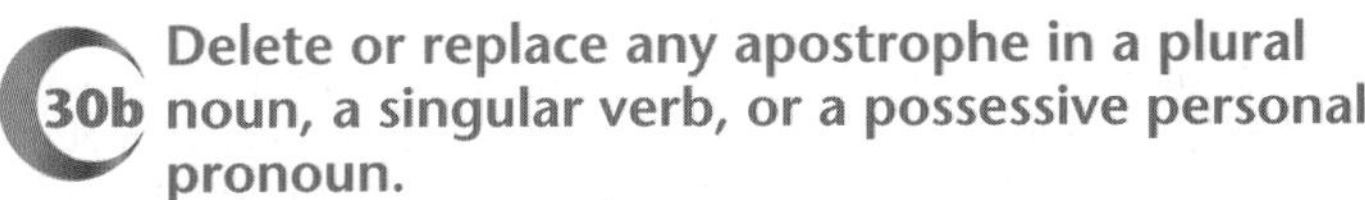

30b Delete or replace any apostrophe in a plural noun, a singular verb, or a possessive personal pronoun.

Not all words ending in *-s* take an apostrophe. Three kinds of words are especially likely to attract unneeded apostrophes.

Plural nouns

The plurals of nouns are generally formed by adding *-s* or *-es* (*boys, Smiths, families, Joneses*). Don't mistakenly add an apostrophe to form the plural:

Faulty The unleashed dog's began traveling in a pack.
Revised The unleashed dogs began traveling in a pack.

Faulty The Jones' and Bass' were feuding.
Revised The Jones**es** and Bass**es** were feuding.

Singular verbs

Do not add an apostrophe to present-tense verbs used with *he, she, it,* and other third-person singular subjects. These verbs always end in *-s* but *never* with an apostrophe:

Faulty The subway break's down less often now.

Revised The subway breaks down less often now.

Possessives of personal pronouns

His, hers, its, ours, yours, theirs, and *whose* are possessive forms of the pronouns *he, she, it, we, you, they,* and *who.* They do not take apostrophes:

Faulty The credit is her's not their's.

Revised The credit is hers, not theirs.

The personal pronouns are often confused with contractions, such as *it's, you're,* and *who's.* See below.

EXERCISE 2
Distinguishing between plurals and possessives

Supply the appropriate form—possessive or plural—of each word given in brackets. Some answers require apostrophes, and some do not.

Example:

A dozen Hawaiian [shirt], each with [it] own loud design, hung in the window.

A dozen Hawaiian shirts, each with its own loud design, hung in the window.

1. Demeter may be the oldest of the Greek [god], older than Zeus.
2. Many prehistoric [culture] had earth [goddess] like Demeter.
3. In myth she is the earth mother, which means that the responsibility for the fertility of both [animal] and [plant] is [she].
4. The [goddess] festival came at harvest time, with [it] celebration of bounty.
5. The [people] [prayer] to Demeter thanked her for grain and other [gift].

30c Use an apostrophe to indicate the omission in a standard contraction.

it is	it's	let us	let's
he is	he's	does not	doesn't
she is	she's	were not	weren't
they are	they're	class of 2004	class of '04
you are	you're	of the clock	o'clock
who is	who's	madam	ma'am

Contractions are common in speech and in informal writing. They may also be used to relax style in more formal kinds of writing, as they are in this handbook. But be aware that many people disapprove of contractions in any kind of formal writing.

Note Contractions are easily confused with the possessive personal pronouns:

Contraction	Possessive pronoun
it's	its
they're	th**eir**
you're	you**r**
who's	who**se**

Faulty Legislators know their going to have to cut the budget to eliminate it's deficit.

Revised Legislators know the**y're** going to have to cut the budget to eliminate its deficit.

If you tend to confuse these forms, search for either spelling throughout your drafts (a word processor can help with this search). Then test for correctness:

- Do you intend the word to contain the sentence verb *is* or *are*, as in *It is a shame, They are to blame, You are right, Who is coming?* Then use an apostrophe: *it's, they're, you're, who's.*
- Do you intend the word to indicate possession, as in *Its tail was wagging, Their car broke down, Your eyes are blue, Whose book is that?* Then don't use an apostrophe.

EXERCISE 3
Forming contractions

Form contractions from each set of words below. Use each contraction in a complete sentence.

Example:

we are: we're
We're open to ideas.

1. she would
2. could not
3. they are
4. he is
5. do not
6. she will
7. hurricane of 1962
8. is not
9. it is
10. will not

EXERCISE 4
Revising: Contractions and personal pronouns

Revise the following sentences to correct mistakes in the use of contractions and personal pronouns. Circle the number preceding any sentence that is already correct.

Example:

The agencies give they're employees their birthdays off.
The agencies give the**ir** employees their birthdays off.

1. In Greek myth the goddess Demeter has a special fondness for Eleusis, near Athens, and it's people.
2. She finds rest among the people and is touched by their kindness.
3. Demeter rewards the Eleusians with the secret for making they're land fruitful.
4. The Eleusians begin a cult in honor of Demeter, whose worshiped in secret ceremonies.
5. Its unknown what happened in the ceremonies, for no participant ever revealed their rituals.

30d An apostrophe is often optional in forming the plurals of abbreviations, dates, and words or characters named as words.

Use the apostrophe with most plural abbreviations that contain periods. With unpunctuated abbreviations, you can omit the apostrophe. (See p. 463 on using periods with abbreviations.)

Ph.D.'s CD-ROMs
B.A.'s BAs

Plural abbreviations for measurements, however, do not take an apostrophe: *ins., gals., lbs.*

The apostrophe for years in a decade is also optional: 1990s or 1990's.

We often refer to a word, letter, or number as the word or character itself, rather than use it for its meaning: *The word* but *starts with a* b. To make such a word or character plural, add an *-s*. An apostrophe is optional as long as you are consistent.

<u>t</u>s or <u>t</u>'s <u>21</u>s or <u>21</u>'s <u>if</u>s or <u>if</u>'s

The sentence has too many <u>but</u>s [or <u>but</u>'s].

Two <u>3</u>s [or <u>3</u>'s] and two <u>&</u>s [or <u>&</u>'s] appeared at the end of each chapter.

30d

Note Words or characters named as words are underlined or italicized, but the added *-s* and any apostrophe are not. (See p. 543 on this use of underlining or italics.)

EXERCISE 5
Forming plurals of abbreviations, dates, and words or characters named as words

Form the plural of each item below by adding *-s*, by using or not using an apostrophe (as appropriate), and by underlining or italicizing appropriately. Use the new plural in a complete sentence.

Example: x

Erase or white out typing mistakes. Do not use <u>x</u>'s [or <u>x</u>s].

1. 7
2. q
3. if
4. and
5. SOS

EXERCISE 6
Revising: Apostrophes

In the following paragraph correct any mistakes in the use of the apostrophe or any confusion between contractions and possessive personal pronouns.

Landlocked Chad is among the worlds most troubled countries. The people's of Chad are poor: they're average per capita income equals $600 a year. Just over 40 percent of Chads population is literate, and every five hundred people must share only two teacher's. The natural resources of the nation have never been plentiful, and now, as it's slowly being absorbed into the growing Sahara Desert, even water is scarce. Chads political conflicts go back to the nineteenth century, when the French colonized the land by brutally subduing it's people. The rule of the French—who's inept government of the colony did nothing to ease tensions among racial, tribal, and religious group's—ended with independence in 1960. But since then the Chadians experience has been one of civil war and oppression, and their also threatened with invasions from they're neighbors.

Note See page 532 for a punctuation exercise involving apostrophes along with other marks of punctuation.

CHAPTER 31

Quotation Marks

Quotation marks—either double (“”) or single (‘’)—mainly enclose direct quotations from speech and from writing. The chart on the next two pages summarizes this and other uses.

Note Always use quotation marks in pairs, one at the beginning of a quotation and one at the end. Most computerized grammar and style checkers will help you use quotation marks in pairs by flagging a lone mark, and many will identify where other punctuation falls incorrectly inside or outside quotation marks. However, the checkers cannot recognize other possible errors in punctuating quotations. You'll need to proofread carefully yourself.

31a Use double quotation marks to enclose direct quotations.

Direct quotations report what someone has said or written in the exact words of the original. Always enclose direct quotations in quotation marks:

> “Fortunately,” said the psychoanalyst Karen Horney, “analysis is not the only way to resolve inner conflicts. Life itself still remains a very effective therapist.”

Indirect quotations report what has been said or written, but not in the exact words of the person being quoted. Indirect quotations are *not* enclosed in quotation marks:

> The psychoanalyst Karen Horney remarked that analysis was not the only solution to inner conflicts, for life was a good therapist.

Indirect quotation often involves a change in the tense of verbs, as in the example here. See pages 324–25.

Advice on punctuating quotations:

http://www.esc.edu/htmlpages/writer/pandg/quote.htm From the State University of New York.

http://leo.stcloudstate.edu/research/puncquotes.html From St. Cloud State University.

Handling quotations from speech or writing

(For explanations, consult the pages in parentheses.)

Direct and indirect quotation

Direct quotation (opposite)

According to Lewis Thomas, "We are, perhaps uniquely among the earth's creatures, the worrying animal. We worry away our lives."

Quotation within quotation (p. 510)

Quoting a phrase by Lewis Thomas, the author adds, "We are 'the worrying animal.'"

Indirect quotation (opposite)

Lewis Thomas says that human beings are unique among animals in their worrying.

Quotation marks with other punctuation marks

Commas and periods (p. 516)

Human beings are the "worrying animal," says Thomas.
Thomas calls human beings "the worrying animal."

Semicolons and colons (p. 517)

Machiavelli said that "the majority of men live content"; in contrast, Thomas calls us "the worrying animal."

Thomas believes that we are "the worrying animal": we spend our lives afraid and restless.

Question marks, exclamation points, dashes (p. 517)

When part of your own sentence:

Who said that human beings are "the worrying animal"?
Imagine saying that we human beings "worry away our lives"!
Thomas's phrase—"the worrying animal"—seems too narrow.

When part of the original quotation:

"Will you discuss this with me?" she asked.
"I demand that you discuss this with me!" she yelled.
"Please, won't you—" She paused.

Altering quotations

Brackets for additions (p. 526)

"We [human beings] worry away our lives," says Thomas.

Brackets for altered capitalization (p. 535)

"[T]he worrying animal" is what Thomas calls us. He says that "[w]e worry away our lives."

(continued)

" "
31a

Handling quotations from speech or writing
(continued)

Ellipsis marks for omissions (p. 527)

MLA style:

"We are **[. . .]** the worrying animal," says Thomas.

Worrying places us "uniquely among the earth's creatures **[. . .]**. We worry away our lives."

Other styles:

"We are **. . .** the worrying animal," says Thomas.

Worrying places us "uniquely among the earth's creatures**. . . .** We worry away our lives."

Punctuating signal phrases with quotations

Introductory signal phrase (p. 483)

He says**,** "We worry away our lives."

An answer is in these words by Lewis Thomas**:** "We are, perhaps uniquely among the earth's creatures, the worrying animal."

Thomas says that "the worrying animal" is afraid and restless.

Concluding signal phrase (p. 483)

We are "the worrying animal**,"** says Thomas.
"Who says**?"** she demanded.
"I do**!"** he shouted.

Interrupting signal phrase (p. 483)

"We are**,"** says Thomas**,** "perhaps uniquely among the earth's creatures, the worrying animal."

"I do not like the idea**,"** she said**;** "however, I agree with it."

Human beings are "the worrying animal**,"** says Thomas**.** "We worry away our lives."

See also:

" "
31a

Special kinds of quoted material

Dialogue (opposite)
Poetry (p. 512)
Prose passages of more than four lines (p. 513)

Using quotations in your own text

Quotations versus paraphrases and summaries (p. 678)
Avoiding plagiarism when quoting (p. 686)
Introducing quotations in your text (p. 693)
Citing sources for quotations (p. 698)

31b Use single quotation marks to enclose a quotation within a quotation.

When you quote a writer or speaker, use double quotation marks (see p. 508). When the material you quote contains yet another quotation, distinguish the two by enclosing the second one in single quotation marks:

> "In formulating any philosophy," Woody Allen writes, "the first consideration must always be: What can we know? Descartes hinted at the problem when he wrote, **'**My mind can never know my body, although it has become quite friendly with my leg.**'"**

Notice that two different quotation marks appear at the end of the sentence—one single (to finish the interior quotation) and one double (to finish the main quotation).

EXERCISE 1
Using double and single quotation marks

Insert single and double quotation marks as needed in the following sentences. Circle the number preceding any sentence that is already correct.

Example:

The purpose of this book, explains the preface, is to examine the meaning of the expression Dance is poetry.

"The purpose of this book,**"** explains the preface, **"**is to examine the meaning of the expression **'**Dance is poetry.**'"**

1. Why, the lecturer asked, do we say Bless you! or something else when people sneeze but not acknowledge coughs, hiccups, and other eruptions?
2. She said that sneezes have always been regarded differently.
3. Sneezes feel more uncontrollable than some other eruptions, she said.
4. Unlike coughs and hiccups, she explained, sneezes feel as if they come from inside the head.
5. She concluded, People thus wish to recognize a sneeze, if only with a Gosh.

31c Set off quotations of dialogue, poetry, and long prose passages according to standard practice.

Dialogue

When quoting conversations, begin a new paragraph for each speaker:

> "What shall I call you? Your name?" Andrews whispered rapidly, as with a high squeak the latch of the door rose.
>
> "Elizabeth," she said. "Elizabeth."
>
> —GRAHAM GREENE, *The Man Within*

Note When you quote a single speaker for more than one paragraph, put quotation marks at the beginning of each paragraph but at the end of only the last paragraph. The absence of quotation marks at the end of each paragraph but the last tells readers that the speech is continuing.

Poetry

When you quote a single line from a poem, a song, or a verse play, run the line into your own text and enclose the line in quotation marks:

> Dylan Thomas remembered childhood as an idyllic time: "About the lilting house and happy as the grass was green" ("Fern Hill" line 2).

(The parenthetical information above and in the following examples provides source citations in MLA style. See pp. 711–18 for an explanation.)

Poetry quotations of two or three lines may be placed in the text or displayed separately. If you place such a quotation in the text, enclose it in quotation marks and separate the lines with a slash surrounded by space:

> An example of Robert Frost's incisiveness is in two lines from "Death of the Hired Man": "Home is the place where, when you have to go there, / They have to take you in" (119–20).

Quotations of more than three lines of poetry should always be separated from the text with space and an indention. *Do not add quotation marks* where the yellow highlights fall in the example:

> Emily Dickinson stripped ideas to their essence, as in this description of "A narrow Fellow in the Grass," a snake:
>
> I more than once at Noon
> Have passed, I thought, a Whip lash
> Unbraiding in the Sun
> When stopping to secure it
> It wrinkled, and was gone – (12-16)

The *MLA Handbook for Writers of Research Papers,* the standard guide to document format in English and some other humanities, recommends the following spacings for displayed poetry quotations:

- Double-space above and below the quotation.
- Indent the quotation one inch from the left margin.
- Double-space the quoted lines.

Unless your instructor specifies otherwise, follow these guidelines for your typewritten or handwritten papers.

Note Be careful when quoting poetry to reproduce faithfully all line indentions, space between lines, spelling, capitalization, and punctuation, such as the capitals and the closing dash in the Dickinson poem on the previous page.

Long prose passages

Use an indention to set off long prose passages from the body of your paper. The guidelines below are from the *MLA Handbook for Writers of Research Papers,* the style manual for English, foreign languages, and some other humanities. If you are writing in history, art history, religion, or philosophy, see page 833. If you are writing in psychology or other social sciences, see pages 857–58. If you are writing in the natural or applied sciences, see pages 876–77.

The *MLA Handbook* recommends setting off all prose quotations of more than four typed lines. Use space and an indention as described in the bulleted list above. *Do not add quotation marks* where the yellow highlights fall in the example:

> In his 1967 study of the lives of unemployed black men, Elliot Liebow observes that "unskilled" construction work requires more experience and skill than is generally assumed.
>
>> A healthy, sturdy, active man of good intelligence requires from two to four weeks to break in on a construction job [. . .]. It frequently happens that his foreman or the craftsman he services is not willing to wait that long for him to get into condition or to learn at a glance the difference in size between a rough 2 x 8 and a finished 2 x 10. (62)

(The parenthetical number at the end of the quotation is a source citation. See pp. 711–18.)

When following MLA style, do not use a paragraph indention for a quotation of a single complete paragraph or a part of a paragraph. Use paragraph indentions only for a quotation of two or more complete paragraphs.

31d Put quotation marks around the titles of works that are parts of other works.

Use quotation marks to enclose the titles of works that are published or released within larger works. (See the box below.) Use single quotation marks for a quotation within a quoted title, as in the second article title and second essay title in the box. And enclose all punctuation in the title within the quotation marks, as in the second article title.

Titles to be enclosed in quotation marks

Other titles should be underlined or italicized. (See p. 541.)

Songs
"Lucy in the Sky with Diamonds"
"Mr. Bojangles"

Short poems
"Stopping by Woods on a Snowy Evening"
"Sunday Morning"

Articles in periodicals
"Comedy and Tragedy Transposed"
"Does 'Scaring' Work?"

Short stories
"The Battler"
"The Gift of the Magi"

Essays
"Politics and the English Language"
"Joey: A 'Mechanical Boy'"

Episodes of television and radio programs
"The Mexican Connection" (on 60 Minutes)
"Cooking with Clams" (on Eating In)

Subdivisions of books
"Voyage to the Houyhnhnms" (Part IV of Gulliver's Travels)
"The Mast Head" (Chapter 35 of Moby-Dick)

Use underlining or italics for all other titles, such as books, plays, periodicals, and movies. (See p. 541.)

Note Some academic disciplines do not require quotation marks for titles within source citations. See pages 845–55 (APA style), 871–76 (CBE style), and 886–91 (Columbia online style for the sciences).

" "
31d

EXERCISE 2
Quoting titles

Insert quotation marks as needed for titles and words in the following sentences. If quotation marks should be used instead of underlining, insert them.

Example:

She published an article titled Marriage in Grace Paley's An Interest in Life.

She published an article titled "Marriage in Grace Paley's 'An Interest in Life.'"

1. In Chapter 8, titled How to Be Interesting, the author explains the art of conversation.
2. The Beatles' song Let It Be reminds him of his uncle.
3. The article that appeared in Mental Health was titled Children of Divorce Ask, "Why?"
4. In the encyclopedia the discussion under Modern Art fills less than a column.
5. One prizewinning essay, Cowgirls on Wall Street, first appeared in Entrepreneur magazine.

31e Quotation marks may be used to enclose words used in a special sense.

On movie sets movable "wild walls" make a one-walled room seem four-walled on film.

Writers often put quotation marks around a word they are using with irony—that is, with a different or even opposite meaning than usual:

With all the "compassion" it could muster, the agency turned away two-thirds of those seeking help.

—Joan Simonson

Readers quickly tire of such irony, though, so use it sparingly.

Note For words you are defining, use underlining or italics. (See p. 543.)

31f Use quotation marks only where they are required.

Don't use quotation marks in the titles of your papers unless they contain or are themselves direct quotations:

Not "The Death Wish in One Poem by Robert Frost"

But The Death Wish in One Poem by Robert Frost

Or The Death Wish in "Stopping by Woods on a Snowy Evening"

Don't use quotation marks to enclose common nicknames or technical terms that are not being defined:

Not As President, "Jimmy" Carter preferred to use his nickname.

But As President, Jimmy Carter preferred to use his nickname.

Not "Mitosis" in a cell is fascinating to watch.

But Mitosis in a cell is fascinating to watch.

Don't use quotation marks in an attempt to justify or apologize for slang and trite expressions that are inappropriate to your writing. If slang is appropriate, use it without quotation marks.

Not We should support the President in his "hour of need" rather than "wimp out" on him.

But We should give the President the support he needs rather than turn away like cowards.

(See pp. 560 and 576 for more discussion of slang and trite expressions.)

31g Place other marks of punctuation inside or outside quotation marks according to standard practice.

The position of another punctuation mark inside or outside a closing quotation mark depends on what the other mark is and whether it appears in the quotation.

1 Place commas and periods inside quotation marks.

Commas or periods fall *inside* closing quotation marks, even when (as in the third example) single and double quotation marks are combined:

Swift uses irony in his essay "A Modest Proposal."

Many first-time readers are shocked to see infants described as "delicious."

"'A Modest Proposal,'" wrote one critic, "is so outrageous that it cannot be believed."

(See pp. 482–84 for the use of commas, as in the last example above, to separate a quotation from a signal phrase such as *she wrote* or *he said.*)

Exception When a parenthetical source citation immediately follows a quotation, place any period or comma *after* the citation:

One critic calls the essay "outrageous" (Olms 26).

Partly because of "the cool calculation of its delivery" (Olms 27), Swift's satire still chills a modern reader.

See page 716 for more on placing parenthetical citations.

2 Place colons and semicolons outside quotation marks.

A few years ago the slogan in elementary education was "learning by playing"; now educators are concerned with teaching basic skills.

We all know what is meant by "inflation"; more money buys less.

3 Place dashes, question marks, and exclamation points inside quotation marks only if they belong to the quotation.

When a dash, question mark, or exclamation point is part of the quotation, put it *inside* quotation marks. Don't use any other punctuation such as a period or comma:

"But must you—" Marcia hesitated, afraid of the answer.

"Go away!" I yelled.

Did you say, "Who is she?" [When both your sentence and the quotation would end in a question mark or exclamation point, use only the mark in the quotation.]

When a dash, question mark, or exclamation point applies only to the larger sentence, not to the quotation, place it *outside* quotation marks—again, with no other punctuation:

One evocative line in English poetry—"After many a summer dies the swan"—was written by Alfred, Lord Tennyson.

Who said, "Now cracks a noble heart"?

The woman called me "stupid"!

EXERCISE 3
Revising: Quotation marks

The underlined words in the following sentences are titles or direct quotations. Remove underlining where appropriate, and insert quotation marks. Be sure that other marks of punctuation are correctly placed inside or outside the quotation marks.

Example:

The award-winning essay is Science and Values.
The award-winning essay is "Science and Values."

1. In the title essay of her book The Death of the Moth and Other Essays, Virginia Woolf describes the last moments of a frail and diminutive body.
2. An insect's death may seem insignificant, but the moth is, in Woolf's words, life, a pure bead.
3. The moth's struggle against death, indifferent, impersonal, is heroic.
4. Where else but in such a bit of life could one see a protest so superb?

5. At the end Woolf sees the moth lying most decently and uncomplainingly composed; in death it finds dignity.

EXERCISE 4
Revising: Quotation marks

Insert quotation marks as needed in the following paragraph.

In one class we talked about a passage from I Have a Dream, the speech delivered by Martin Luther King, Jr., on the steps of the Lincoln Memorial on August 28, 1963:

> When the architects of our republic wrote the magnificent words of the Constitution and the Declaration of Independence, they were signing a promissory note to which every American was to fall heir. This note was a promise that all men would be guaranteed the unalienable rights of life, liberty, and the pursuit of happiness.

What did Dr. King mean by this statement? the teacher asked. Perhaps we should define promissory note first. Then she explained that a person who signs such a note agrees to pay a specific sum of money on a particular date or on demand by the holder of the note. One student suggested, Maybe Dr. King meant that those who wrote and signed the Constitution and Declaration had stated the country's promise that all people in America should have equal political rights and equal opportunity for the pursuit of happiness. He and over 200,000 people had gathered in Washington, DC, added another student. Maybe their purpose was to demand payment, to demand those rights for African Americans. The whole discussion was an eye opener for those of us (including me) who had never considered that those documents make promises that we should expect our country to fulfill.

Note See page 532 for a punctuation exercise involving quotation marks along with other marks of punctuation.

CHAPTER 32

Other Punctuation Marks

This chapter covers the colon (below), the dash (p. 522), parentheses (p. 524), brackets (p. 526), the ellipsis mark (p. 527), and the slash (p. 530).

Note Some computerized grammar and style checkers will flag a lone parenthesis or bracket so that you can match it with another parenthesis or bracket. But most checkers cannot recognize other misuses of the marks covered here. You'll need to proofread your papers carefully for errors.

THE COLON

32a Use the colon to introduce and to separate.

The colon is mainly a mark of introduction: it signals that the words following will explain or amplify. The colon also has several conventional uses, such as in expressions of time.

In its main use as an introducer, a colon is *always* preceded by a complete **main clause**—one containing a subject and a predicate and not starting with a subordinating word (see p. 275 for more on main clauses). A colon may or may not be followed by a main clause. This is one way the colon differs from the semicolon (see the box on the next page). The colon is often interchangeable with the dash, though the dash is more informal and more abrupt (see p. 522).

Note Don't use a colon more than once in a sentence. The sentence should end with the element introduced by the colon.

http://www.esc.edu/htmlpages/writer/pandg/colons.htm Advice and an exercise on the colon, from the State University of New York.

Distinguishing the colon and the semicolon

- The **colon** is a mark of introduction that separates elements of *unequal* importance, such as statements and explanations or introductions and quotations. The first element must be a complete main clause; the second element need not be. (See p. 519.)

  The business school caters to working students**:** it offers special evening courses in business writing, finance, and management.

  The school has one goal**:** to train students to be responsible, competent businesspeople.

- The **semicolon** separates elements of *equal* importance, almost always complete main clauses. (See p. 491.)

  Few enrolling students know exactly what they want from the school**;** most hope generally for a managerial career.

1 Use a colon to introduce a concluding explanation, series, appositive, or long or formal quotation.

Depending on your preference, a complete sentence *after* the colon may begin with a capital letter or a small letter. Just be consistent throughout an essay.

Explanation

Soul food is a varied cuisine**:** it includes spicy gumbos, black-eyed peas, and collard greens.

Soul food has a deceptively simple definition**:** the ethnic cooking of African Americans.

Sometimes a concluding explanation is preceded by *the following* or *as follows* and a colon:

A more precise definition might be the following**:** ingredients, cooking methods, and dishes originating in Africa, brought to the New World by black slaves, and modified or supplemented in the Caribbean and the American South.

Series (p. 479)

At least three soul food dishes are familiar to most Americans**:** fried chicken, barbecued spareribs, and sweet potatoes.

Appositive (p. 280)

Soul food has one disadvantage**:** fat.

Certain expressions commonly introduce appositives, such as *namely* and *that is*. These expressions should *follow* the colon: *Soul food has one disadvantage***:** *namely, fat.*

Long or formal quotation

The comma generally separates a signal phrase from a quotation (see p. 483). But when you introduce a long or formal quotation with a complete sentence, use a colon instead:

> One soul food chef has a solution: "Soul food doesn't have to be greasy to taste good. Instead of using ham hocks to flavor beans, I use smoked turkey wings. The soulful, smoky taste remains, but without all the fat of pork."

2 Use a colon to separate titles and subtitles and the subdivisions of time.

Titles and subtitles	Time
Charles Dickens: An Introduction to His Novels	1:30 AM
Eros and Civilization: An Inquiry into Freud	12:26 PM

3 Use the colon only where required.

Use the colon only at the *end* of a main clause. Do not use it directly after a verb or preposition.

Not Two entertaining movies directed by Steven Spielberg are: *E.T.* and *Raiders of the Lost Ark.*

But Two entertaining movies directed by Steven Spielberg are *E. T.* and *Raiders of the Lost Ark.*

Not Shakespeare possessed the qualities of a Renaissance thinker, such as: humanism and a deep interest in classical Greek and Roman literature.

But Shakespeare possessed the qualities of a Renaissance thinker, such as humanism and a deep interest in classical Greek and Roman literature.

EXERCISE 1
Revising: Colons

Insert colons as needed in the following sentences, or delete colons that are misused.

Example:

Mix the ingredients as follows sift the flour and salt together, add the milk, and slowly beat in the egg yolk.

Mix the ingredients as follows: sift the flour and salt together, add the milk, and slowly beat in the egg yolk.

1. In the remote parts of many Third World countries, simple signs mark human habitation a dirt path, a few huts, smoke from a campfire.
2. In the built-up sections of industrialized countries, nature is all but obliterated by signs of human life, such as: houses, factories, skyscrapers, and highways.

3. The spectacle makes many question the words of Ecclesiastes 1.4 “One generation passeth away, and another cometh; but the earth abideth forever.”
4. Yet many scientists see the future differently they hold that human beings have all the technology necessary to clean up the earth and restore the cycles of nature.
5. All that is needed is: a change in the attitudes of those who use technology.

THE DASH

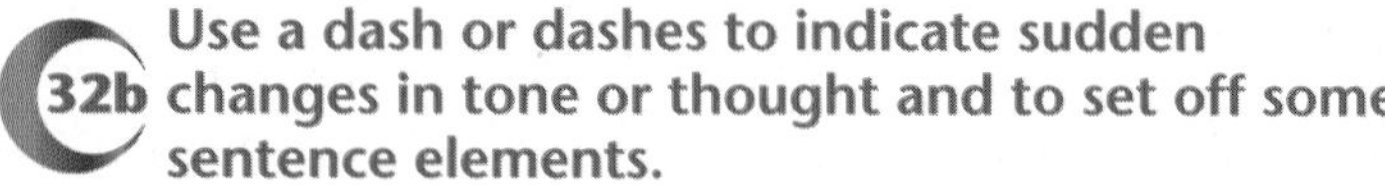

32b Use a dash or dashes to indicate sudden changes in tone or thought and to set off some sentence elements.

The dash is mainly a mark of interruption: it signals an insertion or break.

Note In your papers, form a dash with two hyphens (--), or use the character called an em dash on your word processor. Do not add extra space around or between the hyphens or around the em dash.

1 Use a dash or dashes to indicate shifts and hesitations.

Shift in tone

The novel—if one can call it that—appeared in 1994.

Unfinished thought

If the book had a plot—but a plot would be conventional.

Hesitation in dialogue

“I was worried you might think I had stayed away because I was influenced by—” He stopped and lowered his eyes.

Astonished, Howe said, “Influenced by what?”

“Well, by—” Blackburn hesitated and for an answer pointed to the table. —LIONEL TRILLING

2 Use a dash or dashes to emphasize nonessential elements.

Dashes may be used in place of commas or parentheses to set off and emphasize nonessential elements. (See the box on the facing page.) Dashes are especially useful when these elements are internally punctuated. Be sure to use a pair of dashes when the element interrupts a main clause.

http://www.wisc.edu/writing/Handbook/Dashes.html Advice on using dashes, from the University of Wisconsin at Madison.

Distinguishing dashes, commas, and parentheses

Dashes, commas, and parentheses may all set off nonessential elements.

- **Dashes** give the information the greatest emphasis (this page):

  Many students—including some employed by the college—disapprove of the new work rules.

- **Commas** are less emphatic (p. 473):

  Many students, including some employed by the college, disapprove of the new work rules.

- **Parentheses,** the least emphatic, signal that the information is just worth a mention (p. 525):

  Many students (including some employed by the college) disapprove of the new work rules.

Appositive (p. 280)

The qualities Monet painted—sunlight, rich shadows, deep colors—abounded near the rivers and gardens he used as subjects.

Modifier

Though they are close together—separated by only a few blocks—the two neighborhoods could be in different countries.

Parenthetical expression (p. 525)

At any given time there exists an inventory of undiscovered embezzlement in—or more precisely not in—the country's businesses and banks. —John Kenneth Galbraith

3 Use a dash to set off introductory series and concluding series and explanations.

Introductory series

Shortness of breath, skin discoloration or the sudden appearance of moles, persistent indigestion, the presence of small lumps—all these may signify cancer.

A dash sets off concluding series and explanations more informally and more abruptly than a colon does (see p. 520):

Concluding series

The patient undergoes a battery of tests—CAT scan, bronchoscopy, perhaps even biopsy.

Concluding explanation

Many patients are disturbed by the CAT scan—by the need to keep still for long periods in an exceedingly small space.

4 Use the dash only where needed.

Don't use the dash when commas, semicolons, and periods are more appropriate. And don't use too many dashes. They can create a jumpy or breathy quality in writing.

Not In all his life—eighty-seven years—my great-grandfather never allowed his picture to be taken—not even once. He claimed the "black box"—the camera—would rob him of his soul.

But In all his eighty-seven years my great-grandfather did not allow his picture to be taken even once. He claimed the "black box"—the camera—would rob him of his soul.

EXERCISE 2
Revising: Dashes

Insert dashes as needed in the following sentences.

Example:

What would we do if someone like Adolf Hitler that monster appeared among us?

What would we do if someone like Adolf Hitler—that monster—appeared among us?

1. The movie-theater business is undergoing dramatic changes changes that may affect what movies are made and shown.
2. The closing of independent theaters, the control of theaters by fewer and fewer owners, and the increasing ownership of theaters by movie studios and distributors these changes may reduce the availability of noncommercial films.
3. Yet at the same time the number of movie screens is increasing primarily in multiscreen complexes so that smaller films may find more outlets.
4. The number of active movie screens that is, screens showing films or booked to do so is higher now than at any time since World War II.
5. The biggest theater complexes seem to be something else as well art galleries, amusement arcades, restaurants, spectacles.

PARENTHESES

32c Use parentheses to enclose parenthetical expressions and labels for lists within sentences.

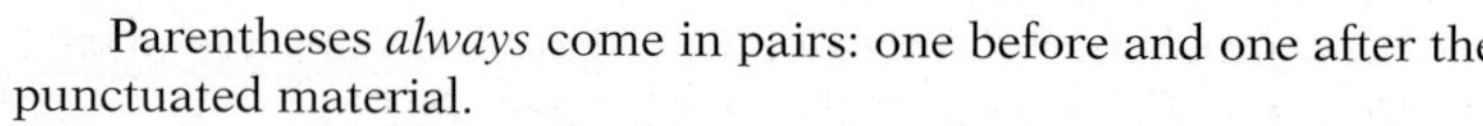

Parentheses *always* come in pairs: one before and one after the punctuated material.

1 Use parentheses to enclose parenthetical expressions.

Parenthetical expressions include explanations, digressions, and examples that may be helpful or interesting but are not essential to meaning. They are emphasized least when set off with a pair of parentheses instead of commas or dashes. (See the box on p. 523.)

> The population of Philadelphia **(**now about 1.5 million**)** has declined since 1950.
>
> *Ariel* **(**published in 1965**)** contains Sylvia Plath's last poems.

Note Don't put a comma before a parenthetical expression enclosed in parentheses:

Not Philadelphia's population compares with Houston's, (just over 1.6 million).

But Philadelphia's population compares with Houston's (just over 1.6 million).

A comma, semicolon, or period falling after a parenthetical expression should be placed *outside* the closing parenthesis:

> Philadelphia has a larger African American population (nearly 40 percent**),** while Houston has a larger Latino population (nearly 28 percent**).**

When it falls between other complete sentences, a complete sentence enclosed in parentheses has a capital letter and end punctuation:

> In general, coaches will tell you that scouts are just guys who can't coach. (But then, so are brain surgeons**.)** —Roy Blount

2 Use parentheses to enclose labels for lists within sentences.

> Outside the Middle East, the countries with the largest oil reserves are **(**1**)** Venezuela (63 billion barrels), **(**2**)** Russia (57 billion barrels), and **(**3**)** Mexico (51 billion barrels).

When you set a list off from your text, do not enclose such labels in parentheses.

( )
32c

EXERCISE 3
Revising: Parentheses

Insert parentheses as needed in the following sentences.

Example:

Students can find good-quality, inexpensive furniture for example, desks, tables, chairs, sofas, even beds in junk stores.

http://www.esc.edu/htmlpages/writer/pandg/paren.htm Advice and an exercise on using parentheses, from the State University of New York.

Students can find good-quality, inexpensive furniture (for example, desks, tables, chairs, sofas, even beds) in junk stores.

1. Many of those involved in the movie business agree that multiscreen complexes are good for two reasons: 1 they cut the costs of exhibitors, and 2 they offer more choices to audiences.
2. Those who produce and distribute films and not just the big studios argue that the multiscreen theaters give exhibitors too much power.
3. The major studios are buying movie theaters to gain control over important parts of the distribution process what gets shown and for how much money.
4. For twelve years 1938–50 the federal government forced the studios to sell all their movie theaters.
5. But because they now have more competition television and videocassette recorders, the studios are permitted to own theaters.

BRACKETS

32d Use brackets within quotations to indicate your own comments or changes.

Brackets have specialized uses in mathematical equations, but their main use for all kinds of writing is to indicate that you have altered a quotation. If you need to explain, clarify, or correct the words of the writer you quote, place your additions in a pair of brackets:

> "That Texaco station [just outside Chicago] is one of the busiest in the nation," said a company spokesperson.

Use brackets if you need to alter the capitalization of a quotation so that it will fit into your sentence. (See also p. 535.)

> "[O]ne of the busiest in the nation" is how a company spokesperson described the station.

[ ] 32d

You may also use a bracketed word or words to substitute for parts of a quotation that would otherwise be unclear. In the sentence below, the bracketed word substitutes for *they* in the original:

> "Despite considerable achievements in other areas, [humans] still cannot control the weather and probably will never be able to do so."

In the style of the Modern Language Association, brackets also surround ellipsis marks that you add to indicate omissions from quotations. (See opposite.)

http://www.esc.edu/htmlpages/writer/pandg/brack.htm Advice on using brackets, from the State University of New York.

The word *sic* (Latin for "in this manner") in brackets indicates that an error in the quotation appeared in the original and was not made by you. Do not underline or italicize *sic* in brackets.

> According to the newspaper report, "The car slammed thru [sic] the railing and into oncoming traffic."

But don't use *sic* to make fun of a writer or to note errors in a passage that is clearly nonstandard or illiterate.

THE ELLIPSIS MARK

32e Use the ellipsis mark to indicate omissions from quotations and pauses in speech.

The **ellipsis mark** consists of three spaced periods (. . .). It usually indicates an omission from a quotation, although it may also show an interruption in dialogue.

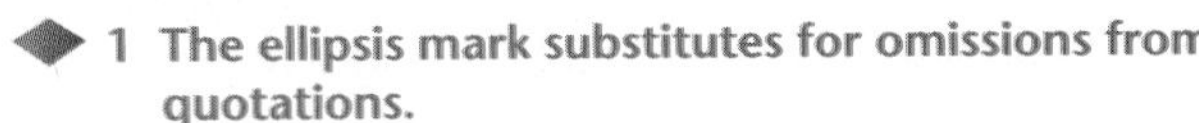

1 The ellipsis mark substitutes for omissions from quotations.

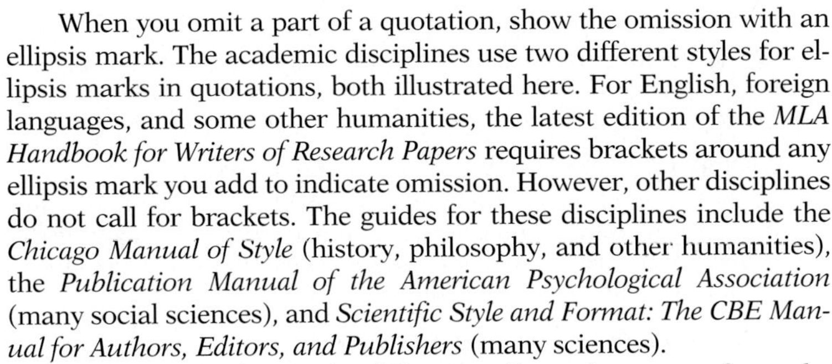

When you omit a part of a quotation, show the omission with an ellipsis mark. The academic disciplines use two different styles for ellipsis marks in quotations, both illustrated here. For English, foreign languages, and some other humanities, the latest edition of the *MLA Handbook for Writers of Research Papers* requires brackets around any ellipsis mark you add to indicate omission. However, other disciplines do not call for brackets. The guides for these disciplines include the *Chicago Manual of Style* (history, philosophy, and other humanities), the *Publication Manual of the American Psychological Association* (many social sciences), and *Scientific Style and Format: The CBE Manual for Authors, Editors, and Publishers* (many sciences).

All the examples in the following discussion quote from the passage below about environmentalism:

Original quotation

"At the heart of the environmentalist world view is the conviction that human physical and spiritual health depends on sustaining the planet in a relatively unaltered state. Earth is our home in the full, genetic sense, where humanity and its ancestors existed for all the millions of years of their evolution. Natural ecosystems—forests, coral reefs, marine blue waters—maintain the world exactly as we would wish it to be maintained. When we debase the global envi-

. . .
32e

http://www.esc.edu/htmlpages/writer/pandg/ellip.htm Advice on using the ellipsis mark, from the State University of New York.

ronment and extinguish the variety of life, we are dismantling a support system that is too complex to understand, let alone replace, in the foreseeable future."

—Edward O. Wilson, "Is Humanity Suicidal?"

MLA style

In MLA style, brackets surround your ellipsis marks to distinguish them from any ellipsis marks the quoted author may have used. Insert one space before the opening bracket. Insert one space after the closing bracket unless it precedes another mark of punctuation. Do not insert space between the brackets themselves and the ellipsis mark.

1. Omission of the middle of a sentence

"Natural ecosystems **[. . .]** maintain the world exactly as we would wish it to be maintained."

2. Omission of the end of a sentence, without source citation

"Earth is our home **[. . .].**" [The sentence period immediately follows the closing bracket.]

3. Omission of the end of a sentence, with source citation

"Earth is our home **[. . .]**" (Wilson 27)**.** [The sentence period follows the source citation.]

4. Omission of the beginning of a sentence

"**[. . .]** [H]uman physical and spiritual health depends on sustaining the planet in a relatively unaltered state." [The brackets around the *H* indicate a change in capitalization from the original.]

5. Omission of parts of two or more sentences

"At the heart of the environmentalist world view is the conviction that human physical and spiritual health depends on sustaining the planet **[. . .]** where humanity and its ancestors existed for all the millions of years of their evolution."

6. Omission of one or more sentences

"At the heart of the environmentalist world view is the conviction that human physical and spiritual health depends on sustaining the planet in a relatively unaltered state**. [. . .]** When we debase the global environment and extinguish the variety of life, we are dismantling a support system that is too complex to understand, let alone replace, in the foreseeable future."

7. Use of a word or phrase

Wilson describes the earth as "our home." [No ellipsis mark needed.]

Note these features of the examples:

- Use an ellipsis mark when it is not otherwise clear that you have left out material from the source, as when the words you quote form a complete sentence that is different in the original (examples 1–5). You don't need an ellipsis mark at the beginning or end of a word or phrase because it will already be obvious that you omitted something (example 7).

- After a grammatically complete sentence, an ellipsis mark either precedes or follows the sentence period (models 2 and 6, respectively). The exception occurs when a parenthetical source citation follows the quotation (example 3), in which case the sentence period falls after the citation.

If you omit one or more lines of poetry or paragraphs of prose from a quotation, use a separate line of ellipsis marks across the full width of the quotation to show the omission:

> In "Song: Love Armed" from 1676, Aphra Behn contrasts two lovers' experiences of a romance:
>
> Love in fantastic triumph sate,
>   Whilst bleeding hearts around him flowed,
> [. . . . .]
> But my poor heart alone is harmed,
>   Whilst thine the victor is, and free. (lines 1-2, 15-16)

(See p. 512 for the format of displayed quotations like this one. And see pp. 717–18 on the source-citation form illustrated here.)

Other styles

When you are following a style guide other than the *MLA Handbook,* do not include brackets around ellipsis marks. Otherwise, the spacing and use of ellipsis marks for different kinds of omissions resembles the MLA style given previously. For instance:

1. Omission of the middle of a sentence
"Natural ecosystems . . . maintain the world exactly as we would wish it to be maintained."

2. Omission of the end of a sentence, without source citation
"Earth is our home. . . ." [Unlike in MLA style, the sentence period, closed up to the last word, precedes the ellipsis mark.]

3. Omission of the end of a sentence, with source citation
"Earth is our home . . ." (Wilson 27). [The sentence period follows the source citation.]

2 The ellipsis mark indicates pauses or unfinished statements.

In your own writing (not when quoting from sources), you can show hesitation or interruption with an ellipsis mark instead of a dash (p. 522). This use of the ellipsis mark occurs most often in reported speech, such as dialogue:

"I wish. . ." His voice trailed off.

Do not add brackets around an ellipsis mark used for this purpose, even if you are following MLA style.

EXERCISE 4
Using ellipsis marks

Use ellipsis marks and any other needed punctuation to follow the numbered instructions for quoting from the following paragraph. Follow MLA style or the style of other disciplines, as required by your instructor.

> Women in the sixteenth and seventeenth centuries were educated in the home and, in some cases, in boarding schools. Men were educated at home, in grammar schools, and at the universities. The universities were closed to female students. For women, "learning the Bible," as Elizabeth Joceline puts it, was an impetus to learning to read. To be able to read the Bible in the vernacular was a liberating experience that freed the reader from hearing only the set passages read in the church and interpreted by the church. A Protestant woman was expected to read the scriptures daily, to meditate on them, and to memorize portions of them. In addition, a woman was expected to instruct her entire household in "learning the Bible" by holding instructional and devotional times each day for all household members, including the servants.
>
> —CHARLOTTE F. OTTEN, *English Women's Voices, 1540–1700*

1. Quote the fifth sentence, but omit everything from *that freed the reader* to the end.
2. Quote the fifth sentence, but omit the words *was a liberating experience that.*
3. Quote the first and sixth sentences.

THE SLASH

32f Use the slash between options, between lines of poetry that are run in to the text, and in electronic addresses.

Option

I don't know why some teachers oppose pass/fail courses.

When used between options, the slash is not surrounded by extra space.

http://webster.commnet.edu/HP/pages/darling/grammar/marks.htm#slash
Advice on using the slash, from the Guide to Grammar and Writing.

Note The options *and/or* and *he/she* should be avoided. (See the Glossary of Usage, pp. 927 and 933.)

Poetry

Many readers have sensed a reluctant turn away from death in Frost's lines "The woods are lovely, dark and deep, / But I have promises to keep" (13–14).

When separating lines of poetry in this way, leave a space before and after the slash. (See p. 512 for more on quoting poetry.)

Electronic addresses

http://www.stanford.edu/depts/spc/spc.html

See page 197 for more on electronic addresses.

EXERCISE 5
Revising: Colons, dashes, parentheses, brackets, ellipsis marks, slashes

Insert colons, dashes, parentheses, brackets, ellipsis marks, or slashes as needed in the following paragraph. When different marks would be appropriate in the same place, be able to defend the choice you make. For ellipsis marks, follow MLA style or the style of other disciplines as required by your instructor.

"Let all the learned say what they can, 'Tis ready money makes the man." These two lines of poetry by the Englishman William Somerville 1645–1742 may apply to a current American economic problem. Non-American investors with "ready money" pour some of it as much as $1.3 trillion in recent years into the United States. The investments of foreigners are varied stocks and bonds, savings deposits, service companies, factories, art works, even the campaigns of political candidates. Proponents of foreign investment argue that it revives industry, strengthens the economy, creates jobs more than 3 million, they say, and encourages free trade among nations. Opponents discuss the risks of heavy foreign investment it makes the American economy vulnerable to outsiders, sucks profits from the country, and gives foreigners an influence in governmental decision making. On both sides, it seems, "the learned say 'Tis ready money makes the man or country." The question is, whose money?

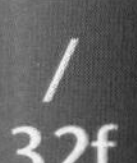

Note See the next page for a punctuation exercise combining colons, dashes, and parentheses with other marks of punctuation, such as commas and semicolons.

EXERCISE ON CHAPTERS 27–32
Revising: Punctuation

The following paragraphs are unpunctuated except for end-of-sentence periods. Insert periods, commas, semicolons, apostrophes, quotation marks, colons, dashes, or parentheses where they are required. When different marks would be appropriate in the same place, be able to defend the choice you make.

Brewed coffee is the most widely consumed beverage in the world. The trade in coffee beans alone amounts to well over $6000000000 a year and the total volume of beans traded exceeds 4250000 tons a year. Its believed that the beverage was introduced into Arabia in the fifteenth century AD probably by Ethiopians. By the middle or late sixteenth century the Arabs had introduced the beverage to the Europeans who at first resisted it because of its strong flavor and effect as a mild stimulant. The French Italians and other Europeans incorporated coffee into their diets by the seventeenth century the English however preferred tea which they were then importing from India. Since America was colonized primarily by the English Americans also preferred tea. Only after the Boston Tea Party 1773 did Americans begin drinking coffee in large quantities. Now though the US is one of the top coffee-consuming countries consumption having been spurred on by familiar advertising claims Good till the last drop Rich hearty aroma Always rich never bitter.

Produced from the fruit of an evergreen tree coffee is grown primarily in Latin America southern Asia and Africa. Coffee trees require a hot climate high humidity rich soil with good drainage and partial shade consequently they thrive on the east or west slopes of tropical volcanic mountains where the soil is laced with potash and drains easily. The coffee beans actually seeds grow inside bright red berries. The berries are picked by hand and the beans are extracted by machine leaving a pulpy fruit residue that can be used for fertilizer. The beans are usually roasted in ovens a chemical process that releases the beans essential oil caffeol which gives coffee its distinctive aroma. Over a hundred different varieties of beans are produced in the world each with a different flavor attributable to three factors the species of plant *Coffea arabica* and *Coffea robusta* are the most common and the soil and climate where the variety was grown.

p

PART VIII

Mechanics

33 Capitals

34 Underlining or Italics

35 Abbreviations

36 Numbers

37 Word Division

CHAPTER 33

Capitals

The conventions for using capital letters change often, but the following pages and a recent dictionary can help you decide whether to capitalize a particular word. The social, natural, and applied sciences require specialized capitalization for terminology, such as *Conditions A and B* or *Escherichia coli.* Consult one of the style guides listed on pages 841 (social sciences) and 869 (natural and applied sciences) for the requirements of particular disciplines.

Note Computerized grammar and style checkers will flag overused capital letters and missing capitals at the beginnings of sentences. They will also spot missing capitals at the beginnings of proper nouns and adjectives—*if* the words are in the checker's dictionary of proper nouns and adjectives. For example, a checker caught *christianity* and *europe* but not *china* (for the country) or *Stephen king.* You'll need to proofread for capital letters on your own as well.

ESL Conventions of capitalization vary from language to language. English, for instance, is the only language to capitalize the first-person singular pronoun (*I*), and its practice of capitalizing proper nouns but not most common nouns also distinguishes it from some other languages.

33a Capitalize the first word of every sentence.

Every writer should own a good dictionary.
Will inflation be curbed?
Watch out!

Information on using capital letters:

http://www.acusysinc.com/English/Capitalization.htm From the Reference Guide to Grammar.

http://webster.commnet.edu/HP/pages/darling/grammar/capitals.htm From the Guide to Grammar and Writing.

http://www.esc.edu/htmlpages/writer/pandg/cap.htm From the State University of New York.

When quoting other writers, you must reproduce the capital letters beginning their sentences or indicate that you have altered the source. Whenever possible, integrate the quotation into your own sentence so that its capitalization coincides with yours:

> "Psychotherapists often overlook the benefits of self-deception," the author argues.
>
> The author argues that "the benefits of self-deception" are not always recognized by psychotherapists.

If you need to alter the capitalization in the source, indicate the change with brackets (see p. 527):

> "[T]he benefits of self-deception" are not always recognized by psychotherapists, the author argues.
>
> The author argues that "[p]sychotherapists often overlook the benefits of self-deception."

Note Capitalization of questions in a series is optional. Both examples below are correct:

> Is the population a hundred? Two hundred? More?
> Is the population a hundred? two hundred? more?

Also optional is capitalization of the first word in a complete sentence after a colon (see p. 520).

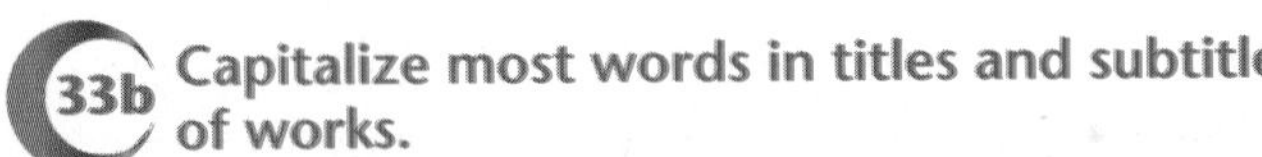

33b Capitalize most words in titles and subtitles of works.

Within your text, capitalize all the words in a title *except* the following: articles (*a, an, the*), *to* in infinitives, and connecting words (prepositions and coordinating and subordinating conjunctions) of fewer than five letters. Capitalize even these short words when they are the first or last word in a title or when they fall after a colon or semicolon.

The Sound and the Fury	*Management: A New Theory*
"Courtship Through the Ages"	"Once More to the Lake"
A Diamond Is Forever	*An End to Live For*
"Knowing Whom to Ask"	"Power: How to Get It"
Learning from Las Vegas	*File Under Architecture*
"The Truth About AIDS"	*Only when I Laugh*

Always capitalize the prefix or first word in a hyphenated word within a title. Capitalize the second word only if it is a noun or an adjective or is as important as the first word.

"Applying Stage Make-up"	*Through the Looking-Glass*
The Pre-Raphaelites	

Note The style guides of the academic disciplines have their own rules for capitals in titles. For instance, MLA style for English and some other humanities capitalizes all subordinating conjunctions but no prepositions. In addition, APA style for the social sciences, CBE style for the sciences, and Columbia online style for the sciences capitalize only the first word and proper names in book and article titles within source citations (see pp. 845–55 on APA, 871–76 on CBE, and 886–91 on Columbia).

33c Always capitalize the pronoun *I* and the interjection *O*. Capitalize *oh* only when it begins a sentence.

I love to stay up at night, but, oh, I hate to get up in the morning.

He who thinks himself wise, O heavens, is a great fool. —VOLTAIRE

33d Capitalize proper nouns, proper adjectives, and words used as essential parts of proper nouns.

Proper nouns name specific persons, places, and things: *Shakespeare, California, World War I.* **Proper adjectives** are formed from some proper nouns: *Shakespearean, Californian.*

1 Capitalize proper nouns and proper adjectives.

Capitalize all proper nouns and proper adjectives but not the articles (*a, an, the*) that precede them.

Proper nouns and adjectives to be capitalized

Specific persons and things

Stephen King	the Leaning Tower of Pisa
Napoleon Bonaparte	Boulder Dam
Doris Lessing	the Empire State Building

Specific places and geographical regions

New York City	the Mediterranean Sea
China	Lake Victoria
Europe	the Northeast, the South
North America	the Rocky Mountains

But: northeast of the city, going south

Days of the week, months, holidays

Monday	Yom Kippur
May	Christmas
Thanksgiving	Columbus Day

Historical events, documents, periods, movements

World War II
the Vietnam War
the Boston Tea Party
the Treaty of Ghent
the Constitution
the Bill of Rights
the Middle Ages
the Age of Reason
the Renaissance
the Great Depression
the Romantic Movement
the Cultural Revolution

Government offices or departments and institutions

House of Representatives
Department of Defense
Appropriations Committee
Polk Municipal Court
Warren County Hospital
Northeast High School

Political, social, athletic, and other organizations and associations and their members

Democratic Party, Democrats
Sierra Club
Girl Scouts of America, Scout
B'nai B'rith
Rotary Club, Rotarians
League of Women Voters
Boston Celtics
Chicago Symphony Orchestra

Races, nationalities, and their languages

Native American
African American
Caucasian
Germans
Swahili
Italian

But: blacks, whites

Religions and their followers

Christianity, Christians
Protestantism, Protestants
Catholicism, Catholics
Judaism, Orthodox Jews
Hinduism, Hindus
Islam, Muslims

Religious terms for the sacred

God
Allah
Christ
Buddha
the Bible [*but* biblical]
the Koran

Note Pronouns referring to God are often capitalized in religious texts. In your writing follow your own preference in capitalizing the pronouns (*God . . . He*) or using small letters (*God . . . he*).

2 Capitalize common nouns used as essential parts of proper nouns.

Common nouns name general classes of persons, places, or things, and they generally are not capitalized. However, capitalize the common nouns *street, avenue, park, river, ocean, lake, company, college, county,* and *memorial* when they are part of proper nouns naming specific places or institutions:

Main Street	Lake Superior
Central Park	Ford Motor Company
Mississippi River	Madison College
Pacific Ocean	George Washington Memorial

3 Capitalize trade names.

Trade names identify individual brands of certain products. When a trade name loses its association with a brand and comes to refer to a product in general, it is not capitalized. Refer to a dictionary for current usage when you are in doubt about a name.

Scotch tape	Xerox
Chevrolet	Bunsen burner

But: nylon, thermos

33e Capitalize most titles of persons only when they precede proper names.

Professor Otto Osborne	Otto Osborne, a professor of English
Doctor Jane Covington	Jane Covington, a medical doctor
Governor Ella Moore	Ella Moore, the governor

Not The Senator supported the bill.

But The senator supported the bill.

Or Senator Carmine supported the bill.

Exception Many writers capitalize a title denoting very high rank even when it follows a proper name or is used alone:

Lyndon Johnson, past President of the United States
the Chief Justice of the United States

33f Capitalize only when required.

In general, modern writers capitalize fewer words than earlier writers did. Capitalize only when a rule says you must, and especially avoid miscapitalizing in the following situations.

1 Use small letters for common nouns replacing proper nouns.

Not I am determined to take an Economics course before I graduate from College.

But I am determined to take an economics course before I graduate from college.

Or I am determined to take Economics 101 before I graduate from Madison College.

2 Capitalize compass directions only when they refer to specific geographical areas.

The storm blew in from the northeast and then veered south along the coast. [Here *northeast* and *south* refer to general directions.]

Students from the South have trouble adjusting to the Northeast's bitter winters. [Here *South* and *Northeast* refer to specific regions.]

3 Use small letters for the names of seasons or the names of academic years or terms.

spring	autumn	senior year
summer	fall quarter	winter term

4 Capitalize the names of relationships only when they form part of or substitute for proper names.

my mother	the father of my friend
John's brother	

I remember how Father scolded us.

Aunt Annie, Uncle Jake, and Uncle Irvin died within two months of each other.

5 Use capitals according to convention in online communication.

Although common in electronic mail and other online communication, messages written in all-capital letters or with no capital letters are difficult to read. Further, messages in all-capital letters may be taken as overly insistent, even rude (see also p. 196). Use capital letters according to rules 33a–33f in all your online communication.

EXERCISE
Revising: Capitals

Capitalize words as necessary in the following sentences, or substitute small letters for unnecessary capitals. Consult a dictionary if you are in doubt. If the capitalization in a sentence is already correct, circle the number preceding the sentence.

Example:

The first book on the reading list is mark twain's *a connecticut yankee in king arthur's court.*

The first book on the reading list is Mark Twain's *A Connecticut Yankee in King Arthur's Court.*

1. San Antonio, texas, is a thriving city in the southwest.
2. The city has always offered much to tourists interested in the roots of spanish settlement of the new world.

3. The alamo is one of five Catholic Missions built by Priests to convert native americans and to maintain spain's claims in the area.
4. But the alamo is more famous for being the site of an 1836 battle that helped to create the republic of Texas.
5. Many of the nearby Streets, such as Crockett street, are named for men who gave their lives in that Battle.
6. The Hemisfair plaza and the San Antonio river link new tourist and convention facilities developed during mayor Cisneros's terms.
7. Restaurants, Hotels, and shops line the River. the haunting melodies of "Una paloma blanca" and "malagueña" lure passing tourists into Casa rio and other excellent mexican restaurants.
8. The university of Texas at San Antonio has expanded, and a Medical Center has been developed in the Northwest part of the city.
9. Sea World, on the west side of San Antonio, entertains grandparents, fathers and mothers, and children with the antics of dolphins and seals.
10. The City has attracted high-tech industry, creating a corridor of economic growth between san antonio and austin and contributing to the texas economy.

Note See page 555 for an exercise involving capitals along with underlining or italics and other mechanics.

CHAPTER 34

Underlining or Italics

Underlining and *italic type* indicate the same thing: the word or words are being distinguished or emphasized. If you underline two or more words in a row, underline the space between the words, too: Criminal Statistics: Misuses of Numbers.

Note Computerized grammar and style checkers cannot recognize problems with underlining or italics. Check your work yourself to ensure that you have used highlighting appropriately.

34a Use underlining or italics consistently and appropriately for your writing situation.

Word processors have made italic type possible in papers and other documents, and it is now used almost universally in business and some academic disciplines. Still, other disciplines continue to prefer underlining, especially in source citations. (The *MLA Handbook for Writers of Research Papers* and the *Publication Manual of the American Psychological Association* both call for underlining.) Ask your instructor for his or her own preferences.

Depending on your instructor's preferences, use either italics or underlining consistently throughout a document. For instance, if you are writing an English paper and following MLA style for underlining in source citations, use underlining in the body of your paper as well.

34b Underline or italicize the titles of works that appear independently.

Within your text, underline or italicize the titles of works, such as books and periodicals, that are published, released, or produced

Information on using underlining or italics:

http://webster.commnet.edu/HP/pages/darling/grammar/italics.htm
From the Guide to Grammar and Writing.

http://www.esc.edu/htmlpages/writer/pandg/italic.htm From the State University of New York.

separately from other works (see the box below). Use quotation marks for all other titles, such as short stories and articles in periodicals. (See p. 514.)

Titles to be underlined or italicized

Other titles should be placed in quotation marks. (See p. 514.)

Books
War and Peace
Psychology: An Introduction

Plays
Hamlet
The Phantom of the Opera

Pamphlets
The Truth About Alcoholism
Plants of the Desert

Long musical works
Tchaikovsky's Swan Lake
The Beatles' Revolver
But: Symphony in C

Television and radio programs
All Things Considered
NBC Sports Hour

Long poems
Beowulf
Paradise Lost

Periodicals
Time
Boston Globe
Yale Law Review

Published speeches
Lincoln's Gettysburg Address
Pericles's Funeral Oration

Movies and videotapes
Schindler's List
How to Relax

Works of visual art
Michelangelo's David
Picasso's Guernica

Note Underline or italicize marks of punctuation only when they are part of the title: *Did you read* Catch-22? (not Catch-22?). In titles of newspapers underline or italicize the name of the city only when it is part of the title:

New York Times — Manchester Guardian

When giving the title of a periodical in your text, you need not capitalize, underline, or italicize the article *the,* even if it is part of the title: *She has the* New York Times *delivered to her in Japan.*

Exceptions Legal documents, the Bible, the Koran, and their parts are generally not underlined or italicized:

Not They registered their deed.
But They registered their deed.

Not We studied the Book of Revelation in the Bible.
But We studied the Book of Revelation in the Bible.

Many sciences do not use underlining or italics for some or all titles within source citations. (See p. 872 on CBE style.)

34c Underline or italicize the names of ships, aircraft, spacecraft, and trains.

Queen Elizabeth 2	*Challenger*	*Orient Express*
Spirit of St. Louis	*Apollo XI*	*Montrealer*

34d Underline or italicize foreign words and phrases that have not been absorbed into English.

English has adopted many foreign words and phrases—such as the French expression "bon voyage"—and these need not be underlined or italicized. A foreign phrase should be underlined or italicized when it has not been absorbed into our language. A dictionary will say whether a phrase is still considered foreign to English.

> The scientific name for the brown trout is *Salmo trutta*. [The Latin scientific names for plants and animals are always underlined or italicized.]
>
> What a life he led! He was a true *bon vivant*.
>
> The Latin *De gustibus non est disputandum* translates roughly as "There's no accounting for taste."

34e Underline or italicize words or characters named as words.

Use underlining or italics to indicate that you are citing a character or word as a word rather than using it for its meaning. Words you are defining fall under this convention:

> The word *syzygy* refers to a straight line formed by three celestial bodies, as in the alignment of the earth, sun, and moon.
>
> Some people say *th*, as in *thought*, with a faint *s* or *f* sound.
>
> Carved into the column, twenty feet up, was a mysterious *7*.

34f Occasionally, underlining or italics may be used for emphasis.

Underlining or italics can stress an important word or phrase, especially in reporting how someone said something:

> "Why on earth would *you* do that?" she cried.

But use such emphasis very rarely. Excessive underlining or italics will make your writing sound immature or hysterical:

> The settlers had *no* firewood and *no* food. Many of them *starved* or *froze* to death that first winter.

34g In online communication, use alternatives for underlining or italics.

Electronic mail and other forms of online communication often do not allow underlining or italics for the purposes described above. The program may not be able to produce the highlighting or may reserve it for a special function. (On World Wide Web sites, for instance, underlining indicates a link to another site.)

To distinguish elements that usually require underlining or italics, type an underscore before and after the element: *Measurements coincide with those in _Joule's Handbook_.* You can also emphasize words with asterisks: *I *will not* be able to attend.*

Avoid using all-capital letters for emphasis. (See also p. 539.)

EXERCISE
Revising: Underlining or italics

Underline or italicize words and phrases as needed in the following sentences, or circle any words or phrases that are underlined unnecessarily. Note that some highlighting is correct as given.

Example:

Of Hitchcock's movies, Psycho is the scariest.
Of Hitchcock's movies, Psycho is the scariest.

1. Of the many Vietnam veterans who are writers, Oliver Stone is perhaps the most famous for writing and directing the films Platoon and Born on the Fourth of July.
2. Tim O'Brien has written short stories for Esquire, GQ, and Massachusetts Review.
3. Going After Cacciato is O'Brien's dreamlike novel about the horrors of combat.
4. The word Vietnam is technically two words (Viet and Nam), but most American writers spell it as one word.
5. American writers use words or phrases borrowed from Vietnamese, such as di di mau ("go quickly") or dinky dau ("crazy").
6. Philip Caputo's gripping account of his service in Vietnam appears in the book A Rumor of War.
7. Caputo's book was made into a television movie, also titled A Rumor of War.
8. David Rabe's plays—including The Basic Training of Pavlo Hummel, Streamers, and Sticks and Bones—depict the effects of the war not only on the soldiers but on their families.
9. Called the poet laureate of the Vietnam war, Steve Mason has published two collections of poems: Johnny's Song and Warrior for Peace.
10. The Washington Post published rave reviews of Veteran's Day, an autobiography by Rod Kane.

Note See page 555 for an exercise involving underlining or italics along with capitals and other mechanics.

CHAPTER 35

Abbreviations

The following guidelines on abbreviations pertain to the text of a nontechnical document. All academic disciplines use abbreviations in source citations, and much technical writing, such as in the sciences and engineering, uses many abbreviations in the document text. Consult one of the style guides listed on pages 822–23, 841, and 869 for the in-text requirements of the discipline you are writing in.

Usage varies, but writers increasingly omit periods from abbreviations of two or more words written in all-capital letters: *US, BA, USMC.* See page 463 on punctuating abbreviations.

Note Computerized grammar and style checkers may flag some abbreviations, such as *in.* (for *inch*) and *st.* (for *street*). A spelling checker will flag abbreviations it does not recognize. But neither checker can tell you whether an abbreviation is appropriate for your writing situation or will be clear to your readers.

Abbreviations for nontechnical writing

- Titles before or after proper names: Dr. *Jorge Rodriguez; Jorge Rodriguez, Ph.D.* (p. 546).
- Familiar abbreviations and acronyms: *USA, AIDS* (p. 546).
- *BC, AD, AM, PM, no.,* and *$* with dates and numbers (p. 546).
- *I.e., e.g.,* and other Latin abbreviations within parentheses and in source citations (p. 547).
- *Inc., Bros., Co.,* and *&* with names of business firms (p. 547).

Information on abbreviations:

http://www.acusysinc.com/English/Abbreviations.htm From the Reference Guide to Grammar.

http://www.esc.edu/htmlpages/writer/pandg/abbrev.htm From the State University of New York.

http://webster.commnet.edu/HP/pages/darling/grammar/abbreviations.htm From the Guide to Grammar and Writing.

35a Use standard abbreviations for titles immediately before and after proper names.

Before the name	**After the name**
Dr. James Hsu	James Hsu, MD
Mr., Mrs., Ms., Hon., St.,	DDS, DVM, Ph.D., Ed.D.,
Rev., Msgr., Gen.	OSB, SJ, Sr., Jr.

Use abbreviations such as *Rev., Hon., Prof., Rep., Sen., Dr.,* and *St.* (for *Saint*) only if they appear with a proper name. Spell them out in the absence of a proper name:

Not We learned to trust the Dr.

But We learned to trust the doctor.

Or We learned to trust Dr. Kaplan.

The abbreviations for academic degrees—*Ph.D., MA, BA,* and the like—may be used without a proper name: *My brother took seven years to get his Ph.D. It will probably take me just as long to earn my BA.*

35b Familiar abbreviations and acronyms are acceptable in most writing.

An **acronym** is an abbreviation that spells a pronounceable word, such as WHO, NATO, and AIDS. These and other abbreviations using initials are acceptable in most writing as long as they are familiar. Abbreviations of two or more words written in all-capital letters may be written without periods (see p. 463):

Institutions	LSU, UCLA, TCU
Organizations	CIA, FBI, YMCA, AFL-CIO
Corporations	IBM, CBS, ITT
People	JFK, LBJ, FDR
Countries	US, USA

Note If a name or term (such as *operating room*) appears often in a piece of writing, then its abbreviation (*OR*) can cut down on extra words. Spell out the full term at its first appearance, give its abbreviation in parentheses, and use the abbreviation from then on.

35c Use *BC, AD, AM, PM, no.,* and *$* only with specific dates and numbers.

44 BC	8:05 PM (*or* p.m.)	no. 36 (*or* No. 36)
AD 1492	11:26 AM (*or* a.m.)	$7.41

Not Hospital routine is easier to follow in the AM than in the PM.

But Hospital routine is easier to follow in the morning than in the afternoon or evening.

Note The abbreviation BC ("before Christ") always follows a date, whereas AD (*anno Domini,* Latin for "in the year of the Lord") precedes a date. Increasingly, these abbreviations are being replaced by BCE ("before the common era") and CE ("common era"), respectively. Both follow the date: *44 BCE, 1492 CE.*

35d Generally, reserve Latin abbreviations for source citations and comments in parentheses.

i.e.	*id est:* that is
cf.	*confer:* compare
e.g.	*exempli gratia:* for example
et al.	*et alii:* and others
etc.	*et cetera:* and so forth
NB	*nota bene:* note well

He said he would be gone a fortnight (i.e., two weeks).
Bloom et al., editors, *Anthology of Light Verse*
Trees, too, are susceptible to disease (e.g., Dutch elm disease).

(Note that these abbreviations are generally not italicized or underlined.)

Some writers avoid these abbreviations in formal writing, even within parentheses:

Informal

The cabs of some modern farm machines (e.g., combines) look like airplane cockpits.

Formal

The cabs of some modern farm machines (for example, combines) look like airplane cockpits.

35e Use *Inc., Bros., Co.,* or & (for *and*) only in official names of business firms.

Not The Santini bros. operate a large moving firm in New York City.

But The Santini brothers operate a large moving firm in New York City.

Or Santini Bros. is a large moving firm in New York City.

Not We read about the Hardy Boys & Nancy Drew.

But We read about the Hardy Boys and Nancy Drew.

35f Generally spell out units of measurement and names of places, calendar designations, people, and courses.

In most academic, general, and business writing, certain words should always be spelled out. (In source citations and technical writing, however, these words are more often abbreviated.)

Units of measurement

The dog is thirty inches [not in.] high.
The building is 150 feet [not ft.] tall.

Exception Long phrases such as *miles per hour* (*m.p.h.*) or *cycles per second* (*c.p.s.*) are usually abbreviated, with or without periods: *The speed limit on that road was once 75 m.p.h.* [or *mph*].

Geographical names

The publisher is in Massachusetts [not Mass. or MA].
He came from Auckland, New Zealand [not NZ].
She lived on Morrissey Boulevard [not Blvd.].

Exceptions The United States is often referred to as the USA or the US. In writing of the US capital, we use the abbreviation DC for District of Columbia when it follows the city's name: Washington, DC.

Names of days, months, and holidays

The truce was signed on Tuesday [not Tues.], April [not Apr.] 16.
The Christmas [not Xmas] holidays are uneventful.

Names of people

Virginia [not Va.] Woolf was British.
Robert [not Robt.] Frost wrote accessible poems.

Courses of instruction

I'm majoring in political science [not poli. sci.].
Economics [not Econ.] is a difficult course.

EXERCISE
Revising: Abbreviations

Revise the following sentences as needed to correct inappropriate use of abbreviations for nontechnical writing. Circle the number preceding any sentences in which the abbreviations are already appropriate as written.

Example:
One prof. lectured for five hrs.
One professor lectured for five hours.

1. In the Sept. 17, 1993, issue of *Science* magazine, Virgil L. Sharpton discusses a theory that could help explain the extinction of dinosaurs.

2. About 65 mill. yrs. ago, a comet or asteroid crashed into the earth.
3. The result was a huge crater about 10 km. (6.2 mi.) deep in the Gulf of Mex.
4. Sharpton's new measurements suggest that the crater is 50 pct. larger than scientists previously believed.
5. Indeed, 20-yr.-old drilling cores reveal that the crater is about 186 mi. wide, roughly the size of Conn.
6. The space object was traveling more than 100,000 m.p.h. and hit earth with the impact of 100 to 300 million megatons of TNT.
7. On impact, 200,000 cubic km. of rock and soil were vaporized or thrown into the air.
8. That's the equivalent of 2.34 bill. cubic ft. of matter.
9. The impact would have created 400-ft. tidal waves across the Atl. Ocean, temps. higher than 20,000 degs., and powerful earthquakes.
10. Sharpton theorizes that the dust, vapor, and smoke from this impact blocked the sun's rays for mos., cooled the earth, and thus resulted in the death of the dinosaurs.

Note See page 555 for an exercise involving abbreviations along with capitals and other mechanics.

CHAPTER 36

Numbers

This chapter addresses the use of numbers (numerals versus words) in the text of a document. All disciplines use many more numerals in source citations.

Note Computerized grammar and style checkers will flag numerals beginning sentences and can be customized to ignore or to look for numerals. But they can't tell you whether numerals or spelled-out numbers are appropriate for your writing situation.

36a Use numerals according to standard practice in the field you are writing in.

Always use numerals for numbers that require more than two words to spell out:

> The leap year has 366 days.
> The population of Minot, North Dakota, is about 32,800.

In nontechnical academic writing, spell out numbers of one or two words:

> Twelve nations signed the treaty.
>
> The ball game drew forty-two thousand people. [A hyphenated number may be considered one word.]

In much business writing, use numerals for all numbers over ten (*five reasons, 11 participants*). In technical academic and business writing, such as in science and engineering, use numerals for all numbers over ten, and use numerals for zero through nine when

Advice on using numbers:

http://webster.commnet.edu/HP/pages/darling/grammar/numbers.htm From the Guide to Grammar and Writing.

http://researchpaper.com/writing_center/23.html From Research-paper.com.

they refer to exact measurements (*2 liters, 1 hour*). (Consult one of the style guides listed on pp. 841 and 869 for more details.)

Note Use a combination of numerals and words for round numbers over a million: *26 million, 2.45 billion.* And use either all numerals or all words when several numbers appear together in a passage, even if convention would require a mixture:

Inconsistent The satellite Galatea is about twenty-six thousand miles from Neptune. It is 110 miles in diameter and orbits Neptune in just over ten hours.

Revised The satellite Galatea is about 26,000 miles from Neptune. It is 110 miles in diameter and orbits Neptune in just over 10 hours.

ESL In American English a comma separates the numerals in long numbers (*26,000*), and a period functions as a decimal point (*2.06*).

36b Use numerals according to convention for dates, addresses, and other information.

Even when a number requires one or two words to spell out, we conventionally use numerals in the following situations:

Days and years

June 18, 2000 AD 12 456 BC 1999

Exception The day of a month may be expressed in words when it is not followed by a year (*June fifth; October first*).

Pages, chapters, volumes, acts, scenes, lines

Chapter 9, page 123
Hamlet, act 5, scene 3, lines 35–40

Decimals, percentages, and fractions

22.5
48% (*or* 48 percent)
$3\frac{1}{2}$

Addresses

RD 2
419 Stonewall Street
Washington, DC 20036

Scores and statistics

21 to 7
a mean of 26
a ratio of 8 to 1

Exact amounts of money

$4.50
$3.5 million (*or* $3,500,000)

The time of day

9:00 AM
2:30 PM

Exceptions Round dollar or cent amounts of only a few words may be expressed in words: *seventeen dollars; fifteen hundred dollars; sixty cents.* When the word *o'clock* is used for the time of day, also express the number in words: *two o'clock* (not *2 o'clock*).

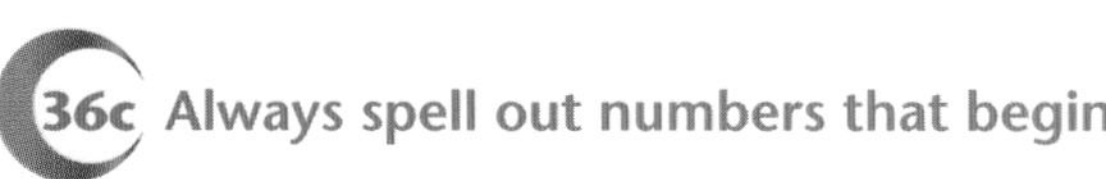

36c Always spell out numbers that begin sentences.

For clarity, spell out any number that begins a sentence. If the number requires more than two words, reword the sentence so that the number falls later and can be expressed as a numeral:

Not 3.5 billion people live in Asia.

But The population of Asia is 3.5 billion.

EXERCISE
Revising: Numbers

Revise the following sentences so that numbers are used appropriately for nontechnical writing. Circle the number preceding any sentence in which numbers are already used appropriately.

Example:
Carol paid two hundred five dollars for used scuba gear.
Carol paid $205 for used scuba gear.

1. The planet Saturn is nine hundred million miles, or nearly one billion five hundred million kilometers, from Earth.
2. A year on Saturn equals almost thirty of our years.
3. Thus, Saturn orbits the sun only two and four-tenths times during the average human life span.
4. It travels in its orbit at about twenty-one thousand six hundred miles per hour.
5. 15 to 20 times denser than Earth's core, Saturn's core measures 17,000 miles across.
6. The temperature at Saturn's cloud tops is minus one hundred seventy degrees Fahrenheit.
7. In nineteen hundred thirty-three, astronomers found on Saturn's surface a huge white spot 2 times the size of Earth and 7 times the size of Mercury.
8. Saturn's famous rings reflect almost seventy percent of the sunlight that approaches the planet.
9. The ring system is almost forty thousand miles wide, beginning 8,800 miles from the planet's visible surface and ending forty-seven thousand miles from that surface.
10. Saturn generates about one hundred thirty trillion kilowatts of electricity.

Note See page 555 for an exercise involving numbers along with abbreviations and other mechanics.

CHAPTER 37

Word Division

To avoid occasional short lines in your documents, you'll probably want to divide some words between the end of one line and the beginning of the next. If you write on a word processor, you can set the program to divide words automatically at appropriate breaks (in the Tools menu, select Language and then Hyphenation). To divide words manually, follow these guidelines:

- Divide words only between syllables. Do not divide one-syllable words, such as *dropped* or *straight*. Consult a dictionary if you're not sure of syllable breaks.
- Put a hyphen at the end of the first line, never at the beginning of the second line.

Not all syllable breaks are appropriate for word division. Use the following rules to decide when and how to divide words.

37a Leave at least two letters at the end of a line and at least three letters at the beginning of a line.

Faulty A newspaper or television editorial for or a-
gainst a candidate can sway an election. A voter may have no other information to draw on.

Revised A newspaper or television editorial for or
against a candidate can sway an election. A
voter may have no other information to draw on.

37b Divide a hyphenated word only at the hyphen.

Faulty If you want to have friends, be good-na-
tured.

Revised If you want to have friends, be good-
natured.

37c Do not divide words in electronic addresses.

If you must break an electronic address—for instance, in a source citation—do so only after a slash. Do not hyphenate, because readers may perceive any added hyphen as part of the address.

Not http://www.library.miami.edu/staff/lmc/soc-
race.html

But http://www.library.miami.edu/staff/lmc/
socrace.html

37d Make sure a word division will not confuse readers.

Some word divisions may momentarily confuse readers because the first or second part by itself forms a pronounceable (or unpronounceable) unit that does not fit with the whole—for example, *poi-gnant, read-dress, her-oism, in-dict*. Avoid word divisions like these.

EXERCISE
Revising: Word division

Revise the following sentences to improve inappropriate word divisions. Consult a dictionary if necessary. Circle the number preceding any sentence in which word division is already appropriate.

Example:

Samuel Johnson, the British essayist and poet, compiled the first English dictionary.

Samuel Johnson, the British essayist and
poet, compiled the first English dictionary.

1. Johnson read books about a wide range of subjects.
2. As a result he was probably the most well-edu-
cated man in England.
3. When he saw a new use for a word, he marked the passage for his secretary to copy.
4. The words were arranged alphabetically in large ledger books, with e-
nough room between words for definitions.
5. For each word the definitions were organized with specialized uses last.

Note See the next page for an exercise involving word division along with capitals and other mechanics.

EXERCISE ON CHAPTERS 33–37
Revising: Mechanics

Revise the paragraphs below to correct any errors in the use of capital letters, underlining or italics, abbreviations, numbers, and word division. (For abbreviations and numbers follow standard practice for nontechnical writing.) Consult a dictionary as needed.

According to many sources—e.g., the Cambridge Ancient History and Gardiner's Egypt of the Pharaohs—the
ancient egyptians devoted much attention to making Life
more convenient and pleasurable for themselves.

Our word pharaoh for the ancient egyptian rulers
comes from the egyptian word pr'o, meaning "great house."
Indeed, the egyptians placed great emphasis on family res-
idences, adding small bedrms. as early as 3500 yrs. b.c.
By 3000 b.c., the egyptians made ice through evaporation
of water at night and then used it to cool their homes. A-
bout the same time they used fans made of palm fronds or
papyrus to cool themselves in the day. To light their
homes, the egyptians abandoned the animal-fat lamps Humans
had used for 50 thousand yrs. Instead, around 1300 b.c.
the people of Egt. devised the 1st oil lamps.

egyptians found great pleasure in playing games. Four
thousand three hundred yrs. ago or so they created one of
the oldest board games known. the game involved racing ivory
or stone pieces across a papyrus playing board. By three
thousand b.c., egyptian children played marbles with semi-
precious stones, some of which have been found in grave-
sites at nagada, EG. Around one thousand three hundred
sixty b.c., small children played with clay rattles covered in silk and shaped like animals.

To play the game of love, egyptian men and women experimented with cosmetics applied to skin and eyelids.
kohl, history's first eyeliner, was used by both sexes
to ward off evil. 5000 yrs. ago egyptians wore wigs
made of vegetable fibers or human hair. In 9 hundred b.c.,
queen Isimkheb wore a wig so heavy that she needed assistance in walking. To adjust their make-up and wigs, e-
gyptians adapted the simple metal mirrors devised
by the sumerians in the bronze age, ornamenting them with
carved handles of ivory, gold, or wood. Feeling that only
those who smelled sweet could be attractive, the egyptians
made deodorants from perfumed oils, e.g., cinnamon and
citrus.

PART IX

Effective Words

CHAPTER 38

Choosing and Using Words

Expressing yourself clearly and effectively depends greatly on what words you choose and how you employ them in sentences. English offers an uncommonly rich and extensive vocabulary from which to select the words that precisely suit your writing situation (below) and your meaning (p. 567). And the language is uncommonly flexible when it comes to pruning unneeded words that make writing weak or inexact (p. 578).

38a Choosing the appropriate word

Appropriate words suit your writing situation—your subject, purpose, and audience. Like everyone, you vary your words depending on the context in which you are speaking and writing. Look, for example, at the underlined words in these two sentences:

> Some patients decide to bag counseling because their shrinks seem strung out.
>
> Some patients decide to abandon counseling because their therapists seem disturbed.

The first sentence might be addressed to friends in casual conversation. The second is more suitable for an academic audience.

The more formal diction of the second example is typical of what's called **standard English.** This is the written English normally expected and used in school, business, the professions, government, newspapers, and other sites where people of diverse backgrounds must communicate with one another. It is "standard" not because it is better than other forms of English, but because it is ac-

Two resources on choosing and using words:

http://www.uottawa.ca/academic/arts/writcent/hypergrammar/diction.html From the University of Ottawa.

http://www.unc.edu/depts/wcweb/handouts/style.html From the University of North Carolina.

Diction in academic and business writing

Always appropriate

Standard English (see facing page)

Sometimes appropriate

Regional words and expressions (p. 560)
Slang (p. 560)
Colloquial language (p. 561)
Neologisms (p. 562)
Technical language (p. 562)
Euphemisms (p. 562)

Rarely or never appropriate

Dialect (below)
Nonstandard language (below)
Archaic and obsolete words (p. 562)
Double talk (p. 563)
Pretentious writing (p. 563)
Biased language: sexist, racist, ethnocentric, etc. (p. 563)

cepted as the common language, much as dimes and quarters are accepted as the common currency.

The vocabulary of standard English is huge, allowing expression of an infinite range of ideas and feelings; but it does exclude words that only some groups of people use, understand, or find inoffensive. Some of those more limited vocabularies should be avoided altogether; others should be used cautiously and in special situations, as when aiming for a special effect with an audience you know will appreciate it. Whenever you doubt a word's status, consult a dictionary (see p. 591).

Note Many computerized grammar and style checkers can be set to flag potentially inappropriate words, such as nonstandard language, slang, colloquialisms, and gender-specific terms (*manmade, mailman*). However, the checker can flag only words listed in its dictionary. And you'll need to determine whether a flagged word is or is not appropriate for your writing situation, as explained below.

1 Revising dialect and nonstandard language

Like many countries, the United States consists of scores of regional, social, or ethnic groups with their own distinct **dialects,** or versions of English. Standard English is one of these dialects, and so are Black English, Appalachian English, Creole, and the English of coastal Maine. All the dialects of English share many features, but each also has its own vocabulary, pronunciation, and grammar.

If you speak a dialect of English besides standard English, you need to be careful about using your dialect in situations where standard English is the norm, such as in academic or business writing.

Otherwise, your readers may not understand your meaning, or they may perceive your usage as incorrect. (Dialects are not wrong in themselves, but forms imported from one dialect into another may still be perceived as wrong.)

Your participation in the community of standard English does not require you to abandon your own dialect. Of course, you will want to use it with others who speak it. You may want to quote it in an academic paper (as when analyzing or reporting conversation in dialect). And you may want to use it in writing you do for yourself, such as journals, notes, and drafts, which should be composed as freely as possible. But edit your academic papers carefully to eliminate dialect expressions, especially those, like the ones below, that dictionaries label "nonstandard":

> hisn, hern, hisself, theirselves
> them books, them courses
> this here school, that there building
> knowed, throwed, hadn't ought, could of
> didn't never, haven't no

2 Using regionalisms only when appropriate

Regionalisms are expressions or pronunciations peculiar to a particular area. Southerners may say they *reckon,* meaning "think" or "suppose." People in Maine invite their Boston friends to come *down* rather than *up* (north) to visit. New Yorkers stand *on* rather than *in* line for a movie.

Regional expressions are appropriate in writing addressed to local readers and may lend realism to regional description, but they should be avoided in writing intended for a general audience.

3 Using slang only when appropriate

All groups of people—from musicians and computer scientists to vegetarians and golfers—create novel and colorful expressions called **slang.** The following quotation, for instance, is from an essay on the slang of "skaters" (skateboarders):

> Curtis slashed ultra-punk crunchers on his longboard, while the Rube-man flailed his usual Gumbyness on tweaked frontsides and lofty fakie ollies. —MILES ORKIN, "Mucho Slingage by the Pool"

http://www.acusysinc.com/English/Slang.htm Advice on slang, from the Reference Guide to Grammar.

"Slang," Orkin goes on to say, "is a convenient, creative, mildly poetic, cohesive agent in many subcultures." It reflects the experiences of a group and binds its members.

Some slang gives new meaning to old words, such as *bad* for "good." Some slang comes from other languages, such as *chow* (food) from the Chinese *chao,* "to stir or fry." The slang of a particular group may also spread to other groups, as *put on ice, funky,* and *dis* have spread beyond their African American origins.

Among those who understand it, slang may be vivid and forceful. It often occurs in dialogue, and an occasional slang expression can enliven an informal essay. Some slang, such as *dropout* (*She was a high school dropout*), has proved so useful that it has passed into the general vocabulary.

But most slang is too flippant and imprecise for effective communication, and it is generally inappropriate for college or business writing. Notice the gain in seriousness and precision achieved in the following revision:

Slang Many students start out pretty together but then get weird.

Revised Many students start out with clear goals but then lose their direction.

4 Using colloquial language only when appropriate

Colloquial language designates the words and expressions appropriate to everyday spoken language. Regardless of our backgrounds and how we live, we all try to *get along with* each other. We play with *kids, go crazy* for something, and in our worst moments try to *get back at* someone who has made us do the *dirty work.*

When you write informally, colloquial language may be appropriate to achieve the casual, relaxed effect of conversation. An occasional colloquial word dropped into otherwise more formal writing can also help you achieve a desired emphasis. But colloquial language does not provide the exactness needed in more formal college, business, and professional writing. In such writing you should generally avoid any words and expressions labeled "informal" or "colloquial" in your dictionary. Take special care to avoid **mixed diction,** a combination of standard and colloquial words:

Mixed diction According to a Native American myth, the Great Creator had a dog hanging around with him when he created the earth.

http://www.acusysinc.com/English/Colloquialisms.htm Advice on colloquial language, from the Reference Guide to Grammar.

Revised According to a Native American myth, the Great Creator was accompanied by a dog when he created the earth.

5 Revising obsolete or archaic words and neologisms

Since our surroundings and our lives are constantly changing, some words pass out of use and others appear to fill new needs. **Obsolete** and **archaic** are dictionary labels for words or meanings of words that we never or rarely use but that appear in older documents and literature still read today. Obsolete words or meanings are no longer used at all—for example, *enwheel* ("to encircle") and *cote* ("to pass"). Archaic words or meanings occur now only in special contexts such as poetry—for example, *fast* ("near," as in *fast by the road*) and *belike* ("perhaps"). Both obsolete and archaic words are inappropriate in nonfiction writing for an academic audience.

Neologisms are words created (or coined) so recently that they have not come into established use. An example is *prequel* (made up of *pre-*, meaning "before," and the ending of *sequel*), a movie or book that takes the story of an existing movie or book back in time. Some neologisms do become accepted as part of our general vocabulary—*motel,* coined from *motor* and *hotel,* is an example. But most neologisms pass quickly from the language. Unless such words serve a special purpose in your writing and are sure to be understood by your readers, you should avoid them.

6 Using technical words with care

All disciplines and professions rely on special words or give common words special meanings. Chemists speak of *esters* and *phosphatides,* geographers and mapmakers refer to *isobars* and *isotherms,* and literary critics write about *motifs* and *subtexts.* Such technical language allows specialists to communicate precisely and economically with other specialists who share their vocabulary. But without explanation these words are meaningless to nonspecialists. When you are writing for nonspecialists, avoid unnecessary technical terms and carefully define terms you must use.

7 Revising indirect or pretentious writing

In most writing, small, plain, and direct words are preferable to big, showy, or evasive words. Avoid euphemisms, double talk, and pretentious writing.

A **euphemism** is a presumably inoffensive word that a writer or speaker substitutes for a word deemed potentially offensive or too blunt, such as *passed away* for *died.* Euphemisms appear whenever a writer or speaker wants to bury the truth, as when a governor mentions the *negative growth* (meaning "decline") in her state. Use euphemisms only when you know that blunt, truthful words would needlessly hurt or offend members of your audience.

A kind of euphemism that deliberately evades the truth is **double talk** (also called **doublespeak** or **weasel words**): language intended to confuse or to be misunderstood. Today double talk is unfortunately common in politics and advertising—the *revenue enhancement* that is really a tax, the *biodegradable* bags that last decades. Double talk has no place in honest writing.

Euphemism and sometimes double talk seem to keep company with fancy writing. Any writing that is more elaborate than its subject requires will sound **pretentious**—that is, excessively showy. Choose your words for their exactness and economy. The big, ornate word may be tempting, but pass it up. Your readers will be grateful.

Pretentious To perpetuate our endeavor of providing funds for our elderly citizens as we do at the present moment, we will face the exigency of enhanced contributions from all our citizens.

Revised We cannot continue to fund Social Security and Medicare for the elderly unless we raise taxes.

8 Revising sexist and other biased language

Even when we do not mean it to, our language can reflect and perpetuate hurtful prejudices toward groups of people, especially racial, ethnic, religious, age, and sexual groups. Such biased language can be obvious—words such as *nigger, honky, mick, kike, fag, dyke,* or *broad.* But it can also bc subtle, generalizing about groups in ways that may be familiar but that are also inaccurate or unfair. For instance, people with physical disabilities are as varied a group as any other: the only thing they have in common is some form of impairment. To assume that people with disabilities share certain attitudes (shyness, helplessness, victimization, whatever) is to disregard the uniqueness of each person.

Biased language reflects poorly on the user, not on the person or persons whom it mischaracterizes or insults. Unbiased language does not submit to false generalizations. It treats people as individuals and labels groups as they wish to be labeled.

http://webster.commnet.edu/HP/pages/darling/grammar/unbiased.htm Advice on using unbiased language, from the Guide to Grammar and Writing.

http://owl.english.purdue.edu/Files/26.html Advice on avoiding sexist language, from the Purdue Online Writing Lab.

Avoiding stereotypes of race, ethnicity, religion, age, and other characteristics

A **stereotype** is a generalization based on poor evidence, a kind of formula for understanding and judging people simply because of their membership in a group:

> Men are uncommunicative.
> Women are emotional.
> Liberals want to raise taxes.
> Conservatives are affluent.

At best, stereotypes betray an uncritical writer, one who is not thinking beyond notions received from others. Worse, they betray a writer who does not mind hurting others, or even *wants* to hurt others.

In your writing, be alert for any general statements about people based on only one or a few characteristics. Be especially cautious about substituting such statements for the evidence you should be providing instead.

Stereotype Immigrants live off the taxes of citizens. [Asserts that all immigrants live on public assistance funded by taxes.]

Revised In 1991 immigrants received $50.8 billion in public assistance and paid $20.3 billion in taxes.

Stereotype Elderly drivers should have their licenses limited to daytime driving. [Implies that all elderly people are poor night drivers.]

Revised Drivers with impaired night vision should have their licenses limited to daytime driving.

Some stereotypes have become part of the language, but they are still potentially offensive.

Stereotype The administrators are too blind to see the need for a new gymnasium.

Revised The administrators do not understand the need for a new gymnasium.

Avoiding sexist language

Among the most subtle and persistent biased language is that expressing narrow ideas about men's and women's roles, position, and value in society. This **sexist language** distinguishes needlessly between men and women in such matters as occupation, ability, behavior, temperament, and maturity. Like other stereotypes, it can wound or irritate readers, and it indicates the writer's thoughtlessness or unfairness. The following box suggests some ways of eliminating sexist language:

Eliminating sexist language

- Avoid demeaning and patronizing language—for instance, identifying women and men differently or trivializing either gender:

  Sexist Dr. Keith Kim and Lydia Hawkins wrote the article.
  Revised Dr. Keith Kim and Dr. Lydia Hawkins wrote the article.
  Revised Keith Kim and Lydia Hawkins wrote the article.

  Sexist Ladies are entering formerly male occupations.
  Revised Women are entering formerly male occupations.

- Avoid occupational or social stereotypes, assuming that a role or profession is exclusively male or female:

  Sexist The considerate doctor commends a nurse when she provides his patients with good care.
  Revised The considerate doctor commends a nurse who provides good care for patients.

- Avoid using *man* or words containing *man* to refer to all human beings. Some alternatives:

businessman	businessperson
chairman	chair, chairperson
congressman	representative in Congress, legislator
craftsman	craftsperson, artisan
layman	layperson
mankind	humankind, humanity, human beings, people
policeman	police officer
salesman	salesperson, sales representative

  Sexist Man has not reached the limits of social justice.
  Revised Humankind [or Humanity] has not reached the limits of social justice.

  Sexist The furniture consists of manmade materials.
  Revised The furniture consists of synthetic materials.

- Avoid the **generic *he*,** the male pronoun used to refer to both genders. (See also p. 344.)

  Sexist The newborn child explores his world.
  Revised Newborn children explore their world. [Use the plural for the pronoun and the word it refers to.]
  Revised The newborn child explores the world. [Avoid the pronoun altogether.]
  Revised The newborn child explores his or her world. [Substitute male and female pronouns.]

  Use the last option sparingly—only once in a group of sentences and only to stress the singular individual.

Using appropriate labels

We often need to label groups: *swimmers, politicians, mothers, Christians, westerners, students.* But labels can be shorthand stereotypes when they generalize about groups of people on the basis of a single characteristic. They can also slight the person labeled and ignore the preferences of the group members themselves. Showing sensitivity when applying labels reveals you to be alert to readers' needs and concerns. Although sometimes dismissed as "political correctness," such sensitivity hurts no one and helps gain your readers' trust and respect.

- Be careful to avoid labels that (intentionally or not) disparage the person or group you refer to. A person with emotional problems is not a *mental patient.* A person with cancer is not a *cancer victim.* A person using a wheelchair is not *wheelchair-bound.*
- Use names for racial, ethnic, and other groups that reflect the preferences of each group's members, or at least many of them. Examples of current preferences include *African American* or *black, latino/latina* (for Americans and American immigrants of Spanish-speaking descent), and *disabled* (rather than *handicapped*). But labels change often. To learn how a group's members wish to be labeled, ask them directly, attend to usage in reputable periodicals, or check a recent dictionary. A helpful reference is Marilyn Schwartz's *Guidelines for Bias-Free Writing* (1995).

EXERCISE 1
Revising: Appropriate words

Rewrite the following sentences as needed for standard written English. Consult a dictionary to determine whether particular words are appropriate and to find suitable substitutes.

Example:

If negotiators get hyper during contract discussions, they may mess up chances for a settlement.

If negotiators <u>become excited or upset</u> during contract discussions, they may <u>harm</u> chances for a settlement.

1. Acquired immune deficiency syndrome (AIDS) is a major deal all over the world.
2. The disease gets around primarily by sexual intercourse, exchange of bodily fluids, shared needles, and blood transfusions.
3. Those who think the disease is limited to homos and druggies are quite mistaken.
4. Stats suggest that one in every five hundred college kids carries the virus.
5. A person with AIDS does not deserve to be subjected to exclusionary behavior or callousness on the part of his fellow citizens. Instead, he has the necessity for all the compassion, med-

ical care, and financial assistance due those who are in the extremity of illness.

6. An AIDS victim often sees a team of doctors or a single doctor with a specialized practice.
7. The doctor may help his patients by obtaining social services for them as well as by providing medical care.
8. The AIDS sufferer who loses his job may need public assistance.
9. For someone who is very ill, a full-time nurse may be necessary. She can administer medications and make the sick person as comfortable as possible.
10. Some people with AIDS have insurance, but others lack the bread for premiums.

38b Choosing the exact word

To write clearly and effectively, you will want to find the words that fit your meaning exactly and convey your attitude precisely. If, like many people, you feel uncertain about words and their meanings, consult the next two chapters, on using a dictionary (39) and improving your vocabulary (40).

Don't worry too much about choosing exact words while you are drafting an essay. If the right word doesn't come to you, leave a blank. Revision (p. 52) or editing (p. 60) is the stage to consider tone, specificity, and precision.

Note A computerized grammar and style checker can provide some help with inexact language. For instance, you can set it to flag commonly confused words (such as *continuous/continual*), misused prepositions in idioms (such as *accuse for* instead of *accuse of*), and clichés. But the checker can flag only words stored in its dictionary. It can't help you at all with using words that have appropriate connotations, making abstract words concrete, or solving other problems discussed in this section. You'll need to read your work carefully on your own.

1 Using the right word for your meaning

Precisely expressing your meaning requires understanding both the denotations and the connotations of words. A word's **denotation** is the thing or idea it refers to, the meaning listed in the dictionary without reference to the emotional associations it may arouse in a reader.

Information on denotation and connotation:

http://www.uottawa.ca/academic/arts/writcent/hypergrammar/conndeno.html From the University of Ottawa.

http://www.esc.edu/htmlpages/writer/style1.htm#denot From the State University of New York.

Using words according to their established denotations is essential if readers are to grasp your meaning. Here are a few guidelines:

- Become acquainted with a dictionary. Consult it whenever you are unsure of a word's meaning.
- Distinguish between similar-sounding words that have widely different denotations:

  Inexact Older people often suffer infirmaries [places for the sick].

  Exact Older people often suffer infirmities [disabilities].

  Some words, called **homonyms** (from the Greek meaning "same name"), sound exactly alike but differ in meaning: for example, *principal/principle* or *rain/reign/rein.* (See pp. 604–05 for a list of commonly confused homonyms.)
- Distinguish between words with related but distinct denotations:

  Inexact Television commercials continuously [unceasingly] interrupt programming.

  Exact Television commercials continually [regularly] interrupt programming.

In addition to their emotion-free denotations, many words also carry associations with specific feelings. These **connotations** can shape readers' responses and are thus a powerful tool for writers. (At the same time they are a potential snare for readers. See p. 151.) Some connotations are personal: the word *dog,* for instance, may have negative connotations for the letter carrier who has been bitten three times. Usually, though, people agree about connotations. The following word pairs are just a few of many that have related denotations but very different connotations:

pride: sense of self-worth
vanity: excessive regard for oneself

firm: steady, unchanging, unyielding
stubborn: unreasonable, bullheaded

lasting: long-lived, enduring
endless: without limit, eternal

enthusiasm: excitement
mania: excessive interest or desire

Understanding connotation is especially important in choosing among **synonyms,** words with approximately, but often not exactly, the same meanings. For instance, *cry* and *weep* both denote the shedding of tears, but *cry* more than *weep* connotes a sobbing sound accompanying the tears. *Sob* itself connotes broken, gasping crying, with tears, whereas *wail* connotes sustained sound, perhaps without tears.

Several resources can help you track down words with the exact connotations you want:

- A dictionary is essential. Many dictionaries list and distinguish among synonyms (see p. 602 for an example).
- A dictionary of synonyms lists and defines synonyms in groups (see p. 589 for a title).
- A thesaurus lists synonyms but does not distinguish among them (see p. 589 for a title).

Note Because a thesaurus lacks definitions, it can only suggest possibilities. You will still need a dictionary to discover the words' exact denotations and connotations. Many computer programs offer thesauruses that make it easy to look up synonyms as you're writing and to insert the chosen word into your text. But with a computerized thesaurus, too, you must choose the word carefully to ensure that it expresses your meaning exactly. If you use such a resource without care, you risk losing your reader's understanding and patience. (See p. 189 for more on electronic thesauruses.)

EXERCISE 2
Revising: Denotation

Revise any underlined word below that is not used according to its established denotation. Circle any word used correctly. Consult a dictionary if you are uncertain of a word's precise meaning.

Example:

Sam and Dave are going to Bermuda and Hauppauge, respectfully, for spring vacation.

Sam and Dave are going to Bermuda and Hauppauge, respectively, for spring vacation.

1. Maxine Hong Kingston was rewarded many prizes for her first two books, *The Woman Warrior* and *China Men*.
2. Kingston sites her mother's tales about ancestors and ancient Chinese customs as the sources of these memoirs.
3. In her childhood Kingston was greatly effected by her mother's tale about a pregnant aunt who was ostracized by villagers.
4. The aunt gained avengeance by drowning herself in the village's water supply.
5. Kingston decided to make her nameless relative infamous by giving her immortality in *The Woman Warrior*.

EXERCISE 3
Considering the connotations of words

Fill the blank in each sentence below with the most appropriate word from the list in parentheses. Consult a dictionary to be sure of your choice.

Example:

Channel 5 _______ Oshu the winner before the polls closed. (*advertised, declared, broadcast, promulgated*)

Channel 5 declared Oshu the winner before the polls closed.

1. AIDS is a serious health ______. (*problem, worry, difficulty, plight*)
2. Once the virus has entered the blood system, it ______ T-cells. (*murders, destroys, slaughters, executes*)
3. The ______ of T-cells is to combat infections. (*ambition, function, aim, goal*)
4. Without enough T-cells, the body is nearly ______ against infections. (*defenseless, hopeless, desperate*)
5. To prevent exposure to the disease, one should be especially ______ in sexual relationships. (*chary, circumspect, cautious, calculating*)

2 Balancing the abstract and concrete, the general and specific

To understand a subject as you understand it, your readers need ample guidance from your words. When you describe a building as beautiful and nothing more, you force readers to provide their own conceptions of the features that make a building beautiful. If readers bother (and they may not), they surely will not conjure up the image you had in mind. You'll be much more likely to achieve your purpose if you tell readers what you want them to know, that the beautiful building is *a sleek, silver skyscraper with blue-tinted windows,* for instance, or *a Victorian brick courthouse with tall, arched windows.*

Clear, exact writing balances abstract and general words, which outline ideas and objects, with concrete and specific words, which sharpen and solidify.

- **Abstract words** name qualities and ideas: *beauty, inflation, management, culture, liberal.* **Concrete words** name things we can know by our five senses of sight, hearing, touch, taste, and smell: *sleek, humming, brick, bitter, musty.*
- **General words** name classes or groups of things, such as *buildings, weather,* or *birds,* and include all the varieties of the class. **Specific words** limit a general class, such as *buildings,* by naming one of its varieties, such as *skyscraper, Victorian courthouse,* or *hut.*

Note that *general* and *specific* are relative terms: the same word may be more general than some words but more specific than others.

Abstract and general words are useful in the broad statements that set the course for your writing:

The wild horse in America has a romantic history.

We must be free from government interference in our affairs.

Relations between the sexes today are only a little more relaxed than they were in the past.

But the sentences following these would have to develop the ideas with concrete and specific details. When your meaning calls for an abstract or general word, make sure you define it, explain it, and narrow it. Look at how concrete and specific information turns vague sentences into exact ones in the examples below:

Vague The size of his hands made his smallness real. [How big were his hands? How small was he?]

Exact Not until I saw his delicate, doll-like hands did I realize that he stood a full head shorter than most other men.

Vague The long flood caused a lot of awful destruction in the town. [How long did the flood last? What destruction did it cause? Why was the destruction awful?]

Exact The flood waters, which rose swiftly and then stayed stubbornly high for days, killed at least six townspeople and made life a misery for the hundreds who had to evacuate their ruined homes and stores.

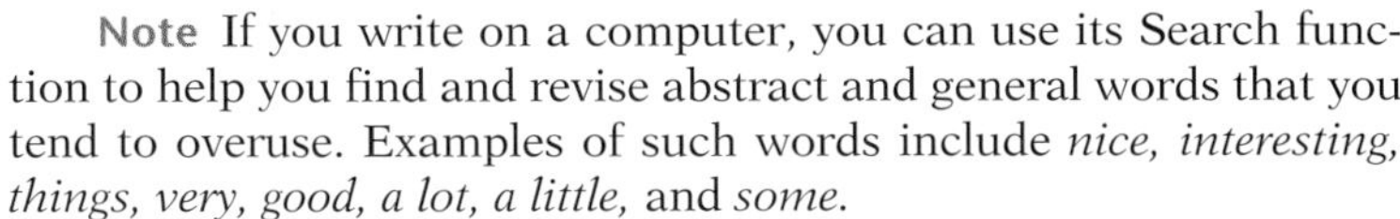

Note If you write on a computer, you can use its Search function to help you find and revise abstract and general words that you tend to overuse. Examples of such words include *nice, interesting, things, very, good, a lot, a little,* and *some.*

EXERCISE 4
Revising: Concrete and specific words

Make the following paragraph vivid by expanding the sentences with appropriate details of your own choosing. Substitute concrete and specific words for the abstract and general ones that are underlined.

I remember clearly how awful I felt the first time I attended Mrs. Murphy's second-grade class. I had recently moved from a small town in Missouri to a crowded suburb of Chicago. My new school looked big from the outside and seemed dark inside as I walked down the long corridor toward the classroom. The class was noisy as I neared the door; but when I entered, everyone became quiet and looked at me. I felt uncomfortable and wanted a place to hide. However, in a loud voice Mrs. Murphy directed me to the front of the room to introduce myself.

EXERCISE 5
Using concrete and specific words

For each abstract or general word below, give at least two other words or phrases that illustrate increasing specificity or concreteness. Consult a dictionary as needed. Use the most specific or concrete word from each group in a sentence of your own.

exact 38b

Example:

tired, sleepy, droopy-eyed

We stopped for the night when I became so droopy-eyed that the road blurred.

1. fabric
2. delicious
3. car
4. narrow-minded
5. reach (*verb*)
6. green
7. walk (*verb*)
8. flower
9. serious
10. pretty
11. teacher
12. nice
13. virtue
14. angry
15. crime

3 Using idioms

Idioms are expressions in any language whose meanings cannot be determined simply from the words in them or whose component words cannot be predicted by any rule of grammar; often, they violate conventional grammar. Examples of English idioms include *put up with, plug away at,* and *make off with.*

Idiomatic combinations of verbs or adjectives and prepositions can be confusing for both native and nonnative speakers of English. A number of these pairings are listed in the box opposite.

ESL If you are learning English as a second language, you are justified in stumbling over its prepositions because their meanings can shift depending on context and because they have so many idiomatic uses. In mastering English prepositions, you probably can't avoid memorization. But you can help yourself by memorizing related groups, such as those below.

At/in/on in expressions of time

Use *at* before actual clock time: at 8:30. Use *in* before a month, year, century, or period: *in April, in 1985, in the twenty-first century, in the next month*. Use *on* before a day or date: *on Tuesday, on August 3, on my daughter's birthday*.

At/in/on in expressions of place

Use *at* before a specific place or address: *at the school, at 511 Iris Street.* Use *in* before a place with limits or before a city, state, country, or continent: *in the house, in a box, in Oklahoma City, in China.* Use *on* to mean "supported by" or "touching the surface of": *on the table, on Iris Street, on page 150.*

http://members.home.net/kayem/idioms/idioms.html Information and exercises on idioms, from English-Zone.Com.

http://www.aitech.ac.jp/~iteslj/quizzes/idioms.html Quizzes on idioms, two-word verbs, and slang, from the *Internet TESL Journal.*

Idioms with prepositions

abide by a rule
abide in a place or state
accords with
according to
accuse of a crime
adapt from a source
adapt to a situation
afraid of
agree on a plan
agree to a proposal
agree with a person
angry with
aware of
based on
capable of
certain of
charge for a purchase
charge with a crime
concur in an opinion
concur with a person
contend for a principle
contend with a person
dependent on
differ about or over a question
differ from in some quality
differ with a person
disappointed by or in a person
disappointed in or with a thing
familiar with
identical with or to
impatient at her conduct
impatient of restraint
impatient for a raise
impatient with a person
independent of
infer from
inferior to
involved in a task
involved with a person
oblivious of or to one's surroundings
oblivious of something forgotten
occupied by a person
occupied in study
occupied with a thing
opposed to
part from a person
part with a possession
prior to
proud of
related to
rewarded by the judge
rewarded for something done
rewarded with a gift
similar to
superior to
wait at a place
wait for a train, a person
wait on a customer

For/since in expressions of time

Use *for* before a period of time: *for an hour, for two years.* Use *since* before a specific point in time: *since 1995, since yesterday.*

A good ESL dictionary is the best source for the meanings of prepositions; see the recommendations on page 587. In addition, some references focus on prepositions. One is *Oxford Dictionary of Current Idiomatic English,* volume 1: *Verbs with Prepositions and Particles.*

EXERCISE 6
Using prepositions in idioms

Insert the preposition that correctly completes each idiom in the following sentences. Consult the box on the previous page or a dictionary as needed.

Example:

I disagree _______ many feminists who say women should not be homemakers.

I disagree with many feminists who say women should not be homemakers.

1. As Mark and Lana waited _______ the justice of the peace, they seemed oblivious _______ the other people in the lobby.
2. But Mark inferred _______ Lana's glance at a handsome man that she was no longer occupied _______ him alone.
3. Angry _______ Lana, Mark charged her _______ not loving him enough to get married.
4. Impatient _______ Mark's childish behavior, Lana disagreed _______ his interpretation of her glance.
5. They decided that if they could differ so violently _______ a minor incident, they should part _______ each other.

4 Using figurative language

Figurative language (or a **figure of speech**) departs from the literal meanings (the denotations) of words, usually by comparing very different ideas or objects:

Literal	As I try to write, I can think of nothing to say.
Figurative	As I try to write, my mind is a slab of black slate.

Imaginatively and carefully used, figurative language can capture meaning more precisely and feelingly than literal language.

Figurative language is commonplace in speech. Having *slept like a log,* you may get up to find it *raining cats and dogs* and to discover that the Yankees *shelled* the Royals last night. But the rapid exchange of speech leaves little time for inventiveness, and most figures of daily conversation, like those above, are worn and hackneyed. Writing gives you time to reject the tired figure and to search out fresh, concrete words and phrases.

The two most common figures of speech are the simile and the metaphor. Both compare two things of different classes, often one abstract and the other concrete. A **simile** makes the comparison explicit and usually begins with *like* or *as:*

> Whenever we grow, we tend to feel it, as a young seed must feel the weight and inertia of the earth when it seeks to break out of its shell on its way to becoming a plant. —Alice Walker

> To hold America in one's thoughts is <u>like</u> holding a love letter in one's hand—it has so special a meaning. —E. B. WHITE

Instead of stating a comparison, a **metaphor** implies it, omitting such words as *like* or *as:*

> I cannot and will not cut my conscience to fit this year's fashions. —LILLIAN HELLMAN

> A school is a hopper into which children are heaved while they are young and tender; therein they are pressed into certain standard shapes and covered from head to heels with official rubber stamps. —H. L. MENCKEN

Two other figures of speech are personification and hyperbole. **Personification** treats ideas and objects as if they were human:

> The economy consumes my money and gives me little in return.
>
> I could hear the whisper of snowflakes, nudging each other as they fell.

Hyperbole deliberately exaggerates:

> She appeared in a mile of billowing chiffon, flashing a rhinestone as big as an ostrich egg.
>
> I'm going to cut him up in small cubes and fry him in deep fat.

To be successful, figurative language must be fresh and unstrained, calling attention not to itself but to the writer's meaning. If readers reject your language as trite or overblown, they may reject your message. One kind of figurative language gone wrong is the **mixed metaphor,** in which the writer combines two or more incompatible figures. Since metaphors often generate visual images in the reader's mind, a mixed metaphor can be laughable:

Mixed Various thorny problems that we try to sweep under the rug continue to bob up all the same.

To revise a mixed metaphor, follow through consistently with just one image:

Improved Various thorny problems that we try to weed out continue to thrive all the same.

EXERCISE 7
Analyzing figurative language

Identify each figure of speech in the following sentences as a simile or a metaphor, and analyze how it contributes to the writer's meaning.

1. A distant airplane, a delta wing out of nightmare, made a gliding shadow on the creek's bottom that looked like a stingray crossing upstream. —ANNIE DILLARD

2. Her roots ran deep into the earth, and from those roots she drew strength enough to hold still against all the forces of chance and disorder. —N. Scott Momaday
3. As a member of the winning team (the graduating class of 1940) I had outdistanced unpleasant sensations by miles. I was headed for the freedom of open fields. —Maya Angelou
4. All artists quiver under the lash of adverse criticism. —Catherine Drinker Bowen
5. Every writer, in a roomful of writers, wants to be the best, and the judge, or umpire, or referee is soon overwhelmed and shouted down like a chickadee trying to take charge of a caucus of crows. —James Thurber

EXERCISE 8
Using figurative language

Invent appropriate figurative language of your own (simile, metaphor, hyperbole, or personification) to describe each scene or quality below, and use the figure in a sentence.

Example:

The attraction of a lake on a hot day
The small waves like fingers beckoned us irresistibly.

1. The sound of a kindergarten classroom
2. People waiting in line to buy tickets to a rock concert
3. The politeness of strangers meeting for the first time
4. A streetlight seen through dense fog
5. The effect of watching television for ten hours straight

5 Using fresh expressions

Trite expressions, or **clichés,** are phrases so old and so often repeated that they have become stale. They include the following:

acid test
add insult to injury
better late than never
beyond the shadow of a doubt
brought back to reality
cold, hard facts
cool, calm, and collected
cool as a cucumber
crushing blow
dyed in the wool
easier said than done
face the music
flat as a pancake
gentle as a lamb
green with envy
hard as a rock
heavy as lead
hit the nail on the head
hour of need
ladder of success

http://webster.commnet.edu/HP/pages/darling/grammar/concise.htm#cliches Information on clichés, with links to lists, from the Guide to Grammar and Writing.

moving experience
needle in a haystack
nose to the grindstone
nutty as a fruitcake
point with pride
ripe old age
sadder but wiser
shoulder the burden
smart as a whip
sneaking suspicion
sober as a judge
stand in awe
strong as an ox
thin as a rail
tired but happy
tried and true
untimely death
wise as an owl

Besides these old phrases, stale writing may also depend on fashionable words that are losing their effect: for instance, *lifestyle, enhance, excellent, fantastic,* and *caring.*

Many of these expressions were once fresh and forceful, but constant use has dulled them. They, in turn, will dull your writing by suggesting that you have not thought about what you are saying and have resorted to the easiest phrase.

Clichés may slide into your drafts while you are trying to express your meaning. In editing, then, be wary of any expression you have heard or used before. Substitute fresh words of your own or restate the idea in plain language:

Trite A healthful lifestyle enhances your ability to go for the gold, allows you to enjoy life to the fullest, and helps you live to a ripe old age.

Revised Living healthfully helps you perform well, enjoy life thoroughly, and live long.

EXERCISE 9
Revising: Trite expressions

Revise the following sentences to eliminate trite expressions.

Example:

The basketball team had almost seized victory, but it faced the test of truth in the last quarter of the game.

The basketball team seemed about to win, but the real test came in the last quarter of the game.

1. The disastrous consequences of the war have shaken the small nation to its roots.
2. Prices for food have shot sky high, and citizens have sneaking suspicions that others are making a killing on the black market.
3. Medical supplies are so few and far between that even civilians who are as sick as dogs cannot get treatment.
4. With most men fighting or injured or killed, women have had to bite the bullet and bear the men's burden in farming and manufacturing.
5. Last but not least, the war's heavy drain on the nation's pocketbook has left the economy in a shambles.

38c Writing concisely

Concise writing makes every word count. Conciseness is not the same as mere brevity: detail and originality should not be cut with needless words. Rather, the length of an expression should be appropriate to the thought.

You may find yourself writing wordily when you are unsure of your subject or when your thoughts are tangled. It's fine, even necessary, to stumble and grope while drafting. But you should straighten out your ideas and eliminate wordiness during revision and editing.

Note Computerized grammar and style checkers will identify at least some wordy structures, such as repeated words, weak verbs, passive voice, and *there is* and *it is* constructions. No checker can identify all these structures, however, nor can it tell you whether the structure is appropriate for your ideas. In short, a checker can't substitute for your own careful reading and editing.

ESL As you'll see in the examples that follow, wordiness is not a problem of incorrect grammar. A sentence may be perfectly grammatical but still contain unneeded words that interfere with your idea.

1 Focusing on the subject and verb

Using the subjects and verbs of your sentences for the key actors and actions will reduce words and emphasize important ideas. (See pp. 419–20 for more on this topic.)

Wordy The reason why most of the country shifts to daylight savings time is that winter days are much shorter than summer days.

Concise Most of the country shifts to daylight savings time because winter days are much shorter than summer days.

Focusing on subjects and verbs will also help you avoid several other causes of wordiness (also discussed further on pages 419–20):

Advice on writing concisely:

http://webster.commnet.edu/HP/pages/darling/grammar/concise.htm From the Guide to Grammar and Writing.

http://leo.stcloudstate.edu/style/wordiness.html From St. Cloud State University.

http://www.acusysinc.com/English/Wordiness.htm From the Reference Guide to Grammar.

http://owl.english.purdue.edu/Files/127.html From the Purdue Online Writing Lab.

Ways to achieve conciseness

Wordy (87 words)

The highly pressured nature of critical-care nursing is due to the fact that the patients have life-threatening illnesses. Critical-care nurses must have possession of steady nerves to care for patients who are critically ill and very sick. The nurses must also have possession of interpersonal skills. They must also have medical skills. It is considered by most health-care professionals that these nurses are essential if there is to be improvement of patients who are now in critical care from that status to the status of intermediate care.

- Focus on subject and verb (facing page), and cut or shorten empty words and phrases (p. 580).
- Avoid nouns made from verbs (below).
- Cut unneeded repetition (p. 581).
- Combine sentences (p. 583).
- Change passive voice to active voice (below).
- Eliminate *there is* constructions (p. 583).
- Cut unneeded repetition (p. 581), and reduce clauses and phrases (p. 583).

Concise (37 words)

Critical-care nursing is highly pressured because the patients have life-threatening illnesses. Critical-care nurses must possess steady nerves and interpersonal and medical skills. Most health-care professionals consider these nurses essential if patients are to improve to intermediate care.

Nouns made from verbs

Wordy The occurrence of the winter solstice, the shortest day of the year, is an event occurring about December 22.

Concise The winter solstice, the shortest day of the year, occurs about December 22.

Weak verbs

Wordy The earth's axis has a tilt as the planet is in orbit around the sun so that the northern and southern hemispheres are alternately in alignment toward the sun.

Concise The earth's axis tilts as the planet orbits around the sun so that the northern and southern hemispheres alternately align toward the sun.

Passive voice

Wordy During its winter the northern hemisphere is tilted farthest away from the sun, so the nights are made longer and the days are made shorter.

Concise During its winter the northern hemisphere tilts away from the sun, making the nights longer and the days shorter.

See also pages 330–31 on changing the passive voice to the active voice, as in the example above.

2 Cutting or shortening empty words and phrases

Empty words and phrases walk in place, gaining little or nothing in meaning. Shorten them to their essential meaning, or cut them entirely. Your writing will move faster and work harder.

Many empty phrases can be cut entirely:

all things considered	in a manner of speaking
as far as I'm concerned	in my opinion
for all intents and purposes	last but not least
for the most part	more or less

Wordy As far as I am concerned, discrimination against women continues to exist in medicine for all intents and purposes.

Revised Discrimination against women continues in medicine.

Other empty words can be cut along with some of the words around them:

angle	character	kind	situation
area	element	manner	thing
aspect	factor	nature	type
case	field		

Wordy The type of large expenditures on advertising that manufacturers must make is a very important aspect of the cost of detergents.

Concise Manufacturers' large advertising expenditures increase the cost of detergents.

Still other empty phrases can be reduced from several words to a single word:

For	Substitute
at all times	always
at the present time	now
at this point in time	now
in the nature of	like
for the purpose of	for
in order to	to
until such time as	until
for the reason that	because
due to the fact that	because
because of the fact that	because
by virtue of the fact that	because
in the event that	if
by means of	by
in the final analysis	finally

Wordy At this point in time, the software is expensive due to the fact that it has no competition.

Revised The software is expensive now because it has no competition.

EXERCISE 10
Revising: Subjects and verbs; empty words and phrases

Revise the following sentences to achieve conciseness by focusing on subjects and verbs and by cutting or reducing empty words and phrases. (See p. 420 for an additional exercise in focusing on subjects and verbs.)

Example:

I made college my destination because of many factors, but most of all because of the fact that I want a career in medicine.

I came to college mainly because I want a career in medicine.

1. *Gerrymandering* refers to a situation in which the lines of a voting district are redrawn so that a particular party or ethnic group has benefits.
2. The name is a reference to the fact that Elbridge Gerry, the governor of Massachusetts in 1812, redrew voting districts in Essex County.
3. On the map one new district was seen to resemble something in the nature of a salamander.
4. Upon seeing the map, a man who was for all intents and purposes a critic of Governor Gerry's administration cried out, "Gerrymander!"
5. At the present time, changes may be made in the character of a district's voting pattern by a political group by gerrymandering to achieve the exclusion of rival groups' supporters.

3 Cutting unnecessary repetition

Planned repetition and restatement can make writing more coherent (p. 86) or emphatic (p. 425). But unnecessary repetition weakens sentences:

Wordy Many unskilled workers without training in a particular job are unemployed and do not have any work.

Concise Many unskilled workers are unemployed.

The use of one word two different ways within a sentence is confusing:

Confusing Preschool instructors play a role in the child's understanding of male and female roles.

Clear Preschool instructors contribute to the child's understanding of male and female roles.

The simplest kind of useless repetition is the phrase that says the same thing twice. In the following examples, the unneeded words are underlined:

biography of his life	habitual custom
circle around	important [basic] essentials
consensus of opinion	large in size
continue on	puzzling in nature
cooperate together	repeat again
few in number	return again
final completion	revert back
frank and honest exchange	square [round] in shape
the future to come	surrounding circumstances

ESL Phrases like those above are redundant because the main word already implies the underlined word or words. The repetition is not emphatic but tedious. A dictionary will tell you what meanings a word implies. *Assassinate,* for instance, means "murder someone well known," so the following sentence is redundant: *Julius Caesar was assassinated and killed.*

EXERCISE 11
Revising: Unnecessary repetition

Revise the following sentences to achieve conciseness. Concentrate on eliminating repetition and redundancy.

Example:

Because the circumstances surrounding the cancellation of classes were murky and unclear, the editor of the student newspaper assigned a staff reporter to investigate and file a report on the circumstances.

Because the circumstances leading to the cancellation of classes were unclear, the editor of the student newspaper assigned a staffer to investigate and report the story.

1. Some Vietnam veterans coming back to the United States after their tours of duty in Vietnam had problems readjusting again to life in America.
2. Afflicted with post-traumatic stress disorder, a psychological disorder that sometimes arises after a trauma, some veterans had psychological problems that caused them to have trouble holding jobs and maintaining relationships.
3. Some who used to use drugs in Vietnam could not break their drug habits after they returned back to the United States.
4. The few veterans who committed crimes and violent acts gained so much notoriety and fame that many Americans thought all veterans were crazy, insane maniacs.
5. As a result of such stereotyping of Vietnam-era veterans, veterans are included into the same antidiscrimination laws that protect other victims of discrimination.

4 Reducing clauses to phrases, phrases to single words

Modifiers—subordinate clauses, phrases, and single words—can be expanded or contracted depending on the emphasis you want to achieve. (See pp. 266–81 on phrases and clauses and 434–36 on working with modifiers.) When editing your sentences, consider whether any modifiers can be reduced without loss of emphasis or clarity:

Wordy The Channel Tunnel, which runs between Britain and France, bores through a bed of solid chalk that is twenty-three miles across.

Concise The Channel Tunnel between Britain and France bores through twenty-three miles of solid chalk.

5 Eliminating *there is* and *it is* constructions

You can postpone the sentence subject with the words *there is* (*there are, there was, there were*) and *it is* (*it was*). (See p. 288.) These constructions can be useful to emphasize the subject (as when introducing it for the first time) or to indicate a change in direction. But often they just add words and create limp substitutes for more vigorous sentences:

Wordy There were delays and cost overruns that plagued the tunnel's builders. It was a fear of investors that they would not earn profits once the tunnel opened.

Concise Delays and cost overruns plagued the tunnel's builders. Investors feared that they would not earn profits once the tunnel opened.

6 Combining sentences

Often the information in two or more sentences can be combined into one tight sentence:

Wordy So far, business has been disappointing. Fewer travelers than were expected have boarded the tunnel train. The train runs between London and Paris.

Concise So far, business has been disappointing, with fewer travelers than expected boarding the tunnel train that runs between London and Paris.

A number of exercises in this handbook give you practice in sentence combining. For a list, see "Sentence combining" in the Index.

http://leo.stcloudstate.edu/style/sentencev.html Advice on combining sentences, from St. Cloud State University.

7 Rewriting jargon

Jargon can refer to the special vocabulary of any discipline or profession (see p. 562). But it has also come to describe vague, inflated language that is overcomplicated, even incomprehensible. When it comes from government or business, we call it *bureaucratese.* It sounds almost as if the writer deliberately ignored every suggestion for clear, concise writing:

Jargon The necessity for individuals to become separate entities in their own right may impel children to engage in open rebelliousness against parental authority or against sibling influence, with resultant confusion of those being rebelled against.

Translation Children's natural desire to become themselves may make them rebel against bewildered parents or siblings.

Jargon The weekly social gatherings stimulate networking among members of management from various divisions, with the aim of developing contacts and maximizing the flow of creative information.

Translation The weekly parties give managers from different divisions a chance to meet and to share ideas.

EXERCISE 12
Revising: Conciseness

Rewrite each passage below into a single concise sentence, using the techniques described in this chapter.

Example:

He was taking some exercise in the park. Then several thugs were suddenly ahead in his path.

He was exercising [or jogging or strolling] in the park when several thugs suddenly loomed in his path.

1. Chewing gum was originally introduced to the United States by Antonio López de Santa Anna. He was the Mexican general.
2. After he had been defeated by the Texans in 1845, the general, who was exiled, made the choice to settle in New York.
3. A piece of chicle had been stashed by the general in his baggage. Chicle is the dried milky sap of the Mexican sapodilla tree.
4. There was more of this resin brought into the country by Santa Anna's friend Thomas Adams. Adams had a plan to make rubber.
5. The plan failed. Then the occasion arose for Adams to get a much more successful idea on the basis of the use to which the resin was put by General Santa Anna. That is, Adams decided to make a gum that could be chewed.

http://www.clearcf.uvic.ca/writersguide/Pages/SentJarg.html Advice on avoiding jargon, from the University of Victoria.

EXERCISE 13
Revising: Conciseness

Make the following passage as concise as possible. Be merciless.

At the end of a lengthy line of reasoning, he came to the conclusion that the situation with carcinogens [cancer-causing substances] should be regarded as similar to the situation with the automobile. Instead of giving in to an irrational fear of cancer, we should consider all aspects of the problem in a balanced and dispassionate frame of mind, making a total of the benefits received from potential carcinogens (plastics, pesticides, and other similar products) and measuring said total against the damage done by such products. This is the nature of most discussions about the automobile. Instead of responding irrationally to the visual, aural, and air pollution caused by automobiles, we have decided to live with them (while simultaneously working to improve on them) for the benefits brought to society as a whole.

CHAPTER 39

Using Dictionaries

A dictionary can answer most of the questions about words you may ask. This chapter will show you how to choose a dictionary that suits your purpose and how to read a dictionary without difficulty.

39a Choosing a dictionary

1 Abridged dictionaries

Abridged dictionaries are the most practical for everyday use. Often called desk dictionaries because of their convenient size, they usually list 150,000 to 200,000 words and concentrate on fairly common words and meanings.

Note Most of the dictionaries listed below are available in both print and electronic form (on diskette and/or CD-ROM), and some are available online as well (see the Web sites below). With an electronic dictionary installed in your word-processing program, you can look up words as you write to check spellings, meanings, synonyms, and other information. You may even be able to customize the dictionary with words and meanings it does not include. But you can use an electronic dictionary only with a computer, of course.

The American Heritage College Dictionary. This dictionary usually lists each word's most common meanings first. It is a more prescriptive dictionary than some of the others listed here, liberally applying usage labels (*slang, informal,* and so on) and including hundreds of usage notes.

Sources for online dictionaries and other language resources:

http://www.iTools.com/research-it/research-it.html From Research-It.

http://www.colostate.edu/depts/WritingCenter/resources/page1.htm From Colorado State University.

http://www.ipl.org/ref/RR/static/ref2000.html From the Internet Public Library.

http://www.encyberpedia.com/glossary.htm From Encyberpedia.

Merriam-Webster's Collegiate Dictionary. Based on the unabridged *Webster's Third New International* (see the next page), this dictionary is more descriptive than prescriptive, emphasizing how the language is actually used. Thus it applies usage labels less frequently than do some other dictionaries. It also emphasizes word histories, arranging meanings in order of their appearance in the language.

The Random House Webster's College Dictionary. Based on the unabridged *Random House Dictionary* (see the next page), this dictionary lists each word's most common meanings first. The dictionary avoids sexist language in definitions and explanations, and its usage notes indicate words or meanings considered offensive or disparaging to groups such as women and minorities. Appendixes include guidelines for avoiding sexist language.

Webster's New World Dictionary. This dictionary arranges meanings in order of their appearance in the language. Usage labels (*colloquial, slang,* and so on) are applied liberally, and words and phrases of American origin are starred.

ESL If English is not your first language, you probably should have a dictionary prepared especially for ESL students in addition to one of the dictionaries listed above. The dictionaries listed below give much more information on such matters as count versus noncount nouns, prepositions with verbs and adjectives, and other concerns of ESL students.

COBUILD English Language Dictionary.

Longman Dictionary of Contemporary English. Longman Dictionary of American English is the American abridgment.

Oxford Advanced Learner's Dictionary. Oxford ESL Dictionary is the American edition.

2 Unabridged dictionaries

Unabridged dictionaries are the most scholarly and comprehensive of all dictionaries, sometimes consisting of many volumes. They emphasize the history of words and the variety of their uses. An unabridged dictionary is useful when you are studying a word in depth, reading or writing about the literature of another century, or looking for a quotation containing a particular word. The following unabridged dictionaries are available at most libraries.

The Oxford English Dictionary, 20 volumes. This is the greatest dictionary of the English language, defining over half a million words. Its entries illustrate the changes in a word's spelling, pronunciation, and meaning with quotations from writers of every century. Some entries span pages. The dictionary focuses on British words and meanings but includes American words and meanings.

The Random House Dictionary of the English Language. This dictionary is smaller (and less expensive) than many unabridged dictionaries. Its entries and definitions are especially up to date, and it includes hundreds of usage notes. Among its appendixes are short dictionaries of French, Spanish, Italian, and German.

Webster's Third New International Dictionary of the English Language. This dictionary attempts to record our language more as it *is* used than as it *should be* used. Therefore, usage labels (such as *slang*) are minimal. The dictionary gives meanings in order of their appearance in the language and provides most acceptable spellings and pronunciations. Plentiful illustrative quotations show variations in the uses of words.

3 Special dictionaries

Special dictionaries limit their attention to a single class of word (for example, slang, engineering terms, abbreviations), to a single kind of information (synonyms, usage, word origins), or to a specific subject (African American culture, biography, history). (See Chapters 49–52 for lists of subject dictionaries in various academic disciplines.)

For guidance on English usage

Usage guides provide help with commonly confused and misused words, phrases, idioms, and other matters:

Follett, Wilson. *Modern American Usage.* Edited by Jacques Barzun.
Morris, William, and Mary Morris. *Harper Dictionary of Contemporary Usage.*
The New Fowler's Modern English Usage. Edited by R. W. Burchfield.

ESL *Practical English Usage,* by Michael Swan, is a usage guide prepared especially for nonnative speakers of English.

For the origins of words

Dictionaries of **etymology,** or word history, explain how words have evolved:

Oxford Dictionary of English Etymology. Edited by Charles T. Onions et al.
Partridge, Eric. *Origins: A Short Etymological Dictionary of Modern English.*

For information on slang

Dictionaries of slang explain the histories and meanings of conversational expressions. They can make entertaining reading.

Partridge's Concise Dictionary of Slang and Unconventional English. Edited by Paul Beale.
Wentworth, Harold, and Stuart Berg Flexner. *Dictionary of American Slang.*

For information about synonyms

A thesaurus like *Roget's* provides extensive lists of words with related meanings. A dictionary of synonyms like *Webster's* contains discussions and illustrations of shades of meaning.

> *Roget's International Thesaurus.* Revised by Robert L. Chapman.
> *Webster's New Dictionary of Synonyms.*

Many electronic dictionaries include a thesaurus as well, and some thesauruses are available independently on diskette, on CD-ROM, or online. Use any thesaurus with care, ensuring that you know the meaning of a synonym before you use it. (See p. 569.)

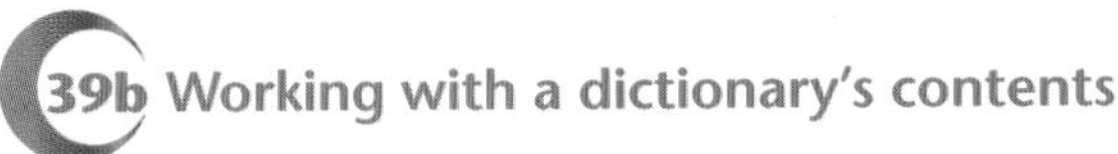

39b Working with a dictionary's contents

Dictionaries use abbreviations and symbols to squeeze a lot of information into a relatively small book. This system of condensed information may at first seem difficult to read. But all dictionaries include in their opening pages detailed information on the arrangement of entries, pronunciation symbols, and abbreviations. And the format is quite similar from one dictionary to another, so becoming familiar with the abbreviations and symbols in one dictionary makes reading any dictionary an easy routine.

Here is a fairly typical entry, from *Merriam-Webster's Collegiate Dictionary.* The labeled parts are discussed on the pages that follow.

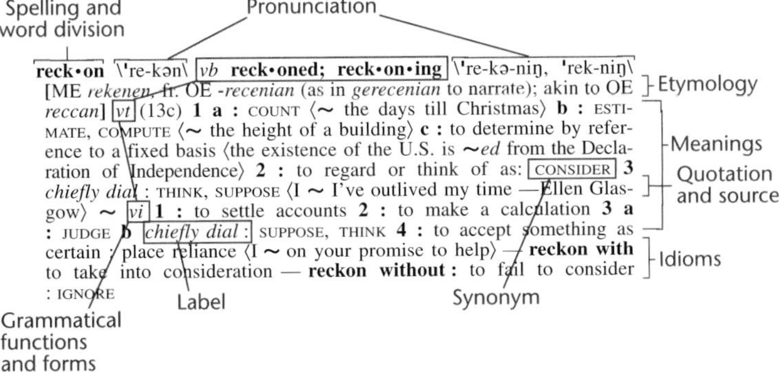

reck•on \'re-kən\ *vb* **reck•oned; reck•on•ing** \'re-kə-niŋ, 'rek-niŋ\ [ME *rekenen,* fr. OE *-recenian* (as in *gerecenian* to narrate); akin to OE *reccan*] *vt* (13c) **1 a :** COUNT ⟨~ the days till Christmas⟩ **b :** ESTIMATE, COMPUTE ⟨~ the height of a building⟩ **c :** to determine by reference to a fixed basis ⟨the existence of the U.S. is ~*ed* from the Declaration of Independence⟩ **2 :** to regard or think of as: CONSIDER **3** *chiefly dial* **:** THINK, SUPPOSE ⟨I ~ I've outlived my time —Ellen Glasgow⟩ ~ *vi* **1 :** to settle accounts **2 :** to make a calculation **3 a :** JUDGE **b** *chiefly dial* **:** SUPPOSE, THINK **4 :** to accept something as certain **:** place reliance ⟨I ~ on your promise to help⟩ — **reckon with :** to take into consideration — **reckon without :** to fail to consider : IGNORE

Spelling and word division

The small initial letters for *reckon* indicate that it is not normally capitalized. (In contrast, *Franklin stove* is capitalized in *Merriam-Webster's* because *Franklin* is a proper noun.)

The centered period in **reck·on** shows the division into syllables. If you are breaking a word at the end of a line, follow the dictionary's division of the word into syllables. (See also Chapter 37.)

For a hyphenated compound word, such as *cross-question,* a dictionary shows the hyphen as part of the spelling: **cross-ques·tion.**

Dictionaries provide any acceptable variant spellings of a word at the beginning of an entry. For the word *dexterous, Merriam-Webster's* has "**dex·ter·ous** *or* **dex·trous.**"

Pronunciation

In *Merriam-Webster's* the pronunciation appears in reversed slashes (\\). The stressed syllable is preceded by an accent mark (ˈre-kən).

Dictionaries use symbols to indicate how to pronounce a word because the alphabet itself does not record all the sounds in the language. (Listen, for example, to the different sounds of *a* in only three words: *far, make,* and *answer.*) Most dictionaries provide a key to the pronunciation symbols at the foot of each page or every two facing pages.

Grammatical functions and forms

Dictionaries give helpful information about a word's functions and forms. The *Merriam-Webster's* entry for *reckon* shows the word to be a verb (*vb*), with the past tense and past participle *reckoned* and the present participle *reckoning,* and with both transitive (*vt*) and intransitive (*vi*) meanings. (For the definitions of these terms, see pp. 259–61 and 301.)

Most dictionaries provide not only the principal forms of regular and irregular verbs but also the plural forms of irregular nouns and the *-er* and *-est* forms of adjectives and adverbs. An adjective or adverb without *-er* and *-est* forms in the dictionary requires the addition of *more* and *most* to show comparison (see p. 352).

Etymology

Dictionaries provide the **etymology** of a word (its history) to indicate its origin and the evolution of its meanings and forms. The dictionary can compress much information about a word into a small space through symbols, abbreviations, and different type fonts. An explanation of these systems appears in the dictionary's opening pages. *Merriam-Webster's* traces *reckon* back most recently to Middle English (ME) and then further back to Old English (OE). The notation "(13c)" before the first definition indicates that the first recorded use of *reckon* to mean "count" occurred in the thirteenth century. When seeking the etymology of a word, be sure to read the entire history, not just the most recent event.

Meanings

Dictionaries divide the general meaning of a word into particular meanings on the basis of how the word is or has been actually used. They arrange a word's meanings differently, either in order of their appearance in the language, earliest first, or in order of their frequency of use, most common first. (*Merriam-Webster's* follows the former practice.) To learn your dictionary's arrangement, consult its opening pages. Then read through a word's entire entry before settling on the meaning that fits the context of what you're reading or writing.

The *Merriam-Webster's* entry for *reckon* ends with two uses of the word in idiomatic expressions (*reckon with* and *reckon without*). These phrases are defined because, as with all idioms, their meanings cannot be inferred simply from the words they consist of (see p. 572).

Labels

Dictionaries apply labels to words or to particular meanings that have a special status or use.

Style labels restrict a word or one of its meanings to a particular level of usage:

- *Slang:* words or meanings inappropriate in writing except for a special effect, such as *crumb* for "a worthless or despicable person."
- *Informal* or *colloquial:* words or meanings appropriate for informal writing but not formal writing, such as *great* to mean "very good," as in *a great movie.*
- *Nonstandard* or *substandard:* words or meanings inappropriate for standard speech and writing, such as *ain't.*
- *Vulgar* or *vulgar slang:* words or meanings considered offensive in speech and writing, as in profanity.
- *Poetic* or *literary:* words or meanings used only in poetry or the most formal writing, such as *eve* for *evening* and *o'er* for *over.*

Subject labels tell us that a word or one of its meanings has a special use in a discipline or profession. In its entry for *relaxation,* for instance, *American Heritage* presents specialized meanings with the subject labels *physiology, physics,* and *mathematics.*

Region labels indicate that a particular spelling, pronunciation, or meaning of a word is not national but limited to an area. A regional difference may be indicated by the label *dialect. Merriam-Webster's* labels as dialect (*dial*) the uses of *reckon* to mean "suppose" or "think" (as in *I reckon I'll do that*). More specific region labels may designate areas of the United States or other countries.

Time labels indicate words or their meanings that the language, in evolving, has discarded. *Obsolete* designates words or meanings that are no longer used; *archaic* designates words or meanings that are out of date but used occasionally.

See pages 558–66 for further discussion of levels of usage and their appropriateness in your writing.

Synonyms

Synonyms are words whose meanings are approximately the same, such as *small* and *little. Merriam-Webster's* defines *reckon* with some words in small capital letters (COUNT, ESTIMATE, CONSIDER, and so on). These are both synonyms and cross-references, in that each word may be looked up in its alphabetical place. Some dictionaries devote separate paragraphs to words with many synonyms. (See pp. 601–02 for a discussion of how to use the synonyms provided by a dictionary to increase your vocabulary.)

Illustrative quotations

Dictionaries are made by collecting quotations showing actual uses of words in all kinds of speech and writing. Some of these quotations, or others that the dictionary makers invent, may appear in the dictionary's entries as illustrations of how a word may be used. Five such quotations illustrate uses of *reckon* in the *Merriam-Webster's* entry (~ in these quotations stands for the word being illustrated).

Unabridged dictionaries usually provide many such quotations, not only to illustrate a word's current uses but also to show the changes in its meanings over time. Abridged dictionaries use quotations more selectively: to illustrate an unusual meaning of the word, to help distinguish between two closely related meanings of the same word, or to show the differences between synonyms.

EXERCISE
Using a dictionary

Consult your dictionary on five of the following words. First find out whether your dictionary lists the oldest or the most common meanings first in its entries. Then, for each word, write down (*a*) the division into syllables, (*b*) the pronunciation, (*c*) the grammatical functions and forms, (*d*) the etymology, (*e*) each meaning, and (*f*) any special uses indicated by labels. Finally, use the word in at least two sentences of your own.

1. depreciation
2. secretary
3. grammar
4. manifest
5. assassin
6. astrology
7. potlatch
8. plain (*adj.*)
9. ceremony
10. toxic
11. steal
12. obelisk

CHAPTER 40

Improving Your Vocabulary

A precise and versatile vocabulary will help you communicate effectively in speech and writing. To a great extent, you can improve your vocabulary by frequent and inquisitive reading, by troubling to notice and learn the interesting or unfamiliar words used by other writers.

This chapter has a twofold purpose: to provide a sense of the potential of English by acquainting you with its history and range of words; and to help you increase the range, versatility, and precision of your own vocabulary.

ESL For nonnative speakers of English, learning the language means not only mastering its words (which this chapter can help with) but also becoming comfortable with its many idioms and other common expressions. For help, consult the ESL preposition guide listed on page 573, the ESL dictionaries listed on page 587, or a reference such as *English Idioms,* by Jennifer Seidl and W. McMordie.

40a Understanding the sources of English

English has over 500,000 words, probably more than any other language. This exceptional vocabulary and the power and range of expression that accompany it derive from its special mix of word sources. Unlike many other languages, English has borrowed a large number of words.

How English drew on its several sources and acquired its large vocabulary is the story of historical changes. The ancestor of English,

http://webster.commnet.edu/HP/pages/darling/grammar/vocabulary.htm Strategies and quizzes for improving vocabulary, from the Guide to Grammar and Writing.

http://www.dictionary.com/Dir/Reference/Dictionaries/Vocabulary_Lists/ Vocabulary resources, from Dictionary.com.

http://www.aitech.ac.jp/~iteslj/quizzes/vocabulary.html Vocabulary-building exercises for ESL writers, from the *Internet TESL Journal.*

Indo-European, was spoken (but not written) perhaps as far back as 5000 BC, and it eventually spread to cover the area from present-day India west to present-day Ireland. In what is now England, an Indo-European offshoot called Celtic was spoken extensively until the fifth century AD. But over the next few centuries, invaders from the European continent, speaking a dialect of Germanic, another Indo-European language, overran the native Britons. The Germanic dialect became the original source of English.

Old English, spoken from the eighth to the twelfth centuries, was a rugged, guttural language. It used a slightly different alphabet from the modern one (including the characters ð and þ for *th*), which has been transcribed in the sample below. The sample shows the opening lines of the Lord's Prayer: "Our Father, who art in heaven, hallowed be thy name. Thy kingdom come. Thy will be done on earth as it is in heaven."

> Fæder ure thu the eart on heofonum, si thin nama gehalgod. Tobecume thin rice. Gewurthe thin willa on eorthan swa swa on heofonum.

Many English nouns—such as *stone, word, gift,* and *foot*—come from Old English. So do most pronouns, prepositions, and conjunctions, some (such as *he, under,* and *to*) without any change in spelling. Other Germanic tribes, using a similar dialect but settling on the European continent instead of in England, fostered two other languages, Dutch and German. As a result, Dutch, German, and English are related languages with some similar traits.

In 1066 the Normans, under William the Conqueror, invaded England. The Normans were originally Vikings who had settled in northern France and had forsaken Old Norse for their own dialect of Old French. They made Norman French the language of law, literature, and the ruling class in England. As a result, English acquired many French words, including many military and governmental words such as *authority, mayor, crime, army,* and *guard.* The common English people kept English alive during the Norman occupation, but they adopted many French words intact (*air, point, place, age*). Eventually, the French influence caused the language to shift from Old to Middle English, which lasted from the twelfth through the fifteenth centuries. During this time a great many Latin words also entered English, for Latin formed the background of Norman French and was the language of the Church and of scholars. English words that entered Middle English directly from Latin or from Latin through French include *language, luminous, memory, liberal,* and *sober.*

Middle English, as the following passage from Geoffrey Chaucer's *Canterbury Tales* shows, was much closer to the modern language than to Old English:

A clerk there was of Oxenford also,
That unto logyk hadde longe ygo.
As leene was his hors as is a rake,
And he nas nat right fat, I undertake,
But looked holwe, and therto sobrely.

Modern English evolved in the fourteenth and fifteenth centuries as the language's sound and spellings changed. This was the time of the Renaissance in Europe. Ancient Latin and Greek art, learning, and literature were revived, first in Italy and then throughout the continent. English vocabulary expanded rapidly, not only with more Latin and many Greek words (such as *democracy* and *physics*) but also with words from Italian and French. Advances in printing, beginning in the fifteenth century, made publications widely available to an increasingly literate audience. Modern American English is four centuries and an ocean removed from the Modern English of sixteenth-century England, but the two are fundamentally the same. The differences and the similarities are evident in this passage from the King James Bible, published in 1611:

> And the Lord God commanded the man, saying, Of euery tree of the garden thou mayest freely eate. But of the tree of the knowledge of good and euill, thou shalt not eate of it: for in the day that thou eatest thereof, thou shalt surely die.

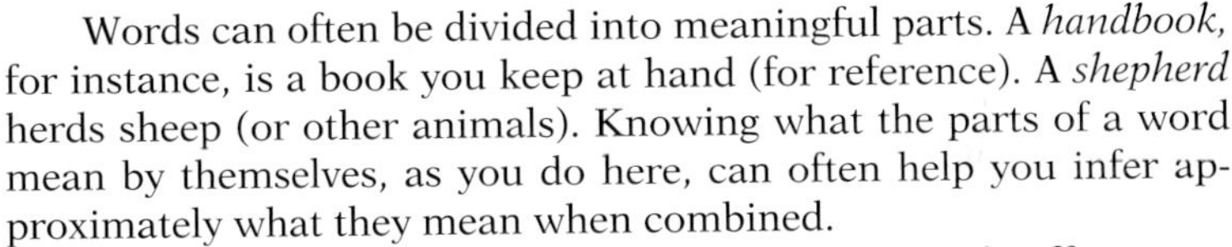

40b Learning the composition of words

Words can often be divided into meaningful parts. A *handbook,* for instance, is a book you keep at hand (for reference). A *shepherd* herds sheep (or other animals). Knowing what the parts of a word mean by themselves, as you do here, can often help you infer approximately what they mean when combined.

The following explanations of roots, prefixes, and suffixes provide information that can open up the meanings of words whose parts may not be familiar or easy to see. For more information, refer to a dictionary's etymologies, which provide the histories of words (see p. 590).

1 Learning roots

A **root** is the unchanging component of words related in origin and usually in meaning. Both *illiterate* ("unable to read and write") and *literal* ("sticking to the facts or to the first and most obvious

http://www.dictionary.com/Dir/Reference/Dictionaries/Etymology/ Information on the sources of words, from Dictionary.com.

meaning of an idea") share the root *liter,* derived from *littera,* a Latin word meaning "letter." A person who cannot understand the letters that make up writing is illiterate. A person who wants to understand the primary meaning of the letters (the words) in a contract is seeking the *literal* meaning of that contract.

At least half the words in English come from Latin and Greek. The list below includes some common Latin and Greek roots, their meanings, and examples of English words containing them:

Root (source)	Meaning	English words
aster, astr (G)	star	astronomy, astrology
audi (L)	to hear	audible, audience
bene (L)	good, well	benefit, benevolent
bio (G)	life	biology, autobiography
dic, dict (L)	to speak	dictator, dictionary
fer (L)	to carry	transfer, referral
fix (L)	to fasten	fix, suffix, prefix
geo (G)	earth	geography, geology
graph (G)	to write	geography, photography
jur, jus (L)	law	jury, justice
log, logue (G)	word, thought, speech	astrology, biology, neologism
luc (L)	light	lucid, translucent
manu (L)	hand	manual, manuscript
meter, metr (G)	measure	metric, thermometer
op, oper (L)	work	operation, operator
path (G)	feeling	pathetic, sympathy
ped (G)	child	pediatrics
phil (G)	love	philosophy, Anglophile
phys (G)	body, nature	physical, physics
scrib, script (L)	to write	scribble, manuscript
tele (G)	far off	telephone, television
ter, terr (L)	earth	territory, extraterrestrial
vac (L)	empty	vacant, vacuum, evacuate
verb (L)	word	verbal, verbose
vid, vis (L)	to see	video, vision, television

EXERCISE 1
Learning roots

Define the following underlined words, using the list of roots above and any clues given by the rest of the sentence. Check the accuracy of your meanings in a dictionary.

1. After guiding me through college, my benefactor will help me start a career.
2. Always afraid of leading a vacuous life, the heiress immersed herself in volunteer work.
3. The posters affixed to the construction wall advertised a pornographic movie.
4. After his auditory nerve was damaged, he had trouble catching people's words.

5. The child empathized so completely with his mother that he felt pain when she broke her arm.

2 Learning prefixes

Prefixes are standard syllables fastened to the front of a word to modify its meaning. For example, the word *prehistory* is a combination of the word *history,* meaning "based on a written record explaining past events," and the prefix *pre-,* meaning "before." Together, prefix and word mean "before a written record explaining past events," or before events were recorded. Learning standard prefixes can help you improve vocabulary and spelling just as learning word roots can.

The following lists group prefixes according to sense so that they are easier to remember. When two or more prefixes have very different spellings but the same meaning, they usually derive from different languages, most often Latin and Greek.

Prefixes showing quantity

Meaning	Prefixes in English words
half	semiannual; hemisphere
one	unicycle; monarch, monorail
two	binary, bimonthly; dilemma, dichotomy
three	triangle, trilogy
four	quadrangle, quartet
five	quintet; pentagon
six	sextuplets; hexameter
seven	septuagenarian; heptarchy
eight	octave, octopus
nine	nonagenarian
ten	decade, decathlon
hundred	century; hectoliter
thousand	millimeter; kilocycle

Prefixes showing negation

Meaning	Prefixes in English words
without, no, not	asexual; illegal, immoral, invalid, irreverent; unskilled
not, absence of, opposing, against	nonbreakable; antacid, antipathy; contradict
opposite to, complement to	counterclockwise, counterweight
do the opposite of, remove, reduce	dehorn, devitalize, devalue
do the opposite of, deprive of	disestablish, disarm
wrongly, bad	misjudge, misdeed

Prefixes showing time

Meaning	Prefixes in English words
before	antecedent; forecast; precede; prologue
after	postwar
again	rewrite

Prefixes showing direction or position

Meaning	Prefixes in English words
above, over	supervise
across, over	transport
below, under	infrasonic; subterranean; hypodermic
in front of	proceed; prefix
behind	recede
out of	erupt, explicit; ecstasy
into	injection, immerse; encourage, empower
around	circumference; perimeter
with	coexist, colloquial, communicate, consequence, correspond; sympathy, synchronize

EXERCISE 2
Learning prefixes

Provide meanings for the following underlined words, using the lists of prefixes and any clues given by the rest of the sentence. Check the accuracy of your meanings in a dictionary.

1. In the twenty-first century some of our oldest cities will celebrate their quadricentennials.
2. Most poems called sonnets consist of fourteen lines divided into an octave and a sestet.
3. When the Congress seemed ready to cut Social Security benefits again, some representatives proposed the countermeasure of increasing Medicare payments.
4. By increasing Medicare payments, the representatives hoped to forestall the inevitable financial squeeze on the elderly.
5. Ferdinand Magellan, a Portuguese sailor, commanded the first expedition to circumnavigate the globe.

3 Learning suffixes

Suffixes are standard syllables fastened to the end of a word to modify its meaning and usually its part of speech. The word *popular* is an adjective. With different suffixes, it becomes a different adjective, an adverb, two different verbs, and a noun:

Adjective	popular populous	**Adverb**	popularly

Verb	populate popularize	**Noun**	population

Many words change suffixes in the same way. In fact, suffixes help us recognize what parts of speech many words are, as the following examples show:

Noun suffixes

misery	miner	internship	randomness
reference	basement	presidency	brotherhood
relevance	nationalist	discussion	kingdom
operator	nationalism	agitation	

Verb suffixes

harden	purify
nationalize	agitate

Adjective suffixes

miserable	presidential	wonderful	useless
edible	gigantic	fibrous	selfish
national	friendly	adoptive	flatulent

The only suffix regularly applied to adverbs is *-ly: openly, selfishly, essentially.*

Note Inflectional endings—such as the plural *-s,* the past tense *-ed,* and the comparative *-er* or *-est*—appear at the ends of words but do not change a word's grammatical function.

EXERCISE 3
Learning suffixes

Identify the part of speech of each word below, and then change it to the part or parts of speech in parentheses by deleting, adding, or changing a suffix. Use the given word and each created word in a sentence. Check a dictionary, if necessary, to be sure suffixes and spellings are correct.

1. magic (*adjective*)
2. durable (*noun; adverb*)
3. refrigerator (*verb*)
4. self-critical (*noun*)
5. differ (*noun; adjective*)
6. equal (*noun; adverb*)
7. conversion (*verb; adjective*)
8. strictly (*adjective; noun*)
9. assist (*noun*)
10. qualification (*verb; adjective*)

40c Learning to use new words

You can learn a new word not only by understanding its composition but also by examining the context in which it appears and by looking it up in a dictionary—both ways to increase your vocabulary by multiplying and varying your experience with language.

1 Examining context

Often, you can guess the meaning of an unfamiliar word by looking at the familiar words around it. This technique is helpful when you don't want to interrupt your reading to look up every unfamiliar word. (When you've finished reading, though, check your guesses in your dictionary.)

Parallelism (Chapter 25) shows you which ideas line up or go together and can often suggest the meaning of a new word. Watch for parallel ideas in the following sentence:

> The kittens see their mother hunt and kill, and they in turn take up predatory behavior.

Context clues suggest the meaning of *predatory:* parallel construction (*kittens see . . . and they . . . take up*); the tip-off phrase *in turn;* and the suggested idea of imitation (kittens watching their mother and taking up her behavior). These clues lead to the correct conclusion that predatory behavior consists of hunting and killing.

The phrase *is called* or the word *is* often signals a definition:

> The point where the light rays come together is called the *focus* of the lens.

Sometimes definitions are enclosed in parentheses or set off by commas or dashes:

> In early childhood these tendencies lead to the development of *schemes* (organized patterns of behavior).
>
> Many Chinese practice *Tai Chi,* an ancient method of self-defense performed as exercise in slow, graceful motions.
>
> At *burnout*—the instant a rocket stops firing—the satellite's path is fixed.

Noticing examples can also help you infer the meaning of a word. The expressions *such as, for example, for instance, to illustrate,* and *including* often precede examples:

> Society often has difficulty understanding nonconformists such as criminals, inventors, artists, saints, and political protesters.

The examples of people who go beyond the average or beyond the rules suggest that *nonconformists* do not adapt themselves to the usual standards and customs of society.

Sometimes an example that reveals the meaning of an unfamiliar word is not announced by a phrase:

> During the first weeks of rehabilitation, Smith exercised as best he could, took his medicine daily, and thought constantly about the physical condition he once possessed.

Guessing the meaning of *rehabilitation* requires considering what occurred during it: (1) exercising "as best he could," as if Smith had some kind of limitation; (2) taking medicine, as if Smith were ill; and (3) thinking about his past physical condition, as if Smith were wishing for the good shape he used to be in. Putting these examples together suggests that *rehabilitation* is returning to a healthy condition, which is one of its meanings.

EXERCISE 4
Examining context

Use context to determine the meanings of the underlined words below. Check the accuracy of your guess by consulting a dictionary.

1. Like America, Michael [Corleone, in *The Godfather*] began as a clean, brilliant young man endowed with incredible resources and believing in a humanistic idealism. Like America, Michael was an innocent who had tried to correct the ills and injustices of his progenitors. —FRANCIS FORD COPPOLA
2. A photograph passes for incontrovertible proof that a given thing happened. The picture may distort; but there is always a presumption that something exists, or did exist, which is like what's in the picture. —SUSAN SONTAG
3. It is not easy to describe or to account for our own culture's particular predilection for butter—a loyalty so fierce and so unreasoning that it is called, by those opposed to it, the "butter *mystique*." —MARGARET VISSER
4. "And this, too, shall pass away." How much [this sentence] expresses! How chastening in the hour of pride! How consoling in the depths of affliction! —ABRAHAM LINCOLN
5. In a community where public services have failed to keep abreast of private consumption, . . . in an atmosphere of private opulence and public squalor, the private goods have full sway. —JOHN KENNETH GALBRAITH

2 Using a dictionary

A dictionary is a quick reference for the meanings of words (see p. 586). It can give the precise meaning of a word whose general meaning you have guessed by examining the word's context. It can also help you fix the word in your memory by showing its spelling, pronunciation, synonyms, and other features.

Although a dictionary of synonyms is the best source for the precise meanings of similar words (see p. 589), an abridged dictionary will supply much information about synonyms. Most abridged dictionaries list a word's common synonyms and either direct you to the entries for the synonyms or distinguish among them in one place. An example of the latter form is the paragraph following, which comes after the main entry for the word *decrease* in *The American Heritage College Dictionary*. By drawing on this information as you edit, you can substitute a more precise word for *decrease* when your meaning calls for one.

> **Syns:** *decrease, lessen, reduce, dwindle, abate, diminish, subside*. These verbs mean to become or cause to become smaller or less. *Decrease* and *lessen* refer to steady or gradual diminution: *Lack of success decreases confidence. His appetite lessens as his illness progresses. Reduce* emphasizes bringing down in size, degree, or intensity: *The workers reduced their wage demands. Dwindle* suggests decreasing bit by bit to a vanishing point: *Their savings dwindled away. Abate* stresses a decrease in amount or intensity and suggests a reduction of excess: *Toward evening the fire began to abate. Diminish* implies taking away or removal: *The warden's authority diminished after the revolt. Subside* implies a falling away to a more normal level: *Our wild enthusiasm did not subside*.

EXERCISE 5
Using the dictionary

Consulting the dictionary entry above (and another dictionary if necessary), write five sentences that make precise use of *decrease* and four of its synonyms.

CHAPTER 41

Spelling and the Hyphen

English spelling is difficult, even for some very experienced and competent writers. You can train yourself to spell better, and this chapter will help you. But you can also improve instantly by acquiring three habits:

- Carefully proofread your writing.
- Cultivate a healthy suspicion of your spellings.
- Compulsively check a dictionary whenever you doubt a spelling.

Note A word processor's spelling checker can help you find and track spelling errors in your papers. But its usefulness is limited, mainly because it can't spot the very common error of confusing words with similar spellings, such as *their/they're/there*. A grammar and style checker may flag commonly confused words, but only the ones listed in its dictionary. You still must proofread your papers yourself. See pages 186–89 for more on spelling checkers and grammar and style checkers.

41a Recognizing typical spelling problems

Spelling well involves recognizing situations that commonly lead to misspelling: pronunciation can mislead you in several ways;

Advice on spelling:

http://webster.commnet.edu/HP/pages/darling/grammar/spelling.htm From the Guide to Grammar and Writing.

http://www.uottawa.ca/academic/arts/writcent/hypergrammar/spelling.html From the University of Ottawa.

Two guides to commonly misspelled words:

http://www.cooper.com/alan/homonym_list.html From All About Homonyms.

http://webster.commnet.edu/HP/pages/darling/grammar/notorious.htm From the Guide to Grammar and Writing.

different forms of the same word may have different spellings; and some words have more than one acceptable spelling.

1 Being wary of pronunciation

In English, unlike some other languages, pronunciation of words is an unreliable guide to their spelling. The same letter or combination of letters may have different sounds in different words. (Say aloud these different ways of pronouncing the letters *ough: tough, dough, cough, through, bough.*) In addition, some words contain letters that are not pronounced clearly or at all, such as the *ed* in *asked,* the silent *e* in *swipe,* or the unpronounced *gh* in *tight.*

Pronunciation is a particularly unreliable guide in spelling **homonyms,** words pronounced the same though they have different spellings and meanings: *great/grate, to/too/two.* Some commonly confused homonyms and near-homonyms, such as *accept/except,* are listed below. (See p. 612 for tips on how to use spelling lists.)

Words commonly confused

accept (to receive)
except (other than)

affect (to have an influence on)
effect (result)

all ready (prepared)
already (by this time)

allude (to refer to indirectly)
elude (to avoid)

allusion (indirect reference)
illusion (erroneous belief or perception)

ascent (a movement up)
assent (agreement)

bare (unclothed)
bear (to carry, or an animal)

board (a plane of wood)
bored (uninterested)

born (brought into life)
borne (carried)

brake (stop)
break (smash)

buy (purchase)
by (next to)

capital (the seat of a government)
capitol (the building where a legislature meets)

cite (to quote an authority)
sight (the ability to see)
site (a place)

desert (to abandon)
dessert (after-dinner course)

discreet (reserved, respectful)
discrete (individual or distinct)

elicit (to bring out)
illicit (illegal)

fair (average, or lovely)
fare (a fee for transportation)

forth (forward)
fourth (after *third*)

gorilla (a large primate)
guerrilla (a kind of soldier)

hear (to perceive by ear)
here (in this place)

heard (past tense of *hear*)
herd (a group of animals)

hole (an opening)
whole (complete)

its (possessive of *it*)
it's (contraction of *it is*)

lead (heavy metal)
led (past tense of *lead*)

lessen (to make less)
lesson (something learned)

meat (flesh)
meet (encounter)

no (the opposite of *yes*)
know (to be certain)

passed (past tense of *pass*)
past (after, or a time gone by)

patience (forbearance)
patients (persons under medical care)

peace (the absence of war)
piece (a portion of something)

plain (clear)
plane (a carpenter's tool, or an airborne vehicle)

presence (the state of being at hand)
presents (gifts)

principal (most important, or the head of a school)
principle (a basic truth or law)

rain (precipitation)
reign (to rule)
rein (a strap for controlling an animal)

raise (to build up)
raze (to tear down)

right (correct)
rite (a religious ceremony)
write (to make letters)

road (a surface for driving)
rode (past tense of *ride*)

scene (where an action occurs)
seen (past participle of *see*)

seam (junction)
seem (appear)

stationary (unmoving)
stationery (writing paper)

straight (unbending)
strait (a water passageway)

their (possessive of *they*)
there (opposite of *here*)
they're (contraction of *they are*)

to (toward)
too (also)
two (following *one*)

waist (the middle of the body)
waste (discarded material)

weak (not strong)
week (Sunday through Saturday)

weather (climate)
whether (*if*, or introducing a choice)

which (one of a group)
witch (a sorcerer)

who's (contraction of *who is*)
whose (possessive of *who*)

your (possessive of *you*)
you're (contraction of *you are*)

2 Distinguishing between different forms of the same word

Spelling problems may occur when the noun form and the verb form of the same word are spelled differently. For example:

Verb	Noun	Verb	Noun
advise	advice	enter	entrance
describe	description	marry	marriage
speak	speech	omit	omission

Sometimes the noun and the adjective forms of the same word differ:

Noun	Adjective	Noun	Adjective
comedy	comic	height	high
courtesy	courteous	Britain	British
generosity	generous		

The principal parts of irregular verbs are usually spelled differently:

begin, began, begun
break, broke, broken
know, knew, known
ring, rang, rung

Irregular nouns change spelling from singular to plural:

child, children
goose, geese
mouse, mice
shelf, shelves
tooth, teeth
woman, women

Notice, too, that the stem of a word may change its spelling in different forms:

four, forty
thief, theft

3 Using preferred spellings ESL

Many words have variant spellings as well as preferred spellings. Often the variant spellings listed in an American dictionary are British spellings.

American	British
color, humor	colour, humour
theater, center	theatre, centre
canceled, traveled	cancelled, travelled
judgment	judgement
realize	realise

41b Following spelling rules

Misspelling is often a matter of misspelling a syllable rather than the whole word. The following general rules focus on troublesome syllables, with notes for the occasional exceptions.

1 Distinguishing between *ie* and *ei*

Words like *believe* and *receive* sound alike in the second syllable, but the syllable is spelled differently. Use the familiar jingle to distinguish between *ie* and *ei:*

> *I* before *e,* except after *c,* or when pronounced "ay" as in *neighbor* and *weigh.*

i **before** *e*	believe grief	bier thief	hygiene friend
ei **after** *c*	ceiling receive	conceive deceit	perceive conceit
ei **sounded as "ay"**	neighbor sleigh	weight freight	eight vein

Exceptions In some words an *ei* combination neither follows *c* nor is pronounced "ay." These words include *either, neither, foreign, forfeit, height, leisure, weird, seize,* and *seizure.* This sentence might help you remember some of them: *The weird foreigner neither seizes leisure nor forfeits height.*

EXERCISE 1
Distinguishing between *ie* and *ei*

Insert *ie* or *ei* in the words below. Check doubtful spellings in a dictionary.

1. br__f	5. for__gn	9. l__surely	13. h__ght
2. dec__ve	6. pr__st	10. ach__ve	14. fr__ght
3. rec__pt	7. gr__vance	11. pat__nce	15. f__nt
4. s__ze	8. f__nd	12. p__rce	16. s__ve

2 Keeping or dropping a final *e*

Many words end with an unpronounced or silent *e: move, brave, late, rinse.* Drop the final *e* when adding an ending that begins with a vowel:

advise + able = advisable surprise + ing = surprising
force + ible = forcible guide + ance = guidance

Keep the final, silent *e* if the ending begins with a consonant:

battle + ment = battlement care + ful = careful
accurate + ly = accurately like + ness = likeness

Exceptions The silent *e* is sometimes retained before an ending beginning with a vowel. It is kept when *dye* becomes *dyeing,* to avoid confusion with *dying.* It is kept to prevent mispronunciation of words like *shoeing* (not *shoing*) and *mileage* (not *milage*). And the final *e* is often retained after a soft *c* or *g,* to keep the sound of the consonant soft rather than hard:

courageous changeable noticeable
outrageous manageable embraceable

The silent *e* is also sometimes *dropped* before an ending beginning with a consonant, when the *e* is preceded by another vowel:

argue + ment = argument
due + ly = duly
true + ly = truly

sp
41b

EXERCISE 2
Keeping or dropping a final *e*

Combine the following words and endings, keeping or dropping a final *e* as necessary to make correctly spelled words. Check doubtful spellings in a dictionary.

1. malice + ious
2. love + able
3. service + able
4. retire + ment
5. sue + ing
6. virtue + ous
7. note + able
8. battle + ing
9. suspense + ion

3 Keeping or dropping a final *y*

Words ending in *y* often change their spelling when an ending is added to them. Change the final *y* to an *i* when it follows a consonant:

beauty, beauties — worry, worried — supply, supplies
folly, follies — merry, merrier — deputy, deputize

But keep the *y* when it follows a vowel, when the ending is *-ing,* or when it ends a proper name:

day, days — cry, crying — May, Mays
obey, obeyed — study, studying — Minsky, Minskys

EXERCISE 3
Keeping or dropping a final *y*

Combine the following words and endings, changing or keeping a final *y* as necessary to make correctly spelled words. Check doubtful spellings in a dictionary.

1. imply + s
2. messy + er
3. apply + ing
4. delay + ing
5. defy + ance
6. say + s
7. solidify + s
8. Murphy + s
9. supply + ed

4 Doubling consonants

Whether to double a word's final consonant depends first on the number of syllables in the word. In one-syllable words, double the final consonant when a single vowel precedes the final consonant. Otherwise, don't double the consonant.

slap, slapping — pair, paired
tip, tipping — park, parking

In words of more than one syllable, double the final consonant when a single vowel precedes the final consonant *and* the consonant ends a stressed syllable once the ending is added. Otherwise, don't double the consonant.

refer, referring — refer, reference
begin, beginning — relent, relented
occur, occurrence — despair, despairing

EXERCISE 4
Doubling consonants

Combine the following words and endings, doubling final consonants as necessary to make correctly spelled words. Check doubtful spellings in a dictionary.

1. repair + ing
2. admit + ance
3. benefit + ed
4. shop + ed
5. conceal + ed
6. allot + ed
7. drip + ing
8. declaim + ed
9. parallel + ing

5 Attaching prefixes

Adding a prefix such as *dis, mis,* and *un* does not change the spelling of a word. When adding a prefix, do not drop a letter from or add a letter to the original word:

uneasy	anti-intellectual	defuse	misstate
unnecessary	disappoint	de-emphasize	misspell
antifreeze	dissatisfied	misinform	

(See also p. 616 on when to use hyphens with prefixes: *prehistory* versus *ex-student.*)

6 Forming plurals

Nouns

Most nouns form plurals by adding *s* to the singular form:

boy, boys
carnival, carnivals
table, tables
Murphy, Murphys

Some nouns ending in *f* or *fe* form the plural by changing the ending to *ve* before adding *s:*

leaf, leaves
life, lives
wife, wives
yourself, yourselves

Singular nouns ending in *s, sh, ch,* or *x* form the plural by adding *es:*

kiss, kisses
wish, wishes
church, churches
Jones, Joneses

(Notice that verbs ending in *s, sh, ch,* or *x* form the third-person singular in the same way. *Taxes* and *lurches* are examples.)

Nouns ending in *o* preceded by a vowel usually form the plural by adding *s:*

ratio, ratios
zoo, zoos

Nouns ending in *o* preceded by a consonant usually form the plural by adding *es:*

hero, heroes
tomato, tomatoes

Exceptions Some very common nouns form irregular plurals:

child, children	man, men
mouse, mice	woman, women

Some English nouns that were originally Italian, Greek, Latin, or French form the plural according to their original language:

analysis, analyses	datum, data
basis, bases	medium, media
beau, beaux	phenomenon, phenomena
crisis, crises	piano, pianos
criterion, criteria	thesis, theses

A few such nouns may form irregular or regular plurals: for instance, *index, indices, indexes; curriculum, curricula, curriculums.* The regular plural is more contemporary.

ESL Noncount nouns do not form plurals, either regularly (with an added *s*) or irregularly. Examples of noncount nouns include *equipment, intelligence,* and *wealth.* (See pp. 356–57.)

Compound nouns

Form plurals of compound nouns in one of two ways. Add *s* to the last word when the component words are roughly equal in importance, whether or not they are hyphenated:

city-states	breakthroughs
painter-sculptors	bucket seats

Add *s* to a noun combined with other parts of speech:

fathers-in-law	passersby

Note, however, that most modern dictionaries give the plural of *spoonful* as *spoonfuls.*

EXERCISE 5
Forming plurals

Make correct plurals of the following singular words. Check doubtful spellings in a dictionary.

1. pile	5. mile per hour	9. Bales	13. thief
2. donkey	6. box	10. cupful	14. goose
3. beach	7. switch	11. libretto	15. hiss
4. summary	8. sister-in-law	12. video	16. appendix

41c Developing spelling skills

The techniques discussed below can help you improve your spelling. In addition, do not overrely on your computer's spelling checker (see p. 186).

1 Editing and proofreading carefully

If spelling is a problem for you, give it high priority while editing your writing (p. 60) and again while proofreading, your last chance to catch misspelled words (p. 63). Reading a draft backward, word by word, can help you spot mistakes such as switched or omitted letters in words you know. Because the procedure forces you to consider each word in isolation, it can also highlight spellings you may be less sure of. A sense of uncertainty is crucial in spotting and correcting spelling errors, even for good spellers who make relatively few errors. Listen to your own uncertainty, and let it lead you to the dictionary.

2 Using a dictionary

How can you look up a word you can't spell? Start by guessing at the spelling and looking up your guess. If that doesn't work, pronounce the word aloud to come up with other possible spellings, and look them up. Unless the word is too specialized to be included in your dictionary, trial and error will eventually pay off.

If you're using a computerized spelling checker, it may do the guessing for you by providing several choices for misspelled words. But you may still need to check a dictionary to verify your choice.

3 Pronouncing carefully

Careful pronunciation is not always a reliable guide to spelling, (see p. 604), but it can keep you from misspelling words that are often mispronounced. For example:

athletics (*not* atheletics)
disastrous (*not* disasterous)
environment (*not* envirnment)
frustrate (*not* fustrate)
government (*not* goverment)
height (*not* heighth)
history (*not* histry)
irrelevant (*not* irrevelant)
laboratory (*not* labratory)
library (*not* libary)
lightning (*not* lightening)
mischievous (*not* mischievious)
nuclear (*not* nucular)
recognize (*not* reconize)
representative (*not* representive)
strictly (*not* stricly)

4 Tracking and analyzing your errors

Keep a list of the words marked "misspelled" or "spelling" or "sp" in your papers. This list will contain hints about your particular spelling problems, such as that you tend to confuse *affect* and *effect* or to form plurals incorrectly. (If you need help analyzing the list, consult your writing instructor.) The list will also provide a personalized study guide, a focus for your efforts to spell better.

5 Using mnemonics

Mnemonics (pronounced with an initial *n* sound) are techniques for assisting your memory. The *er* in *letter* and *paper* can remind you that *stationery* (meaning "writing paper") has an *er* near the end; *stationary* with an *a* means "standing in place." Or the word *dome* with its long *o* sound can remind you that the building in which the legislature meets is spelled *capitol,* with an *o.* The *capital* city is spelled with *al* like *Albany,* the capital of New York. If you identify the words you have trouble spelling, you can think of your own mnemonics, which may work better for you than someone else's.

6 Studying spelling lists

Learning to spell commonly misspelled words will reduce your spelling errors. For general improvement, work with the following list of commonly misspelled words. Study only six or seven words at a time. If you are unsure of the meaning of a word, look it up in a dictionary and try using it in a sentence. Pronounce the word out loud, syllable by syllable, and write the word out. (The list of similar-sounding words on pp. 604–05 should be considered an extension of the one below.)

absence
abundance
acceptable
accessible
accidentally
accommodate
accomplish
accumulate
accuracy
accustomed
achieve
acknowledge
acquire
across
actually
address
admission
adolescent
advice
advising
against
aggravate
aggressive
all right
all together
allegiance

almost
a lot
already
although
altogether
amateur
among
amount
analysis
analyze
angel
annual
answer
apology
apparent
appearance
appetite
appreciate
appropriate
approximately
argument
arrest
ascend
assassinate
assimilation
assistance

associate
atheist
athlete
attendance
audience
average

bargain
basically
because
beginning
belief
believe
beneficial
benefited
boundary
breath
Britain
bureaucracy
business

calculator
calendar
caricature
carrying
cede

ceiling
cello
cemetery
certain
changeable
changing
characteristic
chief
chocolate
choose
chose
climbed
coarse
column
coming
commercial
commitment
committed
committee
competent
competition
complement
compliment
conceive
concentrate
concert

condemn
conquer
conscience
conscious
consistency
consistent
continuous
controlled
controversial
convenience
convenient
coolly
course
courteous
criticism
criticize
crowd
cruelty
curiosity
curious
curriculum

deceive
deception
decide
decision
deductible
definitely
degree
dependent
descend
descendant
describe
description
desirable
despair
desperate
destroy
determine
develop
device
devise
dictionary
difference
dining
disagree
disappear
disappoint
disapprove
disastrous
discipline

discriminate
discussion
disease
disgusted
dissatisfied
distinction
divide
divine
division
doctor
drawer

easily
ecstasy
efficiency
efficient
eighth
either
eligible
embarrass
emphasize
empty
enemy
entirely
entrepreneur
environment
equipped
especially
essential
every
exaggerate
exceed
excellent
exercise
exhaust
exhilarate
existence
expense
experience
experiment
explanation
extremely

familiar
fascinate
favorite
February
fiery
finally
forcibly
foreign

foresee
forty
forward
friend
frightening
fulfill

gauge
generally
ghost
government
grammar
grief
guarantee
guard
guidance

happily
harass
height
heroes
hideous
humorous
hungry
hurriedly
hurrying
hypocrisy
hypocrite

ideally
illogical
imaginary
imagine
imitation
immediately
immigrant
incidentally
incredible
independence
independent
individually
inevitably
influential
initiate
innocuous
inoculate
insistent
integrate
intelligence
interest
interference

interpret
irrelevant
irresistible
irritable
island

jealousy
judgment

kindergarten
knowledge

laboratory
leisure
length
library
license
lieutenant
lightning
likelihood
literally
livelihood
loneliness
loose
lose
luxury
lying

magazine
maintenance
manageable
marriage
mathematics
meant
medicine
miniature
minor
minutes
mirror
mischievous
missile
misspelled
morale
morals
mortgage
mournful
muscle
mysterious

naturally
necessary

neighbor
neither
nickel
niece
ninety
ninth
noticeable
nuclear
nuisance
numerous

obstacle
occasion
occasionally
occur
occurrence
official
omission
omit
omitted
opinion
opponent
opportunity
opposite
ordinary
originally

paid
panicky
paralleled
parliament
particularly
peaceable
peculiar
pedal
perceive
perception
performance
permanent
permissible
persistence
personnel
perspiration
persuade
persuasion
physical
physiology
physique
pitiful
planning
playwright
pleasant
poison
politician
pollute
possession
possibly
practically
practice
prairie
precede
preference
preferred
prejudice
preparation
prevalent
primitive
privilege
probably
procedure
proceed
process
professor
prominent
pronunciation
psychology
purpose
pursue
pursuit

quandary
quantity
quarter
questionnaire
quiet
quizzes

realistically
realize
really
rebel
rebelled
recede
receipt
receive
recognize
recommend
reference
referred
relief
relieve
religious
remembrance
reminisce
renown
repetition
representative
resemblance
resistance
restaurant
rhyme
rhythm
ridiculous
roommate

sacrifice
sacrilegious
safety
satellite
scarcity
schedule
science
secretary
seize
separate
sergeant
several
sheriff
shining
shoulder
siege
significance
similar
sincerely
sophomore
source
speak
specimen
speech
sponsor
stopping
strategy
strength
strenuous
stretch
strict
strictly
studying
succeed
successful
sufficient
summary
superintendent
supersede
suppress
surely
surprise
suspicious

teammate
technical
technique
temperature
tendency
than
then
thorough
though
throughout
together
tomatoes
tomorrow
tragedy
transferred
truly
twelfth
tyranny

unanimous
unconscious
undoubtedly
unnecessary
until
usable
usually

vacuum
vegetable
vengeance
vicious
villain
visible

weather
Wednesday
weird
wherever
whether
wholly
woman
women
writing

yacht

41d Using the hyphen to form compound words

The hyphen (-) is a mark of punctuation used either to divide a word or to form a compound word. Always use a hyphen to divide a word at the end of a line and continue it on the next line, as explained in Chapter 37 on word division. Using a hyphen to form compound words is somewhat more complicated.

Compound words express a combination of ideas. They may be written as a single word (*breakthrough*), as two words (*decision making*), or as a hyphenated word (*cave-in*). Sometimes compound words with the same element are spelled differently—for example, *cross-reference, cross section,* and *crosswalk.* Several generalizations can be made about using the hyphen for compound words. But if you doubt the spelling of a compound word, consult a dictionary.

1 Forming compound adjectives

When two or more words serve together as a single modifier before a noun, a hyphen or hyphens form the modifying words clearly into a unit:

> She is a well-known actor.
> The conclusions are based on out-of-date statistics.
> Some Spanish-speaking students work as translators.

When the same compound adjectives follow the noun, hyphens are unnecessary and are usually left out.

> The actor is well known.
> The statistics were out of date.
> Many students are Spanish speaking.

Hyphens are also unnecessary in compound modifiers containing an *-ly* adverb, even when these fall before the noun: *clearly defined terms; swiftly moving train.*

When part of a compound adjective appears only once in two or more parallel compound adjectives, hyphens indicate which words the reader should mentally join with the missing part:

> School-age children should have eight- or nine-o'clock bedtimes.

Advice on using hyphens in compound words:

http://owl.english.purdue.edu/Files/18.html From the Purdue Online Writing Lab.

http:/webster.commnet.edu/HP/pages/darling/grammar/compounds.htm From the Guide to Grammar and Writing.

2 Writing fractions and compound numbers

Hyphens join the numerator and denominator of fractions and the parts of the whole numbers twenty-one to ninety-nine:

three-fourths	twenty-four
one-half	eighty-seven

3 Forming coined compounds

Writers sometimes create (coin) temporary compounds and join the words with hyphens:

Muhammad Ali gave his opponent a come-and-get-me look.

4 Attaching some prefixes and suffixes

Do not use hyphens with prefixes except as follows:

- With the prefixes *self, all,* and *ex: self-control, all-inclusive, ex-student.*
- With a prefix before a capitalized word: *un-American.*
- With a capital letter before a word: *T-shirt.*
- To prevent misreading: *de-emphasize, anti-intellectual.*

The only suffix that regularly requires a hyphen is *elect,* as in *president-elect.*

5 Eliminating confusion

If you wrote the sentence *Doonesbury is a comic strip character,* the reader might stumble briefly over your meaning. Is Doonesbury a character in a comic strip or a comic (funny) character who strips? A hyphen would prevent any possible confusion: *Doonesbury is a comic-strip character.*

Adding prefixes to words can sometimes create ambiguity. *Recreation* (*creation* with the prefix *re-*) could mean either "a new creation" or "diverting, pleasurable activity." The use of a hyphen, *re-creation,* limits the word to the first meaning. Without a hyphen the word suggests the second meaning.

EXERCISE 6
Using hyphens in compound words

Insert hyphens as needed in the following compounds. Circle all compounds that are correct as given. Consult a dictionary as needed.

1. reimburse
2. deescalate
3. forty odd soldiers
4. little known bar
5. seven eighths
6. seventy eight
7. happy go lucky
8. preexisting
9. senator elect
10. postwar
11. two and six person cars
12. ex songwriter
13. V shaped
14. reeducate

PART X

Research Writing

CHAPTER 42

Planning a Research Project

If you've ever watched a TV detective pursue a culprit, you know that research can be exciting. When an investigator has a goal in sight, the seemingly mundane work of digging through files, interviewing witnesses, and piecing together clues becomes a concentrated and enthusiastic search.

This same excitement can be yours as you conduct research in school. Honest and inquisitive research writing does demand close attention to details, but the work will not be tedious if you see the details as steadily contributing to discoveries about yourself and the world around you. As you consider what others have to say about your subject and build on that to create new knowledge, you will become an expert in your own right. You will have a significant, in-depth understanding of a subject you care about, and you will communicate that understanding to others.

Through research writing, you will also learn skills that will help you in school, in work, and in life:

- Using the library and the Internet for research
- Analyzing and evaluating others' work
- Drawing on others' work to form, support, and extend your own opinions
- Documenting your sources

Your investigation will be influenced by whether you are expected mainly to report, to interpret, or to analyze sources.

Advice on research writing:

http://webster.commnet.edu/mla.htm From Capital Community College.

http://www.ipl.org/teen/aplus/stepfirst.htm From the Internet Public Library.

http://www.wisc.edu/writetest/Handbook/PlanResearchPaper.html From the University of Wisconsin at Madison.

http://karn.ohiolink.edu/~sg-ysu/process.html From Youngstown State University.

- In **reporting,** you survey, organize, and objectively present the available evidence about a topic.
- In **interpreting,** you examine a range of views on a topic in order to answer a question with your own conclusions.
- In **analyzing,** you attempt to solve a problem or answer a question through critical thinking about texts such as scholarly or literary works. (In this context, *analysis* stands for the entire process of critical reading and writing. See pp. 129–36.)

Reporting, interpreting, and analyzing are not exclusive: for instance, a paper analyzing a repeated image in a poet's work would also involve a survey of poems and an interpretation of their meaning. Because the three operations overlap, the research and writing process described in this and the next three chapters can generally serve any one of them.

Throughout Chapters 42–45, we will follow the development of research papers by two students, Edward Begay and Vanessa Haley. Begay's work, emphasizing interpretation, receives somewhat more attention; Haley's work, emphasizing analysis, enters the discussion whenever her process differed significantly from Begay's. Both students' final papers appear in Chapter 47.

42a Starting out

A thoughtful plan and systematic procedures will help you anticipate and follow through on the diverse and overlapping activities of research writing.

As soon as you receive an assignment for a research project, you can begin developing a strategy for completing it. The first step should be making a schedule that apportions the available time to the necessary work. A possible schedule appears on the next page. In it the research-writing process corresponds to the general writing process discussed in Chapters 1–3: planning or developing (steps 1–8), drafting (step 9), and revising and editing (step 10), plus the additional important stage of documenting the sources you use (steps 11–12).

Like any other essay, a research paper evolves gradually, and the steps sometimes overlap and repeat. For instance, while you do research, your reading leads you to organize ideas; and while you organize ideas, you discover where you need to do more research.

Such shifts are inevitable, and allowing for them is one key to successful and rewarding research writing. While working on a project, carry index cards or a notebook with you at all times to use as a

http://www.gmu.edu/departments/writingcenter/handouts/puller.html
Tips on keeping a journal, from George Mason University.

Scheduling steps in research writing

(See the pages in parentheses for discussion of the steps.)

Complete by:

______ 1. Setting a schedule and beginning a research journal (previous page)
______ 2. Finding a researchable topic and question (opposite)
______ 3. Developing a research strategy (p. 624)
______ 4. Finding sources, both print and electronic (p. 633), and making a working bibliography (p. 627)

______ 5. Evaluating and synthesizing sources (pp. 667, 673)
______ 6. Taking notes using summary, paraphrase, and direct quotation (p. 675) and avoiding plagiarism (p. 686)
______ 7. Developing a thesis statement (p. 700)

______ 8. Creating a structure (p. 701)
______ 9. Drafting the paper (p. 704), integrating summaries, paraphrases, and direct quotations into your ideas (p. 693)

______ 10. Revising and editing the paper (p. 707)
______ 11. Citing sources in your text (p. 698)
______ 12. Preparing the list of works cited (p. 698)
______ 13. Preparing and proofreading the final manuscript (p. 708)
______ Final paper due

Each segment marked off by a horizontal line will occupy *roughly* one-fourth of the total time. The most unpredictable segments are the first two, so it's wise to get started early enough to accommodate the unexpected.

research journal, a place to record your activities and ideas. (See pp. 19 and 121 on journal keeping.) In the journal's dated entries, you can keep a record of sources you consult, the leads you want to pursue, any dead ends you reach, and, most important, your thoughts about sources, leads, dead ends, new directions, relationships, and anything else that strikes you. Notes on what your sources actually say should be taken and organized separately—for instance, in the computer files or on the note cards discussed on pages 677–78. The research journal is the place for tracking and developing your own ideas. You will probably find that the very act of writing in it opens your mind and clarifies your thinking, making your research increasingly productive and rewarding.

42b Finding a researchable topic and question

Before reading this section, you may want to review the suggestions given on pages 6–9 for finding and limiting an essay topic. Generally, the same procedure applies to writing any kind of research paper: begin with an assigned subject or one that interests you (perhaps one you've already written about without benefit of research), and then narrow the subject to manageable dimensions by making it specific. However, selecting and limiting a topic for a research paper can present special opportunities and problems. And before you proceed with your topic, you'll want to transform it into a question that can guide your search for sources.

1 Choosing an appropriate topic

A topic for a research paper has four primary requirements, each with corresponding pitfalls:

1. Ample sources of information are available on the topic. Other researchers should have had a chance to produce evidence on the topic, weigh the evidence, and publish their conclusions. And the sources should be accessible.

   Avoid very recent topics, such as a new medical discovery or a breaking story in today's newspaper.

2. The topic encourages research in the kinds and number of sources required by the assignment.

   Avoid (*a*) topics that depend entirely on personal opinion and experience, such as the virtues of your hobby; and (*b*) topics that require research in only one source, such as a straight factual biography or a how-to like "Making Lenses for Eyeglasses." (An exception to *b* is a paper in which you analyze a single work such as a novel or painting.)

3. The topic will lead you to an assessment of sources and to defensible conclusions. Even when a research paper is intended to persuade, the success of the argument will depend on the balanced presentation of all significant points of view.

http://www.ipl.org/teen/aplus/step2.htm Advice on finding a research topic, from the Internet Public Library.

http://www.esc.edu/htmlpages/writer/menus.htm Advice on finding a research question, from the State University of New York.

Checklist for a good research topic

1. Published sources are ample: the topic is not so recent that other researchers will still be discovering it.
2. Sources are diverse: the topic is neither wholly personal nor wholly factual.
3. Sources can be assessed objectively: the topic is not solely a matter of belief, dogma, or prejudice.
4. Sources can be examined thoroughly in the assigned time and length: the topic is not too broad.

Avoid controversial topics that rest entirely on belief or prejudice, such as when human life begins or why women (or men) are superior. Though these topics may certainly be disputed, your own preconceptions could slant your research or conclusions. Further, your readers are unlikely to be swayed from their own beliefs.

4. The topic suits the length of paper assigned and the time given for research and writing.

   Avoid broad topics that have too many sources to survey adequately, such as a major event in history or the collected works of a poet.

2 Posing a research question

Asking a question about your topic can give direction to your research by focusing your thinking on a particular approach. You can even begin asking questions before you find your specific topic, as a way of opening avenues you may not have considered.

The students Edward Begay and Vanessa Haley arrived at their research questions by slightly different paths. For a composition course, Begay's instructor assigned an interpretation with a persuasive purpose but left the selection of subject to the student. Begay had recently read several newspaper articles on a subject that intrigued him: what kind of future computers might bring. Taking this broad subject as his starting point, he used clustering (see p. 25) to pursue some implications. While generating the cluster diagram on the facing page, Begay found himself giving the most thought to the Internet. He posed questions until a cluster about access to the Internet led him to a question that seemed interesting and significant: "Will the poor be excluded from the Internet?"

In developing a topic and question for an analysis paper assigned in a composition course, Vanessa Haley followed a somewhat different procedure. Instead of starting with a general subject, as Begay did, Haley began by looking for an unresolved question, an

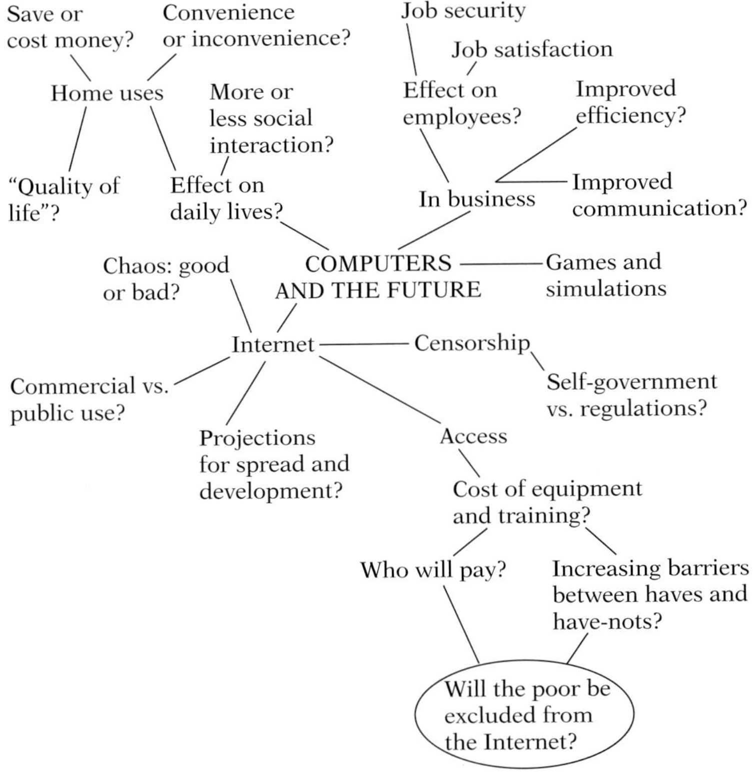

interesting problem, or a disagreement among the experts in some field of study. She had recently been reading an anthology of writings on the environment, and she had been disturbed by how many naturalists and environmentalists view human beings not as part of "nature" but as something separate from it, usually as its destroyer. In her journal, Haley wrote this entry:

> Many writers see nature as a place for humans to retreat to, or a wonderful thing that humans are ruining. Humans aren't considered natural themselves—human civilization isn't considered natural. Human civ. is "anti-natural." Isn't such a separation unrealistic and damaging? We *are* natural. We're here to stay, and we're not going back to the Stone Age, so we'd better focus on the connections between "us" and "it" (nature) rather than just the differences. Dillard seems to do this—seems to connect human and natural worlds. People are neither better nor worse than nature but just bound up in it. "Nature is as careless as it is bountiful, and [. . .] with that extravagance goes a crushing waste that will one day include our own cheap lives" ("Fecundity").

At the end of this entry, Haley refers to and quotes the writer Annie Dillard, one of the authors represented in the anthology. Haley decided to explore Dillard's views further by reading and analyzing more of her work. Haley's opening question for investigation, then, was "How does Annie Dillard see the place of humanity in nature?"

EXERCISE 1
Finding a topic and question

Choose three of the following subjects (or three subjects of your own), and narrow each one to at least one topic and question suitable for beginning work on a research paper. (This exercise can be the first step in a research paper project that continues through Chapters 42–45.)

1. Bilingual education
2. Training of teachers
3. Distribution of music by conventional versus electronic means
4. Dance in America
5. The history of women's suffrage
6. Food additives
7. Immigrants in the United States
8. Space exploration
9. Business espionage
10. The effect of television on professional sports
11. Child abuse
12. African Americans and civil rights
13. Successes in cancer research
14. Computer piracy
15. The European exploration of North America before Columbus
16. Hazardous substances in the workplace
17. Television evangelism
18. Science fiction
19. Treatment or prevention of AIDS
20. Water pollution
21. Women writers
22. Campaign financing
23. Comic film actors
24. An unsolved crime
25. Genetic engineering
26. Male and female heroes in modern fiction
27. Computers and the privacy of the individual
28. Gothic or romance novels in the nineteenth and twentieth centuries
29. The social responsibility of business
30. Trends in popular music

42c Developing a research strategy

Before you start looking for sources, consider what you already know about your subject and where you are likely to find information on it.

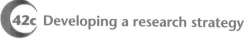

http://webster.commnet.edu/libroot/workbook/design.htm Information on research strategy, with a sample strategy, from Capital Community College.

http://stauffer.queensu.ca/inforef/strategy.htm Advice on developing a research strategy, from Queen's University.

1 Tapping into your own knowledge

Discovering what you already know about your topic will guide you in discovering what you don't know. Take some time to spell out facts you have learned, opinions you have heard or read elsewhere, and of course your own opinions. Use one of the discovery techniques discussed in Chapter 2 to explore and develop your ideas: keeping a journal (p. 19 and also p. 121), observing your surroundings (p. 21), freewriting (p. 22), list making (p. 24), clustering (p. 25), asking the journalist's questions (p. 26), using the patterns of development (p. 26), and thinking critically (p. 28).

When you've explored your thoughts, make a list of questions for which you don't have answers, whether factual (*What is the distribution of computers among affluent and poor schools?*) or more open-ended (*Are computers necessarily a positive force in education?*). These questions will give you clues about the sources you need to look for first.

2 Setting goals for sources

For many research projects, you'll want to consult a mix of sources, as described below. You may start by seeking the outlines of your topic—the range and depth of opinions about it—in reference works and articles in popular periodicals or through a search of the World Wide Web. Then, as you refine your views and your research question, you'll move on to more specialized sources, such as scholarly books and periodicals and your own interviews or surveys. (See pp. 639–65 for more on each kind of source.)

Print and online sources

The sources housed in your library—mainly reference works, periodicals, and books—have two big advantages over most of what you'll find on the Internet: they are cataloged and indexed for easy retrieval; and they are generally reliable, having been screened first by their publishers and then by the library's staff. In contrast, the Internet's retrieval systems are more difficult to use effectively, and online sources tend to be less reliable because most do not pass through any screening before being posted. (There are many exceptions, such as online scholarly journals and reference works and newspapers that are published both in print and online.)

Most instructors expect research writers to consult the print sources found in a library. But they'll accept online sources, too, if you have used them judiciously. Even with its disadvantages, the Internet can be a valuable resource for primary sources, scholarly contributions, current information, and a diversity of views. For guidelines on evaluating both print and online sources, see pages 667–72.

Primary and secondary sources

As much as possible, you should rely on **primary sources,** or firsthand accounts: historical documents (letters, speeches, and so on), eyewitness reports, works of literature, reports on experiments or surveys conducted by the writer, or your own interviews, experiments, observations, or correspondence.

In contrast, **secondary sources** report and analyze information drawn from other sources (often primary ones): a reporter's summary of a controversial issue, a historian's account of a battle, a critic's reading of a poem, a physicist's evaluation of several studies. Secondary sources may contain helpful summaries and interpretations that direct, support, and extend your own thinking. However, most research-writing assignments expect your own ideas to go beyond those in such sources.

Scholarly and popular sources

The scholarship of acknowledged experts is essential for depth, authority, and specificity; the general-interest views and information of popular sources can help you apply more scholarly approaches to daily life.

- *Check the publisher.* Is it a scholarly journal (such as *Education Forum*) or a publisher of scholarly books (such as Harvard University Press), or is it a popular magazine (such as *Time* or *Newsweek*) or a publisher of popular books (such as Random House)?
- *Check the author.* Have you seen the name elsewhere, which might suggest that the author is an expert?
- *Check the title.* Is it technical, or does it use a general vocabulary?

- *Check the electronic address.* Addresses for Internet sources often include an abbreviation that tells you something about the source: *edu* means the source comes from an educational institution, *gov* from a government body, *org* from a nonprofit organization, *com* from a commercial organization such as a corporation. (See pp. 197 and 670 for more on interpreting electronic addresses.)

Older and newer sources

Check the publication date. For most subjects a combination of older, established sources (such as books) and current sources (such as newspaper articles, interviews, or Web sites) will provide both background and up-to-date information. Only historical subjects or very current subjects like Edward Begay's (the Internet) require an emphasis on one extreme or another.

Impartial and biased sources

Seek a range of viewpoints. Sources that attempt to be impartial can offer trustworthy facts and an overview of your subject.

Sources with clear biases can offer a diversity of opinion. Of course, to discover bias, you may have to read the source carefully (see p. 669); but even a bibliographical listing can be informative.

- *Check the author.* You may have heard of the author before as a respected researcher (thus more likely to be objective) or as a leading proponent of a certain view (less likely to be objective).
- *Check the title.* It may reveal something about point of view. (Consider these contrasting titles uncovered by Edward Begay: "Computer Literacy and Ideology" versus "The Process of Introducing Internet-Based Classroom Projects and the Role of School Librarians.")

Note Online sources must be approached with particular care. See pages 670–72.

Sources with helpful features

Depending on your topic and how far along your research is, you may want to look for sources with features such as illustrations (which can clarify important concepts), bibliographies (which can direct you to other sources), and indexes (which can help you develop keywords for electronic searches; see pp. 637–39).

EXERCISE 2
Developing a research strategy

Following the suggestions on page 625, write what you already know about the topic you selected in Exercise 1 (p. 624), and then frame some questions for which you'll need to find answers. Also in writing, consider the kinds of sources you'll probably need to consult, using the categories given on pages 625–27.

42d Making a working bibliography

When you begin searching for sources, it may be tempting to pursue each possibility as you come across it. But that approach would prove inefficient and probably ineffective. Instead, you'll want to find out the full range of sources available and then decide on a good number to consult. For a paper of 1800 to 2500 words, try for ten to thirty promising titles as a start.

To keep track of where sources are and what they are, make a **working bibliography,** a file of books, articles, Web sites, and other possibilities. When you have a substantial file, you can decide which sources seem most promising and look them up first or, if necessary, order them through interlibrary loan.

A working bibliography is your chance to record all the information you need to find your sources and, eventually, to acknowledge them in your paper.

1 Tracking source information

You have several options for making a working bibliography:

- Copy source information by hand on note cards (usually 3″ × 5″), one source to a card. With this system, you can record source information no matter where you are, as long as you have a pen or pencil, and you can easily add, delete, and rearrange sources. Some instructors require that a working bibliography be submitted on note cards.
- Keep the working bibliography on your computer's hard drive or a diskette. (See p. 636 for more on this option.) You'll be able to sort sources by topic or by author and to copy bibliographic data into your paper when you prepare final source citations.
- Combine the previous two systems: print and cut up computer-generated source listings, and then paste or tape each source on a note card.

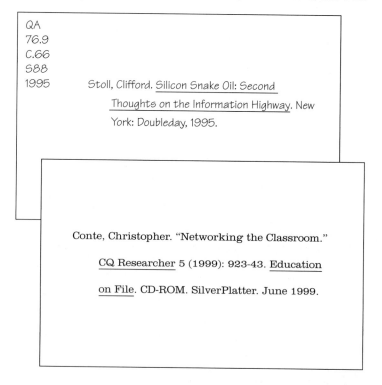

Two samples of source records from Edward Begay's working bibliography appear below. The first, for a book, Begay handwrote on a note card. The second record, for a journal article available on CD-ROM, Begay transferred from a CD-ROM database to his own

QA
76.9
C.66
S88
1995 Stoll, Clifford. Silicon Snake Oil: Second Thoughts on the Information Highway. New York: Doubleday, 1995.

Conte, Christopher. "Networking the Classroom." CQ Researcher 5 (1999): 923-43. Education on File. CD-ROM. SilverPlatter. June 1999.

disk and rewrote in a standard format as discussed below. He then printed the record and pasted it on a note card.

2 Recording source information

When you turn in your paper, you will be expected to attach a list of the sources you have used. So that readers can check or follow up on your sources, your list must include all the information needed to find the sources, in a format readers can understand. The box below shows the information you should record for each type of source so that you will not have to retrace your steps later. (If you keep your working bibliography on your computer, you can download the lists in the box from this book's Web site at *http://www.awlonline.com/littlebrown*. Then copy the appropriate list for each source and fill in the appropriate information.)

Information for a working bibliography

For books

- Library call number
- Name(s) of author(s), editor(s), translator(s), or others listed
- Title and subtitle
- Publication data:
  - Place of publication
  - Publisher's name
  - Date of publication
- Other important data, such as edition or volume number

For periodical articles

- Name(s) of author(s)
- Title and subtitle of article
- Title of periodical
- Publication data:
  - Volume number and issue number (if any) in which article appears
  - Date of issue
  - Page numbers on which article appears

For electronic sources

- Name(s) of author(s)
- Title and subtitle
- Publication data if source is also published in print
- Electronic publication data:
  - Date of release, online posting, or latest revision
  - Name and vendor (or publisher) of a database or name of an online service or network (America Online, Lexis-Nexis, etc.)
  - Medium (CD-ROM, online, etc.)
  - Format of online source (Web page, e-mail, etc.)
- Date you consulted the source
- Search terms used to reach the source (for a database)
- Complete electronic address

For other sources

- Name(s) of author(s) or others listed, such as a government department or a recording artist
- Title of the work
- Format, such as unpublished letter or live performance
- Publication or production data:
  - Publisher's or producer's name
  - Date of publication, release, or production
  - Identifying numbers (if any)

Most academic disciplines require special formats for source citations, and several are presented in this book:

- Modern Language Association (MLA) style, used in English, foreign languages, and some other humanities (pp. 710–42).
- Chicago style, used in history, art history, religion, philosophy, and some other humanities (pp. 822–31).
- American Psychological Association (APA) style, used in psychology and other social sciences (pp. 841–55).
- Council of Biology Editors (CBE) style, used in the biological and other sciences (pp. 869–76).
- Columbia style for online sources in the humanities and the social and natural sciences (pp. 881–91).

Before compiling your working bibliography, ask your instructor what documentation style you should use. Then consult the relevant handbook section to determine what kind of information to include and how to arrange it. (Begay's cards on p. 628 follow MLA style.)

Note Computerized bibliography programs can help you format your source citations in an appropriate academic style. See page 699 for more on such programs.

3 Finding bibliographic information for online sources

Unlike that for printed materials, publication information for online sources can be difficult to find and make sense of. The screen shot opposite shows the first page of a Web site. Circled numbers refer to the numbered explanations following.

1. The source's address, or URL, usually appears in the Web browser's Address or Location field near the top of the screen. If the field does not appear, adjust the settings of the browser so that it displays the field.
2. Use as the source title the title of the page you are consulting. This information usually appears as a heading at the top of the page, but if not it may also appear in the bar along the top of the browser window. When the page heading and the browser title differ, generally choose the browser title because it is the information used for bookmarks and search engines (see pp. 653–56). However, if the browser title conveys no information—for instance, *Home Page*—then use the page heading.
3. Important information often appears at or near the bottom of each page. Look here for (*a*) the name of the author or the sponsoring organization, (*b*) an address for reaching the sponsor or author directly, and (*c*) the publication date or the date of the last revision.

If the page you are reading does not list publication information, look for it on the site's home page. There may be a link to the

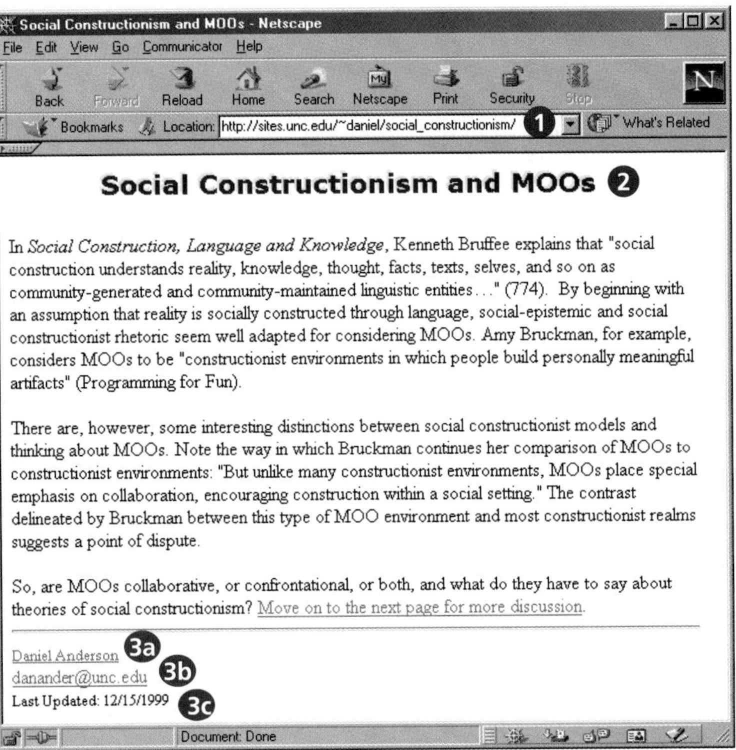

42d

home page, or you can find it by editing the address in the Address or Location field: working backward, delete the end of the address up to the preceding slash; then hit Enter. (For the address in the screen shot, you would delete *social_constructionism/*.) If that action doesn't take you to the home page, delete the end of the remaining address up to the preceding slash and hit Enter. Editing the address in this way, you'll eventually reach the home page.

When scouting a discussion list, Web forum, or newsgroup, save messages that may serve as sources, and keep track of when and where they were posted. You may be able to discover information about the author of a message from the list's archive or from an archive site such as Deja (*http://www.deja.com*). See pages 660–61 for more on these resources.

EXERCISE 3
Compiling a working bibliography

Prepare a working bibliography of at least ten sources for a research paper on one of the following people or on someone of your own choosing. Begin by limiting the subject to a manageable size, posing a question about a particular characteristic or achievement of the person. Then consult the Web, reference works, periodical indexes, and the library's catalog of books. (See pp. 639–58 for more on these resources.) Record complete bibliographic information on note cards or on your computer.

1. Steven Jobs (a founder of Apple Computer), or another business entrepreneur
2. Sandra Day O'Connor, or another Supreme Court justice
3. Emily Dickinson, or another writer
4. Michael Jordan, or another sports figure
5. Isamu Noguchi, or another artist

CHAPTER 43

Finding Sources

Once you have discovered a topic and question for research, have developed a research strategy, and know how to make a working bibliography (all covered in the previous chapter), you're ready to find sources. This chapter discusses electronic searches and the range of sources, both print and electronic, that is available to you.

Note If you require sources that are not available from your own library, you may be able to obtain them from another library, usually by mail, often by fax, sometimes electronically. Ask your librarian for help, and plan ahead: interlibrary loans can take a week or longer.

43a Searching electronically

Computer technology has dramatically altered research methods. Today, most libraries' reference rooms are filled with computer terminals instead of drawers of cards. Electronic catalogs and indexes allow researchers to conduct sophisticated searches with only a few keystrokes, both in the library and from miles away over phone lines. The Internet—a vast network of computers—can supply you with information from around the world: the catalogs of thousands of libraries, the developing ideas of experts, and the texts of newspapers, magazines, and scholarly journals.

http://webster.commnet.edu/libroot/workbook/wrkbk.htm A tutorial for information and library skills, from Capital Community College.

http://lcweb.loc/gov/rr Research tools, online bibliographies, subject lists, and indexes to periodicals and abstracts, from the Library of Congress.

http://www.ipl.org/teen/aplus/library.htm Advice on conducting library searches, from the Internet Public Library.

http://www.uwp.edu/info-services/library/teachslf.htm Advice on using the library, from the University of Wisconsin at Parkside.

http://thorplus.lib.purdue.edu/core A tutorial on searching electronically, from Purdue University.

A tip for researchers

If you are unsure of how to locate or use your library's resources, make an appointment with a reference librarian. This person is very familiar with all the library's resources and with general and specialized research techniques, and it is his or her job to help you and others with research. Even very experienced researchers often consult reference librarians.

The changes brought by computer technology both aid and complicate the research process. You can now rapidly accumulate lists of sources, but they present you with the challenge of deciding which sources are most appropriate for your project. This section explains how to find out what's available to you (below) and offers guidelines for conducting an efficient and productive search (p. 637).

Note If you can reach the Internet and your library's Web site from your home or dorm, you may be tempted to do all of your research online, skipping the resources housed in the library. But don't yield to the temptation. Many of the best resources are on the library's shelves, and most instructors expect research papers to be built on them to some extent. When you spot promising sources while browsing the library's catalogs and indexes online, make records of them and visit the library to look them up.

1 Discovering what's available

Your search for electronic sources will be quicker and more productive if you take the time to find out what kinds of sources you have access to and how you can use them.

Kinds of electronic sources

Your school's library probably offers several kinds of electronic sources:

- The library's catalog of holdings is a database allowing you to search for books and other sources available in the library. You type a subject, an author's name, or a title into a computer terminal, and the screen displays a list of all items matching your request. The catalog may include not only your library's holdings but also those of other schools nearby or in your state. (See pp. 637–39 for more on searching electronic catalogs.)
- Databases on CD-ROM, or compact disk, include indexes, bibliographies, encyclopedias, and other references. You search such a database much as you search a catalog, by author, title, or subject. The CD-ROMs may be available at only certain com-

puters in the library, but some schools distribute the databases over a network within the library or over the library's Web site. (For more on searching CD-ROMs, see pp. 637–39.)

- Online databases and text archives are stored on computers all over the world and are accessible over the Internet, either through your campus network, through a local Internet provider, or through a commercial service such as America Online. The online databases include many indexes, bibliographies, and other references. The text archives, containing the entire contents of sources, include the *New York Times* and other major newspapers, *Time* and other magazines, academic journals, proceedings of professional conferences, reports of government agencies, and files of discussion groups. (See pp. 637–39 and 653–62 for more on searching online sources.)

Your access to sources

Before beginning your research, you will need to find out what resources are available to you and how you can use them. For this, a library orientation is invaluable. Your instructor may arrange one, or the library itself may hold tours. (If so, ask if you must sign up in advance; such sessions can fill up rapidly.) If necessary, conduct your own orientation session: visit your library's reference area, examine any guides available for researchers, and ask questions.

Finding answers to the following sets of questions will give you a head start on your research and help smooth your way.

Computer access to library resources

Computers have changed research locations and times as well as research methods. Depending on your subject and your school's resources, you may even be able to conduct research from home in the middle of the night.

- Which, if any, library resources can be reached from computers elsewhere on campus or from home? If you don't have to be in the library to conduct a search or even to consult certain sources (such as encyclopedias or periodicals), you can budget your time accordingly.
- If you can reach the library from a remote computer, do you need special instructions or an account with a password? Can you gain access through the World Wide Web? (Most libraries have their own Web sites.)
- What software or hardware do you need to reach the library? Usually you'll need special communications software and a modem (a device that lets your computer talk to others over the telephone lines). Is the software provided? How do you install it?
- Whom do you ask for assistance in installing the software and connecting to the library?

Library resources and their formats

No library has all its holdings available in electronic form—books, for example, still occupy shelves and will continue to do so for the predictable future. Knowing what's available and in what form will help you plan and carry out your search.

- Which of the library's books are cataloged electronically? Some libraries list all their books electronically; others list only recent acquisitions—say, books less than ten years old. If your research topic requires you to consult both newer and older sources, you may need to search both the electronic catalog and a catalog bound in books or printed on film. (Few academic libraries still have a card catalog in drawers.)
- Which periodical indexes, bibliographies, and other reference works are available on CD-ROM or in other forms? Many older references have not yet been converted to electronic form, so you may need to consult a printed index for a newspaper dating back ten or fifteen years. In addition, electronic indexes and other sources are expensive, so your library may purchase only some of them. What your library does not have may be available from another library nearby or over the Internet.
- Do certain collections within the library have their own catalogs, either printed or electronic? Some collections of rare or historical documents may not be included in the main catalog. If they might contain sources important to your topic, you will want to know how to reach them.

Recording information

You'll still need a pencil and paper to conduct research, but they aren't necessarily your only tools for recording information. The questions below will help you discover your options:

- Can you print search results in the library? Many libraries provide some printers so that users can print catalog items, periodical listings, and other references located on computer.
- Does the library restrict printing? Some libraries allow users to print only a certain number of references or pages at one session. Some libraries charge a fee for printing.
- Can you save search results on your own floppy disk? Many catalogs and most databases allow users to save copies of references with only a few keystrokes. (The instructions appear on screen or in a separate handbook.) You then have an electronic record of your search, usable outside the library (but see the next question). You can rearrange and supplement source data for your working bibliography (see p. 627).
- Do you need certain hardware or software to "read" the search results you have downloaded on a floppy disk?

2 Making your search efficient and productive

Once you determine what resources are available, you should plan your search. Careful planning is essential: a too-casual search can miss helpful sources while returning hundreds, even thousands, of irrelevant sources.

Probably the most important element in planning a search is to develop **keywords,** or **descriptors,** to describe your subject. Most electronic catalogs and databases and Internet search engines operate by keywords: you type words that define your limited subject (see the box on the following page), and the computer searches for sources indexed by those words or using those words in titles and sometimes in summaries and texts.

To develop keywords, you need to understand what they do when you use them for a search. There are important differences between most databases and the search tools used on the Internet.

- In a database, sources are usually indexed by authors, titles, and publication years and also by keywords that describe the contents of sources. These keywords conform to the database's directory of terms. For the library's catalog, this directory is *Library of Congress Subject Headings* (*LCSH*), which is available in printed form in the library's reference room. Some other databases use *LCSH* as well, but many have their own directory in the form of a thesaurus (available either on the database or in printed form near the computer or at the reference desk). Using the database's own directory will speed your search. (See pp. 643–45 and 647–50 for more on searching databases.)
- For the Internet, which has no overall index like *LCSH,* search engines can help you locate sources. You can use search engines without keywords by following a series of subject directories. But the most powerful search engines can match your keywords with sources that contain those words anywhere—not just in the author's name and the title but also in the full text. The more accurately and specifically your keywords state your topic, the more likely such search engines are to return appropriate sources. One search engine returned more than 34 million listings for Edward Begay's preliminary keywords *Internet access* because these words appeared in that many sources. Begay found that he had to experiment with keywords to retrieve a narrower (and more relevant) list of sources. (See pp. 653–58 for more on search engines, including examples from Begay's search.)

http://www.lib.duke.edu/libguide/key_searching.htm Advice on keyword searches, from Duke University.

43a

Ways to refine keywords

You can refine your keywords in ways now standard, with some variations, among most databases and search engines. When in doubt about whether or how to use any of the following devices, consult the Help section of the resource you are using.

- Use the word *NOT* or the symbol – ("minus") to narrow your search by excluding irrelevant words: for instance, the word *provider* often follows the phrase *Internet access* in discussions of and advertisements for commercial services. Using the keywords *(Internet access) NOT provider* omits such listings from the search.
- Use the word *AND* or the symbol + to narrow your search by indicating that all the terms should appear in the source or its listing: for example, *Internet AND access* or *Internet AND education.*
- Use the word *OR* to broaden your search: *(Internet AND education) OR (cyberspace issues)* would produce sources keyed by either phrase in parentheses. *OR* is especially helpful for words with similar meanings, or synonyms. For instance, *Internet OR cyberspace OR (information highway)* would produce sources containing any of the three terms.
- Use quotation marks or parentheses (as in some of the examples above) to indicate that you want to search for the entire phrase, not the separate words.
- Use the word *NEAR* to indicate that the search words may be close to each other and on either side of each other: for example, *Internet NEAR education.* Depending on the resource you're searching, *NEAR* may specify that the words be directly next to each other or as many as a hundred words apart.
- To indicate that you will accept different versions of the same word, use a so-called wild card, such as *, in place of the optional letters: for example, *wom*n* includes both *woman* and *women; child** includes *child, children, childcare, childhood, childish, childlike,* and *childproof.* The example of *child** suggests that you have to consider all the variations allowed by your wild card and whether it will open up your search too much. If you seek only two or three from many variations, you will be better off using *OR: child OR children AND (Internet use).* (Note that some systems use ?, :, or + for a wild card instead of *.)
- Be sure to spell your keywords correctly. Some search tools will look for close matches or approximations, but correct spelling gives you the best chance of finding relevant sources.

Like Begay, you will probably have to use trial and error in developing your keywords. Because different databases have different directories and many search tools have no directory at all, you should count on occasionally running dry (turning up few or no sources) or hitting uncontrollable gushers (turning up hundreds or thousands of mostly irrelevant sources). But the process is not busy-work—far from it. Besides leading you eventually to worthwhile sources, it can also teach you a great deal about your subject: how you can or should narrow it, how it is and is not described by others, what others consider interesting or debatable about it, what the major arguments are. For example, while Begay's *Internet access* turned up an unmanageable list of sources on the Web, the same keywords produced practically nothing on a CD-ROM database, the *Social Sciences Index*. From misses like these, Begay learned, among other things, that *access* to the Internet did not have the same meaning for him as for most users of the word, and he resolved to make his meaning clear if he used the word in his final paper.

43b Finding reference works

Reference works, often available on CD-ROM or online, include encyclopedias, dictionaries, digests, bibliographies, indexes, atlases, and handbooks. Your research *must* go beyond reference works; indeed, many instructors discourage students from relying on such sources for ideas and information in final papers. But reference works can help you get started:

- They can help you decide whether your topic interests you and whether it meets the requirements for a research paper (p. 621).
- They can direct you to more detailed sources on your topic.
- They can help you refine keywords for electronic searches by giving you the terminology of the field you're researching.
- For an analysis paper, a specialized encyclopedia can identify the main debates in a field and the proponents of each side.

Edward Begay's use of reference works illustrates how helpful such sources can be as a starting point, even for a topic as current as the Internet. Begay first consulted *Bibliographic Guide to the History of Computing, Computers, and the Information Processing Industry* (to get some background on computers and the Internet) and *Encyclopedia of Sociology* (to explore the concept of equality in education).

The following lists give the types of reference works. Ask a reference librarian if you're unsure of where to start. The librarian can also advise you which sources are available on CD-ROM, over the Internet, or in print.

General encyclopedias

General encyclopedias give brief overviews and bibliographies. Covering all fields, they are convenient but very limited.

http://www.ipl.org/ref/RR/static/ref2500.html Links to online editions of general and specialized encyclopedias, from the Internet Public Library.

43b

Index to research sources

Academic American Encyclopedia
Collier's Encyclopedia
The Columbia Encyclopedia
Encyclopedia Americana

Encyclopedia International
The New Encyclopaedia Britannica
Random House Encyclopedia

Specialized encyclopedias, dictionaries, bibliographies

A specialized encyclopedia, dictionary, or bibliography generally covers a single field or subject. These works will give you more detailed and more technical information than a general reference work will, and many of them (especially bibliographies) will direct you to particular books and articles on your subject. Note that many specialized references are available on CD-ROM or online as well as in print.

One general reference work providing information on sources in many fields is the *Essay and General Literature Index* (published since 1900 and now updated semiannually). It lists tens of thousands of articles and essays that appear in books (rather than periodicals) and that might not be listed elsewhere. For a list of specialized reference works in various disciplines, consult the lists elsewhere in this book:

- Literature (p. 800)
- Other humanities, including history, the arts, philosophy, and religion (p. 819)
- Social sciences, such as business and economics, criminal justice, education, and psychology (p. 837)
- Natural and applied sciences, such as biology, engineering, mathematics, and physics (p. 866)

Unabridged dictionaries and special dictionaries on language

Unabridged dictionaries are more comprehensive than college or abridged dictionaries. Special dictionaries give authoritative information on aspects of language. (See Chapter 39 for more on the kinds of dictionaries and how to use them.)

Unabridged dictionaries

A Dictionary of American English on Historical Principles
The Oxford English Dictionary
The Random House Dictionary of the English Language
Webster's Third New International Dictionary of the English Language

Special dictionaries

Cassidy, Frederic G., et al., eds. *Dictionary of American Regional English.*

http://www.ipl.org/ref/RR/static/ref2000.html Links to online dictionaries, from the Internet Public Library.

Chapman, Robert L., ed. *Roget's International Thesaurus.*
Follett, Wilson. *Modern American Usage.* Ed. Jacques Barzun.
The New Fowler's Modern English Usage. Ed. R. W. Burchfield.
Onions, Charles T., et al., eds. *The Oxford Dictionary of English Etymology.*
Partridge, Eric. *A Dictionary of Slang and Unconventional English.* Ed. Paul Beale.
Partridge, Eric. *Origins: A Short Etymological Dictionary of Modern English.*
Webster's Dictionary of English Usage
Webster's New Dictionary of Synonyms
Wentworth, Harold, and Stuart Berg Flexner. *Dictionary of American Slang.*

Biographical reference works

If you want to learn about someone's life, achievements, credentials, or position, or if you want to learn the significance of a name you've come across, consult one of the reference works below.

American Men and Women of Science
Contemporary Authors
Current Biography
Dictionary of American Biography
Dictionary of American Negro Biography
Dictionary of Literary Biography
Dictionary of National Biography (British)
Dictionary of Scientific Biography
McGraw-Hill Encyclopedia of World Biography
Two Thousand Notable American Women
Webster's New Biographical Dictionary
Who's Who in America
World Authors

Atlases and gazetteers

Atlases are bound collections of maps; gazetteers are geographical dictionaries.

Cosmopolitan World Atlas
Encyclopaedia Britannica World Atlas International
National Atlas of the United States of America
National Geographic Atlas of the World
Times Atlas of the World
Times Atlas of World History
Webster's New Geographical Dictionary

http://www.ipl.org/ref/RR/static/ref1000.html Links to online biographies, from the Internet Public Library.

Almanacs and yearbooks

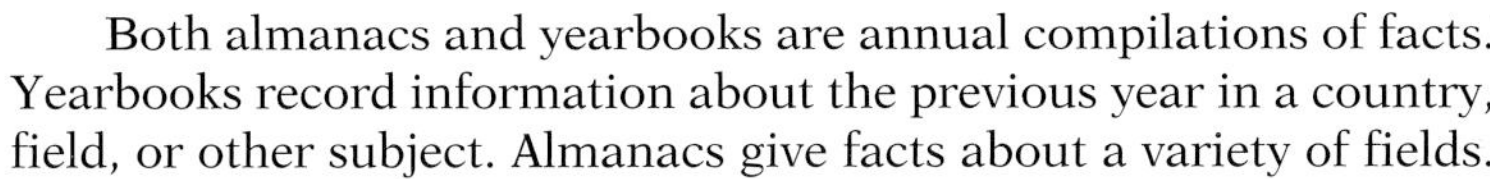

Both almanacs and yearbooks are annual compilations of facts. Yearbooks record information about the previous year in a country, field, or other subject. Almanacs give facts about a variety of fields.

Americana Annual
Britannica Book of the Year
Facts on File Yearbook
Information Please Almanac
US Bureau of the Census. *Statistical Abstract of the United States.*
World Almanac and Book of Facts

43c Finding books

Books can provide background information, subject surveys, popular views of culture, statements of scholarly theory, research results—in short, a broad range of secondary and primary sources (see p. 626).

1 Using the library catalog

The library's catalog lists books alphabetically by authors' names, titles of books, and subjects. If you are starting research on a subject you don't know very well, begin by looking under subject headings. If you know of an expert in the field and you want to find his or her books, look under the author's name. If you know the title of a relevant book but not the author's name, look for the title.

Most academic libraries store their book catalogs on computer; however, older volumes—say, those acquired more than ten or fifteen years ago—may still be cataloged in bound volumes or on microfilm or microfiche (see p. 651). (Few academic libraries today use the once-familiar drawers of cards.) Before you search for books, you'll need to ask a librarian which books are cataloged on computer and which, if any, are not.

You may have access through a specialized computer network or other schools' Web sites to the book catalogs of other libraries in your area or state. You can search these catalogs as you do your own library's, and sometimes you can borrow books from another

http://www.ipl.org/ref/RR/static/ref0500.html Links to online almanacs, from the Internet Public Library.

http://webster.commnet.edu/libroot/workbook/findinfo.htm Advice on finding books, from Capital Community College.

http://lcweb.loc.gov/z3950 Access to hundreds of library catalogs at one site, from the Library of Congress.

library in your area directly through the network or through a librarian. Ask your librarian for assistance with remote searches and loans. And allow time for the book to be sent after your request.

All book catalogs contain similar information, though it may be organized differently from one library to the other. By far the most widely used format derives from the Library of Congress cataloging system and includes author, title, publisher, date of publication, description (number of pages, size, and other data), subject headings the book is listed under, and the library's call number (which directs you to the book's location in the stacks). See opposite for a complete book record showing all this information.

2 Using a search strategy

Unless you seek a specific author or title, your search in the library's catalog will be much more efficient and productive if you zero in on appropriate keywords to describe your subject.

In searching the library's book catalog, you can find such words in *Library of Congress Subject Headings* (*LCSH*). This multivolume work lists headings under which the Library of Congress catalogs books (subject headings but not proper names of people, places, and so on). Consulting this source and following its system of cross-references and headings, you will be able to discover the keywords most likely to lead to appropriate sources.

Edward Begay used *LCSH* to eliminate the keyword *Internet,* which was much too broad for his needs. Instead, he combined *Internet* with some of its *LCSH* subheadings: *Internet and libraries* and *Internet and education.* Begay then used these keywords to search the library's computerized catalog, as illustrated in the following screen shots.

Initial subject search

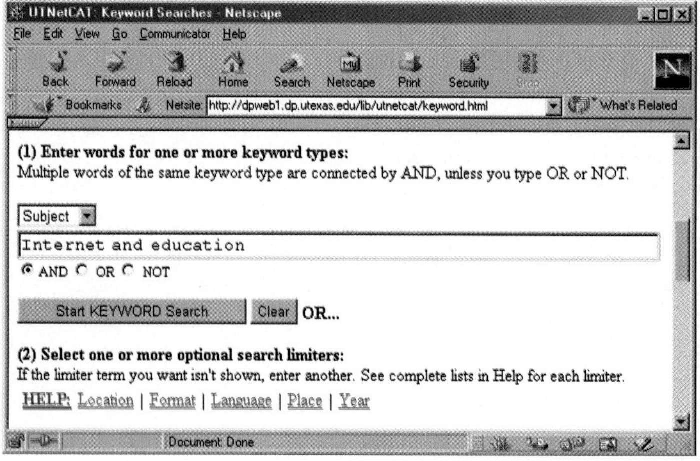

Search results

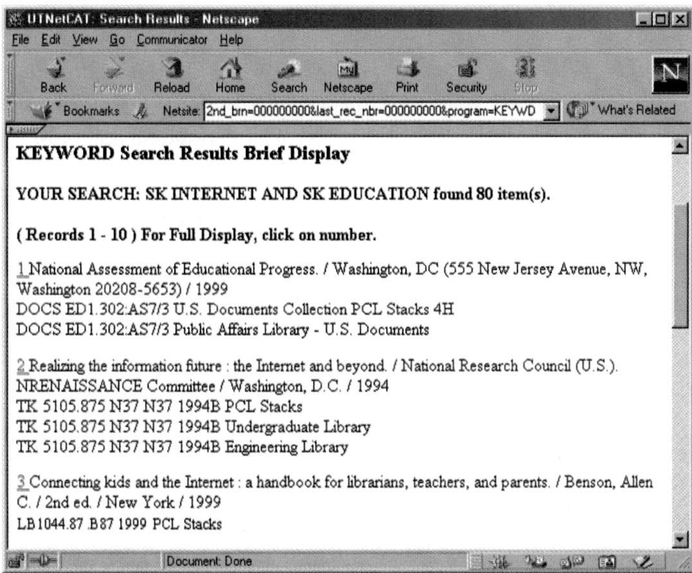

KEYWORD Search Results Brief Display

YOUR SEARCH: SK INTERNET AND SK EDUCATION found 80 item(s).

(Records 1 - 10) For Full Display, click on number.

1 National Assessment of Educational Progress. / Washington, DC (555 New Jersey Avenue, NW, Washington 20208-5653) / 1999
DOCS ED1.302:AS7/3 U.S. Documents Collection PCL Stacks 4H
DOCS ED1.302:AS7/3 Public Affairs Library - U.S. Documents

2 Realizing the information future : the Internet and beyond. / National Research Council (U.S.). NRENAISSANCE Committee / Washington, D.C. / 1994
TK 5105.875 N37 N37 1994B PCL Stacks
TK 5105.875 N37 N37 1994B Undergraduate Library
TK 5105.875 N37 N37 1994B Engineering Library

3 Connecting kids and the Internet : a handbook for librarians, teachers, and parents. / Benson, Allen C. / 2nd ed. / New York / 1999
LB1044.87 .B87 1999 PCL Stacks

Complete book record

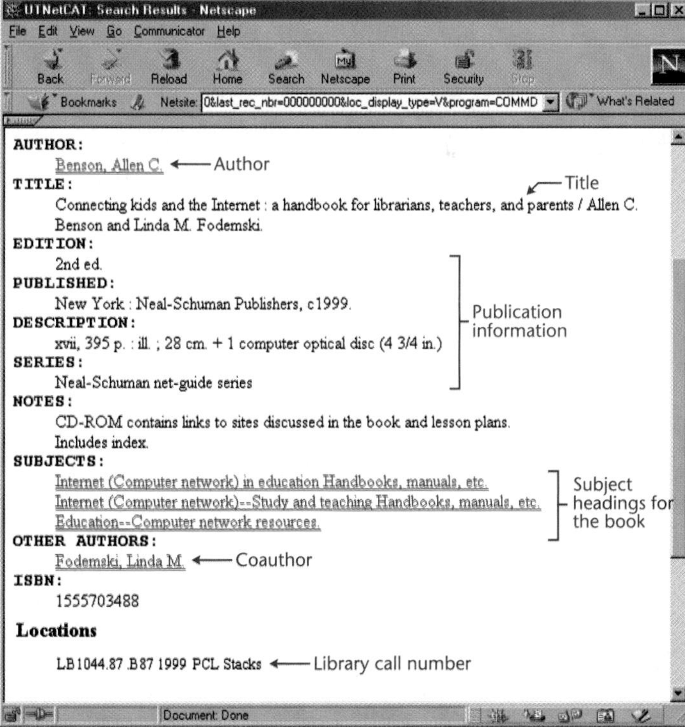

AUTHOR:
Benson, Allen C.
TITLE:
Connecting kids and the Internet : a handbook for librarians, teachers, and parents / Allen C. Benson and Linda M. Fodemski.
EDITION:
2nd ed.
PUBLISHED:
New York : Neal-Schuman Publishers, c1999.
DESCRIPTION:
xvii, 395 p. : ill. ; 28 cm. + 1 computer optical disc (4 3/4 in.)
SERIES:
Neal-Schuman net-guide series
NOTES:
CD-ROM contains links to sites discussed in the book and lesson plans.
Includes index.
SUBJECTS:
Internet (Computer network) in education Handbooks, manuals, etc.
Internet (Computer network)--Study and teaching Handbooks, manuals, etc.
Education--Computer network resources.
OTHER AUTHORS:
Fodemski, Linda M.
ISBN:
1555703488

Locations

LB1044.87 .B87 1999 PCL Stacks

3 Using references to books

Two types of references can help you identify general books that have information about your topic: publishing bibliographies and digests. Publishing bibliographies tell whether a book is still in print, whether a paperback edition is available, what books were published on a certain topic in a certain year, and so on.

Books in Print. Books indexed by author, title, and subject.
Cumulative Book Index
Paperbound Books in Print

You might, for example, want to know if the author of an encyclopedia article has published any relevant books since the date of the encyclopedia. You could look up the author's name in the latest *Books in Print* to find out.

If you want to evaluate a book's relevance to your topic before you search for it, a review index such as the following will direct you to published reviews of the book:

Book Review Digest. Summarizes and indexes reviews of books.
Book Review Index
Current Book Review Citations

For specialized review indexes, see pages 820 (humanities), 839 (social sciences), and 867 (natural and applied sciences).

43d Finding periodicals

Periodicals—journals, magazines, and newspapers—are invaluable sources of information in research. The difference between journals and magazines lies primarily in their content, readership, frequency of issue, and page numbering.

- Magazines—such as *Psychology Today, Newsweek,* and *Rolling Stone*—are nonspecialist publications intended for diverse readers. Most magazines appear weekly or monthly. In print,

http://stauffer.queensu.ca/inforef/bookreview Advice on locating and using book reviews, from Queen's University.

http://webster.commnet.edu/libroot/workbook/journals.htm Advice on finding information in periodicals, from Capital Community College.

http://www.ipl.org/ref/RR/static/ref5300.html Directories of periodicals, from the Internet Public Library.

http://lcweb.loc.gov/rr/main/ab_index.html An extensive list of periodical indexes in every field, from the Library of Congress.

their pages are numbered anew with each issue. Online, their pages are often not numbered.

- Journals often appear quarterly or less frequently and contain scholarly, specialized information intended for readers in a particular field. Examples include *American Anthropologist, Journal of Black Studies,* and *Journal of Chemical Education.* All print and many online journals number their pages. Some page each issue separately, like a magazine. Others page issues sequentially for an entire annual volume, so that issue number 3 (the third issue of the year) may open on page 327. (The method of pagination determines how you cite a journal article in your list of works cited. See p. 728.)

1 Using indexes to periodicals

Several indexes provide information on the articles in journals, magazines, and newspapers. The contents, formats, and systems of abbreviation in these indexes vary widely, and they can be intimidating at first glance. But each one includes an introduction and explanation to aid the inexperienced user.

Many indexes are available on CD-ROM and online. Consult the library's list of databases to find the ones that seem most appropriate for your subject, or use a Web search engine to find online indexes. Edward Begay, for instance, chose to avoid indexes of technical periodicals, such as *Applied Science and Technology Index* and *Computer Database,* because his subject was the social and economic effects of computers rather than the machines themselves. Instead, Begay chose databases such as *Sociofile,* for articles in sociology journals; *PsycLIT,* for articles in psychology journals; and *InfoTrac's National Newspaper Index,* for recent newspaper articles.

Searching electronic periodical indexes is discussed under electronic searches on pages 637–39. To recap, you'll need keywords reflecting the index's own terms for categorizing articles—found either in *Library of Congress Subject Headings* or in the index's thesaurus. You enter these keywords in the space provided on the opening screen of the index; limit the publication dates to be searched, if appropriate; and click on Search or Enter to begin.

Here are the first two listings received by Edward Begay when he searched the *Social Sciences Index* using the keywords *Internet and education.* (The elements of one listing are labeled.)

```
1. ETHNIC differences. Internet--United States  ← Subject heading and subheading
Diversity in a virtual world. By Lack, Jennifer.  ← Article author and title
Ethnicity plays a minor role in determining who is on-
line and who is not, according to a recent study con-
ducted by Forrester Research, Cambridge. The study found   } Summary
that income, education, and the degree of comfort with
```

43d

```
         technology have a greater impact on Internet adoption.
         Accordingly, says Ekaterina Walsh, an analyst at For-
Summary  rester, companies will be more successful by targeting
         people by their hobbies or what is relevant to them at
         the moment than by focusing on ethnicity. The differ-
         ences that do exist among ethnic households as regards
         on-line access and usage are outlined.
         American Demographics, July 1999, Vol. 21 no7 p. 17-18
              Journal title          Date   Volume and issue  Page numbers
         ------------------------------------------------------------------

         2. HIGH technology & education--United States;
            COMPUTER-assisted instruction--United States
         Networking the classroom. By Conte, Christopher
         Questions whether computer technology will reform edu-
         cation. Efforts to link schools to the computer net-
         work; Question of whether computer networking enhances
         learning; Issue of whether teachers are prepared to
         take advantage of computer networking; Impact of com-
         puter networking on gap between poor and affluent
         Americans; High cost of networking; Government initia-
         tives; Bibliography. INSET: Chronology.
         CQ Researcher, 10/20/99, Vol. 5 no39, pp. 923-43,
         1 graph, 1 map, 1bw

         ** FullTEXT Available on CD-ROM **
```

If your first search of a periodical index returns a large number of sources (more than fifty), you should try to narrow your search. Look among the first ten to twenty listings for titles that seem relevant to your subject and then for those titles' subject headings (such as "HIGH technology & education" in the second listing above). Try your search again using one or more of those words or phrases. Experiment with a variety of keywords if necessary to find appropriate sources.

The *Social Sciences Index* is only one of many periodical indexes. Some are general indexes, meaning that their lists are not specialized. These include the following:

InfoTrac. Indexes more than fifteen hundred academic, business, technical, government, and popular publications, including five national newspapers.

NewsBank. Indexes more than five hundred newspapers.

The New York Times Index. Indexes the most comprehensive US newspaper. The index can serve as a guide to national and international events and can indicate what issues of unindexed newspapers to consult for local reactions to such events.

Poole's Index to Periodical Literature. Indexes by subject British and American periodicals of the nineteenth century.

Popular Periodicals Index. Indexes about twenty-five contemporary popular periodicals not listed in major indexes.
ProQuest. Provides both indexes to and the texts of articles in the humanities, education, and the social sciences.
Readers' Guide to Periodical Literature. Indexes articles published in more than a hundred popular magazines. For a current research project, consult several years' listings.
SilverPlatter. Indexes periodicals in psychology, sociology, and nursing.
Wall Street Journal Index. Indexes the leading business newspaper and *Barron's.*

Here, from Edward Begay's research, is a sample from the *Info-Trac* index:

```
Subject: INTERNET Subdivision: DEMOGRAPHIC aspects ← Subject heading and subheading

One Internet, two nations. (Internet usage by ethnic
groups) (Column) Henry Louis Gates Jr. The New York Times
Oct 31, 1999 s0 pWK15(N) pWK15(L) col 2 (20 col in)

What price will be paid by those not on the Net? (poor
minorities denied use of the Internet) Pam Belluck. The
New York Times Sept 22, 1999 pD12(N) pG12(L) col 1 (50
col in)

UNCF Examines Digital Divide On Campus. (United Negro
College Fund) RONALD ROACH. Black Issues in Higher Educa-
tion August 5, 1999 v16 ill p32

A Web That Looks Like the World. (Internet demographics)
(Abstract) Business Week March 22, 1999 i3621 pEB46(1)

Who's on the Internet and why. Dan Johnson. The Futurist
August-Sep 1998 v32 n6 p11(2)

Continental divide. (differences between Silicon Valley,
CA, and Washington DC) (Special Section: The Backbone of
America) Michael Kinsley. Time July 7, 1997 v150 n1 p97(3)
```

Periodical title — Date — Volume, issue number, and page number

For scholarly journals, most libraries have a variety of specialized indexes. Begay also consulted several of these, including the *Social Sciences Index* illustrated on pages 647–48. For lists of scholarly indexes in various academic disciplines, see pages 801 (literature), 820 (other humanities), 838 (social sciences), and 866 (natural and applied sciences).

In addition to the general and specialized indexes, your library may subscribe to online services such as Dialog (for many scholarly indexes as well as entire articles), Nexis (for indexes to newspapers, newsletters, corporate reports, and many other sources, as well as entire articles), and Lexis (for sources in law and litigation such as codes and cases). These services are essentially databases of databases: they gather indexes, periodicals, and other data into huge banks. The services cost money to subscribe to or to use, so your library may restrict access to them, charge for them, or encourage you to use CD-ROM databases instead.

2 Using abstracts and citation indexes

Article summaries—or **abstracts**—can tell you in advance whether you want to pursue a particular article further. Many periodical indexes include abstracts along with bibliographic information, as Edward Begay discovered in *Sociological Abstracts.* One full entry is reproduced below:

```
AUTHOR: Noble, David F.
TITLE: Digital diploma mills: the automation of higher
      education.
SOURCE: Monthly Review (New York, N.Y.) v. 49 no9 (Feb.
      '98) p. 38-52
ABSTRACT: Higher education is entering a new phase that
      is rapidly drawing the halls of academe into the
      age of automation. The headlong rush toward imple-
      menting new technology is spurred in part by the
      incessant pressures of progress, a fear of being
      left behind. However, the process of change does
      not simply involve universities undergoing a tech-
      nological transformation; it is underpinned by the
      growing commercialization of higher education,
      with technology just a vehicle and a disarming
      disguise. The high-tech transformation of higher
      education is being initiated and implemented from
      the top down, either without any involvement by
      students and faculty in decision making or despite
      it. The lines have already been drawn in the
      struggle that will ultimately determine the shape
      of the new age of higher education, with univer-
      sity administrators and their numerous commercial
      partners on one side and those who represent the
      core relation of education--students and teachers
      --on the other.
STANDARD NO: 0027-0520
DATE: 1998
PLACE: United States
RECORD TYPE: art
CONTENTS: feature article
SUBJECT: Distance education. Higher education - United
      States. Internet - Educational use.
```

Abstracts are published in many academic disciplines and are also frequently available on CD-ROM or online. For discipline-specific listings, see pages 801 (literature), 820 (other humanities), 838–39 (social sciences), and 867 (natural and applied sciences).

When you want to trace what has been written *about* an article or book you are consulting, use a **citation index.** This resource lists references to written works after they are published, as when one scientific article comments on an earlier article. Refer to the pages given above for citation indexes in the humanities, social sciences, and natural and applied sciences.

3 Locating and using periodicals

Every library lists its holdings of periodicals (usually called *serials*) either in the main catalog (see p. 643) or in a separate catalog. The listing for each periodical tells how far back the issues go and where and in what form the issues are stored.

Many periodicals are available on CD-ROM or online. If the periodical is not available electronically, its recent issues are probably held in the library's periodicals room. Back issues are usually stored elsewhere, in one of three forms: in bound volumes; on **microfilm,** a filmstrip showing pages side by side; or on **microfiche,** a sheet of film with pages arranged in rows and columns. Consulting periodicals stored on microfilm or microfiche requires using a special machine, or "reader," with which you locate the page and project it on a screen. (Some readers are also attached to coin-operated photocopiers.) Any member of the library's staff will show you how to operate the reader.

If the periodical you seek is not available in your library, you have at least two options:

- You may be able to obtain the article by interlibrary loan. The article may arrive by mail, by fax, or over the Internet, and there may be a fee for the service. Even electronic loans can sometimes take a week or more, so place your order early.
- You may be able to find the periodical online over the Internet. Your library may subscribe to a service such as Project MUSE, which carries dozens of journals online. Or you may be able to locate the periodical on the Web using its title as your keywords.

Note A periodical published both online and in print—especially a newspaper or popular magazine—may differ in its two versions: articles may appear in one form but not the other, or articles may be abridged in the online form. Thus an article you find listed in a periodical index may be shortened or omitted from the online version of the periodical.

43e Finding sources on the World Wide Web

Both for refining your topic and for gathering actual sources, the Web has a number of advantages:

- Since Web publication is faster than print or even CD-ROM publication, you may find more current information on the Web than in your library. For example, many government agencies post their data first online, then in print.
- Many scholarly journals are published online. Some are published *only* online, not in print.
- If your school's library has few resources on your subject, you can search catalogs at other libraries.
- If your library does not have some sources—such as government documents—located by your database searches, you can obtain the documents more quickly over the Internet than by interlibrary loan.

However, the Web has a number of disadvantages, too:

- It provides limited information on the past. Sources dating from before the 1980s or even more recently probably will not appear on the Web.
- It is not all-inclusive. Most books and many periodicals are available only in the library, not via the Web.
- It changes constantly. No search engine can keep up with the Web's daily additions and deletions, and even a source you find today may be different or gone tomorrow. Some sites are designed and labeled as archives: they do not change except with additions. But other sites, such as those for newspapers and magazines, frequently replace old material with new. If you think you'll want to use something from such a site, you should consult it right away. If it seems useful, you should download it to your own computer or take notes from it (see pp. 676–85).
- Because of the Web's constant change, you must record publication information as you are consulting a source. With print sources, if you forget this step you can at least retrace your steps, however tedious that may be. But with Web sources, you often cannot retrace your steps: the site you seek may be gone or may have changed. To track online sources, use the advice and list of elements on page 629.
- The Web is a wide-open network. Anyone with the right hardware and software can place information on the Internet, and even a carefully conceived search can turn up sources with widely varying reliability: journal articles, government documents, scholarly

data, term papers written by high school students, sales pitches masked as objective reports, wild theories. You must be especially diligent about evaluating Internet sources (see p. 670).

Clearly, the Web warrants cautious use. It can provide a wealth of worthwhile information and ideas, but it should not be the only resource you work with.

Note For information on reading Web addresses, or URLs, see pages 197 and 670.

1 Using a search engine

To find sources on the Web, you use a **search engine** that catalogs Web sites in a series of directories and conducts keyword searches (see p. 637). Generally, use a directory when you haven't yet refined your topic or you want a general overview. Use keywords when you have refined your topic and you seek specific information.

Current search engines

Dozens of search engines are available. The box on the next page describes the currently most popular engines. (To reach any of them, enter its address in the Address or Location field of your Web browser.) In addition, several directories that review Web sites and catalog them by topic are good starting places for research projects:

AlphaSearch
http://www.calvin.edu/library/as
BUBL Link
http://bubl.ac.uk/link
Librarians' Index to the Internet
http://slii.org
Internet Public Library
http://www.ipl.org/ref
Scout Select
http://www.ilrt.bris.ac.uk/mirrors/scout/toolkit/bookmarks/index.html
WebGEMS
http://www.fpsol.com/gems/webgems.html

Note No search engine can catalog the entire Web—indeed, even the most powerful engine may not include half the sites available at

http://www.sci.ouc.bc.ca/libr/connect96/search.htm A tutorial for using Web search engines, from Okanagan University College.

http://scout.cs.wisc.edu/toolkit/searching/index.html Information about varying kinds of Web search engines, from the University of Wisconsin at Madison.

Web search engines

The features of search engines change often, and new ones appear constantly. For the latest on search engines, see the links collected by Search Engine Watch at *http://www.searchenginewatch.com/links.*

AltaVista (*http://www.altavista.com*)
AltaVista searches for keywords in the entire text of documents, so it can return very specific results but may also provide many irrelevant results. AltaVista can handle searches in many languages.

AskJeeves (*http://www.askjeeves.com*)
AskJeeves allows searches prompted by questions, such as *Where can I learn about the Internet?* Though appealing, especially to Web beginners, the question prompts produce mixed results.

Dogpile (*http://www.dogpile.com*)
Dogpile queries multiple search engines and allows searches of newsgroups, FTP sites, business news, and other specific resources.

Excite (*http://www.excite.com*)
Excite's advanced search allows searches of news items and in many languages.

Google (*http://google.com*)
Google's search results rank sites based on how many other sites are linked to them, thus providing a measure of sites' usefulness.

HotBot (*http://hotbot.lycos.com*)
Hotbot allows varied kinds of searches and includes a handy feature that searches for URLs that have been linked to a specific page.

Infoseek (*http://infoseek.go.com*)
Infoseek will search newsgroups and other resources and includes a topic option that searches for subject-related information.

Lycos (*http://www.lycos.com*)
Like AskJeeves, Lycos allows question prompts, with the same mixed results. Lycos also allows keyword searches of entire documents or of just document titles, and it supports queries in many languages.

MetaCrawler (*http://www.go2net.com*)
MetaCrawler queries multiple search engines and allows searches within specific categories.

NorthernLight (*http://www.northernlight.com*)
NorthernLight's advanced search permits limiting results by category and sorting results by date and other variables.

WebCrawler (*http://webcrawler.com*)
WebCrawler searches the entire text of documents and can thus return very specific results but also many irrelevant results.

Yahoo! (*http://www.yahoo.com*)
Yahoo!'s advanced search allows queries of specific categories and restrictions in the number of results based on sites' currency.

any given time, and most engines include only a fifth or less. Thus you should try out more than a single engine, perhaps as many as four or five, to cover a good portion of the Web's offerings.

A sample search engine

The screen shot below from the HotBot search engine shows the features common to most engines. The circled numbers are keyed to numbered comments following.

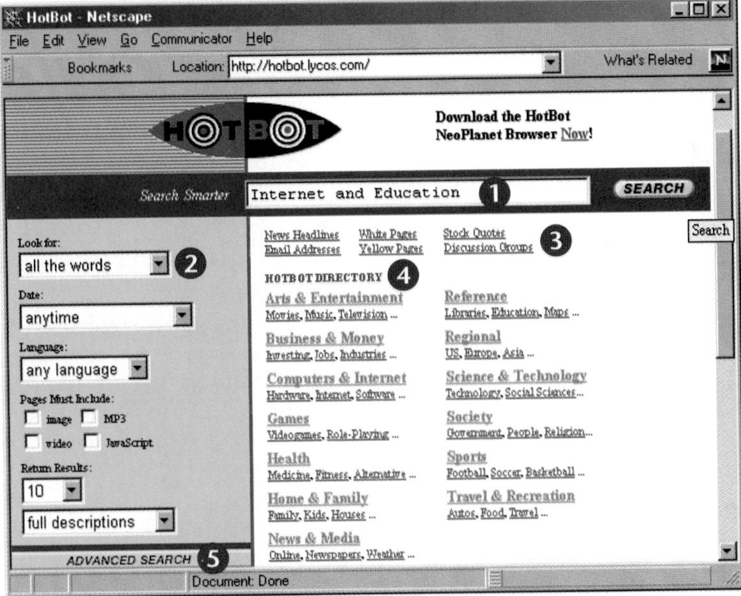

1. To search by keywords, type them into the Search field. (See pp. 637–39 on developing keywords.)
2. Customize your search using menus—for instance, select a date range, a language, or a number of results to see.
3. Click on listings for specific kinds of information and sources—for instance, e-mail addresses or postings to discussion groups.
4. Instead of searching by keywords, browse a subject directory to zero in on your general subject and perhaps your specific topic.
5. Click Advanced Search for more search options and for help using the search engine:

   How to format keyword searches—for instance, whether you need to use *AND*, *NOT*, *OR*, and symbols such as + or –.

   How to search for phrases by using parentheses or quotation marks to link words. A few search engines assume that two or more words in a row without any formatting constitute a phrase to search for.

How to interpret the results of the search. When you perform a search using either keywords or a directory, the search engine generates a list of sites that match your search criteria. The matching sites, or hits, are listed in order of "relevance," which the search engine determines by criteria such as the number of times your search terms appear within a document; whether the terms appear at the beginning, middle, or end of a document; and whether the terms appear in the title or the address of the document. If there are any special ways the search engine determines relevance, its Help information will specify them.

Bookmarks and search histories

Your Web browser probably includes functions that allow you to keep track of Web sources and your search:

- **Bookmarks** save site addresses as links. Click Bookmarks or Favorites near the top of the Web browser screen to add a site you want to return to. A bookmark remains on file until you delete it.
- A browser's search history records the sites you visited over a certain period, such as a single online session or a week's sessions. (After that period, the history is deleted.) If you forgot to bookmark a site, you can click History or Go to locate your search history and recover the site.

2 Following a sample search

For his initial search of the Web, Edward Begay started with the keywords *Internet access* on the search engine AltaVista. But the search returned more than 34 *million* items, as shown in the top screen shot opposite. Begay realized instantly that he needed to alter his search strategy. Checking AltaVista's Advanced Search information, he found that the search engine sorts results based on the number of times keywords appear in a document and on the location of the keywords in the document (title, first paragraph, and so on). When he scanned the first few screens of AltaVista's results, he noticed that most items had to do with commercial providers offering connection to the Internet. Clearly, the keywords *Internet access* were returning the wrong kinds of information.

Begay decided to try another approach and consulted one of the reviewed subject directories listed on page 653. At the Librarians' Index to the Internet, he noticed broad categories such as *Computers* and *Internet Info*. (See the bottom screen shot opposite.) Moving down through *Internet Info,* he located a directory for *Sta-*

First AltaVista results

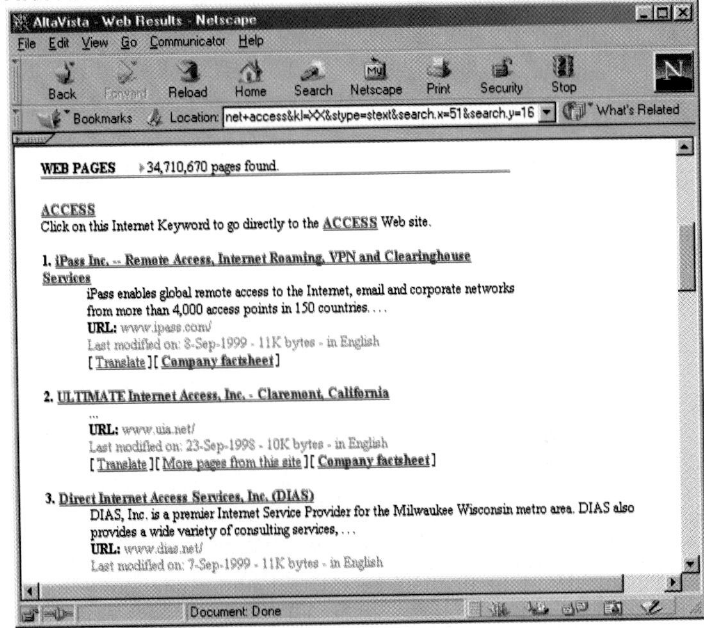

Reviewed subject directory

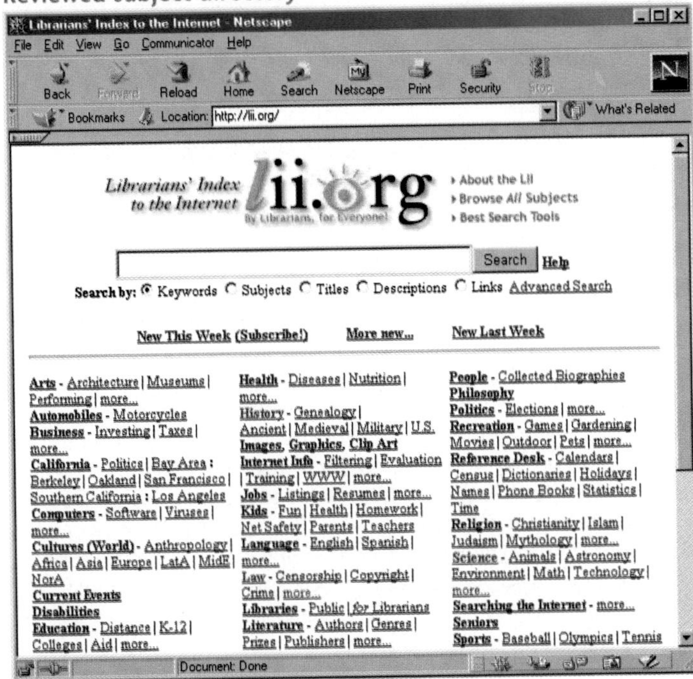

tistics, and there he found links to sites presenting data about Internet users and reporting on Internet access in public schools. The reports covered access to computers, using terms such as *economic access to education* and *digital divide.*

Begay then returned to AltaVista with these new keywords. The keyword *Internet AND (economic access)* proved disappointing, returning hundreds of irrelevant sites. But *Internet AND (economic access) AND education* was much more successful, returning the results shown in the screen shot below. Several of the twenty-four items were directly related to Begay's topic, and Begay bookmarked them for later reference (see p. 656).

Second AltaVista results

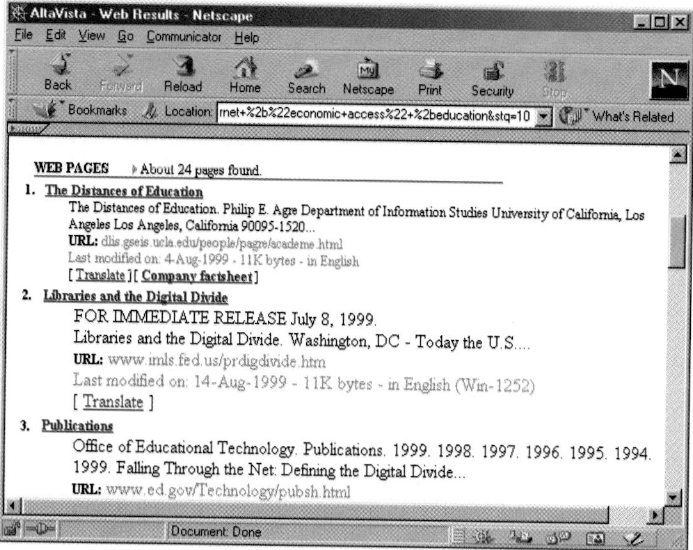

Begay wasn't finished. Knowing that no search engine catalogs every Web site, he decided to try his successful keywords at two other engines, Yahoo! and Dogpile. The Yahoo! search was less productive but did turn up one promising source not listed by AltaVista. The Dogpile search, which worked through multiple search engines, returned a long list of 605 items, including many irrelevant ones but also (among the first twenty-five) three more possible sources.

Begay's Web search illustrates the trial-and-error approach required to refine keywords so that they locate worthwhile sources. Almost any successful Web search will require similar persistence and patience.

43f Finding other online sources

In addition to the Web, several other online resources can aid your research: electronic mail, discussion lists, Web forums, newsgroups, and synchronous communication.

1 Using electronic mail

With e-mail, you can send messages to and receive them from most people who use the Internet, as long as you know their addresses. (See p. 192 for two sources of e-mail addresses.) E-mail skills are an essential component of computer literacy and are discussed in detail on pages 192–97.

As a research tool, e-mail allows you to communicate with others who are interested in your topic. You may, for instance, carry on an e-mail conversation with a teacher at your school or with other students. Or you may interview an expert in another state to follow up on a scholarly article he or she published. (See p. 664 on conducting interviews.)

2 Using discussion lists

A **discussion list** (sometimes called a **listserv** or just a **list**) uses e-mail to connect individuals who are interested in a common subject: subscribers' messages are distributed to the other subscribers' e-mail accounts. (Many college courses use discussion lists for collaboration among students. See p. 243.)

Thousands of discussion lists operate on the Internet, each with a particular purpose and audience. The lists' focus tends to be scholarly or technical: discussions center on building knowledge within the community of subscribers. The discussion on a list may thus be more reliable than that on a Web forum or newsgroup (next two pages). If you find a list relevant to your topic, the discussion might orient you to current issues and debates and might lead you to a particular person who can answer your questions. However,

http://www.pbs.org/uti/begin.html Information about using the Internet, from the Public Broadcasting Service.

http://www.learnthenet.com/english/section/e-mail.html Basic e-mail information, from Learn the Net.

http://tile.net/lists A searchable index of e-mail discussion lists, from Tile.Net.

http://www.liszt.com Searchable indexes of e-mail discussion lists by category, from Liszt.

discussion lists are more difficult than other discussion groups to search because you must subscribe to each one, and you may have more difficulty extracting information from a continuing exchange among specialists.

The best way to find a discussion list that may be appropriate for your project is to search the Tile.Net or Liszt directory given at the bottom of the previous page. These directories provide subscription and other information about particular lists.

When conducting research on a discussion list, follow the guidelines for e-mail etiquette on pages 195–97 as well as those following:

- Many lists have explicit purposes and established conventions. Read the first e-mail message that arrives when you join a list to gather information about its priorities and conventions. Save this message, too, because it usually tells you how to cancel your subscription.
- Check for a file of frequently asked questions (FAQs), which will list the topics covered (and *not* covered) by the list and will answer common questions. Many lists also maintain Web archives of past messages that you can read for information or for a sense of a list's conventions.
- Devote some time to reading the list's messages before sending any questions or comments of your own. By reading but not participating (called **lurking**), you can get a sense of whether the list is relevant to your research topic (and vice versa) and observe the list's conventions.
- List members are usually glad to help with legitimate questions, but they resent messages that rehash familiar debates or that ask them to do someone else's work. Don't ask for information that you can find elsewhere. Instead, query subscribers about their unique knowledge and experiences.
- Evaluate messages carefully. Many list subscribers are passionate experts with fair-minded approaches to their topics, but almost anyone with an Internet connection can post a message to a list. See pages 670–72 on evaluating online sources.

3 Using Web forums

Many Web sites are devoted to discussions of particular issues. Open to everyone, these **forums** organize postings into **threads,** or groups of messages and replies on the same topic. You can visit the site and reach the postings through Web links, or you may be able to

Searchable indexes of Web forums:

http://www.forumone.com From ForumOne.

http://www.remarq.com From RemarQ.

subscribe so that all postings come to you automatically by e-mail. (Web forums are increasingly common as tools for collaboration among the students in a course. See p. 247.)

For indexes and links to Web forums, see the sites given at the bottom of the facing page. Follow the guidelines in the bulleted list opposite for participating in discussion lists. Although Web forums tend to be less scholarly and focused than discussion lists, the participants still expect newcomers to be familiar with the forum's conventions and its threads before they ask questions or contribute opinions.

Because Web forums are open to anyone, you must be especially diligent in evaluating any messages you consider using as sources. See pages 670–72 on evaluating online sources.

4 Using newsgroups

Like Web forums, **newsgroups** are open to everyone and offer discussions on an enormous range of topics. You can search relevant newsgroups at the Web sites listed at the bottom of this page. Investigate the options of the sites' archives as well: the sites may sort messages into threads and may allow you to locate information about the author of a given message, which is key in evaluating the message (see below).

Newsgroups are roughly categorized by subject, indicated by the first letters of the address—for instance, *comp* for computers and computer science, *soc* for social issues, *biz* for business. This prefix will give you an idea of whether the group is relevant to your concerns. When you reach a potentially relevant newsgroup, follow the guidelines for participation given in the bulleted list opposite.

Newsgroup contributions require the same critical evaluation as contributions to discussion lists and Web forums. See pages 670–72 on evaluating online sources.

5 Using synchronous communication

With electronic mail, discussion lists, Web forums, and newsgroups, there's a delay between a message you send and any response you receive. But with **synchronous** (or simultaneous) **communication,** you and others can correspond in real time, as you might talk on the phone. Synchronous programs include IRC (In-

http://sites.unc.edu/ngworkshop Tutorials and exercises for using newsgroups for research, from the University of North Carolina.

http://www.remarq.com Discussions and searchable newsgroup archives, from RemarQ.

http://www.deja.com Discussion and newsgroup archives, from Deja.

ternet relay chat), MUDs (multiuser domains), and MOOs (multiuser domains, object-oriented).

Though used mainly for social purposes, such as games and conversations, synchronous programs are also employed in education and research, as for class discussions, collaborative projects, interviews, and academic debates. Your instructors may ask you to use synchronous communication for coursework or research and will provide the software and instructions you need to get started. You can also discover more about synchronous communication at the first two Web sites given at the bottom of the page.

43g Finding pamphlets and government publications

Organizations such as social-service groups, professional societies, and all branches of government publish booklets, compilations of data, and other sources that usually cannot be retrieved through the library's book catalog or periodicals listings.

Pamphlets, bulletins, and other miscellaneous items are often stored in file drawers, called **vertical files.** To find out what is available in pamphlet form, consult the *Vertical File Index: A Subject and Title Index to Selected Pamphlet Materials.* If your library does not have the item you seek, the index tells you how to order it from its publisher. You'll need to allow extra time for such orders.

Government publications provide a vast array of data, public records, and other historical and contemporary information. For US government publications, by far the most numerous, consult the *Monthly Catalog of US Government Publications,* available on computer. Many federal, state, and local government agencies post important publications—legislation, reports, press releases—on their own Web sites. You can find lists of sites for various federal agencies by using the keywords *United States federal government* with any search engine. Edward Begay took this approach to find statis-

http://www.du.org/cybercomp.html Information about MOOs and MUDs, from Diversity University.

http://www2.famvid.com/i101/chat.html Information about chat on the Internet, including jargon guides, software, and etiquette, from Internet 101.

http://www.fedstats.gov A centralized collection of government statistics, from Fedstats.

http://www.infoplease.com/us.html Links to local, state, and federal government information, from Information Please.

http://www.access.gpo.gov/su_docs Official information from the US Government Printing Office.

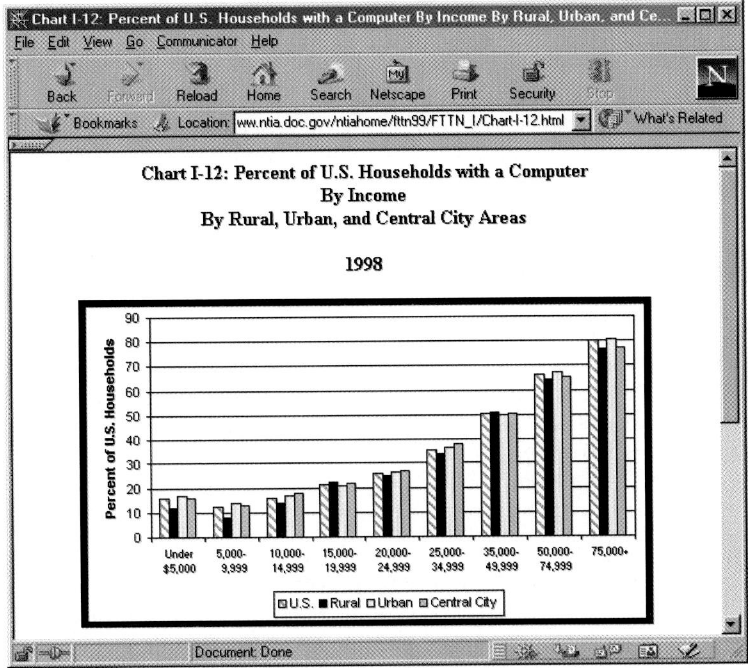

tics from the Department of Commerce on computer use by people at various income levels (see the screen shot above).

Besides what's available online, your library will have a large collection of printed government publications only if it is a depository library (that is, designated to receive such documents). If yours is not a depository library, a librarian may be able to help you obtain a needed publication from another library.

43h Generating your own sources

Many of the sources you consult for a research project—and most of the resources of the library—are likely to be secondary sources whose authors draw their information from other authors. However, academic writing will also require you to consult primary sources and to conduct primary research for information of your own. In many papers this primary research will be the sole basis for your writing, as when you analyze a poem or report on an experiment you conducted. In other papers you will be expected to use your research to support, extend, or refute the ideas of others.

Chapters 48–52 discuss the textual analyses, surveys, experiments, and other primary sources you may use in writing for vari-

ous academic disciplines. One primary source not covered there is the personal interview with an expert in the topic you are researching. Because of the give-and-take of an interview, you can obtain answers to questions precisely geared to your topic, and you can follow up on points of confusion and unexpected leads. In addition, quotations and paraphrases from an interview can give your paper immediacy and authority. Edward Begay used just such an interview in his paper on the Internet (see pp. 760–61).

You can conduct an interview in person, over the telephone, or online using electronic mail (see p. 659) or a form of synchronous communication (see p. 661). A personal interview is probably preferable if you can arrange it, because you can see the person's expressions and gestures as well as hear his or her tone and words. But telephone and online interviews allow you to interview someone who resists a personal interview or who lives far away from you, while still retaining most advantages of interaction.

A few precautions will help you get the maximum information from an interview with the minimum disruption to the person you are interviewing:

- If you do not already know whom to consult for an interview, ask a teacher in the field or do some telephone or library research. Likely sources, depending on your topic, are those who have written about your topic or something closely related, officials in government, businesspeople, even a relative, if he or she is an expert in your topic because of experience, scholarship, or both.
- Call or write for an appointment. Tell the person exactly why you are calling, what you want to discuss, and how long you expect the interview to take. Be true to your word on all points.
- Prepare a list of open-ended questions to ask—perhaps ten or twelve for a one-hour interview. Plan on doing some research for these questions to discover background on the issues and your subject's published views on the issues.
- Give your subject time to consider your questions. Don't rush into silences with more questions.
- Pay attention to your subject's answers so that you can ask appropriate follow-up questions and pick up on unexpected but worthwhile points.
- Take care in interpreting answers, especially if you are online and thus can't depend on facial expressions, gestures, and tone

http://www.askanexpert.com A site that connects users with experts in many fields.

http://www2.rscc.cc.tn.us/~jordan_jj/OWL/Interview2.html Tips for conducting interviews, from Roane State Community College.

of voice to convey the subject's attitudes. Ask for clarification when you need it.

- For in-person and telephone interviews, keep careful notes or, if you have the equipment and your subject agrees, tape-record the interview. For online interviews, save the discussion in a file of its own. (A synchronous discussion may require that you activate a "log" or "archive" function before you begin your interview in order to save it afterward.)
- Before you quote your subject in your paper, check with him or her to ensure that the quotations are accurate.
- Send a thank-you note immediately after the interview. Promise your subject a copy of your finished paper, and send the paper promptly.

EXERCISE 1
Using the library

To become familiar with the research sources available through your library, visit the library and find the answers to the following questions. (Ask a librarian for help whenever necessary.)

1. Which resources are available on computers? Can you print search results? Can you transfer data from the computers to your own disks? What, if any, restrictions are there on the use of library computers for research?
2. Where are reference books stored? How are they cataloged and arranged? Which ones are available on computer? Where and in what format(s) are (*a*) *Contemporary Authors,* (*b*) *Encyclopaedia Britannica,* and (*c*) *MLA International Bibliography of Books and Articles on the Modern Languages and Literatures?*
3. Where is the catalog of the library's periodicals? Where and in what format(s) are the following periodicals stored: (*a*) the *New York Times,* (*b*) *Harper's* magazine, and (*c*) *Journal of Social Psychology?*
4. Where are the library's periodical indexes? Which ones are available on computer? Where and in what format(s) are (*a*) the *New York Times Index,* (*b*) *InfoTrac,* and (*c*) *Social Sciences Index?*
5. What is the format or formats of the library's catalog of books? If any format is incomplete, what is not included? If the catalog (or part of it) is computerized, where are the terminals, and how are they operated?
6. What are the library call numbers of the following books: (*a*) *The Power Broker,* by Robert Caro; (*b*) *Heart of Darkness,* by Joseph Conrad; and (*c*) *The Hero with a Thousand Faces,* by Joseph Campbell?

EXERCISE 2
Finding library sources

Locate at least six promising articles and books for the topic you began working on in the previous chapter (Exercise 1, p. 624, and

Exercise 2, p. 627). Consider the sources "promising" if they seem directly to address your central research question. Following the guidelines on pages 627–31, make a working bibliography of the sources. Be sure to include all the information you will need to acknowledge the sources in your final paper.

EXERCISE 3
Finding Web sources

Use at least three Web search engines to locate six or seven promising sources for your research project. Begin by developing a list of keywords that can be used to query one of the search engines (see p. 637). Check the Advanced Search or Help option of the engine if you need to narrow your search. Then try your refined keywords on the other two search engines as well. How do the results differ? What keyword strategies worked best for finding relevant information?

CHAPTER 44

Working with Sources

The previous chapters helped you lay the groundwork for a research project. This chapter takes you into the most personal, most intensive, and most rewarding part of research writing: using the sources you've found to extend and support your own ideas, to make your topic your own. As before, the work of Edward Begay (on access to the Internet) and Vanessa Haley (on the work of Annie Dillard) will illustrate the activity and thought that go into research writing.

ESL Making a topic your own requires thinking critically about sources and developing independent ideas. These goals may at first be uncomfortable for you if your native culture emphasizes understanding and respecting established authority over questioning and enlarging it. This chapter offers guidance in working with sources so that you can become an expert in your own right and convincingly convey your expertise to others.

44a Evaluating sources

1 Gaining an overview

Once you have a satisfactory working bibliography, scan your list for the sources that are most likely to give you the outlines of your topic, and consult those sources first. Edward Begay, for instance, began investigating titles that seemed to focus on computer use in public schools and libraries, the places where the disadvantaged would be most likely to have access to computers. Vanessa Haley, in contrast, began by reading a book by Annie Dillard, the writer that Haley had decided to focus on, and by looking up some journal articles that seemed to discuss Dillard's views of nature and humanity. For a paper like Haley's that seeks to analyze a writer's work, the work itself is always your starting point, but your own ideas may be supported and extended by those of critics and scholars.

When you first examine your sources, your purpose is to evaluate their usefulness and to develop your thinking, not to collect information. Scanning sources—gauging the kind and extent of ideas and information they offer—can help you determine whether your research is on track. For instance, if all your sources are very technical, assuming more background in the subject than you have, then you may need to search in more general-interest books and periodicals; or if all your sources discuss your subject at a very general level, you probably need to broaden your search—or even revise your topic—before proceeding. Scanning can also suggest the subdivisions of your topic, which will eventually help you structure your paper (pp. 677, 701).

2 Judging relevance and reliability

Not all the sources you find will prove worthwhile: some may be irrelevant to your topic, and others may be unreliable. Gauging the relevance and reliability of sources is the essential task of evaluating them.

In evaluating sources, you need to consider how they come to you. The print sources you find through the library (including books and articles that are also released electronically) have been previewed for you by their publishers and by the library's staff. They still require your critical reading, but you can have some confidence in the information they contain. With online sources, however, you can't assume similar previewing, so your critical reading must be especially rigorous. Special tips for evaluating online sources appear on pages 670–72.

Note Both relevance and reliability can be determined in part by consulting works *about* the source you are considering—that is, the works listed in citation indexes (p. 650) or book review indexes (p. 646). But unless you can dismiss the source on the basis of citations or reviews, you will also need to evaluate it yourself.

Advice on evaluating sources:

http://www.ipl.org/teen/aplus/step5.htm From the Internet Public Library.

http://www.esc.edu/htmlpages/writer/menue.htm From the State University of New York.

http://owl.english.purdue.edu/Files/131.html From the Purdue Online Writing Lab.

http://www.slu.edu/departments/english/research From Saint Louis University.

http://www2.widener.edu/Wolfgram-Memorial-Library/webeval.htm From Widener University.

Guidelines for evaluating sources

For online sources, supplement these guidelines with those on pages 670–72.

Determine **relevance:**

- Does the source devote some attention to your topic?
- Where in the source are you likely to find relevant information or ideas?
- Is the source appropriately specialized for your needs? Check the source's treatment of a topic you know something about, to ensure that it is neither too superficial nor too technical.
- How important is the source likely to be for your writing?

Judge **reliability:**

- How up to date is the source? If the publication date is not recent, be sure that other sources will give you more current views.
- Is the author an expert in the field? Look for an author biography, look up the author in a biographical reference (p. 642), or try to trace the author over the Internet (p. 670).
- What is the author's bias? Check biographical information or the author's own preface or introduction. Use book review indexes (p. 646) or citation indexes (p. 650) to learn what others have written about the author or the source.
- Whatever his or her bias, does the author reason soundly, provide adequate evidence, and consider opposing views? (See pp. 141–60.)

Relevance

To determine whether sources are relevant, scan the introductions to books and articles and the tables of contents of books. You're looking for opinions and facts that pertain directly to your topic. You're also ensuring that your sources are appropriate in level: you can understand them (if with some effort), and they also expand your knowledge. If you don't see what you need or the source is too high-level or too simple, you can drop it from your list.

Reliability

Reliability can be more difficult to judge than relevance. If you haven't already done so, study this book's Chapters 5–7, especially pages 129–36 on analyzing and evaluating texts and pages 141–60 on reading an argument critically. When scanning potential sources, think critically, looking for claims, assumptions, evidence, tone, fairness, and other features discussed on the pages cited. In addition, look for information about the author's background to satisfy yourself that the author has sufficient expertise in your subject. Then try to determine what his or her bias is. For instance, a book on parapsychology by someone identified as the president of the National Organization of Psychics may contain an authoritative explanation of psychic powers, but the author's view is likely to be biased. It should be balanced by research in other sources whose authors are more skeptical of psychic powers.

This balance or opposition is important. You probably will not find harmony among sources, for reasonable people often disagree in their opinions. Thus you must deal honestly with the gaps and conflicts in sources. Old sources, superficial ones, slanted ones—these should be offset in your research and your writing by sources that are more recent, more thorough, or more objective.

3 Evaluating electronic sources

To a great extent, the same critical reading that serves you with print sources will help you evaluate online sources, too (see the box on the previous page). But online sources can range from scholarly works to corporate promotions, from government-sponsored data to the self-published rantings of crackpots. To evaluate an online source, you'll first need to figure out what it is.

Note For more on reading a Web site critically, see pages 129–36. For advice on gathering source information from a Web site, see pages 630–31.

Checking the electronic address

Look for an abbreviation that tells you where the source originates: *edu* (educational institution), *gov* (government body), *org* (nonprofit organization), *mil* (military), or *com* (commercial organization). With a source coming from *compex.com,* you should assume that the contents reflect the company's commercial purposes (although the information may still be helpful). With a source coming from *harvard.edu,* you can assume that the contents are more scholarly and objective (although you should still evaluate the information yourself).

Determining authorship or sponsorship

Many sites list the person(s) or group(s) responsible for the site. A Web site may provide links to information about or other work by an author or group. If not, you can refer to a biographical dictionary or conduct a keyword search of the Web (see p. 637). You should also look for mentions of the author or group in your other sources.

Often you will not be able to trace authors or sponsors or even identify them at all. For instance, someone passionate about the rights of adoptees might maintain a Web site devoted to the subject but not identify himself or herself as the author. In such a case, you'll need to evaluate the quality of the information and opinions by comparing them with sources you know to be reliable.

Guidelines for evaluating online sources

Supplement these guidelines with those on pages 667–70.

- Check the electronic address for an idea of where the source originates.
- Determine who is responsible for the site.
- Gauge the purpose of the site: to build knowledge? to sell something? to create fear? to achieve another goal?
- Evaluate a Web site as a whole, considering its design, its readability, and the value of its links.
- Weigh contributions to discussion groups by putting them in the context of other contributions. Drop sources whose authors will not answer your direct questions.
- Check for references or links to reliable sources, watching especially for balance.
- Compare online sources with tested mainstream sources.

Gauging purpose

Inferring the purpose of an online source can help you evaluate its reliability. Some sources may seem intent on selling ideas or products. Others may seem to be building knowledge—for instance, by acknowledging opposing views either directly or through links to other sites. Still others may seem determined to scare readers with shocking statistics or anecdotes.

Evaluating a Web site as a whole

Consider both the design and the readability of a Web site and the nature of its links. Is the site thoughtfully designed, or is it cluttered with irrelevant material and graphics? Is it carefully written or difficult to understand? Do the links help clarify the purpose of the site—perhaps leading to scholarly sources or, in contrast, to frivolous or indecent sites?

Weighing the contributions to discussion groups

You need to read individuals' contributions to discussion groups especially critically because they are unfiltered and unevaluated. Even on a discussion list (p. 659), whose subscribers are likely to be professionals in the field, you may find wrong or misleading data and skewed opinions. With the more accessible Web forums (p. 660) and newsgroups (p. 661), you should view postings with considerable skepticism.

You can try to verify a contribution to a discussion group by looking at other contributions, which may help you confirm or refute the questionable posting, and by communicating directly with the author to ask about his or her background and publications. If you can't verify the information from a discussion group and the author doesn't respond to your direct approach, you should probably ignore the source.

Checking for references or links to reliable sources

An online source may offer as support the titles of sources that you can trace and evaluate—articles in periodicals, other online sources, and so on. A Web site may include links to these other sources.

Be aware, however, that online sources may refer you only to other sources that share the same bias. When evaluating both the original source and its references, look for a fair treatment of opposing views.

Comparing online and other sources

Always consider online sources in the context of other sources so that you can distinguish singular, untested views from more mainstream views that have been subject to verification.

EXERCISE 1
Evaluating a source

Imagine that you are researching a paper on the advertising techniques that are designed to persuade consumers to buy products. You have listed the following book in your working bibliography:

> Vance Packard, *The Hidden Persuaders,* revised edition, 1981.

On your own or with your classmates (as your instructor wishes), obtain this book from the library and evaluate it as a source for your paper. Use the guidelines on pages 667–70.

EXERCISE 2
Evaluating Web sites

Find and evaluate three Web sites: a commercial site, such as Microsoft's or Apple's; a site for a nonprofit organization, such as the American Medical Association or Greenpeace; and the personal site of an individual. What does each site's design tell you about the author or sponsoring organization? What seems to be the site's purpose or purposes? What do the site's links contribute (or not)? How reliable do you judge the site's information to be? How do the three types of sites differ in these respects?

EXERCISE 3
Evaluating an online discussion

Using the Deja or RemarQ site given on page 661, locate a newsgroup or Web forum on a subject that interests you. (If you already participate in an online discussion group, you can use it instead.) Pick one series of at least ten related messages on a single topic. Write a brief summary of each message (see p. 677 on summarizing). Then analyze and synthesize the messages to develop a one- or two-paragraph evaluation of the discussion. Which messages seem reliable? Which don't? Why?

44b Synthesizing sources

When you begin to locate the differences and similarities among sources, you move into the most significant part of research writing: forging relationships for your own purpose. This **synthesis,** an essential step in critical reading (pp. 133–34), continues through the drafting and revision of a research paper. As you infer connections—say, between one writer's ideas and another's or between two works by the same author—you create new knowledge.

All kinds of connections may occur to you as you work with sources. Edward Begay, researching the potential accessibility of the Internet to both the affluent and the poor, found data in one source to support another source's assertions about a technological gap between private and public schools. He also uncovered a central disagreement among sources over whether the Internet would prove a boon or an obstruction to education. Vanessa Haley, writing about Annie Dillard, sought and found similarities in Dillard's ideas about the place of humanity in nature, ideas expressed in varying contexts throughout Dillard's best-known book. Haley also discovered that her view of Dillard was partly supported by some of the critics she consulted but not supported by others. She knew she would have to take account of these divergent views in her paper.

Your synthesis of sources will grow more detailed and sophisticated as you proceed through the research-writing process. Unless, like Vanessa Haley, you are analyzing primary sources such as the works of a writer, at first read your sources quickly and selectively to obtain an overview of your topic and a sense of how the sources approach it. Don't get bogged down in taking detailed notes, but *do* record your own ideas about sources in your research journal (pp. 619–20).

Responding to sources

Write down what your sources make you think. Do you agree or disagree with the author? Do you find his or her views narrow, or do they open up new approaches for you? Is there anything in the source that you need to research further before you can understand it? Does the source prompt questions that you should keep in mind while reading other sources?

http://www.users.drew.edu/~sjamieso/Synthesis.htm Comprehensive information on synthesizing sources, from Drew University.

Connecting sources

When you notice a link between sources, jot it down. Do two sources differ in their theories or their interpretations of facts? Does one source illuminate another—perhaps commenting or clarifying or supplying additional data? Do two or more sources report studies that support a theory you've read about or an idea of your own?

Heeding your own insights

Apart from ideas prompted by your sources, you are sure to come up with independent thoughts: a conviction, a point of confusion that suddenly becomes clear, a question you haven't seen anyone else ask. These insights may occur at unexpected times, so it's good practice to keep a notebook handy to record them.

Using sources to support your own ideas

As your research proceeds, the responses, connections, and insights you form through synthesis will lead you to answer your starting research question with a statement of your thesis (see p. 700). They will also lead you to the main ideas supporting your thesis—conclusions you have drawn from your synthesis of sources, forming the main divisions of your paper. When drafting the paper, make sure each paragraph focuses on an idea of your own, with the support for the idea coming from your sources. In this way, your paper will synthesize others' work into something wholly your own.

EXERCISE 4
Synthesizing sources

The three passages below address the same issue, the legalization of drugs. What similarities do you see in the authors' ideas? What differences? Write a paragraph of your own in which you use these authors' views as a point of departure for your own view about drug legalization.

Perhaps the most unfortunate victims of drug prohibition laws have been the residents of America's ghettos. These laws have proved largely futile in deterring ghetto-dwellers from becoming drug abusers, but they do account for much of what ghetto residents identify as the drug problem. Aggressive, gun-toting drug dealers often upset law-abiding residents far more than do addicts nodding out in doorways. Meanwhile other residents perceive the drug dealers as heroes and successful role models. They're symbols of success to children who see no other options. At the same time the increasingly harsh criminal penalties imposed on adult drug dealers have led drug traffickers to recruit juveniles. Where once children started dealing drugs only after they had been using them for a few years, today the sequence is often reversed. Many children start using drugs only after working for older drug dealers for a while. Legalization of drugs, like legalization of alcohol in the early 1930s, would drive the drug-dealing business off the streets and out of apartment buildings and into government-regulated, tax-paying stores. It also would force many of the gun-toting dealers out of the business and convert others into legitimate businessmen. —ETHAN A. NADELMANN, "Shooting Up"

Statistics argue against legalization. The University of Michigan conducts an annual survey of twelfth graders, asking the students about their drug consumption. In 1980, 60 percent of those polled said they had used marijuana in the past twelve months, whereas in 1996 only 44 percent had done so. Cocaine use was halved in the same period (15 percent to 7 percent). At the same time, twelve-month use of legally available drugs—alcohol and nicotine-containing cigarettes—remained constant at about 80 percent and 68 percent, respectively. The numbers of illegal drug users haven't declined nearly enough: those teenaged marijuana and cocaine users are still vulnerable to addiction and even death, and they threaten to infect their impressionable peers. But clearly the prohibition of illegal drugs has helped, while the legal status of alcohol and cigarettes has not made them less popular.

—SYLVIA RUNKLE, "The Case Against Legalization"

I have to laugh at the debate over what to do about the drug problem. Everyone is running around offering solutions—from making drug use a more serious criminal offense to legalizing it. But there isn't a real solution. I know that. I used and abused drugs, and people, and society, for two decades. Nothing worked to get me to stop all that behavior except just plain being sick and tired. Nothing. Not threats, not ten-plus years in prison, not anything that was said to me. I used until I got through. Period. And that's when you'll win the war. When all the dope fiends are done. Not a minute before. —MICHAEL W. POSEY, "I Did Drugs Until They Wore Me Out. Then I Stopped."

EXERCISE 5
Evaluating and synthesizing sources

Look up the sources in the working bibliography you made in Chapter 43, Exercise 2 (p. 665). Evaluate the sources for their relevance and reliability. If the sources seem unreliable or don't seem to give you what you need, expand your working bibliography and evaluate the new sources. In your research journal, write down your responses to sources, the connections you perceive among sources, and other original ideas that occur to you.

44c Taking notes using summary, paraphrase, and direct quotation

When you have decided which sources to pursue, you may be ready to gather information, or you may want to step back and get your bearings. Your choice will depend mainly on how familiar you are with the main issues of your topic and whether you have formed a central idea about it.

- If you feel fairly confident that you know what you're looking for in sources, then you might proceed with reading and note taking, as discussed on the following pages.
- If you are attracted to several different main ideas, or you don't see how the various areas of the topic relate, then you might try drafting a thesis statement to focus your thoughts and making an outline to discover relationships. These steps are discussed on pages 700–01 and 702–04, respectively.

The following sections discuss a way of reading sources and systems of taking notes (below); summarizing, paraphrasing, or quoting sources (p. 678); photocopying or downloading sources (p. 683); and using sources accurately and fairly (p. 685).

1 Reading and note taking

The most efficient method of reading secondary sources during research is **skimming,** reading quickly to look for pertinent information. (Primary sources usually need to be read more carefully, especially when they are the focus of your paper.) Follow these guidelines for skimming:

- Read with a specific question in mind, not randomly in hopes of hitting something worthwhile.
- Consult any table of contents, menu, index, or headings to find what you want.
- Concentrate on headings and main ideas, skipping material unrelated to the specific question you are researching.

When you find something relevant, read slowly and carefully to achieve a clear understanding of what the author is saying and to interpret and evaluate the material in the context of your own and others' opinions.

If it is effective, your final paper will show that you have understood and responded critically to your sources—work that can be performed most efficiently in note taking. Taking notes is not a me-

Advice on note taking:

http://www.esc.edu/htmlpages/writer/menun.html From the State University of New York.

http://www.chass.utoronto.ca/~djerz/utwriting/notes.html From the University of Toronto.

chanical process of copying from books and periodicals. Rather, as you read and take notes you analyze and organize the information in your sources. Thus your notes both prompt and preserve your thoughts.

Using a system for taking notes helps simplify the process and later makes writing the paper easier. Before you begin, decide on categories that your subject can be divided into. (If you have previously outlined your preliminary ideas, use outline headings for these categories.) Edward Begay, for instance, divided his general subject of Internet access into these categories:

History of the Internet
Traditional vs. innovative models of education
Business use of the Internet
Differences between rich and poor schools
Training of Internet users
Costs of hooking up to the Internet
Internet and economic inequality
Role of librarians and teachers in Internet use
Role of businesses in Internet use

Headings for your categories will go at the top of each note to cue you about its content.

You can take notes either on note cards or on a computer. (You can also photocopy printed sources or download electronic sources. See p. 683.) Note cards are sometimes easier to rearrange; computer notes are easier to incorporate into your drafts.

Here are a few guidelines for note cards, illustrated by the sample cards beginning on page 679.

- Cards measuring 4″ × 6″ allow more room for notes than those measuring 3″ × 5″.
- Write only one fact or idea on a card so that you can easily rearrange information when you want to.
- If the same source gives you more than one idea or fact, make more than one card.
- Near the top of every card, write the author's last name and the page number(s) of the source so that you will always know where the note came from. (Otherwise, you won't be able to use the note in your paper.) Write a short form of the title as well if you are using two or more sources by the same author.
- Give the note a brief heading corresponding to one of your categories.

If you use a computer for taking notes from sources, follow these guidelines:

- Create one or more files for your notes with headings corresponding to your categories. You can then use your word processor's Search or Find function to locate a particular category and the notes under it.

- Clearly separate consecutive notes with space and perhaps with a horizontal line.
- At the beginning of each note, record the source information: author's last name, title if the author is responsible for two or more sources, and page number(s).
- If a single source provides information relevant to two or more of your headings, sort the information among your categories accordingly.
- To search your notes individually as well as by category, use keywords with the computer's Search or Find function. You might, for instance, search by an author's last name or by a term such as *schools* or *libraries* or *businesses.*
- Print your notes at regular intervals. Then you'll have a paper copy if your instructor asks to see your notes and when you are away from your computer. (Since many computer monitors show less than a full page of text, printouts also allow you to scan your notes more quickly.)

Note A computerized note-taking program can create note "cards" and files and will organize your notes automatically by category. When using such a program, be sure your notes record source information as well.

2 Summarizing, paraphrasing, and quoting sources

As you take notes from sources, you can summarize, paraphrase, quote, or combine methods, depending on why you are using the sources.

Summary

When you **summarize,** you condense an extended idea or argument into a sentence or more in your own words. A full discussion of summary appears on pages 127–28, and you should read that section if you have not already.

Advice on summarizing, paraphrasing, and quoting sources:

http://owl.english.purdue.edu/Files/31.html From the Purdue Online Writing Lab.

http://www.wisc.edu/writing/Handbook/QuotingSources.html From the University of Wisconsin at Madison.

http://www.esc.edu/htmlpages/writer/menusp.htm From the State University of New York.

Summary is most useful when you want to record the gist of an author's idea without the background or supporting evidence. Edward Begay summarized the following quotation from one of his sources, Max Frankel, "The Moon, This Time Around," *New York Times Magazine,* page 42:

> A recent Rand study, with research supported by the Markle Foundation, concluded that in the foreseeable future the free market is likely to deliver e-mail to only half of America. Without induced subsidies, perhaps from Internet access fees, the computer industry may never produce the inexpensive technologies that would enable television sets, telephones and computer games to bring e-mail into the home. Interim subsidies and technologies would also be needed if less-affluent citizens are to get their e-mail outside the home, in apartment lobbies, libraries and schools.

Compare this passage with Begay's one-sentence summary, in which he picks out the kernel of Frankel's idea and expresses it in his own words:

> <u>Internet and economic equality</u>
>
> Frankel 42
>
> Rand study says government direction and subsidy may be required to make e-mail technology universal and accessible to all.

Paraphrase

When you **paraphrase,** you follow much more closely the author's original presentation, but you still restate it in your own words. Paraphrase is most useful when you want to present or examine an author's line of reasoning but don't feel the original words merit direct quotation.

The note card on the next page shows how Begay might have paraphrased the passage by Frankel given above.

http://owl.english.purdue.edu/Files/30.html Advice on paraphrasing, from the Purdue Online Writing Lab.

> Internet and economic equality
>
> Frankel 42
>
> If market forces prevail, according to Rand, e-mail may fail to reach many Americans. The government may have to underwrite the adaptation of household devices to e-mail, possibly by charging for use of the Internet. Similar measures will be required in the short term to make e-mail available to poorer people in public places.

Notice how the paraphrase differs from the Frankel passage in sentence structures and wording, except in the case of terms that lack synonyms such as *government* and *e-mail:*

Frankel's words	**Begay's paraphrase**
A recent Rand study, with research supported by the Markle Foundation, concluded that in the foreseeable future the free market is likely to deliver e-mail to only half of America.	If market forces prevail, according to Rand, e-mail may fail to reach many Americans.
Without induced subsidies, perhaps from Internet access fees, the computer industry may never produce the inexpensive technologies that would enable television sets, telephones and computer games to bring e-mail into the home.	The government may have to underwrite the adaptation of household devices to e-mail, possibly by charging for use of the Internet.
Interim subsidies and technologies would also be needed if less-affluent citizens are to get their e-mail outside the home, in apartment lobbies, libraries and schools.	Similar measures will be required in the short term to make e-mail available to poorer people in public places.

Follow these guidelines when paraphrasing:

- Read the material several times to be sure you understand it.
- Restate the main ideas in your own words and sentence structures. You need not put down in new words the whole passage or all the details. Select what is pertinent and restate only that. If complete sentences seem too detailed or cumbersome, use phrases. Edward Begay might have written this more telegraphic paraphrase of the quotation by Frankel:

Internet and economic inequality

Frankel 42

From Rand: Mkt. forces may leave many Americans without e-mail. Thus govt. role: ensure compatible technology, underwrite adaptation of household devices, make e-mail available to poor in public places.

- Be careful not to distort meaning. Don't change the source's emphasis or omit connecting words, qualifiers, and other material whose absence will confuse you later or cause you to misrepresent the source.

See pages 689–90 for examples of unacceptable (plagiarized) paraphrases.

ESL If English is not your native language, you may have difficulty paraphrasing the ideas in sources because synonyms don't occur to you or you don't see how to restructure sentences. Before attempting a paraphrase, read the original passage several times. Then, instead of "translating" line by line, try to state the gist of the passage without looking at it. Check your effort against the original to be sure you have captured the source author's meaning and emphasis without using his or her words and sentence structures. If you need a synonym for a word, look it up in a dictionary.

Direct quotation

When taking notes, you may be tempted to quote sources rather than take the time to summarize or paraphrase them. But this approach has at least two disadvantages:

- Copying quotations does not encourage you to interact with sources, grappling with their meaning, analyzing them, testing them.
- Copying merely postpones the summarizing and paraphrasing until you are drafting your paper. The paper itself must be centered on *your* ideas, not stitched together from quotations.

Use direct quotation from secondary sources only when the exact words of the original are important (see the box on p. 683). In a paper analyzing primary sources such as literary works, you will use direct quotation extensively to illustrate and support your analysis. (Vanessa Haley used many quotations from her primary source, a book by Annie Dillard; see her final paper on pp. 779–84.)

When recording a quotation from a source, take the following precautions to avoid plagiarism or misrepresentation of the source:

- Copy the material *carefully.* Take down the author's exact wording, spelling, capitalization, and punctuation.
- Proofread every direct quotation *at least twice.*
- Use big quotation marks around the quotation so that later you won't confuse it with a paraphrase or summary.
- If you want to add words for clarity or change the capitalization of letters, use brackets (see pp. 526, 535).
- If you want to omit irrelevant words or sentences, use ellipsis marks, usually three spaced periods (see p. 527). (In MLA style the ellipsis mark is also surrounded by brackets, as illustrated in the note card below.)

The note card below shows how Edward Begay might have quoted part of the passage from Frankel on page 679, using ellipsis marks and brackets to make the quotation more concise and specific.

Internet and economic equality

Frankel 42

"A recent Rand study [. . .] concluded that [. . .] the free market is likely to deliver e-mail to only [the more affluent] half of America [. . .]. [W]ithout induced subsidies, perhaps from Internet access fees, the computer industry may never produce the inexpensive technologies that would enable television sets, telephones and computer games to bring e-mail into the home. Interim subsidies [. . .] would also be needed if less-affluent citizens [who lack home computers] are to get their e-mail outside the home, in apartment lobbies, libraries and schools."

Combination of quotation, summary, and paraphrase

Using quotation in combination with summary or paraphrase can help you shape the material to suit your purposes (although you must be careful not to distort the author's meaning). The card on the facing page shows how Edward Begay might have used a combination of quotation and paraphrase to record the statement by Frankel. Notice that the quotation marks are clearly visible and that the quotations are exact.

Tests for direct quotations

The author's original satisfies one of these requirements:

- The language is unusually vivid, bold, or inventive.
- The quotation cannot be paraphrased without distortion or loss of meaning.
- The words themselves are at issue in your interpretation.
- The quotation represents and emphasizes a body of opinion or the view of an important expert.
- The quotation emphatically reinforces your own idea.
- The quotation is a graph, diagram, or table.

The quotation is as short as possible:

- It includes only material relevant to your point.
- It is edited to eliminate examples and other unneeded material. (For editing quotations, see the bulleted list opposite.)

Internet and economic inequality

Frankel 42

If market forces prevail, according to Rand, e-mail may fail to reach many Americans. The government may have to underwrite the adaptation of household devices "to bring e-mail into the home." Similar measures will be required in the short term "if less-affluent citizens [who lack home computers] are to get their e-mail outside the home, in apartment lobbies, libraries and schools."

Note If the material you are quoting, summarizing, or paraphrasing runs from one page to the next in the source, make a mark (such as a check mark) at the exact spot where one page ends and the next begins. When writing your paper, you may want to use only a part of the material (say, the first or second half). The mark will save you from having to go back to your source to find which page the material actually appeared on.

3 Photocopying or downloading sources

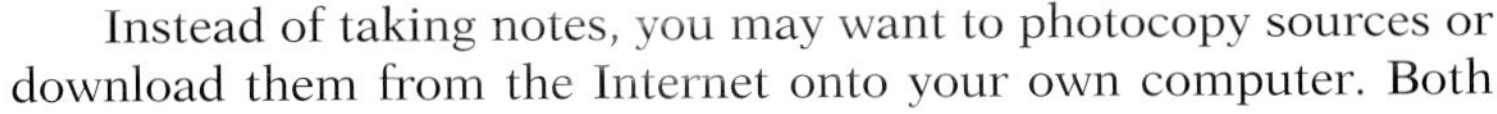

Instead of taking notes, you may want to photocopy sources or download them from the Internet onto your own computer. Both photocopying and downloading have distinct advantages for researchers:

- They are convenient, particularly when material (such as journal articles) can't be removed from the library or requires too much time to examine closely online. You can also print a downloaded document if you prefer to read text on paper.
- Some researchers believe that photocopying or downloading is preferable to taking notes because it reduces the risk of distorting an author's ideas or introducing errors into quotations. With photocopying you need to write out a quotation only once, into your draft; with downloading you can move the quotation directly from source to draft.

But photocopying and downloading have some disadvantages, too:

- Unlike active note taking on cards or on a computer, photocopying or downloading sources may tempt you to glide through an essential stage of research writing: interpreting, analyzing, and synthesizing sources. Once you've copied pages or downloaded a file, your work with a source has just begun.
- Photocopying costs money. To economize, copy only sources you definitely want to use.
- Downloading is usually free as long as your Internet account does not charge for time online. However, you should check the source's copyright notice for any restrictions on downloading or requirements for acknowledging the source. (See also p. 690.)

When you photocopy or download a source, take the following additional steps:

- Make sure that you record complete bibliographical information from the source so that you don't have to retrace your steps for it. (Since online sources can change and disappear, retracing your steps may not even be possible.) Write bibliographic information directly on a photocopy, or add it to a downloaded file. See page 629 for a list of what information to record.
- Read the source as thoughtfully as you would any other. Annotate the relevant passages of a photocopy with underlining, circles, and marginal notes about their significance for your topic. You can accomplish the same work with a downloaded document by opening the downloaded file into your word-processing program and inserting highlights and comments at relevant passages.
- Do not import whole blocks of the source into your draft, especially with downloaded sources that you can excerpt electronically. The guidelines on page 683 for judicious use of quotations apply to sources you photocopy or download as well as to those you take notes from.
- To integrate notes on photocopied or downloaded sources into your other notes, make a cross-reference that briefly summa-

rizes the photocopied or downloaded source—for example, "*Internet and economic equality* / Frankel 42 / Disc. of measures needed for equal e-mail access / See photocopy."

4 Using sources accurately and fairly

In summarizing, paraphrasing, or quoting sources, you must represent the author's meaning exactly, without distorting it. In the following inaccurate summary the writer has stated a meaning exactly opposite that of the original. The original quotation, from the artist Henri Matisse, appears in Jack D. Flam, *Matisse on Art,* page 148.

Original For the artist creation begins with vision. To see is itself a creative operation, requiring an effort. Everything that we see in our daily life is more or less distorted by acquired habits, and this is perhaps more evident in an age like ours when cinema posters and magazines present us every day with a flood of ready-made images which are to the eye what prejudices are to the mind.

Inaccurate summary Matisse said that the artist can learn how to see by looking at posters and magazines (qtd. in Flam 148).

The revision below combines summary and quotation to represent the author's meaning exactly:

Accurate summary Matisse said that the artist must overcome visual "habits" and "prejudices," particularly those developed in response to popular cultural images (qtd. in Flam 148).

EXERCISE 6
Summarizing and paraphrasing

Prepare two source notes, one summarizing the entire paragraph below and the other paraphrasing the first four sentences (ending with the word *autonomy*). Use the format for a note card provided in the preceding section, omitting only the heading.

Federal organization [of the United States] has made it possible for the different states to deal with the same problems in many different ways. One consequence of federalism, then, has been that people are treated differently, by law, from state to state. The great strength of this system is that differences from state to state in cultural preferences, moral standards, and levels of wealth can be accommodated. In contrast to a unitary system in which the central government makes all important decisions (as in France), federalism is a powerful arrangement for maximizing regional freedom and autonomy. The great weakness of our federal system, however, is that people in some states receive less than the best or the most advanced or the least expensive services and policies that government can offer. The federal dilemma does not invite easy solutions, for the costs and benefits of the arrangement have tended to balance out.

—Peter K. Eisinger et al., *American Politics,* p. 44

44d

EXERCISE 7
Combining summary, paraphrase, and direct quotation

Prepare a source note containing a combination of paraphrase or summary and direct quotation that states the major idea of the passage below. Use the format for a note card provided in the preceding section, omitting only the heading.

Most speakers unconsciously duel even during seemingly casual conversations, as can often be observed at social gatherings where they show less concern for exchanging information with other guests than for asserting their own dominance. Their verbal dueling often employs very subtle weapons like mumbling, a hostile act which defeats the listener's desire to understand what the speaker claims he is trying to say (but is really not saying because he is mumbling!). Or the verbal dueler may keep talking after someone has passed out of hearing range—which is often an aggressive challenge to the listener to return and acknowledge the dominance of the speaker.

—PETER K. FARB, *Word Play,* p. 107

44d Avoiding plagiarism

Plagiarism (from a Latin word for "kidnapper") is the presentation of someone else's ideas or words as your own. Whether deliberate or accidental, plagiarism is a serious and often punishable offense.

- *Deliberate* plagiarism:

  Copying a phrase, a sentence, or a longer passage from a source and passing it off as your own.
  Summarizing or paraphrasing someone else's ideas without acknowledging your debt.
  Handing in as your own work a paper you have bought, had a friend write, or copied from another student.

- *Accidental* plagiarism:

  Forgetting to place quotation marks around another writer's words.
  Omitting a source citation for another's idea because you are unaware of the need to acknowledge the idea.
  Carelessly copying a source when you mean to paraphrase.

You do not plagiarize, however, when you draw on other writers' material and acknowledge your sources. That procedure is a

Advice on avoiding plagiarism:

http://www.indiana.edu/~wts/wts/plagiarism.html From Indiana University.

http://owl.english.purdue.edu/Files/151.htm From the Purdue Online Writing Lab.

http://webster.commnet.edu/mla/plagiarism.htm From Capital Community College.

Checklist for avoiding plagiarism

- What type of source are you using: your own independent material, common knowledge, or someone else's independent material? You must acknowledge someone else's material.
- If you are quoting someone else's material, is the quotation exact? Have you inserted quotation marks around quotations run into the text? Are graphs, statistics, and other borrowed data identical to the source? Have you shown omissions with ellipsis marks and additions with brackets?
- If you are paraphrasing or summarizing someone else's material, have you used your own words and sentence structures? Does your paraphrase or summary employ quotation marks when you resort to the author's exact language?
- If you are using someone else's material in your own Web site, have you obtained any needed permission for your use? (See p. 690.)
- Have you acknowledged every use of someone else's material in the place where you use it? Are all your source citations complete and accurate? (See p. 698.)
- Does your list of works cited include all the sources you have used? (See p. 698.)

crucial part of honest research writing, as we have seen. This section shows you how to recognize what you need to acknowledge in order to avoid plagiarism.

ESL More than in many other cultures, teachers in the United States value students' original thinking and writing. In some other cultures, for instance, students may be encouraged to copy the words of scholars without acknowledgment, to demonstrate their mastery of or respect for the scholars' work. But in the United States, use of another's words or ideas without a source citation is plagiarism and is unacceptable. Always use quotation marks around a direct quotation and cite the source. Cite the source as well for any idea you borrow from someone else, even if you state the idea in your own words. When in doubt about the guidelines in this section, ask your instructor for advice.

1 Knowing what you need not acknowledge

Your independent material

You need not acknowledge your own independent material—your thoughts, compilations of facts, or experimental results, expressed in your words or format—to avoid plagiarism. Such material includes observations from your experience (for example, a conclusion you draw about crowd behavior by watching crowds at concerts) as well as diagrams you construct from information you gather yourself. Though you generally should describe the basis for your conclusions so that readers can evaluate your thinking, you need not cite sources for them. However, someone else's ideas and facts are not yours; even when you express them entirely in your words and sentence structures, they require acknowledgment.

Common knowledge

Common knowledge consists of the standard information of a field of study as well as folk literature and commonsense observations.

- Standard information includes the major facts of history, such as the dates of Charlemagne's rule as emperor of Rome (800–814). It does not include interpretations of facts, such as a historian's opinion that Charlemagne was sometimes needlessly cruel in extending his power.
- Folk literature, such as the fairy tale "Snow White," is popularly known and cannot be traced to a particular writer. Literature traceable to a writer is not folk literature, even if it is very familiar.
- A commonsense observation is something most people know, such as that inflation is most troublesome for people with low and fixed incomes. An economist's idea about the effects of inflation on Chinese immigrants is not a commonsense observation.

You may treat common knowledge as your own, even if you have to look it up in a reference book. You may not know, for example, the dates of the French Revolution or the standard definition of *photosynthesis,* although these are considered common knowledge. If you do not know a subject well enough to determine whether a piece of information is common knowledge, make a record of the source as you would for any other quotation, paraphrase, or summary. As you read more about the subject, the information may come up repeatedly without acknowledgment, in which case it is probably common knowledge. But if you are still in doubt when you finish your research, always acknowledge the source.

2 Knowing what you *must* acknowledge

You must always acknowledge other people's independent material—that is, any facts or ideas that are not common knowledge or your own. The source may be anything, including a book, an article, a movie, an interview, a microfilmed document, a computer program, a newsgroup posting, or an opinion expressed on the radio. You must acknowledge summaries or paraphrases of ideas or facts as well as quotations of the language and format in which ideas or facts appear: wording, sentence structures, arrangement, and special graphics (such as a diagram).

You need to acknowledge another's material no matter how you use it, how much of it you use, or how often you use it. Whether you are quoting a single important word, paraphrasing a single sentence, or summarizing three paragraphs, and whether you are using the source only once or a dozen times, you must acknowledge the original author every time. See pages 698–99 for a discussion of how to acknowledge sources.

Copied language: Quotation marks and a source citation

The following example baldly plagiarizes the original quotation from Jessica Mitford's *Kind and Usual Punishment,* page 9. Without quotation marks or a source citation, the example matches Mitford's wording (underlined) and closely parallels her sentence structure:

Original The character and mentality of the keepers may be of more importance in understanding prisons than the character and mentality of the kept.

Plagiarism But the character of prison officials (the keepers) is more important in understanding prisons than the character of prisoners (the kept).

To avoid plagiarism, the writer can paraphrase and cite the source (see the next page) or use Mitford's actual words *in quotation marks and with a source citation* (here, in MLA style):

Revision (quotation) According to one critic of the penal system, "The character and mentality of the keepers may be of more importance in understanding prisons than the character and mentality of the kept" (Mitford 9).

Even with a source citation and with a different sentence structure, the next example is still plagiarism because it uses some of Mitford's words (underlined) without quotation marks:

Plagiarism According to one critic of the penal system, the psychology of the kept may say less about prisons than the psychology of the keepers (Mitford 9).

Revision (quotation) According to one critic of the penal system, the psychology of "the kept" may say less about prisons than the psychology of "the keepers" (Mitford 9).

Paraphrase or summary: Your own words and sentence structure and a source citation

The example below changes Mitford's sentence structure, but it still uses her words (underlined) without quotation marks and without a source citation:

Plagiarism In understanding prisons, we might focus less on the character and mentality of the kept than on those of the keepers.

To avoid plagiarism, the writer can use quotation marks and cite the source (see the previous page) or *use his or her own words* and still *cite the source* (because the idea is Mitford's, not the writer's):

Revision (paraphrase) Mitford holds that we may be able to learn less about prisons from the psychology of prisoners than from the psychology of prison officials (9).

In the next example, the writer cites Mitford and does not use her words but still plagiarizes her sentence structure:

Plagiarism One critic of the penal system maintains that the psychology of prison officials may be more informative about prisons than the psychology of prisoners (Mitford 9).

Revision (paraphrase) One critic of the penal system maintains that we may be able to learn less from the psychology of prisoners than from the psychology of prison officials (Mitford 9).

3 Using and acknowledging online sources

Online sources are so accessible and so easy to download into your own documents that it may seem they are freely available, exempting you from the obligation to acknowledge them. They are not. Acknowledging online sources is somewhat trickier than acknowledging print sources, but no less essential. Further, if you are publishing your work online, you need to take account of sources' copyright restrictions as well.

Note Ask your instructor for advice whenever you are unsure whether and how to cite an online source or whether and how to seek permission for using copyrighted material.

Unpublished projects

When you use material from an online source in a print or online document to be distributed just to your class, your obligation to cite sources does not change: you must acknowledge someone else's independent material in whatever form you find it. With online sources, that obligation can present additional challenges:

- Online sources may change from one day to the next or even be removed entirely. Be sure to record complete source information as noted on page 629 each time you consult the source. Without the source information, you *may not* use the source.
- If you use not only a Web site but also one or more of its linked sites, you must acknowledge the linked sites as well. The fact that one person has used a second person's work does not release you from the responsibility to cite the second work.

- As a courtesy to e-mail correspondents or participants in discussion groups, seek the authors' permission before using their messages. (See p. 670 for advice on tracing online authors.) Obtaining permission advises the authors that their words or ideas are about to be distributed more widely and lets the authors see that in quoting them out of context you have not misrepresented their ideas.

Web compositions and copyrights

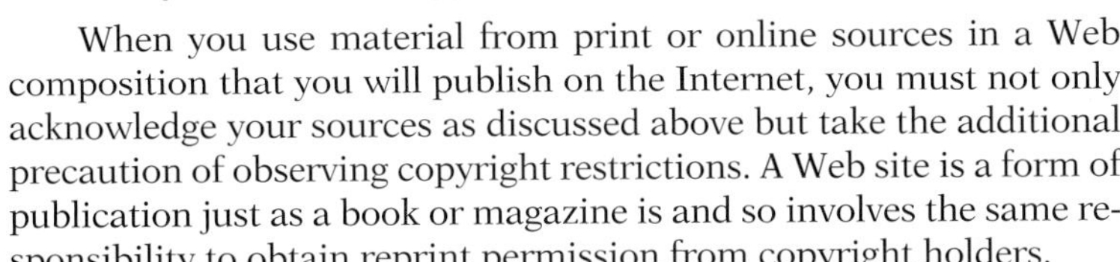

When you use material from print or online sources in a Web composition that you will publish on the Internet, you must not only acknowledge your sources as discussed above but take the additional precaution of observing copyright restrictions. A Web site is a form of publication just as a book or magazine is and so involves the same responsibility to obtain reprint permission from copyright holders.

The legal convention of **fair use** allows an author to quote a small portion of copyrighted material without obtaining the copyright holder's permission, as long as the author acknowledges the source. Applying the principle of fair use is easier with print than with online sources:

- With print sources, a conservative consensus gives this estimate of fair use: quoting fewer than fifty words from an article or fewer than three hundred words from a book. You'll need the copyright holder's permission to use any longer quotation from an article or book; any quotation at all from a play, poem, or song; and any use of an entire work—such as a photograph, chart, or other illustration.
- With online sources such as Web sites, there is less consensus about fair use; indeed, online copyrights are the subject of intense controversy, and the rules are still evolving. To play it safe, seek permission for any text quotation that represents more than a small portion of the whole—for instance, a quotation of forty words out of three hundred. Follow the print guidelines above for plays, poems, songs, and illustrations, adding multimedia elements (audio or video clips) to the list of works that require reprint permission for any use.
- You may also need to seek permission to link your site to another one—for instance, if you rely on the linked site to provide

Information about copyright:

http://lcweb.loc.gov/copyright From the Library of Congress.

http://fairuse.stanford.edu From Stanford University.

http://www.utsystem.edu/OGC/IntellectualProperty/cprtindx.htm From the University of Texas.

substantial evidence for your claims or if you incorporate a linked site's multimedia element (an image or a sound or video clip) into your site.

Generally, you can find information about a site's copyright on the home page or at the bottoms of other pages: look for a notice using the symbol ©. Most worthwhile sites also provide information for contacting the author or sponsor. (See p. 631 for an illustration.) If you don't find a copyright notice, you *cannot* assume that the work is unprotected by copyright. Only if the site explicitly says it is not copyrighted or is available for free use can you exceed fair use without permission.

Note Although most online sources are copyrighted, much valuable material is not: either the creator does not claim copyright, or the copyright has lapsed so that the work is in the public domain. The first category includes most government documents; the second includes most works by authors who have been dead at least fifty years. You do not need permission to reprint from such a source, but *you still must cite the source.*

EXERCISE 8
Recognizing plagiarism

The numbered items below show various attempts to quote or paraphrase the following passage. Carefully compare each attempt with the original passage. Which attempts are plagiarized, inaccurate, or both, and which are acceptable? Why?

> I would agree with the sociologists that psychiatric labeling is dangerous. Society can inflict terrible wounds by discrimination, and by confusing health with disease and disease with badness.
>
> —George E. Vaillant, *Adaptation to Life,* p. 361

1. According to George Vaillant, society often inflicts wounds by using psychiatric labeling, confusing health, disease, and badness (361).
2. According to George Vaillant, "psychiatric labeling [such as 'homosexual' or 'schizophrenic'] is dangerous. Society can inflict terrible wounds by [. . .] confusing health with disease and disease with badness" (361).
3. According to George Vaillant, when psychiatric labeling discriminates between health and disease or between disease and badness, it can inflict wounds on those labeled (361).
4. Psychiatric labels can badly hurt those labeled, says George Vaillant, because they fail to distinguish among health, illness, and immorality (361).
5. Labels such as "homosexual" and "schizophrenic" can be hurtful when they fail to distinguish among health, illness, and immorality.
6. "I would agree with the sociologists that society can inflict terrible wounds by discrimination, and by confusing health with disease and disease with badness" (Vaillant 361).

EXERCISE 9
Taking notes from sources

Continuing from Exercise 5 (p. 675), as the next step in preparing a research paper, make notes from sources you have not photocopied or downloaded. Use summary, paraphrase, direct quotation, or a combination as seems appropriate. Be careful to avoid plagiarism or inaccuracy. Mark each note with the author's name, title, and page number as well as with a heading summarizing its content. Mark this basic information on photocopied or downloaded sources as well, and annotate the sources to highlight and interpret what's significant for your topic.

44e Integrating sources into your text

The evidence of others' information and opinions should *back up* your conclusions. You don't want to let your evidence overwhelm your own point of view and voice. The point of research writing is to investigate and go beyond sources, to interpret them and use them to support your own independent ideas.

1 Deciding when to quote sources directly

Most papers of ten or so pages should not need more than three to four quotations that are longer than a few lines each. Except when you are analyzing literature or other primary sources (see below), favor paraphrases and summaries over quotations. For quotations from secondary sources, use the tests in the box on page 683.

In papers analyzing literature, historical documents, and other sources, quotations will often be both the target of your analysis and the chief support for your ideas. You may need to quote many brief passages, integrated into your sentences, and then comment on the quotations to clarify your analysis and win readers' agreement with it. Examples of such extensive quotation can be seen in Vanessa Haley's analysis of Annie Dillard's writing (pp. 779–84) and in the three literary analyses in Chapter 49 (pp. 807, 811, and 814).

Note Integrating quotations into your sentences involves several conventions discussed elsewhere in this book. See the box on the following page.

Advice on integrating borrowed material:

http://www.english.uiuc.edu/cws/wworkshop/handlingquotations.htm From the University of Illinois at Urbana-Champaign.

http://www.wisc.edu/writing/Handbook/QuoIntroducing.html From the University of Wisconsin at Madison.

Conventions for handling quotations

- For a summary of all conventions regarding quotations, see the chart on pp. 509–10.
- For guidelines on when to quote from sources, see p. 683.
- For the punctuation of signal phrases such as *he insists,* see pp. 482–84.
- For guidelines on when to run quotations into your text and when to display them separately from your text, see pp. 511–13.
- For the use of brackets around your changes or additions in quotations, see pp. 526–27.
- For the use of the ellipsis mark (. . .) to indicate omissions from quotations, see pp. 527–30.

2 Introducing borrowed material

When using a summary, paraphrase, or quotation, work to smooth the transition between your ideas and words and those of thc source.

Note The examples in this section use the MLA style of source documentation, discussed in Chapter 46. The source citations not only acknowledge that material is borrowed but also help to indicate where the borrowed material begins or ends. See page 716 for more on this topic.

Links between borrowed material and your own sentences

Readers will be distracted from your point if borrowed material does not fit into your sentence. In the passage below, the writer has not meshed the structures of her own and her source's sentences:

Awkward One editor disagrees with this view and "a good reporter does not fail to separate opinions from facts" (Lyman 52).

In the following revision the writer adds words to integrate the quotation into her sentence:

Revised One editor disagrees with this view, maintaining that "a good reporter does not fail to separate opinions from facts" (Lyman 52).

Alterations of quotations

To mesh your own and your source's words, you may sometimes need to make a substitution or addition to the quotation, signaling your change with brackets (see pp. 526–27).

Words added

"The tabloids [of England] are a journalistic case study in bad reporting," claims Lyman (52).

Verb form changed

A bad reporter, Lyman implies, is one who "[fails] to separate opinions from facts" (52). [The bracketed verb replaces *fail* in the original.]

Capitalization changed

"[T]o separate opinions from facts" is a goal of good reporting (Lyman 52). [In the original, *to* is not capitalized.]

Noun supplied for pronoun

The reliability of a news organization "depends on [reporters'] trustworthiness," says Lyman (52). [The bracketed noun replaces *their* in the original.]

3 Interpreting borrowed material

Even when it does not conflict with your own sentence structure, borrowed material will be ineffective if you merely dump it in readers' laps without explaining how you intend it to be understood.

Dumped Many news editors and reporters maintain that it is impossible to keep personal opinions from influencing the selection and presentation of facts. "True, news reporters, like everyone else, form impressions of what they see and hear. However, a good reporter does not fail to separate opinions from facts" (Lyman 52).

Reading this passage, we must figure out for ourselves that the writer's sentence and the quotation state opposite points of view. In the following revision, the underlined additions tell us how to interpret the quotation:

Revised Many news editors and reporters maintain that it is impossible to keep personal opinions from influencing the selection and presentation of facts. <u>Yet not all authorities agree with this view. One editor grants that</u> "news reporters, like everyone else, form impressions of what they see and hear." <u>But, he insists,</u> "a good reporter does not fail to separate opinions from facts" (Lyman 52).

Signal phrases

In the revised passage above, the words *One editor grants* and *he insists* are **signal phrases:** they tell readers who the source is and what to expect in the quotations that follow. Signal phrases usually contain (1) the source author's name (or a substitute for it, such as *One editor* and *he*) and (2) a verb that indicates the source author's attitude or approach to what he or she says. In the preceding example, *grants* implies concession and *insists* implies argument. The box below includes a list of verbs for signal phrases. For punctuating signal phrases, see pages 482–84.

44e

Verbs for signal phrases

Use verbs that convey information about source authors' attitudes or approaches. In the sentence *Smith* ______ *that the flood might have been disastrous,* filling the blank with *observes, finds,* or *insists* would create different meanings.

Note Use the present tense of verbs (as in the list below) to discuss the writings of others, including literary works, opinions, and reports of conclusions from research. Use the past tense to describe past events, such as historical occurrences and the procedures used in studies—for example, *In 1993 Holmes stated that he had lied a decade earlier* or *Riley assessed the participants' diets.*

Author is neutral	Author infers or suggests	Author argues	Author is uneasy or disparaging
comments	analyzes	claims	belittles
describes	asks	contends	bemoans
explains	assesses	defends	complains
illustrates	concludes	disagrees	condemns
notes	finds	holds	deplores
observes	predicts	insists	deprecates
points out	proposes	maintains	derides
records	reveals		laments
relates	shows	**Author agrees**	warns
reports	speculates	admits	
says	suggests	agrees	
sees	supposes	concedes	
thinks		concurs	
writes		grants	

Vary your signal phrases to suit your interpretation of borrowed material and also to keep readers' interest. A signal phrase may precede, interrupt, or follow the borrowed material:

Signal phrase precedes

Lyman insists that "a good reporter does not fail to separate opinions from facts" (52).

Signal phrase interrupts

"However," Lyman insists, "a good reporter does not fail to separate opinions from facts" (52).

Signal phrase follows

"[A] good reporter does not fail to separate opinions from facts," Lyman insists (52).

Background information

You can add information to a quotation to integrate it into your text and inform readers why you are using it. Often, you may want to provide the author's name in the text:

Author named

Harold Lyman grants that "news reporters, like everyone else, form impressions of what they see and hear." But, Lyman insists, "a good reporter does not fail to separate opinions from facts" (52).

If the source title contributes information about the author or the context of the quotation, you can provide it in the text:

Title given

Harold Lyman, in his book *The Conscience of the Journalist*, grants that "news reporters, like everyone else, form impressions of what they see and hear." But, Lyman insists, "a good reporter does not fail to separate opinions from facts" (52).

Finally, if the quoted author's background and experience reinforce or clarify the quotation, you can provide these credentials in the text:

Credentials given

Harold Lyman, a newspaper editor for more than forty years, grants that "news reporters, like everyone else, form impressions of what they see and hear." But, Lyman insists, "a good reporter does not fail to separate opinions from facts" (52).

You need not always name the author, source, or credentials in your text. In fact, such introductions may get in the way when you are simply establishing facts or weaving together facts and opinions from varied sources. In the following passage from Edward Begay's paper, the information is more important than the sources, so the sources are mentioned only in a parenthetical acknowledgment:

> Many states organize annual NetDay campaigns designed to bring educators, school boards, community volunteers, and corporations together to wire schools (LA NetDay; MacFarquhar B1).

EXERCISE 10

Introducing and interpreting borrowed material

Drawing on the ideas in the following paragraph and using examples from your own observations and experiences, write a paragraph about anxiety. Integrate at least one direct quotation and one paraphrase from the following paragraph into your own sentences.

In your paragraph identify the author by name and give his credentials: he is a professor of psychiatry and a practicing psychoanalyst.

> There are so many ways in which man is different from all the lower forms of animals, and almost all of them make us uniquely susceptible to feelings of anxiousness. Our imagination and reasoning powers facilitate anxiety; the anxious feeling is precipitated not by an absolute impending threat—such as the worry about an examination, a speech, travel—but rather by the symbolic and often unconscious representations. We do not have to be experiencing a potential danger. We can experience something related to it. We can recall, through our incredible memories, the original symbolic sense of vulnerability in childhood and suffer the feeling attached to that. We can even forget the original memory and still be stuck with the emotion—which is then compounded by its seemingly irrational quality at this time. It is not just the fear of death which pains us, but the anticipation of it; or the anniversary of a specific death; or a street, a hospital, a time of day, a color, a flower, a symbol associated with death.
>
> —WILLARD GAYLIN, "Feeling Anxious," p. 23

44f Documenting sources

Every time you borrow the words, facts, or ideas of others, you must **document** the source—that is, supply a reference (or document) telling readers that you borrowed the material and where you borrowed it from. (For when to document sources, see pp. 686–92.)

Editors and teachers in most academic disciplines require special documentation formats (or styles) in their scholarly journals and in students' papers. All the styles use a citation in the text that serves two purposes: it signals that material is borrowed, and it refers readers to detailed information about the source so that they can locate both the source and the place in the source where the borrowed material appears. The detailed source information appears either in footnotes or at the end of the paper.

Aside from these essential similarities, the disciplines' documentation styles differ markedly in citation form, arrangement of source information, and other particulars. Each discipline's style reflects the needs of its practitioners for certain kinds of information presented in certain ways. For instance, the currency of a source is important in the social and natural sciences, where studies build on and correct each other; thus in-text citations in these disciplines

http://www.colostate.edu/Depts/WritingCenter/references/sources/document/page1.htm Rationale for and advice on documentation, from Colorado State University.

usually include a source's date of publication. In the humanities, however, currency is less important, so in-text citations do not include date of publication.

The disciplines' documentation formats are described in style guides listed elsewhere in this book for the humanities (pp. 822–23), the social sciences (p. 841), and the natural and applied sciences (p. 869). In addition, this book discusses and illustrates five common documentation styles:

- The MLA style, used in English, foreign languages, and some other humanities (p. 710).
- Chicago style, used in history, art history, philosophy, religion, and some other humanities (p. 822).
- APA style, used in psychology and some other social sciences (p. 841).
- CBE style, used in the biological and some other sciences (p. 869).
- Columbia style for online sources in the humanities and in the sciences, which can supplement the other styles (p. 881).

Ask your instructor which style you should use. If no style is required, use the guide that's most appropriate for the discipline you're writing in. Do follow one system for citing sources—and one system only—so that you provide all the necessary information in a consistent format.

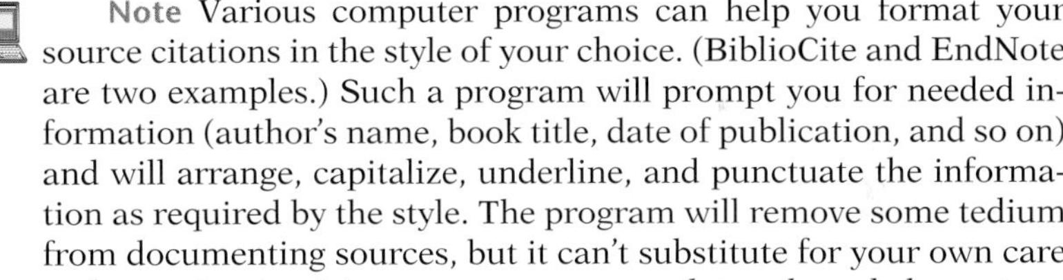

Note Various computer programs can help you format your source citations in the style of your choice. (BiblioCite and EndNote are two examples.) Such a program will prompt you for needed information (author's name, book title, date of publication, and so on) and will arrange, capitalize, underline, and punctuate the information as required by the style. The program will remove some tedium from documenting sources, but it can't substitute for your own care and attention in giving your sources complete acknowledgment using the required form.

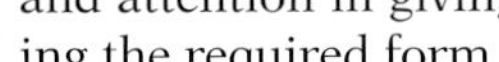

CHAPTER 45

Writing the Paper

Writing a research paper begins when you seek a topic and continues as you evaluate and take notes from your sources. During research, you might even pause to draft paragraphs or sections that pull your sources together to support your ideas. At some point, though, you'll need to turn your attention to the whole paper—ensuring that it has a clear thesis (below), creating a structure (opposite), writing the complete draft (p. 704), revising and editing the paper (p. 707), and preparing the final draft (p. 708). To illustrate these stages, we continue to draw on Edward Begay's and Vanessa Haley's work.

Note This chapter complements and extends the detailed discussion of the writing situation and the writing process in Chapters 1–3, which also include many tips for using a word processor and more links to helpful Web sites. If you haven't already done so, you may want to read Chapters 1–3 before this one.

45a Developing a thesis statement

Perhaps earlier in the research-writing process, but certainly once you have taken notes from your sources, you will want to express your central idea and perspective in a thesis statement of one or two sentences. (See pp. 30–34 if you need guidance on developing a thesis statement.) Drafting a thesis statement will help you see the overall picture and organize your notes.

Edward Begay's and Vanessa Haley's work on their research papers illustrates how a thesis statement evolves to become complete and specific. Before finishing his reading on access to the Internet, Begay wrote the following draft of a thesis statement:

Advice on developing a thesis statement:

http://www.wisc.edu/writetest/Handbook/thesis.html From the University of Wisconsin at Madison.

http://www.esc.edu/htmlpages/writer/menud.htm From the State University of New York.

Tentative thesis statement

Because of the cost of hooking up to the Internet and training people to use it, the nation faces the possibility of a widening gap between rich and poor in information, skills, and income.

This statement captured Begay's preliminary idea that the Internet poses a threat to equality. But with further reading, Begay rethought this idea: many of his sources mentioned Internet access through public schools and libraries, and he began to focus on these institutions as a solution to the problem. The solution opened up new questions: how would schools and libraries have to change, and what would the change cost? With more reading, Begay revised his thesis statement:

Revised thesis statement

To make Internet access universal, public libraries and schools must obtain the necessary resources from government and business to go online.

For Vanessa Haley, framing a thesis statement for her paper on Annie Dillard required drawing together (synthesizing) Dillard's ideas about humanity and nature into a single statement of Haley's own. The first draft merely conveyed Haley's interest in Dillard:

Tentative thesis statement

Unlike many other nature writers, Dillard does not reinforce the separation between humanity and nature.

Haley's revision stated her synthesis of Dillard's ideas:

Revised thesis statement

In her encounters with nature, Dillard probes a spiritual as well as a physical identity between human beings and nature that could help to heal the rift between them.

EXERCISE 1
Developing a thesis statement

Draft and revise a thesis statement for your developing research paper. Make sure the revised version specifically asserts your main idea. (If you need help, consult pp. 30–34.)

45b Creating a structure

Before starting to draft your research paper, organize your ideas and information so that you know the main divisions of your paper, the order you'll cover them in, and the important supporting ideas for each division. The goal is to create a structure that presents your ideas in a sensible and persuasive sequence and that supports ideas at each level with enough explanation and evidence. Consult the discussion of organization on pages 35–46 if you need help distinguishing general and specific information, arranging groups of information, or using a computer effectively for developing a structure.

1 Arranging notes

Creating a structure for a research paper involves almost constant synthesis, the forging of relationships among ideas (see p. 673). As you arrange and rearrange your notes, you find connections among ideas and determine which are most important, which are merely supportive, and which are not relevant at all.

To build a structure, follow these guidelines:

- Arrange your notes in groups of related ideas and information according to the subject headings you wrote on note cards or in computer files. Each of these groups should correspond to a main section of your paper: a key idea of your own that supports the thesis along with the evidence for that idea.
- Review your research journal for connections between sources, opinions of sources, and other thoughts that can help you organize your paper.
- Look objectively at your groups of notes. If some groups are skimpy, with few notes, consider whether you should drop the category or conduct more research to fill it out. If most of your notes fall into one or two groups, consider whether the categories are too broad and should be divided. (Does any of this rethinking affect your thesis statement? If so, revise it accordingly.)
- Within each group, distinguish between the main idea of the group (which should be your own) and the supporting ideas and evidence (which should come from your sources).

2 Using an outline

An outline can help you shape your research and also discover potential problems, such as inadequate support and overlapping or irrelevant ideas.

Advice on outlining:

http://researchpaper.com/writing_center/63.html From Researchpaper.com.

http://owl.english.purdue.edu/Files/132/6-outline.html From the Purdue Online Writing Lab.

http://webster.commnet.edu/mla/outlines.htm From Capital Community College.

Informal outline

For some research projects, you may find an **informal outline** sufficient: you list main points and supporting information in the order you expect to discuss them. Because of its informality, such an outline can help you try out different arrangements of material, even fairly early in the research process.

Edward Begay experimented with an informal outline while examining his sources, in order to see how his developing ideas might fit together:

History of the Internet
  Packet-switching networks—UK, France
  ARPANET—linked US Defense Dept., contractors, universities
  Network of networks—UNIX, NSFNET, and onward

Commercial vs. public use
  1st users universities, libraries, govts.
  Business sees commercial uses
  PCs, modems increase home use

Access to Internet
  Tech. skills needed
  Problems for equality, democracy
  Expense of going online
  Imp. of Internet to democratic society
  Libraries & schools: sites for widespread access
  Libraries & schools need to adapt, find money to go online

This informal outline helped Begay decide not to continue researching the history of the Internet or the conflicts between commercial and public use (the first two sections) because they seemed likely to overwhelm his central concern, equal access to the Internet (last section). Note that Begay did include an endnote in his paper referring to the history of the Internet (p. 772).

Formal outline

Unlike an informal outline, a **formal outline** arranges ideas tightly and in considerable detail, with close attention to hierarchy and phrasing. The example below shows the formal outline's format and schematic content:

I. First main idea
  A. First subordinate idea
    1. First evidence for subordinate idea
      a. First detail of evidence
      b. Second detail of evidence
    2. Second evidence for subordinate idea
  B. Second subordinate idea
II. Second main idea

In this model, main ideas are labeled with Roman numerals, the first sublevel with capital letters, the second with Arabic numerals, and the third with small letters. A fourth sublevel, if needed, is labeled with Arabic numerals enclosed in parentheses. Each level of the outline is indented farther than the one it supports. (Your word processor may be able to help you with the labels and indentions. See p. 36.)

A formal outline can help you decide not only what your main ideas are and how you will arrange them but also how you will support them. Some of this information may not emerge until you are drafting, however, so remain open to revising the outline as you proceed. And consider using a formal outline as a revision tool as well, creating a map of your completed first draft to check and improve the structure (see p. 54).

To be an effective organizer for your thoughts, or an effective revision tool, a formal outline should be detailed and should adhere to several principles of logical arrangement, clarity, balance, and completeness. These are discussed in detail and illustrated on pages 39–41. Briefly:

- The outline should divide material into groups that indicate which ideas are primary and, under them, which are subordinate. A long, undivided list of parallel items probably needs to be subdivided.
- Parallel headings should represent ideas of equal importance and generality and should not overlap one another.
- Single sublevels should be avoided because they illogically imply that something is divided into only one part.

A formal outline is usually written either in phrases—a **topic outline**—or in sentences—**a sentence outline.** A complete topic outline is illustrated on page 39. A complete sentence outline accompanies Edward Begay's research paper on pages 748–49. Either is suitable for a research paper, though a sentence outline, because it requires complete statements, conveys more information.

EXERCISE 2
Creating a structure

Continuing from Exercise 1 (p. 701), arrange your notes into a structure. As specified by your instructor, make an informal outline or a formal sentence or topic outline to guide the drafting of your paper.

45c Drafting the paper

Beginning a draft of what will be a relatively long and complicated paper can be difficult, so it may help to remember that you do not have to proceed methodically from beginning to end. Here are some ideas for writing a draft:

Tips for drafting a research paper

- To get your juices flowing and give yourself a sense of direction, write a quick two- or three-paragraph summary of what the paper will be about. (Pretend you're writing to a friend if that will help loosen you up.) A version of the material you generate in this way may eventually prove useful for your paper's introduction or conclusion.
- Start with the section of the paper you feel most confident about. At first, skip any parts that scare you or give you undue trouble, even the introduction.
- Work in chunks, one unit or principal idea at a time. Fit the sections together only after you begin to see the draft take shape.
- Center each section on an idea of your own, using source material to back up the idea.
- Insert source information (author's name and page number) into the draft as you quote, paraphrase, or summarize.

1 Working section by section

In writing a first draft, remember that a primary reason for doing a research paper is learning how to interpret and evaluate the evidence in sources, draw your own conclusions from the evidence, and weave the two together in a way that establishes your expertise in your subject. The weaving will be easier if you view each principal idea in your outline as a unit. Depending on the importance of the idea to your scheme, on its complexity, and on the amount of evidence needed to support it, a unit may require a single paragraph or a block of several paragraphs.

Compose the units of your paper as if each will stand alone (though of course you will pull the units together before your draft is complete).

- Begin each unit by stating the idea, which should be a conclusion you have drawn from reading and responding to your sources.
- Follow the statement with specific support from your notes: facts and examples; summaries, paraphrases, or quotations of secondary sources; quotations of passages from primary sources with your analysis.

Advice on drafting a research paper:

http://www.ipl.org/teen/aplus/step6.htm#1.3 From the Internet Public Library.

http://www.esc.edu/htmlpages/writer/menub.htm From the State University of New York.

- If your research focuses on or has uncovered a disagreement among experts, present the disagreement fairly and give the evidence that leads you to side with one expert or another.
- As much as possible, try to remain open to new interpretations or new arrangements of ideas that occur to you.

Proceeding in this way will help you avoid a common trap of research writing: allowing your sources to control you, rather than vice versa. Make sure each unit of your paper centers on an idea of your own, not someone else's, and that your paragraphs are pointed toward demonstrating that idea, not merely presenting sources.

2 Tracking source citations

As you draft your paper, insert the source of each summary, paraphrase, and quotation in parentheses in the text—for instance, "(Frankel 42)" referring to page 42 in a work by Frankel. If you are conscientious about inserting these notes and carrying them through successive drafts, you will be less likely to plagiarize accidentally and you will have little difficulty documenting your sources in the final paper. (Documentation is discussed on pp. 698–99.)

3 Drafting on a computer

If you write on a word processor, the following suggestions could ease the transition from developing ideas and reading sources to drafting the paper:

- Copy your preliminary outline into your document file, and compose paragraphs directly under headings, deleting the remnants of the outline and adding transitions as you go along.
- If you have kept your source notes on a computer, you can open both your document file and a copy of your notes file, one above the other. (Leave the original notes file intact in case you accidentally delete a note and need it later.) Then you can import your notes directly into your draft to support your ideas, using the word processor's editing functions to mesh source information into your own ideas and sentences. (See pp. 184–85 for information on editing functions.)
- Instead of working with two files on the same screen, you can copy your notes file into your document file (again, leaving the original notes file intact), arrange the notes under your outline headings, and write the parts of the draft that the notes support. Integrate the notes into your own text using the word processor's editing functions.
- If you do import your notes into your draft, you'll need to rewrite and edit the notes so that they work for your ideas and fit into your sentences. Avoid importing many long quotations from your sources. (See the box on p. 683.)

- Be sure to include source information for every summary, paraphrase, and quotation, as described on pages 686–92.

EXERCISE 3
Drafting your paper

Draft the research paper you have been developing in Chapters 42–45. Before beginning the draft, study your research journal and your notes. While drafting, follow your notes, thesis statement, and outline as closely as you need to, but stay open to new ideas, associations, and arrangements.

45d Revising and editing the paper

When you have written a first draft, take a break for at least a day so that you can gain some objectivity about your work and read the draft critically when you begin to revise.

1 Revising

Evaluate your first draft according to the advice and revision checklist on pages 52–59. Deal with major revisions first, saving editing and formatting for later drafts. Be especially attentive to the following:

- Ensure that your thesis statement accurately describes your topic and your perspective as they emerged during drafting, so that the paper is unified and coherent.
- Be alert for structural problems. (Outlining your draft as suggested on p. 54 can help you see your structure at a glance.)

  Illogical arrangements of ideas.
  Inadequate emphasis of important points and overemphasis of minor points.
  Imbalance between the views of others (support) and your own views (interpretation or analysis).

- Hunt down irrelevant ideas and facts that crept in just because you had notes on them.
- Look for places where supporting evidence is weak.

Advising on revising, editing, and proofreading:

http://webster.commnet.edu/HP/pages/darling/grammar/composition/editing.htm From the Guide to Grammar and Writing.

http://owl.english.purdue.edu/Files/96.html From the Purdue Online Writing Lab.

http://www.ipl.org/teen/aplus/linksrevising.htm From the Internet Public Library.

- Evaluate the reasonableness of your argument (see pp. 165–69).
- Consider where you need to define terms and clarify concepts that readers may be unfamiliar with.

A word processor simplifies the mechanics of revision, making it possible, for instance, to move blocks of text with a few keystrokes or to make side-by-side comparisons of the same passage or section. See pages 53, 54, and 184–85 for tips on revising on a computer.

2 Editing

When you complete your revision—and only then—you are ready to edit. If you do not write on a computer, copy or retype the new draft if possible so that you have a clean copy to work on. If you write on a computer, you can edit directly on screen or print a clean copy. (Some writers find it easier to spot errors on paper than on screen.) For editing, consult the advice and checklist on pages 60–63. Try to read the paper from the point of view of someone who has not spent hours planning and researching but instead has come fresh to the paper. Look for lapses in sense, awkward passages, wordiness, poor transitions between ideas and evidence, unnecessary repetition, wrong or misspelled words, errors in grammar, punctuation, or mechanics—in short, anything that is likely to interfere with a reader's understanding of your meaning.

3 Completing source citations

Before you prepare your final draft (next section), you must insert final source citations into your text and prepare the list of sources for the end of the paper. See pages 698–99 on documenting sources in various disciplines' styles.

> **EXERCISE 4**
> **Revising and editing your paper**
>
> Using the revision and editing checklists on pages 56 and 61 and the pointers above, revise and edit your research paper. Work to improve not only the presentation of ideas but also, if necessary, the ideas themselves. Make sure you have provided an in-text citation for every summary, paraphrase, and direct quotation of a source and that your list of sources is complete.

45e Preparing and proofreading the final draft

Prepare the final draft of your paper when you have edited the text, added the source citations, and written the list of works cited. Most instructors expect research papers to be neatly typed with clear titling, double spacing, standard margins, and minimal handwritten corrections. Your instructor may have additional requirements, suggested by the discipline you are writing in. This book explains four such document formats:

- In English, foreign languages, and some other humanities, use the format of the *MLA Handbook for Writers of Research Papers.* See pages 215–18 for a detailed description and the research papers of Edward Begay and Vanessa Haley (Chapter 47) for illustrations.
- In history, art history, religion, philosophy, and some other humanities, use the Chicago format. See pages 823–24 and 832–33 for a description and illustrations.
- In psychology and other social sciences, use the format of the *Publication Manual of the American Psychological Association.* See pages 845–47 and 855–62 for a description and illustrations.
- In the natural and applied sciences, use the format of *Scientific Style and Format: The CBE Manual for Authors, Editors, and Publishers.* See pages 869–73 and 876–80 for a description and illustration.

In any discipline, you can use a word processor to present your ideas effectively and attractively with readable type fonts, headings, illustrations, and other elements. See pages 200–14 for ideas and illustrations.

Before you submit your paper, proofread it carefully for typographical errors, misspellings, and other slight errors. (See p. 64 for proofreading tips.) Unless the errors are very numerous (more than several on a page), you can correct them by whiting out or crossing out (neatly) and inserting the correction (neatly) in ink. Don't let the pressure of a deadline prevent you from proofreading, for even minor errors can impair clarity or annoy readers and thus negate some of the hard work you have put into your project.

EXERCISE 5
Preparing and proofreading your final draft

Prepare the final draft of your research paper, following your instructor's requirements for document format. If your instructor does not specify a format, follow the guidelines on pages 215–18. Proofread and correct the paper before submitting it.

CHAPTER 46

Documenting Sources in MLA Style

This chapter presents one of the five documentation styles discussed in this book: that of the Modern Language Association, used in English, foreign languages, and some other humanities. The other styles appear later in the book:

- Chicago style for history, art history, philosophy, religion, and some other humanities (p. 822).
- APA style for psychology and other social sciences (p. 841).
- CBE style for the biological and other sciences (p. 869).
- Columbia style for online sources in the humanities and the sciences, supplementing the other four styles (p. 881).

All the styles differ considerably in the form of in-text citation and the formatting of a source list. Ask your instructor which style you should use.

46a Understanding MLA style

The documentation system of the Modern Language Association is detailed in the *MLA Handbook for Writers of Research Papers,* 5th edition (1999). This style employs brief parenthetical citations within the text that direct readers to the list of works cited. For example:

> Only one article mentions this discrepancy (Wolfe 62).

The name Wolfe directs readers to the article by Wolfe in the list of works cited, and the page number 62 specifies the page in the article on which the cited material appears.

The following pages describe this documentation system: what must be included in a citation (opposite), where to place citations

http://www.mla.org/main_stl.htm The MLA Web site, offering occasional updates of MLA style and answers to frequently asked questions.

http://owl.english.purdue.edu/Files/34.html Guidance on using MLA style, from the Purdue Online Writing Lab.

(p. 716), when to use footnotes or endnotes in addition to parenthetical citations (p. 718), and how to create the list of works cited (p. 719). The index below (parenthetical text citations) and the one on pages 720–21 (works-cited entries) provide quick-reference guides to the models.

46b Citing sources in your text: MLA style

1 Writing parenthetical text citations

In-text citations of sources have two requirements:

- They must include just enough information for the reader to locate the appropriate source in your list of works cited.
- They must include just enough information for the reader to locate the place in the source where the borrowed material appears.

Usually, you can meet both these requirements by providing the author's last name and the page(s) in the source on which the material appears. The reader can find the source in your list of works cited and find the borrowed material in the source itself.

Note For most sources, you will provide the author's or authors' last names and a page reference. Do not include the title unless you are citing more than one work by exactly the same author(s) or the source has no listed author (models 8 and 9, p. 714). The examples on the next page cite a book to which neither of these exceptions applies.

MLA parenthetical text citations

Not One text discusses the "ethical dilemmas in public relations practice" (Wilcox, Ault, and Agee, Public Relations 125).

Not One text discusses the "ethical dilemmas in public relations practice" (Public Relations 125).

But One text discusses the "ethical dilemmas in public relations practice" (Wilcox, Ault, and Agee 125).

1. Author not named in your text

When you have not already named the author in your sentence, provide the author's last name and the page number(s), with no punctuation between them, in parentheses.

> One researcher concludes that "women impose a distinctive construction on moral problems, seeing moral dilemmas in terms of conflicting responsibilities" (Gilligan 105).

See models 5 and 6 (p. 713) for the forms to use when the source does not provide page numbers.

2. Author named in your text

If the author's name is already given in your text, you need not repeat it in the parenthetical citation. The citation gives just the page number(s).

> One researcher, Carol Gilligan, concludes that "women impose a distinctive construction on moral problems, seeing moral dilemmas in terms of conflicting responsibilities" (105).

3. A work with two or three authors

If the source has two or three authors, give all their last names in the text or in the citation. Separate two authors' names with "and":

> As Frieden and Sagalyn observe, "The poor and the minorities were the leading victims of highway and renewal programs" (29).

> According to one study, "The poor and the minorities were the leading victims of highway and renewal programs" (Frieden and Sagalyn 29).

With three authors, add commas and also "and" before the final name:

> The text by Wilcox, Ault, and Agee discusses the "ethical dilemmas in public relations practice" (125).

> One text discusses the "ethical dilemmas in public relations practice" (Wilcox, Ault, and Agee 125).

4. A work with more than three authors

If the source has more than three authors, you may list all their last names or use only the first author's name followed by "et al." (the abbreviation for the Latin *et alii,* "and others"). The choice depends on what you do in your list of works cited (see p. 722).

> It took the combined forces of the Americans, Europeans, and Japanese to break the rebel siege of Beijing in 1900 (Lopez et al. 362).

> It took the combined forces of the Americans, Europeans, and Japanese to break the rebel siege of Beijing in 1900 (Lopez, Blum, Cameron, and Barnes 362).

5. A work with numbered paragraphs or screens instead of pages

Some electronic sources number each paragraph or screen instead of each page. In citing passages in these sources, give the paragraph or screen number(s) and distinguish them from page numbers: after the author's name, put a comma, a space, and "par." (one paragraph), "pars." (more than one paragraph), "screen," or "screens."

> Twins reared apart report similar feelings (Palfrey, pars. 6-7).

6. An entire work or a work with no page or other reference numbers

When you cite an entire work rather than a part of it, the citation will not include any page or paragraph number. Try to work the author's name into your text, in which case you will not need a parenthetical citation. But remember that the source must appear in the list of works cited.

> Boyd deals with the need to acknowledge and come to terms with our fear of nuclear technology.

Use the same format when you cite a specific passage from a work with no page or other reference numbers, such as an online source.

If the author's name does not appear in your text, put it in a parenthetical citation.

> Almost 20 percent of commercial banks have been audited for the practice (Friis).

7. A multivolume work

If you consulted only one volume of a multivolume work, your list of works cited will indicate as much (see model 14, pp. 724–25), and you can treat the volume as any book.

If you consulted more than one volume of a multivolume work, give the appropriate volume in your text citation.

> After issuing the Emancipation Proclamation, Lincoln said, "What I did, I did after very full deliberations, and under a very heavy and solemn sense of responsibility" (5: 438).

The number 5 indicates the volume from which the quotation was taken; the number 438 indicates the page number in that volume. When the author's name appears in such a citation, place it before the volume number with no punctuation: (Lincoln 5: 438).

If you are referring generally to an entire volume of a multivolume work and are not citing specific page numbers, add the abbreviation "vol." before the volume number as in (vol. 5) or (Lincoln, vol. 5) (note the comma after the author's name). Then readers will not misinterpret the volume number as a page number.

8. A work by an author of two or more cited works

If your list of works cited includes two or more works by the same author, then your citation must tell the reader which of the author's works you are referring to. Give the title either in the text or in a parenthetical citation. In a parenthetical citation, give the full title only if it is brief; otherwise, shorten the title to the first one or two main words (excluding *A, An,* or *The*).

> At about age seven, children begin to use appropriate gestures with their stories (Gardner, Arts 144-45).

The title *Arts* is shortened from Gardner's full title, *The Arts and Human Development* (see the works-cited entry for this book on p. 722).

9. An unsigned work

Refer to an anonymous source by a full or shortened version of the title, as explained above. In your list of works cited, you will alphabetize an anonymous work by the first main word of the title (see p. 723), so the first word of a shortened title should be the same. This citation refers to an unsigned article titled "The Right to Die."

> One article notes that a death-row inmate may demand his own execution to achieve a fleeting notoriety ("Right").

A page number is unnecessary because the article is no longer than a page (see the entry for the article on p. 729).

10. A government publication or a work with a corporate author

If the author of the work is listed as a government body or a corporation, cite the work by that organization's name. If the name is long, work it into the text to avoid an intrusive parenthetical citation.

> A 1998 report by the Hawaii Department of Education predicts an increase in enrollments (6).

11. An indirect source

When you want to use a quotation that is already in quotation marks—indicating that the author you are reading is quoting someone else—try to find the original source and quote directly from it. (See p. 765). If you can't find the original source then your citation must indicate that your quotation of it is indirect. In the following citation, "qtd. in" ("quoted in") says that Davino was quoted by Boyd:

> George Davino maintains that "even small children have vivid ideas about nuclear energy" (qtd. in Boyd 22).

The list of works cited then includes only Boyd (the work consulted), not Davino.

12. A literary work

Novels, plays, and poems are often available in many editions, so your instructor may ask you to provide information that will help readers find the passage you cite no matter what edition they consult.

For novels, the page number comes first, followed by a semicolon and then information on the appropriate part or chapter of the work.

> Toward the end of James's novel, Maggie suddenly feels "the thick breath of the definite--which was the intimate, the immediate, the familiar, as she hadn't had them for so long" (535; pt. 6, ch. 41).

For poems that are not divided into parts, you can omit the page number and supply the line number(s) for the quotation. To prevent confusion with page numbers, precede the numbers with "line" or "lines" in the first citation; then just use the numbers.

> In Shakespeare's Sonnet 73 the speaker identifies with the trees of late autumn, "Bare ruined choirs, where late the sweet birds sang" (line 4). "In me," Shakespeare writes, "thou seest the glowing of such fire / That on the ashes of his youth doth lie" (9-10).

See pages 811–13 for a sample paper on a poem.

For verse plays and poems that are divided into parts, omit a page number and cite the appropriate part—act (and scene, if any), canto, book, and so on—plus the line number(s). Use Arabic numerals for parts, including acts and scenes (3.4), unless your instructor specifies Roman numerals (III.iv).

> Later in King Lear Shakespeare has the disguised Edgar say, "The prince of darkness is a gentleman" (3.4.147).

See pages 814–16 for a sample paper on a verse play.

For prose plays, provide the page number followed by the act and scene, if any. See the reference to *Death of a Salesman* on page 718.

13. The Bible

When you cite passages of the Bible in parentheses, abbreviate the title of any book longer than four letters—for instance, "Gen." (Genesis), "1 Sam." (1 Samuel), "Ps." (Psalms), "Matt." (Matthew), "Rom." (Romans). Then give the chapter and verse(s) in Arabic numerals.

> According to the Bible, at Babel God "did [. . .] confound the language of all the earth" (Gen. 11.9).

14. An electronic source

Cite an electronic source as you would any other source: usually by author's name or, if there is no author, by title.

> Business forecasts for the fourth quarter tended to be optimistic (White 4).

This example cites a source with page numbers. For a source with paragraph or screen numbers or no numbering, see models 5 and 6 (p. 713).

15. More than one work

If you use a parenthetical citation to refer to more than a single work, separate the references with a semicolon.

> Two recent articles point out that a computer badly used can be less efficient than no computer at all (Gough and Hall 201; Richards 162).

Since long citations in the text can distract the reader, you may choose to cite several or more works in an endnote or footnote rather than in the text. See page 718.

2 Positioning and punctuating parenthetical citations

Position text citations to accomplish two goals:

- Make it clear exactly where your borrowing begins and ends.
- Keep the citation as unobtrusive as possible.

You can accomplish both goals by placing the parenthetical citation at the end of the sentence element containing the borrowed material. This sentence element may be a phrase or a clause, and it may begin, interrupt, or conclude the sentence. Usually, as in the examples below, the element ends with a punctuation mark.

> The inflation rate might climb as high as 30 percent (Kim 164), an increase that could threaten the small nation's stability.

> The inflation rate, which might climb as high as 30 percent (Kim 164), could threaten the small nation's stability.

> The small nation's stability could be threatened by its inflation rate, which, one source predicts, might climb as high as 30 percent (Kim 164).

In the last example the addition of *one source predicts* clarifies that Kim is responsible only for the inflation-rate prediction, not for the statement about stability.

For citations in your running text, generally place the parenthetical citation *before* any punctuation required by your sentence, as in the examples above. If the borrowed material is a quotation, place the citation *between* the closing quotation mark and the punctuation.

> Spelling argues that during the 1970s American automobile manufacturers met consumer needs "as well as could be expected" (26), but not everyone agrees with him.

The exception is a quotation ending in a question mark or exclamation point. Then use the appropriate punctuation inside the closing quotation mark, and follow the quotation with the text citation and a period:

> "Of what use is genius," Emerson asks, "if the organ [. . .] cannot find a focal distance within the actual horizon of human life?" ("Experience" 60). Mad genius is no genius.

When a citation appears after a quotation that ends in a bracketed ellipsis mark, place the citation between the closing quotation mark and the sentence period.

> One observer maintains that "American manufacturers must bear the blame for their poor sales [. . .]" (Rosenbaum 12).

When a citation appears at the end of a quotation set off from the text, place it one space *after* the punctuation ending the quotation. No additional punctuation is needed.

In Arthur Miller's Death of a Salesman, the most poignant defense of Willie Loman comes from his wife, Linda:

> He's not the finest character that ever lived. But he's a human being, and a terrible thing is happening to him. So attention must be paid. He's not to be allowed to fall into his grave like an old dog. Attention, attention must finally be paid to such a person. (56; act 1)

(This citation of a play includes the act number as well as the page number. See p. 716.)

See the two sample research papers starting on pages 746 and 779 for further examples of placing parenthetical references in relation to summaries, paraphrases, and quotations.

3 Using footnotes or endnotes in special circumstances

Occasionally, you may want to use footnotes or endnotes in place of parenthetical citations. If you need to refer to several sources at once, listing them in a long parenthetical citation could be intrusive. In that case, signal the citation with a numeral raised above the appropriate line of text and write a note with the same numeral to cite the sources:

Text At least five studies have confirmed these results.[1]

Note [1] Abbott and Winger 266-68; Casner 27; Hoyenga 78-79; Marino 36; Tripp, Tripp, and Walk 179-83.

You may also use a footnote or endnote to comment on a source or provide information that does not fit easily in the text:

Text So far, no one has confirmed these results.[2]

Note [2] Manter reports spending a year trying to replicate the experiment, but he was never able to produce the high temperatures reported by the original experimenters (616).

In a note the raised numeral is indented five spaces and followed by a space. If the note appears as a footnote, place it at the bottom of the page on which the citation appears, set it off from the text with quadruple spacing, and single-space the note itself. If the note appears as an endnote, place it in numerical order with the other endnotes on a page between the text and the list of works cited; double-space all the endnotes. (See pp. 772–73 for examples of endnotes and the format to use in typing a page of endnotes.)

46c Preparing the list of works cited: MLA style

In the documentation style of the *MLA Handbook,* your in-text parenthetical citations (discussed in 46b) refer the reader to complete information on your sources in a list you title "Works Cited" and place at the end of your paper. The list should include all the sources you quoted, paraphrased, or summarized in your paper. (If your instructor asks you to include sources you examined but did not cite, title the list "Works Consulted.")

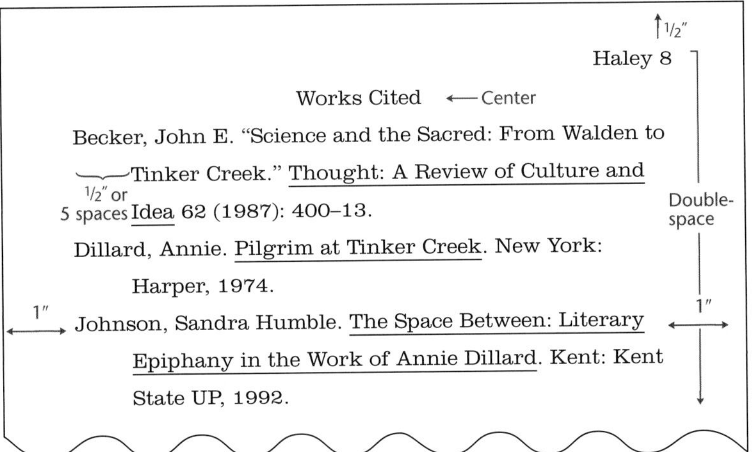
Haley 8

Works Cited

Becker, John E. "Science and the Sacred: From Walden to Tinker Creek." Thought: A Review of Culture and Idea 62 (1987): 400–13.

Dillard, Annie. Pilgrim at Tinker Creek. New York: Harper, 1974.

Johnson, Sandra Humble. The Space Between: Literary Epiphany in the Work of Annie Dillard. Kent: Kent State UP, 1992.

Follow this format for the list of works cited:

- Arrange your sources in alphabetical order by the last name of the author. If an author is not given in the source, alphabetize the source by the first main word of the title (excluding *A, An,* or *The*).
- Type the entire list double-spaced (both within and between entries).
- Indent the second and subsequent lines of each entry one-half inch from the left.

For complete lists of works cited, see the papers by Edward Begay (p. 774) and Vanessa Haley (p. 784).

The box on the next page directs you to the MLA formats for works-cited entries. Use your best judgment in adapting the models to your particular sources. If you can't find a model that exactly matches a source you used, locate and follow the closest possible match. You will certainly need to combine formats—for instance, drawing on model 2 ("A book with two or three authors") and model 26 ("An article in a daily newspaper") for a newspaper article with two authors.

MLA works-cited models

Note Computerized bibliography programs can format your list of works cited in MLA style when you provide the source information. See page 699 for more on such programs.

1 Listing books

The basic format for a book includes the following elements:

① Gilligan, Carol. ② In a Different Voice: Psychological Theory and Women's Development. ③ ⓐ Cambridge: ⓑ Harvard UP, ⓒ 1982.

1. *Author.* Use the author's full name: last name first, followed by a comma, and then the first name and any middle name or initial. Omit any title or degree attached to the author's name, such as Dr. or Ph.D. End the name with a period and one space.
2. *Title.* Give the full title, including any subtitle. Underline the title unless your instructor specifically calls for italics (see p.

541). Capitalize all important words (see p. 535), separate the main title and the subtitle with a colon and one space, and end the title with a period and one space. For citing a part of a book, such as an essay or poem, see model 18 (pp. 725–26).

3. *Publication information.* You can usually find this information on the book's title page or on the copyright page following:

   a. The city of publication, followed by a colon and one space. Use only the first city if the source lists more than one.
   b. The name of the publisher, followed by a comma. Shorten most publishers' names, often to a single word: "Little" for Little, Brown, "Knopf" for Alfred A. Knopf. For university presses, use the abbreviations "U" and "P," as in the example. If the title page lists an imprint and a publisher—for instance, Vintage Books and Random House—give both names with a hyphen: "Vintage-Random."
   c. The date of publication, ending with a period.

When a reference requires other information, generally place it either between the author's name and the title or between the title and the publication information, as specified in the models on the following pages.

1. A book with one author

Gilligan, Carol. In a Different Voice: Psychological Theory and Women's Development. Cambridge: Harvard UP, 1982.

2. A book with two or three authors

Frieden, Bernard J., and Lynne B. Sagalyn. Downtown, Inc.: How America Rebuilds Cities. Cambridge: MIT P, 1989.

Wilcox, Dennis L., Phillip H. Ault, and Warren K. Agee. Public Relations: Strategies and Tactics. 4th ed. New York: Harper, 1999.

Give the authors' names in the order provided on the title page. Reverse the first and last names of the first author *only,* not of any other authors. Separate two authors' names with a comma and "and"; separate three authors' names with commas and with "and" before the third name.

3. A book with more than three authors

Lopez, Robert S., et al. Civilizations: Western and World. Boston: Little, 1975.

You may, but need not, give all authors' names if the work has more than three authors. If you choose not to give all names, provide the name of the first author only, and follow the name with a comma and the abbreviation "et al." (for the Latin *et alii,* meaning "and others").

4. Two or more works by the same author(s)

Gardner, Howard. The Arts and Human Development. New York: Wiley, 1973.

---. The Quest for Mind: Piaget, Lévi-Strauss, and the Structuralist Movement. New York: Knopf, 1973.

Give the author's name only in the first entry. For the second and any subsequent works by the same author, substitute three hyphens for the author's name, followed by a period and one space. Within the set of entries for the author, list the sources alphabetically by the first main word of the title (here "Arts," then "Quest"). Note that the three hyphens stand for *exactly* the same name or names. If the second source above were by Gardner and somebody else, both names would have to be given in full.

5. A book with an editor

Ruitenbeek, Hendrick, ed. Freud as We Knew Him. Detroit: Wayne State UP, 1973.

The abbreviation "ed.," separated from the name by a comma, identifies Ruitenbeek as the editor of the work.

6. A book with an author and an editor

Mumford, Lewis. The City in History. Ed. Donald L. Miller. New York: Pantheon, 1986.

When citing the work of the author, give his or her name first, and give the editor's name after the title, preceded by "Ed." ("Edited by"). When citing the work of the editor, use model 5 for a book with an editor, and give the author's name after the title preceded by "By": Miller, Donald L., ed. The City in History. By Lewis Mumford.

7. A translation

Alighieri, Dante. The Inferno. Trans. John Ciardi. New York: NAL, 1971.

When citing the work of the author, give his or her name first, and give the translator's name after the title, preceded by "Trans." ("Translated by"). When citing the work of the translator, give his or her name first, followed by a comma and "trans."; then follow the title with "By" and the author's name: Ciardi, John, trans. The Inferno. By Dante Alighieri.

When a book you cite by author has a translator *and* an editor, give the translator's and editor's names in the order used on the book's title page. For a translated selection from an edited book, see model 18, pages 725–26.

8. A book with a corporate author

Lorenz Research, Inc. Research in Social Studies Teaching. Baltimore: Arrow, 1997.

List the name of the corporation, institution, or other body as author.

9. An anonymous book

The Dorling Kindersley World Reference Atlas. London: Dorling, 1999.

List an anonymous book by its full title. Alphabetize the book by the title's first main word (here "Dorling"), omitting *A, An,* or *The.*

10. The Bible

The Bible. King James Version.

The New English Bible. London: Oxford UP and Cambridge UP, 1970.

When citing a standard version of the Bible (first example), do not underline the title or the name of the version, and you need not provide publication information. For an edition of the Bible (second example), underline the title and give its full publication information.

11. A later edition

Bollinger, Dwight L. Aspects of Language. 2nd ed. New York: Harcourt, 1975.

For any edition after the first, place the edition number between the title and the publication information. Use the appropriate designation for editions that are named or dated rather than numbered—for instance, "Rev. ed." for "Revised edition."

12. A republished book

James, Henry. The Golden Bowl. 1904. London: Penguin, 1966.

Republished books include paperbound editions of books originally released in hard bindings and books reissued under new titles. Place the original date of publication (but not the place of publication or the publisher's name) after the title, and then provide the full publication information for the source you are using. If the book was originally published under a different title, add this title at the end of the entry and move the original publication date to follow the title—for example, Rpt. of Thomas Hardy: A Life. 1941.

13. A book with a title in its title

Eco, Umberto. Postscript to The Name of the Rose. Trans. William Weaver. New York: Harcourt, 1983.

When a book's title contains another book title (as here: The Name of the Rose), do not underline the second title. When a book's title contains a quotation or the title of a work normally placed in quotation marks, keep the quotation marks and underline both titles: Critical Response to Henry James's "Beast in the Jungle." (Note that the underlining extends under the closing quotation mark.)

14. A work in more than one volume

Lincoln, Abraham. The Collected Works of Abraham Lincoln. Ed. Roy P. Basler. 8 vols. New Brunswick: Rutgers UP, 1953.

Lincoln, Abraham. The Collected Works of Abraham Lincoln. Ed. Roy P. Basler. Vol. 5. New Brunswick: Rutgers UP, 1953. 8 vols.

If you use two or more volumes of a multivolume work, give the work's total number of volumes before the publication information ("8 vols." in the first example). Your text citation will indicate which volume you are citing (see p. 713–14). If you use only one volume, give that volume number before the publication information ("Vol. 5" in the second example). You may add the total number of volumes to the end of the entry ("8 vols." in the second example).

If you cite a multivolume work published over a period of years, give the inclusive years as the publication date: for instance, Cambridge: Harvard UP, 1978-90.

15. A work in a series

Bergman, Ingmar. The Seventh Seal. Mod. Film Scripts Ser. 12. New York: Simon, 1968.

Place the name of the series (not quoted or underlined) just before the publication information. Abbreviate common words such as *modern* and *series.* Add any series number after the series title.

16. Published proceedings of a conference

Watching Our Language: A Conference Sponsored by the Program in Architecture and Design Criticism. 6-8 May 1999. New York: Parsons School of Design, 1999.

Whether in or after the title of the conference, supply information about who sponsored the conference, when it was held, and who published the proceedings. Treat a particular presentation at the conference like a selection from an anthology (model 18).

17. An anthology

Barnet, Sylvan, et al., eds. An Introduction to Literature. 11th ed. New York: Longman, 1997.

When citing an entire anthology, give the name of the editor or editors (followed by "ed." or "eds.") and then the title of the anthology. This anthology has four editors, so "et al." can replace all but the first editor's name. See model 3, page 722.

18. A selection from an anthology

Chekhov, Anton. "Misery." Trans. Constance Garnett. An Introduction to Literature. Ed. Sylvan Barnet et al. 11th ed. New York: Longman, 1997. 58-61.

The essentials of this listing are these: author of selection; title of selection (in quotation marks); title of anthology (underlined); editors' names preceded by "Ed." (meaning "Edited by"); publication information for the anthology; and inclusive page numbers for the selection (without the abbreviation "pp."). In addition, this source requires a translator for the selection and an edition number for the anthology. If you wish, you may also supply the original date of publication for the work you are citing, after its title. See model 12 on page 724.

If the work you cite comes from a collection of works by one author and with no editor, use the following form:

> Auden, W. H. "Family Ghosts." The Collected Poetry of W. H. Auden. New York: Random, 1945. 132-33.

If the work you cite is a scholarly article that was previously printed elsewhere, provide the complete information for the earlier publication of the piece, followed by "Rpt. in" ("Reprinted in") and the information for the source in which you found the piece:

> Reekmans, Tony. "Juvenal on Social Change." Ancient Society 2 (1971): 117-61. Rpt. in Private Life in Rome. Ed. Helen West. Los Angeles: Coronado, 1981. 124-69.

19. Two or more selections from the same anthology

> Auden, W. H. "The Unknown Citizen." Barnet et al. 687-88.
>
> Barnet, Sylvan, et al., eds. An Introduction to Literature. 11th ed. New York: Longman, 1997.
>
> Miller, Arthur. Death of a Salesman. Barnet et al. 1163-231.

When citing more than one selection from the same source, you may avoid repetition by giving the source in full (as in the Barnet et al. entry) and then simply cross-referencing it in entries for the works you used. Thus, instead of full information for the Auden and Miller works, give "Barnet et al." and the appropriate pages in that book. Note that each entry appears in its proper alphabetical place among other works cited.

20. An introduction, preface, foreword, or afterword

> Donaldson, Norman. Introduction. The Claverings. By Anthony Trollope. New York: Dover, 1977. vii-xv.

An introduction, foreword, or afterword is often written by someone other than the book's author. When citing such a piece, give its name without quotation marks or underlining. (But if the work has a title of its own, provide it, in quotation marks, between the name of the author and the name of the piece.) Follow the title of the book with its author's name preceded by "By." Give the inclusive page numbers of the part you cite. (In the preceding example, the small Roman numerals indicate that the cited work is in the front matter of the book, before page 1.)

When the author of a preface or introduction is the same as the author of the book, give only the last name after the title:

Gould, Stephen Jay. Prologue. <u>The Flamingo's Smile: Reflections in Natural History</u>. By Gould. New York: Norton, 1985. 13-20.

21. An article in a reference work

Mark, Herman F. "Polymers." <u>The New Encyclopaedia Britannica: Macropaedia</u>. 15th ed. 1991.

"Reckon." <u>Merriam-Webster's Collegiate Dictionary</u>. 10th ed. 1998.

List an article in a reference work by its title (second example) unless the article is signed (first example). For works with entries arranged alphabetically, you need not include volume or page numbers. For well-known works like those listed above, you may also omit the editors' names and all publication information except any edition number and the year of publication. For works that are not well known, give full publication information:

"Hungarians in America." <u>The Ethnic Almanac</u>. Ed. Stephanie Bernardo. New York: Doubleday, 1991. 109-11.

◆ 2 Listing periodicals: Journals, magazines, and newspapers

The basic format for an article from a periodical includes the following information:

(1) Lever, Janet. (2) "Sex Differences in the Games Children Play." (3) <u>Social Problems</u> (a) 23 (b) (1976) (c): 478-87 (d).

1. *Author.* Use the author's full name: last name first, followed by a comma, and then the first name and any middle name or initial. Omit any title or degree attached to the author's name on the source, such as Dr. or Ph.D. End the name with a period and one space.
2. *Title of the article.* Give the full title, including any subtitle. Place the title in quotation marks, capitalize all important words in the title (see p. 535), and end the title with a period (inside the final quotation mark) and one space.

MLA 46c

3. *Publication information.*
   a. The title of the periodical, underlined, followed by a space. Omit any *A, An,* or *The* from the beginning of the title.
   b. The volume and/or issue number (in Arabic numerals), followed by a space. See the note following.
   c. The date of publication, followed by a colon and a space. See the note following.
   d. The inclusive page numbers of the article (without the abbreviation "pp."). For the second number in inclusive page numbers over 100, provide only as many digits as needed for clarity (usually two): 87–88, 100–01, 398–401, 1026–36, 1190–206. If the article does not run on consecutive pages, provide only the first page number followed by a plus sign: 16+. (See also model 26, opposite.)

Note The treatment of volume and issue numbers and publication dates varies depending on the kind of periodical being cited, as the models indicate. For the distinction between journals and magazines, see pages 646–47.

22. An article in a journal with continuous pagination throughout the annual volume

Lever, Janet. "Sex Differences in the Games Children Play." Social Problems 23 (1976): 478-87.

Some journals number the pages of issues consecutively throughout a year, so that each issue after the first in a year begins numbering where the previous issue left off—say, at page 132 or 416. For this kind of journal, give the volume number after the title ("23" in the example above) and place the year of publication in parentheses. The page numbers will be enough to guide readers to the appropriate issue.

23. An article in a journal that pages issues separately or that numbers only issues, not volumes

Dacey, June. "Management Participation in Corporate Buy-Outs." Management Perspectives 7.4 (1998): 20-31.

Some journals page each issue separately (starting each issue at page 1). For these journals, give the volume number, a period, and the issue number (as in "7.4" in the Dacey entry above). Then readers know which issue of the periodical to consult. When citing an article in a journal that numbers only issues, not annual volumes, treat the issue number as if it were a volume number, as in model 22.

24. An article in a monthly or bimonthly magazine

Tilin, Andrew. "Selling the Dream." Worth Oct. 1999: 94-100.

Follow the magazine title with the month and the year of publication. (Abbreviate all months except May, June, and July.) Don't place the date in parentheses, and don't provide a volume or issue number.

25. An article in a weekly or biweekly magazine

Stevens, Mark. "Low and Behold." New Republic 24 Dec. 1990: 27-33.

Follow the magazine title with the day, the month (abbreviated), and the year of publication. (Abbreviate all months except May, June, and July.) Don't place the date in parentheses, and don't provide a volume or issue number.

26. An article in a daily newspaper

Lewis, Peter H. "Many Updates Cause Profitable Confusion." New York Times 21 Jan. 1999, natl. ed.: D1+.

Give the name of the newspaper as it appears on the first page (but without *A, An,* or *The*). If the name of the city is not in the title of a local newspaper, add the city name in brackets after the title, without underlining: Gazette [Chicago]. Then follow model 25, with two differences: (1) If the newspaper lists an edition at the top of the first page, include that information after the date and a comma. (See "natl. ed." above.) (2) If the newspaper is divided into lettered or numbered sections, provide the section designation before the page number when the newspaper does the same (as in "D1+" above); otherwise, provide the section designation before the colon—for instance, sec. 1: 1+. The plus sign here and with "D1+" in the preceding model indicates that the articles do not run on consecutive pages but start on page 1 or D1 and continue later.

27. An unsigned article

"The Right to Die." Time 11 Oct. 1976: 101.

Begin the entry for an unsigned article with the title of the article. In the list of works cited, alphabetize an anonymous source by the first main word of the title ("Right" in this model).

28. An editorial or letter to the editor

"Bodily Intrusions." Editorial. New York Times 29 Aug. 1990, late ed.: A20.

Add the word "Editorial" or "Letter"—but without quotation marks—after the title if there is one or after the author's name, as follows:

Dowding, Michael. Letter. Economist 5-11 Jan. 1985: 4.

(The numbers "5-11" in this entry are the publication days of the periodical: the issue spans January 5 through 11.)

29. A review

Dunne, John Gregory. "The Secret of Danny Santiago." Rev. of Famous All over Town, by Danny Santiago. New York Review of Books 16 Aug. 1984: 17-27.

"Rev." is an abbreviation for "Review." The name of the author of the work being reviewed follows the title of the work, a comma, and "by." If the review has no title of its own, then "Rev. of . . ." (without quotation marks) immediately follows the name of the reviewer.

30. An abstract of a dissertation or article

Steciw, Steven K. "Alterations to the Pessac Project of Le Corbusier." Diss. U of Cambridge, England, 1986. DAI 46 (1986): 565C.

For an abstract appearing in *Dissertation Abstracts* (*DA*) or *Dissertation Abstracts International* (*DAI*), give the author's name and the title, "Diss." (for "Dissertation"), the institution granting the author's degree, the date of the dissertation, and the publication information.

For an abstract of an article, first provide the publication information for the article itself, followed by the information for the abstract. If the abstract publisher lists abstracts by item rather than page number, add "item" before the number.

Lever, Janet "Sex Differences in the Games Children Play." Social Problems 23 (1976): 478-87. Psychological Abstracts 63 (1976): item 1431.

3 Listing electronic sources

Electronic sources include those available on CD-ROM and those available online, such as through the Internet. Like citations of print sources, citations of online sources require available information such as author, title, and date of publication (date of online posting or last revision for an online source). But online sources also require two special pieces of information:

- Give the date when you consulted the source as well as the date when the source was posted or updated online. The posting date comes first, with other publication information. Your access date falls near the end of the entry, just before the electronic address.
- Give the source's exact electronic address, enclosed in angle brackets (<>). Usually, you'll find the address in your Web browser's Location or Address field near the top of the screen

as you're viewing the source. (Be sure to give the complete address for the specific page you are using, not just for the site's home page.) Place the address at the end of the entry. If you must break an address from one line to the next, do so *only* after a slash, and do not hyphenate.

Try to locate all the information required in the following models, referring to pages 630–31 for help. However, if you search for and still cannot find some information, then give what you can find.

Note You can supplement or replace MLA style for online sources with Columbia online style (Chapter 53). However, there are differences between the two styles (described on pp. 882–83), so ask your instructor which one you should use.

31. A source on a periodical CD-ROM

A source also published in print:

Lewis, Peter H. "Many Updates Cause Profitable Confusion." New York Times 21 Jan. 1999, natl. ed.: D1+. New York Times Ondisc. CD-ROM. UMI-ProQuest. Mar. 1999.

If you cite a source on CD-ROM that's issued periodically (like a journal or magazine), look for information about a print version of the same source. (The information is usually at the beginning of the source.) If there is such information, provide it as in the model above (1), referring to pages 728–30 as needed. Then provide the following information on the CD-ROM version: the title of the CD-ROM (2), underlined; the medium, "CD-ROM" (3), without quotation marks or underlining; the name of the vendor (or distributor) of the CD-ROM (4); and the date of electronic publication (5).

A periodical CD-ROM without information for a print version:

"Vanguard Forecasts." Business Outlook. CD-ROM. Information Access. Mar. 1999.

If a periodical source appears only on CD-ROM (not also in print), give only the CD-ROM title, the medium, the vendor, and the date.

32. A source on a nonperiodical CD-ROM

Shelley, Mary Wollstonecraft. Frankenstein. Classic Library. CD-ROM. Alameda: Andromeda, 1993.

If you cite a single-issue CD-ROM, first provide its author (1) and title (2). Underline titles of books or similarly long works; use quotation marks for short works such as stories or parts of books. Then give the underlined title of the entire disk (3), if there is a title; give the medium (4), without quotation marks or underlining; and end with the disk's place of publication, publisher, and date of publication (5).

If the work you cite or the entire disk has a version or edition number, add it at the appropriate place, as shown in the model below:

> "Sugar." Concise Columbia Encyclopedia. 3rd ed. Microsoft Bookshelf. CD-ROM. 1998-99 ed. Redmond: Microsoft, 1998.

This model also shows citation of a part of a work (in quotation marks) with no author.

33. An online book

A book published independently:

> James, Henry. The Turn of the Screw. New York: Scribner's, 1908-09. 4 Mar. 1999 <http://www.americanliterature.com/TS/TSINDX.HTML>.

For an online book published independently, not as part of a scholarly project or other larger site, provide the author's name (1); the underlined title of the book (2); any publication information for the original print version of the book (3); the date you consulted the source (4); and the electronic address (5). If the book was not published in print before, substitute the date of electronic publication for the print publication information. If the book has an editor or translator, include that information as in the following model.

A book within a scholarly project:

> Austen, Jane. Emma. Ed. Ronald Blythe. Harmondsworth: Penguin, 1972. Oxford Text Archive. 1994. Oxford U. 15 Dec. 1997 <ftp://ota.ox.ac.uk/pub/ota/public/english/Austen/emma.1519>.

For a book published as part of a scholarly project, first list the author and title (1), the name of any editor or translator (2), and any print publication information provided in the source (3). Add the title of the project (4), underlined; the date of electronic publication (5); the name of any sponsoring organization or institution (6); the date of your access (7); and the electronic address (8), which should direct readers to the book rather than to the project as a whole. If the project has an editor, add the name after the project's title (see model 39 on p. 734).

34. An article in an online journal

Palfrey, Andrew. "Choice of Mates in Identical Twins." Modern Psychology 4.1 (1996): 12 pars. 25 Feb. 2000 <http://www.liasu.edu/modpsy/palfrey4(1).htm>.

Follow model 22 or 23 on page 728 for citing a scholarly article (1), but add the date you consulted the source (2) and the electronic address (3). If the journal provides page, paragraph, or other reference numbers, give the inclusive numbers (such as 20-31 for pages, as in model 23) or the total number (such as 12 pars. in the model above). Omit reference numbers if the source does not use them.

35. An online abstract

Palfrey, Andrew. "Choice of Mates in Identical Twins." Modern Psychology 4.1 (1996): 12 pars. Abstract. 25 Feb. 2000 <http://www.liasu.edu/modpsy/abstractpalfrey4(1).htm>.

Treat an online abstract like an online journal article (model 34 above), but add "Abstract" (without quotation marks or underlining) between the publication information and the date of your access.

36. An article in an online newspaper

Still, Lucia. "On the Battlefields of Business, Millions of Casualties." New York Times on the Web 3 Mar. 1999. 17 Aug. 1999 <http://www.nytimes.com/specials/downsize/03down1.html>.

For an online newspaper article, provide the author's name (1); the title of the article (2), in quotation marks; the title of the online newspaper (3), underlined; the date of publication (4); the date you consulted the source (5); and the electronic address for the article (6). Provide section, page, or paragraph numbers if the newspaper does, as in model 26 (p. 729).

37. An article in an online magazine

Palevitz, Barry A., and Ricki Lewis. "Death Raises Safety Issues for Primate Handlers." Scientist 2 Mar. 1998: 1+. 27 Mar. 1998 <http://www.the-scientist.library.upenn.edu/yr1998/mar/palevitz_pl_980302.html>.

Cite an article in an online magazine with the name(s) of the author(s) (1); the title of the article (2), in quotation marks; the title of the periodical (3), underlined; the date of publication (4); any page, paragraph, or other reference numbers (5); the date you consulted the source (6); and the electronic address (7).

38. An online review

Detwiler, Donald S., and Chu Shao-Kang. Rev. of Important Documents of the Republic of China, ed. Tan Quon Chin. Journal of Military History 56.4 (1992): 669-84. 16 Sept. 1997 <http://www.jstor.org/fcgi-bin/jstor/viewitem.fcg/08993718/96p0008x>.

Cite an online review following model 29 on page 730 and the appropriate model on the previous page for an online scholarly journal, newspaper, or magazine (1). Include the date you consulted the source (2) and the electronic address (3).

39. An online scholarly project or database

Scots Teaching and Research Network. Ed. John Corbett. 2 Feb. 1998. U of Glasgow. 5 Mar. 1999 <http://www.arts.gla.ac.uk/www/english/comet/starn/htm>.

When citing an entire project or database, provide the title (1), underlined; the name of any editor (2); the date of publication (3); the name of any organization or institution that sponsors the project or database (4); the date you consulted the source (5); and the electronic address (6). If the project or database has a version number, add it after the editor's name and before the date of publication—for instance, Vers. 3.2.

40. A short work from an online scholarly project or database

Barbour, John. "The Brus." Scots Teaching and Research Network. Ed. John Corbett. 2 Feb. 1998. U of Glasgow. 5 Mar. 1999 <http://www.arts.gla.ac.uk/www/english/comet/starn/poetry/brus/contents/htm>.

For a poem, an article, or another short work published as part of a scholarly project or database, start with the author's name (1) and the title of the short work (2), in quotation marks. Then follow the model above for the complete project (3), but give the specific electronic address for the short work (4).

41. A personal or professional online site

Lederman, Leon. Topics in Modern Physics--Lederman. 12 Dec. 1999 <http://www-ed.fnal.gov/samplers/hsphys/people/lederman.html>.

Cite a personal or professional site with the author's name (1); the title if any (2), underlined; the date you consulted the source (3); and the electronic address (4). If the source has no title, describe it with a label such as "Home page," without quotation marks or underlining. If it has a sponsoring organization or institution, add the name after the title.

42. A work from an online subscription service

Wilkins, Johanna M. "The Myths of the Only Child." Psychology Update 12 Dec. 1999: 16-20. ProQuest Health and Medical Complete. ProQuest Direct. Manhattan Community Coll. Lib., New York. 20 Dec. 1999 <http://www.umi.com/proquest/>.

Online subscription services include those your library subscribes to (such as ProQuest Direct or Lexis-Nexis) and those you subscribe to yourself (such as America Online). If the service you use gives a specific electronic address for your source, you can generally base your works-cited entry on models 33–41, selecting the one that matches your kind of source. However, if the service does not provide the source's specific address, then you need to follow the model above or the one below. The model above, for a library service, begins with author, title, and publication information as appropriate for a magazine article (1). It then adds the name of the database (2), underlined; the name of the service (3), not underlined; the name and location of the subscribing library (4); the date of access (5); and the electronic address of the service's home page (6). You can omit item 2 or 6 if you don't have the information.

Some subscription services ask users to search with keywords or through a directory (or path) of topics:

"China--Dragon Kings." The Encyclopedia Mythica. America Online. 6 Jan. 1999. Path: Research and Learn; Encyclopedia; More Encyclopedias; Encyclopedia Mythica.

This model includes the title of the source and the larger work (1), the name of the service (2), the date of access (3), and then "Path:" (without quotation marks or underlining) and the sequence of topics required to reach the source (4), with the topics separated by semicolons.

If you reached the source with a keyword rather than a path, give that information instead—for instance, Keyword: Mythica.

43. Electronic mail

Millon, Michele. "Re: Grief Therapy." E-mail to the author.
4 May 1997.

For e-mail, give the name of the writer (1); the title, if any, from the e-mail's subject heading (2), in quotation marks; a description of the transmission, including whom it was sent to (3); and the date of posting (4).

44. A posting to a discussion list

The original posting:

Tourville, Michael. "European Currency Reform." Online posting.
6 Jan. 1999. International Finance Discussion List.
12 Jan. 1999 <finance-dl@weg.isu.edu>.

For a list subscribed to via e-mail, give the author's name (1); the title, if any, from the e-mail's subject heading (2), in quotation marks; the words "Online posting" (3), without quotation marks or underlining; the date of the posting (4); the name of the list (5); the date you consulted the source (6); and the electronic address (7). (See pp. 659–61 for more on discussion lists.)

An archived posting:

Tourville, Michael. "European Currency Reform." Online posting.
6 Jan. 1999. International Finance Archive. 2 June 1999
<http://www.weg.isu.edu/finance-dl/46732>.

Whenever possible, cite an archived version of the posting (see p. 660). If the posting has an identifying number, insert it immediately after the list's name—for example, Art Finds Discussion List 22634.

45. A posting to a newsgroup or Web forum

A newsgroup:

Cramer, Sherry. "Recent Investment Practices in U.S. Business."

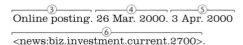

Online posting. 26 Mar. 2000. 3 Apr. 2000 <news:biz.investment.current.2700>.

A newsgroup is not subscriber-based (see p. 661). For a posting to a newsgroup, give the author's name (1); the title from the subject heading (2), in quotation marks; "Online posting" (3), without quotation marks or underlining; the date of posting (4); the date you consulted the source (5); and, in angle brackets, the group's name preceded by "news:" (6), as in the example.

A Web forum:

Franklin, Melanie. Online posting. 25 Jan. 1999. The Creative Process: An Artist's Diary. 27 Jan. 1999 <http://forums/nytimes/com/webin/WebX?14@^182943@eea7>

Give the author (1); the title, if any, in quotation marks (the example has no title); "Online posting" (2), without quotation marks or underlining; the date of posting (3); the name of the forum (4); the date of your access (5); and the address (6).

46. An online graphic, video, or audio file

Hamilton, Calvin J. "Components of Comets." Diagram. Space Art. 1997, 20 Dec. 1999 <wysisiwyg://94/http://spaceart.com/solar/eng/comet.htm>.

In general, you can base citations of online visual or audio sources on models 52–56 and 60 (pp. 739–40, 742), adding information appropriate for an online source. This example includes the creator's name (1); the title of the source (2); a description of the source (3), without quotation marks or underlining; the title of the larger work in which the source appears (4), underlined; the date of the source (5); the date of access (6); and the electronic address (7).

47. A synchronous communication (MUD, MOO, etc.)

Bruckman, Amy. MediaMOO Symposium: Virtual Worlds for Business? 20 Jan. 1998. MediaMOO. 26 Feb. 1998 <http://www.cc.gatech.edu/fac/Amy.Bruckman/MediaMOO/cscw-symposium-98.html>.

Cite a synchronous communication with the name of the speaker (1); a description of the event (2), without quotation marks or underlining; the date of the event (3); the forum (4); the date you consulted the source (5); and the electronic address (6). Whenever possible, cite an archived version of the communication (see model 44 on p. 736).

48. Computer software

(1) Project Scheduler 8000. (2) Vers. 4.1. (3) Orlando: Scitor, 1999.

For software, provide the title (1), underlined; the version number (2); and the publication information (3), including place of publication, publisher, and date. If you consulted or obtained the software online, replace this publication information with the date of your access and the electronic address, as in previous examples.

4 Listing other sources

49. A government publication

Hawaii. Dept. of Education. Kauai District Schools, Profile 1996-97. Honolulu: Hawaii Dept. of Education, 1998.

Stiller, Ann. Historic Preservation and Tax Incentives. US Dept. of Interior. Washington: GPO, 1996.

United States. Cong. House. Committee on Ways and Means. Medicare Payment for Outpatient Occupational Therapy Services. 102nd Cong., 1st sess. Washington: GPO, 1991.

If an author is not listed for a government publication, give the appropriate agency as author, as in the first and last examples. Provide information in the order illustrated, separating elements with a period and a space: the name of the government, the name of the agency (which may be abbreviated), and the title and publication information. For a congressional publication (last example), give the house and committee involved before the title, and give the number and session of Congress after the title. In the second and last examples, "GPO" stands for the US Government Printing Office.

50. A pamphlet

Medical Answers About AIDS. New York: Gay Men's Health Crisis, 1998.

Most pamphlets can be treated as books. In the example above, the pamphlet has no listed author, so the title comes first. If the pamphlet has an author, list his or her name first, followed by the title and publication information as given here.

51. An unpublished dissertation or thesis

Wilson, Stuart M. "John Stuart Mill as a Literary Critic." Diss. U of Michigan, 1970.

The title is quoted rather than underlined. "Diss." stands for "Dissertation." "U of Michigan" is the institution that granted the author's degree.

52. A musical composition or work of art

Fauré, Gabriel. Sonata for Violin and Piano no. 1 in A major, op. 15.

Don't underline musical compositions identified only by form, number, and key. Do underline titled operas, ballets, and compositions (Carmen, Sleeping Beauty).

For a work of art, underline the title and include the name and location of the owner. For a work you see only in a photograph, provide the complete publication information, too, as in the following model. Omit such information only if you examined the actual work.

Sargent, John Singer. Venetian Doorway. Metropolitan Museum of Art, New York. Sargent Watercolors. By Donelson F. Hoopes. New York: Watson, 1976. 31.

53. A film or video recording

Schindler's List. Dir. Steven Spielberg. Perf. Liam Neeson and Ben Kingsley. Universal, 1993.

Start with the title of the work you are citing, unless you are citing the contribution of a particular individual (see the next model). Give additional information (writer, lead performers, and so on) as you judge appropriate. For a film, end with the distributor and date.

For a videocassette, filmstrip, or slide program, include the original release date (if any) and the medium (without underlining or quotation marks) before the distributor's name:

George Balanchine, chor. Serenade. Perf. San Francisco Ballet. Dir. Hilary Bean. 1981. Videocassette. PBS Video, 1987.

54. A television or radio program

Kenyon, Jane, and Donald Hall. "A Life Together." Bill Moyers' Journal. PBS. WNET, New York. 17 Dec. 1998.

As in model 53, start with a title unless you are citing the work of a person or persons. The example above begins with the participants' names, then the episode title (in quotation marks), then the program title (underlined). Finish the entry with the name of the network, the local station and city, and the date.

55. A performance

The English Only Restaurant. By Silvio Martinez Palau. Dir. Susana Tubert. Puerto Rican Traveling Theater, New York. 27 July 1999.

Ozawa, Seiji, cond. Boston Symphony Orch. Symphony Hall, Boston. 25 Apr. 1997.

As with films and television programs, place the title first unless you are citing the work of an individual (second example). Provide additional information about participants after the title, as well as the theater, city, and date. Note that the orchestra name in the second example is neither quoted nor underlined.

56. A recording

Siberry, Jane. "Caravan." Maria. Reprise, 1995.

Brahms, Johannes. Concerto no. 2 in B-flat, op. 83. Perf. Artur Rubinstein. Cond. Eugene Ormandy. Philadelphia Orch. LP. RCA, 1972.

Begin with the name of the individual whose work you are citing. If you're citing a song, give the title in quotation marks. Then provide the title of the recording, underlining the title (first example) unless it identifies a composition by form, number, and key (second example). After the title, provide the names of any other artists it seems appropriate to mention, the manufacturer of the recording, and the date of release. If the medium is other than compact disk, provide it immediately before the manufacturer's name—for instance, LP (as in the second example) or Audiocassette.

57. A letter

Buttolph, Mrs. Laura E. Letter to Rev. and Mrs. C. C. Jones. 20 June 1857. In The Children of Pride: A True Story of Georgia and the Civil War. Ed. Robert Manson Myers. New Haven: Yale UP, 1972. 334-35.

A published letter is listed under the writer's name. Specify that the source is a letter and to whom it was addressed, and give the date on which it was written. Treat the remaining information like that for a selection from an anthology (model 18, p. 725). (See also p. 729 for the format of a letter to the editor of a periodical.)

For a letter in the collection of a library or archive, specify the writer, recipient, and date, as above, and give the name and location of the archive as well:

James, Jonathan E. Letter to his sister. 16 Apr. 1970. Jonathan E. James Papers. South Dakota State Archive, Pierre.

For a letter you receive, give the name of the writer, note the fact that the letter was sent to you, and provide the date of the letter:

Packer, Ann E. Letter to the author. 15 June 1999.

Use the form above for personal electronic mail (e-mail) as well, substituting "E-mail" for "Letter": E-mail to the author (see p. 736).

58. A lecture or address

Carlone, Dennis. "Architecture for the City of the Twenty-First Century." Tenth Symposium on Urban Issues. Cambridge City Hall, Cambridge. 22 May 2000.

Give the speaker's name, the title (in quotation marks), the title of the meeting, the name of the sponsoring organization, the location of the lecture, and the date. If you do not know the title, replace it with "Lecture" or another description, but *not* in quotation marks.

Although the *MLA Handbook* does not provide a specific style for classroom lectures in your courses, you can adapt the preceding format for this purpose:

Ezzy, T. G. Class lectures on the realist novel. Dawson College. 20 Jan. 1999-13 May 1999.

A parenthetical text citation to a particular lecture would require a date: (Ezzy, 12 Mar. 1999).

59. An interview

Graaf, Vera. Personal interview. 19 Dec. 1999.

Christopher, Warren. Interview. <u>Frontline</u>. PBS. WGBH, Boston. 13 Feb. 1998.

Begin with the name of the person interviewed. For an interview you conducted, specify "Personal interview" or the medium (such as "Telephone interview" or "E-mail interview")—without quotation marks or underlining—and then give the date. For an interview you read, heard, or saw, provide the title if any or "Interview" if not, along with other bibliographic information and the date.

60. A map or other illustration

Women in the Armed Forces. Map. Women in the World: An International Atlas. By Joni Seager and Ann Olson. New York: Touchstone, 1999. 44-45.

List the illustration by its title (underlined). Provide a descriptive label ("Map," "Chart," "Table"), without underlining or quotation marks, and the publication information. If the creator of the illustration is credited in the source, put his or her name first in the entry, as with any author.

EXERCISE
Writing works-cited entries

Prepare works-cited entries from the following information. Follow the models of the *MLA Handbook* given in this chapter unless your instructor specifies a different style.

1. An article titled "Credit and Consumer Confidence" by Jocelyn Kim. The article appears in volume 12, issue 4, of *Adaptation to Change,* a journal that pages issues separately. Volume 12 is dated 1998. The article runs from page 101 to page 106.
2. A book called *Black Voices: An Anthology of Afro-American Literature,* published in 1968 by the New American Library in New York, edited by Abraham Clapham.
3. An article you consulted on March 12, 2000, over the Internet. The article is titled "The Meaning of *The Funeral Elegy*" and is by Jane Downing, Bruce Newell, and Laura Suarez. It appears in the online journal *Shakespeare,* volume 4, issue 1, published in 1999. The article is thirty-seven paragraphs long. The address for the article is http://www.shakespeare-cambridge.org/downing.html.
4. An article in *Southern Folklore Quarterly,* volume 24, published in 1960. The article is "The New Orleans Voodoo Ritual Dance and Its Twentieth-Century Survivals," written by John Q. Anderson, on pages 135 through 143. The journal is paged continuously throughout the annual volume.
5. An article on CD-ROM that is also available in print. The author is Susan Chu. The title is "2000 Election Returns May Widen Gender Gap." The article appears in the March 2000 issue of *Politics and Values,* a magazine published monthly, on pages 12 through 26. It also appears on the CD-ROM titled *Resource/One,* released in May 2000 by UMI-ProQuest.

 46d Understanding abbreviations

Most disciplines' documentation styles, including that of the MLA, use as few abbreviations as possible. However, they still use some, and you may encounter many more in your reading. The most common abbreviations found in source citations appear below.

anon.	anonymous
bk., bks.	book(s)
c., ca.	*circa* ("about"), used with approximate dates
ch., chs.	chapter(s)
col., cols.	column(s)
comp., comps.	compiled by, compiler(s)
diss.	dissertation
ed., eds.	edited by, edition(s), editor(s)
et al.	*et alii* ("and others")
ibid.	*ibidem* ("in the same place")
illus.	illustrated by, illustrator, illustration(s)
l., ll.	line(s)
loc. cit.	*loco citato* ("in the place cited")
ms., mss.	manuscript(s)
n., nn.	note(s), as in p. 24, n. 2
n.d.	no date (of publication)
no., nos.	number(s)
n.p.	no place (of publication), no publisher
n. pag.	no pagination
op. cit.	*opere citato* ("in the work cited")
P	Press (UP = University Press)
p., pp.	page(s)
q.v.	*quod vide* ("which see")
rev.	revised, revision, revised by, review
rpt.	reprint, reprinted
sec.	section
supp., supps.	supplement(s)
trans.	translator, translated by
univ., U	university (UP = University Press)
vol., vols.	volume(s)

CHAPTER 47

Two Sample Research Papers

The following pages show the research papers of Edward Begay and Vanessa Haley, whose work we followed in Chapters 42–45. (Begay's paper begins on p. 746, Haley's on p. 779.) Both students followed the style of the *MLA Handbook* for documenting sources (Chapter 46) and formatting their papers (pp. 215–18). Accompanying both students' papers are comments on format, content, source citations, and other matters. The more extensive comments on Begay's paper are indexed below by *italic* page number and **boldface** comment number (in parentheses).

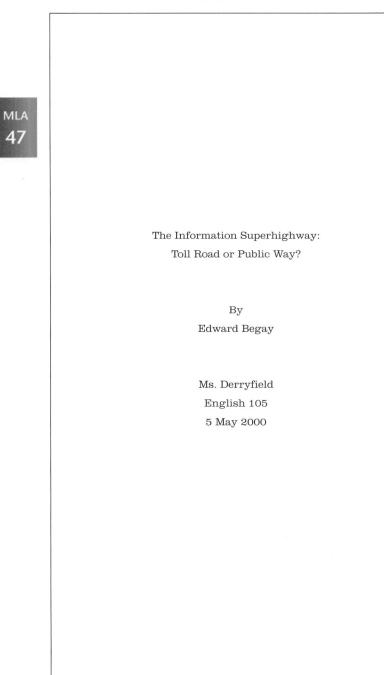

The Information Superhighway:
Toll Road or Public Way?

1

By
Edward Begay

Ms. Derryfield
English 105
5 May 2000

1. **Title page format.** A title page is not required by MLA style but may be required by your instructor. If so, or if you are required to submit an outline with your paper, prepare a title page as shown opposite: the title of the paper about a third of the way down the page; your name (preceded by "By") about an inch below the title; and, starting about an inch below your name, your instructor's name, the course number, and the date. Center all lines in the width of the page and separate them from each other with at least one line of space.

   If your instructor does not require a title page for your paper, follow MLA style: place your name, the identifying information, and the date on the first page of the paper. See Vanessa Haley's paper, page 779, for this format.

Next two pages

2. **Outline format.** If your instructor asks you to include your final outline, place it between the title page and the text, as Begay does on the following pages. Number the pages with small Roman numerals (i, ii), and place your last name just before the page numbers in case the pages of your paper become separated. Place the heading "Outline" an inch from the top of the first page, and double-space under the heading.
3. **Outline content.** Begay includes his final thesis statement as part of his outline so that his instructor can see how the parts relate to the whole. Notice that each main division (numbered with Roman numerals) relates to the thesis statement and that all the subdivisions relate to their main division.

   Begay casts his final outline in full sentences. Some instructors request topic outlines, in which ideas appear in phrases instead of in sentences and do not end with periods. (See p. 39 for this format.).

Begay i

Outline 2

Thesis statement: To make Internet access universal, public libraries and schools must obtain the necessary resources from government and business to go online. 3

I. The "digital divide" is wide: poor people have much less access to computer technology than middle-class and affluent people do.

II. Public libraries can provide Internet access to those who do not own computers, but they face several challenges.

- A. Those who have no access to computers at work or school take advantage of library computers for Internet access.
- B. Providing Internet access creates significant funding challenges for libraries.
- C. Commercialization of the Internet is a threat to libraries but may provide possibilities for funding.
    1. Businesses' spending on Internet infrastructure can benefit libraries.
    2. Businesses can subsidize library access to the Internet, as in the FCC's Universal Services Program.

III. Schools must investigate the role of the Internet in education as well as ways to fund school connections.

- A. Although some experts question the value of technology in the classroom, evidence suggests that computers enhance learning.
    1. Some critics say technology undermines education.

Begay ii

2. Some teachers say that technology fits in well with recent theories of education.
3. Students in schools across the country are using the Internet effectively.

B. Wealthy schools have far greater access to technology than poor ones.

1. Wealthier school systems can fund Internet connections.
2. Poorer systems lack funds for new technology.
3. In poorer systems, outdated computers and lack of Internet access lead to "drill and skill" use of computers.

IV. Libraries and schools must join with businesses and governments in seeking funds to go online and to train teachers and librarians to use technology.

A. Local, state, and federal agencies must step up existing efforts to help put classrooms online and to train teachers.

B. Businesses must also increase assistance to schools and libraries.

1. High-technology companies can provide materials and training.
2. Local businesses can form partnerships with schools.

Begay 1

The Information Superhighway: 4
Toll Road or Public Way?

The "information superhighway," referring to the 5
great communication potential of the Internet, has now
become a familiar term, even among those who are not
yet online. This mass of electronic connections has
grown dramatically in recent years,[1] accompanied by 6
constant predictions of how it will change our lives for
the better. But the superhighway has a serious problem
that receives less attention: its on-ramps--networked
computers and the knowledge to operate them--are not
accessible to everyone. Many observers see a real danger
that the Internet may widen the gap between rich and
poor in this country. According to an important study
by the US Department of Commerce, "The widening gap 7
between those with and without access to the Internet
threatens our democratic society" (xii; emphasis added). 8

The concern expressed by the Department of
Commerce study is fact-based: as discussed below, data
from that study and others do prove a "widening gap"
in access to the Internet. The question, then, is how we
can narrow or even close the gap to ensure that computer technology makes our society more equal rather
than more unequal. In answer, most analysts look to
public libraries and schools because these institutions
are open to all. However, to make Internet access uni- 9
versal, public libraries and schools must obtain the necessary resources from government and business to go
online.

Statistics vary,[2] but all research agrees that people 10
have much greater access to computer technology if they
are middle class or affluent. Recent and very comprehen-

4. **Title.** Begay's title plays on the image of the Internet as a highway to suggest his theme of accessibility. A more descriptive title, such as "Equality on the Internet," would also have been appropriate. **Paper format.** Because he provides a title page as requested by his instructor, Begay does not repeat his full name on the first page of text. For MLA style, which omits a title page, the following would appear in the upper left of this first page:

   Edward Begay

   Ms. Derryfield

   English 105

   5 May 2000

   (See pp. 215–18 for more on MLA format and p. 779 for an example of a research paper without a title page.)

   Even with a title page, Begay centers his title an inch below the top edge of the first page, using no quotation marks or underlining. He provides his last name and the page number on the top right of every page, one-half inch below the top of the paper. The margins of the paper are one inch all around, and everything is double-spaced.
5. **Introduction.** Begay picks up the image of the superhighway from his title to lead into the problem of access. He delays presenting his thesis in order to establish some background about the risks of unequal access. The question at the beginning of the next paragraph sets up the thesis statement at the end of the paragraph.
6. **Using an endnote for supplementary information.** Begay just mentions the growth of the Internet. For readers interested in more, he provides a source in a note at the end of the paper (p. 772). He signals the note with the raised numeral 1.
7. **Citation of a work with no named author.** The government study Begay cites does not list an author, so he gives as its author the name of the sponsoring body.
8. **Citation when the author is named in your text.** Because Begay names the US Department of Commerce in his text, he gives only the page number xii in the parenthetical citation. **Adding emphasis to quotations.** Begay underlines important words in the quotation. He acknowledges this change inside the parenthetical citation with the words "emphasis added," separated by a semicolon from the page number.
9. **Thesis statement.** Begay's introduction has led up to this sentence, which asserts the idea that he will demonstrate in the paper.
10. **Relation to outline.** This paragraph begins part I of Begay's outline (see p. 748). Part II begins on page 752, part III on page 756, and part IV on page 766. **Using an endnote for supplementary information.** Here Begay inserts a reference to a note at the end of the paper in which he explains the difficulty of interpreting statistics about computers in schools.

Begay 2

sive data appear in the Department of Commerce study, which paints the unsettling picture shown in Table 1.

Table 1 11

Computers and Internet Use by Household Income

Household Income	Percentage of Households with Computers	Percentage of Persons Using the Internet
\$5000-\$9999	12.3	12.1
\$15,000-\$19,999	21.2	16.6
\$35,000-\$49,999	50.2	34.7
More than \$75,000	79.9	58.9

Source: United States. Dept. of Commerce. National Telecommunications and Information Admin. Falling Through the Net: Defining the Digital Divide. July 1999. 1 Mar. 2000 <http://www.ntia.doc.gov/ntiahome/digitaldivide/> 17, 43.

Public libraries have long provided free access to information, and many see them as an essential component in broadening access to the Internet. According to the American Library Association, 12

> [. . .] [O]ur nation's libraries are uniquely positioned to serve as the public's means of access to the information superhighway--a place where all people can tap into new technology with the expert assistance of a librarian. (Equity 5) 13 14

11. **Use of a table.** Begay uses a table to present statistics from the Department of Commerce study so that the data are easy to compare and the differences are emphatic. **Table format.** Following MLA style, Begay double-spaces the entire table. **Citation of a source for a table.** Also following MLA style, Begay provides a source note indicating where he obtained the data in the table. The note includes complete information on the source even though Begay also cites the work fully in his list of works cited (see p. 776). The numbers following the electronic address at the end of the note are the pages where Begay found the table's data.
12. **Relation to outline.** This paragraph begins part II of Begay's outline. See page 748.
13. **Format of a long quotation.** This quotation exceeds four typed lines, so Begay sets it off from the text without quotation marks and with double spacing above and below. The quotation is double-spaced and is indented one inch from the left margin. **Editing a quotation with an ellipsis mark and brackets.** Begay uses an ellipsis mark to show that he has omitted the beginning of the quoted sentence (see p. 527), and he adds brackets around the capital *O* to show that the letter was not capitalized in the original (see p. 526). For the ellipsis mark, Begay follows MLA style by supplying brackets around the mark to indicate that it did not appear in the original. (Other disciplines do not use brackets in this way. See p. 529.)
14. **Citation with displayed quotation.** The parenthetical citation after the quotation falls *outside* the sentence period and is separated from the period by one space. **Citation of an unsigned source.** In the absence of an author's name, Begay uses the first main word of the title. (See p. 774 for the source's works-cited entry.)

Begay 3

Most public libraries do have some level of Internet access to serve their patrons: 73.3 percent, according to a recent report (Bertot and McClure 2). And the 15
access specifically benefits those who need it most. The Department of Commerce data show that nearly 30 percent of unemployed adults and 20 percent of those "not in the workforce" take advantage of a public library's computers to use the Internet, whereas fewer than 6 percent of employed adults do so (54).

However, providing Internet access creates signif- 16
icant funding challenges for libraries. For example, at this point almost 75 percent of public libraries have three or fewer computer terminals through which they can offer Internet access (Bertot and McClure 35). Clearly, with the length of time Internet searches can take (not to mention browsing the Internet), three terminals cannot serve many library patrons. Yet terminals are costly and require frequent upgrading.

Many librarians worry that not only cost but also the increasing commercialization of the Internet will prevent libraries from keeping up with the Internet revolution. Early users of the Internet were primarily public institutions, but the network is now dominated by commercial interests. As the Internet becomes more commercialized, market forces rather than public good have begun to dictate Internet services and their cost. For example, cable and telephone companies are merging to take advantage of the profits to be gained by offering various online services to private customers. This focus on profit may pose a threat to public users such as libraries and schools, altering the Internet environment (Bertot and McClure 7).

15. **Citation when the author is not named in your text.** Because Begay has not used Bertot's and McClure's names in the text, he provides them in the parenthetical citation along with the page number.
16. **Revision of a draft.** In his first draft Begay sometimes strung his source information together without interpreting it. In revising he added comments of his own to introduce the information in the context of his ideas:

> *¶However, providing Internet access creates significant funding challenges for libraries. For example,*
> The Department of Commerce data show that nearly 30 percent of unemployed adults and 20 percent of those "not in the workforce" take advantage of a public library's computers to use the Internet, whereas fewer than 6 percent of employed adults do so (54). ~~Yet~~ at this point almost 75 percent of public libraries have three or fewer computer terminals through which they can offer Internet access (Bertot and McClure 35). *Clearly, with the length of time Internet searches can take (not to mention browsing the Internet), three terminals cannot serve many library patrons. Yet terminals are costly and require frequent upgrading.*

Begay 4

Could the profit quest possibly help libraries as
well? Some observers believe it could, either through a 17
kind of trickle-down effect or through business subsidies
of libraries. The librarians Maurice Mitchell and Laverna
Saunders predict that businesses' spending on Internet research and development will ultimately benefit all Internet users, including libraries, especially if businesses can
be persuaded to wire libraries as a way to reach customers
(par. 12). Max Frankel, a New York Times columnist who 18
specializes in the communications media, argues for more
than persuasion: "Rich companies should be charged fees
for profitable private uses of the Internet [. . .] to subsidize
the Net's penetration of every community" (42).

In fact, the US Federal Communications Commis- 19
sion does assess telecommunication providers to fund
the Universal Service Program, which allocates about $2
billion annually to help both libraries and primary and
secondary schools purchase telecommunication services.
However, the fund is modest and does not cover training
of staff or purchases of hardware (computers, modems,
and the like). Libraries need much more help than that if
they are, in the words of Mitchell and Saunders, "to stay
on the [Internet] road and to establish a right-of-way for 20
those who depend upon public transportation" (par. 22).

Of course, the first "public transportation" Ameri- 21
cans take in education is through the public school system. And it is in the schools that the most significant
debates about access to the Internet take place. For the
Internet to be truly democratic, the public schools must
provide all students with access to it. But even more so
in the classroom than in libraries, the questions raised
by technology are complex.

17. **Selecting supporting evidence.** Begay uses two sources in this paragraph to develop his point about possible library benefits from business activity, mixing a paraphrase from professional librarians and a quotation from a newspaper columnist. The use of the authors' names to introduce the paraphrase and quotation clarifies who said what.
18. **Citation of a source using paragraph numbers.** Begay uses "par." ("paragraph") to indicate that the source numbers paragraphs rather than pages. He cites paragraph 12. (See p. 713 for more on this form of citation.)
19. **Omission of a parenthetical citation.** Begay does not provide a parenthetical citation for the Federal Communications Commission report because he names the source in his text and the source had no page or other reference numbers. (See p. 776 for the works-cited entry for this source.)
20. **Adding to a quotation with brackets.** In case readers would misunderstand what kind of road Mitchell and Saunders were discussing, Begay adds a clarifying word to the quotation and surrounds the word with brackets to indicate that it did not appear in the original. (See p. 526.)
21. **Relation to outline.** With this paragraph Begay begins part III of his outline (see p. 748). **Transitional paragraph.** Begay devotes a whole paragraph to his shift in direction, briefly reflecting the ideas in the introduction, summing up the preceding section, and introducing his next point.

Begay 5

Before considering how all students can have
equal access to the Internet, it is necessary to look at
the effect of technology on schools. A noted critic of
computer technology, Clifford Stoll, calls networking 22
"irrelevant to schooling" because "[o]nly a teacher, live
in the classroom, can bring about [. . .] inspiration. This
can't happen over a speaker, a television or a computer
screen" (96). Stoll argues that Internet projects "magnify the computing side, while making the learning
experience seem trivial" and insists that "only human
beings can teach the connection between things"
(108). In a New York Times article on technology 23
in the schools, Neil MacFarquhar reports from interviews
with a number of experts who share Stoll's doubts
about whether technology enhances learning at all.
In the naysayers' views, Internet education is "a cut-
and-paste style of learning," one in which students 24
"[parrot] trivial bites of information found on the computer screen" when they should be "developing the
critical judgment and analysis engendered by culling
through books" (B4).[3] 25

Many educators, however, see the introduction of
technology as a welcome boost to newer education theories. Some theorists argue that the old "transmission" 26
model of education, in which teachers transmit knowledge to passive students, will not prepare students to
live and work in the information age (Conte 923-24). In- 27
stead, these theorists favor a model closer to cognitive
psychology and constructivism, emphasizing active 28
learning and "dealing with complex, real-world problems"--a model well served by computer networking
(Conte 935-36).

22. **Integrating quotations.** Here and elsewhere, Begay establishes his source's credentials in a signal phrase and effectively integrates quotations into his own sentences. (See pp. 693–97.) **Omission of ellipsis marks.** Begay does not use ellipsis marks with the quotations beginning "irrelevant," "magnify," and "only human" because the partial sentences make it clear that he has omitted material from the original. (See p. 529.)
23. **Introducing and citing a discussion of one work.** By mentioning MacFarquhar's name at the beginning of these two sentences, Begay indicates that what follows is from MacFarquhar's work. The page number at the end of the paragraph announces that the citation covers all the intervening material. **Mixing summary, paraphrase, and quotation.** In this paragraph Begay summarizes, paraphrases, and quotes from MacFarquhar's article to give readers a good sense of the issue MacFarquhar raises.
24. **Punctuation with a quotation.** A comma falls inside a closing quotation mark, as here. **Altering a word form in a quotation.** To fit the next quotation into his own sentence, Begay uses brackets to change *parroting* in the original to *parrot*. (See p. 526.)
25. **Punctuation with a parenthetical citation.** The period ending a sentence containing a quotation comes after the citation.
26. **Introducing borrowed material.** Begay here begins paraphrasing and quoting Conte as an expert, so he should have named Conte in the text and identified him with his credentials. (See pp. 695–97.) **Paraphrasing.** Begay paraphrases a quotation by Conte. His note card follows:

> <u>Traditional vs. innovative models of education</u>
>
> Conte 923-24
>
> "[T]he traditional classroom, with its strong central authority and its emphasis on training students to take orders and perform narrow tasks, may have prepared students for work in 20th-century factories. But it can't impart the skills they need in the workplace of the 21st century, where there's a premium on workers who are flexible, creative, self-directed and able to solve problems collaboratively."

27. **Citation of a paraphrase.** Because he does not use Conte's name in the text, Begay correctly gives Conte's name in the citation.
28. **Defining terms.** Begay uses two terms here, *cognitive psychology* and *constructivism,* that he picked up from Conte and other sources. He should have defined the terms to avoid confusing readers.

MLA 47

Begay 6

In fact, many teachers see the Internet as the
most powerful resource in education. Mary E.
McArthur, a veteran teacher in Massachusetts, told me 29
in an online interview that the Internet presents new
possibilities for student learning:

> My students have a much better sense of the
> relevance of their education now that they're
> online. When we were studying ecology, for
> example, some students e-mailed a represen-
> tative of the EPA [Environmental Protection 30
> Agency] in Washington, asking questions
> and offering suggestions about a proposed
> local landfill, and received an immediate re-
> sponse. They took that response to the town's
> planning board when the landfill issue was
> discussed. 31

The Internet, according to McArthur, has made her students not only better learners but better citizens as well.
And contrary to Stoll's vision of dehumanized classrooms, McArthur told me that since her students began
using technology, "conversation is constant. Students
are talking online, to each other, and to me--question-
ing, criticizing, analyzing what they're learning."

McArthur's and her students' experiences are not 32
unique: success stories about education on the Internet
are common in popular and scholarly sources.[4] But
many teachers and students are not discovering what
they might accomplish with the Internet.

The statistics on public schools' access to the
Internet are actually more positive than those for
US households and individuals: according to the US 33
Department of Education, 63 percent of low-income

29. **Primary source: personal interview.** Begay tested his ideas by conducting an e-mail interview of a teacher in a public school. He uses both paraphrase and quotation from the interview, with the subject's permission.
30. **Adding words to quotations.** Begay spells out the full name of the EPA for readers who may not recognize the abbreviation, and he encloses his addition in brackets. (See p. 526.)
31. **Omission of parenthetical citation.** Begay does not use a parenthetical citation at the end of the quotation because the source (an interview) has no page or other reference numbers and the necessary information (McArthur's name) appears in the text before the quotation.
32. **Transitional paragraph.** This paragraph within the section on schools shifts the emphasis from the educational value of technology to its cost. **Summary of sources.** Rather than belabor the Internet success stories, Begay wraps up with a summary. **Using an endnote for citation of several sources.** Begay avoids a lengthy and obtrusive parenthetical citation by referring readers to endnote 4, which lists several sources (see p. 772).
33. **Synthesis of sources.** In this and the next paragraph, Begay integrates information from two sources, drawing his own conclusions about the significance of the data. **Citation of long source names in the text.** To avoid awkwardly long parenthetical citations in this paragraph, Begay gives the names of the government bodies in his text. **Omission of parenthetical citations.** Because the online sources cited in this paragraph have no page or other reference numbers and Begay gives the source names in his text, he does not supply parenthetical citations.

Begay 7

schools now have Internet access. But a distinct "digital divide" still exists, for the same source shows that 94 percent of high-income schools have Internet access. The US General Accounting Office reports that one reason for the discrepancy in low- and high-income schools is that "30 percent of schools in central cities and rural areas have insufficient phone lines, electrical wiring or electrical power to support communications technologies." Whatever the cause, low-income students are clearly less likely to have the hands-on Internet experience that will prepare them for the information age.

The Department of Education reveals another interesting difference between low- and high-income schools as well. The poorer schools dominate the 35 percent of Internet-connected schools that have only a single room devoted to Internet use. In richer schools, more than five such rooms are common. The Department of Education does not comment further, but this difference spells an important difference in the access each student has to the Internet. Even the student who attends a wired school may not be receiving much instruction in Internet use or much time actually working online.

Not only is Internet access unavailable or restricted in many low-income schools, but the computer equipment these schools have is often outdated. An example is Anderson Elementary School in a poor section
of San Jose, California (Poole). Anderson is equipped 34
with computers from the early 1990s that have little processing power and none of the graphical interfaces needed to take advantage of the Internet, especially the Web. With such limited equipment, students at Anderson and other poor schools often cannot match their

34. **Citation of one-page article.** Poole's article appears on only one page of the newspaper it is in, and Begay gives that page number in the list of works cited (see p. 776). Thus he does not need to repeat the page number in the parenthetical citation.

Begay 8

more affluent peers in communicating with experts or
with fellow students from other districts or countries.
Nor can they gain access to many of the resources,
such as up-to-date specialized encyclopedias, that are
available online. Rather than interacting with others 35
through their computers, these students tend to use
computers for "drill and skill" work in reading and
arithmetic: they "learn to do what the computer tells
them," according to Delia Neuman of the University of
Maryland (qtd. in Conte 931).

Students who do not have access to the Internet
may well find themselves left out of a society in which
computer skills will earn a worker 15 percent more
than another worker without such skills ("New Divide" 36
25). And society will suffer as well. According to
Richard W. Riley, secretary of education in the Clinton
administration,

> If the nation continues to ignore the educational needs of [. . .] low-income students [. . .] and continues to [. . .] link up their schools last, it will find itself in an economic bind of the first order. It will have a work force that does not know how to work. (51)

The problem for schools like Anderson Elemen- 37
tary is, of course, money. Leaders in poor school districts are aware of the importance of technology, but
they are also worried about leaking roofs, aging furniture, and overcrowded classrooms. The money to buy
the equipment, make the connections, and train teachers to use and maintain the networks is not easily
found even in middle-class school districts, much less
in poorer districts.

35. **Combining paraphrase and quotation.** Begay had a long quotation by Neuman, but he did not want to devote quite so much space to the side issue of drill-and-skill teaching. Thus he paraphrased Neuman's idea and quoted only the most striking language. The entire quotation appears on the following note card:

> Difference between rich & poor schools
>
> Conte 931
>
> From Delia Neuman, prof., U Maryland Coll. of Library & Information Services: "Economically disadvantaged students, who often use the computer for remediation and basic skills, learn to do what the computer tells them, while more affluent students, who use it to learn programming and tool application, learn to tell the computer what to do."

Citation of an indirect source. With the use of "qtd. in," Begay indicates correctly that he found the quotation by Neuman in the article by Conte. (Neuman is an indirect source; Conte is a direct source.) **Indirect sources.** Indirect sources (and "qtd. in") are appropriate only when the quoted material is not available to consult. But Begay's source, Conte, gave full bibliographic information on Neuman's original article and even an e-mail address for reaching Neuman. Instead of relying on the quotation in Conte, Begay should have gone directly to Neuman's article.

36. **Citation of an unsigned article.** Since Begay is citing an unsigned article, he uses a shortened form of the title for his citation. See the entry for this work in the list of works cited, page 776.
37. **Drawing conclusions.** Rather than leaving it to his readers to figure out the significance of the preceding paragraphs, Begay here wraps up his discussion of schools with his own conclusions about the costs of and thus the limits on technological change in education.

If libraries and schools are to provide widespread 38
access to the Internet, they must find ways not only to integrate technology into their programs but also to pay the bills associated with going online. Adapting the work of libraries and schools to the technological age is the responsibility of the experts within those systems. But finding the money to finance technological advances must involve more elements of society. It will be necessary for government and business to play an active role in wiring libraries and schools and in training professionals to work with the technology.

Governments are already encouraging coopera-
tion. Officials in federal, state, and local governments 39
increasingly urge companies to work with schools to achieve rapid educational access. Many states organize annual NetDay campaigns designed to bring educators, school boards, community volunteers, and corporations
together to wire schools (*LA NetDay*; MacFarquhar B1). 40

It is clear, however, that governments need to offer more than just encouragement. The Universal Services Program of the Federal Communications Commission is a start, but just a start. Divided among nearly 17,000 public libraries and 114,000 primary and secondary schools (*World Almanac* 224, 225), the pro- 41
gram's $2 billion comes to less than $15,000 per institution. Because the fund does not cover hardware or training, schools and libraries must still hustle for these essential (and expensive) components of Internet access. Richard Riley expresses the importance of training in calling for the federal government to "provide every teacher in the United States with the opportunity

38. **Relation to outline.** With this paragraph Begay begins part IV of his outline (see p. 749). **Summary statement.** To introduce this final section of his paper, Begay begins this paragraph with a statement that pulls together libraries and schools and clearly distinguishes the educational from the financial responsiblities for broadening Internet access.
39. **Common knowledge.** In his reading, Begay saw many references to government encouragement of cooperation. Thus he treats the information as common knowledge and does not cite a source for it. (See p. 689 for further discussion of common knowledge.)
40. **Parenthetical citation of more than one work.** Begay discovered information about NetDay campaigns in two sources, so he cites both in parentheses, separating the two with a semicolon.
41. **Use of an almanac.** Begay consulted an almanac for the number of public libraries and primary and secondary schools so that he could calculate the amount of aid each might receive from the Universal Services Program. **Positioning of parenthetical citation.** Because Begay used the almanac only for the number of libraries and schools, not for the calculation, he places the parenthetical citation directly after the almanac data.

to take advantage of first-class training in the latest and most up-to-date technologies available for the classroom" (52). Yet the Department of Education reports that half the teachers it surveyed had to acquire technology skills on their own time, with their own money. In schools and libraries, training staff, wiring, and purchasing equipment must be top priorities. Openly espousing technology is not enough of a role for governments: they must come through with the funds for these priorities if Internet access is to be truly democratic.

Business must also join in. Business has long recognized its responsibility to the larger community, for instance, by supporting youth athletics and contributing to charities through the Chamber of Commerce. Now business needs to help put the community online. Some businesses are already working with schools to increase Internet access. For a number of years IBM 42
and Apple have donated new and used computers to schools. And the 3COM Corporation of Santa Clara, California, regularly provides not only sizable grants to help local schools pay for computer technology but also full-time consultation to help educate teachers and students and "summer technology institutes" for students, teachers, and administrators (Jordahl and Orwig 25). 43

For computer companies, cooperation with schools seems good business, paying off in free advertising, enhanced image, and potential sales. But almost every business has a vested interest in widespread access to technology. As Richard Riley has noted, if today's students are not prepared for tomorrow's world, then businesses will suffer (51). That is one of the rea-

42. **Common knowledge.** Begay already knew of IBM's and Apple's well-publicized programs to place computers in schools; in fact, he had used a donated IBM PC in high school. Thus he treats this information as common knowledge.
43. **Parenthetical citation of a source with two authors**. Begay gives both authors' last names, separating them with "and" and no punctuation.

Begay 11

sons why some noncomputer companies are working to help students become familiar with technology. In Seattle, for example, three local banks assign employee mentors to public school students to help the students learn to use the Internet effectively for schoolwork (Jordahl and Orwig 24). And in South Carolina the Department of Education and the state Chamber of Commerce created school-business networks in which businesspeople help schools with technical knowledge and fund raising (MacFarquhar B1). Such cooperative programs between schools and businesses are essential if students are to be prepared for citizenship in a technological age.

Internet access is or soon will be “access to the 44
central nervous system of our democracy,” says Jeff Chester of the Center for Media Education (qtd. in “New Divide” 26). Providing this access through libraries and schools is perhaps the only way to ensure that both poor and rich have equal access to job opportunities and can participate equally in our democratic processes and institutions. But the schools and libraries cannot do the job alone. They need the strong support of business and government to help make the information superhighway a truly public way.

44. **Conclusion.** In his final paragraph Begay summarizes the main points of his paper to remind readers of both the need for universal Internet access and the ways it can be funded. By referring to the image of the information superhighway from his title and introduction, Begay comes full circle and leaves his readers with a vivid impression of his idea.

Begay 12

Notes 45

[1] For more information on the history of the Inter- 46
net, see Hardy.

[2] The US Department of Commerce study cited here is the most recent and most comprehensive available. Beyond this study, statistics on Internet use are difficult to compare and summarize because they often measure different variables. For example, one study may provide the number of households with Internet access, while another may provide the number of persons or the number of adults. In addition, with a subject this current the data are constantly changing. Nonetheless, all studies agree on the inequities between the affluent and the poor.

[3] For additional criticism of computers in educa- 47
tion, see Goodson et al.

[4] See, for example, MacFarquhar, Conte, and Jordahl and Orwig.

45. **Format of notes.** The word "Notes" is centered one inch from the top of the page. (The heading would be singular—"Note"—if Begay had only one note.) The notes begin two lines (one double space) below the heading. The notes themselves are double-spaced. The first line of each is indented one-half inch and is preceded by a raised number corresponding to the number used in the text. A space separates the number and the note.
46. **Endnotes for additional relevant information.** Begay uses endnotes for sources and information that are somewhat relevant to his thesis but not essential and that don't fit easily into the text. Note 1 refers interested readers to an online article on the history of the Internet. Note 2 provides information on Begay's difficulties interpreting statistics. Note 3 highlights a notable critique of computers in education. And note 4 cites several sources that would be obtrusive in a parenthetical citation. (See p. 718 for more on supplementary notes.)
47. **Citation of a source with more than three authors.** The Goodson citation indicates with "et al." ("and others") that Goodson was a coauthor with at least three others. See the works-cited entry for this source on the next page.

Begay 13

Works Cited 48

Bertot, John Carlo, and Charles R. McClure. The National Survey of U.S. Public Library Outlet Internet Connectivity: Final Report. American Library Association and US National Commission on Libraries and Information Science. Feb. 1999. 15 Mar. 2000 <http://www.ala.org/oitp/survey99.html>.

Conte, Christopher. "Networking the Classroom." CQ 49
Researcher 5 (1999): 923-43.

Equity on the Information Superhighway: Problems 50
and Possibilities. Chicago: ALA, 1996.

Frankel, Max. "The Moon, This Time Around." New 51
York Times Magazine 5 May 1996: 40+. New York Times Ondisc. CD-ROM. UMI-ProQuest. Nov. 1996.

Goodson, Ivor F., et al. "Computer Literacy as Ideology." 52
British Journal of Sociology of Education 17 (1996): 65-80.

Hardy, Henry Edward. "A Short History of the Net." 53
Ocean Home Page. 12 Mar. 2000 <http://www.ocean.ic.net/doc/snethist.html>.

Jordahl, Gregory, and Ann Orwig. "Getting Equipped 54
and Staying Equipped, Part 6: Finding the Funds." Technology & Learning Apr. 1999: 20-26.

LA NetDay99. State of Louisiana. May 1999. 6 Mar. 2000 <http://www.neill.net/netday/issues.html>.

MacFarquhar, Neil. "The Internet Goes to School." 55
New York Times 7 Mar. 1996, late ed.: B1+. New York Times Ondisc. CD-ROM. UMI-ProQuest. Oct. 1996.

48. **Format of list of works cited.** The heading "Works Cited" is centered one inch from the top of the page. The first entry is typed two lines (one double space) below the heading, and the entire list is double-spaced. The first line of each entry begins at the left margin; subsequent lines of the same entry are indented one-half inch. The entries are alphabetized by the last name of the first author or (for sources without authors) by the first main word of the title.
49. Entry for an **article in a journal with continuous pagination throughout an annual volume** (see p. 728).
50. Entry for a **pamphlet** (see p. 938). This entry also cites an **unsigned source** and so is listed and alphabetized by its title (see p. 723).
51. Entry for an **weekly magazine** (see p. 729) and a **source on CD-ROM that also appears in print** (see p. 731). The first date is the publication date of the article; the second is the publication date of the CD-ROM. This entry also illustrates an **article in which pagination is not consecutive.** The "+" indicates that the article does not continue on page 41 but farther back in the issue.
52. Entry for an **article with more than three authors.** A source with more than three authors may be listed with all authors' names or just with the first author's name followed by "et al." ("and others"). (See p. 722.) Begay had all the names in his working bibliography (see below), but he opted not to use them. His text reference is consistent with this decision (see p. 772).

> Goodson, Ivor F., James Mangan, Christina Marshall, and Renee Van Horn. "Computer Literacy as Ideology." British Journal of Sociology of Education 17 (1996): 65-80.

53. Entry for a **personal online site** (see p. 735). In this case, Begay used a part of the site, so he provides the title of the part in quotation marks as well as the title of the site with underlining. For all his online sources, Begay provides the electronic address between angle brackets, as suggested in MLA style.
54. Entry for an **article in a monthly magazine** (see p. 728) and for a **source with two authors** (see p. 722).
55. Entry for an **article in a daily newspaper on CD-ROM.**

MLA 47

Begay 14

McArthur, Mary E. E-mail interview. 20 Mar. 1997. 56

Mitchell, Maurice, and Laverna Saunders. "The National Information Infrastructure: Implications for Libraries." Computers in Libraries 13.10 (Dec. 1993): 22 pars. 21 Mar. 2000 <ftp://netlib.nevada.edu/pub/lib/3246>. 57 58

"A New Divide Between Haves and Have-Nots?" Time Special Issue: Welcome to Cyberspace Spring 1995: 25-26.

Poole, Gary Andrew. "The Widening Digital Divide." New York Times 13 Dec. 1999, late ed.: D3. New York Times Ondisc. CD-ROM. UMI-ProQuest. Feb. 2000.

Riley, Richard W. "Connecting Classrooms, Computers, and Communities." Issues in Science and Technology 12 (1996): 49-52.

Stoll, Clifford. Silicon Snake Oil: Second Thoughts on the Information Highway. New York: Doubleday, 1995. 59

United States. Dept. of Commerce. National Telecommunications and Information Admin. Falling Through the Net: Defining the Digital Divide. July 1999. 1 Mar. 2000 <http://www.ntia.doc.gov/ntiahome/digitaldivide/>. 60

---. Dept. of Education. National Center for Education Statistics. Internet Access in Public Schools. 6 Oct. 1999. 12 Mar. 2000 <http://www.ed.gov/pubs99/98031.html>. 61

---. Federal Communications Comm. Universal Service Program. 28 Sept. 1998. 6 Mar. 2000 <http://www.fcc.gov/Bureaus/Common_Carrier/Public_Notices/1998/da971374.html>.

56. Entry for a **personal interview by e-mail** (see p. 741).
57. Entry for an **article in an online journal.** Online and print journals have similar citation formats (see p. 733). Like many online journals, this one numbers paragraphs rather than pages, so Begay provides the total number of paragraphs where he would otherwise give the inclusive pages ("pars." is short for "paragraphs").
58. Entry for an **unsigned article in a periodical.** This source is listed by its title and alphabetized by the title's first main word. Entry for a **special issue of a periodical.** Begay had to improvise for this special issue of *Time* magazine because the MLA does not specify a format for such a source. In this case, Begay follows the cover of the magazine, where *Special Issue* was treated as part of the magazine's title and *Welcome to Cyberspace* was treated as a subtitle. He works this title into the MLA format for an unsigned magazine article.
59. Entry for a **book with one author** (see p. 722).
60. Entries for **online government publications.** This and the next three entries all cite government publications that Begay found online. Since none of the sources had a named author, Begay lists as author the government body responsible for the source: the government (United States), the department or agency, and (in the first two sources) the group within the department or agency. In each entry, the date of the source comes first, followed by the date Begay consulted the source. Each citation ends with the source's electronic address in angle brackets.
61. Entries for **additional sources by the same author.** Since the previous entry also lists the United States as author, Begay replaces those words in this and the next two entries with three hyphens (see p. 722). He does not replace author information that is unique to each source.

Begay 15

---. General Accounting Off. "Technology in Public Schools." Technology Data. 18 Dec. 1999. 22 Mar. 2000 <http://www.gao.gov/technology/html>.

The World Almanac and Book of Facts 2000. Mahwah: World Almanac, 1999.

Haley 1

Vanessa Haley

Professor Moisan

English 101

24 March 2000

Format of heading and title when no title page is required (see also p. 216)

Annie Dillard's Healing Vision

It is almost a commonplace these days that human arrogance is destroying the environment. Environmentalists, naturalists, and now the man or woman on the street seem to agree: the long-held belief that human beings are separate from nature, destined to rise above its laws and conquer it, has been ruinous.

Introduction of environmental theme

Unfortunately, the defenders of nature tend to respond to this ruinous belief with harmful myths of their own: nature is pure and harmonious; humanity is corrupt and dangerous. Much writing about nature lacks a recognition that human beings and their civilization are as much a part of nature as trees and whales are, neither better nor worse. Yet without such a recognition, how can humans overcome the damaging sense of separation between themselves and the earth? How can humans develop realistic solutions to environmental problems that will work for humanity _and_ the rest of nature?

Focus on issue to be resolved

One nature writer who seems to recognize the naturalness of humanity is Annie Dillard. In her best-known work, the Pulitzer Prize-winning _Pilgrim at Tinker Creek_, she is a solitary person encountering the natural world, and some critics fault her for turning her back on society. But in those encounters with nature, Dillard probes a spiritual as well as a physical identity between human beings and nature that could help to heal the rift between them.

Introduction of Dillard to resolve issue

Thesis statement

Haley 2

Dillard is not renowned for her sense of involvement with human society. Like Henry David Thoreau, with whom she is often compared, she retreats from rather than confronts human society. The critic Gary McIlroy points out that although Thoreau discusses society a great deal in Walden, he makes no attempt "to find a middle ground between it and his experiment in the woods" (113). Dillard has been similarly criticized. For instance, the writer Eudora Welty comments that

Acknowledgment of opposing critical view

> Annie Dillard is the only person in her book, substantially the only one in her world; I recall no outside human speech coming to break the long soliloquy of the author. Speaking of the universe very often, she is yet self-surrounded and, beyond that, book-surrounded. Her own book might have taken in more of human life without losing a bit of the wonder she was after. (37)

It is true, as Welty says, that in Pilgrim Dillard seems detached from human society. However, she actually was always close to it at Tinker Creek. In a later book, Teaching a Stone to Talk, she says of the neighborhood, "This is, mind you, suburbia. It is a five-minute walk in three directions to rows of houses [. . .]. There's a 55 mph highway at one end of the pond, and a nesting pair of wood ducks at the other" (qtd. in McIlroy 111).

First response to opposing view

Rather than hiding from humanity, Dillard seems to be trying to understand it through nature. In Pilgrim she reports buying a goldfish, which she names Ellery Channing. She recalls once seeing through a microscope "red blood cells whip, one by one, through the capillaries" of yet another goldfish (124). Now watching

Second response to opposing view

Haley 3

Ellery Channing, she sees the blood in his body as a bond between fish and human being: "Those red blood cells are coursing in Ellery's tail now, too, in just that way, and through his mouth and eyes as well, and through mine" (125). Gary McIlroy observes that this blood, "a symbol of the sanctity of life, is a common bond between Dillard and the fish, between animal and human life in general, and between Dillard and other people" (115).

Secondary source's analysis of Dillard

For Dillard, the terror and unpredictability of death unify all life. The most sinister image in Pilgrim--one that haunts Dillard--is that of the frog and the water bug. Dillard reports walking along an embankment scaring frogs into the water when one frog refused to budge. As Dillard leaned over to investigate, the frog "slowly crumpled and began to sag. The spirit vanished from his eyes as if snuffed. His skin emptied and dropped; his very skull seemed to collapse and settle like a kicked tent" (6). The frog was the victim of a water bug that injects poisons to "dissolve the victim's muscles and bones and organs" (6). Such events lead Dillard to wonder about a creator who would make all life "power and beauty, grace tangled in a rapture with violence" (8). Human beings no less than frogs and water bugs are implicated in this tangle.

Combination of quotation and Haley's own analysis (next four paragraphs): interprets and synthesizes Dillard's ideas

Mixture of summary and quotation: provides context and keeps quotations trim

Dillard is equally as disturbed by birth as by death. In a chapter of Pilgrim called "Fecundity," she focuses on the undeniable reproductive urge of entire species. Her attitude is far from sentimental:

Discussion of physical identity of all creatures: death and birth

Comment on quotation: advises reader what to look for

> I don't know what it is about fecundity that so appalls. I suppose it is the teeming evidence that birth and growth, which we value,

MLA 47

Haley 4

> are ubiquitous and blind, that life itself is so astonishingly cheap, that nature is as careless as it is bountiful, and that with extravagance goes a crushing waste that will one day include our own cheap lives. (160)

Long quotations, set off from the text: convey Dillard's voice as well as her ideas

The cheapness and brutality of life are problems Dillard wrestles with, wondering which is "amiss": the world, a "monster," or human beings, with their "excessive emotions" (177-78). No matter how hard she tries to leave human society, Dillard has no choice but to "bring human values to the creek" (179). The violent, seemingly pointless birth and death of all life are, spiritually,

Discussion of spiritual identity of all creatures

> two branches of the same creek, the creek that waters the world [. . .]. We could have planned things more mercifully, perhaps, but our plan would never get off the drawing board until we agreed to the very compromising terms that are the only ones that being offers. (180)

For Dillard, accepting the monstrousness as well as the beauty of "being" is the price all living things pay for freedom.

Haley's interpretation of Dillard's ideas

In "The Waters of Separation," the final chapter of <u>Pilgrim</u>, Dillard writes about a winged maple key, or seed. At this point in the book, the critic Sandra Humble Johnson notes, Dillard "has been humbled and emptied; she can no longer apply effort to her search for meaning in a parasitic world" (4). It is the winter solstice--the shortest day of the year. And then Dillard spies the maple key descending to earth and germination. "It rose, just before it would have touched a thistle, and

Resolution of Dillard's concerns

hovered pirouetting in one spot, then twirled on and finally came to rest" (267). The key moved, says Dillard, "like a creature muscled and vigorous, or a creature spread thin to that other wind, the wind of the spirit [. . .] a generous, unending breath" (268). Dillard vows to see the maple key in all of the earth and in herself. "If I am a maple key falling, at least I can twirl" (268).

Conclusion: ties together divergent critical views, environmental theme, and Dillard's work

According to the critic John Becker, "Annie Dillard does not walk out on ordinary life in order to bear witness against it"; instead, she uses the distance from other people "to make meaning out of the grotesque disjointedness of man and nature" (408). Gary McIlroy says, nonetheless, that Dillard "does not succeed in encompassing within her vision any but the most fragmentary consequences for society at large" (116). Possibly both are correct. In Pilgrim at Tinker Creek, Annie Dillard suggests a vision of identity among all living things that could inform modern humanity's efforts to thrive in harmony with its environment, but she does not make the leap to practicalities. Life, she says, "is a faint tracing on the surface of a mystery [. . .]. We must somehow take a wider view, look at the whole landscape, really see it, and describe what's going on here" (9). The description, and acting on it, may take generations. As we proceed, however, we may be guided by Dillard's efforts to mend the disjointedness, to see that human beings and maple keys alike twirl equally.

MLA 47

Haley 6

Works Cited

Becker, John E. "Science and the Sacred: From Walden to Tinker Creek." Thought: A Review of Culture and Idea 62 (1987): 400-13.

Dillard, Annie. Pilgrim at Tinker Creek. New York: Harper, 1974.

Johnson, Sandra Humble. The Space Between: Literary Epiphany in the Work of Annie Dillard. Kent: Kent State UP, 1992.

McIlroy, Gary. "Pilgrim at Tinker Creek and the Social Legacy of Walden." South Atlantic Quarterly 85.2 (1986): 111-16.

Welty, Eudora. Rev. of Pilgrim at Tinker Creek, by Annie Dillard. New York Times Book Review 24 Mar. 1974: 36-37.

PART XI

Writing in the Academic Disciplines

CHAPTER 48

Working with the Disciplines' Goals and Requirements

Writing in the academic disciplines you study in college does much more than simply demonstrate your competence. Writing is actually a way you learn concepts, focus ideas, analyze data, uncover assumptions, interpret patterns, and ask and answer questions.

Academic disciplines both resemble each other and differ in their methods and evidence, assignments, tools and language, and style for source citations and document format. This chapter introduces the goals and requirements common to any academic writing. Then the following chapters enlarge this information for various academic disciplines: literature (49), other humanities (50), the social sciences (51), and the natural and applied sciences (52). The chapters add three documentation styles to MLA style (p. 710): Chicago, APA, and CBE. A fifth style that can supplement any of the others—Columbia style for online sources—appears in Chapter 53.

Note The chapters in this part build on earlier material: Chapters 1–3 on the writing process, Chapters 5–7 on critical thinking and argument, and Chapters 42–45 on research writing.

Guidelines for academic writers

- For the discipline you are writing in, become familiar with the methodology and the kinds of evidence considered appropriate and valid.
- Analyze the special demands of the assignment—the kind of research and sources you need. The questions you set out to answer, the assertions you wish to support, will govern how you choose your sources and evidence.
- Become familiar with the specialized tools and language of the discipline.
- Use the style for source citations and document format customarily used by writers in the discipline.

http://www.cstw.ohio-state.edu/resource/academicdisciplines.htm
Links to advice about writing in the academic disciplines, from Ohio State University.

48a Using the disciplines' methods and evidence

The **methodology** of a discipline is the way its practitioners study their subjects—that is, how they proceed when investigating the answers to questions. Methodology relates to the way practitioners analyze evidence and ideas (see pp. 129–31). For instance, a literary critic and a social historian would probably approach Shakespeare's *Hamlet* quite differently: the literary critic might study the play for a theme among its poetic images; the historian might examine the play's relation to Shakespeare's context, England at the turn of the seventeenth century.

Whatever their approach, academic writers do not compose entirely out of their personal experience. Rather, they combine the evidence of their experience with that appropriate to the discipline, drawing well-supported conclusions about their subjects. The evidence of the discipline comes from research like that described in Chapters 42–44—from primary or secondary sources.

Primary sources are firsthand or original accounts, such as historical documents, works of art, and reports on experiments that the writer has conducted. When you use primary sources, you conduct original research, generating your own evidence. You might analyze a painting and then use examples as evidence for your interpretation of the painting. Or you might conduct a survey of fellow students and then use data from the survey to support your conclusions about students' attitudes.

Many primary sources can be found in the library. But more prevalent among a library's holdings are **secondary sources,** books and articles written *about* primary sources. Much academic writing requires that you use such sources to spark, extend, or support your own ideas, as when you review the published opinions on your subject before contributing conclusions from your original research.

48b Understanding the disciplines' writing assignments

For most academic writing, your primary purpose will be either to explain something to your readers or to persuade them to accept your conclusions. To achieve your purpose, you will adapt your writing process to the writing situation, particularly to the kinds of evidence required by the assignment and to the kinds of thinking you are expected to do. Most assignments will contain key words that tell you what these expectations are—words such as *compare, define, analyze,* and *illustrate* that express customary ways of thinking about and organizing a vast range of subjects. Pages 95–104 and

896 explore these so-called patterns of development. You should be aware of them and alert to the wording in assignments that directs you to use them.

48c Using the disciplines' tools and language

When you write in an academic discipline, you use the scholarly tools of that discipline, including specialized references such as periodical indexes, abstracts, and computerized databases. (See the Web sites given at the bottom of this page and the lists on pp. 801, 821, 843, and 867.) In addition, you may use the aids developed by practitioners of the discipline for efficiently and effectively approaching research, conducting it, and recording the findings. Many of these aids, such as a system for recording evidence from sources, are discussed in Chapters 42–44 and can be adapted to any discipline. Other aids are discussed in the following chapters.

Pay close attention to the texts assigned in a course and any materials given out in class, for these items may introduce you to valuable references and other research aids, and they will use the specialized language of the discipline. This specialized language allows practitioners to write to each other both efficiently and precisely. It also furthers certain concerns of the discipline, such as accuracy and objectivity. Scientists, for example, try to interpret their data objectively, so they avoid *undoubtedly, obviously,* and other words that slant conclusions. Some of the language conventions like this one are discussed in the following chapters. As you gain experience in a particular discipline, keep alert for such conventions and train yourself to follow them.

48d Following the disciplines' styles for source citations and document format

Most disciplines publish journals that require authors to use a certain style for source citations and a certain format for documents. In turn, most instructors in a discipline require the same of students writing papers for their courses.

Resources for writing in the academic disciplines:

http://www.clearinghouse.net From the Argus Clearinghouse.

http://lii.org From the Librarians' Index to the Internet.

http://www.ipl.org/ref From the Internet Public Library.

When you cite your sources, you tell readers which ideas and information you borrowed and where they can find your sources. Thus source citations indicate how much knowledge you have and how broad and deep your research was. They also help you avoid **plagiarism,** the serious offense of presenting the words, ideas, and data of others as if they were your own. (See pp. 686–92 on avoiding plagiarism.)

Document format includes such features as margins and the placement of the title. But it also extends to special elements of the manuscript, such as tables or an abstract, that may be required by the discipline.

Chapters 50–52 direct you to the style guides published by different disciplines and outline the requirements of the ones used most often. If your instructor does not require a particular style, use that of the Modern Language Association, which is described and illustrated at length on pages 710–42 (source citations) and pages 215–18 (document format).

CHAPTER 49 *By Sylvan Barnet*

Reading and Writing About Literature

Why read literature? Let's approach this question indirectly by asking why people *write* literature. A thousand years ago a Japanese writer, Lady Murasaki, offered an answer. Here is one of her characters talking about what motivates a writer:

> Again and again something in one's own life or in the life around one will seem so important that one cannot bear to let it pass into oblivion. There must never come a time, the writer feels, when people do not know about this.

When we read certain works—Murasaki's *The Tale of Genji* is one of them—we share this feeling; we are caught up in the writer's world, whether it is the Denmark of Shakespeare's *Hamlet* or the America of Toni Morrison's *Beloved.* In short, we read literature because it gives us an experience that seems important to us, usually an experience that is both new and familiar. A common way of putting this is to say that reading broadens us and helps us understand our own experience.

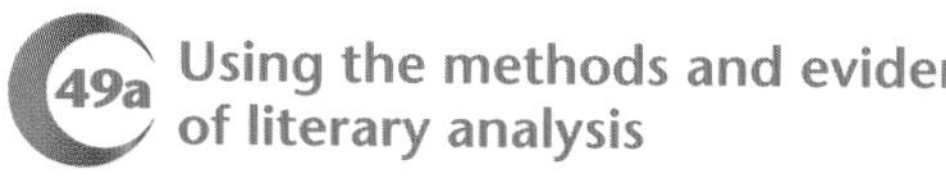

49a Using the methods and evidence of literary analysis

When we read nonliterary writings, it may be enough to get the gist of the argument; in fact, we may have to peer through a good deal of wordiness to find the heart of the matter—say, three claims on behalf of capital punishment. But when we read a story, a poem, or a play, we must pay extremely close attention to what might be called the feel of the words. For instance, the word *woods* in Robert Frost's "Stopping by Woods on a Snowy Evening" has a rural, folksy quality that *forest* doesn't have, and many such small distinctions contribute to the poem's effect.

http://www-english.tamu.edu/wcenter/lit.html Advice on reading and writing about literature, from Texas A&M University.

Literary authors are concerned with presenting human experience concretely, with *showing* rather than *telling*. Consider the following proverb and an unmemorable paraphrase of it:

> A rolling stone gathers no moss.
>
> If a rock is always moving around, vegetation won't have a chance to grow on it.

The familiar original offers a small but complete world: hard (stone) and soft (moss), inorganic and organic, at rest and in motion. The original is also shapely: each noun (*stone, moss*) has one syllable, and each word of motion (*rolling, gathers*) has two syllables, with the accent on the first of the two. Such relationships unify the proverb into a pleasing whole that stays in our minds.

1 Reading a work of literature

Reading literature critically involves interacting with a text. The techniques complement those for critically reading any text, so if you haven't read Chapter 5 on such reading, you should do so. Responding critically is a matter not of making negative judgments but of analyzing the parts, interpreting their meanings, seeing how the parts relate, and evaluating significance or quality.

You can preview a literary text somewhat as you can preview any other text (p. 122). You may gauge the length of the text to determine whether you can read it in one sitting, and you may read a biographical note to learn about the author. In a literary text, however, you won't find aids such as section headings or summaries that can make previewing other texts especially informative. You have to dive into the words themselves.

Do write while reading (pp. 120–21, 123–25). If you own the book you are reading, don't hesitate to underline or highlight passages that especially interest you for one reason or another. Don't hesitate to annotate the margins, indicating your pleasures, displeasures, and uncertainties with remarks such as *Nice detail* or *Do we need this long description?* or *Not believable.* If you don't own the book, make these notes on separate sheets or on your computer.

An effective way to interact with a text is to keep a **reading journal.** A journal is not a diary in which you record your doings but a place to develop and store your reflections on what you read, such as an answer to a question you may have posed in the margin of the text. You could make an entry in the form of a letter to

http://www.gmu.edu/departments/writingcenter/handouts/puller.html
Tips on keeping a reading journal, from George Mason University.

the author or from one character to another. In many literature courses, students collaborate to develop their understanding of a literary work. In such a case, you may want to use your journal to reflect on what other students have said—for instance, why your opinion differs so much from someone else's.

You can keep a reading journal in a notebook or on your computer. Some readers prefer a two-column format like that illustrated on page 125, with summaries, paraphrases, and quotations from the text on the left and with their own responses to these passages on the right. Or you may prefer a less structured format like that illustrated on pages 795.

Here is a very short story by Kate Chopin (1851–1904). (The last name is pronounced in the French way, something like "show pan.") Following the story are a student's annotations and journal entry on the story.

Kate Chopin

The Story of an Hour

Knowing that Mrs. Mallard was afflicted with a heart trouble, great care was taken to break to her as gently as possible the news of her husband's death.

It was her sister Josephine who told her, in broken sentences, veiled hints that revealed in half concealing. Her husband's friend Richards was there, too, near her. It was he who had been in the newspaper office when intelligence of the railroad disaster was received, with Brently Mallard's name leading the list of "killed." He had only taken the time to assure himself of its truth by a second telegram, and had hastened to forestall any less careful, less tender friend in bearing the sad message.

She did not hear the story as many women have heard the same, with a paralyzed inability to accept its significance. She wept at once with sudden, wild abandonment, in her sister's arms. When the storm of grief had spent itself she went away to her room alone. She would have no one follow her.

There stood, facing the open window, a comfortable, roomy armchair. Into this she sank, pressed down by a physical exhaustion that haunted her body and seemed to reach into her soul.

She could see in the open square before her house the tops of trees that were all aquiver with the new spring life. The delicious breath of rain was in the air. In the street below a peddler was crying his wares. The notes of a distant song which some one was singing reached her faintly, and countless sparrows were twittering in the eaves.

http://www.womenwriters.net/domesticgoddess/chopin1.htm Extensive resources for studying Kate Chopin, from the Domestic Goddesses site.

There were patches of blue sky showing here and there through the clouds that had met and piled one above the other in the west facing her window.

She sat with her head thrown back upon the cushion of the chair quite motionless, except when a sob came up into her throat and shook her, as a child who has cried itself to sleep continues to sob in its dreams.

She was young, with a fair, calm face, whose lines bespoke repression and even a certain strength. But now there was a dull stare in her eyes, whose gaze was fixed away off yonder on one of those patches of blue sky. It was not a glance of reflection, but rather indicated a suspension of intelligent thought.

There was something coming to her and she was waiting for it, fearfully. What was it? She did not know; it was too subtle and elusive to name. But she felt it creeping out of the sky, reaching toward her through the sounds, the scents, the color that filled the air.

Now her bosom rose and fell tumultuously. She was beginning to recognize this thing that was approaching to possess her, and she was striving to beat it back with her will—as powerless as her two white slender hands would have been.

When she abandoned herself a little whispered word escaped her slightly parted lips. She said it over and over under her breath: "Free, free, free!" The vacant stare and the look of terror that had followed it went from her eyes. They stayed keen and bright. Her pulses beat fast, and the coursing blood warmed and relaxed every inch of her body.

She did not stop to ask if it were not a monstrous joy that held her. A clear and exalted perception enabled her to dismiss the suggestion as trivial.

She knew that she would weep again when she saw the kind, tender hands folded in death; the face that had never looked save with love upon her, fixed and gray and dead. But she saw beyond that bitter moment a long procession of years to come that would belong to her absolutely. And she opened and spread her arms out to them in welcome.

There would be no one to live for her during those coming years; she would live for herself. There would be no powerful will bending her in the blind persistence with which men and women believe they have a right to impose a private will upon a fellow creature. A kind intention or a cruel intention made the act seem no less a crime as she looked upon it in that brief moment of illumination.

And yet she had loved him—sometimes. Often she had not. What did it matter! What could love, the unsolved mystery, count for in face of this possession of self-assertion which she suddenly recognized as the strongest impulse of her being.

"Free! Body and soul free!" she kept whispering.

Josephine was kneeling before the closed door with her lips to the keyhole, imploring for admission. "Louise, open the door! I beg; open the door—you will make yourself ill. What are you doing, Louise? For heaven's sake open the door."

"Go away. I am not making myself ill." No; she was drinking in the very elixir of life through that open window.

Her fancy was running riot along those days ahead of her. Spring days, and summer days, and all sorts of days that would be her own. She breathed a quick prayer that life might be long. It was only yesterday she had thought with a shudder that life might be long.

She arose at length and opened the door to her sister's importunities. There was a feverish triumph in her eyes, and she carried herself unwittingly like a goddess of Victory. She clasped her sister's waist and together they descended the stairs. Richards stood waiting for them at the bottom.

Some one was opening the front door with a latchkey. It was Brently Mallard who entered, a little travel-stained, composedly carrying his grip-sack and umbrella. He had been far from the scene of accident, and did not even know there had been one. He stood amazed at Josephine's piercing cry; at Richards' quick motion to screen him from the view of his wife.

But Richards was too late.

When the doctors came they said she had died of heart disease—of joy that kills.

A student, Janet Vong, made the following annotations on the first five paragraphs of Chopin's story.

Knowing that Mrs. Mallard was afflicted with a heart trouble, great care was taken to break to her as gently as possible the news of her husband's death.

"heart disease" at end of story

It was her sister Josephine who told her, in broken sentences, veiled hints that revealed in half concealing. Her husband's friend Richards was there too, near her. It was he who had been in the newspaper office when intelligence of the railroad disaster was received, with Brently Mallard's name leading the list of "killed." He had only taken the time to assure himself of its truth by a second telegram, and had hastened to forestall any less careful, less tender friend in bearing the sad message.

Too hasty, it turns out

Would men have heard differently? Is au. sexist?

She did not hear the story as many women have heard the same, with a paralyzed inability to accept its significance. She wept at once with sudden, wild abandonment, in her sister's arms. When the storm of grief had spent itself she went away to her room alone. She would have no one follow her.

old-fashioned style

There stood, facing the open window, a comfortable, roomy armchair. Into this she sank, pressed down by a physical exhaustion that haunted her body and seemed to reach into her soul.

> She could see in the open square before her house the tops of trees that were all aquiver with the new spring life. The delicious breath of rain was in the air. In the street below a peddler was crying his wares. The notes of a distant song which some one was singing reached her faintly, and countless sparrows were twittering in the eaves.

Notices spring: odd in a story of death

Writing in her journal, Vong posed questions about the story—critical points, curiosities about characters, possible implications:

Title nothing special. What might be a better title?
Could a woman who loved her husband be so heartless? *Is* she heartless? *Did* she love him?
What are (were) Louise's feelings about her husband?
Did she want too much? *What* did she want?
Could this story happen today? Feminist interpretation?
Sister (Josephine)—a busybody?
Tricky ending—but maybe it could be true.
"And yet she had loved him—sometimes. Often she had not." Why does one love someone "sometimes"?
Irony: plot has reversal. Are characters ironic too?

Vong's journal entry illustrates brainstorming—the discovery technique of listing ideas (or questions) however they occur, without editing (see p. 24). Another productive journal technique is focused freewriting—concentrating on a single issue (such as one of Vong's questions) and writing nonstop for a set amount of time, again without editing (p. 23).

2 Analyzing a work of literature

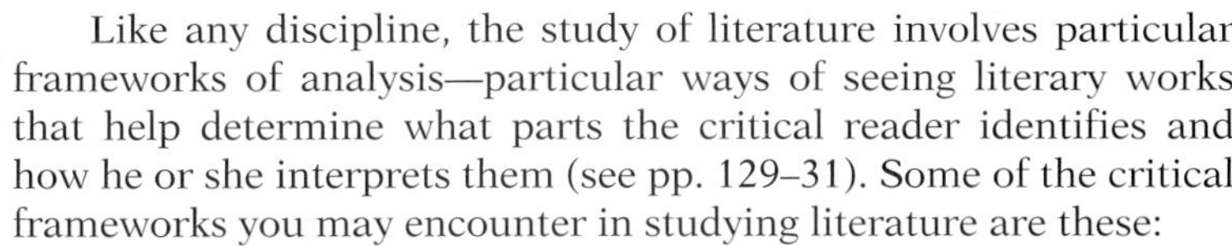

Like any discipline, the study of literature involves particular frameworks of analysis—particular ways of seeing literary works that help determine what parts the critical reader identifies and how he or she interprets them (see pp. 129–31). Some of the critical frameworks you may encounter in studying literature are these:

- **Historical or cultural criticism** focuses on the context in which a literary work was created and how that context affected the work. The critic may examine the author's social, political, and intellectual surroundings or may concentrate on the author's own biography: his or her life experiences or psychological makeup.
- **Feminist criticism** focuses on the representation of gender in literature, often in the literary canon—the body of work repre-

http://www.brocku.ca/english/jlye/criticalreading.html Advice on analyzing literature, from Brock University.

sented in the standard anthologies, discussed in the schools, and examined in the scholarly journals. Feminist critics are especially concerned with the writings of women and with the responses of women to the depiction of both sexes in literature.

- **Reader-response criticism** focuses on the reactions of an audience to a work of literature, asking why readers respond as they do to a text. In this view the meaning of the text lies not just on the page but in how the reader constructs the text.
- **Deconstructive criticism** regards a work of literature skeptically, resisting the obvious meanings and focusing on the ambiguities in the work, especially the internal contradictions. Perceiving that the relationship of words and their meanings is both arbitrary and forever changing—even within the same work—deconstructive critics emphasize multiple meanings and what a text does not say.
- **Formalist criticism** (also called **New Criticism**) focuses primarily on a literary work as a constructed text, as an independent unity understood in itself rather than as an artifact of a particular context or reader response. Beginning with a personal response, the formalist critic tries to account for the response by examining the form of the work (hence *formalist*) and the relations among its elements.

This chapter emphasizes formalist criticism because it engages you immediately in the work of literature itself, without requiring extensive historical or cultural background, and because it introduces the conventional elements of literature that all critical approaches discuss, even though they view the elements differently. The box on the next two pages lists these elements—plot, characters, setting, and so on—and offers questions about each one that can help you think constructively and imaginatively about what you read.

One significant attribute of a literary work is its *meaning,* or what we can interpret to be its meaning. Readers may well disagree over the persuasiveness of someone's argument, but they will rarely disagree over its meaning. With literature, however, disagreements over meaning occur all the time because (as we have seen) literature *shows* rather than *tells:* it gives us concrete images of imagined human experiences, but it usually does not say how we ought to understand the images.

Further, readers bring to their reading not only different critical views, as noted above, but also different personal experiences. To take an extreme case, a woman who has recently lost her husband may interpret "The Story of an Hour" differently from most other readers. Or a story that bores a reader at age fifteen may deeply move him at twenty-five. The words on the page remain the same, but their meaning changes.

In writing about literature, then, we can offer only our *interpretation* of meaning rather than *the* meaning. Still, most people agree that there are limits to interpretation: it must be supported by evidence that a reasonable reader finds at least plausible if not totally convincing. For instance, the student who says that in "The Story of an Hour" Mrs. Mallard does not die but merely falls into a deathlike trance goes beyond the permissible limits because the story offers no evidence for such an interpretation.

Questions for a literary analysis

See later boxes for specific questions on fiction (p. 809), poetry (p. 810), and drama (p. 814).

- **Plot:** the relationships and patterns of events. (Even a poem has a plot, such as a change in mood from bitterness to resignation.)

  What actions happen?
  What conflicts occur?
  How do the events connect to each other and to the whole?

- **Characters:** the people the author creates (including the narrator of a story or the speaker of a poem).

  Who are the principal people in the work?
  How do they interact?
  What do their actions, words, and thoughts reveal about their personalities and the personalities of others?
  Do the characters stay the same, or do they change? Why?

- **Point of view:** the perspective or attitude of the speaker in a poem or the voice who tells a story. The point of view may be **first person** (a participant, using *I*) or **third person** (an outsider, using *he, she, it, they*). A first-person narrator may be a major or a minor character in the narrative and may be **reliable** or **unreliable** (unable to report events wholly or accurately). A third-person narrator may be **omniscient** (knows what goes on in all characters' minds), **limited** (knows what goes on in the mind of only one or two characters), or **objective** (knows only what is external to the characters).

  Who is the narrator (or the speaker of a poem)?
  How does the narrator's point of view affect the narrative?

- **Tone:** the narrator's or speaker's attitude, perceived through the words (for instance, joyful, bitter, or confident).

  What tone (or tones) do you hear? If there is a change, how do you account for it?
  Is there an ironic contrast between the narrator's tone (for instance, confidence) and what you take to be the author's attitude (for instance, pity for human overconfidence)?

(continued)

Questions for a literary analysis
(continued)

- **Imagery:** word pictures or visual details involving the senses (sight, sound, touch, smell, taste).

  What images does the writer use? What senses do they draw on?
  What patterns are evident in the images (for instance, religious or commercial images)?
  What is the significance of the imagery?

- **Symbolism:** concrete things standing for larger and more abstract ideas (for instance, the American flag may symbolize freedom, a tweeting bird may symbolize happiness, or a dead flower may symbolize mortality).

  What symbols does the author use? What do they seem to signify?
  How does the symbolism relate to the other elements of the work, such as character or theme?

- **Setting:** the place where the action happens.

  What does the locale contribute to the work?
  Are scene shifts significant?

- **Form:** the shape or structure of the work.

  What *is* the form? (For example, a story might divide sharply in the middle, moving from happiness to sorrow.)
  What parts of the work does the form emphasize, and why?

- **Theme:** the central idea, a conception of human experience suggested by the work as a whole. Theme is neither plot (what happens) nor subject (such as mourning or marriage). Rather it is what the author says with that plot about that subject.

  Can you state the theme in a sentence? For instance, you might state the following about Kate Chopin's "The Story of an Hour": *Happiness depends partly on freedom.*
  Do certain words, passages of dialogue or description, or situations seem to represent the theme most clearly?
  How do the work's elements combine to develop the theme?

- **Appeal:** the degree to which the work pleases you.

  What do you especially like or dislike about the work?
  Do you think your responses are unique or common to most readers? Why?

3 Using evidence in writing about literature

The evidence for a literary analysis always comes from at least one primary source (the work or works being discussed) and may come from secondary sources (critical and historical works). (See p. 626 for more on primary and secondary sources.) For example, if you were writing about Chopin's "The Story of an Hour," the primary material would be the story itself, and the secondary material (if you used it) might be critical studies of Chopin.

The bulk of your evidence in writing about literature will usually be quotations from the work, although you will occasionally summarize or paraphrase as well (see pp. 678–81). When using quotations, keep in mind the criteria in the box on page 804.

Your instructor will probably tell you if you are expected to consult secondary sources for an assignment. (If so, see pp. 800–01 for lists of research sources in literature.) Secondary sources can help you understand a writer's work, but your primary concern should always be the work itself, not what critics A, B, and C say about it. In general, then, quote or summarize secondary material sparingly. And always cite your sources. (See p. 802.)

49b Understanding writing assignments in literature

A literature instructor may ask you to write one or more of the following types of papers. The first two are the most common.

- **A literary analysis paper** gives your ideas about a work of literature—your interpretation of its meaning, context, or representations based on specific words, passages, and events. For guidelines on analyzing a work of literature, see pages 795–98. (For specific guidelines on analyzing fiction, poetry, and drama, see the boxes on pp. 809, 810, and 814, respectively.)
- **A literary research paper** combines analysis of a literary work with research about the work and perhaps its author. Thus a literary research paper draws on both primary and secondary sources (see opposite). For example, you might respond to what scholars have written about the symbolism in a play by Tennessee Williams, or you might research medieval England as a way to understand the context of Chaucer's *Canterbury Tales*.
- **A personal response** or **reaction paper** gives your thoughts and feelings about a work of literature. For example, you might compare a novel's description of a city with your experience of the same city.
- **A book review** gives a summary of a book and a judgment about the book's value. In a review of a novel, for example, you might discuss whether the plot is interesting, the characters are believable, and the writing style is enjoyable. You might also compare the work to other works by the author.
- **A theater review** gives your reactions to and opinions about a theatrical performance. You might summarize the plot of the play, describe the characters, identify the prominent themes, evaluate the other elements (writing, performances, direction, stage setting), and make a recommendation to potential viewers.

49c Using the tools and language of literary analysis

1 Writing tools

The fundamental tool for writing about literature is reading critically (pp. 791–98 earlier in this chapter and pp. 129–36 in Chapter 5). Asking analytical questions about the work can help you focus your ideas (see the box on pp. 797–98). In addition, keeping a reading journal can help you develop your thoughts (pp. 791–92). Take careful, well-organized notes on any research materials (see pp. 676–78). Finally, discuss the work with others who have read it. They may offer reactions and insights that will help you shape your own ideas.

2 Language considerations

Use the present tense of verbs to describe both the action in a literary work (*Brently Mallard suddenly appears*) and the writing of an author (*Chopin briefly describes the view* or *In his essay he comments that . . .*). Use the past tense to describe events that actually occurred in the past (*Chopin was born in 1851*).

Some instructors discourage students from using the first-person *I* (as in *I felt sorry for the character*) in writing about literature. At least use *I* sparingly to avoid sounding egotistical. Rephrase sentences to avoid using *I* unnecessarily—for instance, *The character evokes the reader's sympathy.*

3 Research sources

In addition to these resources on literature, you may also want to consult some on other humanities (pp. 819–22).

Specialized encyclopedias, dictionaries, and bibliographies

Bibliographical Guide to the Study of the Literature of the U.S.A.
Cambridge Encyclopedia of Language
Cambridge Guide to Literature in English
Dictionary of Literary Biography
Handbook to Literature
Literary Criticism Index
McGraw-Hill Encyclopedia of World Drama
MLA International Bibliography of Books and Articles on the Modern Languages and Literatures
Modern Drama: A Checklist of Critical Literature on Twentieth Century Plays
New Cambridge Bibliography of English Literature
New Princeton Encyclopedia of Poetry and Poetics

Oxford Companion to American Literature
Oxford Companion to the Theatre
Reference Sources in English and American Literature: An Annotated Bibliography
Schomburg Center Guide to Black Literature from the Eighteenth Century to the Present

Periodical indexes

Humanities Index
Literary Criticism Index
MLA International Bibliography of Books and Articles on the Modern Languages and Literatures

Abstracts and citation indexes

Abstracts of English Studies
Abstracts of Folklore Studies
Dissertation Abstracts International (doctoral dissertations). Before 1969, the title was *Dissertation Abstracts.*
Humanities Index

Book reviews

Book Review Digest
Book Review Index
Index to Book Reviews in the Humanities

Web sources

ALEX Catalog of Electronic Texts
http://sunsite.berkeley.edu/alex
English Server
http://eserver.org
Gale Group Literary Index
http://www.galenet.com/servlet/LitIndex
Glossary of Literary Terms
http://www.uky.edu/ArtsSciences/Classics/Harris/rhetform.html
Internet Public Library's Online Literary Criticism Collection
http://www.ipl.org/ref/litcrit
On-Line Books Page
http://digital.library.upenn.edu/books
Literary Resources on the Net
http://andromeda.rutgers.edu/~jlynch/Lit
Top Ten Resources for American Literature
http://www.cwrl.utexas.edu/~daniel/amlit/resources.html
Voice of the Shuttle Drama Page
http://vos.ucsb.edu/shuttle/english2.html#drama
Voice of the Shuttle English Literature Page
http://vos.ucsb.edu/shuttle/english.html
Voice of the Shuttle World Literature Page
http://vos.ucsb.edu/shuttle/litother.html

49d Citing sources and formatting documents in writing about literature

Unless your instructor specifies otherwise, use the style of the Modern Language Association (MLA), detailed in Chapter 46. In this style, parenthetical citations in the text of the paper refer to a list of works cited at the end. Sample papers illustrating this style appear in Chapter 47 as well as in this chapter.

Use MLA format for headings, margins, and other elements. See pages 215–18 for detailed instructions and pages 779–84 for a full paper in this format. For the special formats of poetry and long prose quotations, see pages 511–14.

49e Drafting and revising a literary analysis

The process for writing a literary analysis is similar to that for any other kind of essay: once you've done the reading and thought about it, you need to focus your ideas, gather evidence, draft, and revise.

1 Conceiving a thesis

After reading, rereading, and making notes, you probably will be able to formulate a tentative thesis statement—an assertion of your main point, your argument. (For more on thesis statements, see pp. 30–34.) Clear the air by glancing over your notes and by jotting down a few especially promising ideas—brief statements of what you think your key points may be and their main support. One approach is to seek patterns in the work, such as recurring words,

http://www.unc.edu/depts/wcweb/handouts/literature.html Detailed information on writing about literature, from the University of North Carolina.

http://webster.commnet.edu/HP/pages/darling/grammar/composition/literature.html-ssi Guidance on writing about literature, from the Guide to Grammar and Writing.

http://www.wmich.edu/english/tchg/lit/adv/lit.papers.html Advice on writing a literary analysis, from Western Michigan University.

http://www.cohums.ohio-state.edu/english/programs/writing_center/GENRE07.htm A checklist for writing a literary analysis, from Ohio State University.

http://www.colostate.edu/Depts/WritingCenter/references/litthesis/page.htm Advice on writing a thesis statement for a literature paper, from Colorado State University.

phrases, images, events, symbols, or other elements. (Go back to the work, if necessary, to expand the patterns your notes reveal.) Such patterns can help you see themes both in the work itself and in your ideas about it.

Considering Kate Chopin's "The Story of an Hour," Janet Vong at first explored the idea that Mrs. Mallard, the main character, was unrealistic and thus unconvincing. (See Vong's journal entry on p. 795.) But the more Vong examined the story and her notes, the more she was impressed by a pattern of ironies, or reversals, that actually helped to make Mrs. Mallard believable. In her journal Vong explored the idea that the many small reversals paved the way for Mrs. Mallard's own reversal from grief to joy:

> title? "Ironies in an Hour" (?) "An Hour of Irony" (?) "Kate Chopin's Irony" (?)
> thesis: irony at end is prepared for
> chief irony: Mrs. M. dies just as she is beginning to enjoy life
> smaller ironies:
> 1. "sad message" brings her joy
> 2. Richards is "too late" at end
> 3. Richards is too early at start
> 4. "joy that kills"
> 5. death brings joy and life

From these notes Vong developed her thesis statement:

> The irony of the ending is believable partly because it is consistent with earlier ironies in the story.

This thesis statement asserts a specific idea that can be developed and convincingly argued with evidence from Chopin's story. A good thesis statement will neither assert a fact (*Mrs. Mallard dies soon after hearing that her husband has died*) nor overgeneralize (*The story is an insult to women*).

2 Gathering evidence

In writing about literature, you use mainly evidence gathered from the work itself: quotations and sometimes paraphrases that support your ideas about the work. You can see examples of such quoting and paraphrasing in Janet Vong's final draft on pages 807–08. The box on the next page offers guidelines for using quotations in literary analysis.

You may wonder how much you should summarize the plot of the work. A brief plot summary can be helpful to readers who are unfamiliar with the work. Sometimes plot elements place your ideas in the context of the work or remind readers where your quotations come from. Plot elements may even be used as evidence, as Vong uses the ironic ending of the Chopin story. But plot summary is not

Guidelines for using quotations in literary analysis

- Use quotations to support your assertions, not to pad the paper. Quote at length only when necessary to your argument.
- When you use a quotation, specify how it relates to your idea. Introduce the quotation—for example, *At the outset Chopin conveys the sort of person Richards is: "..."* Sometimes, comment after the quotation. (See pp. 693–97 for more on integrating quotations into your writing.)
- Reproduce spelling, punctuation, capitalization, and all other features exactly as they appear in the source. (See p. 526 for the use of brackets when you need to add something to a quotation, and see p. 527 for the use of an ellipsis mark when you need to omit something from a quotation.)
- Document your sources. (See p. 802.)

literary analysis, and summary alone is not sufficient evidence to support a thesis. Keep any plot summaries brief and to the point.

For a literary research paper, evidence will come from the work itself and from secondary sources such as scholarly works and critical appraisals. The thesis and principal ideas of the paper must still be your own, but you may supplement your reading of the work with the views of respected scholars or critics. Sometimes you may choose to build your own argument in part by disputing others' views. However you draw on secondary sources, remember that they must be clearly identified and documented, even when you use your own words (see pp. 686–92).

Note You can find many student essays about literature on the Web. Such a paper may lead you to other sources or may suggest an idea you hadn't considered. If you want to use another student's paper as a secondary source, you must evaluate it with special care because it will not have passed through a reviewing process, as an article in a scholarly journal does. (See pp. 670–72 on evaluating online sources.) You must also, of course, clearly identify and document the source: borrowing other students' ideas or words without credit is plagiarism. (See pp. 686–92.)

3 Writing a draft

Drafting your essay is your opportunity to develop your thesis or to discover it if you haven't already. (See pp. 48–51 for tips on drafting.) The draft below was actually Janet Vong's second: she deleted some digressions from her first draft and added more evidence for her points. The numbers in parentheses refer to the pages from which she drew the quotations. (See pp. 711–16 on this form of documentation.) Ask your instructor whether you should always give such citations, especially for a short poem or story like Chopin's.

Ironies in an Hour

After we know how the story turns out, if we reread it we find irony at the very start, as is true of many other stories. Mrs. Mallard's friends assume, mistakenly, that Mrs. Mallard was deeply in love with her husband, Brently Mallard. They take great care to tell her gently of his death. The friends mean well, and in fact they <u>do</u> well. They bring her an hour of life, an hour of freedom. They think their news is sad. Mrs. Mallard at first expresses grief when she hears the news, but soon she finds joy in it. So Richards's "sad message" (12), though sad in Richards's eyes, is in fact a happy message.

Among the ironic details is the statement that when Mallard entered the house, Richards tried to conceal him from Mrs. Mallard, but "Richards was too late" (13). This is ironic because earlier Richards "hastened" (12) to bring his sad message; if he had at the start been "too late" (13), Brently Mallard would have arrived at home first, and Mrs. Mallard's life would not have ended an hour later but would simply have gone on as it had been. Yet another irony at the end of the story is the diagnosis of the doctors. The doctors say she died of "heart disease--of joy that kills" (13). In one sense the doctors are right: Mrs. Mallard has experienced a great joy. But of course the doctors totally misunderstand the joy that kills her.

The central irony resides not in the well-intentioned but ironic actions of Richards, or in the unconsciously ironic words of the doctors, but in her own life. In a way she has been dead. She "sometimes" (13) loved her husband, but in a way she has been dead. Now, his apparent death brings her new life. This new life comes to her at the season of the year when "the tops of trees [. . .] were all aquiver with the new spring life" (12). But, ironically, her new life will last only an hour. She looks forward to "summer days" (13), but she will not see even the end of this spring day. Her years of marriage were ironic. They brought her a sort of living death instead of joy. Her new life is ironic too. It grows out of her moment of grief for her supposedly dead husband, and her vision of a new life is cut short.

4 Revising and editing

As in other writing, use at least two drafts to revise and edit, so that you can attend separately to the big structural issues and the smaller surface problems. See pages 56 and 61, respectively, for general revision and editing checklists. The additional checklist below can help you with a literary analysis.

Checklist for revising a literary analysis

- Does the title of your essay give the title and author of the work you discuss and also an idea of your approach to the work?
- Does the introductory paragraph avoid openings such as "In this story . . ."? Name the author and the title so that the reader knows exactly what work you are discussing. Develop your thesis a bit so that readers know where they will be going.
- Is the organization effective? The essay should not dwindle or become anticlimactic; rather, it should build up.
- Do quotations provide evidence and let the reader hear the author's voice?
- Is the essay chiefly devoted to analysis, not to summary? Summarize the plot only briefly and only to further your own ideas. A summary is not an essay.
- Have you used the present tense of verbs to describe both the author's work and the action in the work (for example, *Chopin shows* or *Mrs. Mallard dies*)?
- If you have used the first-person *I* (for instance, *I find the ending highly plausible*), have you avoided using it so often that you sound egotistical?
- Is your evaluation of the work evident? It may be understood (as in Janet Vong's essay on "The Story of an Hour"), or it may be explicit. In either case, give the reasons for judging the work to be effective or not, worth reading or not. Remember that it is not enough to express your likes or dislikes; readers will be interested in an evaluation only if you support it with specific evidence from the work.
- Did you document your sources? (See p. 802.)

Janet Vong's final draft follows. The main changes are explained below and keyed by number to the draft.

1. Vong retitled the paper to incorporate the author and title of the work she was analyzing.
2. Vong added a new introduction to set up the paper. It names the story's author and title, introduces the story's overall irony, very briefly summarizes the story, and states Vong's thesis.
3. At many points, Vong added details and quotations to clarify the ironies in the story by emphasizing the reversals.
4. Vong added a new page for her work cited. (See p. 719 for the format of such a page.)

An essay on fiction (no secondary sources)

Janet Vong

Mr. Romano

English 102

February 20, 2000

Ironies of Life in Kate Chopin's 1
"The Story of an Hour"

Kate Chopin's "The Story of an Hour"--which takes only a few 2
minutes to read--has an ironic ending: Mrs. Mallard dies just when
she is beginning to live. On first reading, the ending seems almost
too ironic for belief. On rereading the story, however, one sees that
the ending is believable partly because it is consistent with other
ironies in the story.

After we know how the story turns out, if we reread it we find
irony at the very start. Because Mrs. Mallard's friends and her sister assume, mistakenly, that she was deeply in love with her husband, Brently Mallard, they take great care to tell her gently of his
death. They mean well, and in fact they *do* well, bringing her an
hour of life, an hour of joyous freedom, but it is ironic that they 3
think their news is sad. True, Mrs. Mallard at first expresses grief
when she hears the news, but soon (unknown to the others) she
finds joy. So Richards's "sad message" (12), though sad in
Richards's eyes, is in fact a happy message.

Among the small but significant ironic details is the statement
near the end of the story that when Mallard entered the house,
Richards tried to conceal him from Mrs. Mallard, but "Richards was
too late" (13). Almost at the start of the story, in the second para- 3
graph, Richards "hastened" (12) to bring his sad news. But if
Richards had arrived "too late" at the start, Brently Mallard would
have arrived at home first, and Mrs. Mallard's life would not have
ended an hour later but would simply have gone on as it had been. Yet
another irony at the end of the story is the diagnosis of the doctors.
They say she died of "heart disease--of joy that kills" (13). In one
sense they are right: Mrs. Mallard has for the last hour experienced a
great joy. But of course the doctors totally misunderstand the joy that
kills her. It is not joy at seeing her husband alive, but her realization 3
that the great joy she experienced during the last hour is over.

All of these ironic details add richness to the story, but the
central irony resides not in the well-intentioned but ironic actions of
Richards, or in the unconsciously ironic words of the doctors, but in
Mrs. Mallard's own life. She "sometimes" (13) loved her husband, but
in a way she has been dead, a body subjected to her husband's will.
Now, his apparent death brings her new life. Appropriately, this new 3
life comes to her at the season of the year when "the tops of trees
[. . .] were all aquiver with the new spring life" (12). But, ironically,
her new life will last only an hour. She is "Free, free, free" (12)--but 3
only until her husband walks through the doorway. She looks forward to "summer days" (13), but she will not see even the end of this
spring day. If her years of marriage were ironic, bringing her a sort
of living death instead of joy, her new life is ironic too, not only because it grows out of her moment of grief for her supposedly dead
husband, but also because her vision of "a long procession of years" 3
(12) is cut short within an hour on a spring day.

[New page.]

Work Cited 4

Chopin, Kate. "The Story of an Hour." <u>Literature for Composition</u>. Ed. Sylvan Barnet et al. 5th ed. New York: Longman, 2000. 12-13.

49f Writing about fiction, poetry, and drama

A work of literature falls into a category, or **genre**—fiction, poetry, or drama—depending on how it is structured. The different genres of literature require different approaches in writing.

1 Writing about fiction

The "Questions for a literary analysis" on pages 797–98 will help you think about any work of literature, including a story or novel, and find a topic to write on. The box on the facing page provides additional questions for thinking about fiction. Not every question is

Advice on writing about fiction:

http://owl.english.purdue.edu/Files/114.html From the Purdue Online Writing Lab.

http://vccslitonline.cc.va.us/vcficweb.htm An online class module from Virginia Community College.

Questions for analyzing fiction

- What happens in the story? For yourself, summarize the plot (the gist of the happenings). Think about what your summary *leaves out.*
- Is the story told in chronological order, or are there flashbacks or flashforwards? On rereading, what foreshadowing (hints of what is to come) do you detect?
- What conflicts does the work include?
- How does the writer reveal character—for instance, by explicit comment or by letting us see the character in action? With which character(s) do you sympathize? Are the characters plausible? What motivates them? What do minor characters contribute to the work?
- Who tells the story? Is the narrator a character, or does the narrator stand entirely outside the characters' world? What does the narrator's point of view contribute to the story's theme? (On narrative points of view, see p. 797.)
- What is the setting, the time and place of the action? What does it contribute to the work?
- Do certain characters or settings or actions seem to you to stand for something in addition to themselves—that is, are they symbolic?
- What is the theme—that is, what does the work add up to? Does the theme reinforce your values, or does it challenge them?
- Is the title informative? Did its meaning change for you after you read the work?

relevant to every story. For an example of writing about fiction, see Janet Vong's essay on pages 807–08.

2 Writing about poetry

Two types of essays on poetry are especially common. One is an analysis of some aspect of the poem in relation to the whole—for instance, the changes in the speaker's tone or the functions of meter and rhyme. The second is an **explication,** a line-by-line (sometimes almost word-by-word) reading that seeks to make explicit every-

Advice on reading and writing about poetry:

http://www.wisc.edu/writing/Handbook/ReadingPoetry.html From the University of Wisconsin at Madison.

http://www.english.uiuc.edu/cws/wworkshop/writtech.poetry.htm From the University of Illinois at Urbana-Champaign.

http://www.hamilton.edu/academics/resource/wc/WritingaboutPoetry.html From Hamilton College.

thing that is implicit in the poem. Thus an explication of the first line of Robert Frost's "Stopping by Woods on a Snowy Evening" (the line goes "Whose woods these are I think I know") might call attention to the tentativeness of the line ("I think I know") and to the fact that the words are not in the normal order ("I think I know whose woods these are"). These features might support the explanation that the poet is introducing—very quietly—a note of the *unusual*, in preparation for the experience that follows. Although one might conceivably explicate a long poem, the method is so detailed that in practice writers usually confine it to short poems or to short passages from long poems.

The "Questions for a literary analysis" on pages 797–98 will help you think about any work of literature, including a poem, and find a topic to write on. The box below provides additional questions for thinking about poetry.

Questions for analyzing poetry

- What parts interest or puzzle you? What words seem especially striking or unusual?
- How would you describe the poem's **speaker** (sometimes called the **persona** or the **voice**)? (The speaker may be very different from the author.) What tone or emotion do you detect—for instance, anger, affection, sarcasm? Does the tone change during the poem?
- What is the structure of the poem? Are there stanzas (groups of lines separated by space)? If so, how is the thought related to the stanzas?
- What is the theme of the poem: what is it about? Is the theme stated or implied?
- What images do you find—evocations of sight, sound, taste, touch, or smell? Is there a surprising pattern of images—say, images of business in a poem about love? What does the poem suggest symbolically as well as literally? (Trust your responses. If you don't sense a symbolic overtone, move on. Don't hunt for symbols.)

An essay on poetry with secondary sources

The following sample paper on a short poem by Gwendolyn Brooks illustrates a literary analysis that draws not only on the poem itself but also on secondary sources—that is, critical works *about* the poem. In the opening paragraph, for instance, the writer uses brief quotations from two secondary sources to establish the problem, the topic that he will address. These quotations, like the two later quotations from secondary material, are used to make points, not to pad the essay.

Note In the paper the parenthetical citations for Brooks's poem give line numbers of the poem, whereas the citations for the secondary sources give page numbers of the sources. See pages 715 and 711, respectively, for these two forms of citation.

Gwendolyn Brooks

The Bean Eaters

They eat beans mostly, this old yellow pair.
Dinner is a casual affair.
Plain chipware on a plain and creaking wood,
Tin flatware.

Two who are Mostly Good.
Two who have lived their day,
But keep on putting on their clothes
And putting things away.

And remembering . . .
Remembering, with tinklings and twinges,
As they lean over the beans in their rented back room that is
  full of beads and receipts and dolls and cloths, tobacco
  crumbs, vases and fringes.

Kenneth Scheff

Professor MacGregor

English 101A

February 7, 2000

Marking Time Versus Enduring in
Gwendolyn Brooks's "The Bean Eaters"

Gwendolyn Brooks's poem "The Bean Eaters" runs only eleven lines. It is written in plain language about very plain people. Yet its meaning is ambiguous. One critic, George E. Kent, says the old couple who eat beans "have had their day and exist now as time-markers" (141). However, another reader, D. H. Melhem, perceives not so much time marking as "endurance" in the old couple (123). Is this poem a despairing picture of old age or a more positive portrait?

"The Bean Eaters" describes an "old yellow pair" who "eat beans mostly" (line 1) off "Plain chipware" (3) with "Tin flatware" (4) in "their rented back room" (11). Clearly, they are poor. Their existence is accompanied not by friends or relatives--children or grandchildren are not mentioned--but by memories and a few possessions (9-11). They are "Mostly Good" (5), words Brooks capitalizes at the end of a line, perhaps to stress the old people's adherence to traditional values as well as their lack of saintliness. They are unexceptional, whatever message they have for readers.

The isolated routine of the couple's life is something Brooks draws attention to with a separate stanza:

> Two who are Mostly Good.
> Two who have lived their day.
> But keep on putting on their clothes
> And putting things away. (5-8)

Brooks emphasizes how isolated the couple is by repeating "Two who." Then she emphasizes how routine their life is by repeating "putting."

A pessimistic reading of this poem seems justified. The critic Harry B. Shaw reads the lines just quoted as perhaps despairing: "they are putting things away as if winding down an operation and readying for withdrawal from activity" (80). However, Shaw observes, the word <u>but</u> also indicates the couple's "determination to go on living, a refusal to give up and let things go" (80). This dual meaning is at the heart of Brooks's poem: the old people live a meager existence, yes, but their will, their self-control, and their connection with another person--their essential humanity--are unharmed.

The truly positive nature of the poem is revealed in the last stanza. In Brooks's words, the old couple remember with some "twinges" perhaps, but also with "tinklings" (10), a cheerful image. As Melhem says, these people are "strong in mutual affection and shared memories" (123). And the final line, which is much longer than all the rest and which catalogs the evidence of the couple's long life together, is almost musically affirmative: "As they lean over the beans in their rented back room that is full of beads and receipts and dolls and cloths, tobacco crumbs, vases and fringes" (11).

What these people have is not much, but it is something.

[New page.]

Works Cited

Brooks, Gwendolyn. "The Bean Eaters." <u>Literature: An Introduction to Fiction, Poetry, and Drama</u>. Ed. X. J. Kennedy and Dana Gioia. 7th ed. New York: Longman, 1999. 732.

Kent, George E. A Life of Gwendolyn Brooks. Lexington: UP of Kentucky, 1990.

Melhem, D. H. Gwendolyn Brooks: Poetry and the Heroic Voice. Lexington: UP of Kentucky, 1987.

Shaw, Harry B. Gwendolyn Brooks. Twayne's United States Authors Ser. 395. Boston: Twayne, 1980.

3 Writing about drama

Because plays—even some one-act plays—are relatively long, analytic essays on drama usually focus on only one aspect of the play, such as the structure of the play, the function of a single scene, or a character's responsibility for his or her fate. The essay's introduction indicates what the topic is and why it is of some importance, and the introduction may also state the thesis. The conclusion often extends the analysis, showing how a study of the apparently small topic helps to illuminate the play as a whole.

The "Questions for a literary analysis" on pages 797–98 will help you think about any work of literature, including a play, and find a topic to write on. The box on the next page provides additional questions for thinking about drama.

An essay on drama (no secondary sources)

The following essay on William Shakespeare's *Macbeth* focuses on the title character, examining the extent to which he is and is not a tragic hero. Although the writer bases the essay on his personal response to the play, he does not simply state a preference, as if saying he likes vanilla more than chocolate; instead, he argues a case and offers evidence from the play to support his claims.

The writer delays stating his thesis fully until the final paragraph: Macbeth is a hero even though he is a villain. But this thesis is nonetheless evident throughout the essay, from the title through the opening three paragraphs (which establish a context and the case the writer will oppose) through each of the five body paragraphs (which offer five kinds of evidence for the thesis).

Note The parenthetical citations in this essay include act, scene, and line numbers—MLA style for citations of verse plays (see pp. 715–16).

http://vccslitonline.cc.va.us/vcdraweb.htm Advice on understanding and writing about drama, an online class module from Virginia Community College.

Questions for analyzing drama

- Does the plot (the sequence of happenings) seem plausible? If not, is the implausibility a fault? If there is more than one plot, are the plots parallel, or are they related by way of contrast?
- Are certain happenings recurrent? If so, how are they significant?
- What kinds of conflict are in the play—for instance, between two groups, two individuals, or two aspects of a single individual? How are the conflicts resolved? Is the resolution satisfying to you?
- How trustworthy are the characters when they describe themselves or others? Do some characters serve as **foils,** or contrasts, for other characters, thus helping to define the other characters? Do the characters change as the play proceeds? Are the characters' motivations convincing?
- What do the author's stage directions add to your understanding and appreciation of the play? If there are few stage directions, what do the speeches imply about the characters' manner, tone, and gestures?
- What do you make of the setting, or location? Does it help to reveal character or theme?
- Do certain costumes (dark suits, flowery shawls, stiff collars) or properties (books, pictures, candlesticks) strike you as symbolic?

Michael Spinter

Professor Nelson

English 211

May 6, 2000

Macbeth as Hero

When we think of a tragic hero, we probably think of a fundamentally sympathetic person who is entangled in terrifying circumstances and who ultimately dies, leaving us with a sense that the world has suffered a loss. For instance, Hamlet must avenge his father's murder, and in doing so he performs certain actions that verge on the wrongful, such as behaving cruelly to his beloved Ophelia and his mother and killing Rosencrantz and Guildenstern; but we believe that Hamlet is fundamentally a decent man and that Denmark is the poorer for his death.

Macbeth, however, is different. He kills King Duncan and Duncan's grooms, kills Banquo, attempts to kill Banquo's son, and finally kills Lady Macduff and her children and her servants. True, the only people whom he kills with his own hands are Duncan and the grooms--the other victims are destroyed by hired murderers--but clearly Macbeth is responsible for all of the deaths. He could seem an utterly unscrupulous, sneaking crook rather than a tragic hero for whom a reader can feel sympathy.

Certainly most of the other characters in the play feel no sympathy for Macbeth. Macduff calls him a "hell-kite," or a hellish bird of prey (4.3.217), a "tyrant" (5.7.14), a "hell-hound" (5.8.3), and a "coward" (5.8.23). To Malcolm he is a "tyrant" (4.3.12), "devilish Macbeth" (4.3.117), and a "butcher" (5.8.69). Readers and spectators can hardly deny the truth of these characterizations. And yet Macbeth does not seem merely villainous. It would be going too far to say that we always sympathize with him, but we are deeply interested in him and do not dismiss him in disgust as an out-and-out monster. How can we account for his hold on our feelings? At least five factors play their parts.

First, Macbeth is an impressive military figure. In the first extended description of Macbeth, the Captain speaks of "brave Macbeth--well he deserves that name" (1.2.16). The Captain tells how Macbeth valiantly fought on behalf of his king, and King Duncan exclaims, "O valiant cousin! Worthy gentleman!" (1.2.2). True, Macbeth sometimes cringes, such as when he denies responsibility for Banquo's death: "Thou canst not say I did it" (3.4.51). But throughout most of the play, we see him as a bold and courageous soldier.

Of course, Macbeth's ability as a soldier is not enough by itself to explain his hold on us. A second reason is that he is in some degree a victim--a victim of his wife's ambition and a victim of the witches. Yes, he ought to see through his wife's schemes, and he ought to resist the witches, just as Banquo resists them, but surely Macbeth is partly tricked into crime. He is responsible, but we can imagine ourselves falling as he does, and his status as a victim arouses our sympathy.

A third source of his hold on us is that although Macbeth engages in terrible deeds, he almost always retains his conscience. For instance, after he murders Duncan he cannot sleep at night. When he tells Lady Macbeth that he has heard a voice saying, "Macbeth does murder sleep" (2.2.35), she ridicules him, but the voice is prophetic: he is doomed to sleepless nights. We in the audience are glad that Macbeth is tormented by his deed, since it shows that he knows he has done wrong and that he still has some decent human feelings.

A fourth reason why we retain some sympathy for Macbeth is that he eventually loses all of his allies, even his wife, and he stands before us a lonely, guilt-haunted figure. On this point, scene 2 of act 3 is especially significant. When Lady Macbeth asks Macbeth why he keeps to himself (line 8), he confides something of the mental stress that he is undergoing. But when she asks, "What's to be done?" (44), he cannot bring himself to tell her that he is plotting the deaths of Banquo and Fleance. Instead of further involving his wife, the only person with whom he might still have a human connection, Macbeth says, "Be innocent of the knowledge, dearest chuck [. . .]" (45). The word chuck, an affectionate form of chick, shows warmth and intimacy that are touching, but his refusal or his inability to confide in his wife and former partner in crime shows how fully isolated he is from all human contact. We cannot help feeling some sympathy for him.

Finally, Macbeth holds our interest, instead of disgusting us, because he speaks so wonderfully. The greatness of his language compels us to listen to him with rapt attention. Some speeches are very familiar, such as "My way of life / Is fall'n into the sear, the yellow leaf [. . .]" (5.3.23-24) and "Tomorrow and tomorrow and tomorrow / Creeps in this petty pace from day to day [. . .]" (5.5.19-20). But almost every speech Macbeth utters is equally memorable, from his first, "So foul and fair a day I have not seen" (1.3.38), to his last:

> Before my body
> I throw my warlike shield. Lay on, Macduff:
> And damned be him that first cries, "Hold, enough!"
>
> (5.8.32-34)

If we stand back and judge Macbeth only by what he does, we of course say that he is a foul murderer. But if we read the play attentively, or witness a performance, and give due weight to Macbeth's bravery, his role as a victim, his tormented conscience, his isolation, and especially his moving language, we do not simply judge him. Rather, we see that, villain though he is, he is not merely awful but also awesome.

[New page.]

Work Cited

Shakespeare, William. The Tragedy of Macbeth. Ed. Sylvan Barnet. Rev. ed. New York: NAL, 1987.

CHAPTER 50

Writing in Other Humanities

The humanities include literature, the visual arts, music, film, dance, history, philosophy, and religion. The preceding chapter discusses the particular requirements of reading and writing about literature. This chapter concentrates on history. Although the arts, religion, and other humanities have their own concerns, they share many important goals and methods with literature and history.

50a Using the methods and evidence of the humanities

Writers in the humanities record and speculate about the growth, ideas, and emotions of human beings. Based on the evidence of written words, artworks, and other human traces and creations, humanities writers explain, interpret, analyze, and reconstruct the human experience.

The discipline of history focuses particularly on reconstructing the past. In Greek the word for history means "to inquire": historians inquire into the past to understand the events of the past. Then they report, explain, analyze, and evaluate those events in their context, asking such questions as what happened before or after the events or how the events were related to then existing political and social structures.

Historians' reconstructions of the past—their conclusions about what happened and why—are always supported with reference to the written record. The evidence of history is mainly primary sources, such as eyewitness accounts and contemporary documents, letters, commercial records, and the like. For history papers, you might also be asked to support your conclusions with those in secondary sources.

In reading historical sources, you need to weigh and evaluate their evidence. If, for example, you find conflicting accounts of the same event, you need to consider the possible biases of the authors. In general, the more a historian's conclusions are supported by public records such as deeds, marriage licenses, and newspaper accounts, the more reliable the conclusions are likely to be.

50b Understanding writing assignments in the humanities

Papers in the humanities generally perform one or more of the following operations:

- Using **explanation,** you might show how a painter developed a particular technique or clarify a general's role in a historical battle.
- Using **analysis,** you might examine the elements of a philosophical argument or break down the causes of a historical event.
- Using **interpretation,** you might infer the meaning of a film from its images or the significance of a historical event from contemporary accounts of it.
- Using **synthesis,** you might find a pattern in a historical period or in a composer's works.
- Using **evaluation,** you might judge the quality of an architect's design or a historian's conclusions.

Most likely, you will use these operations in combination—say, interpreting and explaining the meaning of a painting and then evaluating it. (These operations are discussed in more detail in Chapter 5.)

50c Using the tools and language of the humanities

The tools and language of the humanities vary according to the discipline. Major reference works in each field, such as those listed on pages 819–22, can clarify specific tools you need and language you should use.

1 Writing tools

A useful tool for the arts is to ask a series of questions to analyze and evaluate a work. (A list of such questions for reading literature appears on pp. 797–98.) In any humanities discipline, a journal—a log of questions, reactions, and insights—can help you discover and record your thoughts. (See pp. 120–22 and 619–20.)

In history the tools are those of any thorough and efficient researcher, as discussed in Chapters 42–44: a system for finding and tracking sources (pp. 624–31); a methodical examination of sources, including evaluating and synthesizing them (pp. 667–74); a system for taking notes from sources (pp. 676–78); and a separate system, such as a research journal, for tracking one's own evolving thoughts (pp. 619–20).

2 Language considerations

Historians strive for precision and logic. They do not guess about what happened or speculate about "what if." They avoid trying to influence readers' opinions with words having strongly negative or positive connotations, such as *stupid* or *brilliant* (see p. 568). Instead, historians show the evidence and draw conclusions from that. Generally, they avoid using *I* because it tends to draw attention away from the evidence and toward the writer.

Writing about history demands some attention to the tenses of verbs to maintain consistency. (See pp. 318–25 for explanations of verb tenses.) Generally, historians use the past tense to refer to events that occurred in the past. They reserve the present tense only for statements about the present or statements of general truths. For example:

> Franklin Delano Roosevelt died in 1945. Many of Roosevelt's economic reforms persist in programs such as Social Security, unemployment compensation, and farm subsidies.

3 Research sources

The following lists give resources in the humanities. (Resources for literature appear on pp. 800–01.)

Specialized encyclopedias, dictionaries, and bibliographies

The arts

Architecture: From Prehistory to Post-Modernism
Crowell's Handbook of World Opera
Dance Encyclopedia
Dictionary of Art
Encyclopedia of Pop, Rock, and Soul
Encyclopedia of World Art
Film Research: A Critical Bibliography
Film Review Annual
Guide to the Literature of Art History
International Cyclopedia of Music and Musicians
International Encyclopedia of Communications
International Television and Radio Almanac
New Harvard Dictionary of Music
New Grove Dictionary of Music and Musicians
Oxford Companion to Twentieth-Century Art
Variety's Film Reviews

History

Afro-American Reference
Cambridge Ancient History
Cambridge History of China
Dictionary of American History
Dictionary of American Immigration History

Dictionary of the Middle Ages
Encyclopedia of Asian History
Encyclopedia of Latin-American History
Encyclopedia of World History
Guide to American Foreign Relations Since 1700
Guide to Research on North American Indians
Harvard Guide to American History
History: Illustrated Search Strategy and Sources
Modern Encyclopedia of Russian and Soviet History
New Cambridge Modern History
Oxford Classical Dictionary
The Study of the Middle East: Research and Scholarship in the Humanities and Social Sciences

Philosophy and religion

Catholic Encyclopedia
Concise Encyclopedia of Islam
Dictionary of the History of Ideas
Eastern Definitions: A Short Encyclopedia of Religions of the Orient
Encyclopedia Judaica
Encyclopedia of Ethics
Encyclopedia of Philosophy
Encyclopedia of Religion
Interpreter's Dictionary of the Bible
Library Research Guide to Religion and Theology
New Standard Jewish Encyclopedia
Oxford Dictionary of the Christian Church
Research Guide to Philosophy

Periodical indexes

America: History and Life
Art Index
Avery Index to Architectural Periodicals
Film Literature Index
Humanities Index
Musical Literature International
Music Index
Philosopher's Index
Religion Index

Abstracts and citation indexes

America: History and Life
Arts and Humanities Citation Index
Art Index
Dissertation Abstracts International (doctoral dissertations). Before 1969, the title was *Dissertation Abstracts.*
Historical Abstracts (world history)
Religious and Theological Abstracts

Book reviews

Book Review Digest
Book Review Index

Current Book Review Citations
Index to Book Reviews in the Humanities

Web sources

General

American Studies Web
http://georgetown.edu/crossroads/asw
Arts and Humanities Data Service
http://ahds.ac.uk
Biographies
http://biography.com/find/find.html
Internet Public Library
http://www.ipl.org/ref/RR/static/hum0000.html
Voice of the Shuttle Humanities Gateway
http://humanitas.ucsb.edu/shuttle/general.html#metapages
Oxford University Humanities Gateway
http://users.ox.ac.uk/~humbul

Art

Artnet.Com
http://www.artnet.com
ArtSeek
http://artseek.com
WebGems Art
http://www.fpsol.com/gems/art.html
World Wide Arts Resources
http://wwar.com

Dance

danceonline
http://www.danceonline.com
Sapphire Swan Dance Directory
http://www.SapphireSwan.com/dance

Film

Cinema Sites
http://www.cinema-sites.com
Mining Company's Classic Movies
http://classicfilm.miningco.com/entertainment/classicfilm
MovieWeb
http://www.movieweb.com
Performing Arts Cinema Links
http://www.theatrelibrary.org/links/Cinema.html

History

American and British History Resources on the Internet
http://www.libraries.rutgers.edu/rulib/socsci/hist/amhist3.htm
Gateway to World History
http://www.hartford-hwp.com/gateway
History Place
http://www.historyplace.com

Librarians' Index History Links
http://lii.org/search?title=History&query=History&subsearch=History&searchtype=subject

Music

All Music Guide
http://www.allmusic.com
American Music Resource
http://www.uncg.edu/~flmccart/amrhome.html
ARCANA: Artists' Research, Composers' Aid, and Network Access
http://www.arcananet.org
Web Resources for Study and Research in Music
http://www.ucc.ie/ucc/depts/music/online

Philosophy

Dictionary of Philosophical Terms and Names
http://people.delphi.com/gkemerling/dy/index.htm
Guide to Philosophy on the Internet
http://www.earlham.edu/~peters/philinks.htm
Philosophy Documentation Center
http://www.bgsu.edu/pdc
Resources from the American Philosophical Association
http://www.apa.udel.edu/apa/resources

Religion

American Academy of Religion
http://www.aar-site.org
Internet Resources for the Academic Study of Religion
http://www.academicinfo.net/religindex.html
Religion-Online
http://www.religion-online.org
Virtual Religion Index
http://religion.rutgers.edu/vri

Theater

McCoy's Guide to Theater and Performance Studies
http://www.stetson.edu/departments/csata/thr_guid.html
Queens University Resources
http://stauffer.queensu.ca/inforef/drama
Theater Connections
http://libweb.uncc.edu/ref-arts/theater
theatre-link.com
http://www.theatre-link.com

50d Citing sources in the humanities: Chicago style

Writers in the humanities generally rely on one of the following guides for source-citation style:

The Chicago Manual of Style. 14th ed. 1993.

Gibaldi, Joseph. *MLA Handbook for Writers of Research Papers.* 5th ed. 1999.

Turabian, Kate L. *A Manual for Writers of Term Papers, Theses, and Dissertations.* 6th ed. Rev. John Grossman and Alice Bennett. 1996.

The recommendations of the *MLA Handbook* are discussed and illustrated in Chapter 46. Unless your instructor specifies otherwise, use these recommendations for papers in English and foreign languages. In history, art history, and many other disciplines, however, writers rely on *The Chicago Manual* or the student reference adapted from it, *A Manual for Writers.*

Both books detail two documentation styles. One, used mainly by scientists and social scientists, closely resembles the style of the American Psychological Association, covered in Chapter 51. The other style, used more in the humanities, calls for footnotes or endnotes and an optional bibliography. This style is described below.

1 Using Chicago notes and a list of works cited

In the Chicago note style, a raised numeral in the text refers the reader to source information in endnotes or footnotes. In these notes, the first citation of each source contains all the information readers need to find the source. Thus your instructor may consider a list of works cited optional because it provides much the same information. Ask your instructor whether you should use footnotes or endnotes and whether you should include a list of works cited.

Whether providing footnotes or endnotes, use single spacing for each note and double spacing between notes. Separate footnotes from the text with a short line, as shown in this sample:

In 1901, Madras, Bengal, and Punjab were a few of the huge Indian provinces governed by the British viceroy.[6] British rule, observes Stuart Cary Welch, "seemed as permanent as Mount Everest."[7]

6. Martin Gilbert, *Atlas of British History* (New York: Dorset Press, 1968), 96.

7. Stuart Cary Welch, *India: Art and Culture* (New York: Metropolitan Museum of Art, 1985), 421.

http://www.press.uchicago.edu/Misc/Chicago/cmosfaq.html Answers to frequently asked questions about Chicago style, from the University of Chicago Press.

With endnotes, use the format below for a list of works cited, substituting the heading "NOTES" and numbered entries as for footnotes.

For the list of sources at the end of the paper, use the format below. Arrange the sources alphabetically by the authors' last names.

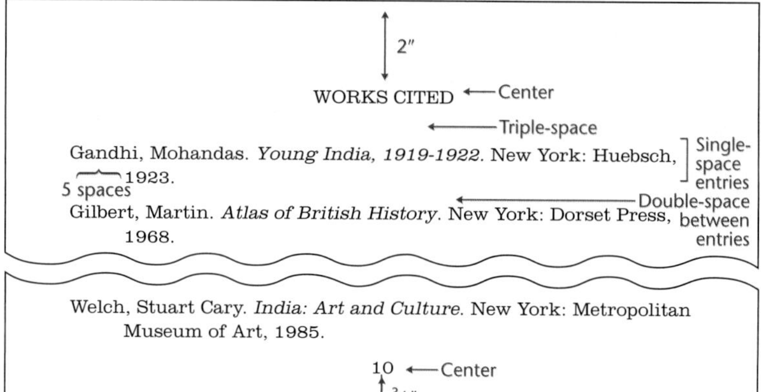

The examples below illustrate the essentials of a note and a works-cited entry.

Note

6. Martin Gilbert, *Atlas of British History* (New York: Dorset Press, 1968), 96.

Works-cited entry

Gilbert, Martin. *Atlas of British History.* New York: Dorset Press, 1968.

Notes and works-cited entries share certain features:

- Italicize or underline the titles of books and periodicals (ask your instructor for his or her preference).
- Enclose in quotation marks the titles of parts of books or articles in periodicals.
- Do not abbreviate publishers' names, but omit "Inc.," "Co.," and similar abbreviations.
- Do not use "p." or "pp." before page numbers.

Notes and works-cited entries also differ in important ways:

Note	Works-cited entry
Start with a number (typed on the line and followed by a period) that corresponds to the note number in the text.	Do not begin with a number.
Indent the first line five spaces.	Indent the second and subsequent lines five spaces.

Note	Works-cited entry
Give the author's name in normal order.	Begin with the author's last name.
Use commas between elements such as author's name and title.	Use periods between elements, followed by one space.
Enclose publication information in parentheses, with no preceding punctuation.	Precede the publication information with a period, and don't use parentheses.
Include the specific page number(s) you borrowed from, omitting "p." or "pp."	Omit page numbers except for parts of books or articles in periodicals.

Many computerized word-processing programs will automatically position footnotes at the bottoms of appropriate pages. Some will automatically number notes and renumber them if you add or delete one or more.

2 Following Chicago models

In these models for common sources, notes and works-cited entries appear together for easy reference. Be sure to use the numbered note form for notes and the unnumbered works-cited form for works-cited entries.

Books

1. A book with one, two, or three authors

1. Carol Gilligan, *In a Different Voice: Psychological Theory and Women's Development* (Cambridge: Harvard University Press, 1982), 27.

Gilligan, Carol. *In a Different Voice: Psychological Theory and Women's Development.* Cambridge: Harvard University Press, 1982.

1. Dennis L. Wilcox, Phillip H. Ault, and Warren K. Agee, *Public Relations: Strategies and Tactics,* 4th ed. (New York: HarperCollins, 1995), 182.

Wilcox, Dennis L., Phillip H. Ault, and Warren K. Agee. *Public Relations: Strategies and Tactics.* 4th ed. New York: HarperCollins, 1995.

2. A book with more than three authors

2. Geraldo Lopez and others, *China and the West* (Boston: Little, Brown, 1990), 461.

Lopez, Geraldo, Judith P. Salt, Anne Ming, and Henry Reisen. *China and the West.* Boston: Little, Brown, 1990.

Chicago note and works-cited models

3. A book with an editor

3. Hendrick Ruitenbeek, ed., *Freud as We Knew Him* (Detroit: Wayne State University Press, 1973), 64.

Ruitenbeek, Hendrick, ed. *Freud as We Knew Him*. Detroit: Wayne State University Press, 1973.

4. A book with an author and an editor

4. Lewis Mumford, *The City in History,* ed. Donald L. Miller (New York: Pantheon, 1986), 216-17.

Mumford, Lewis. *The City in History*. Edited by Donald L. Miller. New York: Pantheon, 1986.

5. A translation

5. Dante Alighieri, *The Inferno,* trans. John Ciardi (New York: New American Library, 1971), 51.

Alighieri, Dante. *The Inferno*. Translated by John Ciardi. New York: New American Library, 1971.

6. An anonymous work

6. *The Dorling Kindersley World Reference Atlas* (London: Dorling Kindersley, 1994), 150-51.

The Dorling Kindersley World Reference Atlas. London: Dorling Kindersley, 1994.

7. A later edition

7. Dwight L. Bollinger, *Aspects of Language,* 2d ed. (New York: Harcourt Brace Jovanovich, 1975), 20.

Bollinger, Dwight L. *Aspects of Language.* 2d ed. New York: Harcourt Brace Jovanovich, 1975.

8. A work in more than one volume

Citation of one volume without a title:

8. Abraham. Lincoln, *The Collected Works of Abraham Lincoln,* ed. Roy P. Basler (New Brunswick: Rutgers University Press, 1953), 5:426-28.

Lincoln, Abraham. *The Collected Works of Abraham Lincoln.* Edited by Roy P. Basler. Vol. 5. New Brunswick: Rutgers University Press, 1953.

Citation of one volume with a title:

8. Linda B. Welkin, *The Age of Balanchine,* vol. 3 of *The History of Ballet* (New York: Columbia University Press, 1969), 56.

Welkin, Linda B. *The Age of Balanchine.* Vol. 3 of *The History of Ballet.* New York: Columbia University Press, 1969.

9. A selection from an anthology

9. Rosetta Brooks, "Streetwise," in *The New Urban Landscape,* ed. Richard Martin (New York: Rizzoli, 1990), 38-39.

Brooks, Rosetta. "Streetwise." In *The New Urban Landscape,* ed. Richard Martin, 37-60. New York: Rizzoli, 1990.

10. A work in a series

10. Ingmar Bergman, *The Seventh Seal,* Modern Film Scripts Series, no. 12 (New York: Simon and Schuster, 1968), 27.

Bergman, Ingmar. *The Seventh Seal.* Modern Film Scripts Series, no. 12. New York: Simon and Schuster, 1968.

11. An article in a reference work

The abbreviation "s.v." in the examples stands for the Latin *sub verbo,* "under the word."

11. *Merriam-Webster's Collegiate Dictionary,* 10th ed., s.v. "reckon."

Merriam-Webster's Collegiate Dictionary, 10th ed., s.v. "reckon."

11. Mark F. Herman, "Polymers," in *The New Encyclopaedia Britannica. Macropaedia,* 16th ed.

Herman, Mark F. "Polymers." In *The New Encyclopaedia Britannica: Macropaedia,* 16th ed.

Periodicals: Journals, magazines, newspapers

12. An article in a journal with continuous pagination throughout the annual volume

12. Janet Lever, "Sex Differences in the Games Children Play," *Social Problems* 23 (1976): 482.

Lever, Janet. "Sex Differences in the Games Children Play." *Social Problems* 23 (1976): 478-87.

13. An article in a journal that pages issues separately

13. June Dacey, "Management Participation in Corporate Buy-Outs," *Management Perspectives* 7, no. 4 (1998): 22.

Dacey, June. "Management Participation in Corporate Buy-Outs." *Management Perspectives* 7, no. 4 (1998): 20-31.

14. An article in a popular magazine

14. Mark Stevens, "Low and Behold," *New Republic,* 24 December 1990, 28.

Stevens, Mark. "Low and Behold." *New Republic,* 24 December 1990, 27-33.

15. An article in a newspaper

15. Peter H. Lewis, "Many Updates Cause Profitable Confusion," *New York Times,* 21 January 1999, national ed., D5.

Lewis, Peter H. "Many Updates Cause Profitable Confusion." *New York Times,* 21 January 1999, national ed., D1, D5.

16. A review

16. John Gregory Dunne, "The Secret of Danny Santiago," review of *Famous All over Town,* by Danny Santiago, *New York Review of Books,* 16 August 1984, 25.

Dunne, John Gregory. "The Secret of Danny Santiago." Review of *Famous All over Town,* by Danny Santiago. *New York Review of Books,* 16 August 1984, 17-27.

Electronic sources

The Chicago Manual offers some models for documenting electronic sources, and *A Manual for Writers* updates these and adds a few more. For other electronic sources and simpler formats, you can use Columbia online style for the humanities, discussed in Chapter 53. Page 883 shows how to adapt Columbia style to Chicago style and details the differences between the two styles. Ask your instructor which style you should use for online sources.

Note Since Chicago style does not specify how to break electronic addresses in notes and works-cited entries, follow MLA style: break only after slashes, and do not hyphenate.

17. A source on a periodical CD-ROM

A source also published in print:

17. Peter H. Lewis, "Many Updates Cause Profitable Confusion," *New York Times,* 21 January 1999, national ed., D5. *New York Times Ondisc* [CD-ROM], UMI-ProQuest, March 1999.

Lewis, Peter H. "Many Updates Cause Profitable Confusion." *New York Times,* 21 January 1999, national ed., D1, D5. *New York Times Ondisc* [CD-ROM]. UMI-ProQuest, March 1999.

A source not published in print:

17. "Vanguard Forecasts," *Business Outlook* [CD-ROM], Information Access, March 1998.

"Vanguard Forecasts." *Business Outlook* [CD-ROM]. Information Access, March 1998.

18. A source on a nonperiodical CD-ROM

18. Mary Wollstonecraft Shelley, *Frankenstein, Classic Library* [CD-ROM] (Alameda, Calif.: Andromeda, 1993).

Shelley, Mary Wollstonecraft. *Frankenstein. Classic Library* [CD-ROM]. Alameda, Calif.: Andromeda, 1993.

19. An online book

19. Jane Austen, *Emma* [book online], ed. Ronald Blythe (Harmondsworth, Eng.: Penguin, 1972, accessed 15 December 1999), *Oxford Text Archive;* available from ftp://ota.ox.ac.uk/public/english/Austen/emma.1519; Internet.

Austen, Jane. *Emma* [book online]. Edited by Ronald Blythe. Harmondsworth, Eng.: Penguin, 1972. Accessed 15 December 1999. *Oxford Text Archive.* Available from ftp://ota.ox.ac.uk/public/english/Austen/emma.1519; Internet.

20. An article in an online periodical

20. Andrew Palfrey, "Choice of Mates in Identical Twins," *Modern Psychology* 4, no. 1 (1996): par. 10 [journal online]; available from http://www.liasu.edu/modpsy/palfrey4(1).htm; Internet; accessed 25 February 2000.

Palfrey, Andrew. "Choice of Mates in Identical Twins." *Modern Psychology* 4, no. 1 (1996): 12 pars. [journal online]. Available from http://www.liasu.edu/modpsy/palfrey4(1).htm; Internet. Accessed 25 February 2000.

21. An online database

21. *Scots Teaching and Research Network* [database online], ed. John Corbett (Glasgow: University of Glasgow, 2 February 1998, accessed 5 March 1999); available from http://www.arts.gla.ac.uk/www/comet/starn.htm; Internet.

Scots Teaching and Research Network [database online]. Edited by John Corbett. Glasgow: University of Glasgow, 2 February 1998. Accessed 5 March 1999. Available from http://www.arts.gla.ac.uk/www/comet/starn.htm; Internet.

Other sources

22. A government publication

22. House, *Medicare Payment for Outpatient Physical and Occupational Therapy Services,* 102d Cong., 1st sess., 1991, H. Doc. 409, 12-13.

U.S. Congress. House. *Medicare Payment for Outpatient Physical and Occupational Therapy Services.* 102d Cong., 1st sess., 1991. H. Doc. 409.

23. A letter

A published letter:

23. Mrs. Laura E. Buttolph to Rev. and Mrs. C. C. Jones, 20 June 1857, *The Children of Pride: A True Story of Georgia and the Civil War,* ed. Robert Manson Myers (New Haven: Yale University Press, 1972), 334.

Buttolph, Mrs. Laura E. Letter to Rev. and Mrs. C. C. Jones, 20 June 1857. In *The Children of Pride; A True Story of Georgia and the Civil War,* ed. Robert Manson Myers. New Haven: Yale University Press, 1972.

A personal letter:

23. Ann E. Packer, letter to author, 15 June 1998.

Packer, Ann E. Letter to author. 15 June 1998.

24. An interview

24. Warren Christopher, interview by William Lindon, *Frontline,* Public Broadcasting System, 13 February 1998.

Christopher, Warren. Interview by William Lindon. *Frontline.* Public Broadcasting System, 13 February 1998.

25. A work of art

25. John Singer Sargent, *In Switzerland,* watercolor, 1908, Metropolitan Museum of Art, New York.

Sargent, John Singer. *In Switzerland,* watercolor, 1908. Metropolitan Museum of Art, New York.

26. A film or video recording

26. *Serenade,* George Balanchine, San Francisco Ballet, PBS Video, 1985, videocassette.

Serenade. George Balanchine. San Francisco Ballet. PBS Video, 1985. Videocassette.

27. A sound recording

27. Johannes Brahms, Concerto no. 2 in B-flat, Artur Rubinstein, Philadelphia Orchestra, Eugene Ormandy, RCA BRC4-6731, 1992.

Brahms, Johannes, Concerto no. 2 in B-flat. Artur Rubinstein. Philadelphia Orchestra. Eugene Ormandy. RCA BRC4-6731, 1992.

Two or more citations of the same source

To minimize clutter and give a quick sense of how often you cite a source, the Chicago style allows a shortened form for subsequent citations of a source you have already cited fully.

You may use the Latin abbreviation "ibid." (meaning "in the same place") to refer to the same source cited in the preceding note:

8. Janet Lever, "Sex Differences in the Games Children Play." *Social Problems* 23 (1976): 482.

9. Ibid., 483.

For any source already cited in your notes, not just immediately before, you may use the author's name and (if the author is responsible for more than one cited source) a shortened form of the title:

1. Carol Gilligan, *In a Different Voice: Psychological Theory and Women's Development* (Cambridge: Harvard University Press, 1982), 27.

2. Carol Gilligan, "Moral Development in the College Years," *The Modern American College,* ed. A. Chickering (San Francisco: Jossey-Bass, 1981), 286.

3. Gilligan, *In a Different Voice,* 47.

Omit the title if you are using only one source by the cited author.

The Chicago style recommends in-text parenthetical citations when you cite one or more works repeatedly. This practice allows you to avoid many notes saying "ibid." or giving the same author's name. In the example following, the note number refers to the complete source information in an endnote; the numbers in parentheses are page numbers in the same source.

British rule, observes Stuart Cary Welch, "seemed as permanent as Mount Everest."[7] Most Indians submitted, willingly or not, to British influence in every facet of life (423-24).

50e Formatting documents in the humanities: Chicago style

In some humanities classes your instructor may ask you to follow MLA style for document format. (See Chapter 46 for a discussion of MLA style.) If your instructor asks you to follow Chicago style, use the guidelines below, which are adapted from Turabian's *Manual for Writers.*

- Provide a title page (not numbered) with at least the full title of the paper, your name, and the date. As in the example below, you may also include other information requested by your instructor, such as the course title and the instructor's name. Use all-capital letters, and center everything horizontally and vertically on the page. Double-space between adjacent lines, adding extra space where shown in the example.

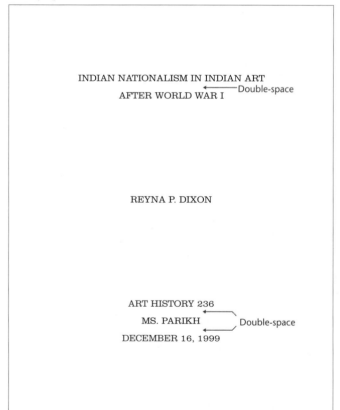

Title page

INDIAN NATIONALISM IN INDIAN ART
AFTER WORLD WAR I

Double-space

REYNA P. DIXON

ART HISTORY 236
MS. PARIKH
DECEMBER 16, 1999

Double-space

- On the paper's first text page, center your title two inches from the top. Type the title in all-capital letters. Treat section titles, such as "NOTES" and "WORKS CITED," the same way (see the illustration on p. 824). Triple-space beneath the title or heading.
- Number text pages with a number only, consecutively from the first page through the entire paper. On the first page of the paper and the first page of any endnotes and the bibliography, place the page number at the bottom of the page, centered (see the illustration on p. 824). On all other pages, place the number at the top, either centered or at the right margin, and double-space to the text below.
- Set long quotations off from your text: poetry quotations of three or more lines and prose quotations of two or more sentences and eight or more lines. (You may display shorter prose quotations to emphasize them or to compare them.) Double-space above and below a displayed quotation, and single-space the quotation itself. Indent the quotation four spaces from the left margin. Do not use quotation marks for a displayed quotation.

CHAPTER 51

Writing in the Social Sciences

The social sciences—including anthropology, economics, education, management, political science, psychology, and sociology—focus on the study of human behavior. As the name implies, the social sciences examine the way human beings relate to themselves, to their environment, and to one another.

51a Using the methods and evidence of the social sciences

Researchers in the social sciences systematically pose a question, formulate a **hypothesis** (a generalization that can be tested), collect data, analyze those data, and draw conclusions to support, refine, or disprove their hypothesis. This is the scientific method developed in the natural sciences (see p. 863).

Social scientists gather data in several ways:

- They make firsthand observations of human behavior and record the observations in writing or on audio- or videotape.
- They interview subjects about their attitudes and behavior, recording responses in writing or on tape. (See pp. 664–65 for guidelines on conducting an interview.)
- They conduct broader surveys using questionnaires that ask people about their attitudes and behavior. (See the box on the facing page.)
- They conduct controlled experiments, structuring an environment in which to encourage and measure a specific behavior.

In their writing, social scientists explain their own research or analyze and evaluate others' research.

The research methods of social science generate two kinds of data:

- **Quantitative data** are numerical, such as statistical evidence based on surveys, polls, tests, and experiments. When public-opinion pollsters announce that 47 percent of US citizens polled approve of the President's leadership, they are offering

Conducting a survey

- Decide what you want to find out—what your hypothesis is. The questions you ask should be dictated by your purpose.
- Define your population. Think about the kinds of people your hypothesis is about—for instance, college men, or five-year-old children. Plan to sample this population so that your findings will be representative.
- Write your questions. Surveys may contain closed questions that direct the respondent's answers (checklists and multiple-choice, true/false, or yes/no questions) or open-ended questions allowing brief, descriptive answers. Avoid loaded questions that reveal your own biases or make assumptions about subjects' answers, such as "Do you want the United States to support democracy in China?" or "How much more money does your father make than your mother?"
- Test your questions on a few respondents with whom you can discuss the answers. Eliminate or recast questions that respondents find unclear, discomforting, or unanswerable.
- Tally the results in actual numbers of answers, including any nonanswers.
- Seek patterns in the raw data that conform or conflict with your hypothesis. Revise the hypothesis or conduct additional research if necessary.

quantitative data gained from a survey. Social science writers present quantitative data in graphs, charts, and other illustrations that accompany their text.

- **Qualitative data** are not numerical but more subjective: they are based on interviews, firsthand observations, and inferences, taking into account the subjective nature of human experience. Examples of qualitative data include an anthropologist's description of the initiation ceremonies in a culture she is studying or a psychologist's interpretation of interviews he conducted with a group of adolescents.

51b Understanding writing assignments in the social sciences

Depending on what social science courses you take, you may be asked to complete a variety of assignments:

- **A summary or review of research** reports on the available research literature on a subject, such as infants' perception of color.

- **A case analysis** explains the components of a phenomenon, such as a factory closing.
- **A problem-solving analysis** explains the components of a problem, such as unreported child abuse, and suggests ways to solve it.
- **A research paper** interprets and sometimes analyzes and evaluates the writings of other social scientists about a subject, such as the effect of national appeals in advertising. An example appears in Chapter 47, page 746.
- **A research report** explains the author's own original research or the author's attempt to replicate someone else's research. A research report begins on page 859.

Many social science disciplines have special requirements for the content and organization of each kind of paper. The requirements appear in the style guides of the disciplines, listed on page 841. For instance, the American Psychological Association specifies the outline for research reports that is illustrated on pages 855–57. Because of the differences among disciplines and even among different kinds of papers in the same discipline, you should always ask your instructor what he or she requires for an assignment.

51c Using the tools and language of the social sciences

The following guidelines for tools and language apply to most social sciences. However, the particular discipline you are writing in, or an instructor in a particular course, may have additional requirements. Many of the research sources listed on pages 837–40 can tell you more about your discipline's conventions.

1 Writing tools

Many social scientists rely on a **research journal** or **log,** in which they record their ideas throughout the research-writing process. Even if a research journal is not required in your courses, you may want to use one. As you begin formulating a hypothesis, you can record preliminary questions. Then in the field (that is, when conducting research), you can use the journal to react to the evidence you are collecting, to record changes in your perceptions and ideas, and to assess your progress. (See pp. 19–21, 120–25, and 619–20 for more on journals.)

To avoid confusing your reflections on the evidence with the evidence itself, keep records of actual data—notes from interviews, observations, surveys, and experiments—separately from the journal.

2 Language considerations

Each social science discipline has specialized terminology for concepts basic to the discipline. In sociology, for example, the words *mechanism, identity,* and *deviance* have specific meanings different from those of everyday usage. And *identity* means something different in sociology, where it applies to groups of people, than in psychology, where it applies to the individual. Social scientists also use precise terms to describe or interpret research. For instance, they say *The subject expressed a feeling of* . . . rather than *The subject felt* . . . because human feelings are not knowable for certain; or they say *These studies indicate* . . . rather than *These studies prove* . . . because conclusions are only tentative.

Just as social scientists strive for objectivity in their research, so they strive to demonstrate their objectivity through language in their writing. They avoid expressions such as *I think* in order to focus attention on what the evidence shows rather than on the researcher's opinions. (However, many social scientists prefer *I* to the artificial *the researcher* when they refer to their own actions, as in *I then interviewed the subjects.* Ask your instructor for his or her preferences.) Social scientists also avoid direct or indirect expression of their personal biases or emotions, either in discussions of other researchers' work or in descriptions of research subjects. Thus one social scientist does not call another's work *sloppy* or *immaculate* and does not refer to his or her own subjects as *drunks* or *innocent victims.* Instead, the writer uses neutral language and ties conclusions strictly to the data.

3 Research sources

Specialized encyclopedias, dictionaries, and bibliographies

General

International Bibliography of the Social Sciences
International Encyclopedia of the Social Sciences
New Dictionary of the Social Sciences

Business and Economics

Accountant's Handbook
Dictionary of Business and Economics
Encyclopedia of Advertising
Encyclopedia of Banking and Finance
Encyclopedia of Business Information Sources
Encyclopedia of Management
Handbook of Modern Marketing
McGraw-Hill Encyclopedia of Economics
The MIT Dictionary of Modern Economics
The New Palgrave: A Dictionary of Economics

Education

Bibliographic Guide to Education
Encyclopedia of American Education
Encyclopedia of Education
Encyclopedia of Educational Research
The Philosophy of Education: An Encyclopedia

Political science and law

Black's Law Dictionary
Guide to American Law
Index to Legal Books
Information Sources of Political Sciences
Political Science: A Guide to Reference and Information Sources

Psychology, sociology, and anthropology

African American Encyclopedia
Afro-American Reference
Asian American Studies
Bibliographic Guide to Psychology
Encyclopedia of Anthropology
Encyclopedia of Crime and Justice
Encyclopedia of Psychology
Encyclopedia of Sociology
Guide to Research on North American Indians
Library Use: A Handbook for Psychology
Race and Ethnic Relations: A Bibliography
Sociology: A Guide to Reference and Information Sources
Sourcebook of Hispanic Culture in the United States

Periodical indexes

ABC: Pol Sci
ABI/INFORM (business)
Business Periodicals Index
Business Publications Index and Abstracts
Criminal Justice Periodicals Index
Education Index
ERIC (Education Resources Information Center). *Current Index to Journals in Education*
Index to Legal Periodicals
Journal of Economic Literature
PAIS International in Print (government publications and political science journals)
Psychological Abstracts
Social Sciences Index
Sociofile
Sociological Index

Abstracts and citation indexes

Abstracts in Anthropology

Business Publications Index and Abstracts
Criminal Justice and Police Science Abstracts
Dissertation Abstracts International (doctoral dissertations). Before 1969, the title was *Dissertation Abstracts.*
Human Resources Abstracts
Index to Legal Periodicals
International Political Science Abstracts
Journal of Economic Literature
PAIS International in Print (government publications and political science journals)
Psychological Abstracts or *PsychLIT*
Social Sciences Citation Index
Social Sciences Index
Sociological Abstracts
Sociological Index
Urban Affairs Abstracts
Wilson Business Abstracts

Book reviews

Index to Book Reviews in the Social Sciences

Web Sources

General

National Council for the Social Sciences
http://www.ncss.org
Social Sciences Data on the Net
http://odwin.ucsd.edu/idata
World Wide Web Virtual Library's Social Science Resources
http://web.clas.ufl.edu/users/gthursby/socsci

Anthropology

American Anthropological Association
http://www.ameranthassn.org
Anthro.Net
http://www.anthro.net
Anthropological Resources on the Internet
http://home.worldnet.fr/clist/Anthro/index.html
ArchNet
http://archnet.uconn.edu

Business and economics

Internet Business Library
http://www.bschool.ukans.edu/IntBusLib
Nyenrode Business Information Services
http://www.library.nijenrode.nl
Scout Report for Business and Economics
http://scout.cs.wisc.edu/report/bus-econ/current/index.html
World Wide Web Resources in Economics
http://www.helsinki.fi/WebEc

Education

AskERIC
http://ericir.syr.edu
EDUCAUSE
http://www.educause.edu
EdWeb
http://edweb.gsn.org
US Department of Education
http://www.ed.gov

Ethnic and gender studies

Ethnic Studies at USC
http://www.usc.edu/isd/archives/ethnicstudies
Race and Race Relations on the Internet
http://www.library.miami.edu/netguides/socrace.html
Voice of the Shuttle Gender Studies Page
http://vos.ucsb.edu/shuttle/gender.html
Women's and Gender Studies Database
http://www.uni-koeln.de/phil-fak/englisch/datenbank/e_index.htm

Political science and law

American Political Science Association Online
http://www.apsanet.org
Internet Legal Resource Guide
http://www.ilrg.com
Librarians' Index Law Resources
http://lii.org/search/file/law
Political Science Resources
http://www.psr.keele.ac.uk

Psychology

American Psychological Association
http://www.apa.org
Mental Health Net
http://mentalhelp.net
PsychCrawler
http://www.psychcrawler.com
University of Houston's Psychology Resources
http://info.lib.uh.edu/indexes/psych.htm

Sociology

American Sociological Association
http://www.asanet.org
Electronic Journals in Sociology
http://www.lib.uwaterloo.ca/discipline/sociology/journals.html
Selected Electronic Journals in Sociology
http://www.library.uiuc.edu/edx/socejour.htm
SocioWeb
http://www.socioweb.com/~markbl/socioweb

51d Citing sources in the social sciences: APA style

As mentioned earlier, some of the social sciences publish style guides that advise practitioners how to organize, document, and type papers. The following is a partial list:

American Anthropological Association. "Style Guide and Information for Authors." *American Anthropologist* (1977): 774–79.
American Political Science Association. *Style Manual for Political Science*. Rev. ed. 1993.
American Psychological Association. *Publication Manual of the American Psychological Association*. 4th ed. 1994.
American Sociological Association. "Editorial Guidelines." Inside front cover of each issue of *American Sociological Review*.
Columbia Law Review. *A Uniform System of Citation*. 16th ed. 1996.
Linguistic Society of America. "LSA Style Sheet." Printed every December in *LSA Bulletin*.

By far the most widely used style is that of the American Psychological Association (APA), so we detail it here. Always ask your instructor in any discipline what style you should use.

Note If you use APA style frequently and write on a computer, you may want to obtain APA-Style Helper, a student's companion to the *Publication Manual of the American Psychological Association* that formats source citations in APA style. It can be downloaded (for a fee) from the APA Web site given at the bottom of this page. Other bibliography programs can also help with APA style. See page 699 for more on such programs.

 1 Using APA parenthetical text citations

In the APA documentation style, parenthetical citations within the text refer the reader to a list of sources at the end of the text. A parenthetical citation contains the author's last name, the date of publication, and sometimes the page number from which material is borrowed. See the next page for an index to the models for various kinds of sources.

http://www.apa.org/journals/acorner.html Answers to frequently asked questions about APA style, from the American Psychological Association.

http://owl.english.purdue.edu/Files/34.html Guidance on using APA style, from the Purdue Online Writing Lab.

APA
51d

APA parenthetical text citations

1. Author not named in your text

> One critic of Milgram's experiments insisted that the subjects "should have been fully informed of the possible effects on them" (Baumrind, 1968, p. 34).

When you do not name the author in your text, place in parentheses the author's name and the date of the source. The APA requires page number(s) preceded by "p." or "pp." for direct quotations (as in the example) and recommends them for paraphrases. Separate the elements with commas. Position the reference so that it is clear what material is being documented *and* so that the reference fits as smoothly as possible into your sentence structure. (See pp. 716–18 for guidelines.) The following would also be correct:

> In the view of one critic of Milgram's experiments (Baumrind, 1968), the subjects "should have been fully informed of the possible effects on them" (p. 34).

2. Author named in your text

> Baumrind (1968) insisted that the subjects in Milgram's study "should have been fully informed of the possible effects on them" (p. 34).

When you use the author's name in the text, do not repeat it in the reference. Place the reference next to the author's name. If you cite the same source again in the paragraph, you need not repeat the reference as long as it is clear that you are using the same source and the page number (if any) is the same. Here is a later sentence from the paragraph containing the preceding example:

> Baumrind also criticized the experimenters' rationale.

3. A work with two authors

Pepinsky and DeStefano (1987) demonstrate that a teacher's language often reveals hidden biases.

One study (Pepinsky & DeStefano, 1987) demonstrates the hidden biases often revealed in a teacher's language.

When given in the text, two authors' names are connected by "and." In a parenthetical citation, they are connected by an ampersand, "&."

4. A work with three to five authors

Pepinsky, Dunn, Rentl, and Corson (1993) further demonstrate the biases evident in gestures.

In the first citation of a work with three to five authors, name all the authors, as in the example above.

In the second and subsequent references to a work with three to five authors, generally give only the first author's name, followed by "et al." (Latin for "and others"):

In the work of Pepinsky et al. (1993), the loaded gestures include head shakes and eye contact.

However, two or more sources published in the same year could shorten to the same form—for instance, two references shortening to Pepinsky et al., 1993. In that case, cite the last names of as many authors as you need to distinguish the sources, and then give "et al.": for instance, (Pepinsky, Dunn, et al., 1993) and (Pepinsky, Bradley, et al., 1993).

5. A work with six or more authors

One study (Rutter et al., 1996) attempts to explain these geographical differences in adolescent experience.

For six or more authors, even in the first citation of the work, give only the first author's name, followed by "et al." If two or more sources published in the same year shorten to the same form, give additional names as explained with model 4, above.

6. A work with a group author

An earlier prediction was even more somber (Lorenz Research, 1997).

For a work that lists an institution, agency, corporation, or other group as author, treat the name of the group as if it were an individual's name.

7. An anonymous work

One article ("Right to Die," 1976) noted that a death-row inmate may crave notoriety.

For an anonymous or unsigned work, use the first two or three words of the title in place of an author's name, excluding an initial *The, A,* or *An.* Underline book and journal titles. Place quotation marks around article titles. (In the list of references, however, do not use quotation marks for article titles. See pp. 850–51.) Capitalize the significant words in all titles cited in the text. (But in the reference list, treat only periodical titles this way. See pp. 850–51.)

8. One of two or more works by the same author(s)

At about age seven, most children begin to use appropriate gestures to reinforce their stories (Gardner, 1973a).

When you cite one of two or more works by the same author(s), the date will tell readers which source you mean—as long as your reference list includes only one source published by the author(s) in that year. If your reference list includes two or more works published by the same author(s) *in the same year,* the works should be lettered in the reference list (see p. 849). Then your parenthetical citation should include the appropriate letter, as in "1973a" above.

9. Two or more works by different authors

Two studies (Herskowitz, 1994; Marconi & Hamblen, 1990) found that periodic safety instruction can dramatically reduce employees' accidents.

List the sources in alphabetical order by the first author's name. Insert a semicolon between sources.

10. An indirect source

Supporting data appear in a study by Wong (cited in Marconi & Hamblen, 1990).

The phrase "cited in" indicates that the reference to Wong's study was found in Marconi and Hamblen. Only Marconi and Hamblen then appears in the list of references.

11. An electronic source

Ferguson and Hawkins (1998) did not anticipate the "evident hostility" of participants (par. 6).

Electronic sources can be cited like printed sources, usually with the author's last name and the publication date. When quoting or paraphrasing electronic sources that number paragraphs instead of pages, provide that information in the text citation, substituting "par." (or "pars.") for "p." (or "pp."). If the source does not have numbering of any kind, provide just the author's name and the date.

2 Using an APA reference list

In APA style, the in-text parenthetical citations refer to the list of sources at the end of the text. This list, titled "References," includes full publication information on every source cited in the paper. The list falls at the end of the paper, numbered in sequence with the preceding pages.

The following sample shows the format of the first page of the APA reference list:

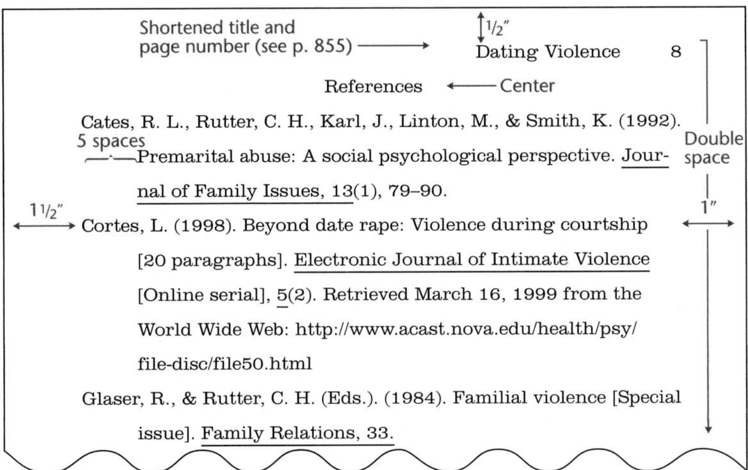

Arrangement

Arrange sources alphabetically by the author's last name or, if there is no author, by the first main word of the title.

Spacing

Double-space all entries.

Indention

Use an appropriate indention for each entry. For papers that will be published, the APA recommends indenting the first line of each entry five to seven spaces, as follows:

Rodriguez, R. (1982). A hunger of memory: The education of Richard Rodriguez. Boston: Godine.

When set into type for publication, the initial indentions are then converted into so-called hanging indentions, in which the first line is not indented while the others are. The hanging indention makes it easier for readers to spot authors' names, so the APA recognizes that students who are preparing final copy (not destined for publication) may wish to use the hanging indention for their references, like so:

Rodriguez, R. (1982). A hunger of memory: The education of Richard Rodriguez. Boston: Godine.

Because it is clearer for readers, the hanging indention is used in the sample on the previous page and in the following models for references, with a five-space indention for the second and subsequent lines of each entry.

Ask your instructor which format he or she prefers.

Punctuation

Separate the parts of the reference (author, date, title, and publication information) with a period and one space. Do not use a final period in references to electronic sources, which conclude with an electronic address (see pp. 851–53).

Authors

List all authors with last name first, separating names and parts of names with commas. Use initials for first and middle names. Use an ampersand (&) before the last author's name.

Publication date

Place the publication date in parentheses after the author's or authors' names, followed by a period. Generally, this date is the year only, though for some sources (such as magazine and newspaper articles) it includes month and sometimes day as well.

Titles

In titles of books and articles, capitalize only the first word of the title, the first word of the subtitle, and proper nouns; all other words begin with small letters. In titles of journals, capitalize all significant words. Unless your instructor specifies italics, underline the titles of books and journals, along with any comma or period following. Do not underline or use quotation marks around the titles of articles.

City of publication

For sources that are not periodicals (such as books or government publications), give the city of publication. The following US cities do not require state names as well: Baltimore, Boston, Chicago, Los Angeles, New York, Philadelphia, and San Francisco.

Follow their names with a colon. For all other cities, add a comma after the city name and give the two-letter postal abbreviation of the state (see p. 906). Then put a colon after the state.

Publisher's name

Also for nonperiodical sources, give the publisher's name after the place of publication and a colon. Use shortened names for many publishers (such as "Morrow" for William Morrow), and omit "Co.," "Inc.," and "Publishers." However, give full names for associations, corporations, and university presses (such as "Harvard University Press"), and do not omit "Books" or "Press" from a publisher's name.

Page numbers

Use the abbreviation "p." or "pp." before page numbers in books and in newspapers, but *not* in other periodicals. For inclusive page numbers, include all figures: "667–668."

Note If the following pages don't provide a model for a kind of source you used, try to find one that comes close, and provide ample information so that readers can trace the source. Often, you will have to combine models to cite a source accurately—for instance, combining "A book with two or more authors" (2) and "An article in a journal" (11) for a journal article with two or more authors.

Books

1. A book with one author

Rodriguez, R. (1982). A hunger of memory: The education of Richard Rodriguez. Boston: Godine.

The initial "R" appears instead of the author's first name, even though the author's full first name appears on the source. In the title, only the first words of title and subtitle and the proper name are capitalized.

2. A book with two or more authors

Nesselroade, J. R., & Baltes, P. B. (1999). Longitudinal research in behavioral studies. New York: Academic Press.

An ampersand (&) separates the authors' names.

3. A book with an editor

Dohrenwend, B. S., & Dohrenwend, B. P. (Eds.). (1994). Stressful life events: Their nature and effects. New York: Wiley.

List the editors' names as if they were authors, but follow the last name with "(Eds.)."—or "(Ed.)." with only one editor. Note the periods inside and outside the final parenthesis.

APA References

APA 51d

4. A book with a translator

Trajan, P. D. (1927). Psychology of animals (H. Simone, Trans.). Washington, DC: Halperin.

The name of the translator appears in parentheses after the title, followed by a comma, "Trans.," a closing parenthesis, and a final period. Note also the absence of periods in "DC."

5. A book with a group author

Lorenz Research. (1997). Research in social studies teaching. Baltimore: Arrow Books.

For a work with a group author—such as a research group, government agency, or corporation—begin the entry with the group name.

In the references list, alphabetize the work as if the first main word (excluding *The, A,* and *An*) were an author's last name.

6. An anonymous book

Merriam-Webster's collegiate dictionary (10th ed.). (1997). Springfield, MA: Merriam-Webster.

When no author is named, list the work under its title, and alphabetize it by the first main word (excluding *The, A, An*).

7. Two or more works by the same author(s) published in the same year

Gardner, H. (1973a). The arts and human development. New York: Wiley.

Gardner, H. (1973b). The quest for mind: Piaget, Lévi-Strauss, and the structuralist movement. New York: Knopf.

When citing two or more works by exactly the same author(s), published in the same year—as in the examples above—arrange them alphabetically by the first main word of the title and distinguish the sources by adding a letter to the date. Both the date *and* the letter are used in citing the source in your text (see p. 844).

When citing two or more works by exactly the same author(s) but *not* published in the same year, arrange the sources in order of their publication dates, earliest first.

8. A later edition

Bollinger, D. L. (1975). Aspects of language (2nd ed.). New York: Harcourt Brace Jovanovich.

The edition number in parentheses follows the title and is followed by a period.

9. A work in more than one volume

Lincoln, A. (1953). The collected works of Abraham Lincoln (R. P. Basler, Ed.). (Vol. 5). New Brunswick, NJ: Rutgers University Press.

Lincoln, A. (1953). The collected works of Abraham Lincoln (R. P. Basler, Ed.). (Vols. 1-8). New Brunswick, NJ: Rutgers University Press.

The first entry cites a single volume (5) in the eight-volume set. The second cites all eight volumes. Use the abbreviation "Vol." or "Vols." in parentheses, and follow the closing parenthesis with a period. In the absence of an editor's name, the description of volumes would follow the title directly: The collected works of Abraham Lincoln (Vol. 5).

10. An article or chapter in an edited book

Paykel, E. S. (1994). Life stress and psychiatric disorder: Applications of the clinical approach. In B. S. Dohrenwend & B. P. Dohrenwend (Eds.), Stressful life events: Their nature and effects (pp. 239-264). New York: Wiley.

Give the publication date of the collection (1994 above) as the publication date of the article or chapter. After the article or chapter title and a period, say "In" and then provide the editors' names (in normal order), "(Eds.)" and a comma, the title of the collection, and the page numbers of the article in parentheses.

Periodicals: Journals, magazines, newspapers

11. An article in a journal with continuous pagination throughout the annual volume

Emery, R. E. (1992). Marital turmoil: Interpersonal conflict and the children of discord and divorce. Psychological Bulletin, 92, 310-330.

See page 647 for an explanation of journal pagination. Note that you do not place the article title in quotation marks and that you capitalize only the first words of the title and subtitle. In contrast, you underline the journal title and capitalize all significant words. Separate the volume number from the title with a comma, and underline the number. Do not add "pp." before the page numbers.

12. An article in a journal that pages issues separately

Dacey, J. (1998). Management participation in corporate buy-outs. Management Perspectives, 7(4), 20-31.

Consult page 647 for an explanation of journal pagination. In this case, place the issue number in parentheses after the volume number without intervening space. Do *not* underline the issue number.

13. An abstract of a journal article

Emery, R. E. (1992). Marital turmoil: Interpersonal conflict and the children of discord and divorce. Psychological Bulletin, 92, 310-330. (From Psychological Abstracts, 69, Item 1320)

When you cite the abstract of an article, rather than the article itself, give full publication information for the article, followed, in parentheses, by the information for the collection of abstracts, including title, volume number, and either page number or other reference number ("Item 1320" above). If it is not otherwise clear that you are citing an abstract (because the word *abstract* does not appear in the title of the periodical or of the abstracts collection), add "[Abstract]" between the source title and the following period. See model 19 on the next page for an example.

14. An article in a magazine

Van Gelder, L. (1996, December). Countdown to motherhood: When should you have a baby? Ms., 37-39, 74.

If a magazine has volume and issue numbers, give them as in models 11 and 12. Also give the full date of the issue: year, followed by a comma, month, and day (if any). Give all page numbers even when the article appears on discontinuous pages, without "pp."

15. An article in a newspaper

Lewis, P. H. (1999, January 21). Many updates cause profitable confusion. The New York Times, pp. D1, D5.

Give month *and* day along with year of publication. Use The in the newspaper name if the paper itself does. For a newspaper (unlike a journal or magazine), precede the page number(s) with "p." or "pp."

16. An unsigned article

The right to die. (1976, October 11). Time, 121, 101.

List and alphabetize the article under its title, as you would an anonymous book (model 6, p. 849).

17. A review

Dinnage, R. (1987, November 29). Against the master and his men [Review of the book A mind of her own: The life of Karen Horney]. The New York Times Book Review, 10-11.

If the review is not titled, use the bracketed information as the title, keeping the brackets.

Electronic sources

The APA *Publication Manual* includes a few models for electronic sources. More recently, the APA Web site (see p. 841) has added new models that extend and in some ways alter those in the *Publication Manual.* The following examples reflect the more recent guidelines when appropriate.

In general, the APA's electronic-source references begin as those for print references do: author(s), date, title. Then you add information on when and how you retrieved the source—for example, Retrieved January 8, 1999 from the World Wide Web: http://www.liasu.edu/finance-dl/46732 (in APA style, no period follows an electronic address at the end of the reference).

Two sources provide more models for electronic sources based on APA style. Each one also differs from APA style, however, so ask your instructor which style you should use.

- Columbia online style for the sciences is discussed in this book's Chapter 53. The differences between APA and Columbia are outlined on page 887.
- Xia Li and Nancy B. Crane's *Electronic Style: A Guide to Citing Electronic Information* (1993) was a source for the APA *Publication Manual.* Li and Crane's formats have since been updated at *http://www.uvm.edu/%7encrane/estyles/apa.html.*

Note Since APA sources do not specify how to break electronic addresses in references, follow MLA style: break only after slashes, and do not hyphenate.

18. A periodical article on CD-ROM

Emery, R. E. (1992). Marital turmoil: Interpersonal conflict and the children of discord and divorce. Psychological Bulletin, 92, 310-330. Retrieved from ERIC database (ERIC Document Reproduction Service, CD-ROM, No. EJ 426 821)

19. An abstract on CD-ROM

Willard, B. L. (1992). Changes in occupational safety standards, 1970-1990 [Abstract]. Retrieved from UMI-ProQuest (Dissertation Abstracts, CD-ROM, Item 7770763)

20. An article in an online journal

Palfrey, A. (1996). Choice of mates in identical twins. Modern Psychology, 4(1). Retrieved February 25, 2000 from the World Wide Web: http://www.liasu.edu/modpsy/palfrey4(1).htm

21. An article in an online newspaper

Still, L. (1996, March 3). On the battlefields of business, millions of casualties. The New York Times on the Web. Retrieved August 17, 1999 from the World Wide Web: http://www.nytimes.com/specials/downsize/03downl.htm

22. A retrievable online posting

Tourville, M. (1999, January 6). European currency reform. International Finance Discussion List. Retrieved January 8, 1999 from the World Wide Web: http://www.liasu.edu/finance-dl/46732

Include postings to discussion lists and newsgroups in your list of references only if they are retrievable by others. The source above is archived and thus retrievable.

23. A nonretrievable online posting

At least one member of the research team has expressed reservations about the design of the study (L. Kogod, personal communication, February 6, 2000).

Personal electronic mail and other online postings that are not retrievable by others should be cited only in your text, as in the example above. If the author's name is given in the text, omit it from the citation: (personal communication, February 6, 2000).

24. A source from an online database

Wilkins, J. M. (1999, December 12). The myths of the only child. Psychology Update, 16-20. Retrieved December 20, 1999 from ProQuest Direct database (ProQuest Health and Medical Complete) on the World Wide Web: http://www.umi.com/proquest/

The retrieval statement includes the online service (here, ProQuest Direct database); the name of the particular database on which you found your source, in parentheses; and the address of the service's home page.

25. Software

Project scheduler 8000 [Computer software]. (1999). Orlando, FL: Scitor.

Other sources

26. A report

Gerald, K. (1958). Medico-moral problems in obstetric care (Report No. NP-71). St. Louis, MO: Catholic Hospital Association.

Treat the report like a book, but provide any report number in parentheses immediately after the title, with no punctuation between them.

For a report from the Educational Resources Information Center (ERIC), provide the ERIC document number in parentheses at the end of the entry:

Jolson, M. K. (1981). Music education for preschoolers (Report No. TC-622). New York: Teachers College, Columbia University. (ERIC Document Reproduction Service No. ED 264 488)

27. A government publication

U.S. House. Committee on Ways and Means. (1991). Medicare payment for outpatient physical and occupational therapy services. 102d Cong., 2d Sess. Washington, DC: U.S. Government Printing Office.

Stiller, A. (1996). Historic preservation and tax incentives. U.S. Department of the Interior. Washington, DC: U.S. Government Printing Office.

Hawaii. Department of Education. (1998). Kauai district schools, profile 1998-99. Honolulu, HI: Author.

If no individual is given as the author, list the publication under the name of the sponsoring agency. When the agency is both the author and the publisher, use "Author" in place of the publisher's name.

28. An abstract of an unpublished dissertation

Steciw, S. K. (1986). Alterations to the Pessac project of Le Corbusier (Doctoral dissertation, University of Cambridge, England, 1986). Dissertation Abstracts International, 46, 565C.

For an abstract of an unpublished doctoral dissertation, give the university and the year of the dissertation in parentheses after the title. Then give the source of the abstract, the volume number, and the page number.

29. An interview

Brisick, W. C. (1988, July 1). [Interview with Ishmael Reed]. Publishers Weekly, 41-42.

List a published interview under the interviewer's name. Provide the publication information for the kind of source the interview appears in (here, a magazine). Immediately after the date, in brackets, specify that the piece is an interview and give the subject's name if necessary. For an interview with a title, follow model 17 (p. 851).

Note that interviews you conduct yourself are not included in the list of references. Instead, use an in-text parenthetical citation, as shown in model 23 (p. 853) for a nonretrievable online posting.

30. A videotape, recording, or other audiovisual source

Spielberg, S. (Director). (1993). Schindler's list [Videotape]. Los Angeles: Viacom.

Siberry, J. (1995). Caravan. On Maria [CD]. Burbank, CA: Reprise.

For audiovisual sources such as films, videotapes, television or radio programs, or recordings, begin with the name of the person whose work you are citing, followed by his or her function, if appropriate, in parentheses. Immediately after the title, give the medium in brackets. Then give the location and name of the distributor.

51e Formatting documents in the social sciences: APA style

The APA *Publication Manual* distinguishes between documents intended for publication (which will be set in type) and those submitted by students (which are the final copy). The guidelines below apply to most undergraduate papers. Check with your instructor for any modifications to this format.

Structure and format

- The title page includes the full title, your name, the course title, the instructor's name, and the date. Include a shortened form of the title along with the page number at the top of this and all other pages. Number the title page 1. The APA allows either the layout below or a centered arrangement like that for Chicago style (see p. 832) but with capital and small letters instead of all capitals and with the addition of the shortened title and page number shown below.

Title Page

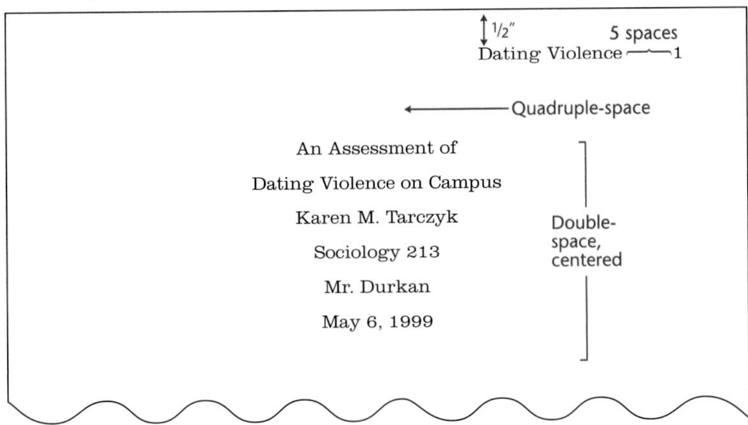

- The first section, labeled "Abstract," summarizes (in about 100 words) your subject, research method, findings, and conclusions. Put the abstract on a page by itself.

Abstract

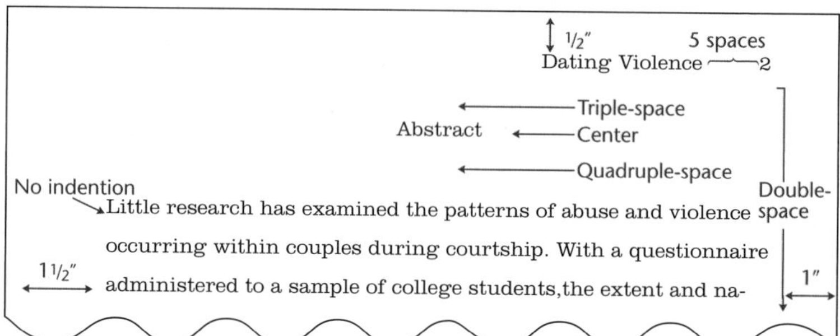

- The body of the paper begins with a restatement of the paper's title and then an introduction (not labeled). The introduction concisely presents the problem you researched, your research method, the relevant background (such as related studies), and the purpose of your research.

First page of body

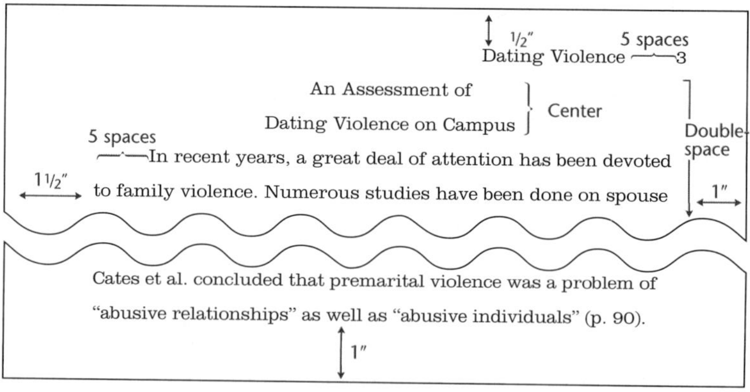

- The next section, labeled "Method," provides a detailed discussion of how you conducted your research, including a description of the research subjects, any materials or tools you used (such as questionnaires), and the procedure you followed. In the illustration on the facing page, the label "Method" is a first-level heading, formatted as in the sample. When you need second- and third-level headings in addition, use these formats, always double-spacing:

APA 51e

First-Level Heading

Second-Level Heading

Third-level heading. Run this heading into the text paragraph.

Later page of body

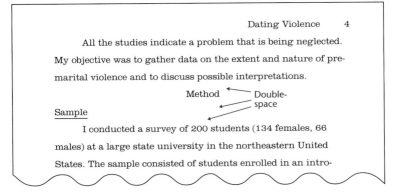

Dating Violence 4

All the studies indicate a problem that is being neglected. My objective was to gather data on the extent and nature of premarital violence and to discuss possible interpretations.

Method

Double-space

Sample

I conducted a survey of 200 students (134 females, 66 males) at a large state university in the northeastern United States. The sample consisted of students enrolled in an intro-

- The "Results" section (labeled with a first-level heading) summarizes the data you collected, explains how you analyzed them, and presents them in detail, often in tables, graphs, or charts.
- The "Discussion" section (labeled with a first-level heading) interprets the data and presents your conclusions. (When the discussion is brief, you may combine it with the previous section under the heading "Results and Discussion.")
- The "References" section, beginning a new page, includes all your sources. See pages 845–47 for an explanation and sample.

Spacing, page numbers, and illustrations

- Use a 1½-inch margin on the left and 1-inch margins on the other sides. (The wider left margin allows for a binder.)
- Number pages consecutively, starting with the title page. Identify each page (including the title page) with a shortened version of the title as well as a page number, as illustrated [opposite.]
- Run into your text all quotations of forty words or less, and enclose them in quotation marks. For quotations of more than forty words, set them off from your text by indenting all lines five spaces, double-spacing above and below. For student papers, the APA allows single-spacing of displayed quotations:

Echoing the opinions of other Europeans at the time, Freud had a poor view of Americans:

> The Americans are really too bad. . . . Competition is much more pungent with them, not succeeding means civil death

> to every one, and they have no private resources apart from their profession, no hobby, games, love or other interests of a cultured person. And success means money. (1961, p. 86)

Do not use quotation marks around a quotation displayed in this way.

- Present data in tables and figures (graphs or charts), as appropriate. (See the sample on p. 861 for a clear format to follow.) Begin each illustration on a separate page. Number each kind of illustration consecutively and separately from the other (Table 1, Table 2, etc., and Figure 1, Figure 2, etc.). Refer to all illustrations in your text—for instance, "(See Figure 3.)." Generally, place illustrations immediately after the text references to them. (See pp. 208–12 for more on illustrations.)

51f Examining a sample social science paper

On the following pages are excerpts from a sociology paper. The student followed the organization described on pages 855–57 both in establishing the background for her study and in explaining her own research. She also followed the APA style of source citation and document format, although page borders and running heads are omitted here and only the required page breaks are indicated. See page 856 for spacing and other format details.

Excerpts from a research report (sociology)

[Title page. See also p. 855.]

An Assessment of
Dating Violence on Campus
Karen M. Tarczyk
Sociology 213
Mr. Durkan
May 6, 1999

[New page.]

Abstract

Little research has examined the patterns of abuse and violence occurring within couples during courtship. With a questionnaire administered to a sample of college students, the extent and nature of such abuse and violence were investigated. The results, some interpretations, and implications for further research are discussed.

[New page.]

An Assessment of
Dating Violence on Campus

In recent years, a great deal of attention has been devoted to family violence. Numerous studies have been done on spouse and child abuse. However, violent behavior occurs in dating relationships as well, yet the problem of dating violence has been relatively ignored by sociological research. It should be examined further since the premarital relationship is one context in which individuals learn and adopt behaviors that surface later in marriage.

The sociologist James Makepeace (1989) contends that courtship violence is a "potential mediating link" between violence in one's family of orientation and violence in one's later family of procreation (p. 103). Studying dating behaviors at Bemidji State University in Minnesota, Makepeace reported that one-fifth of the respondents had had at least one encounter with dating violence. He then extended these percentages to students nationwide, suggesting the existence of a major hidden social problem.

More recent research supports Makepeace's. Cates, Rutter, Karl, Linton, and Smith (1997) found that 22.3% of respondents at Oregon

State University had been either the victim or the perpetrator of premarital violence. Another study (Cortes, 1998) found that so-called date rape, while much more publicized and discussed, was reported by many fewer woman respondents (2%) than was other violence during courtship (21%).

[The introduction continues.]

All these studies indicate a problem that is being neglected. My objective was to gather data on the extent and nature of premarital violence and to discuss possible interpretations.

Method

Sample

I conducted a survey of 200 students (134 females, 66 males) at a large state university in the northeastern United States. The sample consisted of students enrolled in an introductory sociology course.

[The explanation of method continues.]

The Questionnaire

A questionnaire exploring the personal dynamics of relationships was distributed during regularly scheduled class. Questions were answered anonymously in a 30-minute time period. The survey consisted of three sections:

[The explanation of method continues.]

Section 3 required participants to provide information about their current dating relationships. Levels of stress and frustration, communication between partners, and patterns of decision making were examined. These variables were expected to influence the amount of violence in a relationship. The next part of the survey was adopted from Murray Strauss's Conflict Tactics Scales (1982). These scales contain 19 items designed to measure conflict and the means of conflict resolution, including reasoning, verbal aggression, and actual violence.

Results

The questionnaire revealed significant levels of verbal aggression and threatened and actual violence among dating couples. A high number of students, 50% (62 of 123 subjects), reported that they had been the victim of verbal abuse. In addition, almost 14% (17 of 123) of respondents admitted being threatened with some type of violence, and more than 14% (18 of 123) reported being pushed, grabbed, or shoved. (See Table 1.)

[The explanation of results continues.]

[Table on a page by itself.]

Table 1

Incidence of Courtship Violence

Type of violence	Number of students reporting	Percentage of sample
Insulted or swore	62	50.4
Threatened to hit or throw something	17	13.8
Threw something	8	6.5
Pushed, grabbed, or shoved	18	14.6
Slapped	8	6.5
Kicked, bit, or hit with fist	7	5.7
Hit or tried to hit with something	2	1.6
Threatened with a knife or gun	1	0.8
Used a knife or gun	1	0.8

Discussion

Violence within premarital relationships has been relatively ignored. The results of the present study indicate that abuse and force do occur in dating relationships. Although the percentages are small, so was the sample. Extending them to the entire campus population would mean significant numbers. For example, if the nearly 6% incidence of being kicked, bitten, or hit with a fist is typical, then 300 students of a 5,000-member student body might have experienced this type of violence.

[The discussion continues.]

If the courtship period is characterized by abuse and violence, what accounts for it? The other sections of the survey examined some variables that appear to influence the relationship. Level of stress and frustration, both within the relationship and in the respondent's life, was one such variable. The communication level between partners, both the frequency of discussion and the frequency of agreement, was another.

[The discussion continues.]

The method of analyzing the data in this study, utilizing frequency distributions, provided a clear overview. However, more tests of significance and correlation and a closer look at the social and individual variables affecting the relationship are warranted. The courtship period may set the stage for patterns of married life. It merits more attention.

[New page.]

References

Cates, R. L., Rutter, C. H., Karl, J., Linton, M., & Smith, K. (1997). Premarital abuse: A social psychological perspective. Journal of Family Issues, 13(1), 79-90.

Cortes, L. (1998). Beyond date rape: Violence during courtship [20 paragraphs]. Electronic Journal of Intimate Violence. Retrieved March 16, 1999 from the World Wide Web: http://www.acast.nova.edu/health/psy/file-disc/file50.html

Glaser, R., & Rutter, C. H. (Eds.). (1994). Familial violence [Special issue]. Family Relations, 43.

Makepeace, J. M. (1989). Courtship violence among college students. Family Relations, 28, 97-103.

Strauss, M. L. (1982). Conflict Tactics Scales. New York: Sociological Tests.

CHAPTER 52

Writing in the Natural and Applied Sciences

The natural and applied sciences include biology, chemistry, physics, mathematics, engineering, computer science, and their branches. Their purpose is to understand natural and technological phenomena. (A *phenomenon* is a fact or event that can be known by the senses.) Scientists conduct experiments and write to explain the step-by-step processes in their methods of inquiry and discovery.

52a Using the methods and evidence of the sciences

Scientists investigate phenomena by the **scientific method,** a process of continual testing and refinement. (See the box below.) Scientific evidence is almost always quantitative—that is, it consists of numerical data obtained from the measurement of phenomena. These data are called **empirical** (from a Greek word for "experience"): they result from observation and experience, generally in a controlled laboratory setting but also (as sometimes in astronomy or biology) in the natural world. Often the empirical evidence for scientific writing comes from library research into other people's reports of their investigations. Surveys of known data or existing literature are common in scientific writing.

The scientific method

- Observe carefully. Accurately note all details of the phenomenon being researched.
- Ask questions about the observations.
- Formulate a **hypothesis,** or preliminary generalization, that explains the observed facts.
- Test the hypothesis with additional observation or controlled experiments.
- If the hypothesis proves accurate, formulate a **theory,** or unified model, that explains *why.* If the hypothesis is disproved, revise it or start anew.

52b Understanding writing assignments in the sciences

No matter what your assignment, you will be expected to document and explain your evidence carefully so that anyone reading can check your sources and replicate your research. It is important for your reader to know the context of your research—both the previous experimentation and research on your particular subject (acknowledged in the survey of the literature) and the physical conditions and other variables surrounding your own work.

Assignments in the natural and applied sciences include the following:

- A **summary** distills a research article to its essence in brief, concise form. (Summary is discussed in detail on pp. 127–28.)
- A **critique** summarizes and critically evaluates a scientific report.
- A **laboratory report** explains the procedure and results of an experiment conducted by the writer. (An example begins on p. 877.)
- A **research report** reports on the experimental research of other scientists and the writer's own methods, findings, and conclusions.
- A **research proposal** reviews the relevant literature and explains a plan for further research.

A laboratory report has four or five major sections:

1. *Abstract:* a summary of the report. (See p. 856.)
2. *Introduction* or *Objective:* a review of why the study was undertaken, a summary of the background of the study, and a statement of the problem being studied.
3. *Method* or *Procedure:* a detailed explanation of how the study was conducted, including any statistical analysis.
4. *Results:* an explanation of the major findings (including unexpected results) and a summary of the data presented in graphs and tables.
5. *Discussion:* an interpretation of the results and an explanation of how they relate to the goals of the experiment. This section also describes new hypotheses that might be tested as a result of the experiment. If the section is brief, it may be combined with the previous section in a single section labeled *Conclusions.*

In addition, laboratory or research reports may include a list of references (if other sources were consulted). They almost always include tables and figures (graphs and charts) containing the data from the research (see p. 877).

52c Using the tools and language of the sciences

Tools and language concerns vary from discipline to discipline in the sciences. Consult your instructor for specifics about the field you are writing in. You can also discover much about a discipline's tools and language from the research sources listed on pages 866–69.

1 Writing tools

In the sciences a **lab notebook** or **scientific journal** is almost indispensable for accurately recording the empirical data from observations and experiments. Use such a notebook or journal for these purposes:

- Record observations from reading, from class, or from the lab.
- Ask questions and refine hypotheses.
- Record procedures.
- Record results.
- Keep an ongoing record of ideas and findings and how they change as data accumulate.
- Sequence and organize your material as you compile your findings and write your report.

Make sure that your records of data are clearly separate from your reflections on the data so that you don't mistakenly confuse the two in drawing your conclusions.

2 Language considerations

Science writers prefer to use objective language that removes the writer as a character in the situation and events being explained, except as the impersonal agent of change, the experimenter. Although usage is changing, scientists still rarely use *I* in their reports and evaluations, and they often resort to the passive voice of verbs, as in *The mixture was then subjected to centrifugal force.* This conscious objectivity focuses attention (including the writer's) on the empirical data and what they show. It discourages the writer from, say, ascribing motives and will to animals and plants. For instance, instead of asserting that the sea tortoise *evolved* its hard shell *to protect* its body, a scientist would write only what could be observed: that the hard shell *covers and thus protects* the tortoise's body.

Science writers typically change verb tenses to distinguish between established information and their own research. For established information, such as that found in journals and other reliable sources, use the present tense (*Baroreceptors monitor blood pressure*). For your own research, use the past tense (*The bacteria died within three hours*).

Each discipline in the natural and applied sciences has a specialized vocabulary that permits precise, accurate, and efficient communication. Some of these terms, such as *pressure* in physics, have different meanings in the common language and must be handled carefully in science writing. Others, such as *enthalpy* in chemistry, have no meanings in the common language and must simply be learned and used correctly.

3 Research sources

The following lists give resources in the sciences.

Specialized encyclopedias, dictionaries, and bibliographies

American Medical Association Encyclopedia of Medicine
Bibliographic Guide to the History of Computing, Computers, and the Information Processing Industry
Dorland's Illustrated Medical Dictionary
Encyclopedia of Bioethics
Encyclopedia of Chemistry
Encyclopedia of Computer Science and Technology
Encyclopedia of Ecology
Encyclopedia of Electronics
Encyclopedia of Oceanography
Encyclopedia of Physics
Encyclopedic Dictionary of Mathematics
Information Sources in the Life Sciences
Introduction to the History of Science
Introduction to Reference Sources in Health Sciences
Larousse Encyclopedia of Animal Life
McGraw-Hill Encyclopedia of Engineering
McGraw-Hill Encyclopedia of the Geological Sciences
McGraw-Hill Encyclopedia of Science and Technology
Prentice-Hall Encyclopedia of Mathematics
Space Almanac
Van Nostrand's Scientific Encyclopedia
World Resources (environment)

Periodical indexes

ACM Guide to Computing Literature
Applied Science and Technology Index
Bibliography and Index of Geology
Biological and Agricultural Index
Computer Literature Index
Cumulative Index to Nursing and Allied Health Literature
Engineering Index
Environmental Index
General Science Index
Index Medicus
Mathfile

Abstracts and citation indexes

Applied Science and Technology Index
Bibliography and Index of Geology
Biological Abstracts
Chemical Abstracts
Computer Abstracts
Cumulative Index to Nursing and Allied Health Literature
Dissertation Abstracts International (doctoral dissertations). Before 1969, the title was *Dissertation Abstracts.*
Ecology Abstracts
Engineering Index
Environment Abstracts
General Science Index
Mathematical Reviews
Physics Abstracts
Science Citation Index

Book reviews

Technical Book Review Index

Web sources

General

Librarians' Index Science Resources
http://lii.org/search/file/science
National Academy of Sciences
http://www.nas.edu
World Wide Web Virtual Library
http://www.vlib.org/Science.html

Biology

BioLinks
http://www.biolinks.com
BioMedNet
http://www.biomednet.com
BioOnline
http://bio.com/resedu
INFOMINE Biological, Agricultural, and Medical Database
http://ranma.ucr.edu/search/bioagsearch.pl

Chemistry

American Chemical Society ChemCenter
http://www.acs.org:80/index.html
ChemFinder
http://chemfinder.com
University of Houston's Chemistry Resources
http://info.lib.uh.edu/indexes/chem.htm
Virtual Library Chemistry Links
http://www.chem.ucla.edu:80/chempointers.html

Computer science

computer.org
http://www.computer.org
Computing Research Association
http://cra.org
University of Houston's Computer Science Resources
http://info.lib.uh.edu/indexes/compute.htm
Virtual Computer Library
http://www.utexas.edu/computer/vcl

Engineering

American Society of Civil Engineers' Resources
http://www.pubs.asce.org
Engineering Virtual Library
http://www.eevl.ac.uk
Internet Connections for Engineering
http://www.englib.cornell.edu/ice
National Academy of Engineering
http://www.nae.edu

Environmental science

EE-Link
http://eelink.net
EnviroLink
http://www.envirolink.org
Environmental Organization WebDirectory
http://www.webdirectory.com
World Wide Web Virtual Library Resources
http://earthsystems.org/Environment.shtml

Geology

American Geological Institute
http://www.agiweb.org
Cornell University's Geoscience Information System
http://atlas.geo.cornell.edu
Online Resources for Earth Scientists
http://www.gisnet.com/gis/ores
USGS Earth Science Resources
http://www.usgs.gov/network/science/earth/earth.html

Health sciences

American Medical Association
http://www.ama-assn.org
Centers for Disease Control and Prevention
http://www.cdc.gov
MedWeb
http://WWW.MedWeb.Emory.Edu/MedWeb
World Health Organization
http://www.who.int

Mathematics

American Mathematical Society
http://www.ams.org
Mathematical Resources on the Web
http://www.math.ufl.edu/math/math-web.html
Topics in Mathematics
http://archives.math.utk.edu/topics
World Wide Web Virtual Library Resources
http://euclid.math.fsu.edu/Science/Biblo.html

Physics and Astronomy

American Astronomical Society
http://www.aas.org
American Institute of Physics
http://www.aip.org
NASA Space Science Resources
http://spacescience.nasa.gov
PhysicsWeb
http://www.physicsweb.org

Citing sources in the sciences: CBE style

Within the natural and applied sciences, the practitioners of each discipline use a slightly different style of documentation and manuscript format. Following are some of the style guides most often consulted:

American Chemical Society. *ACS Style Guide: A Manual for Authors and Editors.* 2nd ed. 1997.
American Institute of Physics. *Style Manual for Guidance in the Preparation of Papers.* 4th ed. 1990.
American Mathematical Society. *A Manual for Authors of Mathematical Papers.* Rev. ed. 1990.
American Medical Association. *Manual of Style.* 8th ed. 1989.
Bates, Robert L., Rex Buchanan, and Marla Adkins-Heljeson, eds. *Geowriting: A Guide to Writing, Editing, and Printing in Earth Science.* 5th ed. 1992.
Council of Biology Editors. *Scientific Style and Format: The CBE Manual for Authors, Editors, and Publishers.* 6th ed. 1994.

Writers in the life sciences, physical sciences, and sometimes mathematics rely for documentation style on *Scientific Style and Format* from the Council of Biology Editors (CBE). This book de-

http://www.wisc.edu/writing/Handbook/DocCBE6.html Guidance on CBE documentation style, from the University of Wisconsin at Madison.

tails the two styles of in-text citation discussed here: one using author and date and one using numbers. Both types of text citation refer to a list of references at the end of the paper (see opposite). Ask your instructor which style you should use.

1 Using CBE name-year text citations

In the CBE name-year style, parenthetical text citations provide the last name of the author being cited and the source's year of publication. At the end of the paper, a list of references, arranged alphabetically by authors' last names, provides complete information on each source. (See opposite.)

The CBE name-year style closely resembles the APA name-year style detailed on pages 841–45. You can follow the APA examples for in-text citations, making several notable changes for CBE:

- Do not use a comma to separate the author's name and the date: (Baumrind 1968, p. 34).
- For sources with two authors, separate their names with "and" (not "&"): (Pepinsky and DeStefano 1987).
- For sources with three or more authors, use "and others" (not "et al.") after the first author's name: (Rutter and others 1996).
- For anonymous sources, give the author as "Anonymous" both in the citation and in the list of references: (Anonymous 1976).

2 Using CBE numbered text citations

In the CBE number style, raised numbers in the text refer to a numbered list of references at the end of the paper.

Two standard references[1,2] use this term.

These forms of immunity have been extensively researched.[3]

According to one report,[4] research into some forms of viral immunity is almost nonexistent.

Hepburn and Tatin[2] do not discuss this project.

Assignment of numbers

The number for each source is based on the order in which you cite the source in the text: the first cited source is 1, the second is 2, and so on.

Reuse of numbers

When you cite a source you have already cited and numbered, use the original number again (see the last example above, which reuses the number 2 from the first example).

This reuse is the key difference between the CBE numbered citations and numbered references to footnotes or endnotes (pp.

823–31). In the CBE style, each source has only one number, determined by the order in which the source is cited. With notes, in contrast, the numbering proceeds in sequence, so that sources have as many numbers as they have citations in the text.

Citation of two or more sources

When you cite two or more sources at once, arrange their numbers in sequence and separate them with a comma and no space, as in the first example on the previous page.

3 Using a CBE reference list

For both the name-year and the number styles of in-text citation, provide a list, titled "References," of all sources you have cited. Format the page as shown for APA references on page 845 (but you may omit the shortened title before the page number).

Follow these guidelines for references, noting the important differences in name-year and number styles:

Spacing

Single-space each entry, and double-space between entries.

Arrangement

The two styles differ in their arrangement of entries:

Name-year style:

Arrange entries alphabetically by authors' last names.

Number style:

Arrange entries in numerical order—that is, in order of their citation in the text.

Format

In both styles, begin the first line of each entry at the left margin and indent subsequent lines:

Name-year style:

Hepburn PX, Tatin JM. 1995. Human physiology. New York: Columbia Univ Pr. 1026 p.

Number style:

2. Hepburn PX, Tatin JM. Human physiology. New York: Columbia Univ Pr; 1995. 1026 p.

Authors

List each author's name with the last name first, followed by initials for first and middle names. (See the examples above.) Do not use a comma after the last name or periods or space with the initials. Do use a comma to separate authors' names.

CBE References

Placement of dates

The two styles differ, as shown in the examples on the facing page.

Name-year style:

The date follows the author's or authors' names.

Number Style:

The date follows the publication information (for a book) or the title (for a periodical).

Journal titles

Do not underline or italicize journal titles. For titles of two or more words, abbreviate words of six or more letters (without periods) and omit most prepositions, articles, and conjunctions. Capitalize each word. For example, *Annals of Medicine* becomes Ann Med, and *Journal of Chemical and Biochemical Studies* becomes J Chem Biochem Stud. See the Rowell examples on the facing page.

Book and article titles

Do not underline, italicize, or quote a book or an article title. Capitalize only the first word and any proper nouns. See the Rowell and Hepburn and Tatin examples on the facing page.

Publication information for journal articles

Both the name-year and the number styles give the journal's volume number, a colon, and the inclusive page numbers of the article: 28:329-33 in the examples below. (If the journal has an issue number, it follows the volume number in parentheses: 62(2):26-40.) However, the styles differ in the punctuation as well as the placement of the date:

Name-year style:

The date, after the author's name and a period, is followed by a period:

Rowell LB. 1996. Blood pressure regulation during exercise. Ann Med 28:329-33.

Number style:

The date, after the journal title and a space, is followed by a semicolon:

3. Rowell LB. Blood pressure regulation during exercise. Ann Med 1996;28:329-33.

The following examples show both a name-year reference and a number reference for each type of source.

Books

1. A book with one author

Gould SJ. 1987. Time's arrow, time's cycle. Cambridge: Harvard Univ Pr. 222 p.

1. Gould SJ. Time's arrow, time's cycle. Cambridge: Harvard Univ Pr; 1987. 222 p.

2. A book with two to ten authors

Hepburn PX, Tatin JM. 1995. Human physiology. New York: Columbia Univ Pr. 1026 p.

2. Hepburn PX, Tatin JM. Human physiology. New York: Columbia Univ Pr; 1995. 1026 p.

3. A book with more than ten authors

Evans RW, Bowditch L, Dana KL, Drummond A, Wildovitch WP, Young SL, Mills P, Mills RR, Livak SR, Lisi OL, and others. 1998. Organ transplants: ethical issues. Ann Arbor: Univ of Michigan Pr. 498 p.

3. Evans RW, Bowditch L, Dana KL, Drummond A, Wildovitch WP, Young SL, Mills P, Mills RR, Livak SR, Lisi OL, and others. Organ transplants: ethical issues. Ann Arbor: Univ of Michigan Pr; 1998. 498 p.

4. A book with an editor

Jonson P, editor. 1997. Anatomy yearbook. Los Angeles: Anatco. 628 p.

4. Jonson P, editor. Anatomy yearbook. Los Angeles: Anatco; 1997. 628 p.

5. A selection from a book

Krigel R, Laubenstein L, Muggia F. 1997. Kaposi's sarcoma. In: Ebbeson P, Biggar RS, Melbye M, editors. AIDS: a basic guide for clinicians. 2nd ed. Philadelphia: WB Saunders. p 100-26.

5. Krigel R, Laubenstein L, Muggia F. Kaposi's sarcoma. In: Ebbeson P, Biggar RS, Melbye M, editors. AIDS: a basic guide for clinicians. 2nd ed. Philadelphia: WB Saunders; 1997. p 100-26.

6. An anonymous work

[Anonymous]. 1992. Health care for multiple sclerosis. New York: US Health Care. 86 p.

6. [Anonymous]. Health care for multiple sclerosis. New York: US Health Care; 1992. 86 p.

7. Two or more cited works by the same author published in the same year

Gardner H. 1973a. The arts and human development. New York: J Wiley. 406 p.

Gardner H. 1973b. The quest for mind: Piaget, Lévi-Strauss, and the structuralist movement. New York: AA Knopf. 492 p.

(The number style does not require such forms.)

Periodicals: Journals, magazines, newspapers

8. An article in a journal with continuous pagination throughout the annual volume

Ancino R, Carter KV, Elwin DJ. 1983. Factors contributing to viral immunity: a review of the research. Dev Biol 30:156-9.

8. Ancino R, Carter KV, Elwin DJ. Factors contributing to viral immunity: a review of the research. Dev Biol 1983;30:156-9.

9. An article in a journal that pages issues separately

Kim P. 1986 Feb. Medical decision making for the dying. Milbank Quar 64(2):26-40.

9. Kim P. Medical decision making for the dying. Milbank Quar 1986 Feb;64(2):26-40.

10. An article in a newspaper

Krauthammer C. 1986 June 13. Lifeboat ethics: the case of Baby Jesse. Washington Post;Sect A:33(col 1).

10. Krauthammer C. Lifeboat ethics: the case of Baby Jesse. Washington Post 1986 June 13;Sect A:33(col 1).

11. An article in a magazine

Van Gelder L. 1986 Dec. Countdown to motherhood: when should you have a baby? Ms.:37-9.

11. Van Gelder L. Countdown to motherhood: when should you have a baby? Ms. 1986 Dec:37-9.

Electronic sources

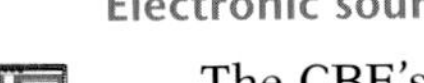

The CBE's *Scientific Style and Format* includes just a few models for electronic sources, and they form the basis of the following examples. For additional models and simpler formats, you can use Columbia online style for the sciences, discussed in Chapter 53. Pages 887–88 show how to adapt Columbia style to the CBE styles (both name-year and number) and detail the differences between the styles. Ask your instructor which style you should use.

Note Since the CBE does not specify how to break electronic addresses, follow MLA style: break only after slashes, and do not hyphenate.

12. A source on CD-ROM

Reich WT, editor. 1998. Encyclopedia of bioethics [CD-ROM]. New York: Co-Health.

12. Reich WT, editor. Encyclopedia of bioethics [CD-ROM]. New York: Co-Health; 1998.

13. An online journal article

Grady GF. 1993 May 2. The here and now of hepatitis B immunization. Today's Med [serial online]. Available from: http://www.fmrt.org/todaysmedicine/Grady050293.html. Accessed 1999 Dec 27.

13. Grady GF. The here and now of hepatitis B immunization. Today's Med [serial online] 1993 May 2. Available from: http://www.fmrt.org/todaysmedicine/Grady050293.html. Accessed 1999 Dec 27.

14. An online book

Ruch BJ, Ruch DB. 1999. Homeopathy and medicine: resolving the conflict [book online]. New York: Albert Einstein Coll of Medicine. Available from: http://www.einstein.edu/medicine/books/ruch.html. Accessed 2000 Jan 28.

14. Ruch BJ, Ruch DB. Homeopathy and medicine: resolving the conflict [book online]. New York: Albert Einstein Coll of Medicine; 1999. Available from: http://www.einstein.edu/medicine/books/ruch.html. Accessed 2000 Jan 28.

15. Computer software

Project scheduler 8000 [computer program]. 1999. Version 4.1. Orlando (FL): Scitor. 1 computer disk: 3 1/2 in. Accompanied by: 1 manual. System requirements: IBM PC or fully compatible computer; DOS 6.0 or higher; Windows 3.1 or higher; 8 MB RAM; hard disk with a minimum of 2 MB of free space.

15. Project scheduler 8000 [computer program]. Version 4.1. Orlando (FL): Scitor; 1999. 1 computer disk: 3 1/2 in. Accompanied by: 1 manual. System requirements: IBM PC or fully compatible computer; DOS 6.0 or higher; Windows 3.1 or higher; 8 MB RAM; hard disk with a minimum of 2 MB of free space.

Other sources

16. A government publication

Committee on Science and Technology, House (US). 1991. Hearing on procurement and allocation of human organs for transplantation. 102nd Cong., 1st Sess. House Doc. nr 409.

16. Committee on Science and Technology, House (US). Hearing on procurement and allocation of human organs for transplantation. 102nd Cong., 1st Sess. House Doc. nr 409; 1991.

17. A nongovernment report

Warnock M. 1992. Report of the Committee on Fertilization and Embryology. Baylor University, Department of Embryology. Waco (TX): Baylor Univ. Report nr BU/DE.4261.

17. Warnock M. Report of the Committee on Fertilization and Embryology. Baylor University, Department of Embryology. Waco (TX): Baylor Univ; 1992. Report nr BU/DE.4261.

18. A sound recording, video recording, or film

Teaching Media. 1993. Cell mitosis [videocassette]. White Plains (NY): Teaching Media. 1 videocassette: 40 min, sound, black and white, 1/2 in.

18. Cell mitosis [videocassette]. White Plains (NY): Teaching Media; 1993. 1 videocassette: 40 min, sound, black and white, 1/2 in.

52e Formatting documents in the sciences: CBE style

The CBE's *Scientific Style and Format* is not specific about margins, spacing for headings, and other elements of document format. Unless your instructor specifies otherwise, you can use the format of the APA (pp. 855–58). The CBE exception to this style is the list of references, which is described and illustrated on pages 871–73.

The most troublesome aspects of manuscript preparation in the sciences are equations or formulas, tables, and figures. When typing equations or formulas, be careful to reproduce alignments, indentions, underlining, and characters accurately. If your typewriter or word processor lacks special characters, write them in by hand. (Stationery and art-supply stores also have sheets of transfer type with special characters in different sizes that can be applied to your manuscript by rubbing.)

Because you will be expected to share your data with your readers, most of your writing for the sciences is likely to require illustrations to present the data in concise, readable form. Tables usually summarize raw data (see p. 879 for an example), whereas figures (mainly charts and graphs) recast the data to show noteworthy comparisons or changes. Follow the guidelines on pages 208–12 for preparing tables and figures.

52f Examining a sample science paper

The following biology paper illustrates the CBE number style for documenting sources. On page 880 passages from the paper and a reformatted list of references show the name-year style. Except for the citations and the references, the paper is formatted in APA style because CBE does not specify a format.

A laboratory report: CBE number style

[Title page.]

Exercise and Blood Pressure

Liz Garson

Biology 161

Ms. Traversa

December 13, 1999

[New page.]

Abstract

The transient elevation of blood pressure following exercise was demonstrated by pressure measurements of twenty human subjects before and after exercise.

[New page.]

Exercise and Blood Pressure

Introduction

The purpose of this experiment was to verify the changes in blood pressure that accompany exercise, as commonly reported.[1,2] A certain blood pressure is necessary for the blood to supply nutrients to the body tissues. Baroreceptors near the heart monitor pressure by determining the degree to which blood stretches the wall of the blood vessel.

[The introduction continues.]

During exercise, the metabolic needs of the muscles override the influence of the baroreceptors and result in an increase in blood pressure. This increase in blood pressure is observed uniformly (irrespective of sex or race), although men demonstrate a higher absolute systolic pressure than do women.[3] During strenuous exercise, blood pressure can rise to 40 percent above baseline.[1]

Method

The subjects for this experiment were twenty volunteers from laboratory classes, ten men and ten women. All pressure measurements were performed using a standard sphygmomanometer, which was tested for accuracy. To ensure consistency, the same sphygmomanometer was used to take all readings. In addition, all measurements were taken by the same person to avoid discrepancies in method or interpretation.

The first pressure reading was taken prior to exercise as the subject sat in a chair. This pressure was considered the baseline for each subject. All subsequent readings were interpreted relative to this baseline.

In the experiment, the subjects ran up and down stairs for fifteen minutes. Immediately after exercising, the subjects returned to the laboratory to have their pressure measured. Thirty minutes later, the pressure was measured for the final time.

Results

Table 1 contains the blood pressure measurements for the male and female subjects. With the exception of subjects 3 and 14, all subjects demonstrated the expected post-exercise increase in blood pressure, with a decline to baseline or near baseline thirty minutes after exercise. The data for subjects 3 and 14 were invalid because the subjects did not perform the experiment as directed.

[Table on a page by itself.]

Table 1. Blood pressure measurements for all subjects (mmHg)

Subject	Baseline[a]	Post-exercise	30-minute reading
Male			
1	110/75	135/80	115/75
2	125/80	140/90	135/85
3	125/70	125/70	125/70
4	130/85	170/100	140/90
5	120/80	125/95	120/80
6	115/70	135/80	125/75
7	125/70	150/80	130/70
8	130/80	145/85	130/80
9	140/75	180/85	155/80
10	110/85	135/95	115/80
Female			
11	110/60	140/85	115/60
12	130/75	180/85	130/75
13	125/80	140/90	130/80
14	90/60	90/60	90/60
15	115/65	145/70	125/65
16	100/50	130/65	110/50
17	120/80	140/80	130/80
18	110/70	135/80	120/75
19	120/80	140/90	130/80
20	110/80	145/90	120/80

[a]Normal blood pressure at rest: males, 110-130/60-90; females, 110-120/50-80.

Discussion

As expected, most of the subjects demonstrated an increase in blood pressure immediately after exercise and a decline to near baseline levels thirty minutes after exercise. The usual pressure increase was 20-40 mmHg for the systolic pressure and 5-10 mmHg for the diastolic pressure.

In the two cases in which blood pressure did not elevate with exercise (subjects 3 and 14), the subjects simply left the laboratory and returned fifteen minutes later without having exercised. The experimental design was flawed in not assigning someone to observe the subjects as they exercised.

CBE 52f

[New page.]

References

1. Guyton AC. Textbook of medical physiology. Philadelphia: WB Saunders; 1997. 998 p.
2. Rowell LB. Blood pressure regulation during exercise. Ann Med 1996;28:329-33.
3. Gleim GW, Stachenfeld NS. Gender differences in the systolic blood pressure response to exercise. Am Heart J 1991;121:524-30.

A laboratory report: CBE name-year style

These excerpts from the preceding paper show documentation in CBE name-year style:

> The purpose of this experiment was to verify the changes in blood pressure that accompany exercise, as commonly reported (Guyton 1997; Rowell 1996).

> This increase in blood pressure is observed uniformly (irrespective of sex or race), although men demonstrate a higher absolute systolic pressure than do women (Gleim and Stachenfeld 1991). During strenuous exercise, blood pressure can rise to 40 percent above baseline (Guyton 1997).

References

Guyton AC. 1997. Textbook of medical physiology. Philadelphia: WB Saunders. 998 p.

Rowell LB. 1996. Blood pressure regulation during exercise. Ann Med 28:329-33.

Gleim GW, Stachenfeld NS. 1991. Gender differences in the systolic blood pressure response to exercise. Am Heart J 121:524-30.

CHAPTER 53

Using Columbia Style for Online Sources

The style manuals in many disciplines do not yet provide detailed guidelines for citing the many kinds of sources available on the Internet. In response, Janice R. Walker and Todd Taylor wrote *The Columbia Guide to Online Style,* published by Columbia University Press in 1998.

The Columbia Guide offers models for both the humanities and the sciences. The humanities models reflect MLA style (Chapter 46), and the science models reflect APA style (Chapter 51)—although there are differences in both cases. The Columbia models can also be adapted for the other two styles covered in this book: Chicago for the humanities (Chapter 50) and CBE for the sciences (Chapter 52).

53a Distinguishing the elements of Columbia style

Columbia style adapts MLA and APA styles, but it also stresses the likely and important elements that allow readers to trace online sources. These elements may be the same as those in conventional printed sources, but often they are not.

Author

The author may be identified only by a login name (such as *jqsmith*) or a fictitious name (such as *c_major*). List the source by this name if it's all you can find, but take special care in evaluating and using such a source. (See pp. 670–72 on evaluating online sources.) Cite a source with no identifiable author by its title.

Title

For the title of a complete work, such as a book or periodical, use italics rather than underlining. If your document were posted on the Web, underlining would signal a hypertext link. Also italicize the titles of online sites and the names of information services.

http://www.columbia.edu/cu/cup/cgos An overview of Columbia online style, with updates, from Columbia University Press.

Date of access

Online sources may change often, so always provide the date of your access so that readers know which version you used. The date falls at the end of the citation, in parentheses, and in the format "day mo. year"—for instance, (31 Aug. 1998). If the source's publication or revision date and your access date are identical, use only the access date.

Electronic address

Always provide an online source's exact and complete electronic address—the complete path for readers to follow in retrieving the source themselves. The address falls just before the access date with no special introduction or additional punctuation—for instance, finance-dl@weg.isu.edu (31 Aug. 1998). Follow MLA style for breaking long addresses: break only after slashes, and do not hyphenate.

53b Citing online sources in the humanities

Columbia online style adapts most elements of MLA documentation (Chapter 46) to provide a thorough system for documenting online sources in the humanities.

- As in MLA style, a citation in the text provides the author's last name and the page or other number where the borrowed material appears—for instance, One researcher disagrees (Johnson 143) or Johnson disagrees (143). (See pp. 711–16 for a variety of examples.) Because many online sources do not use page, paragraph, section, or other numbers, in-text citations of electronic sources may consist only of the author's name.
- Also as in MLA style, a list titled "Works Cited" at the end of your paper arranges your sources alphabetically by the author's last name, or by the first main word of the title if there is no author.

Key differences from MLA style

Columbia online style differs from MLA style (pp. 730–38) in several ways:

Columbia online style	MLA style
Titles of complete works (books, journals) are italicized.	Titles of complete works are underlined.
The electronic address precedes the date of your access and is not enclosed in angle brackets: finance-dl@ weg.isu.edu (23 Feb. 1997).	The electronic address follows the date of your access and is enclosed in angle brackets: 23 Feb. 1997 <finance-dl@ weg.isu.edu>.

Columbia online style	MLA style
The date of access is enclosed in parentheses.	The date of access is not enclosed in parentheses.
The publication medium is not specially identified.	The publication medium—for instance, "Online posting"—sometimes appears after the title.

Ask your instructor which format you should use for online sources.

Chicago style

You can merge Columbia humanities style and Chicago humanities style (Chapter 50) to create citations for online sources that Chicago does not currently cover. The following note and works-cited models show such mergers, drawing on Chicago examples given on page 829.

Footnote or endnote

15. Jane Austen, *Emma,* ed. Ronald Blythe (Harmondsworth, Eng.: Penguin, 1972). *Oxford Text Archive.* ftp://ota.ox.ac.uk/public/english/Austen/emma.1519 (15 Dec. 1999).

Works-cited entry

Austen, Jane. *Emma.* Edited by Ronald Blythe. Harmondsworth, Eng.: Penguin, 1972. *Oxford Text Archive.* ftp://ota.ox.ac.uk/public/english/Austen/emma.1519 (15 Dec. 1999).

These Columbia-Chicago mergers differ from the corresponding Chicago models in several ways:

Columbia online style	Chicago style
The publication medium is not specially identified.	The publication medium—for instance, "book online"—appears after the title in brackets.
The electronic address precedes the date of your access at the end of the entry, and neither is introduced. See the works-cited entry above.	The positions of the electronic address and the access date vary, and both are introduced. In the Chicago works-cited entry for the Austen book, the access date follows the publication date of 1972—Accessed 15 December 1999—and the address falls at the end of the entry—Available from ftp://ota.ox.ac.uk/public/english/Austen/emma.1519; Internet.
The date of access is enclosed in parentheses, and the month is abbreviated.	The date of access is not enclosed in parentheses, and the month is spelled out.

Columbia works-cited models for the humanities

Ask your instructor which format you should use for online sources.

Models of Columbia humanities style

1. A site on the World Wide Web

Lederman, Leon. *Topics in Modern Physics--Lederman.* 10 Oct. 1999. http://www-ed.fnal.gov/samplers/hsphys/people/lederman.html (12 Dec. 1999).

2. A revised or modified site

Ruggira, Wendy. "Chiropractic: Past, Present and Future." *Chiromen.com.* Mod. 30 Sept. 1999. http://chiromen.com/chiropractic.htm (4 Feb. 2000).

3. A book

A book previously published in print:

James, Henry. *The Turn of the Screw.* New York: Scribner's, 1908-09. 1998. *American Literary Classics a Chapter a Day.* http://www.americanliterature.com/TS/TSINDX.HTML (4 Mar. 2000).

An original book:

Cooper, Phoebe, ed. *Sam and Daphne Maeglin: Selected Correspondence, 1940-1964.* 1999. http://www.alphabetica.org/maeglin (21 Mar. 2000).

4. An article in a periodical

Palfrey, Andrew. "Choice of Mates in Identical Twins." *Modern Psychology* 4.1 (1996): 12 pars. http://www.liasu.edu/modpsy/palfrey4(1).htm (25 Feb. 2000).

5. A group or organization as author

Exxon Corporation. "Managing Risk." *Environment, Health and Safety Progress Report.* 1999. http://www.exxon.com/exxoncorp/news/safety_report/index.html (6 Apr. 2000).

United States. Dept. of State. Bureau of Public Affairs. *History of the National Security Council, 1947-1997.* Aug. 1998. http://www.whitehouse.gov/WH/EOP/NSC/html/History.html (6 Feb. 1999).

6. A maintained or compiled site

Scots Teaching and Research Network. Maint. John Corbett. 2 Feb. 1998. U of Glasgow. http://www.arts.gla.ac.uk/www/comet/starn.htm (5 Mar. 2000).

7. A graphic, video, or audio file

Hamilton, Calvin J. "Components of Comets." 1997. *Space Art.* wysisiwyg://94/http://spaceart.com/solar/eng/comet.htm (20 Dec. 1999).

8. Personal electronic mail

Millon, Michele. "Re: Grief Therapy." Personal e-mail (4 May 1999).

9. A posting to a discussion list

Tourville, Michael. "European Currency Reform." 6 Jan. 1999. *International Finance Discussion List.* finance-dl@weg.isu.edu (8 Jan. 1999).

10. A posting to a newsgroup or forum

Cramer, Sherry. "Recent Investment Practices." 26 Mar. 2000. news:biz.investment.current.2700 (3 Apr. 2000).

11. An archived posting

Tourville, Michael. "European Currency Reform." 6 Jan. 1999. *International Finance Discussion List.* http://www.weg.isu.edu/finance-dl/46732 (2 June 1999).

12. An encyclopedia

White, Geoffrey. "Ethnopsychology." *The MIT Encyclopedia of Cognitive Sciences.* Ed. Rob Wilson and Frank Keil. Cambridge: MIT P, 1997. http://mitpress.mit.edu/MITECS/work/whiteg_r.html (26 Mar. 1999).

13. A database

United States. Dept. of Health and Human Services. "Depression Is a Treatable Illness: A Patient's Guide." Apr. 1993. *Health Services Technology Assessment Texts.* No. 93-0533. http://text.nlm.nih.gov/ftrs/pick?collect=930533 (26 Sept. 1999).

14. A gopher or FTP site

Provide directions to a specific source in one of two ways: give the unique address of the file, as in the example above; or give the address of the home page, a space, and the path to the file, as in this example:

Goetsch, Sallie. "And What About Costume?" *Didaskalia: Ancient Theatre Today* 2.2 (1995). gopher://gopher.warwicku.ac.uk Didaskalia/Didaskalia: Ancient Theatre Today/1995/03Features/Goetsch (26 May 1999).

15. A telnet site

Johnson, Earl. "My House: Come In." *Houses of Cyberspace.* 7 Aug. 1999. telnet://edwin.ohms.bookso.com.7777 @go #50827, press 10 (11 Aug. 1999).

16. A synchronous communication

Wendy_Librarian_. "Online Integrity (#421)." *Internet Public Library MOO.* telnet://moo.ipl.org.8888 @go #421 (4 Jan. 1999).

17. Software

Project Scheduler 8000. Vers. 4.1. Orlando: Scitor, 1999.

53c Citing online sources in the sciences

Columbia style adapts most elements of APA style (Chapter 51) to provide a thorough system for documenting online sources in the social, natural, and applied sciences.

- As in APA style, a citation in the text provides the author's last name, the date of publication, and the page or other number where specific borrowings appear—for instance, One researcher called the study "deeply flawed" (Johnson, 1998, p. 143) or Johnson (1998) called the study "deeply flawed" (p. 143). (See pp. 841–45 for a variety of examples.) Because many online sources do not use page, paragraph, or other numbers, citations of specific borrowings from electronic sources often consist only of the author's name and the date.
- Also as in APA style, a list titled "References" at the end of your paper arranges your sources alphabetically by the author's last name, or by the first main word of the title if there is no author.

Key differences from APA style

Though it includes many more kinds of online sources than APA style currently does, Columbia style does differ from APA style (pp. 851–53) in several significant ways:

Columbia online style	APA style
Titles of complete works (books, journals) are italicized.	Titles of complete works are underlined.
A full publication date after the author's name is in the format "year, month day": 1999, December 12. All other dates are in the format "day mo. year": 12 Dec. 1999.	A full publication date after the author's name is in the format "year, month day": 1999, December 12. All other dates are in the format "month day, year": December 12, 1999.
The electronic address precedes the date of your access, with the date in parentheses—for instance, http://www.thinck.com/insec.html (21 Jan. 1998).	The electronic address follows the date of your access, and the two are linked in a statement—for instance, Retrieved January 21, 1998 from the World Wide Web: http://www.thinck.com/insec.html
A period ends the entry.	A period does not end the entry.

Ask your instructor which format you should use for online sources.

CBE style

CBE style (Chapter 52) currently provides few models for citing online sources. By merging Columbia science style and either the CBE name-year style or the CBE number style, you can create citations for kinds of sources not covered by CBE, such as the Web site following.

Columbia reference models for the sciences

Name-year style

Lederman L. 1997 Oct 10. *Topics in modern physics--Lederman.* http://www-ed.fnal.gov/samplers/hsphys/people/lederman.html (12 Dec. 1999).

Number style

4. Lederman L. *Topics in modern physics--Lederman.* 1997 Oct 10. http://www-ed.fnal.gov/samplers/hsphys/people/lederman.html (12 Dec. 1999).

Such mergers of Columbia and CBE styles involve some alterations in the CBE models shown on pages 875–76.

Columbia online style	CBE style
The publication medium is not specially identified.	The publication medium—for instance, "serial online"—appears in brackets after the title.
The electronic address and the date of your access are not introduced—for instance, finance-dl@weg.isu.edu (23 Feb. 1997).	Both the electronic address and the date of your access are introduced—for instance, Available from: finance-dl@weg.isu.edu. Accessed 1997 Feb 23.
The date of access is enclosed in parentheses and is in the format "day mo. year" (the month abbreviated with a period).	The date of access is not enclosed in parentheses and is in the format "year mo day" (the month abbreviated without a period).

Ask your instructor which format you should use for online sources.

Models of Columbia science style

1. A site on the World Wide Web

Lederman, L. (1999, October 10). *Topics in modern physics--Lederman.* http://www-ed.fnal.gov/samplers/hsphys/people/lederman.html (12 Dec. 1999).

2. A revised or modified site

Ruggira, W. (1998). Chiropractic: Past, present and future (Mod. 30 Sept. 1999). *Chiromen.com.* http://chiromen.com/chiropractic.htm (4 Feb. 2000).

3. A book

A book previously published in print:

James, H. (1998). *The turn of the screw.* New York: Scribner's, 1908-1909. *American literary classics a chapter a day.* http://www.americanliterature.com/TS/TSINDX.HTML (4 Mar. 2000).

An original book:

Cooper, P. (Ed.). (1999). *Sam and Daphne Maeglin: Selected correspondence, 1940-1964.* http://www.alphabetica.org/maeglin (21 Mar. 2000).

4. An article in a periodical

Palfrey, A. (1996). Choice of mates in identical twins. *Modern Psychology, 4*(1). http://www.liasu.edu/modpsy/palfrey4(1).htm (25 Feb. 1999).

5. A group or organization as author

Exxon Corporation. (1999). Managing risk. *Environment, health and safety progress report.* http://www.exxon.com/exxoncorp/news/publications/safety_report/index.html (6 Apr. 2000).

U.S. Department of State. Bureau of Public Affairs. (1998, August). *History of the National Security Council, 1947-1997.* http://www.whitehouse.gov/WH/EOP/NSC/html/History.html (6 Feb. 1999).

6. A maintained or compiled site

Scots teaching and research network. (1998, February 2). (J. Corbett, Maint.). University of Glasgow. http://www.arts.gla.ac.uk/www/comet/starn.html (5 Mar. 2000).

7. A graphic, video, or audio file

Hamilton, C. J. (1997). Components of comets [graphic file]. *Space art.* wysisiwyg://94/http://spaceart.com/solar/eng/comet.htm (20 Dec. 1999).

8. Personal electronic mail

Millon, M. Re: Grief therapy [personal e-mail]. (4 May 1999).

Note that APA style calls for citing nonretrievable sources only in your text (see p. 853).

9. A posting to a discussion list

Tourville, M. (1999, January 6). European currency reform. *International finance discussion list.* finance-dl@weg.isu.edu (8 Jan. 1999).

Note that APA style calls for citing nonretrievable sources only in your text (see p. 853). Model 11 shows the format for an archived posting, which is retrievable.

10. A posting to a newsgroup or forum

Cramer, S. (2000, March 26). Recent investment practices. news:biz.investment.current.2700 (3 Apr. 2000).

Note that APA style calls for citing nonretrievable sources only in your text (see p. 853). Model 11 shows the format for an archived posting, which is retrievable.

11. An archived posting

Tourville, M. (1999, January 6). European currency reform. *International finance discussion list.* http://www.weg.isu.edu/finance-dl/46732 (2 June 1999).

12. An encyclopedia

White, G. (1997). Ethnopsychology. In R. Wilson & F. Keil (Eds.), *The MIT encyclopedia of cognitive sciences.* Cambridge, MA: MIT Press. http://mitpress.mit.edu/MITECS/work/whiteg_r.html (26 Mar. 1999).

13. A database

U.S. Department of Health and Human Services. (1993, April). Depression is a treatable illness: A patient's guide. *Health services technology assessment texts* (No. 93-0533). http://text.nlm.nih.gov/ftrs/pick?collect=930533 (26 Sept. 1999).

14. A gopher or FTP site

Provide directions to a specific source in one of two ways: give the unique address of the file, as in the example above; or give the address of the home page, a space, and the path to the file, as in this example:

Goetsch, S. (1995). And what about costume? *Didaskalia: Ancient Theatre Today, 2*(2). gopher://gopher.warwicku.ac.uk Didaskalia/Didaskalia: Ancient Theatre Today/1995/03Features/Goetsch (26 May 1999).

15. A telnet site

Johnson, E. (1999, August 7). My house: Come in. *Houses of cyberspace.* telnet://edwin.ohms.bookso.com.7777 @go #50827, press 10 (11 Aug. 1999).

16. A synchronous communication

Wendy_Librarian_. Online integrity (#421). *Internet Public Library MOO.* telnet://moo.ipl.org.8888 @go #421 (4 Jan. 1999).

17. Software

Project scheduler 8000. (1999). Orlando, FL: Scitor.

PART XII

Special Writing Situations

CHAPTER 54

Essay Examinations

In writing an essay for an examination, you summarize or analyze a topic, usually in several paragraphs or more and usually within a time limit. An essay question not only tests your knowledge of a subject (as short-answer and objective questions do) but also tests your ability to think critically about what you have learned. (If you have not already done so, read this book's Chapter 5 on critical thinking, reading, and writing.)

54a Preparing for an essay examination

To do well on an essay exam, you will need to understand the course content, not only the facts but also the interpretation of them and the relations between them.

- Take careful lecture notes.
- Thoughtfully, critically read the assigned texts or articles.
- Review regularly so the material has time to sink in and stimulate your thinking.
- Create summaries that recast others' ideas in your own words and extract the meaning from notes and texts. (See pp. 127–28 for instructions on summarizing.)
- Prepare notes or outlines that reorganize the course material around key topics or issues. For instance, in a business course you might focus on the advantages and disadvantages of several approaches to management. In a short-story course you might locate a theme running through all the stories you have read by a certain author or from a certain period. In a psychol-

Advice on taking essay exams:

http://www.unc.edu/depts/wcweb/handouts/essay-exams.html From the University of North Carolina.

http://www.cohums.ohio-state.edu/english/programs/writing_center/esyexm4c.htm From Ohio State University.

http://webware.princeton.edu/Writing/essay-ex.htm From Princeton University.

ogy course you might outline various theorists' views of what causes a disorder such as schizophrenia. Any of these examples is a likely topic for an essay question. Thinking of such categories can help you anticipate the kinds of questions you may be asked and increase your mastery of the material.

If you have the opportunity to compose your essay exams on a computer, you'll also need to know the basic operations of computers (see pp. 183–91) and your instructor's procedure for submitting exams. While writing your exam, save your work frequently.

54b Planning your time and your answer

When you first receive an examination, take a few minutes to get your bearings and plan an approach. The time spent will not be wasted.

- Always read an exam all the way through at least once before you start answering any questions.
- As you scan the exam, determine which questions seem most important, which ones are going to be most difficult for you, and approximately how much time you'll need for each question. (Your instructor may help by assigning a point value to each question as a guide to its importance or by suggesting an amount of time for you to spend on each question.)

Planning continues when you turn to an individual essay question. Resist the temptation to rush right into an answer without some planning, for a few minutes can save you time later and help you produce a stronger essay.

- Read the question at least twice. You will be more likely to stick to the question and answer it fully.
- Examine the words in the question and consider their implications. Look especially for words such as *describe, define, explain, summarize, analyze, evaluate,* and *interpret,* each of which requires a different kind of response. Here, for example, is an essay question whose key term is *explain:*

  Question

  Given humans' natural and historical curiosity about themselves, why did a scientific discipline of anthropology not arise until the 20th century? Explain, citing specific details.

See the box on the next page and consult earlier discussions of such terms on pages 95–104 and 129–36.

- After you are sure you understand the question, make a brief outline of the main ideas you want to include in your essay. Use

Sample instructions for essay examinations

Sample instructions	Key words	Strategies for answers	Examples of wrong answers
Define *dyslexia* and compare and contrast it with two other learning disabilities.	Define	Specify the meaning of *dyslexia*—distinctive characteristics, ways the impairment works, etc.	Feelings of children with dyslexia. Causes of dyslexia.
	Compare and contrast	Analyze similarities and differences (severity, causes, treatments, etc.).	Similarities without differences, or vice versa.
Analyze the role of Horatio in *Hamlet*.	Analyze	Break Horatio's role into its elements (speeches, relations with other characters, etc.).	Plot summary of *Hamlet*. Description of Horatio's personality.
Explain the effects of the drug Thorazine.	Explain	Set forth the facts and theories objectively.	Argument for or against Thorazine.
	Effects	Analyze the consequences.	Reasons for prescribing Thorazine.
Discuss term limits for elected officials.	Discuss	Explain and compare the main points of view on the issue.	Analysis of one view. Argument for or against one view.
Summarize the process that resulted in the Grand Canyon.	Summarize	Distill the subject to its main points, elements, or steps	Detailed description of the Grand Canyon.
How do you evaluate the Laffer curve as a predictor of economic growth?	Evaluate	Provide your opinion of significance or value, supported with evidence.	Explanation of the Laffer curve, without evaluation. Comparison of the Laffer curve and another predictor, without evaluation.

the back of the exam sheet or booklet for scratch paper. In the following brief outline, a student planned her answer to the anthropology question on page 895:

1. Unscientific motivations behind 19th-c anthro.

   Imperialist/colonialist govts.
   Practical goals
   Nonobjective and unscientific (Herodotus, Cushing)
2. 19th-c ethnocentricity (vs. cultural relativism)
3. 19th-c anthro. = object collecting

   20th-c shift from museum to univ.
   Anthro. becomes acad. disc. and professional (Boas, Malinowski)

- Write a thesis statement for your essay that responds directly to the question and represents your view of the topic. (If you are unsure of how to write a thesis statement, see pp. 30–34.) Include key phrases that you can expand with supporting evidence for your view. The thesis statement of the student whose outline appears above concisely previews a three-part answer to the sample question:

> Anthropology did not emerge as a scientific discipline until the 20th century because of the practical and political motivations behind 19th-century ethnographic studies, the ethnocentric bias of Western researchers, and a conception of culture that was strictly material.

54c Starting the essay

An essay exam does not require a smooth and inviting opening. Instead, begin by stating your thesis immediately and giving an overview of the rest of your essay. Such a capsule version of your answer tells your reader (and grader) generally how much command you have and also how you plan to develop your answer. It also gets you off to a good start.

The opening statement should address the question directly and exactly, as it does in the successful essay answer beginning on the next page. In contrast, the opening of the unsuccessful essay (pp. 899–900) restates the question but does not answer it, nor does the opening provide any sense of the writer's thesis.

54d Developing the essay

Develop your essay as you would develop any piece of sound academic writing:

- Observe the methods, terms, or other special requirements of the discipline you are writing in (see Chapters 48–52).

- Support your thesis statement with solid generalizations (each one perhaps the topic sentence of a paragraph).
- Support each generalization with *specific, relevant* evidence (see pp. 146–50).

If you observe a few *don't*s as well, your essay will have more substance:

- Avoid filling out the essay by repeating yourself.
- Avoid other kinds of wordiness that pad and confuse, whether intentionally or not. (See pp. 578–84.)
- Avoid substituting purely subjective feelings for real definition, analysis, or whatever is asked of you. (It may help to abolish the word *I* from the essay.)

The following essays illustrate a successful and an unsuccessful answer to the sample essay question on page 895 about anthropology. Both answers were written in the allotted time of forty minutes. Marginal comments on each essay highlight their effective and ineffective elements.

Successful essay answer

Anthropology did not emerge as a scientific discipline until the 20th century because of the practical and political motivations behind 19th-century ethnographic studies, the ethnocentric bias of Western researchers, and a conception of culture that was strictly material.

Gets right to the point with thesis statement.

Answers question directly and previews three-part response.

Before the 20th century, ethnographic studies were almost always used for practical goals. The study of human culture can be traced back at least as far as Herodotus's investigations of the Mediterranean peoples. Herodotus was like many pre-20th-century "anthropologists" in that he was employed by a government that needed information about its neighbors, just as the colonial nations in the 19th century needed information about their newly conquered subjects. The early politically motivated ethnographic studies that the colonial nations sponsored tended to be isolated projects, and they aimed less to advance general knowledge than to solve a specific problem. Frank Hamilton Cushing, who was employed by the American government to study the Zuni tribe of New Mexico, and who is considered one of the pioneers of anthropology, didn't even publish his findings. The political and practical aims of anthropologists and the nature of their research prevented their

Point 1 of thesis: practical aims.

Example.

Example.

work from being a scholarly discipline in its own right.

Anthropologists of the 19th century also fell short of the standards of objectivity needed for truly scientific study. This partly had to do with anthropologists' close connection to imperialist governments. But even independent researchers were hampered by the prevailing assumption that Western cultures were inherently superior. While the modern anthropologist believes that a culture must be studied in terms of its own values, early ethnographers were ethnocentric: they judged "primitive" cultures by their own "civilized" values. "Primitive" peoples were seen as uninteresting in their own right. The reasons to study them, ultimately, were to satisfy curiosity, to exploit them, or to prove their inferiority. There was even some debate as to whether so-called savage peoples were human.

Point 2 of thesis: ethnocentricity.

Finally, the 19th century tended to conceive of culture in narrow, material terms, often reducing it to a collection of artifacts. When not working for a government, early ethnographers usually worked for a museum. The enormous collections of exotica still found in many museums today are the legacy of this 19th-century object-oriented conception of anthropology, which ignored the myths, symbols, and rituals the objects related to. It was only when the museum tradition was broadened to include all aspects of a culture that anthropology could come into existence as a scientific discipline. When anthropologists like Franz Boas and Bronislaw Malinowski began to publish their findings for others to read and criticize and began to move from the museum to the university, the discipline gained stature and momentum.

Point 3 of thesis (with transition *Finally*): focus on objects.

Examples.

In brief, anthropology required a whole series of ideological shifts to become modern. Once it broke free of its purely practical bent, the cultural prejudices of its practitioners, and the narrow conception that limited it to a collection of objects, anthropology could grow into a science.

Conclusion restates thesis supported by essay.

Unsuccessful essay answer

The discipline of anthropology, the study of humans and their cultures, actually began in

Introduction does not answer question.

the early 20th century and was strengthened by the Darwinian revolution, but the discipline did not begin to take shape until people like Franz Boas and Alfred Kroeber began doing scientific research among nonindustrialized cultures. (Boas, who was born in Germany but emigrated to the US, is the father of the idea of historical particularism.)

No thesis statement or sense of direction.

Irrelevant information.

Since the dawn of time, humans have always had a natural curiosity about themselves. Art and literature have always reflected this need to understand human emotions, thought, and behavior. Anthropology is yet another reflection of this need. Anthropologists have a different way of looking at human societies than artists or writers. Whereas the latter paint an individualistic, impressionistic portrait of the world they see, anthropologists study cultures systematically, scientifically. They are thus closer to biologists. They are *social scientists,* with the emphasis on both words.

Adds cliché to the language of the question without answering the question.

Wheel spinning by positioning contemporary anthropology as a scientific discipline.

Another reason why anthropology did not develop until the 20th century is that people in the past did not travel very much. The expansion of the automobile and the airplane has played a major role in the expansion of the discipline.

Not *Another reason* but the first reason given.

Assertion without support.

Cushing's important work among the Zuni Indians in New Mexico is a good example of the transition between 19th-century and 20th-century approaches to anthropology. Cushing was one of the first to develop the method of *participant observation.* Instead of merely coming in as an outsider, taking notes, and leaving, Cushing actually lived among the Zuni, dressing like them and following their customs. In this way, he was able to build a relationship of trust with his informants, learning much more than someone who would have been seen as an outsider.

Next three paragraphs: discussion of pioneers shows familiarity with their work but does not answer question.

Franz Boas, as mentioned earlier, was another anthropology pioneer. A German immigrant, Boas proposed the idea of *historical particularism* as a response to the prevailing theory of *cultural evolution.* Cultural evolution is the idea that cultures gradually evolve toward higher levels of efficiency and complexity. Historical particularism is the idea that every culture is unique and develops differently. Boas developed his theory to counter those who believed in cultural evolution. Working with the

Repetition pads.

Kwakiutl Indians, he was also one of the first anthropologists to use a native assistant to help him gain access to the culture under study.

Information has unclear relevance to subject.

A third pioneer in anthropology was Malinowski, who developed a theory of *functionalism*—that culture responds to biological, psychological, and other needs. Malinowski's work is extremely important and still influential today.

Vague assertion without support.

Anthropologists have made great contributions to society over the course of the past century. One can only hope that they will continue the great strides they have made, building on the past to contribute to a bright new future.

Irrelevant and empty conclusion.

54e Rereading the essay

The time limit on an essay examination does not allow for the careful rethinking and revision you would give an essay or research paper. You need to write clearly and concisely the first time. But try to leave yourself a few minutes after finishing the entire exam for rereading the essay (or essays) and doing touch-ups.

- Correct illegible passages, misspellings, grammatical mistakes, and accidental omissions.
- Verify that your thesis is accurate—that it is, in fact, what you ended up writing about.
- Check to ensure that you have supported all your generalizations. Cross out irrelevant ideas and details, and add any information that now seems important. (Write on another page, if necessary, keying the addition to the page on which it belongs.)

CHAPTER 55

Business Writing

When you write in business, you are addressing busy people who want to see quickly why you are writing and how they should respond to you. A wordy, incoherent letter or memo full of errors in grammar and spelling may prevent you from getting what you want, either because the reader cannot understand your wish or because you present yourself poorly. In business writing, follow these general guidelines:

- State your purpose right at the start.
- Be straightforward, clear, concise, objective, and courteous.
- Observe conventions of grammar and usage, which make your writing clear and impress your reader with your care.

Writing in business demands efficiency, but efficiency does not mean haste. Developing, drafting, and revising—the three overlapping stages of the writing process discussed in Chapters 1–3—apply in business writing as much as in academic writing. Except for brief or routine letters and memos, plan what you want to say; work out your meaning freely, unself-consciously, without stopping to edit; and then revise and edit your draft so that it will achieve your purpose with your reader.

ESL Business writing in your native culture may differ from American business writing. For instance, writers may be expected to begin with polite questions about the addressee or with compliments for the addressee's company. When writing to American businesspeople, get right to the point, even if at first your opening sounds abrupt or even impolite. For examples of appropriate openings, see the sample documents in this chapter.

Advice on business writing in general:

http://www.library.nijenrode.nl From Nyenrode Business Information Services.

http://scout.cs.wisc.edu/report/bus-econ/current/index.html From the Scout Report.

http://www.cohums.ohio-state.edu/english/areas/bizcom.htm From Ohio State University.

55a Writing business letters and job applications

The formats of business letters and résumés are fairly standardized and are thus expected by your correspondents. For more on the specific elements of document design (type fonts and sizes, headings, and so on), see pages 200–14.

1 Using a standard form for letters

Use either unlined white paper measuring $8\frac{1}{2}'' \times 11''$ or what is called letterhead stationery with your address printed at the top of the sheet. Type the letter single-spaced, with double space between elements, on only one side of a sheet. (Unlike the double-spaced papers for your courses, business documents are almost always single-spaced.)

The two most common forms for business letters—the full block and the modified block—are illustrated and described on the following pages.

The letter

Unless you're using letterhead stationery, the **return-address heading** of the letter gives your address (but not your name) and the date. If you are using letterhead, you need add only the date. Place your heading at least an inch from the top of the page, or place the date two lines below the letterhead if there is one. Align all lines of the heading on the left. In the block style, the return-address heading falls at the left margin (see the next page). In the modified block style, it falls to the right of the center of the paper (see p. 908).

The **inside address** shows the name, title, and complete address of the person you are writing to. (See p. 906 for abbreviations of state names.) Place the address at least two lines below the return-address heading. In both block and modified block styles, the address falls at the left margin of the page.

The **salutation** greets the addressee. In both styles it falls at the left margin, two lines below the inside address and two lines above the body of the letter. Follow the salutation with a colon. Whenever possible, address your letter to a specific person. (Call the company

Advice on writing business letters:

http://www.colostate.edu/Depts/WritingCenter/references/documents/bletter/page1.htm From Colorado State University.

http://owl.english.purdue.edu/Files/92.html From the Purdue Online Writing Lab.

Business letter in block style

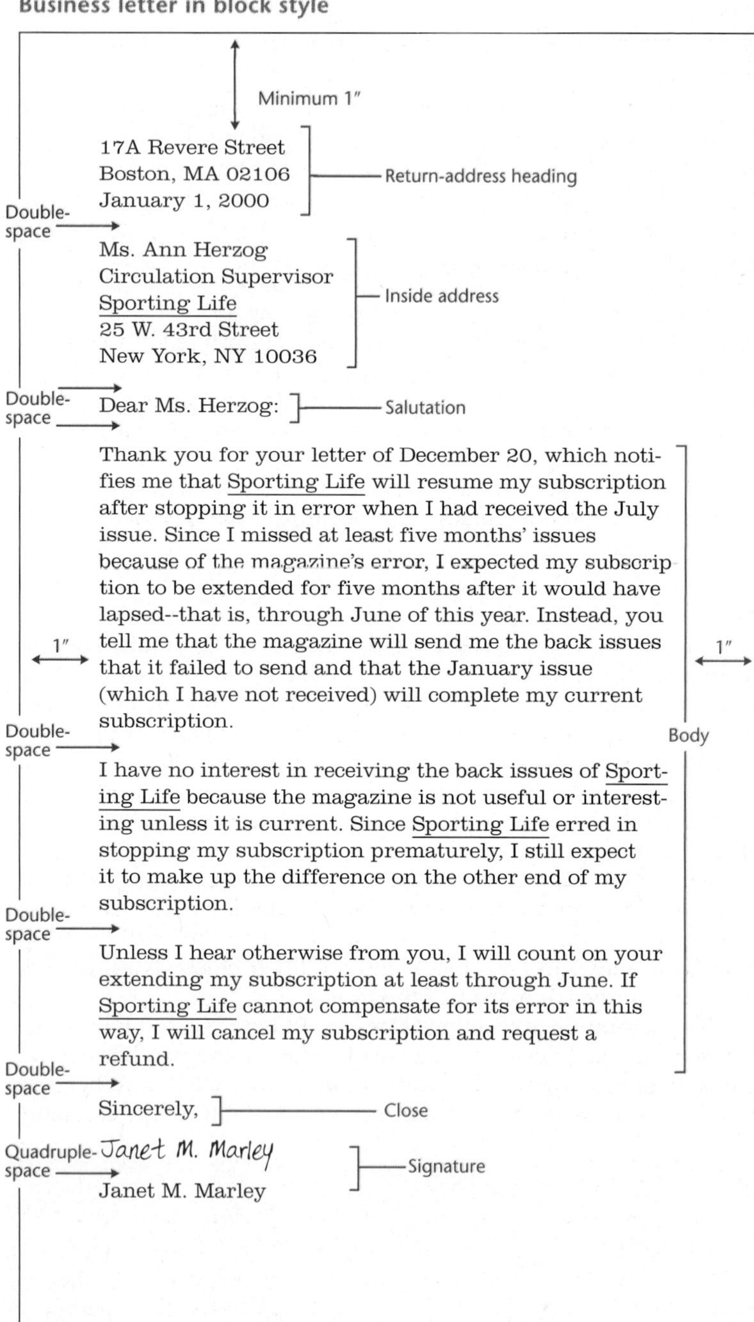
Minimum 1"

17A Revere Street
Boston, MA 02106
January 1, 2000

Return-address heading

Double-space

Ms. Ann Herzog
Circulation Supervisor
Sporting Life
25 W. 43rd Street
New York, NY 10036

Inside address

Double-space

Dear Ms. Herzog:

Salutation

Double-space

Thank you for your letter of December 20, which notifies me that Sporting Life will resume my subscription after stopping it in error when I had received the July issue. Since I missed at least five months' issues because of the magazine's error, I expected my subscription to be extended for five months after it would have lapsed--that is, through June of this year. Instead, you tell me that the magazine will send me the back issues that it failed to send and that the January issue (which I have not received) will complete my current subscription.

1"

1"

Double-space

I have no interest in receiving the back issues of Sporting Life because the magazine is not useful or interesting unless it is current. Since Sporting Life erred in stopping my subscription prematurely, I still expect it to make up the difference on the other end of my subscription.

Body

Double-space

Unless I hear otherwise from you, I will count on your extending my subscription at least through June. If Sporting Life cannot compensate for its error in this way, I will cancel my subscription and request a refund.

Double-space

Sincerely,

Close

Quadruple-space

Janet M. Marley

Janet M. Marley

Signature

55a

or department to ask whom to address.) If you can't find a person's name, then use a job title (*Dear Human Resources Manager, Dear Customer Service Manager*) or use a general salutation (*Dear Smythe Shoes*). Use *Ms.* as the title for a woman when she has no other title, when you don't know how she prefers to be addressed, or when you know that she prefers to be addressed as *Ms.* If you know a woman prefers to be addressed as *Mrs.* or *Miss,* use the appropriate title.

The **body** of the letter, containing its substance, begins at the left margin in both letter styles. Instead of indenting the first line of each paragraph, place an extra line of space between paragraphs so that they are readily visible.

The letter's **close** begins two lines below the last line of the body and aligns with the return-address heading. That is, in the block style the close falls at the left margin (see the facing page), whereas in the modified block style it falls to the right of the center of the page (p. 909). The close should reflect the level of formality in the salutation. For formal letters, *Cordially, Yours truly,* and *Sincerely* are common closes. For less formal letters, you may choose to use *Regards, Best wishes,* or the like. Only the first word of the close is capitalized, and the close is followed by a comma.

The **signature** of a business letter falls below the close and has two parts. One is your name typed on the fourth line below the close. The other is your handwritten signature, which fills the space between the close and your typed name. The signature should consist only of your name, as you sign checks and other documents.

Below the signature at the left margin, you may want to include additional information such as *Enc. 3* (indicating that there are three enclosures with the letter); *cc: Margaret Newton* (indicating that a copy is being sent to the person named); or *CHC/enp* (the initials of the author/the initials of the typist).

The envelope

The envelope of the letter (see below) should show your name and address in the upper-left corner and the addressee's name, title,

JANET M MARLEY
17A REVERE ST
BOSTON MA 02106

MS ANN HERZOG
CIRCULATION SUPERVISOR
SPORTING LIFE
25 W 43RD ST
NEW YORK NY 10036-7146

and address in the center. Use an envelope that will adequately accommodate the letter once it is folded horizontally in thirds.

The United States Postal Service recommends a format for envelopes that makes them easy for machines to read. As illustrated on the previous page, use all capital letters and no punctuation (spaces separate the elements on a line).

The following are the common Postal Service abbreviations for addresses:

Street names

Avenue	AVE	Expressway	EXPY	Road	RD
Boulevard	BLVD	Freeway	FWY	Square	SQ
Circle	CIR	Lane	LN	Street	ST
Court	CT	Parkway	PKY	Turnpike	TPKE

Compass points

North	N	West	W	Southwest	SW
East	E	Northeast	NE	Northwest	NW

State names

Alabama	AL	Kentucky	KY	North Dakota	ND
Alaska	AK	Louisiana	LA	Ohio	OH
Arizona	AZ	Maine	ME	Oklahoma	OK
Arkansas	AR	Maryland	MD	Oregon	OR
California	CA	Massachusetts	MA	Pennsylvania	PA
Colorado	CO	Michigan	MI	Puerto Rico	PR
Connecticut	CT	Minnesota	MN	Rhode Island	RI
Delaware	DE	Mississippi	MS	South Carolina	SC
District of Columbia	DC	Missouri	MO	South Dakota	SD
Florida	FL	Montana	MT	Tennessee	TN
Georgia	GA	Nebraska	NE	Texas	TX
Hawaii	HI	Nevada	NV	Utah	UT
Idaho	ID	New Hampshire	NH	Vermont	VT
Illinois	IL	New Jersey	NJ	Virginia	VA
Indiana	IN	New Mexico	NM	Washington	WA
Iowa	IA	New York	NY	West Virginia	WV
Kansas	KS	North Carolina	NC	Wisconsin	WI
				Wyoming	WY

2 Writing requests and complaints

Letters requesting something—for instance, a pamphlet, information about a product, a T-shirt advertised in a magazine—must be specific and accurate about the item you are requesting. The letter should describe the item completely and, if applicable, include a copy or description of the advertisement or other source that prompted your request.

Letters complaining about a product or a service (such as a

wrong billing from the telephone company) should be written in a reasonable but firm tone. (See the sample letter on p. 904.) Assume that the addressee is willing to resolve the problem when he or she has the relevant information. In the first sentence of the letter, say what you are writing about. Then provide as much background as needed, including any relevant details from past correspondence (as in the sample letter). Describe exactly what you see as the problem, sticking to facts and avoiding discourses on the company's social responsibility or your low opinion of its management. In the clearest and fewest possible words and sentences, proceed directly from one point to the next without repeating yourself. Always include your opinion of how the problem can be solved. Many companies are required by law to establish a specific procedure for complaints about products and services. If you know of such a procedure, be sure to follow it.

3 Writing a job application and résumé

In applying for a job or requesting a job interview, send both a résumé and a cover letter. If you need to submit your application electronically, see page 912.

The cover letter

The cover letter should follow the format guidelines on pages 903–05 and the content guidelines below. See the sample letter on the next page.

- Think of the letter as an interpretation of your résumé for a particular job, not as a detailed account of the entire résumé. Instead of reciting your job history, highlight and reshape only the relevant parts.
- Announce at the outset what job you seek and how you heard about it.

http://www.westwords.com/guffey/job_search.html Resources for job searches, from Communication at Work.

http://www.careermosaic.com/cm/rwc/rwc1.html Information on writing résumés, cover letters, thank you letters, and more, from CareerMosaic.

http://www.quintcareers.com/cover_letters.html A tutorial for writing cover letters, from Quintessential Careers.

http://athena.english.vt.edu/~dubinsky/jobltrcl.htm A checklist for cover letters, from Virginia Polytechnic Institute and State University.

Job-application letter in modified block style

3712 Swiss Avenue
Dallas, TX 75204
March 2, 2000

Raymond Chipault
Human Resources Manager
Dallas News
Communications Center
Dallas, TX 75222

Dear Mr. Chipault:

In response to your posting in the English Department of Southern Methodist University, I am applying for the summer job of part-time editorial assistant for the Dallas News.

I am now enrolled at Southern Methodist University as a sophomore, with a dual major in English literature and journalism. My courses so far have included news reporting, copy editing, and electronic publishing. I worked a summer as a copy aide for my hometown newspaper, and for two years I have edited and written sports stories and features for the university newspaper. My feature articles cover subjects as diverse as campus elections, parking regulations, visiting professors, and speech codes.

As the enclosed résumé and writing samples indicate, my education and practical knowledge of newspaper work prepare me for the opening you have.

I am available for an interview at your convenience and would be happy to show more samples of my writing. Please e-mail me at ianirv@mail.smu.edu or call me at 214-744-3816.

Sincerely,

Ian M. Irvine

Ian M. Irvine

Enc.

- Include any special reason you have for applying, such as a specific career goal.
- Summarize your qualifications for this particular job, including relevant facts about education and employment and emphasizing notable accomplishments. Mention that additional information appears in an accompanying résumé.
- At the end of the letter, mention that you are available for an interview at the convenience of the addressee, or specify when you will be available (for instance, when your current job or classes leave you free).

The résumé

For the résumé that accompanies your letter of application, you can use the guidelines below and on page 912 as well as the samples on the next two pages.

- Provide the following, in table form: your name and address, career objective, education, employment history, any special skills or awards, and information about how to obtain your references.
- Use headings to mark the various sections of the résumé, spacing around them and within sections so that important information stands out.
- Usage varies on capital letters in résumés. Keep in mind that passages with many capitals can be hard to read. Definitely use capitals for proper nouns (pp. 536–38), but consider dropping them for job titles, course names, department names, and the like. (See pp. 538–39.)
- Limit your résumé to one page so that it can be quickly reviewed. However, if your experience and education are extensive, a two-page résumé is preferable to a single cramped, unreadable page.
- If you are submitting a printed résumé, you may want to use some of the techniques of document design discussed on pages 200–14. The sample résumé appears two ways on the next two pages: in a traditional format (one column, serif type) and in a more contemporary design (two columns, sans serif type).

(Text continues on p. 912)

http://owl.english.purdue.edu/bw/resume/resume.html A tutorial for writing résumés, from the Purdue Online Writing Lab.

http://athena.english.vt.edu/~dubinsky/resumec12.htm A checklist for résumés, from Virginia Polytechnic Institute and State University.

Résumé (traditional design)

Ian M. Irvine
3712 Swiss Avenue
Dallas, TX 75204
214-744-3816
ianirv@mail.smu.edu

Position desired
Part-time editorial assistant.

Education
Southern Methodist University, 1998 to present.
Current standing: sophomore.
Major: English literature and journalism.
Journalism courses: news reporting, copy editing, electronic publishing, communications arts, broadcast journalism.

Abilene (Texas) Senior High School, 1994–1998.
Graduated with academic, college-preparatory degree.

Employment history
1998 to present. Reporter, Daily Campus, student newspaper of Southern Methodist University.
Write regular coverage of baseball, track, and soccer teams. Write feature stories on campus policies and events. Edit sports news, campus listings, features.

Summer 1999. Copy aide, Abilene Reporter-News.
Routed copy, ran errands, and assisted reporters with research.

Summer 1998. Painter, Longhorn Painters, Abilene.
Prepared and painted exteriors and interiors of houses.

Special skills
Fluent in Spanish.
Proficient in Internet research and word processing.

References
Available on request:

Placement Office
Southern Methodist University
Dallas, TX 75275

Résumé (contemporary design)

Ian M. Irvine

3712 Swiss Avenue
Dallas, TX 75204
214-744-3816
ianirv@mail.smu.edu

Position desired	Part-time editorial assistant.
Education	*Southern Methodist University,* 1998 to present. Current standing: sophomore. Major: English literature and journalism. Journalism courses: news reporting, copy editing, electronic publishing, communications arts, broadcast journalism. *Abilene (Texas) Senior High School*, 1994-1998. Graduated with academic, college-preparatory degree.
Employment history	1998 to present. Reporter, *Daily Campus*, student newspaper of Southern Methodist University. Write regular coverage of baseball, track, and soccer teams. Write feature stories on campus policies and events. Edit sports news, campus listings, features. Summer 1999. Copy aide, *Abilene Reporter-News.* Routed copy, ran errands, and assisted reporters with research. Summer 1998. Painter, Longhorn Painters, Abilene. Prepared and painted exteriors and interiors of houses.
Special skills	Fluent in Spanish. Proficient in Internet research and word processing.
References	Available on request: Placement Office Southern Methodist University Dallas, TX 75275

Employers often want an electronic version of a résumé so that they can add it to a computerized database of applicants. The employers may scan your printed résumé to convert it to an electronic file, or they may request electronic copy from you in the first place. If you think a potential employer may use an electronic version of your résumé, follow these additional guidelines:

- Keep the design simple so that the résumé can be read accurately by a scanner or transmitted accurately by electronic mail. Avoid images, unusual type, more than one column, vertical or horizontal lines, and highlighting (boldface, italic, or underlining). If its highlighting were removed, the traditionally designed sample on page 910 could probably be scanned or transmitted electronically. The two-column sample on page 911 perhaps could not.
- Use concise, specific words to describe your skills and experience. The employer's computer may use keywords (often nouns) to identify the résumés of suitable job candidates, and you want to ensure that your résumé includes the appropriate keywords. Name your specific skills—for example, the computer programs you can operate—and write concretely with words like *manager* (not *person with responsibility for*) and *reporter* (not *staff member who reports*). Look for likely keywords in the employer's description of the job you seek.

55b Writing business memos

Unlike business letters, which address people in other organizations, business memorandums (memos, for short) address people within the same organization. A memo can be quite long, but more often it deals briefly with a specific topic, such as an answer to a question, a progress report, or an evaluation. Both the content and

Advice on preparing scannable or electronic résumés:

http://www.eresumes.com From Eresumes.com.

http://www.dbm.com/jobguide/eresume.html From the Riley Guide.

http://athena.english.vt.edu/~dubinsky/scantips.htm From Virginia Polytechnic Institute and State University.

Advice on memo writing:

http://owl.english.purdue.edu/Files/99.html From the Purdue Online Writing Lab.

http://www.colostate.edu/Depts/WritingCenter/references/documents/memo/page1.htm From Colorado State University.

the format of a memo aim to get to the point and dispose of it quickly, as indicated in the following guidelines and the sample below.

Content

- State your reason for writing in the first sentence, perhaps outlining a problem, making a request, referring to a request that prompted the memo, or briefly summarizing new findings. Do

Bigelow Wax Company

TO: Aileen Rosen, Director of Sales
FROM: Patricia Phillips, Territory 12 *PP*
DATE: March 17, 2000
SUBJECT: 1999 sales of Quick Wax in Territory 12

Since it was introduced in January 1999, Quick Wax has been unsuccessful in Territory 12 and has not affected the sales of our Easy Shine. Discussions with customers and my own analysis of Quick Wax suggest three reasons for its failure to compete with our product.

1. Quick Wax has not received the promotion necessary for a new product. Advertising—primarily on radio—has been sporadic and has not developed a clear, consistent image for the product. In addition, the Quick Wax sales representative in Territory 12 is new and inexperienced; he is not known to customers, and his sales pitch (which I once overheard) is weak. As far as I can tell, his efforts are not supported by phone calls or mailings from his home office.

2. When Quick Wax does make it to the store shelves, buyers do not choose it over our product. Though priced competitively with our product, Quick Wax is poorly packaged. The container seems smaller than ours, though in fact it holds the same eight ounces. The lettering on the Quick Wax package (red on blue) is difficult to read, in contrast to the white-on-green lettering on the Easy Shine package.

3. Our special purchase offers and my increased efforts to serve existing customers have had the intended effect of keeping customers satisfied with our product and reducing their inclination to stock something new.

Copies: L. Mendes, Director of Marketing
L. MacGregor, Customer Service Manager

not, however, waste words with expressions like "The purpose of this memo is. . . ."

- Devote the first paragraph to a succinct presentation of your solution, recommendation, answer, or evaluation. The first paragraph should be short, and by its end your reader should know precisely what to expect from the rest of the memo: the details and reasoning that support your conclusion.
- Deliver the support in the body of the memo. The paragraphs may be numbered or bulleted so that the main divisions of your message are easy to see. In a long memo, you may need headings (see pp. 207–08).
- Suit your style and tone to your audience. For instance, you'll want to address your boss or a large group of readers more formally than you would a coworker who is also a friend.
- Whatever your style and tone, write concisely. Keep your sentences short and your language simple, using technical terms only when your readers will understand them. Provide only the information that readers need to know.

Format

- The memo has no return address, inside address, salutation, or close. Instead, as shown in the sample memo on the previous page, the heading typically consists of the company's name, the addressee's name, the writer's name, the date, and a subject description or title.
- Type the body of the memo as you would the body of a business letter: single-spaced, double-spaced between paragraphs, and no paragraph indentions.
- Never sign a business memo, but do initial your name in the heading.
- If copies of the memo need to be sent to people not listed in the "To" line, list those people two spaces below the last line.

Note See page 219 for a sample of a business report, which is more formal in expression and format than a memo.

55c Communicating electronically

Communicating via electronic devices, especially electronic mail and fax machines, speeds up correspondence but also creates new challenges. E-mail now plays such a prominent role in commu-

http://www.gooddocuments.com/homepage/homepage.htm Advice on electronic business communication, from Good Documents.

nication of all sorts that we discuss it extensively as part of basic computer literacy (see pp. 192–97). Generally, the standards for business e-mail are the same as for other business correspondence.

Faxes follow closely the formats of print documents, whether letters (p. 903) or memos (p. 912). But there are some key differences:

- Small type, photographs, horizontal lines, and other elements that look fine on your copy may not be legible to the addressee.
- Most faxes require a cover sheet with fax-specific information: the addressee's name, company, and fax number; the date, time, and subject; your own name and fax and telephone numbers (the telephone number is important in case something goes wrong with the transmission); and the total number of pages (including the cover sheet) in the fax.
- Because fax transmissions can go astray, it's often wise to advise your addressee to expect a fax. Such advice is essential if the fax is confidential, because the machine is often shared.
- Transmission by fax can imply that the correspondence is urgent. If yours isn't, consider using the mail. (Swamping your correspondents with needless faxes can make you the child who cried wolf when you really have an urgent message to transmit.)

CHAPTER 56

Oral Presentations

At some point during your education or your work, you will probably be called upon to speak to a group. Oral presentation can be anxiety producing, even for those who are experienced at it. This chapter shows you how you can apply your experiences as a writer to public speaking, and it offers some techniques that are uniquely appropriate for effective oral presentations.

56a Writing and speaking

Writing and speechmaking have much in common: both require careful consideration of your subject, purpose, and audience. Thus the mental and physical activities that go into the writing process can also help you prepare and deliver a successful oral presentation.

Despite many similarities, however, writing for readers is not the same as speaking to listeners. Whereas a reader can go back and reread a written message, a listener cannot stop a speech to rehear a section. Several studies have reported that immediately after hearing a short talk, most listeners cannot recall half of what was said.

Effective speakers adapt to their audience's listening ability by reinforcing their ideas through repetition and restatement. They use simple words, short sentences, personal pronouns, contractions, and colloquial expressions. In formal writing, these strategies might seem redundant and too informal; but in speaking, they improve listeners' comprehension.

Advice for developing and delivering effective oral presentations:

http://www.kumc.edu/SAH/OTEd/jradel/effective.html From the University of Kansas Medical Center.

http://www.ukans.edu/cwis/units/coms2/vpa/vpa.htm From the University of Kansas Communications Department.

http://www.speechwriting.com/speech.htm From Overviews' Speech Writing.

http://www.si.umich.edu/~pne/acadtalk.htm From the University of Michigan.

Checklist for an oral presentation

- **Purpose:** What do you want your audience to know or do as a result of your presentation? How can you achieve your purpose in the time and setting you've been given? (See below.)
- **Audience:** What do you know about the characteristics and opinions of your audience? How can this information help you adapt your presentation to your audience's interests, needs, and opinions? (See below.)
- **Organization and content:** How are your ideas arranged? Where might listeners have difficulty following you? What functions do your introduction and conclusion perform? How relevant and interesting is your supporting material for your topic and your audience? (See p. 918.)
- **Method of delivery:** What method of delivery do you plan: extemporaneous? reading from a text? memorized? a mixture? How does your method suit the purpose, setting, and occasion of your presentation? (See pp. 920–21.)
- **Vocal and physical delivery:** In rehearsing your presentation, what do you perceive as your strengths and weaknesses? Is your voice suitably loud for the setting? Are you speaking clearly? Are you able to move your eyes around the room so that you'll be making eye contact during the presentation? Is your posture straight but not stiff? Do your gestures reinforce your ideas? Do you use visual aids appropriately? (See pp. 921–22.)
- **Confidence and credibility:** What techniques will you use to overcome the inevitable anxiety about speaking? How will you project your confidence and competence? (See pp. 923–24.)

56b Considering purpose and audience

The most important step in developing an oral presentation is to identify your purpose: what do you want your audience to know or do as a result of your speech? Topic and purpose are *not* the

Collections of effective speeches, many on audio:

http://www.historychannel.com/speeches/index.html From the History Channel.

http://debate.uvm.edu/lib.html From the Edwin W. Lawrence Debate Library at the University of Vermont.

http://www.ngsw.org/gallery.html From the National Gallery of the Spoken Word.

http://gos.sbc.edu Women's speeches, from Sweet Briar College's Gifts of Speech.

same thing. Asking "What am I talking about?" is not the same as asking "Why am I speaking?"

In school and work settings, oral presentations may include anything from a five-minute report before a few peers to an hour-long address before a hundred people. Whatever the situation, you're likely to be speaking for the same reasons that you write in school or at work: to explain something to listeners or to persuade listeners to accept your opinion or take an action. See pages 15–17 for more on these purposes.

Adapting to your audience is a critical task in public speaking as well as in writing. You'll want to consider the questions about audience on page 11. But a listening audience requires additional considerations as well:

- Why is your audience assembled? Is it because these people want to hear you, because they are interested in your topic, because they have been required to attend, or because they always meet in this time and place? Listeners who are required to attend may be more difficult to interest and motivate than listeners who attend because they want to hear you and your ideas.
- How large is your audience? With a small group you can be informal. If you are speaking to a hundred or more people, you may need a public address system, a lectern, special lighting, and audiovisual equipment.
- Where will you speak? Your approach should match the setting—more casual for a small classroom, more formal for an auditorium. If the room is large and the audience small, you may ask the audience to fill in the front section of the room.
- How long are you scheduled to speak and when? A long speech early in the morning or late in the afternoon may find your audience too sleepy to listen well. And keep in mind that audiences lose patience with someone who speaks longer than the assigned time.

When speaking, unlike when writing, you can see and hear your audience's responses during your presentation. Thus you have the luxury and challenge of adapting your presentation to an audience as you speak. If you sense that an audience is bored, try to spice up your presentation. If an audience is restless, consult your watch to make sure you have not gone overtime. If you sense resistance, try to make midspeech adjustments to respond to that resistance.

56c Organizing the presentation

An effective oral presentation, like an effective essay, has a recognizable shape. The arrangement of sections guides listeners through a presentation and helps them see how ideas and details are related to each other. The advice in Chapter 2 for organizing and outlining an essay serves the speechmaker as well as the writer (see pp. 35–46). Here are additional considerations for the introduction, conclusion, and supporting material.

1 The introduction

First impressions count. A strong beginning establishes an important relationship among three elements in an oral presentation: you, your topic, and your audience. More specifically, the beginning of an oral presentation should try to accomplish three goals:

- Gain the audience's attention and interest. When you begin to speak, your listeners may not be ready to pay attention: they may be talking to neighbors or be preoccupied with other thoughts. To attract listeners' attention, begin with a question, an unusual example or statistic, or a short, relevant story.
- Put yourself in the speech by demonstrating your expertise, experience, or concern. Your audience will be more interested in what you say and more trusting of you.
- Introduce and preview your topic and purpose. By the time your introduction is over, listeners should know what your topic is and the direction in which you wish to take them as you develop your ideas. This information will give them expectations for your speech on which they can pin the specific points that follow.

In addition to these guidelines for beginning a speech, there are some important pitfalls to avoid:

- Don't try to cram too much into your introduction. Giving only a sneak preview of your speech can pique your audience's curiosity about what you have to say.
- Don't begin with an apology. A statement such as "I wish I'd been given more time to get ready for this presentation" will only undermine your listeners' confidence in you.
- Don't begin with "My speech is about. . . ." The statement is dull, and it does little to clarify purpose.

2 Supporting material

Just as you do when writing, you can and should use facts, statistics, examples, and expert opinions to support spoken arguments (see pp. 146–48). In addition, as a speaker you can draw on other kinds of supporting material:

- Use vivid description to paint a mental image of a scene, a concept, an event, or a person.

- Use well-chosen quotations to add an emotional or humorous moment to your speech.
- Use true or fictional stories to rivet the audience's attention and illustrate your point. Most listeners remember a good story long after they have forgotten other details from a speech.
- Use analogies—comparisons between essentially unlike things, such as a politician and a tightrope walker—to link concepts memorably. (For more on analogy, see p. 101.)

Use a variety of supporting material in your speech. A presentation that is nothing but statistics can bore an audience. Nonstop storytelling may interest listeners but fail to achieve your purpose.

3 The conclusion

Last impressions count as much as first impressions. You may hope that listeners will remember every detail of your speech, but they are more likely to leave with a general impression and a few ideas about you and your message. You want your conclusion to be clear, of course, but you also want it to be memorable. Remind listeners of how your topic and main idea connect to their needs and interests. If your speech was motivational, tap an emotion that matches your message. If your speech was informational, give some tips on how to remember important details.

56d Delivering the presentation

Writing and speaking differ most obviously in the form of delivery: the writer is represented in print; the speaker is represented in person. This section describes the methods and techniques of oral presentation (pp. 920–23) as well as some ways of coping with stage fright (pp. 923–24).

1 Methods of delivery

An oral presentation may be delivered impromptu, extemporaneously, from a text, or from memory. No one technique is best for all speeches; indeed, a single speech may include two or more forms or even all four—perhaps a memorized introduction, an extemporaneous body in which quotations are read from a text, and an impromptu response to audience questions during or after the speech.

- *Impromptu* means "without preparation": an impromptu presentation is one you deliver off-the-cuff, with no planning or practice. You may be called on in a class to express your opinion or to summarize something you've written. You may speak up at a neighborhood meeting. An audience member may ask you a question at the end of an oral presentation. The only way to prepare for such incidents is to be well prepared in general—to be caught up on course reading, for instance, or to know the facts in a debate.

- Extemporaneous speaking—that done with some preparation, but without reading from a text—is the most common form of presentation, typical of class lectures and business briefings. With extemporaneous speaking, you have time to prepare and practice in advance. Then, instead of following a script of every word, you speak from notes that guide you through the presentation. You can look and sound natural while still covering all the material you want to convey.
- Delivering a presentation from a text involves writing the text out in advance and then reading aloud from it. With a text in front of you, you're unlikely to lose your way. However, a reading speaker can be dull for an audience. Try to avoid this form of delivery for an entire presentation. If you do use it, write the text so that it sounds spoken (less formal) rather than written (more formal): for instance, the sentence *Although costs rose, profits remained steady* would sound fine in writing but stiff and awkward in speech because in conversation we rarely use such a structure. In addition, rehearse thoroughly so that you can read with expression and can look up frequently to make eye contact with listeners (see the next page).
- A memorized presentation has a distinct advantage: complete freedom from notes or a text. That means you can look at your audience every minute and can move away from a lectern and even into the audience. However, you may be like most speakers in seeming less relaxed, not more relaxed, when presenting from memory: your mind is too busy retrieving the next words to attend to the responses of the audience. Further, you risk forgetting your place or a whole passage. For these reasons, many experts discourage memorization. At least reserve the method for the introduction, perhaps, or some other part with which you want to make a strong impression. Rehearse not only to memorize the words but, beyond that, to deliver the words fresh, as if for the first time.

2 Vocal delivery

The sound of your voice will influence how your listeners receive you. When rehearsing, consider volume, speed, and articulation.

- Speak loudly. In a meeting with five other people, you can speak in a normal volume. As your audience grows in size, so should your volume. Most speakers can project to as many as a hundred people, but a larger audience may require a microphone. If you can rehearse in the room where you'll be speaking, ask a friend or colleague to sit at the back and tell you what volume is easy to hear. It may seem like shouting to you, but to your audience it will sound confident and clear.

- Speak slowly enough to be understandable. Most audiences prefer speech that's a little fast, around 150 words a minute; but they have difficulty following too-rapid speech at, say, 190 words a minute.
- Speak clearly and correctly. To avoid mumbling or slurring words, practice articulating. Sometimes it helps to open your mouth a little wider than usual. And to avoid mispronouncing words and names, look up questionable ones or ask someone for the correct pronunciation. (See also the tips opposite on practicing your presentation.)

3 Physical delivery

You are more than your spoken words when you make an oral presentation. Your face and body also play a role in how your speech is received.

- Make eye contact with listeners. Looking directly in your listeners' eyes conveys your honesty, your confidence, and your control of your material. Don't look above the heads of the audience or at one friendly face. Instead, move your gaze around the entire room, settle on someone, and establish direct eye contact; then move on to someone else.
- Always stand for a presentation, unless it takes place in a small room where standing would be inappropriate. You can see more audience members when you stand, and they in turn can hear your voice and see your gestures more clearly.
- Stand straight, and move around. Turn your body toward one side of the room and the other, step out from behind any lectern or desk, and gesture appropriately, as you would in conversation. Let your gestures and movement support and draw attention to important words and ideas.

4 Visual aids

Many speakers supplement their oral presentations with visual aids—from words on a chalkboard through posters and models and slides to computer-generated multimedia productions. Visual aids can emphasize key points, organize interrelated concepts, and illustrate complex procedures. They can gain listeners' attention and improve their understanding and memory.

The following guidelines can help you create effective and appropriate visual aids:

- Use visual aids to underscore your points. Short lists of key ideas, illustrations such as graphs or photographs, or objects such as models can make your presentation more interesting and memorable. But use visual aids judiciously: a battery of illustrations or objects will bury your message rather than amplify it.
- Match visual aids and setting. An audience of five people may be able to see a photograph and share a chart; an audience of a hundred will need projected images.
- Coordinate visual aids with your message. Time each visual aid to reinforce a point you're making. Tell listeners what they're looking at—what they should be getting from the aid. Give them enough viewing time so they don't mind turning their attention back to you.
- To regain your audience's attention, remove or turn off any visual aid as soon as you have finished with it.

5 Practice

Practicing an oral presentation is the speechmaker's equivalent of editing and proofreading a written text. You won't gain much by practicing silently in your head; instead, you need to rehearse out loud, with the notes you will be using. For your initial rehearsals, you can gauge your performance by making an audio- or videotape of yourself or by practicing in front of a mirror. A recording will let you hear mumbling, too-rapid delivery, grammatical errors, mispronounced words, and unclear concepts. A mirror or video will reveal your stance, your gestures, and your eye contact. Any of these practice techniques will tell you if your presentation is running too long or too short.

If you plan to use visual aids, you'll need to practice with them, too, preferably in the room where you'll make the presentation and certainly with the help of anyone who will be assisting you. Your goal is to eliminate hitches (upside-down slides, missing charts) and to weave the visuals seamlessly into your presentation.

6 Stage fright

Many people report that speaking in front of an audience is their number-one fear. Even many experienced and polished speakers have some anxiety about delivering an oral presentation, but they use this nervous energy to their advantage, letting it propel them into working hard on each presentation, preparing well in advance, and rehearsing until they're satisfied with their delivery. They know that once they begin speaking and concentrate on their ideas, enthusiasm will quell anxiety. They know, too, that the symptoms of anxiety are usually imperceptible to listeners, who cannot see or hear a racing heart, upset stomach, cold hands, and worried thoughts. Even speakers who describe themselves as nervous usually appear confident and calm to their audiences.

Several techniques can help you reduce your level of anxiety:

- Use simple relaxation exercises, such as deep breathing or tensing and relaxing your stomach muscles, to ease some of the physical symptoms of speech anxiety—stomachache, rapid heartbeat, and shaky hands, legs, and voice.
- Think positively. Try to convert any negative and irrational thoughts about speaking into positive ones about yourself and your behavior. Instead of worrying about the mistakes you might make, concentrate on how well you've prepared and practiced your presentation and how significant your ideas are.
- Don't avoid opportunities to speak in public. Practice and experience build speaking skills and offer the best insurance for success.

Glossary of Usage

This glossary provides notes on words or phrases that often cause problems for writers. The recommendations for standard written English are based on current dictionaries and usage guides such as the ones listed on pp. 586–89. Items labeled **nonstandard** should be avoided in speech and especially in writing. Those labeled **colloquial** and **slang** occur in speech and in some informal writing but are best avoided in the more formal writing usually expected in college and business. (Words and phrases labeled *colloquial* include those labeled by many dictionaries with the equivalent term *informal.*) See Chapter 38, pp. 558–77, for further discussion of word choice and for exercises in usage. See p. 591 for a description of dictionary labels. Also see pp. 604–05 for a list of commonly confused words that are pronounced the same or similarly. The words and definitions provided there supplement this glossary.

The glossary is necessarily brief. Keep a dictionary handy for all your writing, and make a habit of referring to it whenever you doubt the appropriateness of a word or phrase.

a, an Use *a* before words beginning with consonant sounds, including those spelled with an initial pronounced *h* and those spelled with vowels that are sounded as consonants: *a historian, a one-o'clock class, a university.* Use *an* before words that begin with vowel sounds, including those spelled with an initial silent *h: an orgy, an L, an honor.*

The article before an abbreviation depends on how the abbreviation is read: *She was once an AEC undersecretary* (*AEC* is read as three separate letters); *Many Americans opposed a SALT treaty* (*SALT* is read as one word, *salt*).

For the use of *a/an* versus *the,* see pp. 356–58.

accept, except *Accept* is a verb meaning "receive." *Except* is usually a preposition or conjunction meaning "but for" or "other than"; when it is used as a verb, it means "leave out." *I can accept all your suggestions except the last one. I'm sorry you excepted my last suggestion from your list.*

adverse, averse *Adverse* and *averse* both mean "opposed" or "hostile." But *averse* describes the subject's opposition to something, whereas *adverse* describes something opposed to the subject: *The President was averse to adverse criticism.*

advice, advise *Advice* is a noun, and *advise* is a verb: *Take my advice; do as I advise you.*

affect, effect Usually *affect* is a verb, meaning "to influence," and *effect* is a noun, meaning "result": *The drug did not affect his driving; in fact, it seemed to have no effect at all.* But *effect* occasionally is used as a verb meaning "to bring about": *Her efforts effected a change.* And *affect* is used in psychology as a noun meaning "feeling or emotion": *One can infer much about affect from behavior.*

aggravate *Aggravate* should not be used in its colloquial meaning of "irritate" or "exasperate" (for example, *We were aggravated by her constant arguing*). *Aggravate* means "make worse": *The President was irritated by the Senate's indecision because he feared any delay might aggravate the unrest in the Middle East.*

agree to, agree with *Agree to* means "consent to," and *agree with* means "be in accord with": *How can they agree to a treaty when they don't agree with each other about the terms?*

ain't Nonstandard for *am not, isn't,* or *aren't.*

all, all of Usually *all* is sufficient to modify a noun: *all my loving, all the things you are.* Before a pronoun or proper noun, *all of* is usually appropriate: *all of me, in all of France.*

all ready, already *All ready* means "completely prepared," and *already* means "by now" or "before now": *We were all ready to go to the movie, but it had already started.*

all right *All right* is always two words. *Alright* is a common misspelling.

Usage

all together, altogether *All together* means "in unison" or "gathered in one place." *Altogether* means "entirely." *It's not altogether true that our family never spends vacations all together.*

allusion, illusion An *allusion* is an indirect reference, and an *illusion* is a deceptive appearance: *Paul's constant allusions to Shakespeare created the illusion that he was an intellectual.*

almost, most *Almost* means "nearly"; *most* means "the greater number (or part) of." In formal writing, *most* should not be used as a substitute for *almost: We see each other almost* [not *most*] *every day.*

a lot *A lot* is always two words, used informally to mean "many." *Alot* is a common misspelling.

among, between In general, use *among* for relationships involving more than two people or things. Use *between* for relationships involving only two or for comparing one thing to a group to which it belongs. *The four of them agreed among themselves that the choice was between New York and Los Angeles.*

amongst Although common in British English, in American English *amongst* is an overrefined substitute for *among.*

amount, number Use *amount* with a singular noun that names something not countable (a noncount noun): *The amount of food varies.* Use *number* with a plural noun that names more than one of something countable (a plural count noun): *The number of calories must stay the same.*

an, and *An* is an article (see *a, an*). *And* is a coordinating conjunction. Do not accidentally omit the *d* from *and.*

and etc. *Et cetera* (*etc.*) means "and the rest"; *and etc.* therefore is redundant. See also *et al., etc.*

and/or *And/or* indicates three options: one or the other or both (*The decision is made by the mayor and/or the council*). If you mean all three options, *and/or* is appropriate. Otherwise, use *and* if you mean both, *or* if you mean either.

and which, and who *And which* or *and who* is correct only when used to introduce a second clause beginning with the same relative pronoun: *Jill is my cousin who goes to school here and who calls me constantly.* Otherwise, *and* is not needed: *WCAS is my favorite AM radio station, which* [not *and which*] *I listen to every morning.*

ante-, anti- The prefix *ante-* means "before" (*antedate, antebellum*); *anti-* means "against" (*antiwar, antinuclear*). Before a capital letter or *i, anti-* takes a hyphen: *anti-Freudian, anti-isolationist.*

anxious, eager *Anxious* means "nervous" or "worried" and is usually followed by *about. Eager* means "looking forward" and is usually followed by *to. I've been anxious about getting blisters. I'm eager* [not *anxious*] *to get new running shoes.*

anybody, any body; anyone, any one *Anybody* and *anyone* are indefinite pronouns; *any body* is a noun modified by *any; any one* is a pronoun or adjective modified by *any. How can anybody communicate with any body of government? Can anyone help Amy? She has more work than any one person can handle.*

Usage

any more, anymore *Any more* means "no more"; *anymore* means "now." Both are used in negative constructions: *He doesn't want any more. She doesn't live here anymore.*

anyplace Colloquial for *anywhere.*

anyways, anywheres Nonstandard for *anyway* and *anywhere.*

apt, liable, likely *Apt* and *likely* are interchangeable. Strictly speaking, though, *apt* means "having a tendency to": *Horace is apt to forget his lunch in the morning. Likely* means "probably going to": *Horace is leaving so early today that he's likely to catch the first bus.*

Liable normally means "in danger of" and should be confined to situations with undesirable consequences: *Horace is liable to trip over that hose.* Strictly, *liable* means "responsible" or "exposed to": *The owner will be liable for Horace's injuries.*

are, is Use *are* with a plural subject (*books are*), *is* with a singular subject (*book is*).

as Substituting for *because, since,* or *while, as* may be vague or ambiguous: *As we were stopping to rest, we decided to eat lunch.* (Does *as* mean "while" or "because"?) *As* should never be used as a substitute for *whether* or *who. I'm not sure whether* [not *as*] *we can make it. That's the man who* [not *as*] *gave me directions.*

as, like See *like, as.*

as, than In comparisons, *as* and *than* precede a subjective-case pronoun when the pronoun is a subject: *I love you more than he* [*loves you*]. *As* and *than* precede an objective-case pronoun when the pronoun is an object: *I love you as much as* [*I love*] *him.* (See also p. 296.)

assure, ensure, insure *Assure* means "to promise": *He assured us that we would miss the traffic. Ensure* and *insure* often are used interchangeably to mean "make certain," but some reserve *insure* for matters of legal and financial protection and use *ensure* for more general meanings: *We left early to ensure that we would miss the traffic. It's expensive to insure yourself against floods.*

as to A stuffy substitute for *about: The suspect was questioned about* [not *as to*] *her actions.*

at The use of *at* after *where* is wordy and should be avoided: *Where are you meeting him?* is preferable to *Where are you meeting him at?*

at this point in time Wordy for *now, at this point,* or *at this time.*

averse, adverse See *adverse, averse.*

awful, awfully Strictly speaking, *awful* means "awe-inspiring." As intensifiers meaning "very" or "extremely" (*He tried awfully hard*), *awful* and *awfully* should be avoided in formal speech or writing.

Usage

a while, awhile *Awhile* is an adverb; *a while* is an article and a noun. Thus *awhile* can modify a verb but cannot serve as the object of a preposition, and *a while* is just the opposite: *I will be gone awhile* [not *a while*]. *I will be gone for a while* [not *awhile*].

bad, badly In formal speech and writing, *bad* should be used only as an adjective; the adverb is *badly. He felt bad because his tooth ached badly.* In *He felt bad,* the verb *felt* is a linking verb and the adjective *bad* is a subject complement. (See also pp. 349–50.)

being as, being that Colloquial for *because,* the preferable word in formal speech or writing: *Because* [not *Being as*] *the world is round, Columbus never did fall off the edge.*

beside, besides *Beside* is a preposition meaning "next to." *Besides* is a preposition meaning "except" or "in addition to" as well as an adverb meaning "in addition." *Besides, several other people besides you want to sit beside Dr. Christensen.*

better, had better *Had better* (meaning "ought to") is a verb modified by an adverb. The verb is necessary and should not be omitted: *You had better* [not *better*] *go.*

between, among See *among, between.*

bring, take Use *bring* only for movement from a farther place to a nearer one and *take* for any other movement. *First, take these books to the library for renewal, then take them to Mr. Daniels. Bring them back to me when he's finished.*

bunch In formal speech and writing, *bunch* (as a noun) should be used only to refer to clusters of things growing or fastened together, such as bananas and grapes. Its use to mean a group of items or people is colloquial; *crowd* or *group* is preferable.

burst, bursted; bust, busted *Burst* is a standard verb form meaning "to fly apart suddenly" (principal parts *burst, burst, burst*). The past-tense form *bursted* is nonstandard. The verb *bust* (*busted*) is slang.

but, hardly, scarcely These words are negative in their own right; using *not* with any of them produces a double negative (see p. 354). *We have but* [not *haven't got but*] *an hour before our plane leaves. I could hardly* [not *couldn't hardly*] *make out her face.*

but, however, yet Each of these words is adequate to express contrast. Don't combine them. *He said he had finished, yet* [not *but yet*] *he continued.*

but that, but what These wordy substitutes for *that* and *what* should be avoided: *I don't doubt that* [not *but that*] *you are right.*

calculate, figure, reckon As substitutes for *expect* or *imagine (I figure I'll go),* these words are colloquial.

can, may Strictly, *can* indicates capacity or ability, and *may* indicates permission: *If I may talk with you a moment, I believe I can solve your problem.*

can't help but This idiom is common but redundant. Either *I can't help wishing* or the more formal *I cannot but wish* is preferable to *I can't help but wish.*

Usage

case, instance, line Expressions such as *in the case of, in the instance of,* and *along the lines of* are usually unnecessary padding and should be avoided.

censor, censure To *censor* is to edit or remove from public view on moral or some other grounds; to *censure* is to give a formal scolding. *The lieutenant was censured by Major Taylor for censoring the letters her soldiers wrote home from boot camp.*

center around *Center on* is more logical than, and preferable to, *center around.*

climatic, climactic *Climatic* comes from *climate* and refers to weather: *Last winter's temperatures may indicate a climatic change. Climatic* comes from *climax* and refers to a dramatic high point: *During the climactic duel between Hamlet and Laertes, Gertrude drinks poisoned wine.*

complement, compliment To *complement* something is to add to, complete, or reinforce it: *Her yellow blouse complemented her black hair.* To *compliment* something is to make a flattering remark about it: *He complimented her on her hair. Complimentary* can also mean "free": *complimentary tickets.*

compose, comprise *Compose* means "to make up": *The parts compose the whole. Comprise* means "to consist of": *The whole* *comprises the parts.* Thus, *The band comprises* [not *is comprised of*] *twelve musicians. Twelve musicians compose* [not *comprise*] *the band.*

conscience, conscious *Conscience* is a noun meaning "a sense of right and wrong"; *conscious* is an adjective meaning "aware" or "awake." *Though I was barely conscious, my conscience nagged me.*

contact Often used imprecisely as a verb instead of a more exact word such as *consult, talk with, telephone,* or *write to.*

continual, continuous *Continual* means "constantly recurring": *Most movies on television are continually interrupted by commercials. Continuous* means "unceasing": *Some cable channels present movies continuously without commercials.*

convince, persuade In the strictest sense, to *convince* someone means to change his or her opinion; to *persuade* someone means to move him or her to action. *Convince* is thus properly followed by *of* or *that,* whereas *persuade* is followed by *to: Once he convinced Othello of Desdemona's infidelity, Iago easily persuaded him to kill her.*

could care less The expression is *could not* [*couldn't*] *care less. Could care less* indicates some care, the opposite of what is intended.

could of See *have, of.*

couple of Used colloquially to mean "a few" or "several."

credible, creditable, credulous *Credible* means "believable": *It's a strange story, but it seems credible to me. Creditable* means "deserving of credit" or "worthy": *Steve gave a creditable performance. Credulous* means "gullible": *The credulous Claire believed Tim's lies.* See also *incredible, incredulous.*

Usage

criteria The plural of *criterion* (meaning "standard for judgment"): *Our criteria are strict. The most important criterion is a sense of humor.*

data The plural of *datum* (meaning "fact"): *Out of all the data generated by these experiments, not one datum supports our hypothesis.* Usually, a more common term such as *fact, result,* or *figure* is preferred to *datum.* Though *data* is often used as a singular noun, most careful writers still treat it as plural: *The data fail* [not *fails*] *to support the hypothesis.*

device, devise *Device* is the noun, and *devise* is the verb: *Can you devise some device for getting his attention?*

different from, different than *Different from* is preferred: *His purpose is different from mine.* But *different than* is widely accepted when a construction using *from* would be wordy: *I'm a different person now than I used to be* is preferable to *I'm a different person now from the person I used to be.*

differ from, differ with To *differ from* is to be unlike: *The twins differ from each other only in their hair styles.* To *differ with* is to disagree with: *I have to differ with you on that point.*

discreet, discrete *Discreet* (noun form *discretion*) means "tactful": *What's a discreet way of telling Maud to be quiet? Discrete* (noun form *discreteness*) means "separate and distinct": *Within a computer's memory are millions of discrete bits of information.*

disinterested, uninterested *Disinterested* means "impartial": *We chose Pete, as a disinterested third party, to decide who was right. Uninterested* means "bored" or "lacking interest": *Unfortunately, Pete was completely uninterested in the question.*

don't *Don't* is the contraction for *do not,* not for *does not: I don't care, you don't care,* and *he doesn't* [not *don't*] *care.*

due to *Due* is an adjective or noun; thus *due to* is always acceptable as a subject complement: *His gray hairs were due to age.* Many object to *due to* as a preposition meaning "because of" (*Due to the holiday, class was canceled*). A rule of thumb is that *due to* is always correct after a form of the verb *be* but questionable otherwise.

due to the fact that Wordy for *because.*

each and every Wordy for *each* or *every.* Write *each one of us* or *every one of us,* not *each and every one of us.*

eager, anxious See *anxious, eager.*

effect See *affect, effect.*

elicit, illicit *Elicit* is a verb meaning "bring out" or "call forth." *Illicit* is an adjective meaning "unlawful." *The crime elicited an outcry against illicit drugs.*

emigrate, immigrate *Emigrate* means "to leave one place and move to another" (the Latin prefix *e-* means "out of": "migrate out of"): *The Chus emigrated from Korea. Immigrate* means "to move into a place where one was not born" (the Latin prefix *im-* means "into": "migrate into"): *They immigrated to the United States.*

ensure See *assure, ensure, insure.*

enthused Used colloquially as an adjective meaning "showing enthusiasm." The preferred adjective is *enthusiastic: The coach was enthusiastic* [not *enthused*] *about the team's victory.*

especially, specially *Especially* means "particularly" or "more than other things"; *specially* means "for a specific reason." *I especially treasure my boots. They were made specially for me.*

et al., etc. Use *et al.,* the Latin abbreviation for "and other people," only in source citations: *Jones et al.* Avoid *etc.,* the Latin abbreviation for "and other things," in formal writing, and do not use it to refer to people or to substitute for precision, as in *The government provides health care, etc.* See also *and etc.*

everybody, every body; everyone, every one *Everybody* and *everyone* are indefinite pronouns: *Everybody* [or *Everyone*] *knows Tom steals. Every one* is a pronoun modified by *every,* and *every body* a noun modified by *every.* Both refer to each thing or person of a specific group and are typically followed by *of: The game commissioner has stocked every body of fresh water in the state with fish, and now every one of our rivers is a potential trout stream.*

everyday, every day *Everyday* is an adjective meaning "used daily" or "common"; *every day* is a noun modified by *every: Everyday problems tend to arise every day.*

everywheres Nonstandard for *everywhere.*

except See *accept, except.*

except for the fact that Wordy for *except that.*

explicit, implicit *Explicit* means "stated outright": *I left explicit instructions. The movie contains explicit sex. Implicit* means "implied, unstated": *We had an implicit understanding. I trust Marcia implicitly.*

farther, further *Farther* refers to additional distance (*How much farther is it to the beach?*), and *further* refers to additional time, amount, or other abstract matters (*I don't want to discuss this any further*).

feel Avoid this word in place of *think* or *believe: She thinks* [not *feels*] *that the law should be changed.*

fewer, less *Fewer* refers to individual countable items (a plural count noun), *less* to general amounts (a noncount noun, always singular): *Skim milk has fewer calories than whole milk. We have less milk left than I thought.*

field The phrase *the field of* is wordy and generally unnecessary: *Margaret plans to specialize in* [not *in the field of*] *family medicine.*

figure See *calculate, figure, reckon.*

fixing to Avoid this colloquial substitute for "intend to": *The school intends* [not *is fixing*] *to build a new library.*

Usage

flaunt, flout *Flaunt* means "show off": *If you have style, flaunt it. Flout* means "scorn" or "defy": *Hester Prynne flouted convention and paid the price.*

flunk A colloquial substitute for *fail.*

former, latter *Former* refers to the first-named of two things, *latter* to the second-named: *I like both skiing and swimming, the former in the winter and the latter all year round.* To refer to the first- or last-named of three or more things, say *first or last: I like jogging, swimming, and hang gliding, but the last is inconvenient in the city.*

fun As an adjective, *fun* is colloquial and should be avoided in most writing: *It was a pleasurable* [not *fun*] *evening.*

further See *farther, further.*

get This common verb is used in many slang and colloquial expressions: *get lost, that really gets me, getting on. Get* is easy to overuse; watch out for it in expressions such as *it's getting better* (substitute *improving*) and *we got done* (substitute *finished*).

go As a substitute for *say* or *reply, go* is colloquial: *He says* [not *goes*], *"How do you do, madam?"*

good, well *Good* is an adjective, and *well* is nearly always an adverb: *Larry's a good dancer. He and Linda dance well together. Well* is properly used as an adjective only to refer to health: *You look well.* (*You look good,* in contrast, means "Your appearance is pleasing.")

good and Colloquial for "very": *I was very* [not *good and*] *tired.*

had better See *better, had better.*

had ought The *had* is unnecessary and should be omitted: *He ought* [not had ought] *to listen to his mother.*

half Either *half a* or *a half* is appropriate usage, but *a half a* is redundant: *Half a loaf* [not *A half a loaf*] *is better than none. I'd like a half-gallon* [not *a half a gallon*] *of mineral water, please.*

hanged, hung Though both are past-tense forms of *hang, hanged* is used to refer to executions and *hung* is used for all other meanings: *Tom Dooley was hanged* [not *hung*] *from a white oak tree. I hung* [not *hanged*] *the picture you gave me.*

hardly See *but, hardly, scarcely.*

have, of Use *have,* not *of,* after helping verbs such as *could, should, would, may,* and *might: You should have* [not *should of*] *told me.*

he, she; he/she Convention has allowed the use of *he* to mean "he or she": *After the infant learns to creep, he progresses to crawling.* However, many writers today consider this usage inaccurate and unfair because it seems to exclude females. The construction *he/she,* one substitute for *he,* is awkward and objectionable to most readers. The better choice is to make the pronoun plural, to rephrase, or, sparingly, to use *he or she.* For instance: *After infants learn to creep, they progress to crawling. After learning to creep, the infant progresses to crawling. After the infant learns to creep, he or she progresses to crawling.* (See also pp. 344 and 565.)

Usage

herself, himself See *myself, herself, himself, yourself.*

hisself Nonstandard for *himself.*

hopefully *Hopefully* means "with hope": *Freddy waited hopefully for a glimpse of Eliza.* The use of *hopefully* to mean "it is to be hoped," "I hope," or "let's hope" is now very common; but since many readers continue to object strongly to the usage, you should avoid it. *I hope* [not *Hopefully*] *the law will pass.*

idea, ideal An *idea* is a thought or conception. An *ideal* (noun) is a model of perfection or a goal. *Ideal* should not be used in place of *idea: The idea* [not *ideal*] *of the play is that our ideals often sustain us.*

if, whether For clarity, use *whether* rather than *if* when you are expressing an alternative: *If I laugh hard, people can't tell whether I'm crying.*

illicit See *elicit, illicit.*

illusion See *allusion, illusion.*

immigrate, emigrate See *emigrate, immigrate.*

impact Both the noun and the verb *impact* connote forceful or even violent collision. Avoid the increasingly common diluted meanings of *impact:* "an effect" (noun) or "to have an effect on" (verb). The diluted verb (*The budget cuts impacted social science research*) is bureaucratic jargon.

implicit See *explicit, implicit.*

imply, infer Writers or speakers *imply,* meaning "suggest": *Jim's letter implies he's having a good time.* Readers or listeners *infer,* meaning "conclude": *From Jim's letter I infer he's having a good time.*

in, into *In* indicates location or condition: *He was in the garage. She was in a coma. Into* indicates movement or a change in condition: *He went into the garage. She fell into a coma. Into* is also slang for "interested in" or "involved in": *I am into Zen.*

in . . . A number of phrases beginning with *in* are needlessly wordy and should be avoided: *in the event that* (for *if*); *in the neighborhood of* (for *approximately* or *about*); *in this day and age* (for *now* or *nowadays*); *in spite of the fact that* (for *although* or *even though*); and *in view of the fact that* (for *because* or *considering that*). Certain other *in* phrases are nothing but padding and can be omitted entirely: *in nature, in number, in reality,* and *in a very real sense.* (See also pp. 580–81.)

incredible, incredulous *Incredible* means "unbelievable"; *incredulous* means "unbelieving": *When Nancy heard Dennis's incredible story, she was frankly incredulous.* See also *credible, creditable, credulous.*

individual, person, party *Individual* should refer to a single human being in contrast to a group or should stress uniqueness: *The US Constitution places strong emphasis on the rights of the individual.* For other meanings *person* is preferable: *What person* [not *individual*] *wouldn't want the security promised in that advertisement? Party* means "group" (*Can you seat a party of four for dinner?*) and should not be used to refer to an individual except in legal documents. See also *people, persons.*

Usage

infer See *imply, infer.*

in regards to Nonstandard for *in regard to, as regards,* or *regarding.* See also *regarding.*

inside of, outside of The *of* is unnecessary when *inside* and *outside* are used as prepositions: *Stay inside* [not *inside of*] *the house. The decision is outside* [not *outside of*] *my authority. Inside of* may refer colloquially to time, though in formal English *within* is preferred: *The law was passed within* [not *inside of*] *a year.*

instance See *case, instance, line.*

insure See *assure, ensure, insure.*

irregardless Nonstandard for *regardless.*

is, are See *are, is.*

is because See *reason is because.*

is when, is where These are faulty constructions in sentences that define: *Adolescence is a stage* [not *is when a person is*] *between childhood and adulthood. Socialism is a system in which* [not *is where*] *government owns the means of production.* (See also p. 410.)

its, it's *Its* is the pronoun *it* in the possessive case: *That plant is losing its leaves. It's* is a contraction for *it is: It's likely to die if you don't water* *it.* Many people confuse *it's* and *its* because possessives are most often formed with *-'s;* but the possessive *its,* like *his* and *hers,* never takes an apostrophe.

-ize, -wise The suffix *-ize* changes a noun or adjective into a verb: *revolutionize, immunize.* The suffix *-wise* changes a noun or adjective into an adverb: *clockwise, otherwise, likewise.* Avoid the two suffixes except in established words: *The two nations are ready to settle on* [not *finalize*] *an agreement. I'm highly sensitive* [not *sensitized*] *to that kind of criticism. Financially* [not *Moneywise*], *it's a good time to invest in real estate.*

kind of, sort of, type of In formal speech and writing, avoid using *kind of* or *sort of* to mean "somewhat": *He was rather* [not *kind of*] *tall.*

Kind, sort, and *type* are singular and take singular modifiers and verbs: *This kind of dog is easily trained.* Agreement errors often occur when these singular nouns are combined with the plural adjectives *these* and *those: These kinds* [not *kind*] *of dogs are easily trained. Kind, sort,* and *type* should be followed by *of* but not by *a: I don't know what type of* [not *type* or *type of a*] *dog that is.*

Use *kind of, sort of,* or *type of* only when the word *kind, sort,* or *type* is important: *That was a strange* [not *strange sort of*] *statement.*

later, latter *Later* refers to time; *latter* refers to the second-named of two items. See also *former, latter.*

lay, lie *Lay* means "put" or "place" and takes a direct object: *We could lay the tablecloth in the sun.* Its main forms are *lay, laid, laid. Lie* means "recline" or "be situated" and does not take an object: *I lie awake at night. The town lies east of the river.* Its main forms are *lie, lay, lain.* (See also pp. 306–07.)

Usage

leave, let *Leave* and *let* are interchangeable only when followed by *alone; leave me alone* is the same as *let me alone.* Otherwise, *leave* means "depart" and *let* means "allow": *Julia would not let Susan leave.*

less See *fewer, less.*

let See *leave, let.*

liable See *apt, liable, likely.*

lie, lay See *lay, lie.*

like, as In formal speech and writing, *like* should not introduce a full clause (with a subject and a verb) because it is a preposition. The preferred choice is *as* or *as if: The plan succeeded as* [not *like*] *we hoped. It seemed as if* [not *like*] *it might fail. Other plans like it have failed.*

When *as* serves as a preposition, the distinction between *as* and *like* depends on meaning. *As* suggests that the subject is equivalent or identical to the description: *She was hired as an engineer. Like* suggests resemblance but not identity: *People like her do well in such jobs.* See also *like, such as.*

like, such as Strictly, *such as* precedes an example that represents a larger subject, whereas *like* indicates that two subjects are comparable. *Steve has recordings of many great saxophonists such as Ben Webster and*

Lee Konitz. Steve wants to be a great jazz saxophonist like Ben Webster and Lee Konitz.

Many writers prefer to keep *such* and *as* together: *Steve admires saxophonists such as* . . . rather than *Steve admires such saxophonists as*. . . .

likely See *apt, liable, likely.*

line See *case, instance, line.*

literally This word means "actually" or "just as the words say," and it should not be used to qualify or intensify expressions whose words are not to be taken at face value. The sentence *He was literally climbing the walls* describes a person behaving like an insect, not a person who is restless or anxious. For the latter meaning, *literally* should be omitted.

lose, loose *Lose* means "mislay": *Did you lose a brown glove? Loose* means "unrestrained" or "not tight": *Ann's canary got loose. Loose* also can function as a verb meaning "let loose": *They loose the dogs as soon as they spot the bear.*

lots, lots of Colloquial substitutes for *very many, a great many,* or *much.* Avoid *lots* and *lots of* in college or business writing. When you use either one informally, be careful to maintain subject-verb agreement: *There are* [not *is*] *lots of fish in the pond.*

may, can See *can, may.*

may be, maybe *May be* is a verb, and *maybe* is an adverb meaning "perhaps": *Tuesday may be a legal holiday. Maybe we won't have classes.*

may of See *have, of.*

media *Media* is the plural of *medium* and takes a plural verb: *All the news media are increasingly visual.* The singular verb is common, even in the media, but most careful writers still use the plural verb.

might of See *have, of.*

moral, morale As a noun, *moral* means "ethical conclusion" or "lesson": *The moral of the story escapes me. Morale* means "spirit" or "state of mind": *Victory improved the team's morale.*

most, almost See *almost, most.*

must of See *have, of.*

myself, herself, himself, yourself The *-self* pronouns refer to or intensify another word or words: *Paul helped himself; Jill herself said so.* The *-self* pronouns are often used colloquially in place of personal pronouns, but that use should be avoided in formal speech and writing: *No one except me* [not *myself*] *saw the accident. Our delegates will be Susan and you* [not *yourself*].

nohow Nonstandard for *in no way* or *in any way.*

nothing like, nowhere near These colloquial substitutes for *not nearly* are best avoided in formal speech and writing: *That program is not nearly* [not *nowhere near*] *as expensive.*

nowheres Nonstandard for *nowhere.*

number See *amount, number.*

of, have See *have, of.*

off of *Of* is unnecessary. Use *off* or *from* rather than *off of: He jumped off* [or *from,* not *off of*] *the roof.*

OK, O.K., okay All three spellings are acceptable, but avoid this colloquial term in formal speech and writing.

on, upon In modern English, *upon* is usually just a stuffy way of saying *on.* Unless you need a formal effect, use *on: We decided on* [not *upon*] *a location for our next meeting.*

on account of Wordy for *because of.*

on the other hand This transitional expression of contrast should be preceded by its mate, *on the one hand: On the one hand, we hoped for snow. On the other hand, we feared that it would harm the animals.* However, the two combined can be unwieldy, and a simple *but, however, yet,* or *in contrast* often suffices: *We hoped for snow. Yet we feared that it would harm the animals.*

outside of See *inside of, outside of.*

owing to the fact that Wordy for *because.*

party See *individual, person, party.*

Usage

people, persons In formal usage, *people* refers to a general group: *We the people of the United States. . . . Persons* refers to a collection of individuals: *Will the person or persons who saw the accident please notify. . . .* Except when emphasizing individuals, prefer *people* to *persons.* See also *individual, person, party.*

per Except in technical writing, an English equivalent is usually preferable to the Latin *per: $10 an* [not *per*] *hour; sent by* [not *per*] *parcel post; requested in* [not *per* or *as per*] *your letter.*

percent (per cent), percentage Both these terms refer to fractions of one hundred. *Percent* always follows a numeral (*40 percent of the voters*), and the word should be used instead of the symbol (%) in general writing. *Percentage* stands alone (*the percentage of votes*) or follows an adjective (*a high percentage*).

person See *individual, person, party.*

persons See *people, persons.*

persuade See *convince, persuade.*

phenomena The plural of *phenomenon* (meaning "perceivable fact" or "unusual occurrence"): *Many phenomena are not recorded. One phenomenon is attracting attention.*

plenty A colloquial substitute for *very: The reaction occurred very* [not *plenty*] *fast.*

plus *Plus* is standard as a preposition meaning *in addition to: His income plus mine is sufficient.* But *plus* is colloquial as a conjunctive adverb: *Our organization is larger than theirs; moreover* [not *plus*], *we have more money.*

practicable, practical *Practicable* means "capable of being put into practice"; *practical* means "useful" or "sensible": *We figured out a practical new design for our kitchen, but it was too expensive to be practicable.*

precede, proceed The verb *precede* means "come before": *My name precedes yours in the alphabet.* The verb *proceed* means "move on": *We were told to proceed to the waiting room.*

prejudice, prejudiced *Prejudice* is a noun; *prejudiced* is an adjective. Do not drop the *-d* from *prejudiced: I knew that my parents were prejudiced* [not *prejudice*].

pretty Overworked as an adverb meaning "rather" or "somewhat": *He was somewhat* [not *pretty*] *irked at the suggestion.*

previous to, prior to Wordy for *before.*

principal, principle *Principal* is an adjective meaning "foremost" or "major," a noun meaning "chief official," or, in finance, a noun meaning "capital sum." *Principle* is a noun only, meaning "rule" or "axiom." *Her principal reasons for confessing were her principles of right and wrong.*

Usage

proceed, precede See *precede, proceed.*

provided, providing *Provided* may serve as a subordinating conjunction meaning "on the condition (that)"; *providing* may not. *The grocer will begin providing food for the soup kitchen provided* [not *providing*] *we find a suitable space.*

question of whether, question as to whether Wordy substitutes for *whether.*

raise, rise *Raise* means "lift" or "bring up" and takes a direct object: *The Kirks raise cattle.* Its main forms are *raise, raised, raised. Rise* means "get up" and does not take an object: *They must rise at dawn.* Its main forms are *rise, rose, risen.* (See also pp. 306–07.)

real, really In formal speech and writing, *real* should not be used as an adverb; *really* is the adverb and *real* an adjective. *Popular reaction to the announcement was really* [not *real*] *enthusiastic.*

reason is because Although colloquially common, this expression should be avoided in formal speech and writing. Use a *that* clause after *reason is: The reason he is absent is that* [not *is because*] *he is sick.* Or: *He is absent because he is sick.*

reckon See *calculate, figure, reckon.*

regarding, in regard to, with regard to, relating to, relative to, with respect to, respecting Stuffy substitutes for *on, about,* or *concerning: Mr. McGee spoke about* [not *with regard to*] *the plans for the merger.*

respectful, respective *Respectful* means "full of (or showing) respect": *Be respectful of other people. Respective* means "separate": *The French and the Germans occupied their respective trenches.*

rise, raise See *raise, rise.*

scarcely See *but, hardly, scarcely.*

sensual, sensuous *Sensual* suggests sexuality; *sensuous* means "pleasing to the senses." *Stirred by the sensuous scent of meadow grass and flowers, Cheryl and Paul found their thoughts growing increasingly sensual.*

set, sit *Set* means "put" or "place" and takes a direct object: *He sets the pitcher down.* Its main forms are *set, set, set. Sit* means "be seated" and does not take an object: *She sits on the sofa.* Its main forms are *sit, sat, sat.* (See also pp. 306–07.)

shall, will *Will* is the future-tense helping verb for all persons: *I will go, you will go, they will go.* The main use of *shall* is for first-person questions requesting an opinion or consent: *Shall I order a pizza? Shall we dance?* (Questions that merely inquire about the future use *will: When will I see you again?*) *Shall* can also be used for the first person when a formal effect is desired (I *shall expect you around three*), and it is occasionally used with the second or third person to express the speaker's determination (*You shall do as I say*).

should, would *Should* expresses obligation: *I should fix dinner. You should set the table. Jack should wash the dishes. Would* expresses a wish or hypothetical condition: *I would do it. Wouldn't you?* When the context is formal, however, *should* is sometimes used instead of *would* in the first person: *We should be delighted to accept.*

Usage

should of See *have, of.*

since *Since* mainly relates to time: *I've been waiting since noon.* But *since* is also often used to mean "because": *Since you ask, I'll tell you.* Revise sentences in which the word could have either meaning, such as *Since you left, my life is empty.*

sit, set See *set, sit.*

situation Often unnecessary, as in *The situation is that we have to get some help* (revise to *We have to get some help*) or *The team was faced with a punting situation* (revise to *The team was faced with punting* or *The team had to punt*).

so Avoid using *so* alone as a vague intensifier: *He was so late.* So needs to be followed by *that* and a clause that states a result: *He was so late that I left without him.*

some *Some* is colloquial as an adverb meaning "somewhat" or "to some extent" and as an adjective meaning "remarkable": *We'll have to hurry somewhat* [not *some*] *to get there in time. Those are remarkable* [not *some*] *photographs.*

somebody, some body; someone, some one *Somebody* and *someone* are indefinite pronouns; *some body* is a noun modified by *some;* and *some one* is a pronoun or an adjective modified by *some*. *Somebody ought to invent a shampoo that will give hair some body. Someone told Janine she should choose some one plan and stick with it.*

someplace Informal for *somewhere*.

sometime, sometimes, some time *Sometime* means "at an indefinite time in the future": *Why don't you come up and see me sometime? Sometimes* means "now and then": *I still see my old friend Joe sometimes. Some time* means "a span of time": *I need some time to make the payments.*

somewheres Nonstandard for *somewhere*.

sort of, sort of a See *kind of, sort of, type of*.

specially See *especially, specially*.

such Avoid using *such* as a vague intensifier: *It was such a cold winter. Such* should be followed by *that* and a clause that states a result: *It was such a cold winter that Napoleon's troops had to turn back.*

such as See *like, such as*.

supposed to, used to In both these expressions, the *-d* is essential: *I used to* [not *use to*] *think so. He's supposed to* [not *suppose to*] *meet us.*

sure Colloquial when used as an adverb meaning *surely: James Madison sure was right about the need for the Bill of Rights.* If you merely want to be emphatic, use *certainly: Madison certainly was right.* If your goal is to convince a possibly reluctant reader, use *surely: Madison surely was right. Surely Madison was right.*

Usage

sure and, sure to; try and, try to *Sure to* and *try to* are the correct forms: *Be sure to* [not *sure and*] *vote. Try to* [not *Try and*] *vote early to avoid a line.*

take, bring See *bring, take*.

than, as See *as, than*.

than, then *Than* is a conjunction used in comparisons, *then* an adverb indicating time: *Holmes knew then that Moriarty was wilier than he had thought.*

that, which *That* always introduces an essential clause: *We should use the lettuce that Susan bought* (*that Susan bought* limits *lettuce* to a particular lettuce). *Which* can introduce both essential and nonessential clauses, but many writers reserve *which* only for nonessential clauses: *The leftover lettuce, which is in the refrigerator, would make a good salad* (*which is in the refrigerator* simply provides more information about the lettuce we already know of). Essential clauses (with *that* or *which*) are not set off by commas; nonessential clauses (with *which*) are. (See also pp. 473–77.)

that, who, which Use *that* to refer to most animals and to things: *The animals that escaped included a zebra. The rocket that failed cost millions.* Use *who* to refer to people and to animals with names: *Dorothy is* *the girl who visits Oz. Her dog, Toto, who accompanies her, gives her courage.* Use *which* only to refer to animals and things: *The river, which runs a thousand miles, empties into the Indian Ocean.* (See also pp. 386–87.)

their, there, they're *Their* is the possessive form of *they: Give them their money. There* indicates place (*I saw her standing there*) or functions to postpone the sentence subject (*There is a hole behind you*). *They're* is a contraction for *they are: They're going fast.*

theirselves Nonstandard for *themselves.*

then, than See *than, then.*

these kind, these sort, these type, those kind See *kind of, sort of, type of.*

this, these *This* is singular: *this car* or *This is the reason I left. These* is plural: *these cars* or *These are not valid reasons.*

this here, these here, that there, them there Nonstandard for *this, these, that,* or *those.*

thru A colloquial spelling of *through* that should be avoided in all academic and business writing.

thusly A mistaken form of *thus.*

till, until, 'til *Till* and *until* have the same meaning; both are acceptable. *'Til,* a contraction of *until,* is an old form that has been replaced by *till.*

time period Since a *period* is an interval of time, this expression is redundant: *They did not see each other for a long time* [not *time period*]. *Six accidents occurred in a three-week period* [not *time period*].

to, too, two *To* is a preposition; *too* is an adverb meaning "also" or "excessively"; and *two* is a number. *I too have been to Europe two times.*

too Avoid using *too* as an intensifier meaning "very": *Monkeys are too mean.* If you do use *too,* explain the consequences of the excessive quality: *Monkeys are too mean to make good pets.*

toward, towards Both are acceptable, though *toward* is preferred. Use one or the other consistently.

try and, try to See *sure and, sure to; try and, try to.*

type of See *kind of, sort of, type of.* Don't use *type* without *of: It was a family type of* [not *type*] *restaurant.* Or, better: *It was a family restaurant.*

uninterested See *disinterested, uninterested.*

unique *Unique* means "the only one of its kind" and so cannot sensibly be modified with words such as *very* or *most: That was a unique* [not *a very unique* or *the most unique*] *movie.*

until See *till, until, 'til.*

upon, on See *on, upon.*

usage, use *Usage* refers to conventions, most often those of a language: *Is "hadn't ought" proper usage? Usage* is often misused in place of the noun *use: Wise use* [not *usage*] *of insulation can save fuel.*

use, utilize *Utilize* can be used to mean "make good use of": *Many teachers utilize computers for instruction.* But for all other senses of "place in service" or "employ," prefer *use.*

used to See *supposed to, used to.*

wait for, wait on In formal speech and writing, *wait for* means "await" (*I'm waiting for Paul*), and *wait on* means "serve" (*The owner of the store herself waited on us*).

ways Colloquial as a substitute for way: *We have only a little way* [not *ways*] *to go.*

well See *good, well.*

whether, if See *if, whether.*

which, that See *that, which.*

which, who, that See *that, who, which.*

who, whom *Who* is the subject of a sentence or clause (*We don't know who will come*). *Whom* is the object of a verb or preposition (*We do not know whom we invited*). (See also pp. 297–98.)

who's, whose *Who's* is the contraction of *who is: Who's at the door? Whose* is the possessive form of *who: Whose book is that?*

will, shall See *shall, will.*

wise See *-ize, -wise.*

with regard to, with respect to See *regarding.*

would See *should, would.*

would have Avoid this construction in place of *had* in clauses that begin *if* and state a condition contrary to fact: *If the tree had* [not *would have*] *withstood the fire, it would have been the oldest in town.* (See also p. 328.)

would of See *have, of.*

you In all but very formal writing, *you* is generally appropriate as long as it means "you, the reader." In all writing, avoid indefinite uses of *you,* such as *In one ancient tribe your first loyalty was to your parents.* (See also pp. 385–86.)

your, you're *Your* is the possessive form of *you: Your dinner is ready. You're* is the contraction of *you are: You're bound to be late.*

yourself See *myself, herself, himself, yourself.*

Glossary of Terms

This glossary defines terms of grammar, rhetoric, literature, and Internet research. Page numbers in parentheses refer you to sections of the text where the term is explained more fully.

absolute phrase A phrase consisting of a noun or pronoun plus the *-ing* or *-ed* form of a verb (a participle): *Our accommodations arranged, we set out on our journey. They will hire a local person, other things being equal.* An absolute phrase modifies a whole clause or sentence (rather than a single word), and it is not joined to the rest of the sentence by a connector. (See p. 273.)

abstract and concrete Two kinds of language. **Abstract** words refer to ideas, qualities, attitudes, and conditions that can't be perceived with the senses: *beauty, guilty, victory.* **Concrete** words refer to objects, persons, places, or conditions that can be perceived with the senses: *Abilene, scratchy, toolbox.* See also *general and specific.* (See p. 570.)

acronym A pronounceable word formed from the initial letter or letters of each word in an organization's title: NATO (North Atlantic Treaty Organization).

active voice See *voice.*

adjectival A term sometimes used to describe any word or word group, other than an adjective, that is used to modify a noun. Common adjectivals include nouns (*wagon train, railroad ties*), phrases (*fool on the hill*), and clauses (*the man that I used to be*).

adjective A word used to modify a noun (*beautiful morning*) or a pronoun (*ordinary one*). (See Chapter 16.) Nouns, some verb forms, phrases, and clauses may also serve as adjectives: *book sale; a used book; sale of old books; the sale, which occurs annually.* (See *clauses, prepositional phrases,* and *verbals and verbal phrases.*)

Adjectives come in several classes:

- A **descriptive adjective** names some quality of the noun: *beautiful morning, dark horse.*
- A **limiting adjective** narrows the scope of a noun. It may be a **possessive** (*my, their*); a **demonstrative adjective** (*this train, these days*); an **interrogative adjective** (*what time? whose body?*); or a number (*two boys*).
- A **proper adjective** is derived from a proper noun: *French language, Machiavellian scheme.*

Adjectives also can be classified according to position:

- An **attributive adjective** appears next to the noun it modifies: *full moon.*
- A **predicate adjective** is connected to its noun by a linking verb: *The moon is full.* See also *complement.*

adjective clause See *adjective.*

adjective phrase See *adjective.*

adverb A word used to modify a verb (*warmly greet*), an adjective (*only three people*), another adverb (*quite seriously*), or a whole sentence (*Fortunately, she is employed*). (See Chapter 16.) Some verb forms, phrases, and clauses may also serve as adverbs: *easy to stop, drove by a farm, plowed the fields when the earth thawed.* (See *clause, prepositional phrase,* and *verbals and verbal phrases.*)

adverb clause See *adverb.*

adverbial A term sometimes used to describe any word or word group, other than an adverb, that is used to modify a verb, an adjective, another adverb, or a whole sentence. Common adverbials include nouns (*This little piggy stayed home*), phrases (*This little piggy went to market*), and clauses (*This little piggy went wherever he wanted*).

adverbial conjunction See *conjunctive adverb.*

adverb phrase See *adverb.*

Terms

agreement The correspondence of one word to another in person, number, or gender. A verb must agree with its subject (*The chef orders egg sandwiches*), a pronoun must agree with its antecedent (*The chef surveys her breakfast*), and a demonstrative adjective must agree with its noun (*She likes these kinds of sandwiches*). (See Chapter 15.)

Logical agreement requires consistency in number between other related words, usually nouns: *The students brought their books* [not *book*]. (See p. 391.)

analogy A comparison between members of different classes, such as a nursery school and a barnyard or a molecule and a pair of dancers. Usually, the purpose is to explain something unfamiliar to readers through something familiar. (See p. 101.)

analysis The separation of a subject into its elements. Sometimes called **division,** analysis is fundamental to critical thinking, reading, and writing (pp. 129–31) and is a useful tool for developing essays (p. 27) and paragraphs (pp. 98–99).

antecedent The word to which a pronoun refers: *Jonah, who is not yet ten, has already chosen the college he will attend* (*Jonah* is the antecedent of the pronouns *who* and *he*). (See pp. 341–45.)

APA style The style of documentation recommended by the American Psychological Association and used in many of the social sciences. (For discussion and examples, see pp. 841–55.)

appeals Attempts to engage and persuade readers. An **emotional appeal** touches readers' feelings, beliefs, and values. An **ethical appeal** presents the writer as competent, sincere, and fair. A **rational appeal** engages readers' powers of reasoning. (See pp. 171–73.)

appositive A word or phrase appearing next to a noun or pronoun that renames or identifies it and is equivalent to it: *My brother Michael, the best horn player in town, won the state competition* (*Michael* identifies which brother is being referred to; *the best horn player in town* renames *Michael*). (See pp. 280–81.)

argument Writing whose primary purpose is to convince readers of an idea or persuade them to act. (See Chapters 6–7.)

article The word *a, an,* or *the.* Articles are sometimes called **determiners** because they always signal that a noun follows. (See pp. 356–58 for when to use *a/an* versus *the.* See p. 925 for when to use *a* versus *an.*)

assertion See *claim.*

assumption A stated or unstated belief or opinion. Uncovering assumptions is part of critical thinking, reading, and writing (see pp. 131–32). In argument, assumptions connect claims and evidence (see pp. 150–51).

audience The intended readers of a piece of writing. Knowledge of the audience's needs and expectations helps a writer shape writing so that it is clear, interesting, and convincing. (See pp. 10–14, 171–74.)

auxiliary verb See *helping verb.*

balanced sentence A sentence consisting of two clauses with parallel constructions: *Do as I say, not as I do. Befriend all animals; exploit none.* Their balance makes such sentences highly emphatic. (See pp. 423–24.)

belief A conviction based on morality, values, or faith. Statements of belief often serve as assumptions and sometimes as evidence, but they are not arguable and so cannot serve as the thesis in an argument. (See pp. 144–45.)

body In a piece of writing, the large central part where ideas supporting the thesis are presented and developed. See also *conclusion* and *introduction.*

bookmark In Internet use, an electronic address you save for later reference. (See p. 656.)

brainstorming A technique for generating ideas about a topic: concentrating on the topic for a fixed time (say, fifteen minutes), you list every idea and detail that comes to mind. (See pp. 24–25.)

browser A computer program that makes it possible to search the World Wide Web. (See p. 198.)

cardinal number The type of number that shows amount: *two, sixty, ninety-seven.* Contrast *ordinal number* (such as *second, ninety-seventh*).

case The form of a noun or pronoun that indicates its function in the sentence. Most pronouns have three cases:

- The **subjective case** (*I, she*) for the subject of a verb or for a subject complement.
- The **objective case** (*me, her*) for the object of a verb, verbal, or preposition.
- The **possessive case** to indicate ownership, used either as an adjective (*my, her*) or as a noun (*mine, hers*).

(See p. 293 for a list of the forms of personal and relative pronouns.)

Nouns use the subjective form (*dog, America*) for all cases except the possessive (*dog's, America's*).

cause-and-effect analysis The determination of why something happened or what its consequences were or will be. (See pp. 27–28 and 102.)

CBE style Either of two styles of documenting sources recommended by the Council of Biology Editors and frequently used in the natural and applied sciences and in mathematics. (For discussion and examples, see pp. 869–76.)

characters The people in a literary work, including the narrator of a story or the speaker of a poem. (See p. 797.)

Chicago style A style of documentation recommended by *The Chicago Manual of Style* and used in history, art, and other humanities. (For discussion and examples, see pp. 822–31.)

chronological organization The arrangement of events as they occurred in time, usually from first to last. (See pp. 43, 83.)

citation In research writing, the way of acknowledging material borrowed from sources. Most systems of citation are basically similar: a number or brief parenthetical reference in the text indicates that particular material is borrowed and directs the reader to information on the source at the end of the work. The systems do differ, however. (See pp. 710–42 for MLA style, pp. 822–31 for Chicago style, pp. 841–55 for APA style, pp. 869–76 for CBE style, and pp. 881–91 for Columbia style for online sources.)

claim A positive statement or assertion that requires support. Claims are the backbone of any argument. (See pp. 143–46.)

classification The sorting of many elements into groups based on their similarities. (See pp. 27 and 99–100.)

clause A group of related words containing a subject and predicate. A **main (independent) clause** can stand by itself as a sentence. A **subordinate (dependent) clause** serves as a single part of speech and so cannot stand by itself as a sentence.

Main clause	We can go to the movies.
Subordinate clause	We can go if Julie gets back on time.

A subordinate clause may function as an adjective (*The car that hit Fred was speeding*), an adverb (*The car hit Fred when it ran a red light*), or a noun (*Whoever was driving should be arrested*). (See pp. 275–79.)

clichés See *trite expressions.*

climactic organization The arrangement of material in order of increasing drama or interest, leading to a climax. (See pp. 44, 85.)

clip art Drawings and icons available on word processors, CD-ROMs, and the Web, generally used to embellish documents. (See p. 212.)

clustering A technique for generating ideas about a topic: drawing and writing, you branch outward from a center point (the topic) to pursue the implications of ideas. (See p. 25.)

coherence The quality of an effective essay or paragraph that helps readers see relations among ideas and move easily from one idea to the next. (See pp. 45 and 80.)

collaborative learning In a writing course, students working together in groups to help each other become better writers and readers. (See pp. 66–69, 243–52.)

collective noun See *noun.*

colloquial language The words and expressions of everyday speech. Colloquial language can enliven informal writing but is generally inappropriate in formal academic or business writing. See also *formal and informal.* (See p. 561.)

Columbia style The humanities or sciences style of documentation recommended by *The Columbia Guide to Online Style.* (For discussion and examples, see pp. 881–91.)

comma splice A sentence error in which two main clauses are separated by a comma with no coordinating conjunction. (See Chapter 18.)

Comma splice	The book was long, it contained useful information.
Revised	The book was long**;** it contained useful information.
Revised	The book was long**,** <u>and</u> it contained useful information.

common noun See *noun.*

comparative See *comparison.*

comparison The form of an adverb or adjective that shows its degree of quality or amount.

- The **positive degree** is the simple, uncompared form: *gross, shyly.*
- The **comparative degree** compares the thing modified to at least one other thing: *grosser, more shyly.*
- The **superlative degree** indicates that the thing modified exceeds all other things to which it is being compared: *grossest, most shyly.*

The comparative and superlative degrees are formed either with the endings *-er* and *-est* or with the words *more* and *most, less* and *least.* (See pp. 352–53.)

comparison and contrast The identification of similarities (comparison) and differences (contrast) between two or more subjects. (See pp. 27, 100–01.)

complement A word or word group that completes the sense of a subject, an object, or a verb. (See pp. 260–62.)

- A **subject complement** follows a linking verb and renames or describes the subject. It may be an adjective, noun, or pronoun. *I am a lion tamer, but I am not yet experienced* (the noun *lion tamer* and the adjective *experienced* complement the subject *I*). Adjective complements are also called **predicate adjectives.** Noun complements are also called **predicate nouns** or **predicate nominatives.**
- An **object complement** follows and modifies or refers to a direct object. The complement may be an adjective or a noun. *If you elect me president, I'll keep the students satisfied* (the noun *president* complements the direct object *me,* and the adjective *satisfied* complements the direct object *students*).
- A **verb complement** is a direct or indirect object of a verb. It may be a noun or pronoun. *Don't give the chimp that peanut* (*chimp* is the indirect object and *peanut* is the direct object of the verb *give;* both objects are verb complements).

complete predicate See *predicate.*

complete subject See *subject.*

complex sentence See *sentence.*

Terms

compound construction Two or more words or word groups serving the same function, such as a **compound subject** (*Harriet and Peter poled their barge down the river*), **compound predicate** (*The scout watched and waited*) or parts of a predicate (*She grew tired and hungry*), and **compound sentence** (*He smiled, and I laughed*). (See pp. 282–84.) **Compound words** include nouns (*featherbrain, strip-mining*) and adjectives (*two-year-old, downtrodden*).

compound-complex sentence See *sentence.*

compound predicate See *compound.*

compound sentence See *sentence.*

compound subject See *compound construction.*

conciseness Use of the fewest and freshest words to express meaning clearly and achieve the desired effect with readers. (See pp. 578–84.)

conclusion The closing of an essay, tying off the writer's thoughts and leaving readers with a sense of completion. (See pp. 109–11 for suggestions.)

A *conclusion* is also the result of deductive reasoning. See *deductive reasoning* and *syllogism.*

concrete See *abstract and concrete.*

conditional statement A statement expressing a condition contrary to fact and using the subjunctive mood of the verb: *If she were mayor, the unions would cooperate.* See also *mood.*

conjugation A list of the forms of a verb showing tense, voice, mood, person, and number. The conjugation of the verb *know* in present tense, active voice, indicative mood is *I know, you know, he/she/it knows, we know, you know, they know.* (See p. 319 for a fuller conjugation.)

conjunction A word that links and relates parts of a sentence.

- **Coordinating conjunctions** (*and, but, or, nor, for, so, yet*) connect words or word groups of equal grammatical rank: *The lights went out, but the doctors and nurses continued caring for their patients.* (See p. 282.)
- **Correlative conjunctions** or correlatives (such as *either . . . or, not only . . . but also*) are two or more connecting words that work together: *He was certain that either his parents or his brother would help him.* (See p. 283.)
- **Subordinating conjunctions** (*after, although, as if, because, if, when,* and so on) begin subordinate clauses and link them to main clauses: *The seven dwarfs whistle while they work.* (See p. 276.)

conjunctive adverb (adverbial conjunction) An adverb (such as *besides, consequently, however, indeed,* and *therefore*) that relates two main clauses in a sentence: *We had hoped to own a house by now; however, housing costs have risen too fast.* (See pp. 284–85.) The error known as a comma splice results when two main clauses related by a conjunctive adverb are separated only by a comma. (See pp. 377–78.)

connector (connective) Any word or phrase that links words, phrases, clauses, or sentences. Common connectors include coordinating, correlative, and subordinating conjunctions; conjunctive adverbs; and prepositions.

connotation An association called up by a word, beyond its dictionary definition. Contrast *denotation.* (See p. 568.)

construction Any group of grammatically related words, such as a phrase, a clause, or a sentence.

contraction A condensation of an expression, with an apostrophe replacing the missing letters: for example, *doesn't* (for *does not*), *we'll* (for *we will*). (See pp. 504–05.)

contrast See *comparison and contrast.*

coordinate adjectives Two or more adjectives that equally modify the same noun or pronoun: *The camera panned the vast, empty desert.* (See pp. 480–81.)

coordinating conjunction See *conjunction.*

coordination The linking of words, phrases, or clauses that are of equal importance, usually with a coordinating conjunction: *He and I laughed, but she was not amused.* Contrast *subordination.* (See pp. 431–33.)

correlative conjunction (correlative) See *conjunction.*

count noun See *noun.*

courseware A program for online communication and collaboration among the teacher and students in a course. (See p. 246.)

critical thinking, reading, and writing Looking beneath the surface of words and images to discern meaning and relationships and to build knowledge. (See Chapter 5.)

cumulative (loose) sentence A sentence in which modifiers follow the subject and verb: *Ducks waddled by, their tails swaying and their quacks rising to heaven.* Contrast *periodic sentence.* (See p. 421.)

dangling modifier A modifier that does not sensibly describe anything in its sentence. (See pp. 403–05.)

Dangling Having arrived late, the concert had already begun.

Revised Having arrived late, we found that the concert had already begun.

data In argument, a term used for *evidence.* See *evidence.*

database A collection and organization of information (data). A database may be printed, but the term is most often used for electronic sources.

declension A list of the forms of a noun or pronoun, showing inflections for person (for pronouns), number, and case. See p. 293 for a declension of the personal and relative pronouns.

deductive reasoning Applying a generalization to specific circumstances in order to reach a conclusion. See also *syllogism.* Contrast *inductive reasoning.* (See pp. 166–69.)

definition Specifying the characteristics of something to establish what it is and is not. (See pp. 27 and 97–98.)

degree See *comparison.*

demonstrative adjective See *adjective.*

demonstrative pronoun See *pronoun.*

denotation The main or dictionary definition of a word. Contrast *connotation.* (See p. 567.)

dependent clause See *clause.*

derivational suffix See *suffix.*

description Detailing the sensory qualities of a thing, person, place, or feeling. (See pp. 27 and 96.)

descriptive adjective See *adjective.*

descriptor See *keyword(s).*

determiner A word such as *a, an, the, my,* and *your* which indicates that a noun follows. See also *article.* (See pp. 356–60 for the uses of determiners before nouns.)

developing (planning) The stage of the writing process when one finds a topic, explores ideas, gathers information, focuses on a central theme, and organizes material. Compare *drafting* and *revising.* (See Chapters 1–2.)

dialect A variety of a language used by a specific group or in a specific region. A dialect may be distinguished by its pronunciation, vocabulary, and grammar. (See p. 559.)

diction The choice and use of words. (See Chapter 38.)

dictionary form See *plain form.*

direct address A construction in which a word or phrase indicates the person or group spoken to: *Have you finished, John? Farmers, unite.*

direct object See *object.*

direct question A sentence asking a question and concluding with a question mark: *Do they know we are watching?* Contrast *indirect question.*

direct quotation (direct discourse) See *quotation.*

discussion list A mailing list of subscribers who use e-mail to converse on a particular subject. Also called an **e-mail list, listserv,** or **list.** See also *newsgroup* and *Web forum.* (For the use of discussion lists in collaboration among students, see pp. 245–46. For the use of discussion lists for research, see pp. 659–60.)

division See *analysis.*

documentation In research writing, supplying citations that legitimate the use of borrowed material and support claims about its origins. Contrast *plagiarism.* (See pp. 698–99.)

document design The control of a document's elements to achieve the flow, spacing, grouping, emphasis, and standardization that are appropriate for the writing situation. (See Chapter 9.)

domain See *uniform resource locator (URL).*

double negative A generally nonstandard form consisting of two negative words used in the same construction so that they effectively cancel each other: *I don't have no money.* Rephrase as *I have no money* or *I don't have any money.* (See p. 354.)

double possessive A possessive using both the ending *-'s* and the preposition *of: That is a favorite expression of Mark's.*

double talk (doublespeak) Language intended to confuse or to be misunderstood. (See p. 563.)

download To transfer data from another computer.

drafting The stage of the writing process when ideas are expressed in connected sentences and paragraphs. Compare *developing (planning)* and *revising.* (See pp. 48–51.)

editing A distinct step in revising a written work, focusing on clarity, tone, and correctness. Compare *revising.* (See pp. 60–63.)

ellipsis The omission of a word or words from a quotation, indicated by the three spaced periods of an **ellipsis mark:** *"that all . . . are created* *equal."* In MLA style, an added ellipsis mark is surrounded by brackets: *"that all [. . .] are created equal."* (See pp. 527–30.)

elliptical clause A clause omitting a word or words whose meaning is understood from the rest of the clause: *David likes Minneapolis better than [he likes] Chicago.* (See p. 278.)

emoticon Sideways faces made up of punctuation, used to convey emotion or irony in electronic communication. (See p. 196.)

emotional appeal See *appeals.*

emphasis The manipulation of words, sentences, and paragraphs to stress important ideas. (See Chapter 23.)

essay A nonfiction composition on a single subject and with a central idea or thesis.

essential element A word or word group that is necessary to the meaning of a sentence because it limits the thing it refers to: removing it would leave the meaning unclear or too general. Also called a **restrictive element,** an essential element is not set off by punctuation: *The keys to the car are on the table. That man who called about the apartment said he'd try again tonight.* Contrast *nonessential element.* (See pp. 473–75.)

ethical appeal See *appeals.*

etymology The history of a word's meanings and forms.

Terms

euphemism A presumably inoffensive word that a writer or speaker substitutes for a word deemed possibly offensive or too blunt—for example, *passed beyond* for "died." (See p. 562.)

evaluation A judgment of the quality, value, currency, bias, or other aspects of a work. (See pp. 135–36, 667–72.)

evidence The facts, examples, expert opinions, and other information that support the claims in an argument. (See pp. 146–50, 170–71.)

expletive A sentence that postpones the subject by beginning with *there* or *it* and a form of the verb *be: It is impossible to get a ticket. There should be more seats available.* (See p. 288.)

exposition Writing whose primary purpose is to explain something about a topic.

fallacies Errors in reasoning. Some evade the issue of the argument; others oversimplify the argument. (See pp. 155–60.)

faulty predication A sentence error in which the meanings of subject and predicate conflict, so that the subject is said to be or do something illogical: *The installation of air bags takes up space in a car's steering wheel and dashboard.* (See pp. 409–10.)

figurative language (figures of speech) Expressions that suggest meanings different from their literal meanings in order to achieve special effects. (See pp. 573–74.) Some common figures:

- **Hyperbole,** deliberate exaggeration: *The bag weighed a ton.*

- **Metaphor,** an implied comparison between two unlike things: *The wind stabbed through our clothes.*
- **Personification,** the attribution of human qualities to a thing or idea: *The water beckoned seductively.*
- **Simile,** an explicit comparison, using *like* or *as,* between two unlike things: *The sky glowered like an angry parent.*

A **mixed metaphor** is a confusing or ludicrous combination of incompatible figures: *The wind stabbed through our clothes and shook our bones.*

finite verb Any verb that makes an assertion or expresses a state of being and can stand as the main verb of a sentence or clause: *The moose eats the leaves.* (See p. 270.) Contrast *verbal,* which is formed from a finite verb but is unable to stand alone as the main verb of a sentence: *I saw the moose eating the leaves.*

first person See *person.*

flame To attack an online correspondent personally, as in a discussion list or newsgroup. (See p. 196.)

foil A character in a literary work who contrasts with another character and thus helps to define the other character. (See p. 814.)

formal and informal Levels of usage achieved through word choice and sentence structure. More informal writing, as in a letter to an acquaintance or a personal essay, resembles some speech in its colloquial language, contractions, and short, fairly simple sentences. More formal writing, as in academic papers and business reports, avoids these attributes of speech and tends to rely on longer and more complicated sentences.

format In a document such as an academic paper or a business letter, the arrangement and spacing of elements on the page. See also *document design.* (For academic formats, see pp. 215–18. For business formats, see pp. 902–15. See also pp. 200–14 on document design.)

fragment See *sentence fragment.*

frame A window on a computer screen. With two or more frames on the same screen, a Web designer can show two or more documents at once.

freewriting A technique for generating ideas: in a fixed amount of time (say, fifteen minutes), you write continuously without stopping to reread. (See pp. 22–23.)

FTP (file transfer protocol) An Internet standard for transferring files from one computer to another, often used to upload Web pages. (See p. 241.)

function word A word, such as an article, conjunction, or preposition, that serves primarily to clarify the roles of and relations between other words in a sentence: *We chased the goat for an hour but finally caught it.* Contrast *lexical word.*

fused sentence (run-on sentence) A sentence error in which two main clauses are joined with no punctuation or connecting word between them. (See p. 379.)

> **Fused** I heard his lecture it was dull.
>
> **Revised** I heard his lecture**;** it was dull.

future perfect tense See *tense.*

future tense See *tense.*

gender The classification of nouns or pronouns as masculine (*he, boy, handyman*), feminine (*she, woman, actress*), or neuter (*it, typewriter, dog*).

general and specific Terms designating the relative number of instances or objects included in a group signified by a word. The following list moves from most **general** (including the most objects) to most **specific** (including the fewest objects): *vehicle, four-wheeled vehicle, automobile, sedan, Ford Taurus, blue Ford Taurus, my sister's blue Ford Taurus named Hank.* See also *abstract and concrete.* (See p. 570.)

generalization A claim inferred from evidence. See also *inductive reasoning.*

generic *he* *He* used to mean *he or she.* For ways to avoid *he* when you intend either or both genders, see pp. 344 and 565.

generic noun A noun that refers to a typical member of a group rather than to a specific person or thing: *Any person may come. A student needs good work habits. A school with financial problems may shortchange its students.* A singular generic noun takes a singular pronoun (*he, she,* or *it*). (See pp. 343–45.)

Terms

genitive case Another term for possessive case. See *case.*

gerund A verbal that ends in *-ing* and functions as a noun: *Working is all right for killing time* (*working* is the subject of the verb *is; killing* is the object of the preposition *for.*) See also *verbals and verbal phrases.* (See p. 271.)

gerund phrase A word group consisting of a gerund plus any modifiers or objects. See also *verbals and verbal phrases.*

grammar A description of how a language works.

grounds A term used for *evidence* in argument. See *evidence.*

helping verb (auxiliary verb) A verb used with another verb to convey time, obligation, and other meanings: *You should write a letter. You have written other letters.* The **modals** include *can, could, may, might, must, ought, shall, should, will, would.* The other helping verbs are forms of *be, have,* and *do.* (See pp. 303, 308–12.)

homonyms Words that are pronounced the same but have different spellings and meanings, such as *heard/herd* and *to/too/two.* (See pp. 604–05 for a list.)

HTML (hypertext markup language) A computer language used for creating Web pages. An **HTML editor** is a program for coding documents in HTML. (See pp. 235–42.)

hyperbole See *figurative language.*

hypertext Text such as that on the Web that provides links allowing users to move easily and variously within and among documents. Contrast *linear text.* (See pp. 224–26.)

idiom An expression that is peculiar to a language and that may not make sense if taken literally: for example, *dark horse, bide your time,* and *by and large.* See p. 573 for a list of idioms involving prepositions, such as *agree with them* and *agree to the contract.*

illustration or support Supplying examples or reasons to develop an idea. (See pp. 27 and 96–97.)

imagery Pictures created by words that appeal to the sense of sight, hearing, touch, taste, or smell.

imperative See *mood.*

indefinite pronoun See *pronoun.*

independent clause See *clause.*

indicative See *mood.*

indirect object See *object.*

indirect question A sentence reporting a question, usually in a subordinate clause, and ending with a period: *Writers wonder whether their work must be lonely.* Contrast *direct question.*

indirect quotation (indirect discourse) See *quotation.*

inductive reasoning Inferring a generalization from specific evidence. Contrast *deductive reasoning.* (See p. 166.)

infinitive A verbal formed from the plain form of the verb plus the **infinitive marker** *to: to swim, to write.* Infinitives and infinitive phrases may function as nouns, adjectives, or adverbs. See also *verbals and verbal phrases.* (See p. 271.)

infinitive marker See *infinitive.*

infinitive phrase A word group consisting of an infinitive plus any subject, objects, or modifiers. See also *verbals and verbal phrases.*

inflection The variation in the form of a word that indicates its function in a particular context. See *declension,* the inflection of nouns and pronouns; *conjugation,* the inflection of verbs; and *comparison,* the inflection of adjectives and adverbs.

inflectional suffix See *suffix.*

informal See *formal and informal.*

intensifier A modifier that adds emphasis to the word(s) it modifies: for example, *very slow, so angry.*

intensive pronoun See *pronoun.*

interjection A word standing by itself or inserted in a construction to exclaim or command attention: *Hey! Ouch! What the heck did you do that for?*

interpretation The determination of meaning or significance—for instance, in a work such as a poem or in the literature on some issue such as job discrimination. (See pp. 131–33, 796.)

interrogative Functioning as or involving a question.

interrogative adjective See *adjective.*

interrogative pronoun See *pronoun.*

intransitive verb A verb that does not take a direct object: *The woman laughed.* (See pp. 259–60.)

introduction The opening of an essay, a transition for readers between their world and the writer's. The introduction often contains a statement of the writer's thesis. (See pp. 106–09 for suggestions.)

invention The discovery and exploration of ideas, usually occurring most intensively in the early stages of the writing process. (See pp. 9–29 for invention techniques.)

inversion A reversal of usual word order in a sentence, as when a verb precedes its subject or an object precedes its verb: *Down swooped the hawk. Our aims we stated clearly.*

IRC See *synchronous communication.*

irony The use of words to suggest a meaning different from what the words say literally: *What a happy face!* (said to someone scowling miserably); *With that kind of planning, prices are sure to go down* (written with the expectation that prices will rise).

irregular verb A verb that forms its past tense and past participle in some other way than by the addition of *-d* or *-ed* to the plain form: for example, *go, went, gone; give, gave, given.* Contrast *regular verb.* (See pp. 304–05 for a list of irregular verbs.)

jargon In one sense, jargon is the specialized language of any group, such as doctors or baseball players. In another sense, jargon is vague, pretentious, wordy, and ultimately unclear writing such as that found in some academic, business, and government publications. (See p. 584.)

journal A personal record of observations, reactions, ideas, and other thoughts. Besides providing a private place to think in writing, a journal is useful for making notes about reading (pp. 120, 619–20, 791), discovering ideas for essays (p. 19), and keeping track of research (pp. 619–20, 818, 836, 865).

journalist's questions A set of questions useful for probing a topic to discover ideas about it. (See p. 26.)

keyword(s) A word or words that define a subject, used for searching databases such as library catalogs and periodical indexes and for searching the Web. (See pp. 637–39.)

lexical word A word, such as a noun, verb, or modifier, that carries part of the meaning of language. Contrast *function word.*

linear text Text such as a conventional printed document that is intended to be read in sequence. Contrast *hypertext.* (See pp. 224–25.)

linking verb A verb that relates a subject to its complement: *Julie is a Democrat. He looks harmless. The boy became a man.* Common linking verbs are the forms of *be;* the verbs relating to the senses, such as *look* and *smell;* and the verbs *become, appear,* and *seem.* (See p. 261.)

listserv See *discussion list.*

logical agreement See *agreement.*

logical fallacies See *fallacies.*

lurking Reading but not participating in an Internet discussion list, newsgroup, or Web forum. (See p. 660.)

main clause See *clause.*

main verb The part of a verb phrase that carries the principal meaning: *had been walking, could happen, was chilled.* See also *verb phrase.*

mass noun Another term for noncount noun. See *noun.*

mechanics The use of capital letters, underlining or italics, abbreviations, numbers, and divided words. (See Chapters 33–37.)

metaphor See *figurative language.*

misplaced modifier A modifier so far from the term it modifies or so close to another term it could modify that its relation to the rest of the sentence is unclear. (See Chapter 21.)

Misplaced	The boys played with firecrackers that they bought illegally in the field.
Revised	The boys played in the field with firecrackers that they bought illegally.

A squinting modifier could modify the words on either side of it: *The plan we considered seriously worries me.*

mixed construction A sentence containing two or more parts that do not fit together in grammar or in meaning. (See pp. 407–10.)

mixed metaphor See *figurative language.*

MLA style The style of documenting sources recommended by the Modern Language Association and used in many of the humanities, including English. (For explanation and examples, see Chapter 46.)

modal See *helping verb.*

modifier Any word or word group that limits or qualifies the meaning of another word or word group. Modifiers include adjectives and adverbs as well as words, phrases, and clauses that act as adjectives and adverbs.

MOO See *synchronous communication.*

mood The form of a verb that shows how the speaker or writer views the action. (See pp. 327–29.)

- The **indicative mood,** the most common, is used to make statements or ask questions: *The play will be performed Saturday. Did you get the tickets?*

- The **imperative mood** gives a command: *Please get good seats.*
- The **subjunctive mood** expresses a wish, a condition contrary to fact, a recommendation, or a request: *I wish George were coming with us. Did you suggest that he join us?*

MUD See *synchronous communication.*

narration Recounting a sequence of events, usually in the order of their occurrence. (See pp. 26–27 and 95.) Literary narration tells a story. (See Chapter 49.)

narrator The speaker in a poem or the voice who tells a story. (See p. 797.)

neologism A word coined recently and not in established use. (See p. 562.)

netiquette Conventions and courtesies for Internet communication. (See pp. 195–97.)

newsgroup An Internet discussion group with a common site where all postings are recorded. (See p. 661.)

nominal A noun, a pronoun, or a word or word group used as a noun: *Joan and I talked. The rich owe a debt to the poor* (adjectives acting as subject and object). *Baby-sitting can be exhausting* (gerund acting as subject). *I like to play with children* (infinitive phrase acting as object).

nominative Another term for subjective case. See *case.*

noncount noun See *noun.*

nonessential element A word or word group that does not limit the term or construction it refers to and thus is not essential to the meaning of the sentence. Also called a **nonrestrictive element,** a nonessential element is set off by punctuation, usually commas: *The new apartment building, in shades of tan and gray, will house fifty people* (nonessential adjective phrase). *Sleep, which we all need, occupies a third of our lives* (nonessential adjective clause). *His wife, Patricia, is a chemist* (nonessential appositive). Contrast *essential element.* (See pp. 473–77.)

nonfinite verb See *verbals and verbal phrases.*

nonrestrictive element See *nonessential element.*

nonstandard Words and grammatical forms not conforming to standard English. (See p. 559.)

noun A word that names a person, place, thing, quality, or idea: *Maggie, Alabama, clarinet, satisfaction, socialism.* Nouns normally form the possessive case by adding *-'s* (*Maggie's*) and the plural by adding *-s* or *-es* (*clarinets, messes*), although there are exceptions (*men, women, children*). The forms of nouns depend partly on where they fit in certain overlapping groups:

- **Common nouns** name general classes and are not capitalized: *book, government, music.*
- **Proper nouns** name specific people, places, and things and are capitalized: *Susan, Athens, Candlestick Park.*

- **Count nouns** name things considered countable in English (they form plurals): *ounce/ounces, camera/cameras, person/people.*
- **Noncount nouns** name things not considered countable in English (they don't form plurals): *chaos, fortitude, silver, earth, information.*
- **Collective nouns** are singular in form but name groups: *team, class, family.*

noun clause A word group containing a subject and a verb and functioning as a subject, object, or complement: *Everyone wondered how the door opened. Whoever opened it had left.*

number The form of a noun, pronoun, demonstrative adjective, or verb that indicates whether it is singular or plural: *woman, women; I, we; this, these; runs, run.*

object A noun, pronoun, or word group that receives the action of or is influenced by a transitive verb, a verbal, or a preposition. (See pp. 260, 261, 267.)

- A **direct object** receives the action of a verb or verbal and frequently follows it in a sentence: *We sat watching the stars. Emily caught whatever it was you had.*
- An **indirect object** tells for or to whom something is done: *I lent Stan my car. Reiner bought us all champagne.*
- An **object of a preposition** usually follows a preposition and is linked by it to the rest of the sentence: *They are going to New Orleans for the jazz festival.*

object complement See *complement.*

Terms

objective See *case.*

opinion A conclusion based on facts; an arguable, potentially changeable claim. Claims of opinion form the backbone of any argument. (See p. 144.)

ordinal number The type of number that shows order: *first, eleventh, twenty-fifth.* Contrast *cardinal number* (such as *one, twenty-five*).

paragraph Generally, a group of sentences set off by a beginning indention and developing a single idea. That idea is often stated in a **topic sentence.** (See Chapter 4.)

parallelism Similarity of grammatical form between two or more coordinated elements: *Rising prices and declining incomes left many people in bad debt and worse despair.* (See Chapter 25.)

paraphrase The restatement of source material in one's own words and sentence structures, useful for borrowing the original author's line of reasoning but not his or her exact words. Paraphrases must always be acknowledged in source citations. (See pp. 679–81.)

parenthetical citation In the text of a paper, a brief reference, enclosed in parentheses, indicating that material is borrowed and directing the reader to the source of the material. See also *citation.*

parenthetical expression A word or construction that interrupts a sentence and is not part of its main structure, called *parenthetical* because it could (or does) appear in parentheses: *Childe Hassam (1859–1935) was an American painter and etcher. The book, incidentally, is terrible.* (See p. 525.)

participial phrase A word group consisting of a participle plus any objects or modifiers. See also *verbals and verbal phrases.*

participle A verbal showing continuing or completed action, used as an adjective or part of a verb phrase but never as the main verb of a sentence or clause. (See p. 270.)

- A **present participle** ends in *-ing: My heart is breaking* (participle as part of verb phrase). *I like to watch the rolling waves* (participle as adjective).
- A **past participle** most commonly ends in *-d, -ed, -n,* or *-en* (*wished, shown, given*) but sometimes changes the spelling of the verb (*sung, done, slept*): *Jeff has broken his own record* (participle as part of verb phrase). *The closed door beckoned* (participle as adjective).

See also *verbals and verbal phrases.*

particle A preposition or adverb in a two-word verb: *look up, catch on.* (See pp. 316–17.)

parts of speech The classes into which words are commonly grouped according to their form, function, and meaning: nouns, pronouns, verbs, adjectives, adverbs, conjunctions, prepositions, and interjections. See separate entries for each part of speech.

passive voice See *voice.*

past participle See *participle.*

past perfect tense See *tense.*

past tense See *tense.*

path See *uniform resource locator (URL).*

patterns of development Ways of thinking that can help you develop and organize ideas in essays and paragraphs. (See pp. 26–28 and 95–104.)

perfect tenses See *tense.*

periodic sentence A suspenseful sentence in which modifiers precede the main clause, which falls at the end: *Postponing decisions about family while striving to establish themselves in careers, many young adults are falsely accused of greed.* Contrast *cumulative sentence.* (See p. 421–22.)

person The form of a verb or pronoun that indicates whether the subject is speaking, spoken to, or spoken about. In English only personal pronouns and verbs change form to indicate difference in person. In the **first person**, the subject is speaking: *I am* [or *We are*] *planning a party.* In the **second person,** the subject is being spoken to: *Are you coming?* In the **third person,** the subject is being spoken about: *She was* [or *They were*] *going.*

personal pronoun See *pronoun.*

personification See *figurative language.*

phrase A group of related words that lacks a subject or a predicate or both and that acts as a single part of speech. See *absolute phrase, prepositional phrase, verbals and verbal phrases,* and *verb phrase.*

plagiarism The presentation of someone else's ideas or words as if they were one's own. Whether accidental or deliberate, plagiarism is a serious and often punishable offense. (See pp. 686–92.)

plain case Another term for the subjective case of nouns. See *case.*

plain form The dictionary form of a verb: *make, run, swivel.* See also *verb forms.*

planning See *developing (planning).*

plot The pattern of events in a work of literature. (See p. 797.)

plural More than one. See *number.*

point of view The perspective or attitude of the narrator or speaker in a work of literature. See also *person.* (See p. 797.)

positive degree See *comparison.*

possessive See *case.*

predicate The part of a sentence that makes an assertion about the subject. A predicate must contain a finite verb and may contain modifiers, objects of the verb, and complements. The **simple predicate** consists of the verb and its helping verbs: *A wiser person would have made a different decision.* The **complete predicate** includes the simple predicate and any modifiers, objects, and complements: *A wiser person would have made a different decision.* See also *intransitive verb, linking verb,* and *transitive verb.* (See pp. 255, 259–62.)

predicate adjective See *complement.*

predicate noun (predicate nominative) See *complement.*

prefix A letter or group of letters (such as *sub, in, dis, pre*) that can be added at the beginning of a root or word to create a new word: *sub + marine = submarine; dis + grace = disgrace.* Contrast *suffix.* (See pp. 597–98.)

premise Generally, a claim or assumption basic to an argument. In a deductive syllogism, one premise applied to another leads logically to a conclusion. See also *syllogism.* (See pp. 166–69.)

preposition A word that forms a noun or pronoun (plus any modifiers) into a prepositional phrase: *about love, down the steep stairs.* The common prepositions include these as well as *after, before, by, for, from, in, on, to,* and many others. (See pp. 266–67.)

prepositional phrase A word group consisting of a preposition and its object, plus any modifiers. A prepositional phrase usually functions as an adjective (*The boy in green stood up*) or as an adverb (*He walked to the speaker's platform*). (See pp. 267–68.)

present participle See *participle.*

Terms

present perfect tense See *tense.*

present tense See *tense.*

pretentious writing Writing that is more elaborate than the writing situation requires, usually full of fancy phrases and showy words. (See p. 563.)

primary source Firsthand information, such as an eyewitness account of events; a diary, speech, or other historical document; a work of literature or art; a report of a survey or experiment; and one's own interview, observation, or correspondence. Contrast *secondary source.* (See p. 626.)

principal clause A main or independent clause. See *clause.*

principal parts The plain form, past-tense form, and past participle of a verb. See *verb forms.* (See pp. 301–02.)

problem-solution organization The arrangement of material to state and explain a problem and then to propose and explain a solution. (See pp. 44, 85.)

process analysis The explanation of how something works or how to do something. (See pp. 28, 103.)

progressive tense See *tense.*

pronoun A word used in place of a noun. There are eight types of pronouns:

- **Personal pronouns** refer to a specific individual or to individuals: *I, you, he, she, it, we, they.* (See p. 293.)
- **Indefinite pronouns,** such as *everybody* and *some,* do not refer to specific nouns (*Everybody speaks*). (See p. 357.)
- **Relative pronouns**—*who, whoever, which, that*—relate groups of words to nouns or pronouns (*The book that won is a novel*). (See pp. 276–77, 293.)
- **Interrogative pronouns**—*who, whom, whose, which, what*—introduce questions (*Who will contribute?*).
- **Intensive pronouns**—personal pronouns plus *-self* or *-selves*—emphasize a noun or other pronoun (*He himself asked that question*).
- **Reflexive pronouns** have the same form as intensive pronouns. They indicate that the sentence subject also receives the action of the verb (*They injured themselves*).
- **Demonstrative pronouns** such as *this, that,* and *such* identify or point to nouns (*This is the problem*).
- **Reciprocal pronouns**—*each other* and *one another*—are used as objects of verbs when the subjects are plural (*They loved each other*).

proofreading Reading and correcting a final draft for misspellings, typographical errors, and other mistakes. (See pp. 63–64.)

proper adjective See *adjective.*

proper noun See *noun.*

protocol See *uniform resource locator (URL).*

purpose For a writer, the chief reason for communicating something about a topic to a particular audience. Purposes are both general (usually explanation or persuasion) and specific (taking into account the topic and desired outcome). (See pp. 15–17.)

quotation Repetition of what someone has written or spoken. In **direct quotation (direct discourse)**, the person's words are duplicated exactly and enclosed in quotation marks: *Polonius told his son, Laertes, "Neither a borrower nor a lender be."* An **indirect quotation (indirect discourse)** reports what someone said or wrote but not in the exact words and not in quotation marks: *Polonius advised his son, Laertes, not to borrow or lend.*

rational appeal See *appeals.*

reciprocal pronoun See *pronoun.*

reflexive pronoun See *pronoun.*

regional language Expressions common to the people in a particular geographical area. (See p. 560.)

regular verb A verb that forms its past tense and past participle by adding *-d* or *-ed* to the plain form: *love, loved, loved; open, opened, opened.* Contrast *irregular verb.* (See p. 303.)

relative clause A subordinate clause beginning with a relative pronoun such as *who* or *that* and functioning as an adjective.

relative pronoun See *pronoun.*

restrictive element See *essential element.*

Terms

revising The stage of the writing process in which one considers and improves the meaning and underlying structure of a draft. Compare *developing (planning)* and *drafting.* (See pp. 52–59.)

rhetoric The principles for finding and arranging ideas and for using language in speech or writing to achieve the writer's purpose in addressing his or her audience.

rhetorical question A question asked for effect, with no answer expected. The person asking the question either intends to provide the answer or assumes it is obvious: *If we let one factory pollute the river, what does that say to other factories that want to dump wastes there?*

run-on sentence See *fused sentence.*

sans serif See *serifs.*

search engine A computer program that conducts Internet searches from keywords or directories. (See pp. 653–59.)

secondary source A source reporting or analyzing information in other sources, such as a critic's view of a work of art or a sociologist's summary of others' studies. Contrast *primary source.* (See p. 626.)

second person See *person.*

sentence A complete unit of thought, consisting of at least a subject and a predicate that are not introduced by a subordinating word. Sentences can be classed on the basis of their structure in one of four ways. A **simple sentence** contains one main clause: *I'm leaving.* A **compound sentence** contains at least two main clauses: *I'd like to stay, but I'm leaving.* A **complex sentence** contains one main clause and at least one subordinate clause: *If you let me go now, you'll be sorry.* A **compound-complex sentence** contains at least two main clauses and at least one subordinate clause: *I'm leaving because you want me to, but I'd rather stay.* (See pp. 289–90.)

sentence fragment A sentence error in which a group of words is set off as a sentence even though it begins with a subordinating word or lacks a subject or a predicate or both. (See Chapter 17.)

Fragment	She lost the race. Because she was injured. [*Because,* a subordinating conjunction, makes the underlined clause subordinate.]
Revised	She lost the race because she was injured.
Fragment	He could not light a fire. And thus could not warm the room. [The underlined word group lacks a subject.]
Revised	He could not light a fire. Thus he could not warm the room.

sentence modifier An adverb or a word or word group acting as an adverb that modifies the idea of the whole sentence in which it appears rather than any specific word: *In fact, people will always complain.*

series A sequence of three or more items of equal importance: *The children are named John, Hallie, and Nancy.* The items in a series are separated with commas. (See p. 479.)

serifs Small lines on the characters in type fonts, such as the lines along the bottom of this A. **Sans serif** type, such as Arial, does not have serifs. (See p. 205.)

server A computer that links other computers in a network. Servers transfer data and store files.

setting The place where the action of a literary work happens. (See p. 798.)

sexist language Language expressing narrow ideas about men's and women's roles, positions, capabilities, or value. (See pp. 564–65.)

signal phrase Words that indicate who is being quoted: *"In the future," said Andy Warhol, "everyone will be world-famous for fifteen minutes."* (For punctuating signal phrases, see pp. 482–84. For using signal phrases to integrate quotations, see pp. 695–97.)

simile See *figurative language.*

simple predicate See *predicate.*

simple sentence See *sentence.*

simple subject See *subject.*

simple tense See *tense.*

singular One. See *number.*

slang Expressions used by the members of a group to create bonds and sometimes exclude others. Most slang is too vague, short-lived, and narrowly understood to be used in any but very informal writing. (See pp. 560–61.)

spam To send an irrelevant and unsolicited electronic message to many recipients at once, such as all the subscribers to a discussion list. (See pp. 195–96.)

source A place where information or ideas may be found: book, article, Web site, work of art, television program, and so on.

spatial organization In a description of a person, place, or thing, the arrangement of details as they would be scanned by a viewer—for instance, from top to bottom or near to far. (See pp. 43 and 83.)

specific See *general and specific.*

split infinitive The often awkward interruption of an infinitive and its marker *to* by an adverb: *Management decided to immediately introduce the new product.* (See p. 400.)

squinting modifier See *misplaced modifier.*

standard English The English used and expected by educated writers and readers in colleges and universities, businesses, and professions. (See p. 558.)

subject In grammar, the part of a sentence that names something and about which an assertion is made in the predicate. The **simple subject** consists of the noun alone: *The quick brown fox jumps over the lazy dog.* The **complete subject** includes the simple subject and its modifiers: *The quick brown fox jumps over the lazy dog.* (See p. 255.)

subject complement See *complement.*

subjective See *case.*

subjunctive See *mood.*

subordinate clause See *clause.*

subordinating conjunction See *conjunction.*

subordination The use of grammatical constructions to de-emphasize one element in a sentence by making it dependent on rather than equal to another element: *Although I left six messages for him, the doctor failed to call.* Contrast *coordination.* (See pp. 434–38.)

substantive A word or word group used as a noun.

suffix A **derivational suffix** is a letter or group of letters that can be added to the end of a root word to make a new word, often a different part of speech: *child, childish; shrewd, shrewdly; visual, visualize.* (See p. 598.) An **inflectional suffix** adapts a word to different grammatical relations: *boy, boys; fast, faster; tack, tacked.*

summary A condensation and restatement of source material in one's own words and sentence structures, useful in reading for comprehending the material (see pp. 127–28) and in research writing for presenting the gist of the original author's idea (pp. 678–79). Summaries appearing in a paper must always be acknowledged in source citations.

superlative See *comparison.*

syllogism A form of deductive reasoning in which two premises stating generalizations or assumptions together lead to a conclusion. *Premise:* Hot stoves can burn me. *Premise:* This stove is hot. *Conclusion:* This stove can burn me. See also *deductive reasoning.* (See pp. 167–69.)

symbolism The use of a concrete thing to suggest something larger and more abstract, as a red rose may symbolize passion or romance. (See p. 798.)

synchronous communication Real-time, simultaneous communication over the Internet, analogous to a conference call on a telephone. MOOs, MUDs, and IRC (Internet relay chat) are examples. (See pp. 250–51, 661–62.)

synonyms Words with approximately but not exactly the same meanings, such as *snicker, giggle,* and *chortle.* (See p. 568.)

syntax In sentences, the grammatical relations among words and the ways those relations are indicated.

synthesis Drawing connections among the elements within a work (such as the images in a poem) or among entire works (entire poems). Synthesis is an essential skill in critical thinking, reading, and writing (see pp. 133–34) and in research writing (pp. 673–74).

tag question A question attached to the end of a statement and consisting of a pronoun, a helping verb, and sometimes the word *not: It isn't raining, is it? It is sunny, isn't it?*

template A word-processing form for a letter, memo, or other document. (See p. 204.)

tense The form of a verb that expresses the time of its action, usually indicated by the verb's inflection and by helping verbs.

- The **simple tenses** are the **present** (*I race, you go*), the **past** (*I raced, you went*), and the **future,** formed with the helping verb *will* (*I will race, you will go*).
- The **perfect tenses,** formed with the helping verbs *have* and *had,* indicate completed action. They are the **present perfect** (*I have raced, you have gone*), the **past perfect** (*I had raced, you had gone*), and the **future perfect** (*I will have raced, you will have gone*).
- The **progressive tenses,** formed with the helping verb *be* plus the present participle, indicate continuing action. They include the **present progressive** (*I am racing, you are going*), the **past progressive** (*I was racing, you were going*), and the **future progressive** (*I will be racing, you will be going*).

(See p. 319 for a list of tenses with examples.)

theme The main idea of a work of literature. (See p. 798.)

thesis The central, controlling idea of an essay, to which all assertions and details relate. (See p. 30.)

thesis statement A sentence or more that asserts the central, controlling idea of an essay and perhaps previews the essay's organization. (See pp. 30–34.)

third person See *person.*

thread In a discussion list, newsgroup, or Web forum, a series of messages on the same topic. (See pp. 245, 247–48.)

tone The sense of a writer's attitudes toward self, subject, and readers revealed by words and sentence structures as well as by content. (See pp. 10–14, 151–52, 173, 797.)

topic The subject of an essay, narrowed so that it is appropriately specific for the prescribed purpose, length, and deadline.

topic sentence See *paragraph.*

transitional expression A word or phrase, such as *thus* or *for example,* that links sentences and shows the relations between them. (See pp. 89–90 for a list.) The error known as a comma splice occurs when two main clauses related by a transitional expression are separated only by a comma. (See pp. 377–78.)

transitive verb A verb that requires a direct object to complete its meaning. (See pp. 260–61.)

trite expressions (clichés) Stale expressions that dull writing and suggest that the writer is careless or lazy. (See p. 576.)

two-word verb A verb plus a preposition or adverb that affects the meaning of the verb: *jump off, put away, help out.* (See pp. 316–17.)

uniform resource locator (URL) An address for a source on the World Wide Web, specifying **protocol** (the standard for transferring data and files), **domain** (the computer, or **server,** housing the source), and **path** (the location and name of the source). (See p. 197.)

unity The quality of an effective essay or paragraph in which all parts relate to the central idea and to each other. (See pp. 45 and 75.)

upload To transfer data or files from your local computer to another computer.

variety Among connected sentences, changes in length, structure, and word order that help readers see the importance and complexity of ideas. (See Chapter 26.)

verb A word or group of words indicating the action or state of being of a subject. The inflection of a verb and the use of helping verbs with it indicate its tense, mood, voice, number, and sometimes person. See separate listings for each aspect and *predicate.* (See Chapter 14.)

verbals and verbal phrases **Verbals** are verb forms used as adjectives (*swimming children*), adverbs (*designed to succeed*), or nouns (*addicted to running*). The verbals in the preceding examples are a participle, an infinitive, and a gerund, respectively. (See separate entries for each type.) Verbal phrases consist of verbals plus objects or modifiers: *Swimming fast, the children reached the raft. Willem tried to unlatch the gate. Running in the park is his only recreation.* (See pp. 269–72.)

A verbal is a **nonfinite verb:** it cannot serve as the only verb in the predicate of a sentence. For that, it requires a helping verb. (See p. 270.)

verb forms Verbs have five distinctive forms. The first three are the verb's **principal parts:**

- The **plain form** is the dictionary form: *live, swim.*
- The **past-tense form** adds *-d* or *-ed* to the plain form if the verb is regular: *live, lived.* If the verb is irregular, the plain form changes in some other way, such as *swim, swam.*
- The **past participle** is the same as the past-tense form for regular verbs. For irregular verbs, the past participle may differ (*swum*).
- The **present participle** adds *-ing* to the plain form: *living, swimming.*
- The **-s form** adds *-s* or *-es* to the plain form: *lives, swims.*

verb phrase A verb consisting of a helping verb and a main verb: *has started, will have been invited.* A verb phrase can serve as the predicate of a clause: *The movie has started.*

voice The form of a verb that tells whether the sentence subject performs the action or is acted upon. In the active voice the subject acts: *We made the decision.* In the passive voice the subject is acted upon: *The decision was made by us.* (See pp. 329–31.)

warrant A term used for *assumption* in argument. See *assumption.*

Web forum A discussion group on the Web, open to everyone and organized around subjects. (For the use of Web forums in collaboration among students, see pp. 247–48. For the use of Web forums in research, see pp. 660–61.)

wizard A file on many word processors and most desktop publishers that guides the user in designing documents. (See p. 204.)

word order The arrangement of the words in a sentence, which plays a large part in determining the grammatical relation among words in English.

writing process The mental and physical activities that go into producing a finished piece of writing. The overlapping stages of the process—developing or planning, drafting, and revising—differ for different writers and even for the same writer in different writing situations. (See Chapters 1–3.)

writing situation The unique combination of writer, subject, audience, purpose, and other elements that defines an assignment and helps direct the writer's choices. (See pp. 4–5.)

Credits

AltaVista Web page "Internet Access." AltaVista, the AltaVista logo, and the Digital logo are trademarks of Digital Equipment Corporation. Reprinted with the permission of Digital Equipment Corporation.

Blackboard Inc. Use of CourseInfo program in screenshots copyright © 2000 Blackboard, Inc.

Bogdanovich, Peter. Excerpted from "Bogie in Excelsis" in *Pieces of Time*. © 1973 Peter Bogdanovich. Used by permission of Arbor House Publishing Company and the author.

Britt, Suzanne. Excerpt from "That Lean and Hungry Look," *Newsweek*, 9 October 1978. Copyright © 1978, 1988 by Suzanne Britt. Reprinted by permission.

Brooks, Gwendolyn. "The Bean Eaters" from *Blacks* by Gwendolyn Brooks. Copyright © 1991 by Gwendolyn Brooks. Published by Third World Press, Chicago.

Catton, Bruce. From "Grant and Lee: A Study in Contrasts." Copyright © 1956 United States Capitol Historical Society. All rights reserved. Reprinted with permission.

Computer Industry Almanac. Table: "Computers Per 1,000 People in 1998," by Computer Industry Almanac Inc., *www.c-i-a.com*.

Corel Corporation. Wordperfect screenshots and Corel Clipart copyright © 2000 by Corel Corporation and Corel Corporation Limited. Reprinted by permission.

Dillard, Annie. Excerpt from "Sojourner" from *Teaching a Stone to Talk* by Annie Dillard. Copyright © 1982 by Annie Dillard. Reprinted by permission of HarperCollins Publishers, Inc.

Drucker, Peter F. From "How Best to Protect the Environment," *Harper's* Magazine, January 1972. Copyright © 1971 by Minneapolis Star and Tribune Co.

Dyson, Freeman J. Excerpt from *Disturbing the Universe* by Freeman J. Dyson. Copyright © 1979 by Freeman J. Dyson. Reprinted by permission of HarperCollins Publishers, Inc.

Eisinger, Peter, et al. From *American Politics: The People and the Polity*. Copyright © 1978 by Little, Brown and Company. Reprinted by permission.

Farb, Peter. From *Word Play: What Happens When People Talk*. Copyright © 1973 by Peter Farb. Reprinted by permission of Alfred A. Knopf, Inc., and Brandt & Brandt.

Gaylin, Willard. Excerpt from *Feelings: Our Vital Signs* by Willard Gaylin. Copyright © 1979 by Willard Gaylin. Reprinted by permission of HarperCollins Publishers, Inc.

Goreau, Angeline. From "Worthy Women Revisited" by Angeline Goreau. *The New York Times,* December 11, 1986. Copyright © 1986 by *The New York Times*. Reprinted by permission.

Hughes, Emmet John. From "The Presidency vs. Jimmy Carter," *Fortune*, 4 December 1978. Reprinted by permission.

Ik, Kim Yong. From "A Book-Writing Venture" by Kim Yong Ik. Originally published in *The Writer,* October 1965. Copyright © Kim Yong Ik. Reprinted by permission of the author.

Jeffrey, Mac. From "Does Rx Spell Rip-Off?" by Mac Jeffrey, *The New York Times*, August 7, 1978. Copyright © 1978 by *The New York Times*. Reprinted by permission.

Johnston, Lloyd D., Patrick M. O'Malley, and Jerald G. Bachman. *Monitoring the Future National Survey Results on Drug Use, 1975–1999. Volume 1: Secondary School Students.* Rockville, MD: National Institute on Drug Abuse, 2000. Adapted with permission.

Kuralt, Charles. From *Dateline America.* Text copyright © 1979 by CBS, Inc. Reprinted by permission of Harcourt, Inc.

Mayer, Lawrence A. From "The Confounding Enemy of Sleep." *Fortune,* June 1974. Reprinted by permission.

Microsoft Corporation. Use of Microsoft Word and Notepad programs in screenshots reprinted by permission from Microsoft Corporation.

Mobil Oil Corporation. "Myths We Wouldn't Miss" by Mobil Oil Corporation in *The New York Times,* April 11, 1991. Copyright © 1991 by Mobil Corporation. Reprinted by permission.

Mylan, R. "The UN at 50" by R. Mylan. From *Newsweek,* October 18, 1995. Copyright © 1995 Newsweek, Inc. All rights reserved. Reprinted with permission.

Nadelman, Ethan A. From "Shooting Up" by Ethan A. Nadelman in *The New Republic*, June 1988. Reprinted by permission of *The New Republic*. © 1988, The New Republic, Inc.

Netscape Navigator Browser in screenshots. Netscape Communicator browser frame © Netscape Communications Corporation. Screenshots used with permission.

Ouchi, William G. From *Theory Z: How American Business Can Meet the Japanese Challenge,* copyright © Addison Wesley Publishing Company, Inc.

Ornstein, Robert. Excerpt from "A Letter to the Director," *Human Nature*, August 1978. Copyright © 1978 by Human Nature, Inc. Reprinted with permission of the publisher.

Qualcomm Inc. Use of Eudora Light program in screenshots copyright © 2000 Qualcomm, Incorporated.

Reston, James. "You Cannot Refine It" by James Reston. Copyright © 1985 by James Reston. Reprinted by permission of *The New Yorker.*

Rose, Phyllis. Excerpt from "On Shopping." From *Never Say Goodbye* by Phyllis Rose. Copyright © 1991 by Phyllis Rose. Reprinted by permission of Doubleday, a division of Bantam Doubleday Dell Publishing Group, Inc.

Rosen, Ruth. "Search for Yesterday." Todd Gitlin, editor, *Watching Television.* New York: Pantheon Books, 1986.

Sale, Kirkpatrick. "The Environmental Crisis Is Not Our Fault" by Kirkpatrick Sale from *The Nation* Magazine, April 30, 1990. Copyright © 1990 The Nation Company, Inc. Reprinted by permission.

Sowell, Thomas. "Student Loans" from *Is Reality Optional?* by Thomas Sowell. Copyright © 1993 by Thomas Sowell. Reprinted by permission of the author.

Standard & Poor's. Graph: "Five-Year Cumulative Return for Equities in Standard & Poor's 500 Index, 1994–1998." Reprinted by permission.

Staples, Brent. From "Black Men and Public Space" by Brent Staples, as appeared in *Harper's*, December 1986. Copyright © 1986 Brent Staples. Reprinted by permission of the author.

Tan, Amy. From "The Language of Discretion" in *State of Language*. Reprinted by permission of the Sandra Dijkstra Literary Agency.

Tuchman, Barbara. From "The Decline of Quality" by Barbara Tuchman, *The New York Times,* November 2, 1980. Copyright © 1980 by The New York Times Company. Reprinted by permission.

University of Texas Libraries. Use of catalog search results in screenshots © 1995, 1996, 1997, 1998, 1999, 2000. The General Libraries. The University of Texas at Austin.

Walker, Joyce R. "The Computerized Post Office: Sending and Receiving Mail in the Late Age of Print" (hypertext page). Reprinted by permission of the author.

Wax, Judith. From *Starting in the Middle*. Copyright © 1979 by Judith Wax. Reprinted by permission of Henry Holt & Company.

White, Diane. From "At Large" column in *The Boston Globe,* January 27, 1979. Reprinted courtesy of *The Boston Globe*.

Wright, Richard. Excerpt from *Black Boy* by Richard Wright. Copyright © 1937, 1942, 1944, 1945 by Richard Wright. Copyright © renewed 1973 by Ellen Wright. Reprinted by permission of HarperCollins Publishers, Inc.

Zinsser, William. From *The Lunacy Boom* by William Zinsser. Copyright © 1966, 1968, 1969, 1970 by William Zinsser. Reprinted by permission of Carol Brissie.

Index

Index

C

Index

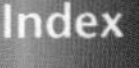
Index

Index

Index

J

M

N

Index

Index

Index

Z

USEFUL LISTS AND SUMMARIES

ESL GUIDE

Throughout the handbook the symbol **ESL** signals topics of special interest to students using English as a second language. This guide arranges these topics for easy reference. ESL material is thoroughly integrated with the rest of the handbook, so any of the page numbers here will also lead to a broader discussion of the topic.